Anacalypsis
(Volume 1 of 2, Part 1 of 2)

By Godfrey Higgins

A Digireads.com Book
Digireads.com Publishing
16212 Riggs Rd
Stilwell, KS, 66085

Anacalypsis (Volume 1 of 2, Part 1 of 2)
By Godfrey Higgins
ISBN: 1-4209-2991-7

Please visit *www.digireads.com*

Preface

It is a common practice with authors to place their portraits in the first page of their books. I am not very vain of my personal appearance, and, therefore, I shall not present the reader with my likeness. But, that I may not appear to censure others by my omission, and for some other reasons which any person possessing a very moderate share of discernment will soon perceive, I think it right to draw my own portrait with the pen, instead of employing an artist to do it with the pencil, and to inform my reader, in a few words, who and what I am, in what circumstances I am placed, and why I undertook such a laborious task as this work has proved.

Respecting my rank or situation in life it is only necessary to state, that my father was a gentleman of small, though independent fortune, of an old and respectable family in Yorkshire. He had two children, a son (myself) and a daughter. After the usual school education, I was sent to Trinity Hall, Cambridge, as a pensioner, and thence to the Temple. As I was expected to pay the fees out of the small allowance which my father made me, I never had any money to spare for that purpose, and I never either took a degree or was called to the bar.

When I was about twenty-seven years of age my father died, and I inherited his house and estate at Skellow Grange, near Doncaster. After some time I married. I continued there till the threatened invasion of Napoleon induced me, along with most of my neighbours, to enter the third West-York militia, of which, in due time, I was made a major. In the performance of my military duty in the neighbourhood of Harwich, I caught a very bad fever, from the effects of which I never entirely recovered. This caused me to resign my commission and return home. I shortly afterward became a magistrate for the West Riding of my native county. The illness above alluded to induced me to turn my attention, more than I had formerly done, to serious matters, and determined me to enter upon a very careful investigation of the evidence upon which our religion was founded. This, at last, led me to extend my inquiry into the origin of all religions, and this again led to an inquiry into the origin of nations and languages; and ultimately I came to a resolution to devote six hours a day to this pursuit for ten years. Instead of *six* hours daily for *ten* years, I believe I have, upon the average, applied myself to it for nearly *ten* hours daily for almost *twenty* years. In the first *ten* years of my search I may fairly say, I found nothing which I sought for; in the latter part of the *twenty*, the quantity of matter has so crowded in upon me, that I scarcely know how to dispose of it.

When I began these inquiries I found it necessary to endeavour to recover the scholastic learning which, from long neglect, I had almost forgotten: but many years of industry are not necessary for this purpose, as far, at least as is useful. The critical knowledge of the Greek and Latin languages, highly ornamental and desirable as it is, certainly is not, in general, necessary for the acquisition of what, in my opinion, may be properly called *real learning*. The ancient poetry and composition are beautiful, but a critical knowledge of them was not my object. The odes of Pindar and the poems of Homer are very fine; but Varro, Macrobius, and Cicero *De Natura Deorum*, were more congenial to my pursuits. The languages were valuable to me only as a key to unlock the secrets of antiquity. I beg my reader, therefore, not to expect any of that kind of learning, which would enable a person to rival Porson in filling up the Lacunæ of a Greek play, or in restoring the famous Digamma to its proper place.

But if I had neglected the study of Greek and Latin, I had applied myself to the study of such works as those of Euclid, and of Locke *on the Understanding*, the tendency of which is to form the mind to a habit of investigation and close reasoning and thinking, and in a peculiar manner to fit it for such inquiries as mine; for want of which habit, a person may possess a considerable knowledge of the Classics, while his mind may be almost incapable of comprehending the demonstration of a common proposition in geometry. In short, we see proofs every day, that a person may be very well skilled in Greek and Latin, while in intellect he may rank little higher than a ploughboy.

Along with the study of the principles of law, whilst at the Temple, I had applied myself also to the acquisition of the art of sifting and appreciating the value of different kinds of evidence, the latter of which is perhaps the most important and the most neglected of all the branches of education. I had also applied myself to what was of infinitely more consequence than all the former branches of study, and in difficulty almost equal to them altogether, namely, to the *unlearning* of the nonsense taught me in youth.

Literary works at the present day have generally one or both of two objects in view, namely, *money* and *present popularity*. But I can conscientiously say, that neither of these has been my leading object. I have become, to a certain extent, literary, because by letters alone could I make known to mankind what I considered discoveries the most important to its future welfare; and no publication has ever been written by me except under the influence of this motive.

When I say that I have not written this work for fame, it must not be understood that I affect to be insensible to the approbation of the great and good: far from it. But if I had my choice, I would rather rank with Epictetus than with Horace, with Cato or Brutus than with Gibbon or Sir Walter Scott. Had either present popularity or profit been my object, I had spared the priests; for, in Britain, we are a priest-ridden race: but though I had died a little richer, I had deserved contempt for my meanness.

My learning has been acquired since I turned forty years of age, for the sole purpose of being enabled to pursue these researches into the antiquities of nations, which, I very early became convinced, were generally unknown or misunderstood. But though I do not pretend to deep classical learning, yet perhaps I may not be guilty of any very inexcusable vanity in saying, that I find myself now, on the score of learning, after twenty years of industry, in many respects very differently circumstanced in relation to persons whom I was accustomed formerly to look up to as learned, from what I was at the beginning of my inquiries; and that now I sometimes find myself qualified to teach those by whom I was at first very willing to be taught, but whom I do not always find disposed to learn, nor to be *untaught* the nonsense which they learned in their youth.

In my search I soon found that it was impossible to look upon the histories of ancient empires, or upon the history of the ancient mythologies, except as pleasing or amusing fables, fit only for the nursery or the fashionable drawing-room table, but totally below the notice of a philosopher. This consideration caused my search into their origin; indefatigable labour for many years has produced the result,—the discovery which I believe I have made, and which in this work I make known to my countrymen.

I am convinced that a taste for deep learning among us is fast declining;* and in this I believe I shall be supported by the booksellers, which is one reason why I have only printed two hundred copies of this work: but I have reason to think the case different in France and Germany; and on this account I have sometimes thought of publishing editions in the languages of those countries. But whether I shall wait till these editions be ready, and till my second volume be finished, before I make public the first, I have not yet determined; nor, indeed, have I determined whether or not I shall publish these editions. This must depend upon the foreign booksellers.

If, like some learned persons, I had commenced my inquiries by believing certain dogmas, and determining that I would never believe any other; or if, like the Rev. Mr. Faber, I had in early life sworn that I believed them, and that I would never believe any other, and that all my comfort in my future life depended upon my *professed* continuance in this belief, I should have had much less trouble, because I should have known what I was to prove; but my story is very different. When I began this inquiry, I was anxious for truth, suspicious of being deceived, but determined to examine every thing as impartially as was in my power, to the very bottom. This soon led me to the discovery, that I must go to much more distant sources for the origin of things than was usual; and, by degrees, my system began to form itself. But not having the least idea in the beginning what it would be in the end, it kept continually improving, in some respects changing, and I often found it necessary to read again and again the same books, for *want of an index*, from beginning to end, in search of facts passed hastily over in the first or second reading, and then thought of little or no consequence, but which I afterwards found most important for the elucidation of truth. On this account the labour in planting the seed has been to me great beyond credibility, but I hope the produce of the harvest will bear to it a due proportion.

I very early found that it was not only necessary to recover and improve the little Greek and Latin which I had learned at school, but I soon found my inquiries stopped by my ignorance of the Oriental languages, from which I discovered that ours was derived, and by which it became evident to me that the origin of all our ancient mythoses was concealed. I therefore determined to apply myself to the study of one of them; and, after much consideration and doubt whether I should choose the Hebrew, the Arabic,

---

* Of this a more decisive proof need not be given than the failure of the Rev. Dr. Valpy's Classical Journal, a work looked up to as an honour to our country by all learned foreigners, which was given up, as well from want of contributors as from want of subscribers.

or the Sanscrit, I fixed upon the first, in the selection of which, for many reasons, which will appear hereafter, I consider myself peculiarly fortunate.

For some time my progress was very slow,—my studies were much interrupted by public business; and, for almost two years together, by a successful attempt into which I was led, in the performance of my duty as a justice of the peace, to reform some most shocking abuses in the York Lunatic Asylum.

In my study of Hebrew, also, a considerable time, I may say, was wasted on the Masoretic points, which at last I found were a mere invention of the modern Jews, and not of the smallest use.*

During this process, I also found it was very desirable that I should consult many works in the libraries of Italy and France, as well as examine the remains of antiquity in those countries, and my reader will soon see that, without having availed myself of this assistance, I should never have been able to make the discoveries of which he will have been apprized. The benefit which I derived from the examination of the works of the ancients, in my two journeys to Rome, and one to Naples, at last produced a wish to examine the antiquities of more Oriental climes, and a plan was laid for travelling in search of WISDOM to the East;—the origin and defeat of this plan I have detailed in the preface to my Celtic Druids. I am now turned sixty; the eye grows dim, and the cholera and plague prevail in the East; yet I have not entirely given up the hope of going as far as Egypt: but what I have finished of my work must first be printed. Could I but ensure myself a strong probability of health and the retention of my faculties, for *ten,* or, I think, even for *seven* years, I should not hesitate on a journey to Samarkand, to examine the library of manuscripts there, which was probably collected by Ulug-Beig. If the strictest attention to diet and habits the most temperate may be expected to prolong health, I may not be very unreasonable in looking forwards for five or six years; and I hope my reader will believe me when I assure him, that the strongest incentive which I feel for pursuing this course of life is the confident hope and expectation of the great discoveries which I am certain I could make, if I could once penetrate into the East, and see things there with my own eyes.

In a very early stage of my investigation, my attention was drawn to the ancient Druidical and Cyclopæan buildings scattered over the world, in almost all nations, which I soon became convinced were the works of a great nation, of whom we had no history, who must have been the first inventors of the religious mythoses and the art of writing; and, in short, that what I sought must be found among them. My book, called the CELTIC DRUIDS, which I published in the year 1827, was the effect of this conviction, and is, in fact, the foundation on which this work is built, and without a perusal

---

* It may be necessary to inform some persons who may read this book, that, in the dark ages, the Jews, in order to fix the pronunciation and the meaning of their Hebrew to their own fancy at the time, invented a system called the Masoretic Points, which they substituted in place of the vowels, leaving the latter in the text; but, where they could not make them stand for consonants and thus form new syllables, leaving them silent and without meaning. The belief in the antiquity of this system has now become with them a point of faith; *of course here the use of reason ends.* On this account I shall add to the appendix to this volume a small tract that I formerly published on this subject, which I doubt not will satisfy reasoning individuals.

of it, this work will, notwithstanding my utmost care, scarcely be understood. It might very well have formed a first volume to this, and I now regret that I did not so arrange it.

I think it right to state here, what I beg my reader will never forget, that in my explanations of words and etymologies I proceed upon the principle of considering all the different systems of letters, Sanscrit excepted, to have formed originally but one alphabet, only varied in forms, and the different written languages but one language, and that they are all mere dialects of one another. This I consider that *I have proved* in my CELTIC DRUIDS, and it will be proved over and over again in the course of the following work.

Numerous are the analyses of the ancient mythology, but yet I believe the world is by no means satisfied with the result of them. There is yet a great blank. That the ancient mythoses have a system for their basis, is generally believed; indeed, I think this is what no one can doubt. But, whether I have discovered the principles on which they are founded, and have given the real explanation of them, others must judge.

The following work is similar to the solution of a difficult problem in the mathematics, only to be understood by a consecutive perusal of the whole—only to be understood after close attention, after an induction of consequences from a long chain of reasoning, every step of which, like a problem in Euclid, must be borne in mind. The reader must not expect that the secrets which the ancients took so much pains to conceal, and which they involved in the most intricate of labyrinths, are to be learned without difficulty. But though attention is required, he may be assured that, with a moderate share of it, there is nothing which may not be understood. But instead of making a consecutive perusal of the work, many of my readers will go to the Index and look for particular words, and form a judgment from the etymological explanation of them, without attending to the context or the arguments in other parts of the volume, or to the reasoning which renders such explanation probable, and thus they will be led to decide against it and its conclusions and consider them absurd. All this I expect, and of it I have no right to complain, unless I have a right to complain that a profound subject is attended with difficulties, or that superficial people are not deep thinkers, or that the nature of the human animal is not of a different construction from what I know it to be. The same lot befel the works of General Vallancey, which contain more profound and correct learning on the origin of nations and languages than all the books which were ever written. But who reads them? Not our little bits of antiquarians of the present day, who make a splashing on the surface, but never go to the bottom. A few trumpery and tawdry daubs on an old church-wall serve them to fill volumes. It is the same with most of our Orientalists. The foolish corruptions of the present day are blazoned forth in grand folios[1] as the works of the Buddhists or Brahmins; when, in fact, they are nothing but what may be called the new religion of their descendants, who may be correctly said to have lost, as they, indeed, admit they have done, the old

---

[1] Vide the works, for instance, published by Akerman

religions, and formed new ones which are suitable to their present state—that is, a state
equal to that of the Hottentots of Africa.

Hebrew scholars have been accused of undue partiality to what is sneeringly called
their *favourite language* by such as do not understand it: and this will probably be
repeated towards me. In self-defence, I can only say, that in my search for the origin
of ancient science, I constantly found myself impeded by my ignorance of the Hebrew;
and, in order to remove this impediment, I applied myself to the study of it. I very
early discovered that no translation of the ancient book of Genesis, either by Jew or
Christian, could be depended on. Every one has the prejudices instilled into him in his
youth to combat, or his prejudged dogma to support. But I can most truly say, that I
do not lie open to the latter charge; for there is scarcely a single opinion maintained in
the following work which I held when I began it. Almost all the latter part of my
life has been spent in unlearning the nonsense I learned in my youth. These considerations I flatter myself will be sufficient to screen me from the sneers of such
gentlemen as suppose all learning worth having is to be found in the Latin and Greek
languages; especially when, in the latter part of this work, they find that I have come to
the conclusion, that the Hebrew language, or that language of which Hebrew, Chaldee,
and Arabic are only dialects, was probably the earliest of the written languages now
known to us.

When I affirm that I think the old synagogue Hebrew the oldest written language,
the philosopher will instantly turn away and say, "Oh! I see this is only the old devoteeism." He may be assured he will find himself mistaken. I believe that I found
my opinion on evidence equally free from modern Christian or ancient Jewish prejudice.
I attribute the preservation of these old tracts (the books of Genesis) from the destruction which has overtaken all other sacred books of the priests of the respective temples
of the world, to the fortunate circumstance that they were made public by Ptolemy Philadelphus. Natural causes, without any miracle, have produced a natural effect, and
thus we have these interesting remains, and have them, too, in consequence of a religious
dogma having operated, nearly uncorrupted, in *their general language*, by modern Jewish and Masoretic nonsense. In the SYNAGOGUE books we have, most fortunately,
several tracts in a language older than any language, as now written, in the world, not
excepting the beautiful and almost perfect Sanscrit. And this I think I shall prove in
the course of the work. That my reader may not run away with a mistaken inference
from what I now say, I beg to observe, that I pay not the least attention to the generally
received ancient chronologies.

In order to arrive at what I believe to be the truth, I have often been obliged to enter
into very abstruse and difficult examinations of the meaning of Hebrew words; but they
are generally words which have undergone the most elaborate discussion, by very great
scholars, and have been the subjects of controversy. This has been a great advantage
to me, as by this means I have been enabled to see every thing which could be said on
the respective points in dispute, and my conclusions may be considered as the summing

up of the evidence on both sides. As the results of my inquiries will sometimes depend upon the meaning of the words, the subjects of these discussions, I have found it necessary to enter, in several instances, into a close and critical examination of their meaning, as I have just said; in which, without care and patience, the reader unlearned in Hebrew will not be able to follow me. But yet I flatter myself that if he will pass over a very few examples of this kind, which he finds too difficult, and go to the conclusion drawn from them, he will, in almost every instance, be able to understand the argument. If, as I believe, the foundations of the ancient mythoses are only to be discovered in the most ancient roots of the languages of the world, it is not likely that such an inquiry into them could be dispensed with.

The letters of the old Synagogue Hebrew language are nearly the same as the English, only in a different form. They are so near that they almost all of them may be read as English, as any person may see in Sect. 46, p. 10, by a very little consideration of the table of letters, and the numbers which they denote. In order that an unlearned reader may understand the etymological conclusions, nearly throughout the whole work every Hebrew word is followed by correspondent letters in English italics, so that a person who does not understand the Hebrew may understand them almost as well as a person who does. Half an hour's study of the table of letters, and attention to this observation, I am convinced is all that is necessary.

In great numbers of places, authors will be found quoted as authority, but whose authority my reader may be inclined to dispute. In every case, evidence of this kind must go for no more than it is worth. It is like interested evidence, which is worth something in every case, though, perhaps, very little. But in many cases, an author of little authority, quoted by me as evidence in favour of my hypothesis, will be found to have come to his conclusion, perhaps, when advocating doctrines directly in opposition to mine, or in absolute ignorance of my theory. In such cases, his evidence, from the circumstance, acquires credibility which it would not otherwise possess: and if numerous instances of evidence of this kind unite upon any one point, to the existence of any otherwise doubtful fact, the highest probability of its truth may be justly inferred. If a fact of the nature here treated of be found to be supported by other facts, and to dovetail into other parts of my system, or to remove its difficulties, its probability will be again increased. Thus it appears that there will be a very great variety in the evidence in favour of different parts of the system, which can only be correctly judged of by a consecutive perusal of the whole. / And, above all things, my reader must always bear in mind, that he is in search of a system, the meaning of which its professors and those initiated into its mysteries have constantly endeavoured in all ages and nations to conceal, and the proofs of the existence of which, the most influential body of men in the world, the priests, have endeavoured, and yet endeavour, by every honest and dishonest means in their power, to destroy./

The following work will be said to be a theory: it is given as a theory. But what is a Theory? Darwin says, "To theorise is to think." The peculiar nature of the subject precludes me from founding my thinkings or reasonings on facts deduced by experiment, like the modern natural philosopher; but I endeavour to do this as far as is in my power. I found them on the records of facts, and on quotations from ancient authors, and on the deductions which were made by writers without any reference to my theory or system. A casual observation, or notice of a fact, is often met with in an author which he considers of little or no consequence, but which, from that very circumstance, is the more valued by me, because it is the more likely to be true.

This book is intended for those only who think that the different mythoses and histories are yet involved in darkness and confusion: and it is an attempt to elucidate the grounds on which the former were founded, and from which they have risen to their present state. It is evident that, if I have succeeded, and if I have discovered the original principles, although, perhaps, trifling circumstances or matters may be erroneously stated, yet new discoveries will every day add new proofs to my system, till it will be established past all dispute. If, on the contrary, I be wrong, new discoveries will soon expose my errors, and, like all preceding theories, my theory will die away, as they are dying away, and it will be forgotten.

I have just said that this work is a theory, and professes, in a great measure, to arrive at probabilities only. I am of opinion that, if ancient authors had attended more to the latter, we should have been better informed than we now are upon every thing relating to the antiquities of nations. The positive assertions, false in themselves, yet not meant to mislead, but only to express the opinions of some authors, together with the intentional falsities of others, have accumulated an immense mass of absurdities, which have rendered all ancient history worse than a riddle. Had the persons first named only stated their opinion that a thing was probable, but which, in composition, it is exceedingly difficult to do, as I have constantly found, their successors would not have been misled by their want of sense or judgment. Every succeeding generation has added to the mass of nonsense, until the enormity is beginning to cure itself, and to prove that the whole, as a system, is false: it is beginning to convince most persons that some new system must be had recourse to, if one can be devised, which may at least have the good quality of containing within itself the *possibility* of being true, a quality which the present *old* system most certainly wants. Now I flatter myself that my *new* system, notwithstanding many errors which it may contain, will possess this quality; and if I produce a sufficient number of known facts that support it, for the existence of which it accounts, and without which system their existence cannot be accounted for, I contend that I shall render it very probable that my system is true. The whole force of this observation will not be understood till the reader comes to the advanced part of my next volume, wherein I shall treat upon the system of the philosophic Niebuhr respecting the history of the ancient Romans.

Of whatever credulity my reader may be disposed to accuse me, in some respects, there will be no room for any charge of this kind, on account of the legends of bards or monks, or the forgeries of the Christian priests of the middle ages; as, for fear of being imposed on by them, I believe I have carried my caution to excess, and have omitted to use materials, in the use of which I should have been perfectly justified. For example I may name the works of Mr. Davies, of Wales, and General Vallancey, both of which contain abundance of matter which supports my doctrines; but even of these, I have used such parts only as I thought could not well be the produce of the frauds of the priests or bards. I endeavour, as far as lies in my power, to regulate my belief according to what I know is the rule of evidence in a British court of law. Perhaps it may be said, that if I am not credulous in this respect of the monks and priests, I am in respect of the ancient monuments. But these ancient unsculptured stones or names of places, are not like the priests, though with many exceptions in all sects, regular, systematic liars, lying *from interest*, and boldly defending the practice on principle—a practice brought down from Plato, and continued to our own day. Witness the late restoration of the annual farce of the liquefaction of the blood of St. Januarius, and the fraudulent title to what is called the Apostles' Creed in our Liturgy.

Some years ago a fraud was attempted by a Brahmin on Sir William Jones and Major Wilford. These two gentlemen being totally void of any suspicion were deceived, but in a very little time the latter detected the fraud, and instantly published it to the world in the most candid and honourable manner. This has afforded a handle to certain persons, who dread discoveries from India, to run down every thing which Wilford wrote, not only up to that time, but in a long and industrious life afterward. I have been careful, in quoting from his works, to avoid what may have been fraudulent; but so far from thinking that Wilford's general credit is injured, I think it was rather improved by the manner in which he came forward and announced the fraud practised on him. There was no imputation of excessive credulity previously cast upon him, and I consider it likely that this instance made him more cautious than most others against impostures in future. I cannot help suspecting, that this fraud was the cause of much true and curious matter being rendered useless.

It has been said, that the more a person inquires, the less he generally believes. This is true; and arises from the fact that he soon discovers that great numbers of the priests, in every age and of every religion, have been guilty of frauds to support their systems, to an extent of which he could have had no idea until he made the inquiry. Many worthy and excellent men among our priests have been angry with me, because I have not more pointedly excepted the ORDER in the British empire from the general condemnation expressed in my CELTIC DRUIDS, though I there expressly stated that I *did* except many individuals. The fraudulent title of the Apostles' Creed, which I have just named, would alone justify me.

The following *rational* account of the corruption of religion is given by the cool and philosophical Basnage:[1] " Divines complain that the people have always a violent pro-' pensity to sensible objects and idolatry; and I do not deny it; but in the mean time

---

[1] Bk. iii. ch. xix. p. 217.

" divines of all ages have been more to blame than the people, since they conducted
" them to the adoration of creatures : that they might be able to discourse longer, and to
" distinguish themselves from the crowd, they have disguised religion with obscure
" terms, emblems and symbols; as if they were alive ; as if they were persons ; and have
" dressed them up like men and women.   This has trained up and encouraged the peo-
" ple in their carnal notions.   They thought that they might devote themselves to
" the symbols, which were furnished with a wondrous efficacy, and treated of more than
" the Deity himself.   Whereas they ought to give the people the simplest ideas of
" God, and talk soberly of him : they embellish, they enrich, and magnify their ideas of
" him, and this is what has corrupted religion in all ages, as is manifest from the in-
" stance of the Egyptians.   By veiling religion under pretence of procuring it respect,
" they have buried and destroyed it."

Though the labour which I have gone through in the production of this volume of my
work has been very great, yet it has been sweetened by many circumstances, but by
none so much as the conviction, that in laying open to public view the secret of the
mythoses of antiquity, I was performing one of the works the most valuable to my fellow-creatures which was ever completed,—that it was striking the hardest blow that ever
was struck at the tyranny of the sacerdotal order,—that I was doing more than any man
had ever done before to disabuse and enlighten mankind, and to liberate them from the
shackles of prejudice in which they were bound.

Another thing which sweetened the labour was, the perpetual making of new discoveries,—the whole was a most successful voyage of discovery.

No doubt, in order to prevent females from reading the following work, it will be accused of indecency.   Although I have taken as much care as was in my power to remove any good grounds for the charge, it is certainly open to it, in the same way as are
many works on comparative anatomy.   But these, in fact, are indecent only to persons of
indecent and filthy imaginations—to such persons as a late Lord Mayor of London, who
ordered the Savoyard statue-dealers out of the city, until they clothed their Venus de
Medicis with drapery.

In all cases brevity, as far as clearness of expression would admit, has been my object ;
and I can safely say, though the reason for many passages may not be obvious to a reader who has not deeply meditated on the subject as I have done, yet I believe scarcely
one is inserted in the book which has not appeared to me at the time to be necessary to
elucidate some subject which was to follow.

It has been observed, that persons who write a bad style, generally affect to despise a
good one.   Now whatever may be thought of mine, I beg to observe, that I regret it is
not better ; I wish I had been more attentive to it in early life ; but I must freely confess,
that my mind has been turned to the discovery of truth almost to the entire neglect of
style.

I fear some repetitions will be found which would not have occurred had I been better
skilled in the art of book-making ; but in many cases I do not know how they could

have been avoided, as a new consequence will often be shewn to flow from a statement formerly made for a different purpose. However, I justify myself by the example of the learned and popular Bryant, who says,

" As my researches are deep and remote, I shall sometimes take the liberty of repeat-
" ing what has preceded, that the truths which I maintain may more readily be perceived.
" We are oftentimes, by the importunity of a persevering writer, teazed into an unsatis-
" factory compliance and yield a painful assent: but upon closing the book, our scruples
" return; and we lapse at once into doubt and darkness. It has, therefore, been my
" rule to bring vouchers for every thing which I maintain; and though I might, upon
" the renewal of my argument, refer to another volume and a distant page; yet I many
" times choose to repeat my evidence, and bring it again under immediate inspection.
" And if I do not scruple labour and expense, I hope the reader will not be disgusted by
" this seeming redundancy in my arrangement. What I now present to the public,
" contains matter of great moment, and should I be found in the right, it will afford a
" sure basis for a future history of the world. None can well judge either of the labour
" or utility of the work, but those who have been conversant in the writings of chrono-
" logers and other learned men upon these subjects, and seen the difficulties with which
" they are embarrassed. Great undoubtedly must have been the learning and perspicacity
" of many who have preceded me. Yet it may possibly be found at the close, that a
" feeble arm has effected what those prodigies in science have overlooked."[1]

I conceive the notice which I have taken of my former work cannot be considered impertinent, as it is, indeed, the foundation on which this is built. The original habita-tion of the first man, and the merging of nearly all ancient written languages into one system, containing sixteen letters, which in that work I have shewn and proved, pave the way for the more important doctrines that will be here developed, and form an essential part of it. The whole taken together, will, I trust, draw aside the veil which has hitherto covered the early history of man,—the veil, in fact, of Queen Isis, which she, I hope erroneously, boasted should never be withdrawn. If, in this undertaking, it prove that I have spent many years, and bestowed much labour and money in vain, and have failed, Mr. Faber may then have to comfort himself that his failure is not the last. I think it no vanity to believe that I have succeeded better than he has done, because I have come to the task with the benefit of the accumulated labours of Mr. Faber, and of all my pre-decessors. So that if there be merit in the work, to them, in a great degree, it must be attributed. I have the benefit both of their learning and of their errors.

In the fifth book a number of astronomical calculations are made. But every thing like scientific parade and the use of technical terms, to which learned men are generally very partial, are studiously avoided; and I apprehend that even the little knowledge of astronomy which any well-educated school-girl may possess, will be sufficient for under-standing these calculations. Close attention to the argument will doubtless be re-

[1] Bryant, Anal. Pref. p. vii

quired; but, with less than this, my reader will not expect to solve the problem which has hitherto set at defiance the learning and talent of all scientific inquirers. When my reader comes to this part of my work he will find, that to make my calculations come right, I have constantly been obliged to make a peculiar use of the number 2160, and in many cases to deduct it. For this he will find no *quite satisfactory* reason given. But though I could not account for it, the coincidence of numbers was so remarkable, that I was quite certain there could, in the fact, be no mistake. In the second volume this will be satisfactorily accounted for; and I flatter myself it will be found to form, not a blemish, but the apex, necessary to complete the whole building.

How I may be treated by the critics on this work, I know not; but I cannot help smiling when I consider that the priests have objected to admit my former book, *the Celtic Druids*, into libraries, because it was antichristian; and it has been attacked by Deists, because it was superfluously religious. The learned deist, the Rev. R. Taylor, has designated me as *the religious* Mr. Higgins. But God be thanked, the time is come at last, when a person may philosophise without fear of the stake. No doubt the priests will claim the merit of this liberality. It is impossible, however, not to observe what has been indiscreetly confessed by them a thousand times, and admitted as often both in parliament and elsewhere by their supporters, that persecution has ceased, not because the priests wished to encourage free discussion, but because it is at last found, from the example of Mr. Carlile and others, that the practice of persecution, at this day, only operates to the dissemination of opinion, not to the secreting of it. In short, that the remedy of persecution is worse than the disease it is meant to cure.

On the subject of criticism Cleland has justly observed, " The judging of a work, not " by the general worth of it, but by the exceptions, is the scandal of criticism and the " nuisance of literature; a judgment that can dishonour none but him who makes it."[1] In most cases where I have known the characters of the priests who have lost their temper, and taken personal offence at what I have said against the order, in that work, I have thought I could discover a reason for it which *they* did not assign. As the subjects there treated of may be considered to be continued here, the objections of my opponents will be found to be refuted without the odious appearance of a polemical dispute. As for those attacks which were evidently made by the priests merely for the purpose, as far as possible, of preventing their followers from reading the *Celtic Druids*, and not for the purpose of refuting that work, they are of no consequence. Although it was published in great haste, I am happy to have it in my power to state, that no error of any importance has been pointed out, some few overlooked errors of the press excepted. Various attacks upon it are characterized by the obvious vexation and anger of my opponents, rather than by argument. But the attack of one gentleman I think it right to notice.

The Rev. Hugh James Rose, B. D., Christian Advocate of Cambridge, has honoured

---

[1] Preface to Specimen, p. xi.

it with his notice ; but it is gratifying to me to be able to say, that except one proverbial expression, *in toto cœlo* PERHAPS, improperly used, and a mistake in writing Plato for Herodotus, and Herodotus for Plato, which, in a great part of the impression, was corrected with the pen, and in all was ordered to be so corrected with it, before the book left the printer's, and a mistake in writing παρ' εξοχην instead of κατ' εξοχην, he has not found any other fault, though I think he has shewn no want of inclination.   With respect to the latter error, as I certainly never discovered the *gross* and *shocking* inadvertency until a great part of this work was printed, I should not be at all surprised if somewhere, as I wrote for Greek παρ' εξοχην instead of κατ' εξοχην, I should have written for French *kat'* excellence instead of *par* excellence.

A writer in the Bishop's review accuses me of being in *a rage* with priests.   I flatter myself I am never in a rage with any thing ; but, I never have scrupled and never shall scruple to express my detestation of an order which exists directly in opposition to the commands of Jesus Christ—which in no case is of use to mankind, but which has produced more demoralisation and misery in the world than all other causes put together. With this conviction it would be base in me to withhold my opinion, and not even the fear of the auto-da-fé shall prevent me from expressing it.

As long as the art of writing and reading was a secret confined to a few select persons, priests might be thought to be wanted to say the prayers for the ignorant ; but as most persons can read now, they are no longer necessary; and the prayer which Jesus Christ taught is so very short and simple, that no person, above the class of an idiot, can be in any difficulty about it ; and there can be little doubt that Jesus Christ taught that simple and short form that priests might no longer be necessary.

Matthew vi. 5, 6, 7, 9, makes Jesus say, " When thou prayest, thou shalt not be as the " Hypocrites, for they love to pray standing in the synagogues" [they go in great form to church and have their pew made with high walls and lined with crimson cloth], "and in " the corners of the streets, that they may be seen of men ;" [attend Bible and Missionary meetings ;] " verily they have their reward.   But thou, when thou prayest, enter " into thy closet, and when thou hast shut thy door, pray to thy Father which is in " secret, and thy Father which seeth in secret, shall reward thee openly.   But when ye " pray, use not vain repetitions as the heathen do, for they think that they shall be heard " for their much speaking.   After this manner, therefore, pray ye," &c.

Here priesthoods and priests, *vipers* as Jesus often called them, are expressly forbidden.   *In giving directions what a person is to do when he prays*, he directly countermands every other mode of proceeding.   In strict keeping with this, not a single word of his can be pointed out in any one of the gospels, which can be construed into even a toleration of priests ; and in the *vain repetitions* liturgies are evidently implied.

In the prayer which Jesus gave, he gave a liturgy and directions for the use of it, and no human being who has learned to repeat this prayer can ever want any priest or other apparatus.

Had Jesus considered any symbol or confession of faith necessary, he would have given one.   As he has not given one, and as he did take upon himself to legislate in the case, on every principle of sound reasoning it must be held, that he did not think a belief in this or in that *faith*, as it is called, (which his profound wisdom well knew never can be a merit or demerit,) was necessary to salvation.   This justifies its name, *the poor man's religion*.   The poor man's whole duty to God is contained in this prayer, and the whole moral part of his duty to *man* is contained in the direction to every one to do to his neighbour as he would wish his neighbour to do to him.   Its founder left nothing in writing, because the poor man's religion does not require it.

This great simplicity makes the pure, unadulterated Christian religion the most beautiful religion that ever existed.   Restore it to this pure and simple state, and ninety-nine out of every hundred of all the philosophers in the world will be its friends, instead of its enemies.   In the accounts which we read of Jesus's preaching, he is made to say, that if they believed on him they should be saved.   In order to find some pretext for *their own nonsense*, the priests, by a gross, fraudulent mistranslation, have made *him talk nonsense* and say, if ye believe oɴ ᴍᴇ, instead of ɪɴ ᴍᴇ, or *in my words*, ye shall be saved.   On this they found the necessity of faith in their dogmas.   Some persons will think this a merely *trifling* critical emendation ; but so far is it from being trifling, that it is of the very greatest importance, and on it some most important doctrines depend.   All this tends to support the doctrines of the celebrated Christian philosopher Ammonius Saccas, of which I shall have much to say in the following work.

But it is necessary to observe, that this simple view of the religion leaves *untouched* every dogma of every sect.   It shews that the religion damns no person for an opinion. It leaves every one to enjoy his own opinions.   It censures or condemns the opinions of no one ; but I fear that it will be liked almost by no one, because it prevents every one from condemning the opinion of his neighbour.   If Jesus can be said to have established any rite, it will be found in the adoption of the *very ancient* ceremony of the Eucharistia, the most beautiful of all the religious ceremonies ever established, and of which I shall often have to treat in the course of my work.   Jesus Christ was put to death, if the four gospel histories can be believed, merely for teaching what I have no doubt he did teach, that Temples, Priests, Mysteries, and Cabala, were all unnecessary.   Mohamed, by abolishing priests, liturgies, and symbols, and by substituting a simple hymn in praise of the Creator, was a much more consistent Christian than the modern Paulite ; and this, and nothing but this, was the religion of Mohamed.   The Koran was none of his.

The priest to whom I lately alluded has called me misosierist.   This he may do as long as he pleases.[1]   How is it possible for a person who, like me, is a sincere friend of religion, not to be indignant at an order which has, by its frauds, rendered the history of all religions, and of every thing connected with them, doubtful—by frauds systematically practised in all ages, and continued even to the present day, and in our own country ?

---

[1] My work called *The Celtic Druids* has never been noticed in any way which can be called *a review*, except in the fifth and sixth numbers of the Southern Review of North America, printed at Charleston.   In that periodical it is reviewed by a very learned man, with whom I first became acquainted in consequence of his critique.

I consider that when the Bishop's review called me a misosierist, it paid me the greatest of compliments. To be called a misosierist is the same as to be called Philanthropist. I am proud of the epithet.

I have been accused of being fond of paradox. The word *paradox* means, *beyond common opinion*. When common opinion tells me to believe that God, the Supreme First Cause, walked in the garden, or that he, as Jupiter, carried Io away on his back to Crete, I am not afraid of being paradoxical or doing wrong in adopting the opinion of all the first fathers of the church, and in seeking some meaning which the original words do not literally possess.

If the priests can refute the doctrines which I teach, they will not lose a moment in doing it; if they cannot, they will have recourse to turning selected passages and parts of arguments *into ridicule*. To this they are welcome. I shall rejoice in the proof of my victory.

I have come to one resolution—never to attempt to vindicate myself from any unfounded charge of ignorance or misquotation in this book; but, only to notice such real errors in the work, as may be pointed out, and to correct them, of whatever kind they may be.

Like my learned friend Eusebe de Salverte, I shall be accused of rationalism.[1] I, beforehand, plead guilty to the charge. I can be of no religion which does not appear to be consistent with sound reason, and I cannot stoop, with the advocates of priestcraft and idiotism, to lend my hand to continue the degradation of my fellow-creatures. Since the priests and their abettors have thought proper to convert the exercise of the highest gift of God to man *reason* into a term of reproach—rationalism—I know not how to return the compliment, though I do not like to render *evil* for evil, better than by designating their attempted opposition to reason, *idiotism*.

To guard myself against being accused of the disgusting practice of using abusive epithets, I beg that the term *devotee*, which will often occur, as of course it conveys no meaning against any one's moral character, may not be considered to mean a bigot, but merely a person very much, or rather more than usually religious, which is its true and correct meaning. I leave the use of abusive language, such as *infidel*, to persons who, feeling that their arguments are weak, try to strengthen them by violence.

In the execution of this work I have endeavoured to place myself above all religions and sects, and to take a bird's-eye view of them all; and, as I have favoured none, I know I shall be favoured by none. A few and very few persons, those persons who are really philosophers *will* read it. The generality of mankind will read no further than to that part where it begins to touch their own prejudices or their own religion; then they will throw it down. It is very seldom indeed that a religious person is capable of reasoning respecting matters connected with his religion. This is the cause why, on this subject, no two persons scarcely ever agree. And I beg my reader to recollect, that if he take the opinion of a religious person on any matter connected with such a work as this, as

---

[1] *Foreign Quarterly Review, No.* XII

there are numbers of religions, the chances are very great, that in some part it must have attacked the religion of the person whose opinion he takes ; whence it follows, that the chances are in proportion to the whole numbers of religions which exist to one, that he depends on a prejudiced person, and is deceived. All this will operate against the the book ; but how can I expect any better ?—for the immediate effect of my theory, if universally received, would be, to render obsolete nine-tenths of all the literature of the world, and to overthrow almost every prevailing system of history, chronology, and religion. But founding my opinion on a thorough conviction that I have solved the great problem and have discovered the long-lost truths of antiquity which have been so long sought for in vain, I feel no doubt that the time will come when my discovery will be adopted, when the errors in the work or in the system will be corrected, and the truth it contains will be duly appreciated, and that, if I have succeeded in developing the origin of religions, nations, and languages, it will by degrees make its way. Besides, the schoolmaster is abroad. Tempora mutantur, et veritas prævalebit.

I shall be found frequently to express *a suspicion ;* as for instance, *I have a suspicion,* or *I have a strong suspicion.* I think it right to apprize my reader, that when I use these words, I really mean that *I suspect* or *conjecture,* and that however numerous may be the proofs which I produce, I yet admit a doubt, and by no means intend to place the credit of my work upon the absolute truth of the doctrines so doubtfully advanced by me. Of course among such an innumerable number of references contained in the notes, errors would have been found, even if my eyes had not begun to fail me, and to verify them it is impossible to travel again over all the libraries from Glasgow to Naples. I shall be thankful for any corrections.

In many places the explanations of words will be found to be given in numbers. This has been generally treated by the learned with contempt. I think it right to give notice to the reader, that before this work is finished, this *buffoonery,* as it has been called by those who did not understand it, and who were too idle or too proud to inquire what could be the cause that the *most learned of the ancients* used such a practice, will be found of the very first importance, and to be any thing but buffoonery.

It is also necessary to observe, that if an observation or notice of an ancient custom should sometimes appear, which may be thought to be introduced without good cause, it is not therefore to be concluded that all persons will be of that opinion. I think it right to warn my reader, that there are more passages than one in the book, which are of that nature, which will be perfectly understood by my masonic friends, but which my engagements prevent my explaining to the world at large.

My masonic friends will find their craft very often referred to. I believe, however, that they will not find any of their secrets betrayed ; but I trust they will find it proved, that their art is the remains of a very fine ancient system, or, perhaps, more properly, a branch of the fine and beautiful system of WISDOM which, in this work, I have developed.

In the latter part of the work many facts are stated and observations made which ought to have had a place in the earlier parts of it ; this arose from the fact, that when I commenced printing, I thought I had finished my first volume: but, as it proceeded, I continued my researches, and in consequence met with many new circumstances tending to complete or strengthen my system.   Was I to leave them unnoticed?   This would have been a kind of infanticide.   Their late introduction may injure the work ; but my object is not to make a book, but to develop great truths, respecting ancient Language, Religion, and the Origin of Nations.

Sometimes a quotation will be found to contain bad grammar, as for instance, in Book X. Chapter VI. Sect. 11, pp. 716, 717 ; but I have thought it better to leave it as I found it, than run the risk of making an author say what he did not intend, by my correction.   Schoolmasters think such things of consequence.   They are certainly better avoided.   It is a common practice of our scholars to endeavour to tie down inquirers to the niceties which the old languages acquired when they had arrived at their highest state of perfection, prohibiting any licence, and making no allowance for their uncertain state before grammars or lexicons were written.   For instance, Buddha and Buda, between which they now make some very nice distinctions ; saying, one is the Planet Mercury, and the other is Wisdom, a distinction adopted evidently in later times.   This is the counterpart of the Sun and the planet Mercury of the Greeks, both of which, I shall shew, meant the Sun and the Planet also.   The same is the case with the Greek words Eρως and Eρος, one of which I shall be told means *hero* and the other Love ; but which I shall prove must have been originally the same, and each must have had both meanings, before the later Greeks fixed the meaning of every word in their language. These puny criticisms are calculated for nothing but the concealment of truth, and are founded upon a total forgetfulness or ignorance of the principles or history of all languages.   This will be discussed much at large in my second volume, but I have thought it right thus slightly to notice it here, in order to assuage the anger of those small critics, in the mean time.

I think it right to make an observation upon an effect of prejudice, which has operated for the concealment of truth in modern times more than almost any other cause whatever, and it is this : it constantly happens that circumstances are met with, to all appearance closely connected with the history of the Jews, and yet in places so remote from Judea, and so unconnected with it, that our inquirers have not been able to admit even the possibility of any connexion having existed between them ; and, in order that they might not expose themselves to ridicule for what has appeared even to themselves to be absurd credulity, they have, without any dishonest motive, disguised and corrupted words without number.   Thus we find, instead of Solomon,[1] Soleimon and Suleimon ; instead of David, Daoud, and, as the learned Dr. Dorn calls it, Davudze ; and instead of Jacob, *Yucoob*, when the name was clearly meant, in the original, to be what we call Jacob.

---

[1] It is true that, properly speaking, neither person ought to have been called Solomon ; but, as the same name of a person was originally meant in both cases, they ought both to be represented by the same letters.

In a similar manner, in Hamilton's Gazetteer, the word which, in old maps, is properly called Adoni, is changed by him into Adavani, and Salem into Chelam. Vide Book x. Chap. vii. Sec. 8, p. 758.

Another evil consequence has arisen out of this union of ignorance and prejudice, which is, that many works, because they contain passages relating to matters which have been thought to be comparatively modern, have hastily been decided to be modern forgeries, and cast away. The force of this argument my reader cannot now estimate, but he will understand it as he advances in the work; on this account the question respecting the genuineness of almost every writing which has been deemed spurious deserves reconsideration. Now I would produce, as examples of this, some of the books of the Apocrypha, and, for one, the book of *Jesus, the son of Sirach*. Something which has caused them to be thought modern, will be found respecting this personage in my next volume. The fact, as my reader will see, is rather a proof of the genuineness of that book at least. The effect of this prejudice has been totally to prevent any approximation towards the truth. The discoveries which I have made have been effected by pursuing a course diametrically opposite. If not merely as much care had been taken to discover the truth as has been taken to conceal it, but only a *fair* and *impartial care* had been taken, the true character of the ancient histories and mythologies would have been discovered long since. This I beg my reader always to bear in mind. It is of the very first importance. When I began my inquiries, I was the dupe of this superstition. This is an example of the many things which I have stated that I found so difficult to unlearn.

For a very long time, and during the writing of the greater part of my work, I abstained from the practice of many etymologists, of exchanging one letter for another, that is, the letter of one organ for another of the same organ; such, for instance, as Pada for Vada, (p. 759,) or Beda for Veda, in order that I might not give an opportunity to captious objectors to say of me, as they have said of others, that by this means I could make out what I pleased. From a thorough conviction that this has operated as a very great obstacle to the discovery of truth, I have used it rather more freely in the latter part of the work, but by no means so much as the cause of truth required of me. The practice of confining the use of a language while in its *infancy* to the strict rules to which it became tied when in its *maturity*, is perfectly absurd, and can only tend to the secreting of truth. The practice of indiscriminately changing *ad libitum* a letter of one organ for another of the same organ, under the sanction of a grammatical rule,—for instance, that B and V are permutable, cannot be justified. It cannot, however, be denied, that they are often so changed; but every case must stand upon its own merits. The circumstances attending it must be its justification.

I have no doubt that the professed Oriental scholars will nearly all unite to run down my work. The moment I name Irish literature and several other subjects, they will curl up the corner of the lip, as they have often done before. Oriental scholars are no ways different from the remainder of mankind, and it is not likely that they should receive with pleasure the rude shock which this work will give to many of their preju-

dices. It is not likely that they will hear with pleasure, that in all their researches
into the history of antiquity they have been in the wrong track. All this is natural, and
I find no fault with it—it is what I ought to expect,—it is what has happened in almost
every case where an individual has attacked old prejudices. Was it not the case with
Locke? Was it not the case with Newton? some of whose best works did not go to a
second edition in less than thirty years! If these *master minds* were so treated, would it
not be absurd in *me* to hope to escape without illiberal attacks or censures? But there is
one thing of which I must complain in Orientalists,—they always appear to speak on the
subjects to which they have directed their studies with authority, as if they did not admit
of any doubt. But if a person will carefully attend to them, he will find, nevertheless,
that scarcely any two of them agree on a single point.

I must also make another observation which I fear will give offence. Some of them,
I think, prize too highly the knowledge of the ancient Oriental dead languages,—
they seem to think that these once acquired, all wisdom is acquired also as a necessary
consequence. They seem to forget that the knowledge of these languages is of no other
value than as a key to unlock the treasuries of antiquity. I wish to recall this to their
recollection, and to remind them of the story of the Chameleon, that *others can see as
well as themselves.* In making these observations, I hope they will not consider that I
wish to depreciate their Oriental learning; far from it. I think it has not been so much
appreciated as it deserves by their countrymen, and though I think they cannot pretend
to compete in learning with the Jesuits or the priests of the *propaganda*, whose whole
lives were spent in the acquisition of Oriental learning, and almost in nothing else; yet
I think that the proficiency which great numbers of them have made in the learning of
the East, in the midst of the performance of numerous arduous labours of civil or
military life, is above all praise, and has laid their countrymen under the greatest obligation to them.

Before I conclude, I feel myself bound to acknowledge my obligations to my Printer,
Mr. Smallfield, not only for his punctuality and attention, but for many orthographical
and other suggestions, which have greatly improved the work. It would have been still
more worthy of the reader's perusal, if, like the monks in their works, I could have called
a brotherhood to my assistance, or if, like Mr. Bryant,[1] I could have had a learned and
confidential friend to advise and assist me.

After having spent many years upon this work, I have long doubted, as I have already
intimated, whether I should make it public or not. I will not deny that I feel cowardly.
I flatter myself that I am esteemed by many valuable friends, some of whom I may
probably lose by my publication. What shall I gain by it? Nothing.—Posthumous
fame? Perhaps so. Is this worth having? Pliny and Cicero so thought. Is the
work worth publishing? I flatter myself the answer may be *in the affirmative.* Is it
calculated to do good? Is it calculated to reduce the power and influence of priests,

[1] Vide his Preface to the third Volume of the 4to edition.

and to enlighten mankind? It surely is. The discussion alone, supposing I am mistaken, must tend to elicit and to establish truth; and truth is good. Supposing that I believe the publication to be for the good of mankind, am I justified in suppressing it? In this case, am I doing to the rest of mankind as I would wish them to do to me? A sentiment of the great and good Epictetus is so appropriate to my situation and circumstances, that I think I cannot do better than conclude with his words, except, indeed, it be humbly to imitate their author, and to endeavour, as far as lies in me, to profit by his example.

" If you resolve to make wisdom and virtue the study and business of your life, you " must be sure to arm yourself beforehand against all the inconveniences and discourage- " ments that are likely to attend this resolution. I imagine that you will meet with " many scoffs and much derision; and that people will upbraid you with turning phi- " losopher all on the sudden. But be not you affected or supercilious; only stick close " to whatever you are in your judgment convinced is right and becoming: and consider " this as your proper station, assigned you by God, which you must not quit on any " terms. And remember, that if you persevere in goodness, those very men who derided " you at first will afterward turn your admirers. But if you give way to their re- " proaches, and are vanquished by them, you will then render yourself doubly and most " deservedly ridiculous." (Stanhope.) Yes, indeed, I am resolved I will endeavour to imitate thee, immortal slave, and will repeat the words of the modern poet,

> " Steadfast and true to Virtue's sacred laws,
> " Unmoved by vulgar censure or applause,
> " Let the world talk, my friends; that world, we know,
> " Which calls us *guilty*, cannot make us so.
> " With truth and justice support Nature's plan,
> " Defend the cause, or quit the name of man."

GODFREY HIGGINS

SKELLOW GRANGE, NEAR DONCASTER
May 1, 1833

CHAPTER III.

CHAPTER IV.

CHAPTER V.

CHAPTER VI.

CHAPTER VII.

CHAPTER VIII.

CHAPTER IX.

CHAPTER X.

CHAPTER XI.

CHAPTER XII.

CHAPTER XIII.

BOOK VI. CHAPTER I.

CHAPTER VI.

CHAPTER VII.

CHAPTER VIII.

CHAPTER IX.

CHAPTER I

Probable Origin of Numbers and Letters, and of the adoption of the Number 28 for the former, and 16 for the latter——They both preceded Hieroglyphics

1. In the following preliminary observations, I have repeated much of what may be found in my work, entitled THE CELTIC DRUIDS, but it is so much enlarged, and I hope improved, by additional evidence in its support, that I have found it impossible to avoid the repetition to do justice to my subject. Therefore I hope it will be excused: more particularly as I consider that the removal of all doubt respecting the antiquity of the 16 or Cadmean letter system is necessary, several very important consequences being drawn from it, which have an intimate relation to the doctrines developed in the following work.

2. In an inquiry into the origin of nations, or into the early history of mankind, one of the very first objects which offers itself to our attention is the invention of letters and numbers. Of this we have no actual information to which the least attention can be paid; for I suppose no one listens to such stories as those of their invention by Hermes or Mercury in Egypt, or Hercules in Gaul; it is therefore evident that to theory, and to theory alone, we must have recourse for the solution of the difficulty. A bare probability is the utmost at which we can ever expect to arrive in the investigation of this very interesting subject.

3. There is no likelihood that man would be endowed with these sciences at his creation; therefore it follows as a matter of course, that we must suppose the knowledge of them to have been the result of his own ingenuity, and of the gradual development of his faculties. This being admitted, it surely becomes a matter of great curiosity to ascertain the probable line of conduct, and the gradual steps which he would pursue for their acquisition.

4. After he had arrived at the art of speaking with a tolerable degree of ease and fluency, without being conscious that he was reasoning about it, he would probably begin to turn his thoughts to a mode of recording or perpetuating some few of the observations which he would make on surrounding objects, for the want of which he would find himself put to inconvenience. This I think was the origin of Arithmetic. He would probably very early make an attempt to count a few of the things around him, which interested him the most, perhaps his children; and his ten fingers would be his first reckoners; and thus by them he would be led to the decimal instead of the more useful octagonal calculation which he might have adopted; that is, stopping at 8 instead of 10. Thus, 8 + 1, 8 + 2, 8 + 3, instead of 10 + 1 or 11; 10 + 2 or 12; 10 + 3 or 13. There is nothing natural in the decimal arithmetic; it is all artificial, and must have arisen from the number of the fingers; which, indeed, supply an easy solution to the whole enigma. Man would begin by taking a few little stones, at first in number five, the number of fingers on one hand. This would produce the first idea of numbers. After a little time he would increase them to ten. He would, by placing them in order, and making them into several parcels, by degrees acquire a clear idea of ten numbers. He would divide them into two, and compare them with one another and with the fingers on each hand, and he would observe their equality; and thus by varying his parcels in different ways, he would begin to do what we call calculate, and acquire the idea of what we call a calculation. To these heaps or parcels of stones, and operations by means of them, he would give names; and I suppose that he called each of the stones a calculus, and the operation a calculation.

5. The ancient Etruscans have been allowed by most writers on the antiquities of nations, to have been among the oldest civilized people of whom we have any information. In my Essay on *the Celtic Druids*, I have shewn that their

language, or that of the Latins, which was in fact their language in a later time, was the same as the Sanscrit of India. This I have proved not merely by the uncertain mode of shewing that their words are similar, but by the construction of the language. The absolute identity of the modes of comparison of the adjective, and of the verb impersonal, which in my proof I have made use of, cannot have been the effect of accident. The words which I have used above for the first calculation, and for the instruments used in its performance, *calculus*[1] and *calculation*, are Latin, the language of the descendants of the Etruscans, and thus may have been readily derived from the earliest people of the world, whether Asiatic or European. I name this to shew that there is no objection to the names merely because they are the names of a modern language.

6. During the time that man was making this calculation, his attention would be turned to the Sun and Moon. The latter he would perceive to increase and decrease; and after many moons he would begin to think it was what we call periodical; and though he had not the name of period, he would soon have the idea in a doubtful way, and with his calculi he would begin a calculation. He would deposit one every day for twenty-eight days, being nearly the time one moon lived, and is the mean between the time of her revolution round the earth, twenty-nine days twelve hours and forty-four minutes, and the time she takes to go round her orbit, twenty-seven days, seven hours and forty-three minutes. Any thing like accuracy of observation it would be absurd to expect from our incipient astronomer. After a few months' observation he would acquire a perfect idea of a period of twenty-eight days, and thus he would be induced to increase his arithmetic to twenty-eight calculi. He would now try all kinds of experiments with these calculi. He would first divide them into two parts of equal number. He would then divide them again, each into two parts, and he would perceive that the two were equal, and that the four were equal, and that the four heaps made up the whole twenty-eight. He would now certainly discover (if he had not discovered before) the art of adding, and the art of dividing, in a rude way, by means of these calculi, probably at first without giving names to these operations. He would also try to divide one of the four parcels of calculi into which the Moon's age was divided still lower, but here for the first time he would find a difficulty. He could halve them or divide them into even parcels no lower than seven, and here began the first cycle of seven days, or the week. This is not an arbitrary division, but one perfectly natural, an effect which must take place, or result from the process which I have pointed out, and which appears to have taken place in almost every nation that has learned the art of arithmetic. From the utmost bounds of the East, to the Ultima Thule, the septenary cycle may be discovered. By this time, which would probably be long after his creation, man would have learned a little geometry. From the shell of the egg, or the nut, he would have found out how to make an awkward, ill-formed circle, or to make a line in the sand with his finger, which would meet at both ends. The spider, or experiment, would certainly have taught him to make angles, though probably he knew nothing of their properties.

7. A very careful inquiry was made by Dr. Parsons some years ago into the arithmetical systems of the different nations of America, which in these matters might be said to be yet in a state of infancy, and a result was found which confirms my theory in a very remarkable manner. It appears, from his information, that they must either have brought the system with them when they arrived in America from the Old World, or have been led to adopt it by the same natural impulse and process which I have pointed out.

8. The ten fingers with one nation must have operated the same as with the other. They all, according to their several languages, give names to each unit, from one to ten, which is their determinate number, and proceed to add an unit to the ten; thus, ten *one*, ten *two*, ten *three*, &c., till they amount to two tens, to which sum they give a peculiar name, and so on to three tens, four tens, and till it comes to ten times ten, or to any number of tens. This is also practised among the Malays, and indeed all over the East: but to this among the Americans there is one curious exception, and that is, the practice of the Caribbeans. *They* make their determinate period at five, and add one to the name of each of these fives, till they complete ten, and they then add two fives, which bring them to twenty, beyond which they do not go. They have no words to express ten or twenty, but a periphrasis is made use of. From this account of Dr. Parsons', it seems pretty clear that these Americans cannot have brought their figures and system of notation with them from the Old World, but must have invented them; because if they had brought it, they would have all brought the decimal system, and some of them would not have stopped at the quinquennial, as it appears the Caribbees did. If they had come away after the invention of letters, they would have brought letters with them: if after the invention of figures, but before letters, they would all have had the decimal notation. From this it follows, that they must have migrated either before the invention of letters or figures, or, being ignorant persons, they did not bring the art with them. If this latter were the case, then the mode of invention according to my theory must have taken place entirely and to its full extent with the Americans, (which proves my assumed natural process in the discovery

---

[1] In the same way we have *annus* and *annulus*, *circus* and *circulus*.

to be correct,) and in part, though not to the full extent, with the Caribbees : but the same *natural* process must have influenced both, which proves that my theory is rational and probable, and really has a principle of human nature for its foundation. I think the fact of the Caribbees having proceeded by the same route, but having only gone part of the way, is a strong circumstance to confirm my hypothesis.

9. *The natives of Java have the quinary system, or calculation by fives.* And it is remarkable that the word *lima*, which means *five*, means also the *hand*. It appears from Mr. Crawford, that in early times they had only the quinary system, which by degrees they improved to the denary.

10. In support of the idea which I have suggested above relative to the period of twenty-eight days, several circumstances or historical facts of the earliest nations of whom we have any account, may be cited. The almost *universal adoption* of the septenary cycle, which as a *religious ordinance* was certainly not known to the Israelites before the time of Moses, can in no other way be accounted for, and is in itself not of trifling moment. When man advanced in astronomical science, and parcelled the path of the moon in the heavens into divisions, he did not choose for this purpose twenty-nine or twenty-seven, but twenty-eight ; and, accordingly, this was the number of mansions of the moon into which the Lunar Zodiac was divided by the astrologers of Egypt, of Arabia, of Chaldea, and of India. It was not, in my opinion, until a late date, comparatively speaking, that the mansions in India were more correctly divided into twenty-seven ; but I do not state this as a fact, because I think it is not clearly made out which of the two Indian divisions, twenty-seven or twenty-eight, with which we meet, was the most ancient. If it were twenty-seven, I should consider this as a circumstance strongly tending to support the doctrine of Bailly, advocated by me in my Celtic Druids, that a highly civilized nation had formerly existed, of which the learning of India and Egypt was a remnant. I think, from various circumstances which will be noticed in the following work, the reader will be induced to believe that the Indian division was originally the same as those of the Chaldees and Arabians. All the three Zodiacs differ in the figures on them in such a manner as to make it likely that they are not copies from one another, but that they have each given their own figures to the divisions previously made into twenty-eight, from some common source. A learned astronomer, Mr. Bentley, in his work lately published, called *Ancient and Modern Hindoo Astronomy*,[1] states them to have been originally *twenty-eight*.

11. The Chinese also have a Lunar Zodiac divided into twenty-eight parts or mansions, and seven classes, four of which are assigned to each of the seven planets. But they do not, like the Hindoos, the Chaldees, and the Arabians, give them the forms of animals.[2] Here is evidently the same system, which so completely accords with my theory of the first lunar observations of uncivilised or infant man. And the circumstance of their Zodiac being without the forms of animals seems to confirm my idea, that the Hindoo, the Chaldean, the Arabic, and Egyptian Zodiacs, must have been drawn from some common source which originally was without them. There must have been some common reason for all these different nations adopting a Zodiac of twenty-eight divisions. I know not any so probable as the supposed length of the Moon's period. The animals in those Zodiacs are many of them natives of low latitudes : for instance, the elephant of Africa and India—which shews where the persons lived who gave them these animals. The Solar Zodiac, which has not the elephant, shews that it is not the produce of any nation where the elephant was indigenous. If the elephant and camel had been natives of the country where the Solar Zodiac was invented, they would not have been left out, to substitute goats or sheep. The modern astronomer, Mr. Bentley, was told by a learned Mohamedan, that the Lunar Zodiacs originally came from a country north of Persia and north-west of China—*the evident birth-place of the Solar Zodiac*.[3]

12. My opinion on this subject is confirmed by that of the learned Professor Playfair, who says, " It is also to the " phases of the Moon that we are to ascribe the common division of time into weeks, or portions of seven days, which " seems to have prevailed almost over the whole earth."[4]

13. It has been observed by Bishop Doyly, in an attack upon Sir W. Drummond, that the Zodiac is not of Indian extraction, but of Greek, because the animals of which it is composed are not natives of India.[5] The argument seems fair, for it is not credible that the elephant should have been omitted in an Indian composition. The same argument applies to Egypt and the remainder of Africa. But this is by no means a proof that it is the invention of the Greeks. The climate of Samarcand, in Tartary, is the same as that of Greece, and as I consider that the latter is quite out of the question, I maintain that it tends strongly to confirm my hypothesis.

---

[1] P. 5.   [2] Encyclop. Brit.   [3] Bentley on Hind. Ast., p. 251.   [4] Trans. Roy. Soc. Edin. Vol. II. p. 140.

[5] The whimsical sign called Capricorn, in the Indian Zodiac, is an entire goat and an entire fish ; in the Greek and Egyptian, the two are united and form one animal. It has been observed, that this is itself a presumptive proof that the Indian is the older of the two. And the Indian name, as noticed by Mons. Dupuis, (Tome III. p. 332,) is, as he has justly observed, probably taken from a primeval language whence both the Greek and Indian have been formed.

14. The Bishop says,[1] " The first astronomers were not calculators, but observers. Now the Moon is *seen* in the " Zodiac, and her place is obvious to the eye of the most rude observer : the Sun is not *seen* in it, and its place is only " known by comparison and calculation. Thus the division of the Zodiac with respect to the Moon was probably " among the earlier results of attention to the heavenly appearances, and its division with respect to the Sun among " the results comparatively later." This is probable ; but it seems to follow that it could not have been invented by the Greeks till they were far advanced in science ; and if this be admitted, it seems absolutely incompatible with the ignorance of the Greek authors of its origin. Their fabulous nonsense clearly proves their ignorance, but Phornutus and other authors admit it. In several passages, Bishop Doyly[2] states quite enough to prove that the Zodiac could be invented neither by the Chaldeans, by whom he always means the Babylonians, nor by the Egyptians, nor the Greeks. It is absolutely certain that the inventors of the Neros and the Metonic cycle must have been infinitely more learned than any of these three at any period of their histories before the birth of Christ. It is also proved from the number of the pillars in the Druidical circles of Britain, that the builders of them must have been acquainted with these cycles. The Phenniche and Phan, noticed in Chap. V. sect. xiv. Chap VI. sect. xxv. of the Celtic Druids, and the note on it, Appendix, p. 307, prove that the Irish were acquainted with these cycles.

15. It has been observed by Bishop Doyly,[3] " That we may rest assured that the duodecimal division of the Zodiac " was formed in correspondence with the twelve lunations of the year. Since the Sun completed one apparent period " while the Moon completed twelve periods, the distribution of the Zodiac into twelve parts, so as to afford one man- " sion for the Sun during each of the twelve revolutions of the Moon, was by far the most obvious and natural." This is remarkably confirmed by what I have just now observed, and by the well-known historical fact that the Indians, the Chinese, Persians, Arabians, Egyptians, and Copts, had a lunar Zodiac divided into twenty-eight parts, called the man- sions of the Moon, from immediate reference to the Moon's motion through the several days of her period. The universality of this division is a proof of its extreme antiquity.[4]

16. Again the Bishop says, " As has been already mentioned, the appointment of the twelve signs of the Zodiac was " probably a result of some advanced state of astronomy: men must then have been not merely observers of the " heavenly appearances, but must have begun to calculate and compare with some degree of science. Now we have " every reason to know that many nations, the Chaldeans and Egyptians especially, were diligent observers in astro- " nomy from very early times. They partitioned out the sphere into many constellations; noted the risings and " settings of the stars; kept accounts of the eclipses, &c.; and, in many instances, determined the calendar with sur- " prising exactness, considering the means which they employed. But then these means were such as to shew that " they had made little or no advance in the science of astronomy, properly so called. Lalande mentions a number of " particulars respecting the early efforts of the Chaldeans and Egyptians in astronomy, which seem to prove decidedly " that they had made no progress beyond rude observation, although they certainly accomplished, in this manner, " more than could have been supposed. Among other things, he mentions,[5] that the Chaldeans ascertained the dura- " tion of the year by the very artificial method of measuring the length of a shadow of a raised pole. The Egyptians, " too, settled their years merely by observing the risings and settings of stars.[6] He thinks the latter have been unduly " celebrated for astronomical knowledge, because we hear of them only from the Greeks, who were comparatively " ignorant. He expressly calls the astronomy of the Egyptians very moderate, 600 years B. C."[7] All this shews that the science of the Babylonians and Egyptians was but the débris of former systems, lost at that time by them, as it is known to have been in later times lost by the Hindoos.

17. Hyde gives the following account of the lunar mansions among the Arabians: " The stars or asterisms they " most usually foretold the weather by, were those they call Anwà, or the Houses of the Moon. These are twenty-eight " in number, and divide the Zodiac into as many parts, through one of which the moon passes every night : as some " of them set in the morning, others rise opposite to them, which happens every thirteenth night." To these the Arabs ascribe great power.[8]

18. All these superstitions appear to us very foolish, but yet we retain some of them. How many Englishmen believe that the Moon regulates the weather, or rather how few disbelieve it ! A moment's reflection ought to teach them, that if the moon had any influence, it would be exerted regularly and periodically, like that upon the tides. But

---

[1] Remarks on Œd. Jud. p. 189.   [2] Ibid. p. 191.   [3] Ibid. p. 190.

[4] Sir W. Jones's Works, Vol. I. p. 330 ; Hyde on the Tables of Ulug. Beg. ; Bailly's Astron. Anc. pp. 109, 126, 476, 475, 491 ; Goguet, Vol. II. p. 401.

[5] See Lalande's Astron., Vol. I. p. 89.   [6] Ib. 93.   [7] Ib. p. 102 ; Doyley, p. 192.

[8] Hyde in Not. ad Tabulas Stellar. ; Ulugh Beigh, p. 5 ; Sale's Prel. Disc., p. 41.

our prejudices, like those of the Arabian, will not permit us to see the folly of our own superstitions. Over each day and month the Persians and Arabians, as well as all the followers of the Magi or Magians, believed that a genius or angel presided, giving to each day or month the name of one of them. They had the same names as those of the Jews,—Gabriel, Michael, &c. The Jews say they took them from the Persians.

19. If my reader possess my Celtic Druids, I beg him to turn to the first chapter, section vi., and consider what is there said respecting the Lunar Cycle of twenty-eight days, and what is said afterward respecting the antiquity of the Chaldeans or Culdees, the priests of the first of the nations of the world, with their 360 crosses in Iona, their Metonic Cycles, &c., and the information afforded by Mr. Maurice in his Observations on the Ruins of Babylon, p. 29, that the Chaldeans of Babylon had a LUNAR ZODIAC consisting of twenty-eight mansions or houses, in which her orb was supposed to reside during the twenty-eight nights of her revolution, and I think he must be struck with the surprising manner in which my theory is supported by circumstances.

20. Plutarch, in his Treatise *de Iside et Osiride*,[1] states, that the division of Osiris into fourteen parts was a mythological mode of expression for the different phases of the moon, during the increase and decrease of that orb. Mr. Maurice observes, that this "manifestly alludes to the different degrees of light which appear in the moon, and to the "number of days in which she performs her course round the earth."[2]

21. Porphyry distinctly notices the period of twenty-eight days with the Egyptians,[3] which he also observes was a Lunar period.

22. A traveller of the ancients, of the name of *Jambulus*, who visited Palibothra, and who resided seven years in one of the oriental islands, supposed to be Sumatra, states, that the inhabitants of it had an alphabet consisting of twenty-eight letters, divided into seven classes, each of four letters. There were seven original characters which, after undergoing four different variations each, constituted these seven classes. I think it is very difficult not to believe that the origin of the Chinese Lunar Zodiac and of these twenty-eight letters was the same, namely, the supposed length of the Lunar revolution. The island of Sumatra was, for many reasons, probably peopled from China.[4]

23. The Burmas keep four Sabbaths at the four phases of the moon, which shews the cycle of twenty-eight days.[5]

24. Astrologers had also in India another Lunar division. Mr. Colebrooke says, "Astrologers also reckon twenty-"eight *yogas*, which correspond to the twenty-eight nacshatras or divisions of the moon's path."[6] These different astronomical systems are among the oldest of the records of the world which we possess, and come nearest to the time when the science of letters and arithmetic must have been discovered, and tend strongly to support my theory of man's division of time into weeks, and the formation of his first arithmetic from the moon's age.

25. During the time that man was making his observations on the motions of the Moon, he would also be trying many experiments on his newly-discovered circle. He would divide it into two, then into four; thus he would make radii. Whilst he was doing this, he would begin to observe that the Sun was like the Moon, in the circumstance that it was periodical; that it changed continually, and continually returned to what it was before, producing summer and winter, spring and autumn; that after it had blessed him for a certain time with warmth and comfort, and the supply of fruits necessary for his subsistence, it gradually withdrew; but that in a certain number of days it returned, as the Moon had always returned, nearly to its former situation. He would do as he had done with respect to the Moon, collect calculi, and deposit one for every day; and he would find that there were, as he supposed, three hundred and sixty days in a period of the Sun's revolution. About this time, probably, he would hit upon the comparison of his period constantly returning into itself with his circle—the Sun's endless period with his endless circle. He would deposit his calculi about the circumference of his circle. He would divide it by means of these calculi into two parts. He would then halve them cross-ways, thus making four pieces or segments of circles, each having ninety stones. He would halve the nineties, but he could go no lower with halving, than making his ninety into two; therefore after many experiments he would divide his ninety into three divisions, placed in the circumference of the circle, or into thirties: each thirty again he would divide into three, and he would find each little division to contain ten calculi, the exact number of his fingers, and the most important number in his arithmetic, and the whole number would equal the days of a supposed solar revolution—three hundred and sixty days. By this time he must have made considerable progress in arithmetic and geometry. He must have learned the four common rules of the former, and how to make a square, a right-angled triangle, a correct circle, and other useful knowledge in these sciences. To all this there is nothing which can be objected, except it be the assumption, that he would reckon the Sun's period at three hundred and sixty days. But we are justified in assuming this from the well-known fact, that the ancients, even within the reach of history, actually believed the year to consist of only three hundred and sixty days.

[1] P. 93.   [2] Hist. Hind. Vol. I. p. 135.   [3] De Abstin. Lib. iv.; Taylor, p. 145.
[4] Asiat Res. Vol. X. p. 151.   [5] Ibid. Vol. VI. p. 297.   [6] Ibid. Vol. VIII. p. 366.

26. From the circumstances here pointed out, I suppose it to have happened, that the circle became divided into 360 parts or degrees. Philosophers, or perhaps I should say astrologers, now began to exercise all their ingenuity on the circle. They first divided it into two parts of 180 degrees each; then into four of 90 degrees each; then each 90 into three; and they observed that there were in all twelve of these, which afterward had the names of animals and other things given to them, came at length to be called signs of the Zodiac, and to be supposed to exercise great influence on the destinies of mankind. They then divided each of the 12 into three parts, called Decans, and these decans again into two, called Dodecans; then there would be

A Circle consisting of 360 degrees,
2 Semicircles of . . . 180 degrees each,
4 Quadrants of . . . 90 degrees each,
12 Signs of . . . . . . 30 degrees each,
36 Decans of . . . . 10 degrees each, or 24 parts of 15 degrees each, and each 15 into 3 fives or Dodecans, and
72 Dodecans of . . 5 degrees each.

27. In a way somewhat analogous to this, they would probably proceed with the division of the year. As it consisted of the same number of days as the circle of degrees, they divided it into halves and quarters, then into twelve months,[1] and these months into thirty days each; and as each day answered to one degree of the circle, or to each calculus laid in its circumference, and each degree of the circle was divided into sixty minutes, and each minute into sixty seconds, the day was originally divided in the same manner, as Bailly shews. Of this our sixty minutes and sixty seconds are a remnant.

28. The following, I believe, was the most ancient division of time:

1 Year	12 Months	1 Circle	12 Signs
1 Month . . .	30 Days	1 Sign.	30 Degrees
1 Day	60 Hours	1 Degree. . . .	60 Hours
1 Hour	60 Minutes	1 Hour	60 Minutes
1 Minute . . .	60 Seconds	1 Minute. . . .	60 Seconds.

29. About the time this was going on, it would be found that the Moon made thirteen lunations in a year, of twenty-eight days each, instead of twelve only of thirty: from this they would get their Lunar year much nearer the truth than their Solar one. They would have thirteen months of four weeks each. They would also soon discover that the planetary bodies were seven; and after they had become versed in the science of astrology, they allotted one to each of the days of the week; a practice which we know prevailed over the whole of the Old World. A long course of years probably passed after this, before they discovered the great Zodiacal or precessional year of 25,920 years. In agreement with the preceding division, and for other analogical reasons connected with the Solar and Lunar years above-named, and with a secret science now beginning to arise, called Astrology, they divided it by sixty, and thus obtained the number 432—the base of the great Indian cycles. When they had arrived at this point they must have been extremely learned, and had probably corrected innumerable early errors, and invented the famous cycles called the Neros, the Saros, the Vans, &c.

30. In another way they obtained the same result. It seems to have been a great object with the ancient astrologers to reduce these periods to the lowest point to which it was possible to reduce them, without having recourse to fractions; and this might perhaps take place before fractions were invented. Thus we find the dodecan, five, was the lowest to which they could come. This, therefore, for several reasons, became a sacred number. In each of the twelve signs of the Zodiac of thirty degrees each, they found there were six of these dodecans of five degrees, and that there were of course 6 × 12 = 72, and 72 × 6 = 432, in the whole circle, forming again the base of their most famous cycle. It was chiefly for these reasons that the two numbers five and six became sacred, and the foundations of cycles of a very peculiar kind, and of which I shall have occasion to treat much at large in the course of this work.

31. After man had made some progress, by means of his calculi, in the art of arithmetic, he would begin to wish for an increased means of perpetuating his ideas, or recording them for his own use, or for that of his children. At first, I conceive, he would begin by taking the same course with right lines marked on a stone, or on the inner rind of a tree, which he had adopted with his calculi. He would make a right line for one, two lines for two, and so on until he got five, the limit of one hand. He here made a stop, and marked it by two lines, meeting at the bottom thus, V: after this he began anew for his second series thus, V and I or VI, and so on till he came to VIIII, the end of the

[1] What induced the ancient Egyptians and Chaldees to throw two signs into one, and thus make only eleven, it is now perhaps impossible to determine.

second series, and he then made two fives thus, $\begin{smallmatrix}V\\\Lambda\end{smallmatrix}$ X, or ten. This was with him a most important number, and became in process of time of the greatest importance also, as we shall hereafter find, in the concerns of mankind. It was called the perfect, or complete number, evidently from completing the number of the fingers of the hands. When man began to follow up his arithmetic to his number of twenty-eight, he proceeded with this as he had done with his calculi and number ten, and added units thus, XI, XII, &c., until he arived at twenty, and then he wrote two tens thus, XX. After this he again proceeded in the same way till he arrived at his XXVIII. Nothing can be more simple than this, and this is what we find among the Latins, the same nation in which we found our calculi, and the Etruscans, and it is what (except with respect to the X) was used, according to General Vallancey,[1] by the ancient Irish, among whom indeed, if any where, we may expect to find the first traces of civilized man. How the X came to be varied, or its use left off by the Irish, I know not; but it was probably from a religious motive similar to that which made the Hebrews substitute a letter for their Jod, of which more hereafter.

32. General Vallancey observes, That from the X all nations began a new reckoning, because it is the number of fingers on both hands, which were the original instruments of numbering: hence יד (id) ied in Hebrew means both the *hand* and the number *ten*;[2] and in the same manner the word *lamb* means *hand* and *ten* with the Buddhists of Tartary, whose first arithmetic stopped at ten; and *lima* means *hand* and *five* with the Malays, whose first arithmetic stopped at five. We can scarcely believe that this coincidence of practice is the effect of accident.

33. Among the Hebrews the name of the perfect number, i. e. ten, was Jod or I, their name of God. Among the Arabs, it was Ya, the ancient Indian name of God (as in the course of this work I shall prove), and among the Greeks it was I or EI, the same as the Hebrew name of God. By the Etruscans, whatever might be its name, it was described by the X or T, and for the sake of an astrological meaning I have no doubt the Greeks contrived that the X should stand for 600. But relative to this I shall have much to say hereafter.

34. In the Chinese language the twenty-fourth radical, the Shih, is in the shape of the cross thus +, and means ten. It also means *complete, perfect, perfectly good*.[3] Thus the same system is universally found.

35. What I have said respecting the origin of numbers, and the importance which I have attached to them, must not be considered merely a theory, totally without support from history, for the historical accounts of most nations shew us that the superstitious regard to numbers was carried to almost an inconceivable length. I think the doctrines of Pythagoras may be considered as among the oldest of any which we find in the Western world, and whatever they were, thus much we know, that they were all founded on numbers. We also know that the astronomical system which is confessed to have been obtained by him in the East was the true one, in its great features—the revolving motions of the planets; then have we not reason to believe that these very numbers, which we find recurring every where in the Eastern and Western systems, were the same? We find the numbers five and six continually recurring in both systems, as the basis of the sacred 60, 360, 3600, and 432, 4320, &c. Then how can we doubt that they became *sacred* for the reasons which I have given? There must have been some cause for the effect, and what other can be assigned than that which I have supposed?

36. We will now return to our incipient astronomers' twenty-eight calculi.

37. I feel little doubt that the system I have here developed was the origin of arithmetic, that it preceded the art of writing, and was its cause or precursor. It led the way to this most useful discovery. Mr. Bryant supports my opinion so far as to allow that the use of arithmetic must have been known long before letters.

38. After man had found by this combination of right lines the art of writing down the few limited ideas appertaining to these twenty-eight signs for numbering the days, he would begin to entertain the desire of extending the art of writing to other objects. For this purpose he would naturally try to use these same right lines. This experiment we have in full view in the Irish Oghams, and it is particularly exemplified in an Irish inscription called the Callan inscription, which is given in the Celtic Druids, in the second table of Alphabets. The total unfitness of this kind of writing for the conveyance of complicated chains of reasoning, or indeed of ideas generally, is there exhibited. Dr. Aikin says, " fifteen lines are required to express the first five letters of this alphabet, and this may be translated in five dif-" ferent ways; consequently nothing can be more uncertain than its true meaning." Here I think we find the origin of the Ogham writing and of the Northern Runes. Thus these simple lines at angles would constitute the first letters or figures or signs used by mankind for the conveyance of ideas. This is confirmed by the result of our researches into the earliest inscriptions and letters on ancient monuments.

39. The Oghams, or secret alphabets, of the Irish, all consist of right lines, and the ancient Runes of the same; and it would be very easy to select several complete alphabets, consisting of nothing but right lines, at various angles, from

---

Collect. de Reb. Hib. No. XII. p. 571.   [2] Vall. Col. Vol. V. p. 177.   [3] Morrison's Chinese Dict. p. 299.

the letters on the oldest Greek and Etruscan coins. The old Runes were inscribed on sticks or staves of wood, cut or shaved so as to expose three plain surfaces, and on these the right-lined letters were engraved with a stylus. These are what are alluded to by Aulus Gellius,[1] when he states the laws of Solon to have been engraved *axibus ligneis*, which have been mistranslated *table* or *board*. These two Latin words will bear no such construction.[2] They mean the staves or stems of trees used by the ancient Druids, as well as by the Greeks. And on them were inscribed the letters of the Ionian Greeks, which Herodotus says were originally composed of right lines.[3]

40. These inscribed stems were in part the origin of a vast variety of interesting allegories respecting trees, letters, and science, particularly among the Arabians and a numerous class of oriental philosophers called Gnostics.

41. The Greek system of notation is nearly the same as the Latin. The numbers are as follow: I, II, III, IIII, Π, ΠΙ, ΠΙΙ, ΠΙΙΙ, ΠΙΙΙΙ, Δ, ΔΙ, ΔΙΙ, ΔΙΙΙ, ΔΙΙΙΙ, ΔΠ, ΔΔ 20, ΔΔΙ 21, ΔΔΠ 25, ΔΔΔ 30, &c. The principle is evidently the same, and all the letters consist of right lines easily made axibus ligneis; and though the ten, the sacred number, does not consist of an X, it does of an equilateral triangle, Δ, which I have no doubt was adopted for a mysterious reason, hereafter pointed out.

42. Pliny the Elder says, that the Ionian letters were the oldest of Greece, and that the most ancient Grecian letters were the same as the Etruscan; and as he produces the example of an ancient inscription to justify his assertion, it seems more worthy of attention than most of the idle, gossiping stories which he has collected together. We have just now seen that the most ancient of the Greek and Italian alphabets have a strong tendency to the right-lined practice. Now the question very naturally arises, who were, and whence came, the Ionians? This is a question which it is very easy to ask, but very difficult to answer,—a question which will be most intimately connected in the answer with some very abstruse and profound oriental doctrines into which I must enter in the course of the following work, and which will require much previous investigation. I shall, therefore, beg to suspend it for the present, but the reader will please to bear it in mind.

43. My reader is not to suppose that I imagine the process of the invention of letters took place literally by one pair of persons as I have here represented. What is meant is only to shew generally the nature of the process. The steps by which the result was obtained it is not possible, in the nature of things, to describe with accuracy. Various persons would from time to time be employed, or perhaps a society, on whom the natural causes which I have pointed out, or other causes similarly natural, would operate to produce the effect; for example, the number of the fingers of the hand creating the first class of numbers, the two hands the second class, &c.

44. From General Vallancey I learn a fact which strongly confirms my theory. He says, "The Phœnicians had nu-"merals before they had letters. Their first numerals were similar to the Irish Ogham, marks consisting of straight, "perpendicular lines, from one to nine, thus: I, II, III, IV, &c. *Ten* was marked with an horizontal line—; and "these they retained after they had adopted the Chaldean alphabetic numerals."[4]—"There cannot be a stronger proof "that numerals preceded letters, than the Hebrew word ספר *Spr, sepher*, which properly signifies to number, to "cipher: numeration, numbering: but after numerals were applied as literary characters, the same word denoted, as it "does at this day, a scribe, a letter, a book, a literary character."[5] Bates says, the word *sepher* has all the senses of the Latin *calculus*. Mr. Hammer, of Vienna, found in Egypt an Arabic manuscript which is written in Arabic words, but in a character which is evidently the same as the tree Ogham of Ireland. See Plate I. Fig. I. The word Ogham or Agham is Indian, and means secret or mysterious.

45. From various circumstances it is not improbable that these right-lined figures had originally the names of trees. In the infant state of society, so large a number of letters or signs for an alphabet as twenty-eight, would be rather an incumbrance than an advantage. It would take a long time for man to discover the advantage of a correct sign for every vocal sound which he was capable of uttering, and he probably made a selection of sixteen of them: the first sixteen, perhaps. In our names of numbers there is not now the least appearance of the names of the letters or trees:

[1] The words of Gellius are, *In Legibus Solonis, illis antiquissimis, quas Athenis, axibus ligneis incisæ erunt.* Some learned men, not understanding the nature of the ancient staves on which letters were accustomed to be inscribed, have wished to substitute *assibus* for *axibus*. Had they succeeded, they would have completely changed the sense of the author, and have concealed the interesting fact, that the ancient Irish and the Greeks used the same mode of writing. The emendations of Editors have done infinite mischief to science. I have no objection to emendations suggested in notes, but scarcely ever ought they to be carried into the text. By emendations, as *authentic records*, the Old and New Testaments have, in innumerable instances, been rendered doubtful as to their real meaning.

[2] See Celtic Druids, Chap. I. Sect. xxxi.   [3] Ibid. Sect. xxxi. xxxii.
[4] Vall. Col. Vol. V. pp. 183—186.   [5] Ibid. p. 175.

and the names of many of our numbers may be found in almost all languages. So that if they ever had the names of trees, a change must have taken place at a very early period.

46. The first notice which we have of letters being called by the names of trees is found in one of the alphabets of the ancient Irish, called the Beth-luis-nion. It consists of the seventeen letters in the table, in column No. 4, in the order in which they stand in the Irish grammar, with the meaning of each placed opposite to it:

1	2	3	4	5	6	7
	B	Boibel		B	Beith	Birch
	L	Loth		L	Luis	Quicken
	F	Foran		N	Nuin	Ash
	S	Salia		F	Fearan	Alder
	N	Neaigadon		S	Suil	Willow •
	D	Daibhoith		D	Duir	Oak
	T	Teilmon		T	Tinne	Furze •
	C	Casi		C	Coll	Hazel
	M	Moiria		M	Muin	Vine
	G	Gath		G	Gort	Ivy
	P			P	Poth	Dwarf Elder •
	R	Ruibe		R	Ruis	Elder
	A	Acab		A	Ailim	Elm
	O	Ose		O	On, or Oir	Spindle
	U	Ura		U	Ux	White-thorn or Heath
	E	Esu		E	Eactha or Eadha	Aspen
	J	Jaichim		J	Jodha	Yew

Column No. 1 is another Irish alphabet, of which the letters had a different shape and different names, but it was in number the same.

47. In the following Table the column No. 1 contains the names of the letters of the ancient Samaritan and Hebrew or Chaldee alphabets. No. 2 contains the Samaritan letters. No. 3, the Hebrew or Chaldee letters used after the Babylonish captivity. No. 4 contains the Hebrew or Chaldee final letters, opposite to their powers of notation. No. 5 contains the powers of notation of the Samaritan, the Chaldee, and the Greek letters. No. 6 contains the Greek letters. In No. 7, the asterisks shew the letters first brought to Greece from Phœnicia by Cadmus. No. 8 contains the names of the Greek letters. No. 9 contains the Celtic Irish letters in English characters, placed opposite to the letters in the other alphabets to which they correspond. No. 10 contains the names of the Celtic Irish letters; and No. 11, their meanings.

• Logan, Scottish Gael, Vol. II. p. 390.

ALPHABETS

1	2	3	4	5	6	7	8	9	10	11
Aleph	ℵ	א		1	A α	•	Alpha	A	Ailm	Elm tree
Beth	ℶ	ב		2	B β	•	Beta	B	Beth	Birch
Gimel	ℷ	ג		3	Γ γ	•	Gamma	G	Gort	Ivy
Daleth	ℸ	ד		4	Δ δ	•	Delta	D	Duir	Oak
He	ℷ	ה		5	E ε	•	Epsilon	E	Eadha	Aspen
Vau	ℸ	ו		6	F	•	Digamma	Fv	Fearn	Alder
Zain		ז		7	Z ζ		Zeta			
Heth		ח		8	H η		Eta			
Teth		ט		9	Θ θ		Theta			
Jod		'		10	I ι	•	Iota	I	Jodha	Yew
Caph		כ	ך	20	K κ	•	Kappa	C	Coll	Hazle
Lamed		ל		30	Λ λ	•	Lambda	L	Luis	Quicken
Mem		מ	ם	40	M μ	•	Mu	M	Muin	Vine
Nun		נ	ן	50	N ν	•	Nu	N	Nuin	Ash
Samech		ס		60	Ξ ξ		Xi			
Oin		ע		70	O ο	•	Omicron	O	Oir	Spindle
Pe		פ	ף	80	Π π	•	Pi	P	Pieth Bhog	Dwarf elder
Tzaddi		צ	ץ	90	Ϛ		Episemon bau			
Koph		ק		100			Επσημαυ ϛαυ			
				100	P ρ	•	Rho	R	Ruis	Elder
Resh		ר		200						
				200	Σ σ	•	Sigma	S	Suil	Willow
Shin		ש		300						
				300	T τ	•	Tau	T	Teine	Furze
Tau		ת		400						
				400	T υ	•	Upsilon	U	Uath* / Heath / aspirate	White-thorn

		Initials	Finals							
Caph	K	כ	ך	500	Φ φ		Phi			
Mem	M	מ	ם	600	X χ		Chi			
Nun	N	נ	ן	700	Ψ ψ		Psi			
Pe	P	פ	ף	800	Ω ω		Omega			
Tzaddi	Z	צ	ץ	900	⁊		Sanpi			

* No doubt the Tau or Teine ought to be the last letter, but the Uath has been obliged to be put here instead of at the sixth place, to make room for the Digamma, an anomaly, in the Greek language, not understood.

48. In the treatise called The Celtic Druids, I have proved, by a great variety of circumstantial and positive evidence, that the sixteen or seventeen letter-alphabet here given of the Irish, in its principle or system, was the same as those of the ancient Samaritan, the Phœnician, the Hebrew or Chaldee, the Persian, the Etruscan, the Greek, and the Latin. I have shewn that, however numerous the letters of these languages may be at this day, different learned men, without any intercourse with one another, or any idea that an universal system prevailed among them, have reduced them to, or proved that they were originally, only sixteen or seventeen in number. And these are, in all of them, the very same letters, as is ascertained by their having the powers of notation in a manner so similar as to put the identity of the principle or system out of all question.

49. Bishop Burgess, in his Introduction to the Arabic Language, without having the least idea of the general system which I have pointed out, has confirmed it in a very remarkable manner.[1] He has shewn that the Arabic had originally only seventeen letters, including the Digamma. The near approximation of the powers of notation, and the similarity of the names of the letters, shew that they are the same as the Irish, the Greek, and the Hebrew.

Arabic		Hebrew	Greek		Irish
1	Alef	Aleph	Alpha	1	Ailm.
2	Ba	Beth	Beta	2	Beth.
3	Gim	Gimel	Gamma	3	Gort.
4	Dal	Daleth	Delta	4	Duir.
200	Ra	Resh	Ro	100	Ruis.
300	Shin	Shin	Sigma	200	Suil.
90	Sad	Tzadi			
400	Ta	Tau	Tau	300	Teine.
70	Ain	Oin	Omicron	70	Oir.
80	Fa	Pe	Pi	80	Pieth-Bhog.
20	Caf	Caph	Kappa	20	Coll.
30	Lam	Lamed	Lambda	30	Luis.
40	Mim	Mem	Mu or Mui	40	Muin.
50	Nun	Nun	Nu or Nui	50	Nuin.
6	Wau	Vau	F, formerly Vau, pronounced U, then V, afterwards Digamma	6	Fearn.
5	Ha	He	Epsilon	5	Eadha.
10	Ya	Yod	Iota	10	Jodha.
			Upsilon		Uath.

50. The Shin, Shin, and Sigma, I have substituted for the Sin, Samech, and Xi, which are in the Bishop's table, and which is evidently a mistake, the Greek X, being one of the new, and not one of the Cadmean or ancient Greek letters. This mistake is a most fortunate circumstance, because it proves that the Bishop did not know the principle of these alphabets which I have been explaining, and therefore cannot be suspected of having made his original letters to suit it. And it also renders it impossible for any one to say, that he has been contriving his seventeen primary letters to make them suitable to the Irish, whose letters he probably looked on with too much contempt to have considered them even for a single moment. This adds very materially to the value of his opinion.

51. The powers of notation are the same in all the ancient alphabets, with their increased number of letters, *till they get to the nineteenth letter, Ra or Resh,* when a variation takes place, which I have shewn probably arose in after times from the coming into use of the Greek Digamma.[2]

52. The following is the table of the Arabian system of numbers given by Bishop Burgess:

Alif	1		Ya	10	10	Kaf	100	19
Ba	2		Caf	20	11	Ra	200	20
Gim	3		Lam	30	12	Shin	300	21
Dal	4		Mim	40	13	Ta	400	22
Ha	5		Nun	50	14	Tha	500	23
Wav	6		Sin	60	15	Rha	600	24
Za	7		Ain	70	16	Dhal	700	25
Hha	8		Fe	80	17	Dad	800	26
Ta	9	9	Sad	90	18	Da	900	27
						Ghain	1000	28

---

[1] See Celtic Druids, Ch. VI. Sect. xxvi.   [2] See Ibid.

53. Here, I think, is as triumphant a proof of the truth of the system as can well be desired. Here is the exact number of the Calculi 28, and here they are interwoven into the decimal calculation in a very wonderful manner; the 1000 exactly answering to the number of 28 figures. If I be told that the present Arabic alphabet is, comparatively speaking, modern, I reply, however the forms of its letters may have been changed by the Califs, the principle, the system, is evidently ancient, both of the letters and figures. No one can for a moment believe that they *invented a new alphabet* and *system of notation* which, by mere accident, coincided with all the old systems of the world; the idea is ridiculous; it involves a contradiction in terms.

54. Some persons have pretended that the Irish selected their letters from the Latin and Greek. How came they to select the identical letters which Cadmus brought to Greece, and no others? This at once disposes of this pretence, and proves to a certainty, that, if the Irish received their letters from Greece, they must have received them before the time of Homer; if from Syria, before the time of Moses, whose Pentateuch contains twenty-two letters. This carries back Irish literature to a time surprisingly ancient.

55. The alphabets of ancient nations have attracted the attention of several learned men at different times and places, and they have endeavoured, with very great care, to ascertain the original number of letters in those alphabets. Nearly all their investigations have terminated in demonstrating the same facts, viz. that the different systems of letters agree within one; that they all amount to sixteen or to seventeen letters; that they have a striking similarity in their names; and that the correspondent letters have the same numerical powers; and, from incidental circumstances, it is very evident that the learned men to whom I allude, Morton, Chishull, Burgess, &c., have had no intention of making the different alphabets systematically agree with one another. This I have most clearly proved in my essay on THE CELTIC DRUIDS, to which, for the complete proof of the truth of these assertions, I must refer.

56. I now beg my reader to refer back to page 5, to the account given by the ancient traveller *Jambulus* of the alphabet of Sumatra, and I think when he has read it with attention he will be obliged to believe that it must have been the same in system as the Arabic, and both to have come from the first system of notation founded on the supposed age of the Moon; and I also beg him to consider the tree alphabet found in the Arabic language by professor Hammer in Egypt; in fact, an Arabic treatise *written in an Irish Ogham letter*. Before I finish I shall trace these Arabians to the borders of China.

57. The Sanscrit alphabet consists of not less than fifty letters, but the number of simple articulations may be reduced to twenty-eight, (the number of the Arabic and of my first numbers,) five vowels and twenty-three consonants. May not the original twenty-eight numerals have been adopted by the Indians for their letters, and sixteen only of them selected by the Arabs? And may not this have been the reason why the difference between the Arabic and Sanscrit appears to be greater than that between the Sanscrit and all the other Western languages? if indeed there be this difference, a fact which I very much doubt.

58. Though I am ignorant of the Sanscrit language, a close attention to great numbers of its proper names had made me strongly suspect that its system of letters was originally the same as that of the Western nations. The following two passages which I have discovered will shew that I had good grounds for my suspicion. Colonel Wilford says, " The Sanscrit alphabet, after striking off the double letters, and such as are used to express sounds peculiar to that " language, has a surprising affinity with the old alphabets used in Europe, and they seem to have been originally the " same."[1] In another place Col. Wilford says, " I have observed that gradual state of decay in the Sanscrit language, " through the dialects in use in the Eastern parts of India down to the lowest, in which last, though all the words are " Sanscrit more or less corrupted, the grammatical part is poor and deficient, exactly like that of our modern languages " in Europe, whilst that of the higher dialects of that country is at least equal to that of the Latin language. From " such a state of degradation no language can recover itself: all the refinements of civilization and learning will never " retrieve the use of a lost case or mood. The improvements consist only in borrowing words from other languages, " and in framing new ones occasionally. This is the remark of an eminent modern writer, and experience shews that " he is perfectly right. Even the Sanscrit alphabet, when stripped of its double letters, and of those peculiar to that " language, is THE PELASGIC, and every letter is to be found in that, or the other ancient alphabets, which obtained " formerly all over Europe, and I am now preparing a short essay on that interesting subject."[2]

59. This is confirmed by Col. Van Kennedy, who says, " In all essential respects, the Greek, Latin, and Sanscrit " alphabetical systems are similar."[3]

60 In THE CELTIC DRUIDS I have pointed out a very curious circumstance of a Sanscrit sentence being found at Eleusis. This is confirmed by an observation of Col. Van Kennedy's, that there are 339 Sanscrit words in the poems of Homer.[4] I shall resume the subject of the Sanscrit language hereafter.

---

[1] Asiat. Res. Vol. X. p. 152.   [2] Ibid. Vol. VIII. 8vo, p. 265.   [3] Res. into the Orig. of Lang., p. 131.   [4] Ibid. p. 209.

61. If more than sixteen or seventeen letters be found in the Amiclean or Eugubean inscriptions, I think they prove, either that these inscriptions are forgeries, or that their date has been mistaken. For after the detection of the frauds of the rascals *Ennius* and *Fourmont*, I think they cannot be permitted to overturn the positive assertion of Pliny, that Cadmus brought only sixteen letters, supported as the assertion is by the varieties of authorities and reasonings which I have given, and the independent examination and opinions of learned modern inquirers, that all these languages are reduceable to sixteen letters. Before the conclusion of this work the reader will find, that consequences of the most important nature follow the reduction of the different written languages to one system, consisting of that number of letters.

62. The decimal system of which the last table (Sect. 52) consists, has every appearance of being founded on the original simple twenty-eight units. After civilization had advanced, a higher notation than the twenty-eight would be wanted, and the Arabians appear to have adopted the decimal system, keeping as near as possible to the ancient twenty-eight letters, as a close examination will prove; for what is the 20 but two *tens*, the 30 but *three* tens, the 100 but *ten* tens, the 1000 but *one hundred* tens? Perhaps it may be said, that the coincidence of the decimal numbers to the twenty-eight calculi is accidental. But is it accidental that the powers of notation in the Arabic, Hebrew, Greek, and Irish letters are the same till they come to nineteen; that is, similar in eighteen instances in succession? It is a very singular ACCIDENT that in each of the eighteen cases the letters and numbers should agree in the different languages. It is also a most fortunate *accident* which should cause the elements of the Irish names of letters, the Muin, Nuin, &c., as I shall now shew, to be found in the Arabic. By a careful comparison of the names of the different letters in the Irish Beth-luis-nion, with the Samaritan, Hebrew, and Greek, it will appear almost certain that they have all been called after the trees which now grow in the latitude of England, or else that the trees have been named after them.[1] But it is proper to observe, that great allowance ought to be made for the change necessarily arising from the lapse of perhaps thousands of years. It seems to me impossible to doubt the original identity of the Samaritan, the Greek, and the Hebrew letters; and how wonderfully are they changed! Then if we do not find the English names of trees differ more from the Irish names of letters, and the names of the Greek, Hebrew, and Samaritan letters, than the alphabets differ from each other, we shall have a similarity as great as, perhaps greater than, can be expected. It is not at all probable that the similarity should continue till this time in all the letters: very few will be sufficient to establish the fact, if they only possess a sufficient degree of similarity. The Arabic system of notation or arithmetic, which is so intimately connected with their system of letters, is believed, by all Orientalists, to have come from India. I trust I shall be able to prove that they came together from India.

63. The Aleph, Alpha, and Ailm, are not strikingly similar; but there is a very obvious resemblance between the words Ailm and Elm; the first letter of the word Ailm being pronounced as we pronounce the A in our A, B, C, or in the word *able*.

64. The Beth or Beith of the Samaritan and Hebrew is the identical Beth or Beith, the Birch-tree of the Irish. Pliny calls Betulla the Birch, a Gaulish tree. In one of the dialects of Britain, the Welsh, it is called Bedw.

65. In the next three names of letters, the similarity is lost, except that they begin with the same consonant.

66. The Digamma forms an exception to all rules.

67. The Jod, or Iod or Iota, and Iodha and Yew, are all clearly the same, or as near as can be expected. This will be immediately found on pronouncing the Y in the word Yew by itself, instantly followed by the other letters.

68. The name of this tree is, as I have shewn in my Celtic Druids, one of the names of Jehovah, *Ieu*. It is considered by our country people to be in its wood the most durable of all trees.

69. There is nothing more which is striking till we come to the Mem, Mu, Muin, vine. The *vine* may have readily come from the word Muin—the letter M being dropped for some unknown cause; or the M may have been prefixed to the Vin, and be what Hebrew grammarians call *formative*; or it may have been prefixed for a reason which will be given hereafter.

70. The Nun is the Nu and Nuin without difficulty, though it has no relation to the Ash in sound or in letters. Yet the Nun of the Hebrew is evidently the same as the Irish tree Nuin.

71. The Oin and the Irish Oir have a similarity, but have no relation to the Spindle or the Oir, except in the first letter of the latter name.

72. The Samaritan and Hebrew Resh is the Irish Ruis.

73. The Shin and Tau are only similar in the first letters to the Suil and Teine.

74. The similarity, it is true, is not found in many of the sixteen letters, but there is sufficient similarity to prove

---

[1] It has been observed in the CELTIC DRUIDS, that the vine which is found among the trees in this alphabet is neither of Indian nor of British origin; for though it grows in both, it is common in neither; but it is indigenous in the same latitude in the country which I suppose was the birth-place of the human race, that is, between 45 and 50 degrees of North latitude, where all the other trees of this alphabet are to be found.

that the Irish have not merely culled letters out of the Roman alphabet and given them the names of trees: for although the examples of similarities are now become oddly and unsystematically arranged, yet their present situation can have arisen from nothing but an original identity, destroyed by various accidents. If the Ailm have nothing to do with the Aleph, it is evidently the same as the English Elm; and if the Beth or Beith has little or nothing to do with the English Birch, it is evidently identical with the Hebrew Beth. How came an Irish tree to bear the name of a Hebrew letter? Thus again, the Jod, Iod, Iota, Jodha, and Yew, are *all* nearly allied, and the Jod and Jodha identical. Again, how came this Irish name of a tree and a letter of their alphabet to be the same as the Hebrew name of this letter? Can any one look at the Greek Mu, the Irish Muin, and the English vine, and not be convinced (all the other letters and circumstances considered) that they are the same? Vine is evidently the three last letters of the Irish *Muin*.

75. The Irish name of the Ash, Nuin, is the same as the Hebrew and Samaritan *Nun* and the Greek *Nu*.

76. Lastly, the Samaritan and Hebrew Resh is unquestionably the Irish *Ruis*, the Elder. Again I ask, how came these Hebrew letters to bear the name of Irish trees? Did the Irish literati understand Hebrew several thousand years ago, and call their trees after Hebrew and Samaritan letters on purpose to puzzle the learned men of the present day? There is no way of accounting for these extraordinary coincidences and circumstances except by supposing an original alphabet called after trees, and changed by accident in long periods of time. Bigots may ridicule this, but they cannot refute it.

77. It is a singular circumstance, that though the Irish names of letters, for instance the Mem or Muin, and the Beith, are the Irish names of trees, they are not the *known* Hebrew names of trees. It is impossible to believe that the Asiatics *by accident* called their sixteen letters after the Irish names of trees. I think it is pretty clear that the Hebrew letters, and of course the Greek or Cadmean taken from them, were originally called after the Beth-luis-nion of the Irish, *or after some language whence that was taken.*

78. The ancient Rabbis had a tradition, that the names of the Hebrew letters had the meaning of the names of different trees, and General Vallancey attempts to specify them. But he does not seem to have succeeded. His information is taken from the old Jewish writers, who appear to give rather what they surmise than what they found in the synagogue copies of the Pentateuch. But their opinion is very important indeed, as a record of an old tradition. It seems that the Rabbis had received a tradition that the names of their letters had the meaning of the names of trees, which they wished, but wished in vain, to *verify.*

79. The General quotes the authority of Bayer, " that each of the Chaldean or Hebrew letters derives its name " from some tree or shrub; as ב *Beth*, a thorn; ד *Daleth*, a vine; ה *He*, the pomegranate; ו *Vau*, the palm; י *Jod*, " ivy; ט *Teth*, the mulberry-tree; ס *Samech*, the apple-tree; פ *Pe*, the cedar; ר *Resh*, the pine," &c.[1]

80. There is, as I have said, the strongest probability that the art of figuring or of arithmetic took precedence of the art of writing. The figures would evidently be the first wanted, and probably, in the way I have stated, the names of trees were given to them. The Mexicans had the knowledge of figures—the decimal calculation, but not of letters: the natives of Otaheite had the same.[2] From the use of the first ten or fifteen figures for numbers of the calculi, a transition to letters would not be very difficult, and probably took place and gave them their names of leaves. And I think it very probable that (what is commonly called) the accidental discovery of letters, may have been the original cause of the Old World having attained so superior a state of refinement and civilization—notwithstanding some persons may think this a cause too small for so large an effect. It would, I conceive, operate by geometrical progression.

81. From all these considerations, there is a strong probability that the first alphabet was denoted by the names of trees; and, from a passage of Virgil's, one might be induced to believe that the leaves themselves were actually used:

> Arrived at Cumæ, when you view the flood
> Of black Avernus, and the sounding wood,
> The mad prophetic Sibyl you shall find
> Dark in a cave, and on a rock reclined.
> She sings the fates, and in her frantic fits
> The notes and names, inscribed TO LEAVES COMMITS.
> What she commits to leaves, in order laid,
> Before the cavern's entrance are display'd.
> Unmoved they lie: but if a blast of wind
> Without, or vapours issue from behind,
> The leaves are borne aloft in liquid air;
> And she resumes no more her museful care,

---

[1] Pref. and Prospect. for an Irish Dict. by Gen. Vallancey; Davies' Cel. Res., p. 305.   [2] Astle, p. 182.

Nor gathers from the rocks her scatter'd verse,
Nor sets in order what the winds disperse.
Thus many, not succeeding, most upbraid
The madness of the visionary maid,
And with loud curses leave the mystic shade.

Æn. Lib. III. ver. 445.

But, oh! commit not thy prophetic mind
To flitting leaves, the sport of every wind,
Lest they disperse in air our empty fate:
Write not, but, what the powers ordain, relate.

Lib. vi. L. 116—129.

82. I think if any sense is to be made of this poetical description, we must understand that each leaf had or was a letter.

———————— foliisque notas et nomina mandat.
Quaecumque in foliis descripsit carmina virgo,
Digerit in numerum, atque antro seclusa relinquit:
Illa manent immota locis, neque ab ordine cedunt:
Verum eadem verso tenuis cum cardine ventus
Impulit et teneras turbavit janua frondes,
Nunquam deinde curo volitantia prendere saxo,
Nec revocare situs, aut jungere carmina, curat:
Inconsulti abeunt, sedemque odere Sibyllae.

It seems pretty clear that if whole words had been written, each word upon a leaf, and these words in verse, the inquirer might easily have put them together. From this it may fairly be inferred, that if letters were written at all, there could only have been one on each leaf.

83. In the religious rites of a people I should expect to find the earliest of their habits and customs, and the above passage relating to this Celtic Sibyl can mean nothing except that the leaves themselves were used either as letters (each leaf standing for a letter) or the names of letters, each written on a leaf which the wind might easily blow away. But it is probable that the leaves themselves may have been used, and that this practice may have been derived from the letters having the names of trees, and may have been adopted for the sake of mystery, which we know was greatly affected in all the old religions. The way in which this passage is connected by Virgil, a native of Cisalpine Gaul, with the Celtic or Cimmerian Sibyl of Cuma, where he died and was buried, *and the misletoe of the Druids*, carries it back to a period antecedent to any ancient Italian history which we possess. I cannot help believing that it has a close connexion with the Irish practice of calling their letters after the names of trees.[1]

84. There have been authors who have wasted their time in inquiries into the mode in which the inventor of the alphabet proceeded to divide the letters into dentals, labials, and palatines. There surely never was any such proceeding. The invention was the effect of unforeseen circumstance—what we call accident; and when I consider the proofs, so numerous and clear, of the existence of the oldest people of whom we have any records, the Indian Buddhists in Ireland, and that in that country their oldest alphabet has the names of trees, I cannot be shaken in my opinion that the trees first gave names to letters, and that the theory I have pointed out is the most probable.

85. I suspect that, some how or other, our practice of calling the parts of our books *leaves* came from this custom. The bark of the Irish birch-tree, the Papyrus, or the *roll* of skin, had no leaves.

86. From Mr. Davies I learn that the Welsh bards had a similar alphabet to that of the Irish. He says, "The Anti-
" quarians claim an alphabet of their own, which, in all its essential points, agrees with that of the bards in Britain.
" 1 It was Druidical. 2 It was a magical alphabet, and used by those Druids in their divinations and their decisions
" by lot. 3. It consisted of the same radical sixteen letters which formed the basis of the Druidical alphabet in Britain.
" 4. Each of these letters received its name from some tree or plant of a certain species, regarded as being, in some
" view or other, descriptive of its power, and these names are still retained.

87. "So far the doctrine of the British Druids is exactly recognized in the *Western island*. The same identical system
" is completely ascertained and preserved. Yet there are circumstances which point out a very ancient and remote
" period for the separation of these alphabets from each other " Mr. Davies then observes, that " among other things
" the order of the letters is different." He says, there are three kinds of writing; and adds, "The third, which is said

---

[1] If it were consistent with the object of this dissertation, I think I could prove by strong circumstantial evidence, that Virgil was initiated into the order of Druids or Chaldeans or Culdees. I am not the first person who has held this opinion. I believe it was held by the great ROGER BACON, but being too profound for his ignorant compeers, like the circular orbits of Pythagoras, it was turned into ridicule.

" to be *(no doubt)* the remains of an old *magical* alphabet, is called *Beth-luis-nion na Ogma*, or the alphabet of *magical*
" or *mysterious letters*; the first *three* of which are *Beth*, *Luis*, *Nion*, whence it is named."[1] In my CELTIC DRUIDS I
have maintained that our islands were peopled by two swarms from a common Eastern hive, one coming by Gaul, the
other in ships through the straits of Gibraltar. This account of the appearance of the two alphabets of Ireland and
Britain seems to support *my system*.

88. I am quite of opinion that the Welsh are right ; but that not only *their* letters, but all letters, were once magical
and astrological, and known only to the sacred caste of priests for many generations. I am of opinion that our common
playing cards once formed an astrological instrument of the same kind.

89. The Greek, the Hebrew, and the Arabic systems are evidently the same, though in their latter letters, from
some unknown cause, a change takes place, and the powers of notation vary ; but they do not vary till they get to the
nineteenth letter, as observed above, where the hundreds begin ; and in the mode of variation after it takes place the
same system is continued. From all this I am inclined to think, that the old Arabic language, which I shall shew is
really Hebrew, as all the roots of Hebrew and Chaldee words are found in it, was a language before the present Hebrew, Greek, Sanscrit, and Deva Nagari letters were invented ; that the first SYSTEM of arithmetic was that now
possessed by the Arabians, *though not invented by them in their present country at least* ; and that the inventors of the
first alphabet made it of right lines and lines joined at angles, and called its component parts after certain names of
numbers, which, at that time, probably, in the first lost language, had the names of trees ; and that from this came all
the allegories of Gnosticism, respecting the trees in the Garden of Eden, held by the Valentinians, Basilideans, Barde-
sanians, &c, allegories which have been acknowledged by very learned men to have been the produce of a very ancient
oriental system, in existence long previous to the birth of Christ—such as that of the tree bearing twelve sorts of fruit,
one in each month, &c., &c. The alphabet was the wood or the forest—the tree was the system—the upright stem, the
אלף Alpha, the Chaldee name for the trunk of a tree (as I am informed by General VALLANCEY).—The words were
the branches—the letters were the leaves growing out of the stem or branches—and the fruits were the doctrines and
knowledge of good and evil, learned by means of receiving these doctrines from letters. In this manner a prodigious
number of allegories were invented. In the old Irish, the words *wood* and *alphabet* are described by the same letters—
Aus, which also signify both a tree and knowledge.

90. Taliesin, a Welsh bard of the sixth century, has written a poem on the battle of the trees, which is yet in
existence, and in which he compares the words in the secret letters of the Welsh to twigs or branches of trees. The
subject is the battle between good and evil, light and darkness, Oromasdes and Arimanius. Mr. Davies thinks this is
an allusion to the original system.[1]

91. Apollonius Rhodius says, that when Orpheus played on the lyre, the trees of Pieria came down from the hills to
the Thracian coast, and ranged themselves in due order at Zona.[1] This is a Grecian allegory, of the same kind, perhaps
copied from the Orientals. Virgil has given an account of an elm-tree, which Æneas found growing at the side of the
road to the infernal regions, loaded with dreams. This tree had the name of the elm, the first letter of the alphabet,
the alpha, the trunk which bears all the rest, loaded with every kind of science and learning :

> Full in the midst of this infernal road
> An elm displays her dusky arms abroad :
> The god of sleep there hides his heavy head ;
> And empty dreams on every leaf are spread.

92. The following extract from a work of a Chaldean Rabbi is given by Kircher : Arbor magna in medio Paradisi,
cujus rami, *dictiones*, ulterius in ramos parvos et folia, quæ sunt *literæ*, extenduntur : the great tree in the garden of
Eden, whose leaves were letters, and whose branches were words.

93. It is agreed by all authors that the Druids pretended to perform various operations by means of sticks, sprigs, or
branches of trees, which are commonly called magical. Some account of this may be seen in Tacitus *de Moribus
Germanorum*. But, in fact, all the old native authors are full of these accounts : and it is impossible to read or consider them for a moment, without seeing the extraordinary similarity of the practice to that of Jacob with respect to
the sheep of Laban, named in Gen. xxx. 37. The rod of Moses, and that of Aaron throwing out sprouts, &c., afford
additional instances of similarity

94. The letters of these magical alphabets, all which answered to the leaves of trees, were engraved on the surface of
the rods, or sticks, cut square or triangular, to which the straight and simple form of the letters was peculiarly
favourable. Hence the letters and the alphabets came to be considered magical, and the whole system of writing
compared to a tree bearing leaves and fruits. And hence, also, came the celebrated *Sortes Virgilianæ*, which had this

---

[1] Celtic Rev. p. 275.   [1] Ibid., p. 274.   [1] Argonaut, Lib. I. ver. 29.

name from the belief that Virgil was a Chaldean magician or astrologer.   He was of the order of men who were banished by Marcus Aurelius, under the name of Mathematici and Chaldei, of whom I shall have much to say hereafter.

95. From these leaf letters, or letters having the names of trees, and from the right-lined letters inscribed on the boles of trees, the ancients, particularly the Arabians, invented their almost innumerable allegories, an account of which, much more detailed than I think it necessary to give, may be found in the fifth volume of Gen. Vallancey's *Collectanea Hibernica*.

96. On this subject General Vallancey observes, " And hence the Sephiroth-tree, or tree of numbers, of the Caba-
" listical Jews: and this tree contained ten names, viz corona, sapientia, prudentia, clementia, gravitas, ornatus, tri-
" umphus, confessio laudis, fundamentum, regnum.   The number ten seems to have been fixed on because, as relating
" to numerals, ten was called perfection, as from thence all nations began to count anew.   For this reason the Egyptians
" expressed the number ten by the word *mid*, that is, perfection; and the Irish call it *deag*, a word of like meaning:
" and for this reason the Chaldeans formed the word *jod*, or number ten, by an equilateral triangle thus Δ,[1] which was
" the symbol of perfection with the Egyptians.   The Egyptians doubled the triangle thus X, and then it became a cross
" of St. Andrew, or the letter X or ten, that is, *perfection*, being the perfect number, or the number of figures on both
" hands: hence it stood for ten with the Egyptians, Chinese, Phœnicians, Romans, &c., and is so used with us at this
" day.   The Mexicans also use the same figure in their secular calendars.   The Tartars call it *lumh*, from the Scythian
" *lumh*, a hand, synonymous to the *jod* of the Chaldeans, and thus it became the *name of a cross*, and of the high priest
" of the Tartars; and with the Irish, *luam* signifies the head of the church, an abbot, &c.   Ce qu'il y a de remarkable
" c'est que le grand prêtre des Tartares port le nom de *lama* qui, en langue Tartare, signifie *la croix*: et les *Bogdoi* qui
" conquirent la Chine en 1644, et qui sont soumis au *dalai-lama* dans les choses de la religion, ont toujours des *croix*
" sur eux, qu'ils appellent aussi *lamas*."[2]

97. It has been observed by General Vallancey, that " it seems natural and universal to man to have entertained
" the idea of numbering from his fingers, and it does not appear extraordinary that, when man led an agrestic life, (as
" the Chaldeans and Scythians, the parents of numerals, did,) and had occasion to carry numbers higher than the fin-
" gers on his hands, that, before he had assigned arbitrary marks for numbers, he should have adopted the names of
" trees—objects immediately surrounding him, some of which grew more luxuriantly than others—and that having
" invented an arbitrary mark for such a number, he should give it the name of the tree which stood for it: and thus,
" having formed a numerical alphabet, these numerals at length became letters, as I have shewn in the preceding pages,
" still bearing the original names."[3]

98. I think it very probable that from the use of leaves as letters, the hieroglyphics may have taken their rise.   Sup-
pose letters in the shape of the leaves of trees to have been made of thin laminæ of gold or tin, and strung on a cord, something like the tripods of the ancient Peruvians, a magical letter would thus be invented which could be deciphered by none but those who understood the secret; and it might be made extremely complicated by the addition of leaves not in the alphabet, or by the forms of other things, between the words or real letters, which would not, to the initiated, increase the difficulty of reading it, but rather the contrary, and at the same time would render it perfectly unintelligible to those not initiated.   After some time these leaf letters would be drawn on plain surfaces, and again; with a little more experience, all other kinds of objects would be added to increase the difficulty and mystery, until the leaves would be lost sight of altogether, and the hieroglyphics come to what we find them.

99. Much has been said respecting the picture-writing of the Mexicans, sent to Cortes, by the Emperor's messengers. They made drawings of the horses, ships, &c., because they had never seen such objects before, and of course their language could convey no idea of them.   But this had no resemblance, in reality, to the Egyptian hieroglyphics. The intention of the ancient hieroglyphics was to enable one person to convey to another information relating to something already known to both, and of which, therefore, they possessed an idea common to both.   But the pictures of Mexico were intended, by the persons drawing them, to convey a new idea respecting something wholly unknown to the beholder, for whose use they were intended, and of which, consequently, he had never formed an idea before.

100. Mr. Astle, on the Origin and Progress of Writing, supports my opinion that hieroglyphics were not the origin of writing.[4] " The subject of this chapter (Origin of Letters) hath engaged the attention and perplexed the sagacity

---

[1] I know not where Gen. Vallancey got his triangle for the Chaldaic ten, but the triangle was the ten of the Greeks.

[2] Voyage de la Chine, par Avril, Liv. iii. p. 194.   [3] Vall. Col. Heb. Vol. V. p. 187.

[4] Ch. ii. p. 10.

" of many able and judicious persons for many centuries: some of the most respectable writers have reasoned upon
" erroneous principles, and, by their works, have obscured the true path which might have led to the discovery of
" letters. Mons. Fourmont, Bishop Warburton, and Mons. Gebelin, have endeavoured to shew that alphabets were
" originally made up of hieroplyphic characters; but it will presently appear that the letters of an alphabet were essen-
" tially different from the characteristic marks deduced from hieroglyphics, which last are marks for things and ideas,
" in the same manner as the ancient and modern characters of the Chinese; whereas the former are only marks for
" sounds; and though we should allow it an easy transition from the Egyptian hieroglyphics to the characteristic
" marks of the Chinese, which have been demonstrated by Du Halde and others to be perfectly hieroglyphic, yet it
" doth not follow that the invention of an alphabet must naturally succeed these marks. It is true there is a sufficient
" resemblance between the Mexican picture-writing, the Egyptian hieroglyphics, and the Chinese characters; but these
" are foreign to alphabetic letters, and, in reality, do not bear the least relation to them."

101. From a consideration of certain historical facts which cannot be denied, I think I can shew that hieroglyphics
did not precede the invention of letters, as has been generally imagined.

102. It has been observed by almost every philosopher who has visited the pyramids of Egypt, that they are placed
exactly to face the four cardinal points of the compass, from which astronomers know that their builders must have
possessed a very considerable skill in the science of astronomy. This affords a strong presumption that the art of
writing must have been known to their builders; they can scarcely be believed to have possessed so much science as
the fact seems to require, without it. Now, in the next place, it may be observed, that there is not on any one of the
larger pyramids the least appearance of any thing like a hieroglyphic. This fact, combined with the evident knowledge
possessed by their builders of astronomy, justifies the presumption that they were built before hieroglyphical writing
was known, though perhaps after our mode of writing was discovered. Though the two facts may not be considered
to amount to a decisive proof, I maintain that taken together they afford strong presumptive evidence. On the subject
of hieroglyphics,

103. Mr. Maurice says, " Before we quit the pyramids, I must be permitted to make one reflection. On no part
" of the three great pyramids, internal or external, does there appear the least sign of those hieroglyphic sculptures
" which so conspicuously and so totally cover the temples, the obelisks, and colossal statues, of Upper Egypt. This
" exhibits demonstrative proof, that at the period of the construction of those masses, that kind of hieroglyphic
" decoration was not invented, for, had that sacerdotal character been then formed, they would undoubtedly not have
" been destitute of them." [1]

104. Some of the smaller pyramids have been built out of the ruins or stones of temples on which have been
hieroglyphics. This shews these particular pyramids to be of modern date. No doubt they have been tombs. All
our churches are tombs; but they are also places of worship.

105. After the celebrated Mr. Belzoni and Lieut.-Col. Fitzclarence had with great labour obtained admission to the
inner chamber of the second in size of the pyramids, Mr. Belzoni discovered, from an inscription, that it had been
opened before by one of the Califs. It appeared that the contents of the sarcophagus which he discovered had been
thrown out, and were lying on the floor at its side. He preserved part of them, which were bones, and brought them
to England, never letting them go out of his own possession. These were carefully and publicly examined by several
of the first natural philosophers in London, who, to their great surprise, discovered that they were the remains of an
animal of the Beeve kind.[2] Respecting these facts there never has been any dispute. They are perfectly notorious;
and neither Mr. Belzoni, nor the natural philosophers, had any theory, interest, or system, to influence their judgments
respecting them. Part of the bones may yet be seen, where I have seen them, at the house of Lieut.-Colonel
Fitzclarence.

106. I suppose no one will doubt that these were the bones of an exemplar of the famous God Apis, on which some
foolish and absurd priest-ridden king must have been weak enough to lavish such immense labour and treasure. This Bull
Apis has been proved by many philosophers to have been the Bull of the Zodiac; in fact, the Sun, when he entered
the sign of the Bull in the Zodiac, at the vernal equinox, concerning which I shall shortly make some observations,
and of which I shall have much to say in the following work. This being, for the sake of argument, at the present
moment admitted, it follows that the Zodiac must have been invented before one of its signs, the Bull, can have become
the object of adoration.

107. Now I think no person can believe that the Zodiac, with its various signs, and divided and subdivided as
it necessarily is into many parts, was invented before writing. Then it seems to follow, if this be admitted, that

[1] Maur. Ant. Hind. Vol. III. p. 95.   [2] Class. Journal, Vol. XXI. p. 16.

the art of writing must have been known before the pyramids, the burial-place of the Bull, were built; and as the hieroglyphics were not invented till after the building of the pyramids, it seems to follow, that they were not invented till after the invention of writing, consequently that they were not, as it has generally been thought, the origin of writing.

108. The intimate relations between India and Egypt, in some ancient period, cannot possibly be doubted. But what is the reason that there are no hieroglyphics in India? The days of the week are dedicated in each to the same Gods. The adoration of the Bull of the Zodiac or the Sun, in the sign Taurus, is common to both. The same Zodiac is, with a trifling variation, also common to both. Then how came they not both to have hieroglyphics, if hieroglyphics were invented before writing, or figures in arithmetic?

109. I conclude that this connexion or intercourse (which will be proved over and over again in the course of the following work) must have existed before the invention of hieroglyphics, and must also, in a great measure, have ceased before their invention, because, if the contrary had been the case, hieroglyphics would, in some degree, have been common to the two countries. When the religion went from one to the other, the hieroglyphical system, if in existence, would have gone also. From which it almost necessarily follows, that hieroglyphics are, comparatively speaking, a modern invention.

110. In their endeavours to prove that hieroglyphics were the originals or parents of letters and writing, philosophers have done every thing which ingenuity could devise to establish the fact; but I think their arguments are founded upon no sufficient data, and therefore have always appeared to me unsatisfactory. For my theory I have a great number of facts and circumstances which cannot be disputed, and I think my arguments founded upon them are sound.[1]

111. From the whole investigation there can be no doubt, whether the leaf alphabets were the origin of hieroglyphics or not, that the latter were invented after the discovery of the art of writing, and were a secret and sacred system invented for the purpose of concealing certain religious or historical truths from the vulgar eye.

112. Before I quit this subject I think it proper to recall my reader's attention to the observation, that whether Egypt was colonized from India or India from Egypt, it is very clear that the intercourse of colonization must have ceased before hieroglyphics were invented, or they would certainly have been found among the priests in both countries. And it is also probable that they were invented after Moses and the Hebrew tribe left Egypt, or we should have found some notice of them in the books of Moses—the Pentateuch. I only say *it is probable*; but it is by no means certain.

113. M. Denon[2] has given a description of a painting in one of the tombs of the kings of Thebes, in which, among other things, is described the sacrifice of a child, and he has these words: " Incense is offered to him in honour of these " victories; a priest writes his annals, and consigns them to sacred memorial. It is, therefore, proved, that the ancient " Egyptians had written books: the famous *Thoth* was then a book, and not inscribed tablets sculptured on walls, as has " been often supposed. I could not help flattering myself that I was the first to make so important a discovery: but I " was much more delighted when, some hours after, I was assured of the proof of the discovery by the possession of a " manuscript itself, which I found in the hand of a fine mummy that was brought to me. In its right hand, and resting " on the left arm, was a roll of papyrus, on which was the manuscript." And here, with respect to this MS., end Mons. Denon's observations; not another word of what became of the papyrus, or of the language or letters in which it was written. But in plate LV. a short description is given of a manuscript found upon a papyrus which, I suppose, is meant for it. Nothing can be made out from it except that it reads from right to left. In plate LVI. is a copy of another manuscript equally unintelligible, which was found upon a papyrus in a mummy.

114. In consequence of the attempts of Mr. Bankes to prove, from the style of building of the temples, confirmed by the explanations of M. Champollion, that many of the hieroglyphics on them relate to the Roman emperors, these manuscripts cannot be made use of to prove the antiquity of letters; but they prove that letters were known before the hieroglyphics on the temples, in which these mummies were found used, or, that hieroglyphics were continued in use after the invention of the art of writing, and along with it. I have no doubt that some of the buildings in Egypt were erected by the Roman emperors, that many others of them were partly their work, and that still more of them were erected by the monarchs of Egypt after the time of Cambyses. But the sepulchres, and many parts of the temples of Thebes and other temples of Upper Egypt, I have no doubt existed before Cambyses's time, and escaped his fury.

115. I have *no doubt* that the churches of Notre Dame and St. Denis, at Paris, were both the workmanship of the

---

[1] The text of the Bible itself proves that letters were well known in the time of Moses, therefore the author does not attempt to refute the arguments of those who pretend that he was the inventor of them.

[2] Vol. III. Chap. xx. Aik. Trans. p. 70.

middle ages, but I think that the Zodiac on the former, and the Mosaic pavement found in the latter, of a Bacchanal filling a wine vessel, were the works of an age long prior.

116. My view of the subject is considerably strengthened by an observation of Belzoni's, I think, that some of the smaller pyramids have been built with stones, the ruins of old temples, on which are hieroglyphics broken and worked into them. And Mons. Denon found in the bases of some of the oldest pillars at Medinet Abou, near Thebes, Carnac, numerous hieroglyphics. On which he asks, " How many preceding ages of civilization would it require to be able to " erect such buildings? How many ages again, before these would have fallen into ruins, and served as materials for " the foundations of other temples, which themselves have existed for so many centuries?" The questions are interesting : but it would not require a long period for the buildings to have decayed, if the *decay* were produced by the violent hand of a *Cambyses.* On the subject of *the Origin of Letters,* I must refer my reader to the first chapter of THE CELTIC DRUIDS, where it is treated of at large.

CHAPTER II

Etymology and its Use

1. A LITTLE time ago two systems of Etymology were published, one by the Rev. Mr. Whiter, of Cambridge, and the other by Mr. James Gilchrist. The former called his work *Etymologicon Universale.* It is very large, and was printed by the University of Cambridge, at its press. The object is to prove that ALL the words of every language may be traced back to the word *Earth.*[1] Great learning and ingenuity are displayed, and incredible labour must have been bestowed on the production. The work of the latter gentleman, entitled *Philosophic Etymology,* is not so large, and in its doctrine is directly in opposition to the former. Mr. Gilchrist contends, that CL, CR, LC, or RC, is the primary simple word of written language, and that all the *copia verborum* are merely varieties and combinations of that one simple word, or rather sign.

2. He says, "There is nothing arbitrary about language. All the dialects, as Hebrew, Celtic, Greek, Latin, &c., are " essentially but one language. They have such diversities as may be termed idioms ; but with all their circumstantial " varieties, they have substantial uniformity : they proceed on the same principles, and have the same origin. The " philosophic grammar and lexicography of one, is in reality that of all."[2] In this I perfectly agree with Mr. Gilchrist: I also agree with him that there is a wide difference between a scholar and a philosopher, but I cannot think with him that men in the first instance conversed wholly by *looking,* not by *listening ;* and that the different modifications of sound, emitted from the mouth, were a subsequent step of improvement and conveniency, not contemplated when the mouth was first applied to curiologic signs; which application of the mouth was not anticipated when these signs were first employed, and which signs were not contemplated when hieroglyphics were invented : that thus, in the use of signs, men were led on step by step from hieroglyphics or picture-writing to curiologics, an abridged form of the preceding ; from curiologics engraved or drawn on any substance, to the expression of them by the mouth ; and from the expression of them by the mouth to the eye, to the expression of them by sound to the ear, enabling men to converse in the dark as well as in the light. If I understand Mr. Gilchrist, he supposes both hieroglyphics and letters to have been invented before speech. This does, indeed, surprise me very much. On reflecting on the first situation of man, I cannot help believing that he would not perceive his mate many minutes before he would utter some kind of a sound or sounds, which would soon grow into monosyllabic words.

3. I lay it down as a principle, that there were no such persons as *Aborigines* (as this word is often used)—that man did not rise into existence by accident, or without cause : but that he was the effect of a cause, a creation, or formation by a Being possessing power. This admitted, I consider that he must have acquired his knowledge of speech either by experience, or have such knowledge of it given to him by his Creator, as would enable him to communicate his ideas to his mate, and that in each case his Creator gave him the power of using his voice at the same time that he gave him the power of using his teeth and other organs. And if I admit the former, that man acquired *by experience* the

---

[1] See his Prelim. Diss. p. 77.   [2] Phil. Etymol. p. xx.

use of speech, which of course every philosopher will do, I must think that both Mr. Whiter and Mr. Gilchrist go to causes far too scientific to account for it. Speech would be very much the effect of circumstance—there would not be any thing like system in its first formation.

4. Mr. Gilchrist's idea that the first letters arose from *curved* lines, seems to me not only not to be so probable as that of *right* lines, which I have unfolded above, but it seems to me to be actually against all the *early* and, what is more, *well*-founded historical facts which we possess. For the fact *of the oldest letters and figures which we possess consisting of right lines* does not depend, alone, on the relations of writers, but upon their existing at this day on old coins and stones: in which latter fact, therefore, we cannot be deceived. I think my theory *as rational* as Mr. Gilchrist's; in addition to which, I have the evidence of the oldest inscriptions, and, as I have shewn, analogy also, on my side; for the higher we ascend the more *right-lined* the alphabets become.

5. As I have just now said, if I understand Mr. Gilchrist aright,[1] he maintains that hieroglyphics were invented before letter-writing. We know of only one nation, the Egyptians, among whom hieroglyphics ever existed, and I think I have proved that they were not invented by that nation till after letters were in use. I make no account of the Mexican paintings, for our information respecting them is too scanty to draw any conclusions from them; and that part of our information which we do possess, namely, the painting of Cortes's ships and horses, is against hieroglyphics being the origin of letters, rather than in favour of it; because, as I have observed above, these drawings were not to convey ideas of known things, but ideas of unknown things—new things, and new ideas.

6. The plan or theory proposed by Mr. Whiter and Mr. Gilchrist, of resolving all words into one, or nearly into one, seems to me to be not only contrary to the analogy of nature, but to clog their philological researches with insuperable and unnecessary difficulties. Let us for a moment consider man to have newly started into existence, by what means does not signify, and to exist alone. I will suppose this to have happened in a beautiful valley in upper Tibet, about latitude 35, at the vernal equinox, a fig-tree growing near him, bearing its early crop of fruit. The olfactory nerves, I think, would speedily draw him to the tree; he would take of the fruit, and what is vulgarly called instinct would teach him to put it into his mouth and to eat it. Before he ate the fig, he would have become master of several ideas; but as he would have had no occasion to communicate them, he probably would not have made any effort at speech.

7. We will now suppose this being, in the state of about twenty years of age, to awake and find a beautiful young woman close to him and touching him. Instinct would again begin to move him; love would ensue and its consequences, and very speedily afterward the wish to communicate happiness; for it is all a mistake that man is born to *evil* as the smoke flies upwards. He is born to good, and all his NATURAL tendencies are to good, though he possesses passions and is a fallible being, from which circumstances partial evil has naturally arisen. Much time would not elapse before he would, in order to communicate happiness, wish to call the attention of his mate to something—perhaps to partake with him of some fruit—and, to awaken this attention, an attempt to speak or make a sound would be made; after this, another and another attempt; and thus a few monosyllabic words would be formed, such as were easiest made by the organs of speech, and thus from this kind of process the first language would arise. It would probably consist of arbitrary sounds, not formed in any way from one another or from one word; and had Mr. Gilchrist tried to trace all language to these primitive words, he would, I think, have perfectly succeeded.

8. But after some time a second race of original words would have arisen, which would a little increase the first language, and which must not be neglected. The voice of love would have been heard, and would not have been heard in vain. A child would make its appearance, and would have a little language of its own, which would never be lost, which would grow with its growth, strengthen with its strength, and which we actually find yet existing in every language on earth—exemplified in the words Ma, Mater, Moder, Muder, Pa, Pater, Fater, Fader, &c., &c.; and thus from these two sources came to be formed the first original language. It would probably consist of monosyllabic roots, which would be very simple: and to these, I think, all language may be reduced.[2]

9. It is necessary to guard myself from being misunderstood in what I have said above, that the language of the eyes was not the *first* language, because I believe that it *was*; but what I mean is, that this language would last but for a very short time:—a very few hours, perhaps only a few minutes. The first man and his mate, surrounded as M. Cuvier has shewn that they probably were, by animals, formed long before, young and old, in every state, and, like these animals, possessing animal sensations, and being, in addition, imitative creatures, would in a very few hours, perhaps minutes, perform all the animal functions, exercise all the animal powers, do as other animals did: and until they

---

[1] Philosophic Etymol. p. 33.

[2] I wish Mr. Gilchrist had undertaken the task of so reducing them, for no man is better qualified. Had he and Mr. Whiter attempted to re-form or re-discover the ancient first language or collection of words, and their systems had been left unfinished, other learned men would have continued them, perhaps, till they had been completed.

had thus exercised these powers, perhaps the eyes, the most eloquent eyes, would continue to be the medium of the communication of ideas; but eloquent as they are, they would not continue to be so much longer; for an attempt to emit sound would be made, and thus would arise the first words.

10. I beg my reader to attend to the beings of the animal creation. He cannot suppose man, though inferior to them in many respects, to be much inferior to them in those which we are considering. How long is it before the dove or the partridge learns to call its mate with the voice of love, or its young about it, when it has found a nest of ants? Has man any language more significant than that which these birds possess? When the hen chucks her first chickens around her, can any language be more intelligible?[1] and she has no profound philosophers to make grammars for her, or divines to write creeds for her. Can the animal man be supposed to have been worse endowed than these fowls? I think not. Grant but these advantages of the animals around him, and it is all which I ask for my system, and I think it must be established.

11. If these philosophers had undertaken to prove that all languages might be resolved into one, consisting of a certain number of monosyllables or roots, they would have undertaken to prove what I am persuaded is perfectly true; and they would, I doubt not, have succeeded in their undertaking. But I think neither of their theories tenable. If their theories had been well founded, the abilities which they have displayed would not have failed to establish them. But though I think they have both failed, I beg to be understood not to have any wish to detract from their merit. Nor do I wish to enter into controversy with either of them. I should not have noticed their treatises but that I felt it would be a great reflection on myself to let it be supposed that I was ignorant of them.

12. I now take my leave of these two gentlemen, to whom, with Bacon, Hobbes, Locke, and Tooke, we are all under great obligation. I enter not more into their systems, because my object and theirs is different. Their systems are only auxiliary to mine. I feel perfectly confident that it will not be long before some ingenious man, with the assistance of Mr. Tooke, Mr. Whiter, and Mr. Gilchrist, will, upon the foundation which I have laid, erect the edifice of the true philosophy of grammar. If in this I am mistaken, I shall be only like hundreds of my predecessors.

13. Perhaps it will be said that my system depends too much on the explanation of words. The observation does not cause me much uneasiness. For if my system be founded in the truth, it must shew itself in the words of all languages, in an infinite variety of ways; in which case the observation will never do it any injury, or be able to prevent its reception when it comes to be known. If it be not true, it will fall, as others have done before it, whether depending on explanation of words, etymology, or not. As among the ancient Greeks and Romans, and the modern Europeans, we have a great number of systems, in like manner there was the same variety among the Orientalists; but I feel confident I shall be able to shew that they all flowed from one fountain; that one refined and beautiful system was not only the foundation, but that, however varied the systems which branched from it might be, yet in many respects the parent, the original, is every where to be seen, even in the Western systems of the present day.

14. It will probably also be objected by those who wish not to discover truth, but to throw discredit upon this work, that I often make etymological deductions in one word from two languages. This would have been more plausible if I had not first proved, most *unquestionably*, (as I believe,) the intimate *connexion*—indeed, I feel I am quite justified in saying the absolute *identity*, of the Western and Oriental languages in a very remote period. And this observation will apply to all the languages in which the sixteen-letter system has obtained. It is impossible to doubt that one original language has extended over all the old world, which is the reason that we find Hebrew and Hindoo words in Britain, and words of the most remote countries and climates intermixed, in a manner in no other way to be accounted for. All the sixteen-letter languages are but dialects of an original language.

15. But my practice of explaining words from what are at this day two languages, will be objected to by enemies of inquiry, because it has a tendency to discover hidden truths. But if there have been one language upon which several have been founded or built, what is so natural as that the roots of a compound word should be found in several of them? Suppose two colonies emigrated, the one to Europe and the other to Africa, from Chaldea, and that each carried a certain word; this word might change, by being compounded with other words, in both cases, so as to become in each case a new word. Is it not evident that the roots of the word may reasonably be sought in either or both the new languages?

16. In etymological inquiries a mere corruption no doubt may sometimes be admitted; but this must be done with great caution, and when there is strong extra evidence to support it. For proof of this, our own language affords innumerable examples. Of this kind of corruption I need to produce only one instance from our Liturgy—*prevent* us in all our doings. Here we have not a change in one or two radicals only, but in a whole word. Again in the Latin word *hostis*.

---

[1] The common barn-door hen has at least two clear and distinct words, one which she commonly uses to her chickens, and another when she calls them to her on having discovered any unexpected hoard of food.

17. Etymology may be considered in another point of view. What is a written word but an effect—an effect arising from an unknown cause? What we want is, to find the cause—to ascertain if there were one original written language —by what steps any given word descended from that first parent to its present state. In many cases this may be difficult, in others it may be impossible to make it out; but is there not the same difficulty with translations? Does not one word often mean several different and often opposite things? There is scarcely a word in Parkhurst's Hebrew Lexicon which has not four or five different meanings; and how do we proceed to find out which, in any case, is the one intended, but by comparing it with the context? Most words may be derived from several others, but the variety or uncertainty, great as I admit it is, is generally not greater than in mere translations.

18. Sir William Jones says, "I beg leave, as a philologer, to enter my protest against conjectural etymology in his- "torical researches, and principally against the licentiousness of etymologists in transposing and inserting letters, in " substituting at pleasure any consonant for another of the same order, and in totally disregarding the vowels." I most heartily join in the protest, though I think etymology the grand and only telescope by means of which we can discover the objects of far distant and remote antiquity. But Sir William afterward says, "When we find, indeed, the " same words, letter for letter, and in a sense precisely the same, in different languages, we can scarce hesitate in " allowing them a common origin."[1] To shew how little he attended to his own sound and sensible remarks respecting the changing of letters, in a page or two preceding he had been observing, that the word Moses ought to have been Musah, not Moses. It is written in the Hebrew משה Mse. I cannot admit this to be either Musah or Moses. If, in compliance with modern authority, I admit the u to be supplied, I cannot admit the ה e, the fifth letter, to be changed into א a, the first, and the letter ה h, without authority, to be added. I have shewn in my Celtic Druids, that the Hebrew system of letters is the same as the English and Greek; and when it is desired to write the Hebrew letters משה Mse in the English characters, the same letters which the order and the power of notation shew to be identical, ought to be used, and no others. The practice of substituting one consonant for another can very seldom be admitted; it can be subjected to no rule, but in every instance where such a liberty is taken each case must stand upon its own merits, and be left to the judgment of the reader. I do not mean to say that a letter may never be changed, but it ought never to be changed except for a very good reason; and when it is so changed, the doctrine to be deduced from it will stand on a much worse foundation than if it had not been so changed. But after all, the practice of changing letters cannot possibly be denied. For instance, do we not see sovereigns in India sometimes called Nawab, and sometimes Nabob—the w and b interchanged; and so on in other cases?

19. But uncertain as the nature of etymological science is supposed to be in researches into the early learning of the world, it is the best fountain from which we can draw. Let those of a different opinion pursue their own plan, and continue to believe the histories of Greece that Cadmus founded Thebes by means of men raised from sowing the teeth of serpents; or that Jupiter, in the form of a Bull, ran away with Europa from her father Agenor, by whom he had three sons—Minos, Sarpedon, and Radamanthus, who were really all living persons.

20. As reason cannot be made effectual against etymology, the power of ridicule has been applied, and it has had the success it will always have against truth—it will fail. A pickled cucumber has been derived from Jeremiah King (e. g. Jeremiah King—Jer. King—Girkin). Now this is very good, and whenever similar licences are taken under the same or similar circumstances as this, the result deserves nothing but ridicule, and the persons who depend upon such deduc- tions are really ridiculous. Forced allegories are equally ridiculous; and pray what are our orthodox impugners of ety- mology better in their literal explanations of the Old-Testament writings? What shall I say to the wrestling of God with Jacob and wounding him in the thigh? What of his ineffectual attempt to kill Moses at an inn? These gentlemen run down etymology in order that they may open the door to their literal meanings. But the truth is, the abuse of either is ridiculous, as every thing must be when not kept within the bounds of sense and reason. And with respect to etymo- logy, however uncertain it may be, it is the only instrument left us for the investigation of ancient science, all others having failed us, and the certainty of facts discovered by its agency will depend upon the reason and probability which the etymological deduction will possess, in every individual case; and of each case the reader must be the judge. But the real truth is, that etymology is not run down because it is not calculated to discover truth, but because it is calcu- lated to discover too much truth.

21. Very certain I am that if we are not willing to receive the learning of the ancients through the medium of etymo- logy, and a comparison of the words of one language with another, we must remain in ignorance. The early historical accounts are all little better than fables. Every word, in every language, has, no doubt, originally had a meaning, whether a nation has it by inheritance, by importation, or by composition. It is evident, then, if we can find out the original meaning of the words which stand for the names of objects, great discoveries may be expected.

---

[1] Asiat. Res. Vol. III. 4to. p. 489.

22. I repeat, the science of etymology is the standing *but* for the shafts of every fool. If a witling be so foolish that he can ridicule nothing else, he can succeed against etymology. The true and secret reason of the opposition to etymology is, that the priests knowing it is by its aid only that ancient science can be discovered, have exerted every nerve to prejudice the minds of youth against it. After all, what is it but the science of explaining the meaning of words? Its uncertainty every one must admit. But in this it is only like the words of all languages, in almost every one of which every noun has a great number of meanings. On the meaning of the words, as selected judiciously or injudiciously, depends the value of the translation, which is, of course, sometimes sense, sometimes nonsense. But, I think, one is scarcely less doubtful, or subject to fewer mistakes, than the other. Are there not at least two meanings given to almost every important text of the Bible? The same is the case with etymological deductions.[1] The devotee, as in duty bound, will take the construction of his priest, the philosopher of his reason. And when an etymologist finds out a new derivation, we are as much obliged to him as we are to a lexicographer when he discovers a new meaning in a word which has been before overlooked.

23. The first word of Genesis may furnish an example of what I mean. We have great authorities to justify the rendering of the word either by *wisdom* or *beginning*, or both. And it must be for the reader to decide whether it has one or the other, or both—the double meaning.

24. When a translator finds a word with several meanings, than which nothing is more common, it is his duty to compare it with the context and to consider all the circumstances under which it is placed, and his prudence and judgment are displayed, or his want of them, in the selection which he makes. It is precisely the same with etymology. There is no argument which can be brought against etymology which may not be advanced with equal force against translations. In the course of the following work I shall have occasion to return to this subject several times.

CHAPTER III

Origin of the Adoration of the Bull, and of the Phallic and Vernal Festivals

1. THE Rev. Mr. Maurice, in his *learned* work on the Antiquities of India, has shewn, in a way which it is impossible to contradict, that the May-day festival and the May-pole of Great Britain, with its garlands, &c , known to us all, are the remains of an ancient festival of Egypt and India, and probably of Phœnicia, when these nations, in countries very distant, and from times very remote, have all, with one consent, celebrated the entrance of the sun into the sign of Taurus, at the vernal equinox; but which, in consequence of the astronomical phenomenon, no longer disputed, of the precession of the equinoxes, is removed far in the year from its original situation. This festival, it appears from a letter in the *Asiatic Researches*,[1] from Colonel Pearce, is celebrated in India on the first of May, in honour of Bhavani (a personification of vernal nature, the Dea Syria of Chaldea, and the Venus Urania of Persia). A May-pole is erected, hung with garlands, around which the young people dance, precisely the same as in England. The object of the festival, I think with Mr. Maurice, cannot be disputed; and that its date is coeval with the time when the equinox actually took place on the first of May. To account for these facts consistently with received chronology, he says, " When " the reader calls to mind what has already been observed, that owing to the precession of the equinoxes, after the rate " of seventy-two years to a degree, a total alteration has taken place through all the signs of the ecliptic, insomuch that " those stars which formerly were in Aries have now got into Taurus, and those of Taurus into Gemini: and when he " considers also the difference before mentioned, occasioned by the reform of the calendar, he will not wonder at the " disagreement that exists in respect to the exact period of the year on which the great festivals were anciently kept, " and that on which, in imitation of primeval customs, they are celebrated by the moderns. Now the vernal equinox, " after the rate of that precession, certainly could not have coincided with the first of May less than four thousand years " before Christ, which nearly marks the æra of the creation, which, according to the best and wisest chronologers,

---

[1] I beg my reader to look in Mr. Whiter's *Etymologicon* for the meaning of *argo*. It has scores of meanings, some as opposite as the poles.

[1] Vol. II. p. 333.

" began at the vernal equinox, when all nature was gay and smiling, and the earth arrayed in its loveliest verdure, and
" not, as others have imagined, at the dreary autumnal equinox, when that nature must necessarily have its beauty
" declining, and that earth its verdure decaying. *I have little doubt, therefore, that May-day, or at least the day on*
" *which the Sun entered Taurus, has been immemorially kept as a sacred festival from the creation of the earth and man,*
" *and was originally intended as a memorial of that auspicious period and that momentous event.*" He afterwards
adds, " on the general devotion of the ancients to the worship of the BULL, I have had frequent occasion to remark,
" and more particularly in the Indian history, by their devotion to it at that period,

———— aperit cum cornibus annum
Taurus,

" ' When the Bull with his horns opened the Vernal year.' I observed that all nations seem anciently to have vied
" with each other in celebrating that blissful epoch; and that the moment the sun entered the sign Taurus, were dis-
" played the signals of triumph and the incentives to passion: that memorials of the universal festivity indulged at that
" season are to be found in the records and customs of people otherwise the most opposite in manners and most remote
" in situation. I could not avoid considering the circumstance as a strong additional proof, that mankind originally
" descended from one great family, and proceeded to the several regions in which they finally settled, from one com-
" mon and central spot: that the Apis, or Sacred Bull of Egypt, was only the symbol of the sun in the vigour of vernal
" youth; and that the Bull of Japan, breaking with his horn the mundane egg, was evidently connected with the same
" bovine species of superstition, founded on the mixture of astronomy and mythology."[1]

2. Mr. Maurice in a previous part of his work had shewn that the May-day festival was established to celebrate the
generative powers of nature, called by the ancient Greeks φαλλοφορις—that φαλλος, in Greek, signifies a pole, and that
from this comes our May-pole.

3. After the equinox (in consequence of the revolution of the pole of the equator round the pole of the ecliptic)
ceased to be in Taurus, and took place in Aries, the equinoctial festivals were changed to the first of April, and were
celebrated on that day equally in England and India: in the former, every thing but the practice of making April
fools has ceased; but in the latter, the festival is observed as well as the custom of making April fools; that is, the
custom of sending persons upon ridiculous and false errands to create sport and merriment, is one part of the rites of
the festival. In India this is called the *Nauruts* and the *Huli*[2] festival. This vernal festival was celebrated on the day
the ancient Persian year began, which was on the day the sun entered into the sign of Aries; and Mr. Maurice says,
" The ancient Persian coins, stamped with the head of a ram, which, according to D'Ancarville, were offered to
" Gemshid, the founder of Persepolis, and first reformer of the solar year amongst the Persians, are an additional
" demonstration of the high antiquity of this festival." When Sir Thomas Roe was ambassador at Delhi, this festival
was celebrated by the Mogul with astonishing magnificence and splendour: it has the name of Nauruts both in India
and Persia, and was celebrated in both alike.[3] And in the ambassador's travels the writer acquaints us, " That some
" of their body being deputed to congratulate the Schah on the first day of the year, they found him at the palace of
" Ispahan, sitting at a banquet, and having near him the *Minatsin*, or astrologer, who rose up ever and anon, and
" taking his astrolobe went to observe the sun; and at the very moment of the sun's reaching the equator, he published
" aloud the new year, the commencement of which was celebrated by the firing of great guns both from the castle and
" the city walls, and by the sound of all kinds of instruments."

4. It is not only in Persia and India that this worship of the Bull is to be found; there is no part of the old world,
from the extremest East to the West, where the remains of it are not to be found.[4]

5. The reader will observe in the whole of the above quotations from Mr. Maurice the style of the Christian apologist,
who is endeavouring to account for a disagreeable circumstance which he cannot deny, and to shew that it is not
inconsistent with his religious system. He will see that it is the evidence of an unwilling witness, and on this account
evidence of the greatest importance. The learning and talent of Mr. Maurice are unquestionable, and it cannot for a
moment be doubted, that he would have denied the fact if he could have done it honestly. But in the teeth of the
most clear evidence of its existence *that* was absolutely impossible. I do not, however, mean to insinuate that he was
dishonest enough to have attempted it if he could have done so with a chance of success, for I believe no book was
ever more honestly written. The reality, close connexion, and object, of the Tauric and Phallic worship, have been so
clearly and fully proved by D'Ancarville, Payne Knight, Maurice, Parkhurst in his Hebrew Lexicon, Bryant, Faber,
Dupuis, Drummond, and many others, that there is no room left for a moment's doubt. It would therefore only be an

---

[1] Maurice's Ind. Ant. Vol. VI. pp. 91—93.
[2] The word Huli, I apprehend, is derived from, or is the same as, the ancient Celtic word Yule.
[3] Ind. Ant. Vol. VI. p. 76.   [4] Celtic Druids, Chap. v. Sect. ii.

idle waste of time to attempt to prove it. I could only repeat an immense mass of facts, now well known, from these authors, without adding any thing new. I have therefore determined not to attempt it, but to trust that any reader who may not have studied this subject, will depend upon the irreproachable testimony of Mr. Maurice. If he be not satisfied, he may consult the works above-named, where he will find much instruction, if not amusement. For these reasons I hope I shall be excused going into the proof of the antiquity of the Phallic and Tauric festivals, although their ancient existence is of the very first importance to my system.—My system, in fact, is founded upon them, and upon them I rest my foot as upon a foundation from which I am convinced nothing can remove me. The fact that the May-day festivals of India and Britain are admitted to have been instituted to celebrate the entrance of the sun into the sign Taurus at the vernal equinox, overthrows all our learned men's systems of chronology, root and branch; it leaves scarcely a wreck behind, and will enable me nearly to explain the origin and meaning of all the Mythoses of antiquity, and, indeed, of almost all those of modern times also.

ANACALYPSIS

BOOK I

CHAPTER I

Age of the World—Flood—Planets and Days of the Week—The Moon

1. On looking back into antiquity, the circle of vision terminates in a thick and impenetrable mist. No end can be distinguished. There seems reason to believe that this is an effect of that cause, whatever it may be, which first produced and gave law to the revolving motions of the planets, or other phenomena of nature, and therefore cannot be impugned, perhaps ought not to regretted. At all events, *if this obscurity be regretted,* it is pretty evident that there is little hope of its being removed. But in endeavouring to stretch our eye to the imaginary end of the prospect, to the supposed termination of the hitherto to us unbounded space, it is unavoidably arrested on its way by a variety of objects, of a very surprising appearance; and it is into their nature that I propose to inquire. When I look around me, on whatever side I cast my eyes, I see the ruins of a former world—proofs innumerable of a long-extended period of time. Perhaps among all the philosophers no one has demonstrated this so clearly as Mons. Cuvier. I apprehend these assertions are so well known and established that it is unnecessary to dwell upon them.

The great age of the world must be admitted; but the great age of man is a different thing. The latter may admit of doubt, and it is man with whom, in the following treatise, I propose to concern myself, and not his habitation. On man, his folly, his weakness, and, I am sorry I must add, his wickedness, I propose to treat: his habitation I leave to the geologists.

In the most early history of mankind I find all nations endeavouring to indulge a contemptible vanity, by tracing their origin to the most remote periods; and, for the gratification of this vanity, inventing fables of every description. *Of this weakness they have all, in reality, been guilty;* but the inhabitants of the oriental countries occupy rather a more prominent place than those of the western world; and I believe it will not be denied that, in the investigation of subjects connected with the first race of men, they are entitled on every account to claim a precedence. If, since the creation of man, a general deluge have taken place, their country was certainly the situation where he was preserved: therefore to the eastern climes I apply myself for his early history, and this naturally leads me into an inquiry into their ancient records and traditions.

2. All nations have a tradition of the destruction of the world by a flood,[1] and of the preservation of man from its effects. Here are two questions. Of the affirmative of the former no person

---

[1] The nature of this flood I shall discuss in a future chapter.—June, 1830.

who uses his eyes can doubt. But the latter is in a different predicament. A question may arise whether man existed before the flood above spoken of, or not. If the universality of a tradition of a fact of this nature would prove its truth, there would be scarcely room for doubt, and the previous creation of man would be established. But I think in the course of the following inquiry we shall find that universal tradition of a fact of this kind is not enough by itself for its establishment. It appears to me that the question of the existence of the human race previous to the flood will not much interfere with my inquiries, but will, if it be admitted, only oblige me to reason upon the idea that certain facts took place before it, and that the effects arising from them were not affected by it.

If I speak of persons or facts before the deluge, and it should be determined that the human species did not exist before that event, then the form of speech applied erroneously to the ante-diluvians must be held to apply to the earliest created of the post-diluvians; and this seems to me to be the only inconvenience which can arise from it. I shall therefore admit, for the sake of argument, that an universal flood took place, and that it happened *after* the creation of man.

Much difference of opinion has arisen upon the question whether the flood to which I have alluded was universal or not. The ancient records upon which Christians found their religion, as generally construed, maintain the affirmative; but no one who gives even a very slight degree of consideration to the circumstances of the Americas can deny that probability leans the contrary way. It is a very difficult question, but I do not consider that it has much concern with the object of this work.

Though it be the most probable, if man were created before the last general deluge, that a portion of the human race was saved along with the animals in the new, as well as a portion in the old world, yet it is equally probable that one family, or at most only a very small number of persons, were saved in the latter.

The strongest argument against the descent of the present human race from one pair has hitherto been found in the peculiar character of the Negro. But it is now admitted, I believe, that Mr. Lawrence has removed that difficulty, and has proved that man is one genus and one species, and that those who were taken by some philosophers for different species are only varieties. I shall assume this as a fact, and reason upon it accordingly. If there were any persons saved from the deluge except those before spoken of, who were found near the Caspian Sea, they do not appear to have made any great figure in the world, or to have increased so as to form any great nations. They must, I think, soon have merged and been lost in the prevailing numbers of the oriental nation. But I know not in history any probable tradition or circumstance, the existence of the Negro excepted, which should lead us to suppose that there ever were such persons. If they did exist, I think they must have been situated in China. It is possible that they may have been in that country, but it is a bare possibility, unsupported by any facts or circumstances known to us. No doubt the Chinese are entitled to what they claim—a descent from very remote antiquity. But it is acknowledged that one of their despots destroyed all their authentic and official records, in consequence of which little or no dependence can be placed upon the stories which they relate, of transactions which took place any length of time previous to that event.

The cautious way in which I reason above respecting the universal nature of the flood, and the conditional style of argument which I adopt in treating the question of man's creation before or after it, no doubt will give offence to a certain class of persons who always go to another class, called priests, for permission to believe, without using their own understandings. I am sorry that I should offend these good people, but as I cannot oblige them by taking for granted the truth of alleged facts, the truth or falsity of which is, at least in part, the object of this work, it is clearly not fit, as it is not intended, for their perusal.

3. Of the formation of our planetary system, and particularly of our world and of man, a vast variety of accounts were given by the different philosophers of Greece and Rome, a very fair description of which may be met with in the first volume of the Universal History, and in Stanley's History of Philosophy. Many of these cosmogonists have been highly celebrated for their wisdom; and yet, unless we suppose their theories to have been in a great degree allegorical, or to have contained some secret meaning, they exhibit an inconceivable mass of nonsense. But some of them, for instance that of Sanchoniathon, so largely discussed by Bishop Cumberland, are clearly allegorical: of course all such must be excepted from this condemnation.

If a person will apply his mind without prejudice to a consideration of the characters and doctrines of the ancient cosmogonists of the western part of the world, he must agree with me that they exhibit an extraordinary mixture of sense and nonsense, wisdom and folly—views of the creation, and its cause or causes, the most profound and beautiful, mixed with the most puerile conceits—conceits and fancies below the understanding of a plough-boy. How is this to be accounted for? The fact cannot be denied. Of the sayings of the wise men, there was not one, probably, more wise than that of the celebrated Γνώθι σεαυτόν, Know thyself, and probably there was not one to which so little regard has been paid. It is to the want of attention to this principle that I attribute most of the absurdities with which the wise and learned, perhaps in all ages, may be reproached. Man has forgotten or been ignorant that his faculties are limited. He has failed to mark the line of demarcation, beyond which his knowledge could not extend. Instead of applying his mind to objects cognizable by his senses, he has attempted subjects above the reach of the human mind, and has lost and bewildered himself in the mazes of metaphysics. He has not known or has not attended to what has been so clearly proved by Locke, that no idea can be received except through the medium of the senses. He has endeavoured to form ideas without attending to this principle, and, as might well be expected, he has run into the greatest absurdities, the necessary consequence of such imprudence. Very well the profound and learned Thomas Burnet says,[1] "Sapientia prima est stultitia caruisse;" "primusque ad veritatem gradus præcavere errores." Again he says, "Sapientis enim est, non tantum ea quæ sciri possunt, scire: sed etiam quæ sciri non possunt, discernere et discriminare."[2]

It must not be understood from what I have said, that I wish to put a stop to all metaphysical researches; far from it. But I do certainly wish to controul them, to keep them within due bounds, and to mark well the point beyond which, from the nature of our organization, we cannot proceed. Perhaps it may not be possible to fix the exact point beyond which the mind of man can never go, but it may be possible to say without doubt, of some certain point, beyond this he has not yet advanced. By this cautious mode of proceeding, though we may *pretend* to *less* knowledge, we may in fact *possess more*.

For these various reasons I shall pass over, without notice, the different theories of the formation of the world by the sages of Greece and Rome. In general they seem to me to deserve no notice, to be below the slightest consideration of a person of common understanding. As a curious record of what some of the wise men of antiquity were, they are interesting and worthy of preservation: as a rational exposé of the origin of things, they are nothing.

Among the subjects to which I allude as being above the reach of the human understanding are Liberty and Necessity, the Eternity of Matter, and several other similar subjects.

4. Our information of the historical transactions which it is supposed took place previous to the catastrophe,[3] and its attendant flood, which destroyed the ancient world, is very small. Mons.

---

[1] Arch. Phil. cap. vii.   [2] Ibid. p. 95.

[3] This catastrophe has been thought by many of the moderns to have arisen from a change of the direction of the

Bailly has observed, that the famous cycle of the Neros, and the cycle of seven days, or the week, from their peculiar circumstances, must probably have been of antediluvian invention. No persons could have invented the Neros who had not arrived at much greater perfection in astronomy than we know was the state of the most ancient of the Assyrians, Egyptians, or Greeks. The earliest of these nations supposed the year to have consisted of 360 days only, when the inventors of the Neros must have known its length to within a few seconds of time—a fact observed by Mons. Bailly to be a decisive proof that science was formerly brought to perfection, and therefore, consequently, must have been afterward lost. There are indeed among the Hindoos proofs innumerable that a very profound knowledge of the sciences was brought by their ancestors from the upper countries of India, the Himmalah mountains, Thibet or Cashmir. These were, I apprehend, the first descendants of the persons who lived after the deluge. But this science has long been forgotten by their degenerate successors, the present race of Brahmins. The ancient Hindoos might be acquainted with the Neros, but I think it probable that Josephus was correct in saying it is of antediluvian discovery; that is, that it was discovered previous to the time allotted for the deluge. And it is a curious circumstance that we receive this tradition from the people among whom we find the apparently antediluvian part of the book, or the first tract of the book, called Genesis, about which I shall have much more to observe in the course of this work.

The other cycle just now named, of the seven days or the week, is also supposed by Bailly to be, from its universal reception, of equal antiquity. There is no country of the old world in which it is not found, which, with the reasons which I will now proceed to state, pretty well justify Mons. Bailly in his supposition.

5. In my *Preliminary Observations*, and in my treatise on *The Celtic Druids*, I have pointed out the process by which the planetary bodies were called after the days of the week, or the days of the week after them. I have there stated that the septennial cycle would probably be among the earliest of what would be called the scientific discoveries which the primeval races of men would make.

Throughout all the nations of the ancient world, the planets are to be found appropriated to the days of the week. The seven-day cycle, with each day named after a planet, and universally the same day allotted to the same planet in all the nations of the world, constitute the first proof, and leave no room to doubt that one system must have prevailed over the whole. Here are the origin and the reason of all judicial astrology, as well as the foundation upon which much of the Heathen mythology was built. The two were closely and intimately connected.

It is the object of this work to trace the steps by which, from the earliest time and small beginnings, this system grew to a vast and towering height, covering the world with gigantic monuments and beautiful temples, enabling one part of mankind, by means of the fears and ignorance of the other part, to trample it in the dust.

Uncivilized man is by nature the most timid of animals, and in that state the most defenceless. The storm, the thunder, the lightning, or the eclipse, fills him with terror. He is alarmed and trembles at every thing which he does not understand, and that is almost every thing that he sees or hears.

If a person will place himself in the situation of an early observer of the heavenly bodies, and consider how they must have appeared to him in his state of ignorance, he will at once perceive that it was scarcely possible that he could avoid mistaking them for animated or intelli-

---

earth's axis, and a simultaneous, or perhaps consequent, change of the length of the year from 360 to 365 days. The change of the axis was believed among the ancients by Plato, Anaxagoras, Empedocles, Diogenes, Leucippus, and Democritus. Vide book ii. ch. iv. of Thomas Burnet's *Archæologia Philosophica*.

gent beings. To us, with our prejudices of education, it is difficult to form a correct idea of what his sensations must have been, on his first discovering the five planets to be different from the other stars, and to possess a locomotive quality, apparently to him subject to no rule or order. But we know what happened; he supposed them animated, and to this day they are still supposed to be so, by the greatest part of the world. Even in enlightened England judicial astrologers are to be found.

I suppose that after man first discovered the twenty-eight day cycle, and the year of 360 days, he would begin to perceive that certain stars, larger than the rest, and shining with a steady and not a scintillating light, were in perpetual motion. They would appear to him, unskilled in astronomy, to be endowed with life and great activity, and to possess a power of voluntary motion, going and coming in the expanse at pleasure. These were the planets. A long time would pass before their number could be ascertained, and a still longer before it could be discovered that their motions were periodical. The different systems of the ancient philosophers of Greece and other countries, from their errors and imperfections, prove that this must have been the state of the case. During this period of ignorance and fear arose the opinion, that they influenced the lot of man, or governed this sublunary world; and very naturally arose the opinion that they were intelligent beings. And as they appeared to be constantly advancing towards and receding from the sun, the parent of life and comfort to the world, they were believed to be his ministers and messengers. As they began in some instances to be observed to return, or be visible in the same part of the heavens, they would naturally be supposed by the terrified barbarian to have duties to perform; and when the very ancient book of Job[1] represents the morning stars to have sung together, and all the sons of God to have shouted for joy, it probably does not mean to use merely a figurative expression, but nearly the literal purport of the language.

In contemplating the host of heaven, men could not fail soon to observe that the fixed stars were in a particular manner connected with the seasons—that certain groups of them regularly returned at the time experience taught them it was necessary to commence their seed-time or their harvest; but that the planets, though in some degree apparently connected with the seasons, were by no means so intimately and uniformly connected with them as the stars. This would be a consequence which would arise from the long periods of some of the planets—Saturn, for instance. These long periods of some of the planets would cause the shortness of the periods of others of them to be overlooked, and would, no doubt, have the effect of delaying the time when their periodical revolutions would be discovered; perhaps for a very long time: and, in the interim, the opinion that they were intelligent agents would be gaining ground, and receiving the strengthening seal of superstition; and, if a priesthood had arisen, the fiat of orthodoxy.

From these causes we find that, though in judicial astrology or magic the stars have a great influence, yet that a great distinction is made between them and the planetary bodies; and I think that, by a minute examination of the remaining astrological nonsense which exists, the distinction would be found to be justified, and the probability of the history here given confirmed.

As it has been observed, though the connexion between the planets and the seasons was not so intimate as that between the latter and the stars, yet still there was often an apparent connexion, and some of the planets would be observed to appear when particular seasons arrived, and thus after a certain time they were thought to be beneficent or malevolent, as circumstances appeared to justify the observers' conclusions.

6. Of the different histories of the creation, that contained in the book, or collection of books,

---

[1] Chap. xxxviii. ver. 7.

called Genesis, has been in the Western parts of the world the most celebrated, and the nonsense which has been written respecting it, may fairly vie with the nonsense, a little time ago alluded to, of the ancient learned men of Greece and Rome.

This book professes to commence with a history of the creation, and in our vulgar translation it says, " *In the beginning God created the heavens and the earth.*" But I conceive for the word *heavens* the word *planets* ought to be substituted. The original for the word *heavens* is of great consequence. Parkhurst admits that it has the meaning of *placers* or *disposers*. In fact, it means the planets as distinguished from the fixed stars, and is the foundation, as I have said, and as we shall find, upon which all judicial astrology, and perhaps much of the Heathen mythology, was built.

After man came to distinguish the planets from the stars, and had allotted them to the respective days of the week, he proceeded to give them names, and they were literally the Dewtahs of India, the Archangels of the Persians and Jews, and the most ancient of the Gods of the Greeks and Romans, among the vulgar of whom each planet had a name, and was allotted to, or thought to be, a God.

The following are the names of the Gods allotted to each day: Sunday to the Sun, Monday to the Moon, Tuesday to Mars, Wednesday to Mercury, Thursday to Jupiter, Friday to Venus, and Saturday to Saturn : and it is worthy of observation, that neither Bacchus nor Hercules is among them; on which I shall have an observation to make in a future part of this work. In almost every page we shall have to make some reference to judicial astrology, which took its rise from the planetary bodies.

The Sun, I think I shall shew, was unquestionably the first object of the worship of all nations. Contemporaneously with him or after him succeeded, for the reasons which I have given, the planets. About the time that the collection of planets became an object of adoration, the Zodiac was probably marked out from among the fixed stars, as we find it in the earliest superstitions of the astrologers. Indeed, the worship of the equinoctial sun in the sign Taurus, the remains of which are yet found in our May-day festivals, carries it back at least for 4,500 years before Christ . How much further back the system may be traced, I pretend not to say.

7. After the sun and planets it seems, on first view, probable that the moon would occupy the next place in the idolatrous veneration of the different nations ; but I am inclined to think that this was not the case. Indeed, I very much doubt whether ever he or she, for it was of both genders, was an object of adoration at all in the very early periods. I think it would be discovered so soon that its motions were periodical, that there would be scarcely any time for the error to happen ; for I cannot conceive it possible that it should have been thought to be an intelligent being after once its periodical nature was discovered.

This doctrine respecting the Moon will be thought paradoxical and absurd, and I shall be asked what I make of the goddess Isis. I reply, that it is the inconsistencies, contradictions, and manifest ignorance of the ancients respecting this goddess, which induce me to think that the Moon never was an object of worship in early times, and that it never became an object of adoration till comparatively modern times, when the knowledge of the ancient mysteries was lost, and not only the knowledge of the mysteries, but the knowledge of the religion itself, or at least of its origin and meaning, were lost. The least attention to the treatises of Plato, Phornutus, Cicero, Porphyry, and, in short, of every one of the ancient writers on the subject of the religion, must convince any unprejudiced person that they either were all completely in the dark, or pretended to be so. After the canaille got to worshipping onions, crocodiles, &c., &c., &c., no doubt

---

' *Celtic Druids*, p. 291.

the moon came in for a share of their adoration ; but all the accounts of it are full of inconsistency and contradiction : for this reason I think it was of late invention, and that Isis was not originally the moon, but the mother of the gods. Many other reasons for this opinion will be given in the course of the work, when I come to treat of Isis and the Moon.

CHAPTER II

First God of the Ancients—The Sun—Double Nature of the Diety—Metempsychosis and the Renewal of Worlds—Moral Evil—Eternity of Matter—Buddha —Genesis

1. I SHALL now proceed to shew, in a way which I think I may safely say cannot be refuted, that all the Gods of antiquity resolved themselves into the solar fire, sometimes itself as God, or sometimes as emblem or shekinah of that higher principle, known by the name of the creative Being or God. But first I must make a few observations on his nature, as it was supposed to exist by the ancient philosophers.

On the nature of this Being or God the ancient oriental philosophers entertained opinions which took their rise from a very profound and recondite course of reasoning, (but yet, when once put in train, a very obvious one,) which arose out of the relation which man and the creation around him were observed by them to bear, to their supposed cause—opinions which, though apparently well known to the early philosophers of all nations, seem to have been little regarded or esteemed in later times, even if known to them, by the mass of mankind. But still they were opinions which, in a great degree, influenced the conduct of the world in succeeding ages ; and though founded in truth or wisdom, in their abuse they became the causes of great evils to the human race.

The opinions here alluded to are of so profound a nature, that they seem to bespeak a state of the human mind much superior to any thing to be met with in what we have been accustomed to consider or call ancient times. From their philosophical truth and universal reception in the world, I am strongly inclined to refer them to the authors of the Neros, or to that enlightened race, supposed by Mons. Bailly to have formerly existed, and to have been saved from a great catastrophe on the Himmalah mountains. This is confirmed by an observation which the reader will make in the sequel, that these doctrines have been like all the other doctrines of antiquity, gradually corrupted—incarnated, if I may be permitted to compose a word for the occasion.

Sublime philosophical truths or attributes have become clothed with bodies and converted iuto living creatures. Perhaps this might take its origin from a wish in those professing them to conceal them from the vulgar eye, but the cause being forgotten, all ranks in society at last came to understand them iu the literal sense, their real character being lost ; or perhaps this incarnatiou might arise from a gradual falling away of mankind from a high state of civilization, at which it must have arrived when those doctrines were discovered, into a state of ignorance,—the produce of revolutions, or perhaps merely of the great law of change which in all nature seems to be eternally in operation.

2. The human animal, like all other animals, is in his mode of existence very much the child of accident, circumstance, habit : as he is moulded in his youth he generally continues. This is in nothing, perhaps, better exemplified than in the use of his right hand. From being carried in

the right arm of his nurse, his right hand is set at liberty for action and use, while his left is at rest: the habit of using the right hand in preference to the left is thus acquired and never forgotten. A similar observation applies to the mind. To natural causes leading men to peculiar trains or habits of thinking or using the mind, may be traced all the recondite theories which we find among the early races of man. If to causes of this kind they are not to be ascribed, I should be glad to know where their origins are to be looked for. If they be not in these causes to be found, we must account for them by inventing a history of the adventures of some imagined human being, after the manner of the Greeks and many others, whose priests never had a difficulty, always having a fable ready for the amusement of their credulous votaries.

In opposition to this, I, perhaps, may be asked, why the inhabitants of the new world have not arrived at the high degree of civilization,—at the same results, as the inhabitants of the old? The answer is, Accident or circumstances being at first different, they have been led to a different train of acting or thinking; and if they branched off from the parent stock in very early times, accident or circumstances being after their separation different, are quite sufficient to account for the difference of the results. It seems probable, that from their knowledge of figures and their ignorance of letters, they must have branched off in a very remote period. Although the peculiar circumstance, that few or none of the animals of the old world were found in the new one, or of the animals of the new one in the old, seems to shew a separate formation of the animal creation; yet the identity of many of the religious rites and ceremonies of the inhabitants of the two worlds, and other circumstances pointed out by Mr. Faber and different writers, seem to bespeak only one formation or creation of man.

The rise of the doctrine respecting the nature of God named above, is said to be lost in the most remote antiquity. This may be true; but perhaps a little consideration will enable us to point out the natural cause from which, as I have observed, it had its origin. Like the discovery of figures or arithmetic, the septennial cycle, &c., it probably arose among the first philosophers or searchers after wisdom, from their reflecting upon the objects which presented themselves to their observation.

3. That the sun was the first object of the adoration of mankind, I apprehend, is a fact, which I shall be able to place beyond the reach of reasonable doubt. An absolute proof of this fact the circumstances of the case put it out of our power to produce; but it is supported by reason and common sense, and by the traditions of all nations, when carefully examined to their foundations. The allegorical accounts or mythoses[1] of different countries, the inventions of an advanced state of society, inasmuch as they are really only allegorical accounts or mythoses, operate nothing against this doctrine.

When, after ages of ignorance and error, man became in some degree civilized, and he turned his mind to a close contemplation of the fountain of light and life—of the celestial fire—he would observe among the earliest discoveries which he would make, that by its powerful agency all nature was called into action; that to its return in the spring season the animal and vegetable creation were indebted for their increase as well as for their existence. It is probable that for this reason chiefly the sun, in early times, was believed to be the creator, and became the first object of adoration. This seems to be only a natural effect of such a cause. After some time it would

---

[1] This is nothing against the Mosaic account, because it is allowed by all philosophers, as well as most of the early Jews and Christian fathers, to contain a mythos or an allegory—by Philo, Josephus, Papias, Pantænus, Irenæus, Clemens Alex., Origen, the two Gregories of Nyssa and Nazianzen, Jerome, Ambrose, Spencer de Legibus Hebræorum, Alexander Geddes, the Romish translator of the Bible, in the Preface and Critical Remarks, p. 49. See also Marsh's Lectures, &c., &c. Of this I shall say more hereafter.

be discovered that this powerful and beneficent agent, the solar fire, was the most potent destroyer, and hence would arise the first idea of a Creator and Destroyer united in the same person. But much time would not elapse before it must have been observed, that the destruction caused by this powerful being was destruction only in appearance, that destruction was only reproduction in another form—regeneration; that if he appeared sometimes to destroy, he constantly repaired the injury which he seemed to occasion—and that, without his light and heat, every thing would dwindle away into a cold, inert, unprolific mass.' Thus at once, in the same being, became concentrated, the creating, the preserving, and the destroying powers,—the latter of the three being, at the same time, both the destroyer and regenerator. Hence, by a very natural and obvious train of reasoning, arose the creator, the preserver, and the destroyer—in India, *Brahma, Vishnu,* and *Siva;* in Persia, *Oromasdes, Mithra,* and *Arimanius;* in Egypt, *Osiris, Neith,* and *Typhon:* in each case *Three Persons and one God.* And *thus* arose the TRIMURTI, or the celebrated Trinity. On this Mr. Payne Knight says, "The hypostatical division and essential unity of the " Deity is one of the most remarkable parts of this system, and the farthest removed from " common sense and reason: and yet this is perfectly reasonable and consistent, if considered " together with the rest of it, for the emanations and personifications were only figurative abstrac- " tions of particular modes of action and existence, of which the primary cause and original essence " still continued one and the same. The three hypostases being thus only one being, each " hypostasis is occasionally taken for all, as is the case in the passage of Apuleius before cited, " where Isis describes herself as the universal deity.'"

The sun himself, in his corporeal and visible form of a globe of fire, I do not doubt was, for a long time, the sole trinity. And it would not be till after ages of speculation and philosophizing that man would raise his mind to a more pure trinity, or to a trinity of abstractions,—a trinity which would probably never have existed in his imagination if he had not first had the more gross corporeal igneous trinity, with its effects, for its prototype, to lead him to the more refined and sublime doctrine, in which the corporeal and igneous trinity gave way among philosophers to one of a more refined kind; or to a system of abstractions, or of attributes, or of emanations, from a superior being, the creator and preserver of the sun himself.

It has been said in reply to this, Then this fundamental doctrine on which, in fact, all the future religion and philosophy of the world was built, you attribute to accident! The word accident means, by us unseen or unknown cause; but I suppose, that when an intelligent Being was establishing the present order of the universe, he must know how the unseen cause or accident which he provided would operate,—this accident or unseen cause being only a link in a chain, the first link of which begins, and the last of which ends, in God.

That the sublime doctrine of emanations, or abstractions as it was called, above alluded to, prevailed among the oriental nations, cannot be doubted; but yet there may be a doubt whether they were ever entirely free from an opinion that the creative Deity consisted of a certain very refined substance, similar, if not the same, as the magnetic, galvanic, or electric fluid. This was the opinion of all the early Christian fathers, as well, I think, as of the Grecians. But still, I think, certain philosophers arose above this kind of materialism, among whom must have been the Buddhists and Brahmins of India; but of this we shall see more in the sequel. We shall find this a most difficult question to decide.

' Described in Genesis by the words ובהו תהו *thu-u-bhu,* which mean a mass of matter effete, unproductive, unprolific, ungenerating, and itself devoid of the beautiful forms of the animal, vegetable, and mineral kingdoms,—the mud or Ilus of Sanchoniathon. The words of our Bible, as here used, *without form and void,* have not any meaning.

' Knight, p. 163.

4. The Trinity described above, and consisting of abstractions or emanations from the divine nature, will be found exemplified in the following work in a vast variety of ways; but in all, the first principle will be found at the bottom of them. I know nothing in the works of the ancient philosophers which can be brought against them except a passage or two of Plato, and one of Numenius, according to Proclus.

Plato says, "When, therefore, that God, who is a perpetually reasoning divinity, cogitated " about the god who was destined to subsist at some certain period of time, he produced his body " smooth and equable; and every way from the middle even and whole, and perfect from the " composition of perfect bodies." [1]

Again Plato says, "And on all these accounts he rendered the universe a happy God." [2] Again he says, " But he fabricated the earth, the common nourisher of our existence; which being " conglobed about the pole, extended through the universe, is the guardian and artificer of night " and day, and is the first and most ancient of the gods which are *generated* within the heavens. " But the harmonious progressions of these divinities, their concussions with each other, the revo- " lutions and advancing motions of their circles, how they are situated with relation to each other " in their conjunctions and oppositions, whether direct among themselves or retrograde, at what " times and in what manner they become concealed, and, again emerging to our view, cause " terror, and exhibit tokens of future events to such as are able to discover their signification; of " all this to attempt an explanation, without suspecting the resemblances of these divinities, " would be a fruitless employment. But of this enough, and let this be the end of our discourse " concerning the nature of the visible and *generated* gods." [3]

How from these passages any ingenuity can make out that Plato maintained a trinity of the Sun, the Moon, and the Earth, as the Supreme God or the Creator, I do not know, and I should not have thought of noticing them if I had not seen an attempt lately made in a work not yet published, to depreciate the sublime doctrines of the ancients by deducing from these passages that consequence.

The other passage is of Numenius the Pythagorean, recorded by Proclus, who says that he taught, that the world was the third God, ὁ γαρ κοσμος κατ᾽ αυτον ὁ τριτος ἐστι Θεος.[4]

This is evidently nothing but the hearsay of hearsay evidence, and can only shew that these doctrines, like all the other mythoses, had become lost or doubtful to the Greeks. The latter quotation of this obscure author will be found undeserving of attention, when placed in opposition to the immense mass of evidence which will be produced in this work. And as for the passage of Plato, I think few persons will allow it to have any weight, when in like manner every construction of it is found to be directly in opposition to his other doctrines, as my reader will soon see.[5]

5. The doctrine as developed above by me, is said to be too refined for the first race of men. Beautifully refined it certainly is: but my reader will recollect that I do not suppose that man arrived at these results till after many generations of ignorance, and till after probably almost innumerable essays of absurdity and folly. But I think if the matter be well considered, the Pan-

---

[1] Plato's Tim., Taylor, p. 483.   [2] Ibid. p. 484.   [3] Ibid. p. 499, 500.
[4] Comment. in Tim. of Plat. II. 93.

[5] In the seventh chapter of the 2nd book of Arch. Phil. by Thomas Burnet, who was among the very first of modern philosophers, may be seen an elaborate and satisfactory proof that the ancient philosophers constantly held two doctrines, one for the learned, and one for the vulgar. He supports his proofs by an example from Jamblicus and Laertius, relative to some notions of Pythagoras, which accorded with the vulgar opinion of the Heavens, but which were contrary to his REAL opinions. He has completely justified the ancients from the attempts of certain of the moderns to fix upon them their simulated opinions. The fate of Socrates furnishes an admirable example of what would happen to those who in ancient times taught true doctrines to the vulgar, or attempted to draw aside the veil of Isis.

theistic scheme (for it is a part of a pantheism) of making the earth the creator of all, will require much more refinement of mind than the doctrine of attributing the creation to the sun. The first is an actual refinement run into corruption, similar to Bishop Berkley's doctrine,—refinement, indeed, carried to a vicious excess, carried to such an excess as to return to barbarism; similar, for instance, to what took place in the latter ages of Greece and Rome in the fine arts, when the beautiful Ionic and Corinthian orders of architecture were deserted for the Composite.

We may venture, I think, to presume that adoration must first have arisen either from fear or admiration; in fact, from feeling. As an object of feeling, the sun instantly offers himself. The effect arising from the daily experience of his beneficence, does not seem to be of such a nature as to wear away by use, as is the case with most feelings of this kind. He obtrudes himself on our notice in every way. But what is there in the earth on which we tread, and which is nothing without the sun, which should induce the half-civilized man to suppose it an active agent—to suppose that it created itself? He would instantly see that it was, in itself, to all appearance תֹהוּ te̅u, ובֹהוּ ube̅u,[1] an inert, dead, unprolific mass. And it must, I think, have required an exertion of metaphysical subtlety, infinitely greater than my trinity must have required, to arrive at a pantheism so completely removed from the common apprehension of the human understanding. In my oriental theory, every thing is natural and seductive; in the other, every thing is unnatural and repulsive.

My learned friend who advocates this degrading scheme of Pantheism against my sublime and intellectual theory, acknowledges what cannot be denied, that the doctrines held in these two passages of Numenius and Plato, are directly at variance with their philosophy as laid down in all their other works. Under these circumstances, I think I may safely dismiss them without further observation, as passages misunderstood, or contrivances to conceal their real opinions.

6. Of equal or nearly equal date, and almost equally disseminated throughout the world with the doctrine of the Trinity, was that of the Hermaphroditic or Androgynous character of the Deity. Man could not help observing and meditating upon the difference of the sexes. He was conscious that he himself was the highest in rank of all creatures of which he had any knowledge, and he very properly and very naturally, as far as was in his power, made God after the being of highest rank known to him, after himself; thus it might be said, that in his own image, in idea, made he his God. But of what sex was this God? To make him neuter, supposing man to have become grammarian enough to have invented a neuter gender, was to degrade him to the rank of a stone. To make him female was evidently more analogous to the general productive and prolific characters of the author of the visible creation. To make him masculine, was still more analogous to man's own person, and to his superiority over the female, the weaker vessel; but still this was attended with many objections. From a consideration of all these circumstances, an union of the two was adopted, and he was represented as being Androgynous.

Notwithstanding what I have said in my last paragraph respecting the degradation of making God of the neuter gender, I am of opinion that had a neuter gender been known it would have been applied to the Deity, and for that reason would have been accounted, of the three genders, the most honourable. For this, among other reasons, if I find any very ancient language which has not a neuter gender, I shall be disposed to consider it to be probably among the very oldest of the languages of the world. This observation will be of importance hereafter.

7. Of all the different attributes of the Creator, or faculties conferred by him on his creature, there is no one so striking or so interesting to a reflecting person as that of the generative power.

---

[1] Gen. chap. i.

This is the most incomprehensible and mysterious of the powers of nature. When all the adjuncts or accidents of every kind so interesting to the passions and feelings of man are considered, it is not wonderful that this subject should be found in some way or other to have a place among the first of the human superstitions. Thus every where we find it accompanying the triune God, called Trimurti or Trinity, just described, under the very significant form of the single obelisk or stone-pillar, denominated the Lingham or Phallus,[1] and the equally significant Yoni or Cteis, the female organ of generation : sometimes single, often in conjunction. The origin of the worship of this object is discussed at large in my *Celtic Druids*, and will be found in the index by reference to the words Phallus, Linga, Lithoi.

8. The next step after man had once convinced himself of the existence of a God would be, I think, to discover the doctrine of the immortality of the soul. Long before he arrived at this point, he must have observed, and often attempted to account for, the existence of moral evil. How to reconcile this apparent blot in the creation to the beneficence of an all-powerful Creator, would be a matter of great difficulty : he had probably recourse to the only contrivance which was open to him, a contrivance to which he seems to have been driven by a wise dispensation of Providence, the doctrine of a future state of existence, where the ills of this world would find a remedy, and the accounts of good and evil be balanced ; where the good man would receive his reward, and the bad one his punishment. This seems to me to be the probable result of the contemplation of the existence of evil by the profound primeval oriental philosophers, who first invented the doctrine of the Trinity.

9. Other considerations would lend their assistance to produce the same result. After man had discovered the doctrine of the immortality of the soul, the metempsychosis followed the doctrine of the reproduction or regeneration by the third person of the triune God, by a very natural process, as the doctrine of the triune God had before arisen by an easy process from the consideration by man of the qualities of the beings around him. Everywhere, throughout all nature, the law that destruction was reproduction appeared to prevail. This united to the natural fondness for immortality, of which every human being is conscious, led to the conclusion, that man, the élite of the creation, could not be excepted from the general rule; that he did but die to live again, to be regenerated; a consciousness of his own frailty gradually caused a belief, that he was regenerate in some human body or the body of some animal as a punishment for his offences, until by repeated penances of this kind, his soul had paid the forfeit of the crimes of its first incarnation, had become purified from all stain, and in a state finally to be absorbed into the celestial influence, or united to the substance of the Creator. As it happens in every sublunary concern, the law of change corrupted these simple principles in a variety of ways ; and we find the destroyer made into a demon or devil, at war with the Preserver or with the Creator. Hence arose the doctrine of the two principles opposed to each other, of Oromasdes and Arimanius in perpetual war, typified by the higher and lower hemisphere of the earth, of winter and summer, of light and darkness, as we shall find developed in a variety of ways. What could be so natural as to allot to the destroyer the lower hemisphere of cold and darkness, of winter, misery, and famine? What so natural as to allot to the beneficent Preserver the upper hemisphere of genial warmth, of summer, happiness, and plenty? Hence came the festivals of the equinoxes and of the solstices, much of the complicated machinery of the heathen mythology, and of judicial astrology.

From similar trains of reasoning arose the opinion that every thing in nature, even the world itself, was subject to periodical changes, to alternate destructions and renovations—an opinion,

---

[1] Religion de l'Antiquité, par Cruizer, Notes, Introd. p. 525.

perhaps, for sublimity not to be equalled in the history of the different philosophical systems of the world, the only doctrine which seemed, in the opinion of the ancients, to be capable of reconciling the existence of evil with the goodness of God.

10. A little time ago I said, that the first philosophers could not account for the existence of moral evil without the doctrine of the immortality of the soul. I am induced to make another observation upon this subject before I leave it. In the modern Christian system, this difficulty has been overcome, as most theological difficulties usually are, among devotees, by a story. In this case by a story of a serpent and a fruit tree, of which I shall not here give my opinion, except that, like most of the remainder of Genesis, it was anciently held to have an allegorical meaning, and, secondly, that I cannot do Moses the injustice of supposing that he, like the modern priests, could have meant it, at least by the higher classes of his followers, to be believed *literally*.

Moral evil is a relative term; its correlative is moral good. Without evil there is no good; without good there is no evil. There is no such thing known to us as good or evil *per se*. Here I must come to Mr. Locke's fine principle, so often quoted by me in my former book, the truth of which has been universally acknowledged, and to which, in their reasoning, all men seem to agree in forgetting to pay attention,—that we know nothing except through the medium of our senses, which is experience. We have no experience of moral good or of moral evil except as relative and correlative to one another; therefore, we are with respect to them as we are with respect to God. Though guided by experience we confidently believe their existence in this qualified form, yet of their nature, independent of one another, we can know nothing. God having created man subject to one, he could not, without changing his nature, exclude the other. All this the ancients seem to have known; and, in order to account for and remove several difficulties, they availed themselves of the metempsychosis, a renewal of worlds, and the final absorption of the soul or the thinking principle into the Divine substance, from which it was supposed to have emanated, and where it was supposed to enjoy that absolute and uncorrelative beatitude, of which man can form no idea. This doctrine is very sublime, and is such as we may reasonably expect from the school where Pythagoras studied;[1] but I do not mean to say that it removes all difficulties, or is itself free from difficulty. But absolute perfection can be expected only by priests who can call to their aid apples of knowledge. Philosophers must content themselves with something less. Of the great variety of sects or religions in the world there is not one, if the priests of each may be believed, in which any serious difficulties of this kind are found.

11. Modern divines, a very sensitive race, have been much shocked with the doctrine of the ancients, that nothing could be created from nothing, *ex nihilo nihil fit*. This is a subject well deserving consideration. The question arises how did the ancients acquire the knowledge of the truth of this proposition. Had they any positive experience that matter was *not* made from nothing? I think they had not. Then how could they have any knowledge on the subject? As they had received no knowledge through the medium of the senses, that is from experience, it was rash and unphilosophical to come to any conclusion.

The ancients may have reasoned from analogy. They may have said, Our experience teaches that every thing which we perceive has pre-existed before the moment we perceive it, therefore it is fair to conclude that it must always have existed. A most hasty conclusion. All that

---

[1] Carmel, close to the residence of Melchizedek, where was the temple of Iao, without image. See Jamblicus, chap. iii., Taylor's translation. When I formed the table of additional errata to my Celtic Druids, I had forgotten where I found the fact here named relating to the residence of Pythagoras, which caused the expression of the doubt which may be seen there respecting it.

they could fairly conclude was, that, for any thing which they knew to the contrary, it *may* have existed from eternity, not that it *must* have existed. But this amounts not to knowledge.

Are the modern priests any wiser than the ancient philosophers? Have they any knowledge from experience of matter having ever been created from nothing? I think they have not.[1] Then how can they conclude that it was created from nothing? They cannot know any thing about it; they are in perfect ignorance.

If matter *have* always existed, I think we may conclude that it will always exist. But if it *have not* always existed, will it always continue to exist? I think we may conclude it to be probable that it will. For if it have not always existed it must have been created (as I will assume) by God. God would not create any thing which was not good. He will not destroy any thing that is good. He is not changeable or repents what he has done: therefore he will not destroy the matter which he has created. From which we may conclude, that the change of form which we see daily taking place is periodical; at least there is in favour of this what the Jesuits would call a probable opinion; and this brings us to the alternate creations and destructions of the ancients. A learned philosopher says, " The bold and magnificent idea of a creation from nothing was reserved for the more " vigorous faith and more enlightened minds of the moderns, who seek no authority to confirm " their belief; for as that which is self-evident admits of no proof, so that which is in itself impos- " sible admits of no refutation."[2]

This doctrine of the renewal of worlds, held by the ancient philosophers, has received a great accession of probability from the astronomical discoveries of La Place, who has demonstrated, that certain motions of the planetary bodies which appeared to Newton to be irregular, and to portend at some future period the destruction of the solar system, are all periodical, and that after certain immensely elongated cycles are finished, every thing returns again to its former situation. The ancient philosophers of the East had a knowledge of this doctrine, the general nature of which they might have acquired by reasoning similar to the above, or by the same means by which they acquired a knowledge of the Neros.

This is not inconsistent with the doctrine of a future judgment and a state of reward and punishment in another world. Why should not the soul transmigrate, and after the day of judgment (a figure) live again in the next world in some new body? Here are all the leading doctrines of the ancients. I see nothing in them absurd—nothing contrary to the moral attributes of God —and nothing contrary even to the doctrines of Jesus of Nazareth. It has been thought that the doctrine of the pre-existence of souls may be found in the New Testament.

Many of the early fathers of the Christians held the doctrine of the Metempsychosis, which they defended on several texts of the New Testament.[3] It was an opinion which had a very general circulation both in the East and in the West. It was held by the Pharisees or Persees, as they ought to be called, among the Jews; and among the Christians by Origen,[4] Chalcidius, (if he were a Christian,) Synesius, and by the Simonians, Basilidians, Valentiniens, Marcionites, and the Gnostics in general. It was held by the Chinese, and, among the most learned of the Greeks, by Plato and Pythagoras. Thus this doctrine was believed by nearly all the great and good of every religion, and of every nation and age; and though the present race has not the smallest information more than its ancestors on this subject, yet the doctrine has not now a single votary in the Western part of the world. The Metempsychosis was believed by the celebrated Christian apologist, Soame Jenyns, perhaps the only believer in it of the moderns in the Western parts.

---

[1] The book of Genesis, when properly translated, says nothing on the subject.
[2] Knight, p. 131.   [3] Beausobre, *Hist. Manich.* L. vii. c. v. p. 491.   [4] Ib. p. 492.

The following observations tend not only to throw light on the doctrine of the Indians, the earliest philosophers of whom we have any genuine records, but they also shew that their doctrine is identically the same as that of certain individuals of the Western philosophers, who, recorded traditions inform us, actually travelled in very remote ages to the country of the Brahmins to learn it.

"Pythagoras, returning from his Eastern travels to Greece, taught the doctrine of the "Metempsychosis, and the existence of a Supreme Being, by whom the universe was created, and "by whose providence it is preserved; that the souls of mankind are emanations of that Being. "Socrates, the wisest of the ancient philosophers, seems to have believed that the soul existed "before the body; and that death relieves it from those seeming contrarieties to which it is "subject, by its union with our material part. Plato (in conformity to the opinions of the learned "Hindoos) asserted, that God infused into matter a portion of his divine spirit, which animates "and moves it: that mankind have two souls of separate and different natures—the one cor- "ruptible, the other immortal: that the latter is a portion of the Divine Spirit: that the mortal "soul ceases to exist with the life of the body; but the divine soul, no longer clogged by its union "with matter, continues its existence, either in a state of happiness or punishment: that the souls "of the virtuous return, after death, into the source whence they flowed; while the souls of the "wicked, after being for a certain time confined to a place destined for their reception, are sent "back to earth to animate other bodies. Aristotle supposed the souls of mankind to be portions "or emanations of the divine spirit; which at death quit the body, and, like a drop of water falling "into the ocean, are absorbed into the divinity. Zeno, the founder of the Stoic sect, taught that "throughout nature there are two eternal qualities; the one active, the other passive: that the "former is a pure and subtle æther, the divine spirit; and that the latter is in itself entirely inert, "until united with the active principle. That the divine spirit, acting upon matter, produced "fire, air, water, earth: that the divine spirit is the efficient principle, and that all nature is moved "and conducted by it. He believed also that the soul of man, being a portion of the *universal* "*soul*, returns after death to its first source. The opinion of the soul being an emanation of the "divinity, *which is believed by the Hindoos*, and was professed by Greeks, seems likewise to have "been adopted by the early Christians. Macrobius observes, Animarum originem emanare de "cœlo, inter recte philosophantes indubitatæ constant esse fidei. SAINT JUSTIN says, the soul is "incorruptible, because it EMANATES from God; and his disciple Tatianus, the Assyrian, observes, "that man having received a portion of the divinity, is immortal as God is. Such was the "system of the ancient philosophers, Pythagoreans, Brachmans, and some sects of the Chris- "tians."[1]

Thus *from trains of reasoning* similar to what I have briefly described, and from natural causes, I think arose all the ancient doctrines and mythologies.

12. The oldest philosophy or mythology of which we have any certain history, is that of the Buddha of the Eastern nations, in which are to be found the various doctrines to which I have just alluded. From the Metempsychosis arose the repugnance among the Buddhists to the slaughter of animals,—a necessary consequence of this doctrine uncorrupted and sincerely believed. From this circumstance in the first book of Genesis, or book of Wisdom, which is probably a work of the Buddhists, the slaughter of animals is prohibited or not allowed. After a time the mild doc- trines of Buddha came to be changed or corrupted and superseded by those of Crishna. Hence in the second book of Genesis, or the book of the Generations, or Re-generations[2] of the planetary

[1] Forbes, Orient. Mem. Vol. III. Ch. xxxiii. p. 261.   [2] Parkhurst, in voce, ילד ild.

bodies, which is, I think, a Brahmin work, they are allowed to be used for sacrifice. In the third book, or the book of the Generations, or Re-generations[1] of the race of man, the Adam, they are first allowed to be eaten as food.

How long a time would elapse before man would arrive at the point I here contemplate—the knowledge of the doctrines which I have described—must evidently depend, in a great measure, upon the degree of perfection in which he was turned out from the hand of his Creator. On this point we are and we must remain in ignorance. I argue upon the supposition that man was created with only sufficient information for his comfortable existence, and, therefore, I must be considered to use merely a conditional argument. If any person think it more probable that man was turned out of his Creator's hand in a state of perfection, I have no objection to this; but my reasoning does not apply to him. If he will condescend to reason with me, he must conditionally admit my premises.

13. It is not to be supposed, that I imagine these profound philosophical results respecting the Trinity, &c., to have been arrived at by the half civilized or infant man all at once—in a day, a week, or a year. No, indeed! many generations, perhaps thousands of years may have elapsed before he arrived at this point; and I think the discovery of several of them in every part of the world, new as well as old, justifies the inference that they were the doctrines of a race, in a high state of civilization, either immediately succeeding or before the flood, which has so evidently left its traces everywhere around us. Before these profound results were arrived at, innumerable attempts must have been made to discover the origin of things. Probably every kind of absurdity imaginable may have been indulged in. All this we may readily suppose, but of its truth we cannot arrive at absolute certainty. At the same time, for any thing we know to the contrary, man may have been created in such a state as easily to have arrived at these conclusions. It is scarcely possible for us at this day to be able to appreciate the advantages which the first races of mankind would possess, in not having their minds poisoned, and their understandings darkened, and enervated by the prejudices of education. Every part of modern education seems to be contrived for the purpose of enfeebling the mind of man. The nurse begins with bobgoblins and ghosts, which are followed up by the priests with devils and the eternal torments of hell. How few are the men who can entirely free themselves from these and similar delusions in endless variety instilled into the infant mind!

A learned philosopher has said, " It is surprising that so few should have perceived how " destructive of intellect, the prevailing classical system of education is; or rather that so few " should have had courage to avow their conviction respecting classical absurdity and idolatry. " Except Bacon and Hobbes, I know not that any authors of high rank have ventured to question " the importance or utility of the learning which has so long stunned the world with the noise of " its pretensions; but sure it does not require the solid learning or philosophic sagacity of a " Bacon or a Hobbes to perceive the ignorance, nonsense, folly, and *dwarfifying* tendency of the " kind of learning which has been so much boasted of by brainless pedants."

All the doctrines which I have stated above, are well known to have been those of the most ancient nations; the theory of the origin of those doctrines is my own. But I beg leave to observe, that whether the theory of their origin be thought probable or not, the fact of the existence of the doctrines will be proved beyond dispute in a great variety of ways; and it is on the fact of their existence that the argument of this work is founded. The truth or falsity of the theory of their origin will not affect the argument. But of such persons as shall dispute the mode

---

[1] These are the names which the books give to themselves.

above described, by which the ancients are held to have arrived at their knowledge, I request the statement of a more rational theory.

I shall now proceed to shew, that the doctrines which I have here laid down were disseminated among all nations, and first that the Sun or solar fire was the sole object of the worship of all nations either as God himself, or as emblem or shekinah of the Supreme Being.

CHAPTER III

The Sun the first object of Adoration of all Nations—The Gods not deceased Heroes—The Chinese have only one God—Hindoo Goddesses—Toleration and Change in Religions

1. On the first view of the mythological systems of the Gentiles, the multitude of their gods appears to be infinite, and the confusion inextricable. But if a person will only consider the following chapters carefully, and without prejudice, he will probably discover a system which, in some degree, will unravel their intricacies, will reconcile their apparent contradictions, will explain the general meaning of their mysteries, and will shew the reason why, among the various religions in later times, toleration so universally prevailed. But yet it is not intended to attempt, as some persons have done, a complete development of the minutiæ of the mysteries, or to exhibit a perfect system attended with an explanation of the ceremonies and practices which the Heathens adopted in the secret recesses of their temples, which they guarded from the prying eye of the vulgar with the greatest care and the most sacred oaths; and which have long since been buried amidst the ruins of the finest buildings of antiquity—lamentable sacrifices to the zeal, bigotry, and fury of the Iconoclasts, or of the professors of Christianity.

Few persons have exhibited more learning or ingenuity on the subject of the ancient worship than Mr. Bryant and M. Dupuis: and whatever opinion people may entertain of different parts of their works, or of some of their hypotheses, yet they can scarcely refuse assent to their general assertions, that all the religions of antiquity, at least in their origin, are found to centre in the worship of the Sun, either as God the Creator himself, or as the seat of, or as the emblem of Creator.

Socrates, Pythagoras, Plato, Zoroaster or Zeradust, &c., and all those initiated in the most secret mysteries, acknowledged one supreme God, the Lord and First Cause of all. And perhaps, though it can never be *certainly* known, those who only received the lesser mysteries,[1] might confine their worship to the sun and the host of heaven; but it was only the vulgar and ignorant who bent the knee to the stone, wood, or metal idols of the gods, perhaps only a *little more* numerous than the images of the Christian saints.

2. It has until lately been the general opinion, that the gods of the ancients were nothing but the heroes or the benefactors of mankind, living in very illiterate and remote ages, to whom a grateful posterity paid divine honours. This appears at first sight to be probable; and as it has

---

[1] An interesting account of the mysteries of the Heathens will be found in Part II. of Vol. II. of Dupuis's History of all Religions.

served the purpose of the Christian priests, to enable them to run down the religion of the ancients, and, in exposing its absurdities, to contrast it disadvantageously with their own, it has been, and continues to be, sedulously inculcated, in every public and private seminary. The generality of schoolmasters know no better; they teach what they have learned and what they believe. But, as this rank of men increase in talent and learning, this is gradually wearing away.

· Although the pretended worship of Heroes appears at first sight plausible, very little depth of thought or learning is requisite to discover that it has not much foundation in truth. It was not in the infant state of society, that men were worshiped; it was not, on the contrary, until they arrived at a very high and advanced state of civilization. It was not Moses, Zoroaster, Confucius, Socrates, Solon, Lycurgus, Plato, Pythagoras, or Numa, that were objects of worship; the benefactors of mankind in all ages have been oftener persecuted than worshiped. No, divine honours (if such they can be called) were reserved for Alexander of Macedon, the drunkard, for Augustus Cæsar, the hypocrite, or Heliogabalus, the lunatic. A species of civil adoration, despised by all persons of common understanding, and essentially different from the worship of the Supreme Being, was paid to them. It was the vice of the moment, and soon passed away. How absurd to suppose that the elegant and enlightened Athenian philosopher could worship Hercules, because he killed a lion or cleaned a stable! Or Bacchus, because he made wine or got drunk! Besides, these deified heroes can hardly be called Gods in any sense. They were more like the Christian Saints. Thus we have Divus Augustus, and Divus Paulus, and Divus Petrus. Their nature has been altogether misunderstood; it will afterward be explained.

3. After a life of the most painful and laborious research, Mr. Bryant's opinion is, that all the various religions terminated in the worship of the Sun. He commences his work by shewing, from a great variety of etymological proofs, that all the names of the Deities were derived or compounded from some word which originally meant the Sun. Notwithstanding the ridicule which has been thrown upon etymological inquiries, in consequence of the want of fixed rules, or of the absurd length to which some persons have carried them, yet I am quite certain it must, in a great measure, be from etymology at last that we must recover the lost learning of antiquity.

Macrobius[1] says, that in Thrace they worship the Sun or Solis Liber, calling him Sebadius; and from the Orphic poetry we learn that all the Gods were one :

$$\text{Εις Ζευς, εις Αιδης, εις Ηλιος, εις Διονυσος,}$$
$$\text{εις Θεος εν παντεσσι. [2]}$$

Diodorus Siculus says, that it was the belief of the ancients that Osiris, Serapis, Dionusos, Pluto, Jupiter, and Pan, were all one. [3]

Ausonius represents all the deities to be included under the term Dionusos. [4]

Sometimes Pan [5] was called the God of all, sometimes Jupiter. [6]

Nonnus also states, that all the different Gods, whatever might be their names, Hercules, Ammon, Apollo, or Mithra, centred in the Sun.

Mr. Selden says, whether they be called Osiris, or Omphis, or Nilus, or Siris, or by any other name, they all centre in the Sun, the most ancient deity of the nations. [7]

Basnage[8] says, that Osiris, that famous God of the Egyptians, was the Sun, or rather the Sun was the emblem of the beneficent God Osiris.

---

[1] Sat. L. i. 18.   [2] Orphic Fragm. iv. p. 364, Gesner, Ed.   [3] L. i. p. 23.
[4] Auson. Epigram. 30; Bryant, Vol. I. p. 310, 4to.   [5] 4 Orp. Hym. x. p. 200, Gesner.
[6] Euphorion.   [7] Selden de Diis Syriis, p. 77.   [8] B. iii. Ch. xviii. Sect. xxii.

Serapis was another name for the Sun. Remisius gives an inscription to Jupiter the Sun, *the invincible Serapis.*

Mithras was likewise the Sun, or rather was but a different name, which the Persians bestowed on the Egyptian Osiris.

Harpocrates also represented the Sun. It is true, he was also the God of Silence ; he put his finger upon his mouth, because the Sun was worshiped with a reverential silence, and thence came the Sigè of the Basilidians, who had their origin from Egypt. [1]

By the Syrians the Sun and Heat were called חמה *hme,* Chamha ;[2] and by the Persians Hama.[3] Thus the temple to which Alexander so madly marched in the desert, was called the temple of the Sun or of Ammon. Mr. Bryant shews that Ham was esteemed the Zeus of Greece, and the Jupiter of Latium.

Αμμος ὁ Ζευς Αριστελει. [4]

Αμμων γαρ Αιγυπτιοι καλεουσι τον Δια. [5]

Ham, sub Jovis nomine, in Africa cultus.[6]

Ζευ Διζυης Αμμων, κιρα τη φορε κικλυθι Μαντι.[7]

Mr. Bryant says, " The worship of Ham, or the Sun, as it was the most ancient, so it was the " most universal of any in the world. It was at first the prevailing religion of Greece ; and was " propagated over all the sea-coast of Europe, from whence it extended itself into the inland pro- " vinces. It was established in Gaul and Britain ; and was the original religion of this island, " which the Druids in after times adopted." [8]

This Ham was nothing but a Greek corruption of a very celebrated Indian word, formed of the three *letters* A U M, of which I shall have much to say hereafter.

Virgil gives the conduct of the year to Liber or Bacchus, [9] though it was generally thought to be in the care of Apollo. It also appears from the Scholia in Horace,[10] that Apollo and *Dionusos* were the same. In fact, they were all three the same, the Sun.

'Ηλιε παγγωστωρ παναιλε χρυσοφεγγες. [11]

4. It is allowed that the grand mysteries of the Grecian religion were brought by way of Thrace from Assyria, Persia, Egypt, or other Eastern parts, by a person of the name of Orpheus, or at least that it came from those parts, whoever brought it into Greece. And in the doctrines attri- buted to this philosopher, we may reasonably expect to find the ground-works of the religion, in fact, the religion unadulterated by the folly of the populace, and the craft of the priests. And here we shall find a pure and excellent religion.

Proclus says of the religion, Ζευς κεφαλη, Ζευς μεσσα· Διος δ'εκ παντα τετυκται—Jove is the head and middle of all things ; all things were made out of Jove.

According to Timotheus, in Cedrenus, Orpheus asserted the existence of an eternal, incom- prehensible Being, Δημιουργον απαντον, και αυτυ τυ αιθερος, και παντων των επ' αυτον τον αιθερα, the Creator of all things, even of the æther itself, and of all things below that æther. According to him, this Δημιουργος is called ΦΩΣ, ΒΟΥΛΗ, ΖΩΗ, Light, Counsel, Life. And Suidas says, that these three names express one and the same power, ταυτα τα τρια ονοματα μιαν δυναμιν απεφηνατο : and Timotheus concludes his account by affirming that Orpheus, in

[1] Basnage, B. iii. Ch. xviii.   [2] Selden de Diis Syriis Syntag. II. C. viii. p. 247.
[3] Gale's Court of the Gentiles, Vol. I. Ch. xi. p. 72.   [4] Hesychius.   [5] Herodotus, L. ii. C. xlii.
[6] Bochart, Geog. Sac. L. i. C. i. p. 5.   [7] Pind. Pyth. Ode iv. 28, Schol.
[8] Bryant, Vol. I. 4to. p. 284.   [9] Georg. L. i. v. 6.   [10] Lib. ii. Ode xix.
[11] Orphic Fragm. in. Macrob. Sat. L. i. C. xxiii.

his book, declared, διὰ τῶν αὐτῶν ὀνομάτων μιᾶς Θεότητος τὰ πάντα ἐγένετο, καὶ αὐτὸς ἐςι τὰ πάντα : That all things were made by one Godhead, in three names, and this God is all things. Proclus gives us the following as one of the verses of Orpheus :

Ζεὺς βασιλεὺς, Ζεὺς αὐτὸς ἀπάντων ἀρχιγενέθλος
'Εν κράτος, εἷς δαίμων γένετο μέγας ἀρχὸς ἁπάντων.

Jupiter is the king, Jupiter himself is the original source of all things ; there is one power, one god, and one great ruler over all.[1] But we have seen that Jupiter and all the other Gods were but names for the Sun ; therefore it follows that the Sun, either as emblem or as God himself, was the object of universal adoration.

The Heathens, even in the later days of their idolatry, were not so gross in their notions, but that they believed there was only one supreme God. They did, indeed, worship a multitude of deities, but they supposed all but one, to be subordinate deities. They always had a notion of one deity superior to all the powers of heaven, and all the other deities were conceived to have different offices or ministrations under him—being appointed to preside over elements, over cities, over countries, and to dispense victory to armies, health, life, and other blessings to their favourites, if permitted by the Supreme Power. Hesiod supposes one God to be the Father of the other deities ;

———— Θεῶν Πατὴρ ἠδὲ καὶ Ἀνδρῶν·

and Homer, in many passages of the Iliad, represents one Supreme Deity as presiding over all the others ;[2] and the most celebrated of their philosophers always endeavoured to assert this theology.[3]

5. Dr. Shuckford has shewn that the Egyptians originally worshiped the Supreme God, under the name of Cneph, affirming him to be without beginning or end. Philo Biblius says, that they represented him by the figure of a serpent with the head of a hawk, in the middle of a circle—certainly a very mythological emblem ; but then he represents them to have given to this Being all the attributes of the Supreme God the Creator, incorruptible and eternal. Porphyry calls him τὸν Δημιουργὸν, the Maker or Creator of the universe.[4]

The opinion entertained by Porphyry may be judged of from the following extract :

" We will sacrifice," says he, " but in a manner that is proper, bringing choice victims with the " choicest of our faculties ; burning and offering to God, who, as a wise man observed, is above " all—nothing sensual: for nothing is joined to matter, which is not impure ; and, therefore, " incongruous to a nature free from the contagion belonging to matter ; for which reason, neither " speech, which is produced by the voice, nor even internal or mental language, if it be infected " with any disorder of the mind, is proper to be offered to God ; but we worship God with an " unspotted silence, and the most pure thoughts of his nature."[5]

---

[1] Maurice, Ind. Ant. Vol. IV. p. 704.

[2] Vide Iliad, vii. ver. 202, viii. vers. 5—28, &c. See also Virgil, Æn., ii. ver. 777.

———— non hæc sine numine Divûm
Eveniunt: non te huic comitem asportare Creüsam
Fas, aut ille sinit superi regnator Olympi.

Jupiter is here supposed to be the numen divûm, and his will to be the fas or fate, which no one might contradict : Fatum est, says Cicero, non id quod superstitiosè sed quod physicè dictum causa æterna rerum. De Divin. L. i. C. xxxv. Deum—interdum necessitatem appellant, quia nihil aliter possit atque ab eo constitutem sit. Id. Academ. Quæst. L. iv. C. xliv.

[3] Cic. in lib. de Nat. Deorum, in Acad. Quæst. L. i. C. vii., Ibid. C. xxxiv.; Plato de Legib. L. x. in Phil. in Cratyl. &c.; Aristot. L. de Mundo, C vi.; Plutarch de Placit. Philos. L. i.; Id. in lib. de E. I. apud Delphos, p. 393. See Shuckford, B. ix. Vol. II. p. 394.

[4] Plut. de Iside and Osiride, p. 359; and Euseb. Præp. Evan. L. i. C. x.; Shuckford Con. B. v. p. 312.

[5] Val. Col. Vol. III. p. 466.

Shuckford says, " But if we look into Italy we not only find in general that the writers of their
" antiquities[1] remark, that their ancient deities were of a different sort from those of Greece, but
" according to Plutarch,[2] Numa, the second King of Rome, made express orders against the use of
" images in the worship of the Deity; nay, he says further, that the first 170 years after the
" building of the city, the Romans used no images, but thought the Deity invisible, and reputed
" it unlawful to make representations of him from things of an inferior nature; so that, according
" to this account, Rome being built about A. M. 3256,[3] the inhabitants were not greatly corrupted
" in their religion, even so late as A. M. 3426, which falls when Nebuchadnezzar was King of
" Babylon, and about 169 years after the time where I am to end this work. It is remarkable
" that Plutarch does not represent Numa as correcting or refining the ancient idolatry of Italy;
" but expresses, that this people never had these grosser deities, either before or for the
" first 170 years of their city; so that it is more than probable, that Greece was not thus cor-
" rupted when the Pelasgi removed from thence into Italy: and further, that the Trojans were
" not such idolaters at the destruction of their city, because, according to this account, Æneas
" neither brought with him images into Italy, nor such Gods as were worshiped by the adoration
" of images; and, therefore, Pausanias,[4] who imagined that Æneas carried the Palladium into
" Italy, was as much mistaken as the men of Argus, who affirmed themselves to have it in their
" city., The times of Numa are about 200 years after Homer, and very probably the idolatry so
" much celebrated in his writings might by this time begin to appear in Italy, and thereby
" occasion Numa to make laws and constitutions against it."[6]

After the above observations, Shuckford goes on to assert, in a style rather democratical for a
Doctor of Divinity, that the first corruptions of religion were begun by kings and rulers of nations!
And he produces several examples to support his assertion, which are not much in point. If he
had said, that these corruptions had been produced by the knavery of his own order, the priests,
working upon the timidity and weakness of timid and weak kings, and making them its tools, he
would have been perfectly correct. For this is the mode by which half the miseries of mankind
have been produced by this pernicious order of men. And when he says that the inhabitants of
Italy were not greatly corrupted, he goes too far; he ought to have confined his observations to the
Romans. But perhaps to them only he alluded.

6. The Chinese, with all their apparent idolatry, had only one God.

Speaking of the religion of the Chinese, Sir W. Jones[7] says, " Of the religious opinions enter-
" tained by Confucius and his followers, we may glean a general notion from the fragments of
" their works, translated by Couplet: they professed a firm belief in the Supreme God, and gave
" a demonstration of his being and of his providence, from the exquisite beauty and perfection of
" the celestial bodies, and the wonderful order of nature in the whole fabric of the visible world.
" From this belief they deduced a system of ethics, which the philosopher sums up in a few words
" at the close of the Lunyn. He" (says Confucius) " who shall be fully persuaded that the
" Lord of Heaven governs the universe, who shall in all things choose moderation, who shall
" perfectly know his own species, and so act among them, that his life and manners may conform
" to his knowledge of God and man, may be truly said to discharge all the duties of a sage, and to
" be exalted above the common herd of the human race!"

Marco Paulo[8] informs us, that in his time the Chinese paid their adoration to a tablet fixed
against the wall in their houses, upon which was inscribed the name of the high, celestial, and

[1] Dionys. Halicar., Lib. vii.   [2] In Numa, and Clem. Alexand. Stromat. Lib. i.   [3] Usher's Annals.
[4] In Corinthiacis.   [5] Ibid.   [6] Shuckford Con. B. v. p. 352, 8vo. Ed.
[7] Diss. VII. p. 227.   [8] B. ii. Ch. xxvi. Ed. of W. Marsden, 4to.

supreme God ; to whose honour they burnt incense, but of whom they had no image. The words, Mr. Marsden says, which were on the tablet were three, *tien,* heaven; *hoang-tien,* supreme heaven; and *Shang-ti,* sovereign Lord. De Guignes tells us, that the word *tien* stands indifferently for the visible heaven and the Supreme Deity.[1] Marco Paulo tells us, that from the God whose name was on the tablet the Chinese only petition for two things, *sound intellect* and *health of body,* but that they had another God, of whom they had a statue or idol called *Natigai,* who was the God of all terrestrial things ; in fact, God, the Creator of this world, (inferior or subordinate to the Supreme Being,) from whom they petition for fine weather, or whatever else they want—a sort of Mediator. Here is evidently a striking similarity to the doctrines of some of the early Christian heretics.

It seems pretty clear from this account, that originally, and probably at this time also, like all the ancients of the West in the midst of their degrading idolatry, they yet acknowledged one Supreme God, with many subordinate agents, precisely the same as the Heathens of Greece and Rome, and modern Christians, under the names of inferior gods, angels, demons, saints, &c. In fact they were Deists.

7. In addition to the authorities which have been produced to prove that the whole of the different Gods of antiquity resolve themselves at last, when properly examined, into different names of the God Sol, it would be easy, if it were necessary, to produce as many more from every quarter of the world ; but what, it may be asked, will you do with the Goddesses ? The reader shall now see ; and first from the learned and Rev. Mr. Maurice.

" Whoever will read the Geeta with attention will perceive in that small tract the outlines of " nearly all the various systems of theology in Asia. That curious and ancient doctrine of the " Creator being both male and female, mentioned in a preceding page to be designated in Indian " temples by a very indecent exhibition of the masculine and feminine organs of generation in " union, occurs in the following passages : ' I am the *father* and *mother* of this world; I plant myself " upon my own nature, and create again and again this assemblage of beings ; I am generation " and dissolution, the place where all things are deposited, and the inexhaustible seed of all " nature ; I am the beginning, the middle, and the end of all things.' " In another part he more directly says, " The great Brahme is the womb of all those various forms which are conceived in " every natural womb, and I am the father that soweth the seed.' "[2] Herodotus informs us that the Persian Mithras was the same with the Assyrian Venus Mylitta or Urania, and the Arabian Alitta.[3] Mr. Cudworth shews that this must have been the Aphrodita Urania, by which was meant the creating Deity. It is well known that the Venus Aphrodite was a Phœnician Deity, worshiped particularly at Citium, and was of both the male and female gender,—the Venus Genitrix.

Proclus describes Jupiter, in one of the Orphic Hymns, to be both male and female, αρρενοθηλυν, Hermaphroditic. And Bishop Synesius adopts it in a Christian hymn.[4] The Priapus of the Etruscans was both male and female. (See Table LVIII. of Gorius.) He has the membrum virile, with the female breasts.

Damascius, treating of the fecundity of the Divine Nature, cites Orpheus as teaching, that the Deity was at once both male and female, αρσενοθηλυν αυτην υπεςησατο, προς ενδειξιν των παντων γεννητικης εσιας, to shew the generative power by which all things were formed. Proclus, upon the Timæus of Plato, cites the following :

Ζευς αρσην γενετο. Ζευς αμβροτος πελετο νυμφη·

Jupiter is a man ; Jupiter is also an immortal maid. And in the same commentary, and the same page, we read that all things were contained εν γαςερι Ζηνος, in the womb of Jupiter.

---

[1] Tom. II. p. 360.   [2] Maurice Ind. Ant. Vol. IV. p. 705.   [3] Hyde de Rel. Pers. Cap. iii. p. 95.   [4] Ubi sup. p. 304.

8. Manichæus, according to Theodoret, said, in his allegorical language, " That a male-virgin " gave light and life to Eve," that is, created her. And the Pseudo-Mercurius Trismegistus in Pæmander said, that God being male and female, (αρρενοθηλυς ων,) because he is light and life, engendered by the word another intelligence, which was the Creator. The male-virgin, Theodoret says, was called Joel, or Ιαηλ, which Beausobre thinks was " EL, God, and Joha, life-making, " vivifying, life-giving, or the generating God." (So far my friend Beverley.) But which was probably merely the יו Ieu, אל al, or God Iao, of which we shall treat hereafter. Again, Mr. Beverley says, " In Genesis it is written, ' God said, Let us create man after our own image and " likeness.' This, then, ought in strictness of language to be a male and female God, or else it " would not be after the likeness proposed."

" The male-virgin of the Orientals is, I know, considered the same by Plato as his 'Εςια, or " Vesta, whom he calls the soul of the body of the universe. This Hestia, by the way, is in my " view a Sanscrit lady, whose name I take to have been EST, or she that is, or exists, having " the same meaning as the great name of the Jewish Deity. Est is shewn in the Celtic Druids to " be a Sanscrit word, and I do not doubt of this her derivation. The A terminal is added by the " Greek idiom to denote a female, as they hated an indeclinable proper name, such as HEST or " EST would have been." Extract from a letter from Mackenzie Beverley, Esq.[1]

Apuleius makes the mother of the Gods of the masculine gender, and represents her describing herself as called Minerva at Athens, Venus at Cyprus, Diana at Crete, Proserpine in Sicily, Ceres at Eleusis: in other places, Juno, Bellona, Hecate, Isis, &c.;[2] and if any doubt could remain, the philosopher Porphyry, than whom probably no one was better skilled in these matters, removes it by acknowledging that Vesta, Rhea, Ceres, Themis, Priapus, Proserpine, Bacchus, Attis, Adonis, Silenus, and the Satyrs, were all the same.[3]

Valerius Soranus calls Jupiter the mother of the Gods:

Jupiter omnipotens, Regum Rex ipse Deûmque
Progenitor, Genetrixque Deûm ; Deus et idem.

Synesius speaks of him in the same manner :

Συ Πατηρ, συ δ εσσι Μητηρ,
Συ δ αρσην, συ δι θηλυς.[4]

The like character is also given to the ancient deity Μητις, or Divine Wisdom, by which the world was framed :

Μητις-ερμηπευεται, Βολη, Φως, Ζωοδοτηρ.[5]
Αρσην μεν και θηλυς εφυς, πολυωνυμε Μητι.[6]

And in two of the Orphic Fragments all that has been said above seems to be comprehended. This Deity, like the others, is said to be of two genders, and to be also the Sun.[7]

Μητις, Mr. Bryant says, is a masculine name for a feminine deity,[8] and means Divine Wisdom. I suspect it was a corruption of the Maia or Mia of India.

In Cyprus, Venus is represented with a beard, and called Aphrodite.[9]

Calvus, the poet, calls her masculine, as does also Macrobius.[10]

---

[1] The A at the end of the word EST may be the Chaldee emphatic article; then Vesta would be the Est or the Self-existent.

[2] Apuleii Metamorph. L. ii. p. 241.   [3] Porphyry ap. Eusebium, Evan. Præp. L. iii. C. xi.
[4] Bryant, Anal. Vol. I. p. 315.   [5] Orpheus, Eusebii Chronicon.   [6] Orphic Hymn, xxxi. 10, p. 224.
[7] Bryant, Vol. I. p. 204. Ed. 4to.   [8] Bryant, Anal. Vol. II. p. 25.
[9] Hesychius Servius upon Virgil's Æneid, L. ii. 632.   [10] Satur. L. iii. C. viii.

Jupiter is called feminine, and the genetrixque Deûm,[1] by Augustine.

The Orphic verses make the Moon both male and female. [2]

9. The following extract from Sir W. Jones's Dissertation on the Gods of Greece and India, will, perhaps, be of some weight with the very large class of mankind, who prefer authority to reason ; and may serve to justify or excuse the opinions here expressed, by shewing them that they are neither new nor unsupported : " We must not be surprised at finding, on a close examination, " that the characters of all the Pagan Deities, male and female, melt into each other, and at last " into one or two ; for it seems a well founded opinion, that the whole crowd of Gods and God- " desses in ancient Rome and modern Váránes, mean only the powers of nature, and principally " those of the *Sun*, expressed in a variety of ways, and by a multitude of fanciful names."

In a future part of this work I shall have much more to say of the Goddesses or the female generative power, which became divided from the male, and in consequence was the cause of great wars and miseries to the Eastern parts of the world, and of the rise of a number of sects in the Western, which have not been at all understood.

Thus, we see, there is in fact an end of all the multitude of the Heathen Gods and Goddesses, so disguised in the Pantheons and books of various kinds, which the priests have published from time to time to instil into the minds of their pupils—that the ancient Heathen philosophers and legislators were the slaves of the most degrading superstition ; that they believed such nonsense as the metamorphoses described by Ovid, or the loves of Jupiter, Venus, &c., &c. That the rabble were the victims of a degrading superstition, I have no doubt. This was produced by the knavery of the ancient priests, and it is in order to reproduce this effect that the modern priests have misrepresented the doctrines of their predecessors. By vilifying and running down the religion of the ancients, they have thought they could persuade their votaries that their new religion was *necessary* for the good of mankind : a religion which, in consequence of their corruptions, has been found to be in practice much worse and more injurious to the interests of society than the old one. For, from these corruptions the Christian religion—the religion of purity and truth when uncorrupted—*has not brought peace but a sword.*

After the astrologers had parcelled out the heavens into the forms of animals, &c., and the annual path of the Sun had become divided into twelve parts, each part designated by some animal, or other figure, or known emblem, it is not surprising that they should have become the objects of adoration. This M. Dupuis has shewn,[3] was the origin of the Arabian and Egyptian adoration of animals, birds, &c. Hence, in the natural progress of events, the adoration of images arose among the Heathens and Christians.

10. The same tolerating spirit generally prevailed among the votaries of the Heathen Gods of the *Western world*, which we find among the Christian saints. For though in some few instances the devotees in Egypt quarrelled about their Gods, as in some few instances the natives of Christian towns have quarrelled about their Divi or tutelar saints, yet these petty wars never created much mischief.[4] They were evidently no ways dangerous to the emoluments of the priests, and therefore they were not attended with very important consequences.

A great part of the uncertainty and apparent contradictions which we meet with in the history of the religions of antiquity, evidently arises from the inattention of the writers to the changes which long periods of time produce.

It is directly contrary to the law of nature for any thing to remain stationary. The law of

---

[1] August. de Civit. Dei, L. iv. C. xi. and L. vii. C. ix.   [2] Hymn viii. 4.
[3] Ch. i. Rel. Univ.
[4] See Mosheim, who shews that the religious wars of the Egyptians were not like those of the Christians.

perpetual motion is universal; we know of no such thing as absolute rest. Causes over which man has no controul overturn and change his wisest institutions. Monuments of folly and of wisdom, all, all crumble into dust. The Pyramids of Egypt, and the codes of the Medes or of Napoleon, all will pass away and be forgotten.

M. Dupuis, in his first chapter, has shewn that probably all nations first worshiped, as we are told the Persians did, without altars or temples, in groves and high places. After a certain number of years, in Persia, came temples and idols, with all their abuses; and these, in their turn, were changed or abolished, and the worship of the Sun restored, or perhaps the worship of the Sun only as emblem of the Creator. This was probably the change said to have been effected by Zoroaster.

The Israelites at the *exodus* had evidently run into the worship of Apis the Bull, or the Golden Calf of Egypt, which it was the object of Moses to abolish, and in the place thereof to substitute the worship of one God—*Iao*, Jehovah—which, in fact, was only the Sun or the Solar Fire, yet not the Sun, as Creator, but as emblem of or the shekinah of the Divinity. The Canaanites, according to the Mosaic account, were not idolaters in the time of Abraham; but it is implied that they became *so* in the long space between the time he lived and that of Moses. The Assyrians seem to have become idolaters early, and not, as the Persians, to have had any reformer like Zoroaster or Moses, but to have continued till the Iconoclasts, Cyrus and Darius, reformed them with fire and sword; as their successor Cambyses soon afterward did the Egyptians. The observations made on the universality of the solar worship, contain but very little of what might be said respecting it; but yet enough is said to establish the fact. If the reader wish for more, his curiosity will be amply repaid by a perusal of Mr. Bryant's Analysis of the Heathen Mythology. He may also read the fourth chapter of Cudworth's Intellectual System, which is a most masterly performance.

CHAPTER IV

Two Ancient Ethiopias—Great Black Nation in Asia—The Buddha of India a Negro—The Arabians were Cushites—Memnon—Shepherd Kings—Hindoos and Egyptians similar—Syria peopled from India

1. In taking a survey of the human inhabitants of the world, we find two classes, distinguished from each other by a clear and definite line of demarkation, the *black* and *white* colours of their skins. This distinguishing mark we discover to have existed in ages the most remote. If we suppose them all to have descended from one pair, the question arises, Was that pair *black* or *white?* If I were at present to say that I thought them black, I should be accused of a fondness for paradox, and I should find as few persons to agree with me, as the African negroes do when they tell Europeans that the Devil is *white*. (And yet no one, except a West-India planter, will deny that the poor Africans have reason on their side.) However, I say not that they were *black*, but I shall, in the course of this work, produce a number of extraordinary facts, which will be quite sufficient to prove, that a black race, in *very* early times, had more influence over the affairs of the world than has been lately suspected; and I think I shall shew, by some very striking circumstances yet existing, that the effects of this influence have not entirely passed away.

2. It was the opinion of *Sir William Jones*, that a great nation of Blacks[1] formerly possessed the dominion of Asia, and held the seat of empire at Sidon.[2] These must have been the people called by Mr. Maurice Cushites or Cuthites, described in Genesis; and the opinion that they were Blacks is corroborated by the translators of the Pentateuch, called the Seventy, constantly rendering the word *Cush* by Ethiopia. It is very certain that, if this opinion be well founded, we must go for the time when this empire flourished to a period anterior to all our regular histories. It can only be known to have existed from accidental circumstances, which have escaped amidst the ruins of empires and the wrecks of time.

Of this nation we have no account; but it must have flourished after the deluge. And, as our regular chronological systems fill up the time between the flood and what is called known, undoubted history; if it be allowed to have existed, its existence will of course prove that no dependence can be placed on the early parts of that history. It will shew that all the early chronology is false; for the story of this empire is not told. It is certain that its existence can only be known from insulated circumstances, collected from various quarters, and combining to establish the fact. But if I succeed in collecting a sufficient number to carry conviction to an impartial mind, the empire must be allowed to have existed.

3. The religion of Buddha, of India, is well known to have been very ancient. In the most ancient temples scattered throughout Asia, where his worship is yet continued, he is found *black as jet*, with the flat face, thick lips, and curly hair of the Negro. Several statues of him may be met with in the Museum of the East-India Company. There are two exemplars of him brooding on the face of the deep, upon a coiled serpent. To what time are we to allot this Negro? He will be proved to have been prior to the god called Cristna. He must have been prior to or contemporaneous with the black empire, supposed by Sir William Jones to have flourished at Sidon. The religion of this Negro God is found, by the ruins of his temples and other circumstances, to have been spread over an immense extent of country, even to the remotest parts of Britain, and to have been professed by devotees inconceivably numerous. I very much doubt whether Christianity *at this day* is professed by more persons than yet profess the religion of Buddha. Of this I shall say more hereafter.

4. When several cities, countries, or rivers, at great distances from each other, are found to be called by the same name, the coincidence cannot be attributed to accident, but some specific cause for such an effect must be looked for. Thus we have several cities call Heliopolis, or the city of the Sun; the reason for which is sufficiently obvious. Thus, again, there were several Alexandrias; and on close examination we find two Ethiopias alluded to in ancient history—one above the higher or southern part of *Egypt*, and the other somewhere to the east of it, and, as it has been thought, in Arabia. The people of this latter are called Cushim in the Hebrew text of the Old Testament, and Ethiopians by the text of the Septuagint, or the Seventy. That they cannot have been the Ethiopians of Africa is evident from a single passage,[3] where they are said to have invaded Judah in the days of Asa, under Zerah, their king or leader. But the Lord smote the Cushim; and Asa and the people that were with him pursued them unto Gerar; and the Ethiopians were overthrown, and they (i. e. Asa and his people) smote all the cities round about Gerar, &c. Whence it plainly follows, that the Cushim here mentioned, were such as inhabited the parts adjoining to Gerar, and consequently not any part of the African Ethiopia, but Arabia.

---

[1] I do not use the word Negro, because they MAY not have been *Negroes* though *Blacks*, though it is probable that they were so; and I wish the distinction to be remembered.

[2] But why should not Babylon have been the place?   [3] 2 Chron. xiv. 9—15.

When it is said that Asa smote the Cushites or Ethiopians, in number a million of soldiers, as far as Gerar, and despoiled all the cities round about, it is absurd to suppose that the Gerar in the lot of the tribe of Simeon is meant. The expression all the cities and the million of men cannot apply to the little town of that tribe. Probably the city in Wilkinson's Atlas, in the *Tabula Orientalis*, at the side of the Persian gulf, which is called Gerra, is the city meant by the word Gerar; and, that Saba was near where it is placed by Dr. Stukeley, or somewhere in the Peninsula, now called Arabia.

In 2 Chron. xxi. 16, it is said, *And of the Arabians that were near the Ethiopians*. This again shews that the Ethiopians were in the Peninsula, or bordered on it to the eastwards. They could not have lived to the west, because the whole land of Egypt lay between them, if they went by land; and the Red Sea lay between the two nations westwards.

In Habakkuk iii. 7, the words Midian and Cushan are used as synonymes: *I saw the tents of Cushan in affliction : the curtains of the land of Midian did tremble.*

It is said in Numbers xii. 1, " *And Miriam and Aaron spake against Moses, because of the Ethiopian woman whom he had married; for he had married an Ethiopian woman.*" אשה cusit. It appears that this Ethiopian woman was the daughter of Jethro, priest of Midian, near Horeb, in Arabia. [1]

5. Dr. Wells has justly observed, that the Cush spoken of in scripture is evidently Arabia, from Numbers xii. 1, just cited; and that it is also certain, from Exod. ii. 15—21, that the wife of Moses was a Midianitish woman; and it is proved that Midian or Madian was in Arabia, from Exod. iii. 1, &c.: consequently the Cush here spoken of, and called Ethiopia, must necessarily mean Arabia. He also proves, from Ezek. xxix. 10, that when God says he " will make the land " desolate from the tower of Syene to the borders of Ethiopia," *Cush*, he cannot mean an African Cush, because he evidently means *from one boundary of Egypt to the other*: and as Syene is the southern boundary between the African Ethiopia and Egypt, it cannot possibly be that he speaks of the former, but of the other end of Egypt, which is Arabia.

The circumstance of the translators of the Septuagint version of the Pentateuch having rendered the word Cush by the word Ethiopia, is a very decisive proof that the theory of two Ethiopias is well founded. Let the translators have been who they may, it is totally impossible to believe that they could be so ignorant as to suppose that the African Ethiopia could border on the Euphrates, or that the Cushites could be African Ethiopians.

From all the accounts which modern travellers give of the country above Syene, there does not appear, either from ruins or any other circumstance, reason to believe that it was ever occupied by a nation strong enough to fight the battles and make the great figure in the world which we know the people called Cushites or Ethiopians did at different times. The valley of the Nile is very narrow, not capable of containing a great and powerful people. Sheba and Saba were either one or two cities of the Cushites or Ethiopians, and Pliny says, that the Sabæans extended from the Red Sea to the Persian Gulf, thus giving them the whole of Arabia; one part of which, it is well known, is called from its fertility of soil and salubrity of climate, Felix, or The Happy.

---

[1] Vide Exod. ch. ii. and iii. It is not to be supposed that this great tribe of Israelites had not laws before those given on Sinai. It is perfectly clear that great numbers of those in Leviticus were only re-enactments of old laws or customs. The marriage of Moses with an Ethiopian woman, against which Miriam and Aaron spoke, was a breach of the law, and the children were illegitimate. This was the reason why Aaron succeeded to the priestly office, instead of the sons of Moses. This also furnishes an answer to what a learned author has written about the disinterested conduct of Moses proving his divine mission. The conduct of Moses, in this instance, proves nothing, and all the labour of the learned gentleman has been thrown away. But Moses had two wives, both Ethiopians—one of Meroe, called Tharbis, and the other of Midian, in Arabia. Josephus' Antiq. L. ii. ch. x.

Dr. Wells states, that the Ethiopians of Africa alone are commonly called *Lubim*, both by ancient and modern writers.[1]

But the country east of the Euphrates was called Cush, as well as the country west of it; thus giving the capital of Persia, Susan or Susiana, which was said to be built by Memnon, to the Cushites or Ethiopians, as well as Arabia.

Mr. Frey, in his vocabulary, gives the word בוש, *cus*, as a word whose meaning is unknown; but the Septuagint tells us it meant *black*. Mr. Hyde shews, that it was a common thing for the Chaldeans to substitute the Tau for the Shin, thus בות *cut*, for בוש *cus*. Thus, in their dialect, the Cuthites were the same as the Cushites.

If my reader will examine all the remaining passages of the Old Testament, not cited by me, where the words Ethiopia and Ethiopians are used, he will see that many of them can by no possibility relate to the African Ethiopia.

6. Eusebius[2] states the Ethiopians to have come and settled in Egypt, in the time of Amenophis. According to this account, as well as to the account given by Philostratus,[3] there was no such country as Ethiopia beyond Egypt until this invasion. According to Eusebius these people came from the river Indus, and planted themselves to the south of Egypt, in the country called from them Ethiopia. The circumstance named by Eusebius that they came from the Indus, at all events, implies that they came from the East, and not from the South, and would induce a person to suspect them of having crossed the Red Sea from Arabia: they must either have done this, or have come round the northern end of the Red Sea by the Isthmus of Suez; but they certainly could not have come from the present Ethiopia.

But there are several passages in ancient writers which prove that Eusebius is right in saying, not only that they came from the East, but from a very distant or very eastern part.

Herodotus[4] says, that there were two Ethiopian nations, one in India, the other in Egypt. He derived his information from the Egyptian priests, a race of people who must have known the truth; and there seems no reason either for them or Herodotus to have mis-stated the fact.

Philostratus[5] says, that the Gymnosophists of Ethiopia, who settled near the sources of the Nile, descended from the Bramins of India, having been driven thence for the murder of their king.[6] This, Philostratus says, he learnt from an ancient Brahmin, called Jarchas.

Another ancient writer, Eustathius, also states, that the Ethiopians came from India. These concurring accounts can scarcely be doubted; and here may be discovered the mode and time also when great numbers of ancient rites and ceremonies might be imported from India into Egypt: for, that there was a most intimate relation between them in very ancient times cannot be doubted; indeed, it is not doubted. The only question has been, whether Egypt borrowed from India, or India from Egypt. All probability is clearly, for a thousand reasons, in favour of the superior antiquity of India, as Bailly and many other learned men have shewn—a probability which seems to be reduced to a certainty by Herodotus, the Egyptians themselves, and the other authors just now quoted. There is not a particle of proof, from any historical records known to the author, that any colony ever passed from Egypt to India, but there is, we see, direct, positive historical evidence, of the Indians having come to Africa. No attention can be paid to the idle stories of the conquest of India by Bacchus, who was merely an imaginary personage, in short, the God Sol.

Dr. Shuckford gives an opinion that Homer and Herodotus are both right, and that there were two Ethiopias, and that the Africans came from India.[7]

[1] Wells, Vol. I. p. 200.   [2] In Chron. ad Num. 402.   [3] In vita Apollon. Tyanei.
[4] L. vii. C. lxx.   [5] Vita Apoll. C. vi.   [6] Crawford, Res. Vol. II. p. 193.   [7] B. ix. p. 334.

7. The Bishop of Avranches thinks he has found three provinces of the name of *Chus*; Ethiopia, Arabia, and Susiana.[1] There were three Ethiopias, that is, countries of Blacks, not three *Chusses*; and this is perfectly consistent with what M. Bochart[2] has maintained, that Ethiopia (of Africa) is not named Chus in any place of scripture; and this is also consistent with what is said by both Homer and Herodotus.[3] The bishop shews clearly, that the ancient Susiana is the modern *Chuzestan* or Elam, of which Susa was the capital. The famous Memnon, probably the Sun, was said to be the son of Aurora. But Eschylus informs us, that Cissiene was the mother of Memnon, and to him the foundation of Susa is attributed; and its citadel was called Memnonium, and itself the city of Memnon. This is the Memnon who was said to have been sent to the siege of Troy, and to have been slain by Achilles; and who was also said, by the ancient authors, to be an Ethiopian or a Black. It seems the Egyptians suppose that this Memnon was their king Amenophis. The Ethiopians are stated by Herodotus to have come from the Indus; according to what modern chronologers deduce from his words, about the year 1615 B. C., about four hundred years after the birth of Abraham, in (1996,) and about a hundred years before Moses rebelled against the Egyptians and brought the Israelites out of Egypt. Palaces were shewn which belonged to this Memnon at Thebes and other places in Egypt, as well as at Susa, which from him were called in both places Memnoniums; and to him was erected the famous statue at Thebes, which is alleged to have given out a sound when first struck by the rays of the morning sun. Bishop Huet thinks, (probably very correctly,) that this statue was made in imitation of similar things which the Jewish traveller Rabbi Benjamin found, in the country where the descendants of Chus adore the sun; and this he shews to be the country of which we speak. It lies about Bussora, where the Sabeans are found in the greatest numbers, and who are the people of whom he speaks.

The bishop thinks this Memnon cannot have been Amenophis, because he lived very many years before the siege of Troy, in which he is said to have been an actor. It seems to me to be as absurd to look to Homer or Virgil for the chronology of *historical facts*, as to Shakespeare, Milton, or any other epic poet. These poems *may* state facts, but nothing of a historical or chronological kind can be received without some collateral evidence in confirmation. It never was supposed to be incumbent on any epic poet to tie himself down to mere historical matters of fact. And wherever it is evident, either from the admission of a later historical author or from any other circumstance, that he is relating facts from the works of the poets without any other authority, he can be as little depended upon as they can.

The bishop has shewn that the accounts of modern authors, George Syncellus, Suidas, Pausanias, Dionysius *Periegites*, &c., &c., are full of contradictions; that they are obliged to suppose two Memnons. All this arises from these persons treating the poem of Homer as a history, instead of a poem. *We shall never have an ancient history worthy of the perusal of men of common sense, till we cease treating poems as history, and send back such personages as Hercules, Theseus, Bacchus, &c., to the heavens, whence their history is taken, and whence they never descended to the earth.*

It is not meant to be asserted that these epic poems may not be of great use to a historian. It is only meant to protest against their being held as authority by themselves, when opposed either to other histories or to known chronology. This case of Memnon is in point. Homer wanted a hero to fill up his poem; and, without any regard to date, or any thing wrong in so doing, he accommodated the history to his poem, making use of Amenophis or Memnon, or the religious tradition whichever it was, as he thought proper. These poems may also be of great

---

[1] Diss. on Parod. Ch. xiii.   [2] Phaleg. L. iv. C. ii.
[3] Homer, Odyss. δ; Herod. Polymn. Cap. lxix. lxx.; also Steph. in 'Ομηρίται.

use as evidence of the customs and manners of the times, both of when they were written and previously, and very often of dry unconnected facts which may turn out to be of consequence. Thus Virgil makes Memnon *black*,[1] as does also Pindar.[2] That Pindar and Virgil were right, the features of the bust of Memnon in the British Museum prove, for they are evidently those of the Negro.

8. It is probable that the Memnon here spoken of, if there ever were such a man, was the leader of the Shepherds, who are stated by Manetho and other historians to have come from the East, and to have conquered Egypt. The learned Dr. Shuckford thinks, that the troubles caused in Egypt by the shepherd kings appear to have happened about the time the Jews left it under Moses. He places these events between the death of Joseph and the birth of Moses.[3] And he supposes that the Jews left the country in consequence of the oppressions of these shepherd kings. It is very clear that much confusion has arisen in this part of ancient history from these eastern shepherds having been confounded with the Israelites, and also from facts relating to the one having been attributed to the other. Josephus takes the different accounts to relate to the same people. This is attended with great difficulty. The shepherds are said by Manetho, after a severe struggle with the old inhabitants, to have taken refuge in a city called Avaris or Abaris,[4] where they were a long time besieged, and whence at last they departed, two hundred and forty thousand in number, together with their wives and children, (in consequence of a capitulation,) into the deserts of Syria.

If there were two races of people who have been confounded together, one of which came from India and overran Arabia, Palestine, and Egypt, and brought thence its religion to the Egyptians, and was in colour black, it must have come in a very remote period. This may have been the race of shepherd kings, of whom Josephus speaks when he says, they oppressed the Israelites : but the assertion of Josephus can hardly have been true, for they must have been expelled long before the Israelites came. The second race were the Arabian shepherd tribe called captives, who, after being settled some time in the land of Goshen, were driven or went out into the open country of Arabia. They at last, under the command of Joshua, conquered Palestine, and finally settled there. Bishop Cumberland has proved that there was a dynasty of Phenician shepherd kings, who were driven out three hundred years before Moses. These seem to have been the black or Ethiopian, Phenician Memnonites. They may have exactly answered to this description, but to his date of three hundred years I pay no attention, further than that it was a great length of time.

Josephus says that the copies of Manetho differed, that in one the Shepherds were called *Captives*, not *kings*, and that he thinks this is more agreeable to ancient history; that Manetho also says, the nation called Shepherds were likewise called Captives in their sacred books; and that after they were driven out of Egypt, they journied through the wilderness of Syria, and built a city in Judea, which they called Jerusalem.[5]

Josephus[6] says, that Manetho was an Egyptian by birth, but that he understood Greek, in which he wrote his history, translating it from the old Egyptian records.

If the author understand Mr. Faber rightly in his Horæ Mosaicæ,[7] he is of opinion that these

---

[1] Æneid, Lib. i.   [2] Olymp. Od. ii.; vide Diss. of Bishop Huet, ch. xiii. p. 185.
[3] Shuckford, Conn. pp. 233, 234.

[4] We read of a person coming from the Hyperboreans to Greece, in the time of Pythagoras, called Abaris or Avaris. Josephus also tells us that the city in the Saite Nomos, (Seth-roite,) i. e. *Goshen*, where the oriental Shepherds resided, was called Avaris. Now I suspect that this man was called from the Hebrew word עברי *ober*, as was also the name of the city, and that they both meant stranger or foreigner : the same as the tribe of Abraham, in Syria.

[5] Jos. vers. Apion, B. i. § xiv., Whiston, p. 291.   [6] Ut sup. § xiv.   [7] Ch. ii. Sect. xi. p. 23.

Shepherd Captives were the Israelites. The accounts of these two tribes of people are confused, as may naturally be expected, but there are certainly many striking traits of resemblance between them. Mr. Shuckford, with whom in this Mr. Volney agrees, thinks there were two races of Shepherd kings, and in this opinion he coincides with most of the ancients; but most certainly, in his treatise against Apion, Josephus only names one. [1] We shall have much to say hereafter respecting these shepherds, under the name of Palli.

The only objection which occurs against Amenophis or Memnon being the leader of the Hindoo race who first came from the Indus to Egypt is, that according to our ideas of his chronology, he could scarcely be sufficiently early to agree with the known historical records of India. But our chronology is in so very vague and uncertain a state, that very little dependance can be placed upon it. And it will never be any better till learned men search for the truth and fairly state it, instead of sacrificing it to the idle legends or allegories of the priests, which cannot by any possible ingenuity be made consistent even with themselves.

Mr. Wilsford, in his treatise on Egypt and the Nile, in the Asiatic Researches, informs us, that many very ancient statues of the God Buddha in India have crisp, curly hair, with flat noses and thick lips; and adds, " nor can it be reasonably doubted, that a race of Negroes formerly had power " and pre-eminence in India."

This is confirmed by Mr. Maurice, who says, " The figures in the Hindoo caverns are of a very " different character from the present race of Hindoos : their countenances are broad and full, the " nose flat, and the lips, particularly the under lip, remarkably thick." [2]

This is again confirmed by Colonel Fitzclarence in the journal of his journey from India. And Maurice, in the first volume of his Indian Antiquities, states, that the figures in the caves in India and in the temples in Egypt, are absolutely the same as given by Bruce, Niebuhr, &c.

Justin states, that the Phœnicians being obliged to leave their native country in the East, they settled first near the Assyrian Lake, which is the Persian Gulf; and Maurice says, " We find an " extensive district, named Palestine, to the east of the Euphrates and Tigris. The word Pales- " tine seems derived from Pallisthan, the seat of the Pallis or Shepherds." [3] Palli, in India, means Shepherd.

This confirms Sir William Jones's opinion, in a striking manner, respecting a black race having reigned at Sidon.

9. It seems to me that great numbers of circumstances are producible, and will be produced in the following work, to prove that the mythology, &c., &c., of Egypt were derived from India, but which persons who are of a different opinion endeavour to explain away, as inconclusive proofs. They, however, produce few or no circumstances tending towards the proof of the contrary, viz. that India borrowed from Egypt, to enable the friends of the superior antiquity of India, in their turn, to explain away or disprove.

It is a well-known fact that our Hindoo soldiers when they arrived in Egypt, in the late war, recognized the Gods of their country in the ancient temples, particularly their God Cristna.

The striking similarity, indeed identity, of the style of architecture and the ornaments of the ancient Egytian and Hindoo temples, Mr. Maurice has proved[4] beyond all doubt. He says, " Travellers, who have visited Egypt in periods far more recent than those in which the above- " cited authors journeyed thither, confirm the truth of their relation, in regard both to the number " and extent of the excavations, the beauty of the sculptures, and their similitude to those carved " in the caverns of India. The final result, therefore, of this extended investigation is, that, in

---

[1] Jos. vers. Apion, C. i. § xiv. B. i.   [2] Maurice, Hind. Ant. Vol. II. pp. 374—376.

[3] Maurice, Hist. Vol. II. p. 146.   [4] Antiquities of Hindostan, Vol. I. Sect. viii.

" the remotest periods, there has existed a most intimate connexion between the two nations, and
" that colonies emigrating from Egypt to India, or from India to Egypt, transported their deities
" into the country in which they respectively took up their abode." This testimony of the Rev.
Mr. Maurice's is fully confirmed by Sir W. Jones, who says,

" The remains of architecture and sculpture in India, which I mention here as mere monuments
" of antiquity, not as specimens of ancient art, seem to prove an early connexion between this
" country and Africa: the pyramids of Egypt, the colossal statues described by Pausanias and
" others, the Sphinx, and the Hermes Canis, which last bears a great resemblance to the Varáhá-
" vatar, or the incarnation of Vishnou in the form of a Boar, indicate the style and mythology
" of the same indefatigable workmen who formed the vast excavations of Canara, the various
" temples and images of Buddha, and the idols which are continually dug up at Gayá, or in its
" vicinity. The letters on many of those monuments appear, as I have before intimated, partly
" of Indian, and partly of Abyssinian or Ethiopic, origin: and all these indubitable facts may
" induce no ill-founded opinion, that Ethiopia and Hindostan were peopled or colonized by the
" same extraordinary race; in confirmation of which it may be added, that the mountaineers of
" Bengal and Bahar, can hardly be distinguished in some of their features, particularly their lips
" and noses, from the modern Abyssinians, whom the Arabs call the children of Cush: and the
" ancient Hindus, according to Strabo, differed in nothing from the Africans but in the straight-
" ness and smoothness of their hair, while that of the others was crisp or woolly; a difference
" proceeding chiefly, if not entirely, from the respective humidity or dryness of their atmospheres:
" hence the people who *received the first light* of the rising sun, according to the limited knowledge
" of the ancients, are said by Apuleius to be the Arii and Ethiopians, by which he clearly meant
" certain nations of India; where we frequently see figures of Buddha with curled hair, apparently
" designed for a representation of it in its natural state."[1]

Again, Sir W. Jones says, " Mr. Bruce and Mr. Bryant have proved that the Greeks gave the
" appellation of Indians to the nations of Africa, and to the people among whom we now live."[2] I
shall account for this in the following work.

Mons. de Guignes maintains, that the inhabitants of Egypt, in very old times, had unquestionably a common origin with the old natives of India, as is fully proved by their ancient monuments, and the affinity of their languages and institutions, both political and religious.[3]

Many circumstances confirming the above, particularly with respect to the language, will be
pointed out hereafter.

10. It is curious to observe the ingenuity exercised by Sir W. Jones to get over obstacles which
oppose themselves to his theological creed, which he has previously determined nothing *shall*
persuade him to disbelieve. He says, " We are told that the Phenicians, like the Hindus, adored
" the Sun, and asserted water to be the first of created things; *nor can we doubt that Syria,*
" *Samaria, and Phenice,* or the long strip of land on the shore of the Mediterranean, *were*
" *anciently peopled by a branch of the Indian stock,* but were afterwards inhabited by that race
" which, for the present we call Arabian." Here we see he admits that the ancient Phœnicians
were Hindoos: he then goes on to observe, that " In all three *the oldest religion* was the Assyrian,
" as it is called by Selden, and the Samaritan letters appear to have been the same at first with
" those of Pheuice."[4] Now, with respect to which was the oldest religion, as their religions
were all, at the bottom, precisely the same, viz. the worship of the Sun, there is as strong a
probability that the earliest occupiers of the land, the Hindoos, were the founders of the solar
worship, as the contrary.

---

[1] Diss. III. on Hind., by Sir W. Jones, p. 111.   [3] Jones's Eighth An. Diss. Asiatic Res.
[2] Diss. VII. of Sir W. Jones on the Chinese, p. 220.   [4] Sir W. Jones's Eighth An. Diss.

When the various circumstances and testimonies which have been detailed are taken into consideration, there can be scarcely any doubt left on the mind of the reader, that, by the word Ethiopia, two different countries have been meant. This seems to be perfectly clear. And it is probable that by an Ethiopian, a *negro*, correctly speaking, may have been meant, not merely a *black* person; and it seems probable that the following may have been the real fact, viz. that a race either of Negroes or Blacks, but probably of the former, came from India to the West, occupying or conquering and forming a kingdom on the two banks of the Euphrates, the eastern Ethiopia alluded to in Numbers, chap. xii.; that they advanced forwards occupying Syria, Phœnicia, Arabia, and Egypt; that they, or some tribe of them, were the shepherd kings of Egypt; that after a time the natives of Egypt rose against them and expelled part of them into Abyssinia or Ethiopia, another part of them into Idumea or Syria, or Arabia, and another part into the African desert of Lybia, where they were called Lubim.

The time at which these people came to the West was certainly long previous to the exodus of the Israelites from Egypt; but how long previous to that event must remain doubtful. No system of chronology can be admitted as evidence; every known system is attended with too many difficulties. Perhaps chronology may be allowed to instruct us, in relation to facts, as to which preceded or followed, but certainly nothing more. No chronological date can be depended on previous to the capture of Babylon by Cyrus: whether we can depend upon it quite so far back seems to admit of doubt.

Part of the ancient monuments of Egypt may have been executed by these people. The memnoniums found in Persia and in Egypt leave little room to doubt this. In favour of this hypothesis all ancient sacred and profane historical accounts agree; and poetical works of imagination cannot be admitted to compete as evidence with the works of serious historians like Herodotus. This hypothesis likewise reconciles all the accounts which at first appear discordant, but which no other will do. It is also confirmed by a considerable quantity of circumstantial evidence. It is, therefore, presumed by the writer, he may safely assume in his forthcoming discussions, that there were two Ethiopias, one to the East of the Red Sea, the other to the West of it; and that a very great nation of *blacks* from India, did rule over almost all Asia in a very remote æra, in fact beyond the reach of history or any of our records.

This and what has been observed respecting judicial astrology will be retained in recollection by my reader; they will both be found of great importance in our future inquiries. In my Essay on *The Celtic Druids,* I have shewn, that a great nation called Celtæ, of whom the Druids were the priests, spread themselves almost over the whole earth, and are to be traced in their rude gigantic monuments from India to the extremity of Britain. Who these can have been but the early individuals of the *black* nation of whom we have been treating I know not, and in this opinion I am not singular. The learned Maurice says, " Cuthites, i. e. Celts, built the great temples in India " and Britain, and excavated the caves of the former." [1]   And the learned Mathematician, Reuben Burrow, has no hesitation in pronouncing Stonehenge to be a temple of the black, curly-headed Buddha.

I shall leave the further consideration of this *black* nation for the present. I shall not detain my reader with any of the numerous systems of the Hindoos, the Persians, the Chaldeans, Egyptians, or other nations, except in those particular instances which immediately relate to the object of this work,—in the course of which I shall often have occasion to recur to what I have here said, and shall also have opportunities of supporting it by additional evidence.

---

[1] Maurice, Hist. Hind. Vol. II. p. 249.

BOOK II

CHAPTER I

The Ancient Persians of the Religion of Abraham—First Books of Genesis—Disingenuous conduct in the Translatory of the Bible—Abraham acknowledged more than one God

1. THE religion and ancient philosophy of the Chaldeans, by whom are meant the Assyrians, as given by Stanley,[1] at first view exhibit a scene of the utmost confusion. This may be attributed in part to the circumstance, that it is not the history of their religion and philosophy at any one particular æra, but that it is extended over a space of several thousand years, during which, perhaps, they might undergo many changes. To this circumstance authors have not paid sufficient attention; so that what may have been accurately described in the time of *Herodotus* may have been much changed in the time of *Porphyry*. Thus different authors appear to write in contradiction to each other, though each may have written what was strictly true at the time of which he was writing.

Under the name of the country of the Chaldeans several states have at different periods been included. It has been the same with respect to Persia. When an author speaks of Persia, sometimes Persia only is meant, sometimes Bactria, sometimes Media, sometimes all three; and Assyria is very often included with them. Here is another source of difficulty and confusion.

After the conquest of Babylon and its dependent states, the empire founded by its conquerors, the Persians, was often called, by writers of the Western part of the world, the Assyrian or Chaldean empire. In all these states or kingdoms the religion of the Persians prevailed; and the use of the indiscriminate terms, Persian, Assyrian, and Chaldean, by Porphyry, Plutarch, &c., when treating of that empire, has been the cause of much of the uncertainty respecting what was the religion of the Persians and Assyrians. Thus, when one historian says, the Chaldeans, meaning the Assyrians, worshiped the idol Moloch; and another says, they worshiped fire, as the emblem of the Deity; they are probably both correct: one assertion is true before the time of Cyrus, the other afterward.

Although it may not be possible to make out a connected and complete system, yet it will be no difficult matter to shew, that, at one particular time, the worship of the Assyrians, Chaldeans, Persians, Babylonians, was that of one Supreme God; that the Sun was worshiped as an emblem only of the divinity, and that the religions of Abraham, of the children of Israel, and of these Eastern nations were originally the same. The Christian divines, who have observed the identity, of course maintain that the other nations copied from Moses, or the natives of Palestine, i. e. that several great and mighty empires, copied from a small and insignificant province. No doubt this is possible: whether probable or not must be left to the judgment of the reader, after he has well considered all the circumstances detailed in the following work.

2. The very interesting and ancient book of Genesis, on which the modern system of the

---

[1] Part XIX.

reformed Christian religion is chiefly founded, has always been held to be the production of Moses. But it requires very little discernment to perceive, that it is a collection of treatises, probably of different nations. The first ends with the third verse of the second chapter—the second with the last verse of the fourth.

In the first verse of the first book, the ALEIM, which will be proved to be the Trinity, being in the plural number, are said by Wisdom to have formed, from matter previously existing, the םימש *smim*, or planetary bodies, which were believed by the Magi to be the rulers or directors of the affairs of men. This opinion I shall examine by and by. From this it is evident, that this is in fact a Persian, or still more Eastern, mythos.

The use of animals for food being clearly not allowed to man, in chap. i. vers. 29, 30, is a circumstance which bespeaks the book of Buddhist origin. It is probably either the parent of the Buddhist religion, or its offspring. And it is different from the next book, which begins at the fourth verse of the second chapter, and ends with the last verse of the fourth; because, *among other reasons* in it, the creation is said to have been performed by a different person from that named in the first,—by Jehovah Aleim, instead of Aleim. Again, in the first book, man and woman are created at the same time; in the second, they are created at different times. Again, in the first book, the fruit of ALL the trees is given to the man; in the second, this is contradicted, by one tree being expressly forbidden. These are in fact two different accounts of the creation.

. The beginning of the fifth chapter, or third tract, seems to be a repetition of the first, to connect it with the history of the flood. The world is described as being made by God, (Aleim,) and not as in the second by Jehovah or the God Jehovah or Jehovah Aleim; and, as in the first, the man and woman are made at one time, and not, as in the second, at different times. The account of the birth of Seth, given in the twenty-fifth verse of the fourth chapter, and the repetition of the same event in the third verse of the fifth chapter, or the beginning of the third tract, are a clear proof that these tracts are by different persons; or, at least, are separate and distinct works. The reason why the name of Seth is given here, and not the names of any of the later of Adam's children, is evidently to connect Adam with Noah and the flood, the object of the third tract. The permission, in the third tract, to eat animals implying that it was not given before, is strictly in keeping with the denial of it in the first.

The histories of the creation, both in the first and in the second book of Genesis, in the sacred books of the Persians, and in those of the Chaldeans, are evidently different versions of the same story. The Chaldeans state the world to have been created not in six days, but in six periods of time—the lengths of the periods not being fixed. The Persians, also, divide the time into six periods.

In the second book, a very well-known account is given of the origin of evil, which is an affair most closely interwoven with every part of the Christian system, but it is in fact nothing more than an oriental mythos, which may have been taken from the history of the ancient Brahmins, in whose books the principal incidents are to be found; and, in order to put this matter out of doubt, it will only be necessary to turn to the plates, to Figs. 2, 3, 4, taken from icons in the very oldest of the caves of Hindostan, excavated, as it is universally agreed, long prior to the Christian æra. The reader will find the first to be the seed of the woman bruising the serpent's head; the second, the serpent biting the foot of her seed, the Hindoo God Cristna, the second person of their trinity; and the third, the spirit of God brooding over the face of the waters. The history in Genesis is here so closely depicted that it is impossible to doubt the identity of the two.

Among the Persians and all the oriental nations it has been observed, that the Creator or God was adored under a triple form—in fact in the form of a trinity. In India, this was Bramah,

Cristna or Vishnu, and Siva; in Persia, it was Oromasdes, Mithra, and Arhimanius; in each case the Creator, the Preserver, and the Destroyer.

I shall now proceed to shew that, in this particular, the *religion of Abraham* and the Israelites was accordant with all the others.

3. But before I proceed, I must point out an example of very blameable disingenuousness in every translation of the Bible which I have seen. In the original, God is called by a variety of names, often the same as that which the Heathens gave to their Gods. To disguise this, the translators have availed themselves of a contrivance adopted by the Jews in rendering the Hebrew into Greek, which is to render the word הוה *Ieue*, and several of the other names by which God is called in the Bible, by the word Κυριος or Lord, which signifies one having authority, the sovereign. In this the Jews were justified by the commandment, which forbids the use of the name *Ieue*. But not so the Christians, who do not admit the true and evident meaning adopted by the Jews—*Thou shalt not take the name of Ieue, thy God, in vain.* And, therefore, they have no right, when pretending to give a translation, to call God by any other name than that in the original, whether it be *Adonis*, or *Ie*, or *Ieue*, or any other. This the reader will immediately see is of the first importance in obtaining a correct understanding of the book. The fact of the names of God being disguised in all[1] the translations tends to prove that no dependence can be placed on any of them. The fact shews very clearly the temper or state of mind with which the translators have undertaken their task. God is called by several names. How is the reader of a translation to discover this, if he find them all rendered by one name? He is evidently deceived. It is no justification of a translator, to say it is of little consequence. Little or great, he has no right to exercise any discretion of this kind. When he finds God called Adonai, he has no business to call him Jehovah or Elohim.

4. The fact that Abraham worshiped several Gods, who were, in reality, the same as those of the Persians, namely, the creator, preserver, and the destroyer, has been long asserted, and the assertion has been very unpalatable both to Jews and many Christians; and to obviate or disguise what they could not account for, they have had recourse, in numerous instances, to the mistranslation of the original, as will presently be shewn.

The following texts will clearly prove this assertion. The Rev. Dr. Shuckford pointed out the fact long ago; so that this is nothing new.

In the second book of Genesis the creation is described not to have been made by Aleim, or the Aleim, but by a God of a double name—יְהֹוָה אלהים *Ieue Aleim*; which the priests have translated LORD God. By using the word LORD, their object evidently is to conceal from their readers several difficulties which arise afterward respecting the names of God and this word, and which shew clearly that the books of the Pentateuch are the writings of different persons.

Dr. Shuckford has observed, that in Genesis xii. 7, 8, Abraham did not call upon the name of the LORD as we improperly translate it; but invoked God in the name of the Lord (i. e. Ieue) whom he worshiped, and who appeared to him; and that this was the same God to whom Jacob prayed when he vowed that the Lord should be his God.[2] Again, in Gen. xxviii. 21, 22, יהוה יהוה לי לאלהים erit Dominus mibi in Deum; and he called the place בית אלהים (*Bit aleim*), Domus Dei. Again, Shuckford says,[3] that in Gen. xxvi. 25, Isaac invoked God as Abraham did in the name of this Lord, יהוה Ieue or Jehovah. On this he observes, "It is very evident that Abraham "and his descendants worshiped not only the true and living God, but they invoked him in the "name of the Lord, and they worshiped the Lord in whose name they invoked, so that two per- "sons were the object of their worship, God and this Lord: and the Scripture has distinguished

---

[1] At least I have never seen an exception.   [2] Shuckford, Book vii. pp. 130, 131.   [3] Book vii. p. 130.

" these two persons from one another by this circumstance, that *God no man hath seen at any*
" *time nor can see,*[1] but the Lord whom Abraham and his descendants worshiped was the person
" who appeared to them."[2]

In the above I need not remind my reader that he must insert the name of *Ieue* or *Jehovah* for
the name of Lord.

Chapter xxi. verse 33, is wrong translated: when properly rendered it represents Abraham to
have invoked *(in the name of Jehovah)* the everlasting God.[3] That is, to have invoked the everlasting God, or to have prayed to him in the name of Jehovah—precisely as the Christians do at
this day, who invoke God in the name of Jesus—who invoke the first person of the Trinity in the
name of the second.

The words of this text are, ויקרא-שם יהוה בשם אל עולם et *invocavit ibi in nomine* IEUE *Deum
æternum.*

The foregoing observations of Dr. Shuckford's are confirmed by the following texts :

Gen. xxxi. 42, " Except the God of my father, the God of Abraham, and the fear of Isaac," &c.

Gen. xxxi. 53, " The Gods of Abraham, and the Gods of Nahor, the Gods of their father, judge
betwixt us, אלהי אביהם. Dii patria eorum, that is, the Gods of Terah, the great-grandfather of
both Jacob and Laban. It appears that they went back to the time when there could be no dispute
about their Gods. They sought for Gods that should be received by them both, and these were
the Gods of Terah. Laban was an idolater, (or at least of a different sect or religion—Rachel stole
his Gods,) Jacob was not ; and in consequence of the difference in their religion, there was a
difficulty in finding an oath that should be binding on both.

In Gen. xxxv. 1, it is said, *And* (אלהים *Aleim) God said unto Jacob, Arise, go up to Bethel, and
dwell there; and make there an altar unto God* (לאל LAL) *that appeared unto thee, when thou fleddest
from the face of Esau thy brother.* If two Gods at least, or a plurality in the Godhead, had not
been acknowledged by the author of Genesis, the words would have been, *and make there an altar
unto me, that,* &c. ; or, *unto me, because I appeared,* &c.

Genesis xlix. 25, מאל אביך ויעזרך ואת שדי ויברכך, a Deo tui patris et adjuvabit te ; et omnipo-
tente benedicet tibi. By the God (Al) of thy father *also* he[4] will help thee, and the Saddai (Sdi)
also shall bless thee with blessings, &c.

It is worthy of observation, that there is a marked distinction between the *Al* of his father who
will help him, and the *Saddi* who will bless him. Here are two evidently clear and distinct Gods,
and neither of them the destroyer or the evil principle.

Even by the God (אל *Al) of thy father, who shall help thee : and by the Almighty,* שדי *omnipo-
tente, who shall bless thee with blessings of heaven above, blessings of the deep that lieth under,
blessings of the breasts and of the womb.* The Sdi or Saddi are here very remarkable ; they seem
to have been peculiarly Gods of the blessings of this world.

Deut. vi. 4, יהוה אלהינו יהוה אחד. This, Mr. Hales has correctly observed, ought to be rendered Jehovah our Gods is one Jehovah.

The doctrine of a plurality, shewn above in the Pentateuch, is confirmed in the later books of the
Jews.

Isaiah xlviii. 16, ועתה אדני יהוה שלחני ורוחו. Et nunc Adonai Ieue misit me et spiritus ejus :
And now the Lord (Adonai) Jehovah, hath sent me and his spirit.

---

[1] Exod. xxxiii. 20.
[2] Shuckford, Con. Book v. p. 292.
[3] Gen. xii. 11 ; Shuckford, Book ix. p. 379, Ed. 3, also p. 400.
[4] The mighty one named in the former verse, the אביר *Abir*.

Again Isaiah li. 22, בה-אמר אדניך יהוה ואלחיך ריב עמו. Thus thy Adonai Jehovah spoke, and thy Aleim reprimanded his people. Sic dixit tuus Adoni Ieue, et tuus Aleim litigabit suo populo.

Two persons of the Trinity are evident in these texts. The third is found in the serpent, which tempted Eve in its evil character, and in its character of regenerator, healer, or preserver, in the brasen serpent set up by Moses, in the wilderness, to be adored by the Israelites, and to which they offered incense from his time through all the reigns of David and Solomon, to the time of Hezekiah, the name of which was Nehushtan.[1] Numbers xxi. 8, 9; 2 Kings xviii. 4. The destroyer or evil spirit may also probably be found in the *Aub* named Lev. xx. 27; Deut. xviii. 11.

There are many expressions in the Pentateuch besides those already given, which cannot be accounted for without a plurality of Gods or the Trinity, a doctrine which was not peculiar to Abraham and his descendants, but was common to all the nations of the ancient world from India to Thule, as I have before observed, under the triple title of creator, preserver, and destroyer—Brama, Vishnu, and Siva, among the Hindoos; Oromasdes, Mithra, and Arhimanius, among the Persians.

We shall see in the next chapter, that the Trinity will be found in the word Aleim of the first verse of Genesis, which will tend to support what I have asserted, viz. that it is an Indian book.

CHAPTER II

On the word ALEIM or Jewish Trinity—Saddai Adonis—Trinity of the Rabbis —Meaning of the words AL and EL

1. Perhaps there is no word in any language about which more has been written than the word Aleim; or, as modern Jews corruptly call it, Elohim.[2] But all its difficulties are at once removed by considering it as a representation of the united Godhead, the Trinity in Unity, the three Persons and one God. It is not very unlike the word Septuagint—of which we sometimes say, *it* gives a word such or such a sense, at other times *they* give such a sense, &c. A folio would be required to contain all that has been said respecting this word. The author believes that there is no instance in which it is not satisfactorily explained by considering it, as above suggested, as the representation of the Trinity.

The root אל *al*, the root of the word Aleim, as a verb, or in its verbal form, means to mediate, to interpose for protection, to preserve;[3] and, as a noun, a mediator, an interposer. In its feminine it has two forms, אלה *ale*, and אלה *alue*. In its plural masculine it makes אלים *alim*, in its plural feminine אלהים *aleim*. In forming its plural feminine in ים *im*, it makes an exception to the general Hebrew rule, which makes the plural masculine in ים *im*. But though an exception, it is by no means singular. It is like that made by עזים *ozim*, she-goats, דבים *dbim*, she-bears, &c.[4] In the second example in its feminine form, it drops the u or *vau*, according to a common practice of the Hebrew language.

---

[1] This has been observed by Mr. Maurice, Hind. Ant. Vol. III. p. 209.
[2] In the Synagogue copies it is always Aleim.
[3] Parkhurst in voce.   [4] Parkhurst's Grammar, p. 8.

A controversy took place about the middle of the last century between one Dr. Sharpe and several other divines upon the word Aleim. The Doctor was pretty much of my opinion. He says; " If there is no reason to doubt, as I think there is none, that אלה *ale* and אלוה *alue* are the " same word, only the *vau* is suppressed in the one, and expressed in the other, why may not " אלהים *aleim* be the plural of one as well as of the other? If it be said it cannot be the plural " of אלה *alue*, because it is wrote without the *vau*; I answer, that קרבים *qrbim*, רחקים *rhqim*, " נברים *gbrim*, גדלים *gdlim*, &c., are frequently wrote without the vau: are they not, therefore, " the plurals of קרוב *qrub*," &c.? Again, he says,

" When, therefore, Mr. Moody tells us that אלהים *aleim* may be the plural masculine of אלה " *ale*, as אדנים *adnim*, and אדני *adni*, are also plurals of אדון *adun*, Lord, so may אלהים *aleim* and " אלהי *alei* be plural of אלוה *Alue*, God." [1]

In the course of the controversy it seems to be admitted by all parties, that the word has the meaning of mediator or interposer for protection, and this is very important.

I cannot quite agree with Mr. Moody, because, according to the genius of the Hebrew language, it is much more in character for אלהים *aleim* to be the plural feminine of אלה *ale*, a feminine noun, than the plural masculine; and for אלים *alim* to be the plural masculine, of the masculine noun אל *al*.

But it does not seem to have ever occurred to any of those gentlemen, that the words in question, אלה *ale*, or אלוה *alue*, and אל *al*, might be one the masculine, and the two others the feminine, of the same word—like God and Goddess. They never seem to have thought that the God of the Hebrews could be of any sex but their own, and, therefore, never once gave a thought to the question. The observation of Mr. Moody is very just, if אלה *ale* be a masculine noun. But it is much more according to the genius of the language that it should be feminine. If אלה *ale* be masculine, it is an exception. I beg the reader to observe, that the Arabians, from whose language the word *al* properly comes, have the word for the Sun, in the *feminine*, and that for the moon, in the *masculine* gender; and this accounts for the word being in the feminine plural. From the androgynous character of the Creator, the noun of multitude, Aleim, by which we shall now see that he was described, probably was of the common gender: that is, either of one gender or the other, as it might happen.

From the plural of this word, אל *al*, was also formed a noun of multitude used in the first verse of Genesis: exactly like our word *people*, in Latin *populus*, or our words nation, flock, and congregation. Thus it is said, ברא אלהים *bura aleim*, *Aleim formed the earth;* as we say, the nation consumes, a flock strays, or the congregation sings psalms, or a triune divinity, or a trinity blesses or forms. It is used with the emphatic article: " Their cry came up to THE Gods," האלהים *e-aleim*. In the same way we say, wolves got to THE sheep, or THE flock, or THE congregation sing or sings. Being a noun of multitude, according to the genius of the language, the verb may be either in the singular or plural number.

Parkhurst says, that " the word *Al* means God, the Heavens, Leaders, Assistance, Defence, " and Interposition; or, to interpose for protection." He adds, " that אלל *All*, with the ל *l* doubled, has the meaning, in an excessive degree, of *vile*, the denouncing of *a curse: nought*, " *nothing, res nihili*." Mr. Whiter [2] says, that it has the same meaning in Arabic. and that AL AL, also means Deus optimus maximus. Thus we have the idea of creating, preserving, and destroying.

The meaning of mediator, preserver, or intervener, joined to its character of a noun of multitude, at once identifies it with the Trinity of the Gentiles. Christians will be annoyed to find their God

[1] Sharpe, on Aleim, pp. 179, 180.   [2] Etymol. Univ. Vol. I. p. 512.

called by the same name with that of the Heathen Gods; but this is only what took place when he was called שדי *Sdi*, Saddi, Saddim, or אדני *adni*, Adonai, or Adonis, אדן *adun*, or בעל *bol*, Baal: so that there is nothing unusual in this.

The Jews have made out that God is called by upwards of thirty names in the Bible; many of them used by the Gentiles, probably before they fell into idolatry.

The word אל *al*, meaning preserver; of course, when the words יהוה ה אלהים *ieue-e-aleim* are used, they mean *Ieue the preserver*, or the *self-existent preserver*—the word *Ieue*, as we shall afterward find, meaning self-existent.

When the אלהים *aleim* is considered as a noun of multitude, all the difficulties, I think, are removed.

It seems not unlikely that by the different modes of writing the word אל *al*, a distinction of sexes should originally have been intended to be expressed. The Heathen divinities, Ashtaroth and Baal-zebub, were both called Aleim.[1] And the Venus Aphrodite, Urania, &c., were of both genders. The God Mithra, the Saviour, was both male and female. Several exemplars of him, in his female character, as killing the bull, may be seen in the Townly Collection, in the British Museum. By the word Aleim the Heathen Gods were often meant, but they all resolved themselves at last into the Sun, as triune God, or as emblem of the three powers—the Creator, the Preserver, and the Destroyer—three Persons but one God—he being both *male and female*. Without doubt Parkhurst and the divines in the controversy with Dr. Sharpe, do not give, till after much research, as meanings of the verb אל *al*, *to mediate, to interpose, or intervene*; and of the noun *the mediator, interposer, or intervener*. But here we evidently have the preserver or saviour. At first it might be expected that the gender of the word *Aleim* and of the other forms from its root would be determined by the genders of the words which ought to agree with it: but from the extraordinary uncertain state of this language nothing can be deduced from them—as we find nouns feminine and plural joined to verbs masculine and singular (Gen. i. 14); and nouns of multitude, though singular, having a verb plural—and, though feminine, having a verb masculine (Gen. xli. 57). But all this tends, I think, to strengthen an observation I shall have occasion to make hereafter, that the Hebrew language shews many marks of almost primeval rudeness or simplicity; and, that the Aleim, the root whence the Christian Trinity sprung, is the real trinity of the ancients—the old doctrine revived. Nothing could be desired more in favour of my system than that the word *Aleim* should mean preserver, or intervener, or mediator.

At first it seems very extraordinary that the word אל *al* or אלה *ale*, the name of the beneficent Creator, should have the meaning of curse. The difficulty arises from an ill-understood connexion between the Creator, Preserver, and Destroyer—the Creator being the Destroyer, and the Destroyer the Creator. But in this my theory is beautifully supported.

2. It appears that in these old books, God is called by names which are sometimes singular, sometimes plural, sometimes masculine, and sometimes feminine. But though he be occasionally of each gender, for he must be of the masculine or feminine gender, because the old language has no neuter; he is not called by any name which conveys the idea of Goddess or a feminine nature, as separable from himself. My idea is very abstruse and difficult to explain. He is, in fact, in every case Androgynous; for in no case which I have produced is a term used exclusively belonging to one sex or the other. He is never called Baaltes, or Asteroth, or Queen of Heaven. On this subject I shall have much to say hereafter.

Many Christians no doubt, will be much alarmed and shocked at the idea of the word *ale* being of the feminine gender. But why should not the Hebrew language have a feminine to the word

[1] Sharpe, p. 224.

אל *al*, as the English have a feminine to the word God, in Goddess, or the Romans in the words Deus and Dea? And why should not God be of the feminine gender as easily as of the masculine? Who knows what gender God is of? Who at this day is so foolish as to fancy that God is of any gender? We have seen that all the Gods of the Gentiles were of both genders. We find God called *Al, Ale, Alue, Alim,* and *Aleim*—more frequently *Aleim* than any other name. It must be observed, that God nowhere calls himself by any of those names, as he does by the name יה *Ie* or *Jah,* or יהוה *Ieue,* which is the only name by which he has ever denominated himself. Dr. Shuckford, on Genesis xxvi. 25, makes Ieue, [1] mean Preserver or Mediator.

The God Baal was both masculine and feminine, and the God of the Jews was once called Baal. The learned Kircher [2] says, " Vides igitur dictas Veneris Uraniam, Nephtem, et Momemphitam, " nihil aliud esse quam Isidem, quod et vaccæ cultis satis superque demonstrat proprius Isidi " certe hanc eandem quoque esse, quæ in historia Thobiæ Dea Baal dicitur quæ vacca colebatur ; " sic enim habetur, C. i. 5, Εθυον τη Βααλ τη δαμαλει. Scilicet faciebant sacra τη Βααλ " juvencæ seu vaccæ, quod et alio loco videlicet L. iii. Reg. C. xix. ubi Baal legitur feminino " genere ; Ουκ εκαμψαν γονατα τη Βααλ—non incurvaverunt genu Baali. Hesychius autem " Βηλθης inquit, ή 'Ηρα ή Αφροδιτη, Belthes, Juno sive Venus, est cuicum juvencam sacrificârint " Phœnices, veresimile est, eandem esse cum Venere Ægyptia, seu Iside, seu Astartbe Assyrio- " rum, sicut enim Baal est Jupiter, sic Baalis seu Belthis est Juno seu Venus, cui parallela sunt, " Adonis seu Thamus, et Venus seu Astaroth ; (quorum ille Baal Assyriorum hæc eorum *Beltis* " est ;) quibus respondent Osiris et Isis, Jupiter et Juno seu Venus Ægyptiorum ; eternum " secuti שמים בעל *Baal samim* est Jupiter Olympius, ita שמים בלת *Baalet samaim* est Juno " Olympia, scilicet, Domina cœli seu Regina : quemadmodum Jerem. vii. 44, eam vocant Septua- " ginta Interpretes, quod nomen Isidi et Astarthi et Junoni Venerive proprie convenit : uti ex " variis antiquarum inscriptionum monumentis apud Janum Gruterum videre est." [3]

Parkhurst says, [4] " *But* AL *or* EL *was the very name the Heathens gave to their God Sol, their Lord or Ruler of the hosts of heaven.*"

The word Aleim אלהים has been derived from the Arabic word *Allah* God, by many learned men ; but Mr. Bellamy says this cannot be admitted ; for the Hebrew is not the derived, but the primitive language. Thus the inquiry into the real origin or meaning of this curious and important word, and of the language altogether, is at once cut short by a dogmatical assertion. This learned Hebraist takes it for granted from his theological dogma, that the two tribes of Israel are the favourites of God, exclusive of the ten other tribes—that the language of the former must be the original of all other languages ; and then he makes every thing bend to this dogma. This is the mode which learned Christians generally adopt in their inquiries ; and for this reason no dependance can be placed upon them : and this is the reason also why, in their inquiries, they seldom arrive at the truth. The Alab, articulo emphatico alalah (Calassio) of the Arabians, is evidently the אל *Al* of the Chaldees or Jews ; whether one language be derived from the other I shall not give an opinion at present : but Bishop Marsh, no mean authority as all will admit, speaking of the Arabic, [5] says, " Its importance, therefore, to the interpretation of Hebrew is apparent.

---

[1] Which means self-existent. Vide Celtic Druids, Ch. v. Sect. xxxvii. and xxxviii.

[2] Œd. Æg. Synt. iv. Cap. xiii. Vol. I. p. 319.

[3] Proserpine, in Greek Περσεφονη, was styled by Orpheus, (in his Hymn Εις Περσεφονη,) Ζωη και Θανατις, both Life and Death. He says of her—φερεις γαρ αιει και παντα φονευεις, Thou both *producest* and *destroyest* all things.

Porphyry and Eusebius say, she said of herself, " I am called of a *three-fold* nature, and *three-headed.*" Parkhurst, p. 347.

[4] Lex. p. 20.   [5] Lecture XIV. p. 28.

" It serves, indeed, as a key to that language; for it is not only allied to the Hebrew, but is at the
" same time so copious, as to *contain the roots of almost all the words in the Hebrew Bible*." If this
be true, it is evident that the Arabian *language* may be of the greatest use in the translating of the
Scriptures; though the Arabian version of them, in consequence of its having been made from the
Greek Septuagint or some other Greek version, (if such be the fact,) instead of the original, may
be of no great value. And if I understand his Lordship rightly, and it be true, that the Arabic
contains the roots of the Hebrew, it must be a more ancient language than the Hebrew. But,
after all, if the two languages be dialects of the same, it is nonsense to talk of one being derived
from the other.

In the first verse of Genesis the word Aleim is found without any particle before it, and, therefore, ought to be literally translated *Gods formed;* but in the second chapter of Exodus and 23d
verse, the emphatic article ח *e* is found, and therefore it ought to be translated, that " their cry
" came up to THE *Gods*," or THE Aleim. In the same manner the first verse of the third chapter
ought to have *the mountain of the Gods*, or *of the Aleim, even to Horeb*, instead of *the mountain of
God*. Mr. Bellamy has observed that we cannot say Gods he created, but we can say Gods or
Aleim created; and the fact, as we see above, of the word Aleim being sometimes preceded by
the emphatic article ח *e* shews, that where it is omitted the English article ought to be omitted,
and where it is added the English article ought to be added.

Perhaps the word Septuagint may be more similar to the word Aleim. But if there be no idiom
in our language, or the Latin, or the Greek, *exactly similar* to the Hebrew, this is no way
surprising.

3. Persons who have not given much consideration to these subjects will be apt to wonder that
any people should be found to offer adoration to the evil principle; but they do not consider that,
in all these recondite systems, the evil principle, or the destroyer, or Lord of Death, was at the
same time the regenerator. He could not destroy, but to reproduce. And it was probably not
till this principle began to be forgotten, that the evil being, *per se*, arose; for in some nations this
effect seems to have taken place. Thus Baal-Zebub is in Iberno Celtic, Baal *Lord*, and Zab *Death*,
Lord of Death; but he is also called *Aleim*, the same as the God of the Israelites;[1] and this is
right, because he was one of the Trimurti or Trinity.

If I be correct respecting the word Aleim being feminine, we here see the Lord of Death of the
feminine gender; but the Goddess Ashtaroth or Astarte, the Eoster of the Germans,[2] was also
called Aleim.[3] Here again Aleim is feminine, which shews that I am right in making Aleim the
plural *feminine*. Thus we have distinctly found Aleim the Creator, (Gen. i. 1,) Aleim the Preserver, and Aleim the Destroyer, and this not by inference, but literally expressed. We have also
the Apis or Bull of Egypt expressly called Aleim, and its plurality admitted on authority not
easily disputed. Aaron says, אלה אלהיך *ale aleik, these are thy Aleim who brought thee out of the
land of Egypt.*[4]

Mr. Maurice says,[5] Moses himself uses this word Elohim, with verbs and adjectives in the
plural. Of this usage Dr. Allix enumerates two, among many other glaring instances, that might
be brought from the Pentateuch; the former in Genesis xx. 13, Quando errare *fecerunt* me Deus;
the latter in Gen. xxxv. 7, Quia ibi *revelati sunt* ad eum Deus; and by other writers in various
parts of the Old Testament. But particularly he brings in evidence the following texts: Job
xxxv. 10; Josh. xxiv. 19; Psa. cxix. 1.

The 26th verse of the first chapter of Genesis completely establishes the plurality of the word

---

[1] Sharpe, p. 224.   [2] See Ancient Universal History, Vol. II. pp. 334—346.
[3] Sharpe, p. 221.   [4] Parkhurst, p. 81.   [5] Ind. Ant. Vol. IV. p 81.

Aleim. *And then said Aleim, we will make man in* OUR *image according to* OUR *likeness.* To rebut this argument it is said, that this is nothing but a dignified form of speech adopted by all kings in speaking to their subjects, to give themselves dignity and importance, and on this account attributed to God. This is reasoning from effect to cause, instead of from cause to effect. The oriental sovereigns, puffed up with pride and vanity, not only imitated the language of God in the sacred book; but they also went farther, and made their base slaves prostrate themselves before them in the same posture as they used in addressing their God. In this argument God is made to use incorrect language in order that he may imitate and liken himself to the vainest and most contemptible of human beings. We have no knowledge that God ever imitated these wretches; we do know that *they* affected *to* imitate and liken themselves to Him. This verse proves his plurality: the next, again, proves his unity: for there the word *bara* is used—whence it is apparent that the word has both a singular and plural meaning.

On the 22d verse of the third chapter of Genesis, my worthy and excellent old friend, Dr. A. Geddes, Vicar Apostolic of the Roman See in London, says,[1] " *Lo! Adam—or man—is become* " *like one of us.* If there be any passage in the Old Testament which countenances a plurality of " persons in the Godhead; or, to speak more properly, a plurality of Gods, it is this passage. " He does not simply say, *like us;* but like *one of us* כמנו כאחד. This can hardly be explained as " we have explained נעשׂה *Let us make,* and I confess it has always appeared to me to imply a " plurality of Gods, in some sense or other. It is well known that the *Lord* or *Jehovah,* is called " in the Hebrew Scriptures, ' The God of Gods.' He is also represented as a Sovereign sitting " on his throne, attended by all the heavenly host;" in Job called *the sons of God.* Again he says, " Wherever Jehovah is present, whether on Sinai or Sion, there he is attended by twenty " thousand angels, of the Cherubic order. When he appeared to Jacob, at Bethel, he was " attended by angels, and again when he wrestled with the same patriarch."

The first verse of the twelfth chapter of Ecclesiastes is strongly in favour of the plurality of Aleim—Remember thy Creators, not Creator—בוראיך את זכר. But many copies have the word בוראך and others בראך without the י. " But," as Parkhurst observes, " it is very easy to account " for the transcribers dropping the plural י I, in their copies, though very difficult to assign a " reason why any of them should insert it, unless they found it in their originals."[2] The Trinitarian Christians have triumphed greatly over the other Christian sects and the Jews, in consequence of the plurality of the Aleim expressed in the texts cited above. It appears that they have justice on their side.

There would have been no difficulty, with the word Aleim, if some persons had not thought that the plurality of Aleim favoured the doctrine of the Christian Trinity, and others that the contrary effect was to be produced by making Aleim a noun singular. But whatever sect it may favour or oppose, I am clearly of opinion that it conveys the idea of plurality, just as much as the phrase Populus laudavit Deum, or, in English, The Congregation sings.

4. It has already been observed that the God of the Jews was also called by a very remarkable name שדי אל *al sdi.* The proper name *Sdi* is constantly translated *God Almighty.*[3]

In Gen. xlix. 25, שדי *Sdi* is put for the *Almighty,* (as it is translated,) not only without the word אל *al* preceding it, as usual, but in opposition to it.

In Deut. xxxii. 17, the Israelites are said to have sacrificed to שדים *sdim* and not to אלה *ale*—as it is translated in our version, " to devils and not to God," אלהים לא ידעום eos noverunt non diis, *to Gods whom they did not know.* Here is a marked distinction between the Sadim and the Aleim.

---

[1] Crit. Rem. Gen. iii., pp. 48, 49.   [2] Parkhurst, Lex. p. 82.

[3] Gen. xxviii. 3, xxxv. 11, xliii. 14, xlviii. 3; Exod. vi. 3.

Here is *Ale* in the singular number, God; *Aleim* in the plural number, Gods: and here is *Sadim*, the plural number of another name of the Deity, which is both of the masculine and feminine gender.

In Gen. xiv. 3, the kings are said to have *combined*, " *in the vale of Siddim, which is the salt* " *sea.*" This shews that the Gods called Saddai were known and acknowledged, by the Canaanites, before the time of Abraham. This word Siddim is the plural of the word used, in various places, as the name of the true God—both by itself as *Saddi* and *El* Saddi. In Exodus vi. 3, the Israelites are ordered to call God *Ieue ;* but before that time he had been only known to their fathers as *Al Saddi*, God Almighty.

Now, at last, what does this word *Sadi, Saddim,* or *Shaddai,* שדי *Sdi,* really mean ? Mr. Park- hurst tells us, it means *all-bountiful—the pourer forth of blessings ;* among the Heathen, the *Dea Multimammia ;* in fact, the Diana of Ephesus, the Urania of Persia, *the Jove of Greece,* called by Orpheus the mother of the Gods, each male as well as female—the Venus Aphrodite ; in short, the genial powers of nature. [1] And I maintain, that it means also the figure which is often found in collections of ancient statues, most beautifully executed, and called the *Hermaphrodite.* See Gallery of Naples and of Paris.

The God of the Jews is also often known by the name of Adonai אדני [2] But this is nothing but the God of the Syrians, Adonis or the Sun, the worship of whom is reprobated under the name of *Tammuz,* in Ezekiel viii. 14.

From these different examples it is evident that the God of the Jews had several names, and that these were often the names of the Heathen Gods also. All this has a strong tendency to shew that the Jewish and Gentile systems were, at the bottom, the same.

Why we call God masculine I know not, nor do I apprehend can any good reason be given. Surely the ancients, who described him as of both genders, or of the doubtful gender, were more reasonable. Here we see that the God of the Jews is called שדי *Sdi,* and that this Sdi is the Dea *Multimammia,* who is also in other places made to be the same as the אל *al* or אלה *ale.* Therefore it seems to follow, that the Gods of the Israelites and of the Gentiles were in their originals the same. And I think by and by my reader will see evident proof, that the religion of Moses was but a sect of that of the Gentiles ; or, if he like it better, that the religion of the Gentiles was but a sect of the religion of Jehovah, *Ieue,* or of Moses.

It may be here observed that these names of God of two genders are almost all in the old tracts, which I suppose to have been productions of the Buddhists or Brahmins of India, for which I shall give more reasons presently.

5. From what I may call the almost bigoted attachment of the modern Jews to the unity of God, it cannot for a moment be supposed, that they would forge any thing tending to the proof of the Trinity of the Christians ; therefore, if we can believe father Kircher, the following fact furnishes a very extraordinary addition to the proofs already given, that the Jews received a trinity like all the other oriental nations. It was the custom among them, to describe their God Jehovah or Ieue, by three jods and a cross in a circle, thus : ⊕. Certainly a more striking illustration of the doctrine I have been teaching can scarcely be conceived : and it is very curious that it should be found accompanied with the cross, which the learned father, not understanding, calls the Mazoretic *Chametz.* This mistake seems to remove all suspicion of Christian forgery ; for I can hardly believe that if the Christian priests had forged this symbol, the learned Father would not have availed himself of it to support the adoration of the Cross, as well as of the Trinity. The

---

[1] Parkhurst, Lex. pp. 720, 721.   [2] Vide Parkhurst, p. 141 and p. 788.

the jods were also disposed in the form of a crown, thus ⅄☥Ɩ, to signify the mystical name of Jehovah or Ieue. The reader may refer to the Œdipus Ægyp. Vol. II. Cap. ii. pp. 114, 115, where he will find the authorities at length, and where, among the reasons given by the father to prove the Christian Trinity, is proof enough of that of the Jews. He will find also an observation of Galatinus's that the three letters יהו *ieu* were the symbol of Jehovah, an observation made by me in the Celtic Druids, [1] though for a different reason, and accounted for in a different manner; but the fact is admitted. The cross here seems to be united to the Trinity—but more of this hereafter.

Dr. Alix, on Gen. i. 10, says, that the Cabalists constantly added the letter jod, being the first letter of the word *Ieue* to the word Aleim *for the sake of a mystery*. The Rabbi Bechai says, it is to shew that there is a divinity in each person included in the word. [2] This is, no doubt, part of the Cabala, or esoteric religion of the Jews. Maimonides says, the vulgar Jews were forbidden to read the history of the creation, for *fear* it should lead them into idolatry; [3] probably for fear they should worship the Trimurti of India, or the Trinity of Persia. The fear evidently shews, that the fearful persons thought there was a plurality in Genesis.

6. It is a very common practice with the priests not always to translate a word, but sometimes to leave it in the original, and sometimes to translate it as it may suit their purpose: sometimes one, sometimes the other. Thus they use the word *Messiah* or *Anointed* as they find it best serves their object. Thus, again, it is with the word EL, in numerous places. For instance, in Gen. xxviii. 19, *And he called the name of the place Beth-el*, instead of *he called the place The House of the Sun*. The word Beth means *House*, and El *Sun*. [4]

" Ai was situated between Bith-Avon (read Bith-On) and Bith-El; and these were temples of " the Sun, under his different titles of On and El." [5]

Speaking of the word Jabneel, Sir W. Drummond says, " El, in the composition of these " Canaanite names does not signify Deus but Sol." [6] This confirms what I have before observed from Parkhurst.

" Thus Kabzeel, literally means The Congregation of the Sun." [7]

" Messiah-El a manifest corruption of the word Messiah—The Anointed of El, or the Sun. [8]

" Carmel, The Vine of El, or of the Sun." [9]

" Migdal-El Horem, The Station of the Burning Sun." [10]

" Amraphel, Ammon, or the Sun in Aries, here denominated Amraphel, Agnus Mirabilis." [11]

" El-tolad signifies the Sun, or The God of Generation." [12]

In all the above-named examples the word El ought to be written Al. In the original it is אל *Al*; and this word means the God Mithra, the Sun, as the Preserver or Saviour.

---

[1] Ch. v. Sect. xxxviii.   [4] Maur. Ind. Ant. Vol. IV. p. 86.   [3] Ibid. p. 89.
[4] See Œdip. Jud. p. 250.   [5] Ibid. p. 221.   [6] Ibid. p. 270.
[7] Ibid. p. 272.   [8] Ibid. p. 280.   [9] Ibid. p. 334.   [10] Ibid. 338.
[11] Ibid. p. 76.   [12] Ibid. p. 286.

CHAPTER III

Esdras and the Ancient Jewish Cabala—Emanations, what—Meaning of the word
Berasit—Sephiroths and Emanations continued—Origin of Time—Planets or
Samim—Observations on the preceding Sections

1. As all the ancient Heathen nations had their mysteries or secret doctrines, which the priests carefully kept from the knowledge of the vulgar, and which they only communicated to a select number of persons whom they thought they could safely trust; and as the Jewish religion was anciently the same as the Persian, it will not be thought extraordinary, that, like the Persian, it should have its secret doctrines. So we find it had its Cabala, which, though guarded like all ancient mysteries, with the most anxious care, and the most solemn oaths, and what is still worse, almost lost amidst the confusion of civil brawls, cannot be entirely hidden from the prying curiosity of the Moderns. In defiance of all its concealment and mischances, enough escapes to prove that it was fundamentally the same as that of the Persian Magi; and thus adds one more proof of the identity of the religions of Abraham and of Zoroaster.

The doctrine here alluded to was a secret one—more perfect, the Jews maintain, than that delivered in the Pentateuch; and they also maintain, that it was given by God, on Mount Sinai, to Moses *verbally* and not written, and that this is the doctrine described in the fourth book of Esdras, ch. xiv. 6, 26, and 45, thus:

These words shalt thou declare, and these shalt thou hide.

And when thou hast done, some things shalt thou publish, and some things shalt thou shew secretly to the WISE.

.... the Highest spake, saying, The first that thou hast written publish openly, that the worthy and the unworthy may read it: but keep the seventy last, that thou mayest deliver them only to such as be WISE *among the people. For in them is the spring of understanding, the fountain of* WISDOM.

Now, though the book of Esdras be no authority in argument with a Protestant Christian for any point of doctrine, it may be considered authority in such a case as this. If the Jews had had no secret doctrine, the writer never would have stated such a fact, in the face of all his countrymen, who must have known its truth or falsity. No doubt, whatever might be pretended, the real reason of the Cabala being unwritten, was concealment. But the Jews assert that, from the promulgation of the law on Mount Sinai, it was handed down, pure as at first delivered. In the same way they maintain, that their written law has come to us unadulterated, without a single error. One assertion may be judged of by the other. For, of the tradition delivered by memory, one question need only be asked: What became of it, when priests, kings, and people, were all such idolaters, viz. before and during the early part of the reign of the good King Josiah, that the law was completely forgotten—not even known to exist in the world? To obviate this difficulty, in part, the fourth book of Esdras was probably written.

2. The following passage may serve, at present, as an outline of what was the general nature of the Cabala:

" The similarity, or rather the coincidence, of the Cabalistic, Alexandrian, and Oriental philo-
" sophy, will be sufficiently evinced by briefly stating the common tenets in which these different
" systems agreed; they are as follow: All things are derived by emanation from one principle:
" and this principle is God. From him a substantial power immediately proceeds, which is the

" image of God, and the source of all subsequent emanations. This second principle sends forth,
" by the energy of emanation, other natures, which are more or less perfect, according to their
" different degrees of distance, in the scale of emanation, from the First Source of existence, and
" which constitute different worlds, or orders of being, all united to the eternal power from which
" they proceed. Matter is nothing more than the most remote effect of the emanative energy of
" the Deity. The material world receives its form from the immediate agency of powers far
" beneath the First Source of being. Evil is the necessary effect of the imperfection of matter.
" Human souls are distant emanations from Deity, and after they are liberated from their
" material vehicles, will return, through various stages of purification, to the fountain whence
" they first proceeded." [1]

From this extract the reader will see the nature of the oriental doctrine of emanations, which,
as here given in most, though not in all, respects, coincides with the oriental philosophy: [2] and
the honest translation given by the Septuagint of Deut. xxxiii. 2—*he shined forth from Paran with
thousands of saints, and having his angels on his right hand,* [3] proves that the Cabala was as old or
older than Moses.

The ancient Persians believed, that the Supreme Being was surrounded with angels, or what
they called Æons or Emanations, from the divine substance. This was also the opinion of the
Manicheans, and of almost all the Gnostic sects of Christians. As might be expected, in the
particulars of this complicated system, among the different professors of it a great variety of
opinions arose; but all, at the bottom, evidently of the same nature. These oriental sects were
very much in the habit of using figurative language, under which they concealed their metaphysical doctrines from the eyes of the vulgar. This gave their enemies the opportunity, by construing them literally, of representing them as wonderfully absurd. All these doctrines were also
closely connected with judicial astrology. To the further consideration of the above-cited text I
shall return by and by.

3. Perhaps in the languages of the world no two words have been of greater importance than the
first two in the book of Genesis, ראשית ב B-RASIT; (for they are properly *two* not *one* word;)
and great difference of opinion has arisen, among learned men, respecting the meaning of them.
Grotius renders them, *when first;* Simeon, *before;* Tertullian, *in power;* Rabbi Bechai and
Castalio, *in order before all;* Onkelos, the Septuagint, Jonathan ben Uzziel, and the modern
translators, *in the beginning.*

But the official or accredited and admitted authority of the Jewish religion, the JERUSALEM
TARGUM, renders them BY WISDOM.

It may be observed that the Targum of Jerusalem is, or was formerly, the received orthodox
authority of the Jews: the other Targums are only the opinions of individuals, and in this
rendering, the Jewish Cabala and the doctrine of the ancient Gnostics are evident; and, it is, as I
shall now shew, to conceal *this* that Christians have suppressed its true meaning. To the celebrated and learned Beausobre I am indebted for the most important discovery of the secret doctrine
contained in this word. He says, " The Jews, instead of translating Berasit by the words *in the
" beginning*, translate it by *the Principle* (par le Principe) *active and immediate of all things, God
" made*, &c., that is to say, according to the Targum of Jerusalem, BY WISDOM, (PAR LA SA-
" GESSE,) God made, &c." [4]

---

[1] Dr Rees' Encyclopedia, art. Cabala.
[2] See Hist. Phil. Enfield, Vol. II. Ch. iii.; Phil. Trans. No. CCI. p. 800; Burnet's Archæol. Lib. i. Cap. vii.
[3] See Beausobre, Liv. ix.
[4] " Il y a encore une réflexion à faire sur cette matière. Elle roule sur l'explication du mot Rasit, qui à la tête
" de la Genèse, et qui, si l'on en croit d'anciens Interprètes Juifs, ne signifie pas *le commencement*, mais *le Principe*

Beausobre also informs us, Maimonides maintains, that this is the only LITERAL and TRUE meaning of the word. And Maimonides is generally allowed to have been one of the most learned of modern Jews. (He lived in the twelfth century.) Beausobre further says, that CHALCIDIUS, METHODIUS, ORIGEN, and CLEMENS ALEXANDRINUS, a most formidable phalanx of authorities, give it this sense. The latter quotes a sentence as authority from the work of St. Peter's now lost. Beausobre gives us as the expression of Clemens, " This is what St. Peter says, who has very " well understood this word: ' God has made the heaven and the earth by the Principle. (Dieu " 'a fait le Ciel et la Terre dans le Principe.) This principle is that which is called Wisdom by " ' all the prophets.'" [1] Here is evidently the doctrine of the Magi or of Emanations.

Of this quotation from Peter, by Clemens, the Christian divine will perhaps say, It is spurious. I deny his right to say any such thing. He has no right to assume that Peter never wrote any letters but the two in our canon; or that Clemens is either mistaken or guilty of fraud in this instance, without some proof.

The following passage of Beausobre's shews that St. Augustine coincided in opinion with the other fathers whom I have cited on the meaning of the word רֵאשִׁית Rasit : " Car si par Reschit " on entend le Principe actif de la création, et non pas le commencement, alors Moïse n'a plus dit " que le Ciel et la Terre furent les premières des œuvres de Dieu. Il a dit seulement, que Dieu " créa le ciel et la terre par le Principe, qui est son Fils. Ce n'est pas l'époque, c'est l'auteur " immédiat de la création qu'il enseigne. Je tiens encore cette pensée de St. Augustin. Les " anges, dit il, ont été faits avant le Firmament, et même avant ce qu'est rapporté par Moïse, " Dieu fit le ciel et la terre par le Principe ; car ce mot de Principe ne veut pas dire, que le ciel et " la terre furent faits avant toutes choses, puisque Dieu avoit déjà fait les anges auparavant; il " veut dire, que Dieu a fait toutes choses par SAGESSE, qui est son Verbe, et que l'Écriture a " nommée le Principe." [2]

By Wisdom, I have no doubt, was the secret, if not the avowed, meaning of the words; and I also feel little doubt that, in the course of this work, I shall prove that the word Αρχη used by the Seventy and by Philo had the same meaning. But the fact that the LXX. give Αρχη as the rendering of Berasit, which is shewn to have the meaning of WISDOM by the authorities cited above, is of itself quite enough to justify the assertion that one of the meanings of the word Αρχη was WISDOM, and in any common case it would be so received by all Lexicographers.

WISDOM is one of the three first of the Eight Emanations which formed the eternal and ever-happy Octoade of the oriental philosophers, and of the ten Sephiroth of the Jewish Cabala. See Parkhurst's Hebrew Lexicon, p. 668, and also his Greek one in voce Αρχη, where the reader will find that, with all his care, he cannot disguise the fact that ראש ras means wisdom. See also Beausobre, [3] where, at large, may be found the opinions of the greatest part of the most learned of the Fathers and Rabbis on the first verse of Genesis.

The Jerusalem Targum, as already stated, is the orthodox explanation of the Jews : it used to be read in their synagogues, and the following is its rendering of this celebrated text, which com-

---

" actif et immediat de toutes choses. Ainsi au lieu de traduire, Au commencement Dieu fit le Ciel et la Terre, ils " traduisoient, Dieu fit le Ciel et la Terre PAR LE PRINCIPE, c'est à-dire, selon l'explication du Targum de Jerusalem. " PAR LA SAGESSE : Maimonide soutient, que cette explication est la seule LITTÉRALE ET VÉRITABLE. Elle passa " d'abord chez les Chrétiens. On la trouve non seulement dans Chalcidius, qui marque qu'elle venoit des Hébreux, " mais dans Méthodius, dans Origène, et dans Clement d'Alexandrie, plus ancien que l'un et l'autre." Beausobre. Hist. Manich. Liv. vi. Ch. i. p. 290.

[1] Beausobre, Hist. Manich. Liv. vi. Ch. i. p. 290.   [2] Hist. Manich. Liv. vi. Ch. i. p. 291.

[3] Hist. Manich. Liv. v. Ch. iii. and Liv. vi. Ch. i.

pletely justifies that which I have given of it : בחבמה ברא אלהא ית שמיא ית ארעא   In sapientia creavit Deus cœlum et terram. [1]

It is said in Proverbs viii. 22, " Jehovah possessed me," *wisdom*, ראשית *rasit* ; but not בראשית *b-rasit*, which it ought to be, to justify our vulgar translation, which is, " The Lord possessed me " IN *the beginning*." The particle ב *b*, the sign of the ablative case, is wanting ; but it is interpolated in our translation, to justify the rendering, because it would be nonsense to say the Lord possessed me, *the beginning*. [2]

The Targum of Jerusalem says that God made man by his Word, or Λογος, Gen. i. 26. So says Jonathan, Es. xlv. 12 ; and in Gen. i. 27, he says, that the Λογος created man after his image. See Allix's Judgment of the Jewish Church, p. 131. From this I think Dr. Allix's assertion is correct, that the Targum considered the ראשית *rasit*, and the Λογος to be identical.

And it seems to me to be impossible to form an excuse for Parkhurst, as his slight observation in his Greek Lexicon shews that he was not ignorant. Surely supposing that he thought those authorities given above to be mistaken, he ought, in common honesty, to have noticed them, according to his practice with other words, in similar cases.

4. According to the Jewish Cabala a number of Sephiroths, being Emanations, issued or flowed from God—of which the chief was *Wisdom*. In Genesis it is said, by *Wisdom* God created or formed, &c. Picus, of Mirandula, confirms my rendering, and says, " This *Wisdom* is the Son." [3] Whether the Son or not, this is evidently the first emanation, MINERVA—the Goddess of *Wisdom* emanating or issuing from the head of Jove, (or Iao or Jehovah,) as described on an Etruscan brass plate in the Cabinet of Antiquities at Bologna. [4] This is known to be Etruscan, from the names being on the arms of the Gods in Etruscan letters, which proves it older than the Romans, or probably than the Grecians of Homer.

M. Basnage says, " Moses Nachmanides advanced three Sephiroths above all the rest ; *they* " *have never been seen by any one ; there is not any defect in them nor any disunion*. If any one " should add another to them, he would deserve death. There is, therefore, nothing but a dispute " about words : you call three *lights* what Christians call Father, Son, and Holy Ghost. That " first eternal number is the Father : the WISDOM by which God created the heavens is the Son : " and Prudence or Understanding, which makes the third number of the Cabalists, is the Christian " Holy Ghost." [5]

5. The word *Rasit*, as we might expect, is found in the Arabic language, and means, as our Lexicographers, who are the same class of persons that made our Hebrew Lexicons, tell us, *head*, *chief*—and is used as a term of honour applied to great persons : for instance, Aaron-al-raschid. Al is the emphatic article. Abd-al-raschid, i. e. Abdallah-al-raschid, &c.

For a long time I flattered myself that I might set down Parkhurst as one of the very few Polemics, with whose works I was acquainted, against whom I could not bring a charge of pious fraud, but the way in which he has treated the first word of Genesis puts it out of my power. It seems to me impossible to believe that this learned man could be ignorant of the construction which had been given to the word ראשית *rasit*.

Again, I repeat, it is impossible to acquit Parkhurst of disingenuousness in suppressing, in his Hebrew Lexicon, the opinions held respecting the meaning of this word by CLEMENS ALEXANDRINUS, CHALCIDIUS, METHODIUS, ORIGEN, ST. AUGUSTINE, MAIMONIDES, and by the authors of

---

[1] Kircher, Œd. Ægypt. Syntag. II. Cap. vii.
[2] Kircher, Œd. Egypt. Syntag. II. Cap. vii.
[3] Book iv. Ch. v. Sect. vii.

[4] Vide Parkhurst, p. 668.
[5] A copy of the plate may be seen in Montfaucon.

the TARGUM OF JERUSALEM, the accredited exposition of the Jewish church, and in the slight and casual way in which he has expressed a disapprobation of the rendering of the Targum, in his Greek Lexicon. It is really not to be believed that he and the other modern Lexicographers— Bates, Taylor, Calassio, &c., should have been ignorant, for I believe they all suppress the rendering. It ought to serve as a warning to all inquirers that they never can be too much on their guard. How true is the dictum of Bacon, that every thing connected with religion is to be viewed with suspicion !

Wisdom was the first emanation from the Divine power, the protogonos, the beginning of all things, the Rasit of Genesis, the Buddha of India, the Logos of Plato and St. John, as I shall prove. *Wisdom* was the beginning of creation. *Wisdom* was the primary, and *beginning* the secondary, meaning of the word. Of its rendering in the LXX., by the word Αρχη, I shall treat presently at great length. The fact was, Parkhurst saw that if the word had the meaning of *Wisdom* it would instantly establish the doctrine of Emanations ; and if he had given, as he ought to have done, the authority of the Jerusalem Targum and of Maimonides, no person would have hesitated for a moment to prefer it to his sophistry. But as the doctrine of emanations must, at all events, be kept out of sight, he suppressed the authorities.

The meaning of *wisdom*, which the word *Ras* bore, I can scarcely doubt was, in fact, secret, sacred, and mystical ; and in the course of the following work my reader will perceive, that wherever a certain mythos, which will be explained, was concerned, two clear and distinct meanings of the words will be found : one for the initiated, and one for the people. This is of the first importance to be remembered. If the ancients really had a secret system it was a practice which could not well be dispensed with, and innumerable proofs of it will be given ; but among them there will not be found one more important, nor more striking, than that of the word רש *ras* or בראשית *b-rasit*. To the reconsideration of the meaning of this word I shall many times have occasion to revert. I shall now return to the text of Deuteronomy, from which I have digressed.

That the angels are in fact emanations from the Divine substance, according to the Mosaic system, is proved from Deut. xxxiii. 2. Moses says, according to the Septuagint, *The Lord is come from Sinai : he has appeared to us from Seir ; he shined forth from Paran with thousands of saints, and having his* ANGELS ON HIS RIGHT HAND. But M. Beausobre[1] has shewn, (and which Parkhurst, p. 149, in voce, דת *dt*, confirms,) that the Hebrew word אשדת *asdt*, which the Septuagint translates *angels*, means *effusions*, that is, *emanations*, from the Divine substance. According to Moses and the Seventy translators, therefore, the Angels were Emanations from the Divine substance. Thus we see here that the doctrines of the Persians and that of the Jews, and we shall see afterward, of the Gnostic and Manichean Christians, were in reality the same.

The fact has been established that the Septuagint copy which we now possess is really a copy of that spoken of by Philo and the Evangelists, though in many places corrupted, so that no more need be said about it. But if any one be disposed to dispute this passage of the LXX., it may be observed to him, that the probability is strongly in favour of its being genuine.

It is not a disputed text. It is found in these words in the ancient Italic version, which was made from the Septuagint,[2] which shews that it was there in a very early period, and it did not flatter the prejudice or support the interest either of the modern Jews or the ruling power of the Christians to corrupt it, but the contrary. As M. Beausobre properly observes, if the question

---

[1] Hist. Manich. Liv. ix. Ch. ii.
[2] Qui avoit été fait sur les LXX. Beausobre, Hist. Manich. Liv. ix. Ch. ii. p. 621 ; and Sim. Hist. Crit. du V. Test. Liv. ii. Ch. xi.

be decided by authority, the authority of the Septuagint is vastly preferable to that of the Masorets, who lived many ages after the makers of the Septuagint. And, as he says, if reason be admitted to decide it, a person inclined to favour the system of emanations, would urge, in the first place, that אשרת *asdt* is a Hebrew word, one entire word, which cannot be divided; and that it is evident from the Septuagint, that the ancient Hebrews did not divide it. Secondly, he would say, that *Dat*, which signifies *law, commandment*, is not a Hebrew but a Median[1] word, which the Hebrews took from the Medes, and is not to be found in any of their books, but such as were written after the captivity; so that there is no reason to suppose it had been used by Moses in Deuteronomy. Thirdly, he would say, that the fire of the law, or the law of fire, as our English has it, is unnatural; and that although it is said the law was given from the middle of the fire, there is nothing to shew that it was from the right hand of God. In fine, he would urge that the explanation of the LXX. is much more natural. God comes with thousands of saints, and the angels, the principal angels, those who are named Emanations were at his right hand. These proofs would have been invincible in the first ages of Christianity, when the version of the Septuagint was considered to be inspired, and had much greater authority given to it than to the Hebrew.

In many of Dr. Kennicot's Hebrew codices, the word אשרת *adst*, is written in one word, but not in all: it is likewise the same in three of the Samaritan; and in two of the latter it is written אשרת *asdut*. The following are the words of the Septuagint:

Κυριος εκ Σινα ηκει, και επεφανεν εκ Σηειρ ημιν, και κατεσπευσεν εξ ορυς Φαραν, συν μυριασι Καδης· εκ δεξιων αυτη Αγγελοι μετ' αυτη.[2]

Nothing can be more absurd than the vulgar translation, which is made from a copy in which the words have been divided by the Masorets. But it was necessary to risk any absurdity, rather than let the fact be discovered that the word meant angels or emanations, which would so strongly tend to confirm the doctrine of the Gnostics, and also prove that the religions of Moses and the Persians were the same. M. Beausobre has satisfactorily explained the contrivance of the Masorets to disguise the truth by dividing the word *Asdt* אשרת, or, as he calls it, *Eschdot*, into two, Esch-Dot. And his observations respecting the authority of the Italic versions and the Septuagint, written so many centuries before the time of the Masorets, when the language was a living one, is conclusive on the subject. The very fact of adopting the use of the points, is a proof either that the language was lost or nearly so, or that some contrivance, after the time of Jerom, was thought necessary by the Jews, to give to the unpointed text such meaning as they thought proper.

6. But to return to the word Berasit, or more properly the word ראשית *Rasit*, the particle ב *beth* being separated from it. A curious question has arisen among Christian philosophers, whether Time was in existence before the creation here spoken of, or the beginning, if it be so translated.

The word cannot mean the beginning of creation, according to the Mosaic account, because the context proves that there were created beings before the creation of our world—for instance, the angels or cherubim who guarded the gate of paradise after the fall.[3]

In common language, the words, *In the beginning*, mean some little time after a thing has begun; but this idea cannot be applied to the creation. The expression cannot be applied to any period of time *after* the universe began to exist, and it cannot be applied to any period *before* it began to exist. If the words *at first* be used, they are only different words for precisely the same

---

[1] He says he owes this remark to Mons. de la Croze, à qui je serois bien fâché de la dérober.

[2] Deut. xxxiii. 2, LXX. juxt. Exemp. Vatic.; Beausobre, Hist. Manich. Liv. ix. Ch. ii. p. 621.

[3] See St. Agustine above, in section 3 and Job xxxviii. 7.

idea. The translators of the Septuagint and Onkelos are undoubtedly entitled to high respect. In this case, however, they advocate an untenable opinion, if they both do advocate the meaning of *beginning*, because our system was not the first of created things ; and they make the divine penman say what was not true—in fact, to contradict himself in what follows. But if we adopt the explanation of the Jerusalem Targum and of the other learned Jews, and of the earliest of the fathers of the church, there is nothing in it inconsistent with the context ; but, on the contrary, it is strictly in accordance with it, and with the general system of oriental philosophy, on which the whole Mosaic system was founded.

I think the author of Genesis had more philosophy than to write about the *beginning* of the world. I cannot see any reason why so much anxiety should be shewn, by some modern translators, to construe this word as meaning *beginning*. I see clearly enough why others of them should do so, and why the ancient translators did it. They had a preconceived dogma to support, their partiality to which blinded their judgment, and of philosophy they did not possess much. However, it cannot be denied that, either in a primary or secondary sense, the word means *wisdom* as well as *beginning*, and, therefore, its sense here must be gathered from the context.

I will now return to the word *Samim*, as I promised in the early part of this book.

7. The two words called in the first chapter of Genesis השמים *e-smim* , the heavens, ought to be translated *the planets*. In that work the sun, and moon, and the earth, are said to be formed, and also separately from them the samim or planets ; and afterward the stars also. Dr. Parkhurst has very properly explained the word to mean *disposers*. They are described in the Chaldean Oracles as a septenary of living beings. By the ancients they were thought to have, under their special care, the affairs of men. Philo was of this opinion, and even Maimonides declares, that they are endued with life, knowledge, and understanding ; that they acknowledge and praise their Creator. On this opinion of the nature of the planets, all judicial astrology, magic, was founded—a science, I believe, almost as generally held by the ancients, as the being of a God is by the moderns.[1]

Phornutus, Περι Ουρανυ,[2] says, " For the ancients took those for Gods whom they found to " move in a certain regular manner, thinking them to be the causers of the changes of the air and " the *conservation of the universe*. These, then, are Gods (Θεοι) which are the disposers (Θετηρες) " and formers of all things."

The word איתשמיא *itsmia* is used by the Targum of Jerusalem for the word את שמם *at smim* of Genesis, and I think fully justifies my rendering of that word by *planets* instead of the word *heavens*. It comes from the root שם *sm*, which signifies to fix, to enact, *pono, sancior*—and means *placers, fixers, enactors*.

With respect to the שמם *smim*, Parkhurst is driven to a ridiculous shift, similar to the case of the first word ראשית *rasit*. It was necessary to conceal the truth from his Christian reader, but this was very difficult without laying himself open to a charge of pious fraud. In this instance he will be supported by the Jews, because *at this day* neither Jews nor Christians will like to admit that the very foundation of their religions is laid in judicial astrology. But such I affirm is the fact, as any one may at once see, by impartially considering what Parkhurst has unwillingly been obliged to allow in his Lexicon. He does not admit that the singular of the word means *a disposer* or *placer*, or *the* disposer or *placer*, but he takes the plural and calls them the disposer*s* or placer*s*. And, shutting his eyes to the planetary bodies and to the word רקיע *rqio*, which means the space, air, or firmament, and which can have no other meaning, he calls the שמם *smim*, *the firmament*, and says it is the disposers. It is absurd to speak of the air, or space, or firmament, in the plural ; and that Parkhurst must have known. In some author (I yet believe somewhere in

---

[1] See Faber, Vol. II. p. 226.   [2] Ap. Parkhurst, in voce שם *sm*, p. 745.

Parkhurst) I found the שמים *smim*, called *the disposers of the affairs of men*, and by mistake, if it were a mistake, I quoted it as from Parkhurst in my Celtic Druids. It is of little consequence where I got the quotation, as the fact itself is true. The planets in ancient times were always taken to be the superintendants and regulators of the affairs of mankind, and this is the meaning of Genesis. This idea, too, was the foundation of all judicial astrology : which is as visible as the noonday sun in every part of the Old and New Testament. The word רקיע *rqio* means the firmament or ethereal space ; the word ככב *ccb* means a star : and though the word שמים *smim* sometimes means stars, as we call the planets *stars*, yet its primary meaning is *the disposers* or *planets*. Originally the fixed stars were not regarded as disposers.

For proof that the word שמים *smim* means *placers* or *disposers*, see Hutchinson, " Of the " Trinity of the Gentiles,"[1] and Moses's Principia.[2] They shew that the essential meaning of the word שמים *smim* is disposers or placers of other things. If they were not to dispose or place the affairs or conduct of men, pray what were they to place ? Were they to dispose of the affairs of beasts, or of themselves ? They were the צבא *Zba*, or Heavenly Host, and I have no doubt the original word was confined to the wandering stars, whatever it might be afterward. Parkhurst and Hutchinson shew great unwillingness to allow that they mean disposers, but they are both obliged to confess it, and in this confession, admit, in fact, the foundation of judicial astrology.

It is very certain that the ancient philosophers knew the difference between the stars and planets, as well as the moderns. This is the only place where the formation of the planets is named ; the formation of the sun, moon, and stars, is described in the 14th verse. As I have just said, השמים *esmim* does not mean the vast expanse, because this is afterward described in the 6th verse by the word רקיע *rqio*.

In the eighth verse the word *rqio* is used. In our translation it is said, he called the expanse heavens. But before the word רקיע *rqio* the particle ל *l*, the sign of the dative case is written, which shews that a word is understood to make sense. Thus, And he called the שמים *smim*, in the *rqio* or expanse, planets. This merely means, and he gave to the *smim* the name which they now bear, of smim. This explanation of mine is justified by the Jerusalem Targum, in its use of the word ןישמיא *itsmia*, placers.

Persons are apt to regard with contempt the opinion, that the planetary bodies are animated or rational beings. But let it not be forgotten that the really great Kepler believed our globe to be endowed with living faculties ; that it possessed instinct and volition—an hypothesis which Mons. Patrin has supported with great ingenuity.[3] Among those who believed that the planets were intelligent beings, were Philo, Origen, and Maimonides.[4]

The first verse of Genesis betrays the Persian or Oriental philosophy in almost every word. The first word *rasit* ראשית or *wisdom* refers to one, or probably to the chief, of the emanations from the Deity. This is allowed by most of the early fathers, who see in it the second person of the Trinity. The word בארא *bara* in the singular number, followed by אלהים *Aleim* in the plural, or a noun of multitude, refers to the Trinity, three Persons and one God ; and does not mean that the Aleim created, but that it formed, εποιησεν, fecit, as the Septuagint says, out of matter previously existing. On the question of the eternity of matter it is perfectly neutral : it gives no opinion. The word חשמים *esmim* in the Hebrew, and ןימשה *esmin* in the Chaldee, do not mean the heavens or heavenly bodies generally, but the planets only, the disposers, as Dr. Parkhurst, after the Magi, calls them.

This is all perfectly consistent, and in good keeping, with what we know of the Jewish Cabala.

---

[1] In voce, p. 20.   [2] Part II. p. 56.
[3] Vide Jameson's Cuvier, p. 45, and Nouveau Dict. d'Histoire Naturelle.   [4] Faber, Pag. Idol. Vol. I. p. 32.

And it is surely only reasonable to expect, that there should be something like consistency between this verse and the Cabala, which we know was founded, in some degree, perhaps entirely, upon it.

The conduct of Christian expositors, with respect to the words שמים *smim* and ראשית *rasit*, has been as unfair as possible. They have misrepresented the meaning of them in order to prevent the true astrological character of the book from being seen. But, that the first does mean *disposers*, the word *heavens* making nonsense, and the words relating to the stars, in the 16th verse, shewing that they cannot be meant, put it beyond a question. My reader may, therefore, form a pretty good judgment how much Parkhurst can be depended upon for the meaning of the second, from the striking fact that, though he has filled several columns with observations relating to the opinions of different expositors, he could not find room for the words, *the opinion of the Synagogue is, that the word means* WISDOM, or *the Jerusalem Targum says it means* WISDOM. But it was necessary to conceal from the English reader, as already stated, the countenance it gives to judicial astrology and the doctrine of emanations.

Indeed, I think the doctrine of Emanations in the Jewish system cannot be denied. This Mr. Maurice unequivocally admits : " The Father is the great fountain of the divinity ; the Son and " the Holy Spirit are EMANATIONS from that fountain." Again, " The Christian Trinity is a " Trinity of subsistences, or persons joined by an indissoluble union." [1] The reader will please to recollect that *hypostasis* means subsistence, which is a Greek word—ὑποϛασις, from ὑπο *sub*, and ιϛημι, *sto, existo*.

In the formation of an opinion respecting the real meaning of such texts as these, the prudent inquirer will consider the general character of the context; and, in order that he may be the better enabled to do this, I request him to suspend his judgment till he sees the observations which will be made in the remainder of this work.

Whatever trifling differences or incongruities may be discovered between them, the following conclusions are inevitable, viz. that the religion of Abraham and that of the Magi, were in reality the same ; that they both contained the doctrine of the Trinity ; and that the oriental historians who state this fact, state only what is true.

Dr. Shuckford gives other reasons to shew that the religions of Abraham and of the Persians were the same. He states, that Dr. Hyde was of his opinion, and thus concludes : " The first " religion, therefore, of the Persians, was the worship of the true God, and they continued in it " for some time after Abraham was expelled Chaldæa, having the same faith and worship as " Abraham had, except only in those points concerning which he received instruction after his " going into Haran and into Canaan." [2]

8. I must now beg my reader to review what has been said respecting the celebrated name of God, *Al*, Ale, Aleim; and to observe that this was in all the Western Asiatic nations the name both of God and of the Sun. This is confirmed by Sir W. Drummond and Mr. Parkhurst, as the reader has seen, and by the names given by the Greeks to places which they conquered. Thus : בית אל *Bit Al*, House of the Sun, became Heliopolis. I beg my reader also to recollect that when the Aleim appeared it was generally in the form of fire, thus he appeared to Moses in the bush. Fire was, in a particular manner, held sacred by the Jews and Persians ; a sacred fire was always burning in the temple of Jerusalem. From all this, and much more which the reader will find presently, he will see that though most undoubtedly the Sun was not the object of the adoration of Moses, it is very evident that it had been closely allied to it. In the time of Moses, not the sun, but the higher principle thought to reside in the sun, perhaps the Creator of the sun himself, had

[1] Maurice, Ind. Ant. Vol. IV. p. 49.   [2] Shuckford, Book v. p. 308, Ed. 3.

become the object of adoration, by the Gentiles if not by Moses (but of the latter it may be matter of doubt) ; and it is probable that it had arisen as I have supposed and described in my last book.

Thus if a person was to say, that the God of Moses resolved himself at last into the Sun, he would not be correct ; but he would be very near it. The object of this observation will be seen hereafter.

I must also beg my reader's attention to the observation at the end of Chapter II. Sect. 4, of this book relating to the word ᴇʟ, as used by Sir W. Drummond. In the Asiatic language, the first letter of the word is the first letter of the alphabet and not the fifth, as here written by Sir William, and this shews the importance of my system of reducing the alphabets to their originals : for here, most assuredly, this name of the Sun is the same as the Hebrew name of God. But by the mistake of Sir William this most important fact is concealed. No doubt dialectic variations in language will take place [1] between neighbouring countries, which occasion difficulties, and for which allowance must be made : but, by not attending to my rule, we increase them, and create them, where they are not otherwise to be found.

But we do not merely increase *difficulties*, we disguise and conceal absolute *facts*. Thus it is a fact that the Sun and the God of Moses had the same names ; that is, that the God of Moses was called by the same word which meant Sun, in the Asiatic language : but by miscalling one of them *El* instead of Al, the fact is concealed, and it is an important fact, and will lead to important results.

We must also recollect, that when I translate the first word of Genesis by the word *Wisdom*, I am giving no new theory of my own, but only the orthodox exposition of the Jewish religion, as witnessed in the Jerusalem Targum, read in their synagogues, supported by the authorities of the most eminent of the Jewish Rabbis, Maimonides, &c., and the most learned of the Christian fathers, Clemens, Origen, &c. All this is of importance to be remembered, because a great consequence will be deduced from this word *Wisdom*. It was, as it were, the foundation on which a mighty structure was erected.

It was by what may be called a peculiar Hypostasis, denominated *Wisdom*, that the *higher principle* operated when it formed the world. This is surely quite sufficient to shew its great importance—an importance which we shall see demonstrated hereafter, when I treat of the celebrated Buddha of India.

CHAPTER IV

Why Cyrus restored the Temple—Melchizedek—Abraham, what he was—Abraham the Father of the Persians—Daniel—Book of Esther, Persian—Zoroaster—Variation between Persians and Israelites—Sacrifices—Religion of Zoroaster—Religion of Zoroaster continued—Zendavesta—Observations on the Religion of Jews and Persians—All ancient Religions Astrological

1. Fʀᴏᴍ the striking similarity between the religion of Moses and that of the Persians, it is not difficult to see the reason why Cyrus, Darius, and the Persians, restored the temples of Jerusalem

---

[1] With the Syrians the A changed into the O.

and Gerizim, when they destroyed the temples of the idolaters in Egypt and other places, which, in fact, they did wherever they came. It appears probable that the temple on Gerizim was built or restored within a few years of the same time with that at Jerusalem : and for the same reason —because the religion was that of the Persians, with such little difference as distance of country or some peculiar local circumstances in length of time might produce.

In Genesis xiv. 20, we read, that when Abraham returned from the pursuit of the five kings who were smitten by him as far as Hobah and Damascus, he received gifts from Melchizedek, King of Salem, and paid him tithes of all he had taken from his enemies. The situation of this Salem has been much disputed, and concerning it I shall have much to say hereafter : but it was evidently somewhere West of the Jordan, in the country of the Canaanites. Now this king and priest is said to have been a priest of the most high God. And as the Canaanites *were then in the land*, (Gen. xii. 6,) or were then its inhabitants, it is evident that he could be no other than their priest. There is nothing in the sacred history which militates against this in the slightest degree. It is quite absurd to suppose that there should be priests without a people, and there were no others besides the Canaanites. There is no expression which would induce us to believe that they were idolaters in the time of Abraham. The covenants and treaties of friendship which Abraham entered into with them, raise a strong presumption that they could not then have been so wicked as they are represented to have been in the time of Moses, five hundred years afterward. As the history supplies no evidence that the Canaanites were idolaters in the time of Abraham, the fact of a priest of the true God, and this priest a king, being in the midst of them, almost proves that they were not idolaters. The conduct of Abimelech, (Genesis xx.,) in restoring Sarah to her husband, as soon as he found her to be a married woman, and his reproof of Abraham for his deceit, shew, whatever his religion might be, that his morality was at least as good as that of the father of the faithful. But several circumstances named in the context, prove him of the same religion.

Dr. Shuckford not only agrees with me that Abraham and the Canaanites were of the same religion, and that Melchizedek was their priest, but he also shews that Abimelech and the Philistines were at that time of the same religion.[1] He also gives some reason to suppose that the Egyptians were the same.[2]

The circumstance that the old inhabitants of Palestine (Palli-stan) were of the same religion as the tribe which came with Abraham, will be seen by and by to be of consequence. This can scarcely be accounted for, except we suppose them to have come from the same country from which he came.

Joseph could hardly have married a daughter of the priest Potiphar, if he had been an idolater. And it is curious that he was priest of On or Heliopolis, a place which will be found to be of great importance in the following observations. Shuckford says,

" Melchizedec, the King of Salem, was a priest of the most high God, and he received and " entertained Abraham as a true servant and particular favourite of that God, whose priest he " himself was ; *blessed* (said he) *be Abraham*, servant of the most high God, possessor of heaven " and earth."[3]

Respecting the rites or ceremonies performed by this priest, few particulars are known. It appears his votaries paid him tithes. Abraham, we have seen, paid him tithes of all the plunder which he took from the five kings whom he had defeated. This contribution is enforced in the religion of the ancient Persians, and also in the religious ordinances of the Jews. It is very singular that the exact *tenth* should be found in all the three religions to be paid. It might be asked,

---

[1] Book v. pp. 309, 310.   [2] Ibid. pp. 312, 313.   [3] Gen. xiv. 19 ; Shuckford, Book v. p. 310.

If they were not the *same* religions, how came they all to fix upon the exact number of ten, and not the number of eight or twelve? There is nothing in the number, that should lead their adherents to it, rather than to any other. The second of the rites of Melchizedek's religion which is known, is the offering or sacrifice of bread and wine, about which more will be said hereafter.

It is not possible to determine from *Genesis* where the Salem was of which Melchizedek was priest. (I pay no attention to the *partisan Josephus.*) Taking advantage of this uncertainty the Christians have settled it to be Jerusalem. But it happens in this case that a Heathen author removes the difficulty. Eupolemus states that Abraham received gifts from Melchizedek in the Holy City of Hargarizim, or of Mount Gerizim. Har, in the ancient language, signifies mount. This proves that there was a place holy to the Lord upon Gerizim, long before Joshua's time, whatever the Jews may allege to the contrary against the Samaritans.

There is much reason to believe that this Melchizedek was the priest of the Temple of Jove, Jupiter, or Iao, without image, spoken of by the Greeks, to which Pythagoras and Plato are said to have resorted for study; the place where Joshua placed his unhewn stones. The mountain Carmel, probably, extended over a considerable extent of country. Hargerizim was probably looked on as a mount of Carmel, as Mount Blanc is a mount of the Alps.

Melchizedek (Gen. xiv. 19) ought to be written צדק מלכי *mlki-zdq*, and means literally *Kings of Justice;* but it is evidently a proper name. The proper translation is, " And Melchizedek, " king of peace, brought forth bread and wine, because he (*was*, understood) priest *to the most* " high God. And he blessed him (or he bestowed his benediction upon him, first addressing a " prayer to God) and said, Blessed be Abram, by the most high God, possessor of heaven and " earth; (he then addresses Abraham;) and blessed be the most high God who hath delivered " thine enemies into thine hand," &c. I cannot conceive how any person who comes to the consideration of this text with an impartial and candid mind can find any difficulty.

When David and the priests removed the holy place from Gerizim to the city of the Jebusites, they then, perhaps, first called it *Jerusalem;* and to justify themselves against the charges of the Samaritans, they corrupted the text in Joshua, as some of the most eminent Protestant divines are obliged to allow, substituting Ebal for Gerizim, and Gerizim for Ebal. The whole is a description of the sacrifice of bread and wine, repeated by Jesus Christ a few hours previous to his crucifixion: the same, probably, as was offered by Pythagoras at the shrine of the bloodless Apollo. It was sometimes celebrated with wine, sometimes with water. The English priests, in the time of Edward the Sixth, not knowing what to make of it, ordered it in the rubric to be celebrated with both, mixing them together. It is still continued by the Jews at their pascal feast, and is altogether, when unaccompanied by nonsense not belonging to it, the most beautiful religious ceremony that ever was invented. It is found in the Buddhist rites of Persia before they were corrupted, in the rites of Abraham, of Pythagoras, and, in a future page I shall shew, of the ancient Italians, and of Jesus Ναζωραιος, the Nazarite, of the city of Nazarites, or of Nazareth. Of this city of Nazareth it might be said, that it was nothing, in fact, but a suburb of the sacred city *which God had chosen to place his name there.* (Deut. xii. 5—14.) It was a convent of Essenian Monks, or Carmelites, for all monks were Carmelites before the fifth century after Christ. If Pythagoras were one of them, in this very place, it is probable that he took the vows, *Tria vota substantialia,* Poverty, Chastity, and Obedience, still taken by the Buddhists in India, and Carmelites in Rome. These constituted the companies of prophets named in 1 Sam. xix. 20, and I see no reason why Jesus may not have been the head of the order, though I admit we have no proof of it; but of this more hereafter.

Melchizedek could not be king of the city of Jerusalem in the time of Abraham, because it was

not built; for it was in the *thicket* in this place, Mount Moriah, where he found the ram fast by
the horns, when he prepared to sacrifice his son Isaac. It therefore follows, that the city of the
Jebusites must have been built between the time fixed for the sacrifice by Abraham, and the time
of David; or rather, perhaps, between the time of Moses and of David; and for this to have
been effected, there was a space of about five hundred years. By building an altar here it might
be made a holy place, and thus a city might be drawn to it. If there had been a city here in the
time of Abraham, the history would have said, that he went to the *town* to sacrifice, not to the
mount. The whole context implies that there was no town.

2. It is very clear that Abraham is represented in the history as a rich and powerful shepherd
king, what we should now call an Arab or Tartar chieftain, constantly migrating with his tribe
from place to place to seek pasture for his flocks and herds. He probably never remained long in
one situation, but dwelt in the mountains in summer, and in the plains in winter. How formidable, and indeed ruinous, wandering tribes of this description have been in later times to the Romans
and other civilized nations is well known. And though the distance from Canaan to Persia is considerable, it is not greater than migratory shepherd tribes often pass, and by no means equal to
Abraham's journey which we learn from Genesis that he did take from Haran, in the upper part of
Mesopotamia, to Egypt. Terah, the father of Abraham, seems to have been of the same migratory
character, for he removed from Ur in Chaldea, to Haran in Mesopotamia—no little distance.
(Gen. xi. 31.)

Palestine is now nearly in the same situation in which it was in the time of Abraham. The
nomade tribes under the patriarchal government of their Sheiks, ramble about the country, sometimes attacking the towns, sometimes making treaties and confederacies with them.

When I speak of Abraham I mean the tribe which became known by the name of Israelites.
Whether there was such a man as Abraham, and whether the tribe did not come from much more
eastern countries, will be discussed hereafter.

It appears that Abraham attacked the confederate kings, and drove them before him, (Gen.
xiv. 15,) and that the war raged (ver. 6) from near Damascus to Mount Seir: from which it is
evident, that it must have been a very great one. When, therefore, it is said that Abraham divided his 318 trained servants against the confederate kings, the literal meaning cannot be intended. Some very learned persons have supposed, that the whole of this account is an astronomical allegory, and every one must confess that this is not destitute of probability. But
allowing all that Sir W. Drummond has said to be true, it is still evident from the terms used,
such as Damascus, Mount Seir, &c., &c., the names of places must have been used in the allegory
(and if the names of *places* be used, why should not the names of *persons?*) by way of accommodation: and whether it be all allegory or not, the argument will not be affected, because it
is only here undertaken to produce such probable proofs that the worship of Abraham and his family and that of the Persians were the same, as that no unprejudiced person can refuse his assent
to them.

Dr. Hyde[1] not being able to account for the great similarity, which could not be denied,
between the religion of Moses and of Zoroaster, (without any authority,) supposes, that the latter
was a slave or servant in the family of Daniel or of Ezra, at Babylon, during the captivity; and
that he was by birth a Jew. This ridiculous fancy is supported by Prideaux;[2] but as it is completely laughed down by Maurice,[3] no more need be said about it, except merely that the similarity, indeed identity, of the two religions being clearly seen by the learned doctor, it was neces-

[1] Hist. Rel. Vet. Pers. Chap. xxiv. p. 314.   [2] Con. Vol. I. p. 213.   [3] Ind. Ant. Vol. II. p. 118.

sary to find some plausible reason for it. Dr. Hyde observed also, that a marked similarity was to be found between Abraham and the Brahma of the Hindoos, but I reserve that point for another chapter.

3. The Persians also claim Ibrahim, i. e. Abraham, for their founder, as well as the Jews. Thus we see that according to all ancient history the Persians, the Jews, and the Arabians, are descendants of Abraham.

But Abraham was not merely the founder of the Persians, but various authors assert, that he was a great Magician, at the head of the Magi, that is, he was at the head of the priesthood, as our king is, and as the Persian kings always were, and as the Roman Emperors found it necessary to become in later days: no doubt a sound and wise policy. His descendants, Jacob for instance, continued to occupy the same station. The standards of the tribes of the Israelites, the ornaments of the Temple, the pillars *Joachim* and *Boaz*, the latter with its orrery or sphere at the top of it, the Urim and Thummim, in short, the whole of the Jewish system betrays judicial astrology, or, in other words, magic, in every part. The Magi of Persia were only the order of priests—Magi in Persia, Clergymen in England. It must not be supposed that the word Magus or Magi, conveyed the vulgar idea attached to modern Magicians, persons dealing with the devil, to work mischief. They probably became objects of detestation to the Christians in the eastern nations from opposing their religion, and in consequence were run down by them, and held up to public odium, in the same way as philosophers are now endeavoured to be, and not without some success. To be versed in *magic* is something horrid, not to be reasoned about. It is to be as bad as Voltaire, or as Lord Byron.

There can be no doubt that judicial astrology, or the knowledge of future events by the study of the stars, was received and practised by all the ancient Jews, Persians, and many of the Christians, particularly the Gnostics and Manicheans. The persons now spoken of, thought that the planets were the signs, that is, gave information of future events, not that they were the causes of them [1] —not that the events were controlled by them: for between these two there is a great difference. Eusebius tells us, on the authority of Eupolemus, that Abraham was an astrologer, and that he taught the science to the priests of *Heliopolis* or *On*. This was a fact universally asserted by the historians of the East. Origen was a believer in this science as qualified above; and M. Beausobre observes, it is thus that he explained what Jacob says in the prayer of Joseph: *He has read in the tables of heaven all that will happen to you, and to your children.* [2]

4. When the Jews were carried away to Babylon, Daniel is said to have been one of the prisoners, and to have risen to a very high situation at the court of the great king; and in fact to have become almost his prime minister. (Dan. ii. 48.) On the taking of the city, he appears to have been a principal performer: he was occupied in explaining the meaning of the writing on the wall at the very moment that the city was stormed. After the success of the Persians, we find him again in great power with the new king, who was of his own sect or religion, and as bitter against idolaters as himself. We also find that the Jews were again almost immediately restored to their country.

If Daniel opened the gates of Babylon to admit the enemy, certainly of all men he must have been the best qualified to tell Belshazzar that his city was taken. If he were a Jew, he had been carried away and reduced to slavery by the enemy of his country, and under all the circumstances,

---

[1] It is not meant to say that, at a very early period, the planets were not believed to be the active agents of a superior power: they probably were.

[2] " Il a lu dans les tables du ciel, tout ce qui doit vous arriver, et à vos enfans ." Beausobre, Hist. Manich. Liv. vii. ch. i. p. 429.

if he made the restoration of his countrymen the price of what in him can hardly be called his treason, very few people will be found to condemn him.

There can be no doubt, but that if the story of Daniel had been met with in a history of the Chinese or the Hindoos, or of any nation where religious prejudice had not beclouded the understanding, all historians would have instantly seen, that the Assyrian despot was justly punished for his egregious folly, in making a slave, whose country he had ruined, one of his prime ministers, and for entrusting him with the command of his capital when besieged by his enemies—by persons professing the same religion as his minister. Upon any other theory, how are we to account for Daniel's being, soon after the capture of Babylon, found to be among the ministers of its conqueror?

I suspect that Daniel was a Chaldee or Culdee or Brahmin priest—a priest of the same order of which, in former times, Melchizedek had been a priest.

The gratification of that spirit which induced Darius, Cyrus, and their successors, to wage a war of extermination wherever they came against the temples, &c., of idolaters, would probably greatly aid Daniel in pleading the cause of his country. But it is worthy of observation that, although the temples, altars, and priests, were restored, both in Judæa and Samaria, yet the country was kept in a state of vassalage to the Persian kings. They had no more kings in Judæa or Samaria, till long after the destruction of the Persian empire by Alexander.[1]

5. Perhaps in the Old Testament there is not a more curious book than that of Esther. It is the only remaining genuine specimen of the ancient chronicles of Persia.

The object of putting this book into the canon of the Jews is to record, for their use, the origin of their feast of Purim. Michaelis is of opinion, from the style of the writing and other circumstances, that the last sixteen verses of this book were added at Jerusalem. This seems very probable. It is pretty clear, from this book, that the religion of Persia in the time of Ahasuerus, as he is named in scripture, had begun to fall into idolatry; and that it was reformed by Mordecai, who slew seventy-five thousand of the idolaters, and restored it to its former state, when it must have been in all its great features like that of the Jews, if not identically the same. A very ingenious writer in the old Monthly Magazine,[2] supposes, " that Ezra was the only Zoroaster, and " that the twenty-one books of Zertusht were the twenty-one books of our Hebrew Bible; with " the exception, indeed, that the canon of Ezra could not include Nehemiah, who flourished after " the death of Ezra, or the extant book of Daniel, which dates from Judas Maccabeus, or the Ec- " clesiastes, which is posterior to Philo: and that it did include the book of Enoch, now retained " only in the Abyssinian canon."

6. No person who has carefully examined will deny, I think, that all the accounts which we have of Zoroaster are full of inconsistencies and contradictions. Plato says, he lived before him 6000 years. Hyde or Prideaux and others, make him contemporary with Darius Hystaspes, or Daniel. By some he is made a Jew; this opinion arose from the observation of the similarity of many of his doctrines to those of the Jews. Now, what is the meaning of the complicated word

---

[1] Cyrus is described as a Messiah or Saviour. He restored the temple, but not the empire. He saved the priests, though he kept the country in slavery; therefore, he was a Messiah, a holy one of God. This is natural enough, and gives us the clue to all the Jewish sacred books. They were the writings of the priests and prophets or monks, not of the nation. An established priesthood generally cares nothing for the nation; it only cares for itself. Though the nation be kept in slavery, if the tithes and altars be restored, all is well; and its conquerors are Saviours, Messiahs. When Alexander conquered Palestine and arrived at Jerusalem, (if he ever did arrive there,) we are told, that the high priest went out to meet him with the keys of the city,—thus renouncing the race of Messiahs who had formerly restored his temple and religion. And in this *treachery* the pious *Rollin* sees great merit: thus what weak people miscal religion obscures the understandings of the best of men.

[2] No. CCCLXXXV. Aug. 1823.

Zoroaster, or Zoradust ? Of the latter I can make nothing; but of the former, which is the name by which he was generally called in ancient times, Mr. Faber (I think) has made *Astre, Zur*, or *Syr*. Here is the star or celestial body *Syr* or *Sur*, which we shall presently find, is, without any great violence, the celestial body, the Bull or the Sun. Hence we arrive at an incarnation of the Deity, of the Sun, or of Taurus—a renewed incarnation. This accounts for the antiquity assigned to him by Plato, and for the finding of him again under Darius Hystaspes. In short, he is a doctrine, or a doctrine taught by a person. He was the founder of the Magi, who were priests of the religion of the Sun, or of that Being of whom the Sun was the visible form or emblem.

Dr. Hyde, after allowing that the religion of the Persians was originally the same with that of Abraham, and that it fell into Sabiism, says, he thinks that it was reformed by him. He adds, that the ancient accounts call it the *religion of Ibrahim or Abraham*. The idea of its reformation by Abraham, seems to be without any proof. However, we may safely admit that it consisted in the worship of the one true God, or of the sun, merely as an emblem ; and, that it was really reformed and brought back to this point, from which it had deviated, by some great man, whether he were Abraham or Zoroaster; as that of the Jews was, from the worship of Apis or the Calf, by Moses. Hyde says, they had a true account of the creation of the world, [1] meaning hereby the account in Genesis. This may be very true if the religion of the Jews came from Persia, and was, in fact, identically the same. How, indeed, could it be essentially different, if, as Dr. Hyde believed, they both worshiped the same God, with nearly the same ceremonies ? [2]

There can be no doubt that the Persians and Assyrians had their religion originally from the same source; but that the latter, in the time of Cyrus, had degenerated into idolatry, from which the former were at that time free. This greater purity was probably owing to the reformation which is related by several authors to have been effected by Zoroaster, by whom it had been brought back to its first principles. It had probably degenerated before his time as much as that of the Assyrians. The authorities in proof of the fact of some one having reformed the Persian religion, are so decided as to make it almost unquestionable.

7. Notwithstanding the general similarity between the two religions, there are several particulars in which they so pointedly differ, after the time of Moses, that unless the reason of the difference could be shewn, they might be thought to invalidate the argument already adduced. But as we happen to know, in most cases, the precise reasons for the difference, this very discrepancy rather tends to confirm than to weaken the argument, as they are, in fact, for particular reasons, exceptions to a general rule.

When it is said that the religions of the descendants of Abraham and of the Persians were the same, considerable allowance must be made for the peculiar circumstances in which they were then placed, and in which they are viewed by us. We see them in records or histories, whose dates are acknowledged to be long after the time of Abraham, written by persons, strangers, probably, to the religion and language of both these nations. The Persians have a sacred book, called *Sohfi Ibrahim*, or the book of Abraham, but which ought to be called *the book of the* wisdom *of Abraham*. [3] The Jews also have a sacred book, called the book of Moses, and the first of which, known to us under the name of Genesis, is called by them רשית *rasit*, or *the book of wisdom*. Now, supposing them to have been the same in the time of Abraham, we may reasonably suppose considerable changes and additions would be made, [4] to both religions in the space of five or six hundred years, merely from the natural effects of time: but besides this,

---

[1] Rel. Vet. Pers. Cap. iii.   [2] See Shuckford, Book v. p. 309.

[3] Sohfi is nothing but a word represented by the Greek Σοφια, and by the *Sophoun* of the Arabians

[4] Shuckford, Book v.

we know that they both underwent a great change, one by Zoroaster and the other by Moses, who reformed or formed them anew. The two chiefs or reformers resided at a great distance from each other, and unless they had had some communication it is evident that in their reforms they would not establish the same rites and ceremonies. This may account for several ordinances being found in the law of Moses which are not found in the law of Zoroaster, and *vice versâ*.

After the migration of Moses and his tribes from Egypt, before he undertook the invasion of the beautiful country of Palestine, he spent many years in rambling about the deserts or uncultivated pasture lands bordering on the Northern end of the Red Sea, and Arabia Petræa. The settled natives of these countries were sunk into the grossest and most degrading idolatry and superstition, much worse than even that of the Assyrians, or that of the Persians, before it was reformed by Zoroaster. In order to prevent his people from being contaminated by this example, Maimonides informs us, *on the authority of the old Jewish authors*, that Moses made many of his laws in direct opposition to the customs of these people. And for this same reason we are told, in Exodus, that he punished the alliance of his people with any of the natives of these countries, with the most horrible severity: a policy, though sufficiently cruel and unjust, as exercised by him in several cases, certainly wisely contrived for the object he had in view.

The observance of the Sabbath on the *seventh* instead of the *first* day of the week, and in its extreme degree of strictness, was ordained effectually to separate the Jews from the neighbouring nations:[1] and experience has shewn that nothing could have been better contrived for that purpose.

The learned Maimonides says, "they [the Arabians] worshiped the sun at his rising; for which "reason, as our Rabbins expressly teach in Gemara, Abraham our father designed the West for "the place of the Sanctum Sanctorum, when he worshiped in the mountain Moriah. Of this ido-"latry they interpret what the Prophet Ezekiel saith of the men with their backs toward the "temple of the Lord and their faces toward the East, worshiping the Sun toward the East." (Ezek. viii. 16.) Perhaps a better knowledge of the Arabian superstitions might enable us to account for many other of the ordinances of Moses, which appear to us unmeaning and absurd.[2] In this instance of adoration toward the rising Sun, we see that the religion of the Magi had become corrupted by the Arabians, and that in order to avoid this very corruption, and preserve the worship of one God, (which was the great object of Moses, that to which all the forms and ordinances of discipline, both of the Magi and Moses, were subservient,) he established a law directly in opposition to that whence his religion had originally sprung. For the Persians always worshiped turning their faces to the East, which the Jews considered an abomination, and uniformly turned to the West when they prayed. And certainly this would be against the author's hypothesis, if we did not know exactly the reason for it.

Though Maimonides says that Abraham designed the *West* for the place of adoration, he does not say that he ordered it; if he had, it would have been mentioned in the Pentateuch. It seems much more likely to have been ordered by Moses, for the same reason that he made the several laws as observed above, in opposition to the corruptions of the Persians or Arabians; but it might be adopted by Moses for the same reason also that he adopted very many other religious rites of the Egyptians,[3] who sometimes worshiped towards the West, as well as Jews.

---

[1] See my Horæ Sabbaticæ, in the British Museum.

[2] Vide Stanley's Hist. Phil. Chal. Part xix. Ch. ii. pp. 38, 801, 4to.

[3] Perhaps it was not ordained by either Moses or Abraham, as no directions relating to it are to be found in the Pentateuch, but by the builders of the temple, in which the Sacred part, or Kebla, was placed in the West. Beaus. Hist. Manich. Vol. II. Liv. vi. Ch. viii. p. 385; Windet de vit. Func. Stat. Sect. vii. p. 77; Pirke, Eliez. p. ii.; Porph. de Ant. Nymp p. 268.

The third chapter and twenty-fourth verse of Genesis informs us, that a tabernacle was erected to the East of Eden. This tends to prove that this book was of Persian origin, and of a date previous to the time when the Exodus was written; and that the people whose sacred book it was originally worshiped towards the East. See Parkhurst,[1] who shews that there were tabernacles before that erected by Moses. He also shews that at a time not long after the Exodus the idolaters had the same things.

There can be no doubt that when ignorant fanatics, like the early fathers, Papias, Hegisippus, &c., were travelling, as we know that they did, to find out the true doctrines of the gospel, they would make the traditions bend in some respects to their preconceived notions. Thus the Jewish sects of Nazarenes and Ebionites kept the Sabbath, and other Jewish rites; and thus, men like Justin, converts from Heathenism, who had no predilection for Judaism, abolished them. Hence we find, at a very early period of the Christian era, the advocates of these opposite opinions persecuting one another, each calling the other *heretic.* The converts from Heathenism, taking their traditions from the Persian fountain, abolished the Sabbath, but adopted the custom of turning to the East in prayer, and the celebration of the Dies Solis or Sunday; as well as some other days, as will afterward be shewn, sacred among the Heathens to that luminary. It is curious to observe the care shewn in every part of the Gospels and the Epistles of the orthodox to discourage the pharasaical observance of the Sabbath, so much and so inconsistently cried up by modern Puritans. Whenever the commandments are ordered to be kept, the injunction is always followed by an explanation of what commandments are meant, and the Sabbath in every instance is omitted.

8. Learned men have exercised great ingenuity in their endeavours to discover the origin and reason of sacrifices, (a rite common to both Jews and Heathens,) in which they have found great difficulty. They have sought at the bottom of the well what was swimming on the surface. The origin of sacrifice was evidently a gift to the priest, or the cunning man, or the Magus or Druid,[2] to induce him to intercede with some unknown being, to protect the timid or pardon the guilty; a trick invented by the rogues to enable them to cheat the fools; a contrivance of the idle possessing brains to live upon the labour of those without them. The sacrifice, whatever it might be in its origin, soon became a feast, in which the priest and his votary were partakers; and if, in some instances, the body of the victim was burnt, for the sake of deluding the multitude, with a show of disinterestedness on the part of the priest, even then, that he might not lose all, he reserved to himself the skin. See Lev. vii. 8.

But it was in very few instances that the flesh was really burnt, even in burnt-offerings. Deut. xii. 2: *And thou shalt* OFFER *thy* BURNT-OFFERINGS, *the flesh and the blood, upon the altar of the* LORD *thy God: and the blood of thy sacrifices shall be poured out upon the altar of the* LORD *thy God, and thou shalt* EAT *the flesh:* not *burn* it. At first the sacrifice was a feast between the priest and devotee, but the former very soon contrived to keep it all for himself; and it is evident from Pliny's letter to Trajan, that when there was more than the priest could consume, he sent the overplus to market for sale.

It is difficult to account for the very general reception of the practice of sacrifice, it being found among almost all nations. The following is the account given of it by the Rev. Mr. Faber:

" Throughout the whole world we find a notion prevalent, that the Gods could only be appeased " by bloody sacrifices. Now this idea is so thoroughly arbitrary, there being no obvious and " necessary connexion, in the way of cause and effect, between slaughtering a man or a beast, and " recovering of the divine favour by the slaughterer, that its very universality involves the neces- " sity of concluding that all nations have borrowed it from some common source. It is in vain to

[1] Lex. p. 634.   [2] Druid is a Celtic word and has the meaning of *Absolver from Sin.*

" say, that there is nothing so strange, but that an unrestrained superstition might have excogi-
" tated it. This solution does by no means meet the difficulty. If sacrifice had been in use only
" among the inhabitants of a *single* country, or among those of some few neighbouring countries,
" who might reasonably be supposed to have much mutual intercourse; no fair objection could be
" made to the answer. But what we have to account for is, the universality of the practice; and
" such a solution plainly does not account for such a circumstance; I mean not merely the exist-
" ence of sacrifice, but its *universality*. An apparently irrational notion, struck out by a wild
" fanatic in one country and forthwith adopted by his fellow-citizens, (for such is the hypothesis
" requisite to the present solution,) is yet found to be equally prevalent in all countries. There-
" fore if we acquiesce in this solution, we are bound to believe, either that all nations, however
" remote from each other, borrowed from that of the original inventor; or that by a most marvel-
" lous subversion of the whole system of calculating chances, a great number of fanatics, severally
" appearing in every country upon the face of the earth, without any mutual communication,
" strangely hit upon the self-same arbitrary and inexplicable mode of propitiating the Deity. It
" is difficult to say which of the two suppositions is the most improbable. The solution therefore
" does not satisfactorily account for the fact of the *universality*. Nor can the fact, I will be bold to
" say, be satisfactorily accounted for, except by the supposition, that no one nation borrowed the
" rite from another nation, but that all alike received it from a common origin of most remote
" antiquity."

Such is the account given of this disgusting practice. Very well has the Rev. Mr. Faber
described it, *as apparently an irrational notion struck out by a wild fanatic,—an arbitrary and
inexplicable mode hit upon by fanatics of propitiating the Deity.* As he justly says, *why should that
righteous man* (meaning Abel) *have imagined that he could please the Deity, by slaying a firstling
lamb, and by burning it upon an altar ? What connexion is there betwixt the means and the end ?
Abel could not but have known, that God, as a merciful God, took no pleasure in the sufferings of
the lamb. How, then, are we to account for his attempting to please such a God, by what abstractedly
is an act of cruelty ?*[1] Very true, indeed, Reverend Sir, an act of cruelty, as a type of an infinitely
greater act of cruelty and injustice, in the murder, by the Creator, of his only Son, by the hands
of the Jews : an act not only of injustice and cruelty to the sufferer, but an act of equal cruelty
and injustice to the perpetrators of the murder, whose eyes and understandings were blinded lest
they should see and not execute the murder—and lest they should repent *and their sins be for-
given them.* What strange beings men, in all ages, have made their Gods ! ! !

I cannot ascribe such things to *my* God. This may be *will* worship; but belief is not in my
power. I am obliged to believe it more probable that men may lie, that priests may be guilty of
selfish fraud, than that the wise and beneficent Creator can direct such irrational, fanatical, cruel
proceedings, to use Mr. Faber's words. The doctrine of the Atonement, with its concomitant
dogmas, is so subversive of all morality, and is so contrary to the moral attributes of God, that it is
totally incredible : as the Rev. Dr. Sykes justly observes of actions contrary to the moral attributes
of God, that they are incredible even if supported by miracles themselves. However, I am happy
to say that belief in this doctrine is no part of the faith declared by Jesus Christ to be necessary to
salvation—no part in short of his gospel, though it may be of the gospel of Bishop Magee.

That in later times the practice of sacrifice was very general cannot be denied; but I think a
time may be perceived when it did not exist, even among the Western nations. We read that it
was not always pratised at Delphi. Tradition states that in the earliest time no bloody sacrifice
took place there, and among the Buddhists, who are the oldest religionists of whom we have any

---

[1] See Faber, Pagan Idol. B. ii. Ch. viii. pp. 466, 482.

sacred traditions, and to whom the first book of Genesis probably belongs, no bloody sacrifices ever prevailed. With Cristna, Hercules, and the worshipers of the Sun in Aries, they probably arose. The second book of Genesis I think came from the last. No doubt the practice took its rise in the Western parts of the world, (after the sun entered Aries,) even among the followers of the Tauric worship, and was carried to a frightful extent. But the prevalence of the practice, as stated by Mr. Faber, is exaggerated. It never was practised by the followers of Buddha, though they have constituted, perhaps, a majority of the inhabitants of the world.

I believe the history of Cain and Abel is an allegory of the followers of Cristna, to justify their sacrifice of the firstling of the flock—of the Yajna or Lamb in opposition to the Buddhist offering of bread and wine or water, made by Cain and practised by Melchizedek.

9. Dr. Shuckford has satisfactorily shewn that the sacrifices and ceremonies of purification of the Heathens, and of Abraham and his family and descendants, were in fact all identical, with such trifling changes as distance of countries and length of time might be expected to produce. [1] Moses can hardly be said to have copied many of his institutions from the Gentiles. The Israelites had them probably before the time of Moses. The prohibition of marrying out of the tribe was one of these. The custom was evidently established by Abraham, Isaac, and Jacob, with their wives.—But to return to my subject.

How many Zoroasters there were, or whether more than one, it is difficult to determine; but one of them was thought by Hyde, as we have already shewn, to have lived in the time of Darius Hystaspes; but whether he really lived then or not is of no consequence, except that the account given of him shews what the religion of the Persians at that time was. Sir W. Drummond thinks he really lived much earlier, as does also Mr. Moyle. [2] He is said to have been deeply skilled in the Eastern learning, and also in the Jewish Scriptures. Indeed, so striking is the similarity between his doctrines and those of Moses, that Dean Prideaux is almost obliged to make a Jew of him: and this he really was, in religion. But why he should abuse him, and call him many hard names it is difficult to understand. He does not appear to have formed a new religion, but only to have reformed or improved that which he found.

The following is Dean Prideaux's account of the religion of Zoroaster: " The chief reformation " which he made in the Magian religion was in the first principle of it; for whereas before they " had held the being of two first causes, the first light, or the good god, who was the author of all " good; and the other darkness, or the evil god, who was the author of all evil; and that of the " mixture of those two, as they were in a continued struggle with each other, all things were " made; he introduced a principle superior to them both, one supreme God who created both " light and darkness, and out of these two, according to the alone pleasure of his own will, made " all things else that are, according to what is said in the 45th chapter of Isaiah, ver. 5—7.—In " sum, his doctrine, as to this particular, was, that there was one Supreme Being, independant " and self-existing from all eternity; that under him there were two angels, one the angel of light, " who is the author and director of all good; and the other the angel of darkness, who is the author " and director of all evil; and that these two, out of the mixture of light and darkness, made all " things that are; and that they are in a perpetual struggle with each other; and that where the " angel of light prevails, there the most is good, and where the angel of darkness prevails, there " the most is evil; that this struggle shall continue to the end of the world; that then there shall " be a general resurrection, and a day of judgment, wherein just retribution shall be rendered to " all according to their works: after which, the angel of darkness and his disciples shall go into a

[1] Shuckford, Con. Book v. p. 314.
[2] Pliny mentions a Zoroaster who lived sex millibus annorum ante Platonis mortem. Maurice, Vol. II. p. 124.

" world of their own, where they shall suffer in everlasting darkness the punishment of their evil
" deeds ; and the angel of light, and his disciples, shall also go into a world of their own, where they
" shall receive in everlasting light the reward due unto their good deeds : and that after this they
" shall remain separated for ever, and light and darkness be no more mixed together to all eternity.
" And all this the remainder of that sect which is now in Persia and India, do, without any varia-
" tion, after so many ages, still hold even to this day. And how consonant this is to the truth
" is plain enough to be understood without a comment. And whereas he taught that God origi-
" nally created the good angel only, and that the other followed only by the defect of good, this
" plainly shews, that he was not unacquainted with the revolt of the fallen angels, and the en-
" trance of evil into the world that way, but had been thoroughly instructed how that God at first
" created all his angels good, as he also did man, and that they that are now evil became such
" wholly through their own fault, in falling from that state which God first placed them in. All
" which plainly shews the author of this doctrine to have been well versed in the sacred writing
" of the Jewish religion, out of which it manifestly appears to have been all taken." [1]

Another reformation which Zoroaster is said to have introduced, was, the building of temples,
for before his time the altars were all erected upon hills and high places in the open air. Upon
those the sacred fire was kept burning, but to which they denied that they offered adoration, but
only to God in the fire. [2] It is said that Zoroaster pretended to have been taken up into heaven,
and to have heard God speak from the midst of a flame of fire ; that, therefore, fire is the truest
shekinah of the Divine presence ; and that the sun is the most perfect fire—for which reason he
ordered them to direct their worship towards the sun, which they called Mithra. He pretended
to have brought fire from heaven along with him, which was never permitted to go out. It was
fed with clean wood, and it was deemed a great crime to blow upon it, or to rekindle it except
from the sun or the sacred fire in some other temple. Thus the Jews had their shekinah or sacred
fire in which God dwelt, and which came down from heaven upon their altar of burnt-offerings :
and Nadab and Abihu were punished with death for offering incense to God with other fire. The
Jews used clean peeled wood for the fire, and, like the Persians, would not permit it to be blown
upon with the mouth.

To feed the sacred fire with unhallowed fuel, was punishable with death ; to blow upon it the
same. But though it was thus treated with the most profound veneration, as a part of the glorious
luminary of heaven, it was not worshiped ; though the Lord Jehovah, who shrouded himself in
the sacred fire, or took up his residence in the sun, was worshiped. Thus God upon Sinai or
Horeb, or in the bush, appeared in a flame of fire to Moses, who fell down on his face to it. Yet
the text means to represent that he worshiped God, not fire.

A very ingenious and learned critic, [3] in his controversy with Dean Prideaux, has maintained,
that the Persians destroyed the temples in Egypt, because they disapproved the worshiping of
God in temples, when the whole earth was his temple ; and that they had only *two* Principles
and never acknowledged a *third*, superior to the Good and Evil ones, till about the time of the
Christian æra. He seems to be mistaken in both these respects. The fact that the Persians had
no closed temples in the time of Herodotus, may be very true, and cannot well be disputed, as he
affirms it : but notwithstanding this, it is plain that though they did not choose to have temples
of their own, they had no objection to the temple-worship of others ; because if they had, they
would not have restored the temples of the Jews and Samaritans at Jerusalem and Gerizim. This

[1] Prid. Con. Part I. Lib. iv. p. 267. 8vo.
[2] These are nothing but the Hill-altars of the Canaanites, (of which we often read in the Old Testament,) the ancient
circles of the Druids, which I have lately discovered are as common in India, Persia, and Syria, as in Britain.
[3] Moyle, Works, Vol. II.

fact proves that their enmity was against the temples of idolaters, not against those of the true God, nor against temples merely as temples. For the same reasons the pious Theodosius destroyed the temples at Alexandria; but he had no objection to temple-worship, or worship in buildings.

The Israelites had no temple till the time of Solomon, but they had circles of stone pillars at Gerizim and Gilgal, exactly the same as those at the Buddhist temple of Stonehenge.

10. Zoroaster retired to a cavern where he wrote his book, and which was ornamented on the roof with the constellations and the signs of the Zodiac; whence came the custom among his followers of retiring to caves which they called Mithriatic caves, to perform their devotions, in which the mysteries of their religion were performed. Many of these caves of stupendous size and magnificence exist at this day in the neighbourhood of Balck, and in different parts of upper India and Persia.

They had several orders of priests like our parochial priests and bishops, and at the head of them an Archimagus or Archpriest, the same as the Pope or the High Priest of the Jews: the word Magus, in the Persian language, only meant priest: and they did not forget that most useful Jewish rite, the taking of tithes and oblations. At stated times the priests read part of their sacred writings to the people. The priests were all of the same family or tribe, as among the Jews.

Dr. Pococke and Hyde acknowledge that many things in their sacred books are the same as those in the Pentateuch, and in other parts of the Bible. Of course they easily account for this by the assertion, that they were taken from the Jews. But the fact of the identity is not denied: which copied from the other is not *now* the question. All that it is necessary to shew is, that they were the same. They contain many of the Psalms, called by the Jews and Christians, absurdly enough, *the Psalms of David*, and nearly the same account of Adam and Eve, the deluge, &c. The creation is stated, as already mentioned, to have taken place in *six* periods, which together make up a year; and Abraham, Joseph, Moses, and Solomon, are all spoken of in the same manner as in the Jewish Scriptures. In these books are inculcated similar observances about beasts, clean and unclean,—the same care to avoid pollution, external and internal,—the same purifyings, washings, &c., &c. Zoroaster called his book *the book of Abraham*, because he pretended that, by his own reformation, he had only brought back the religion to the state in which it was in the time of Abraham. [1] Can any one, after this, doubt the identity of the two religions? If they were not the same, what would make them so?

The Zendavesta which we have, and which was translated by Anquetil Du Perron, is said, by Sir W. Jones, to be spurious; but it is admitted by the best authors to agree with the ancient one, at least "in its tenets and the terms of religion." [2] Upon the question of its genuineness it is not necessary to give an opinion. Probably Sir W. Jones would find anachronisms in it, such as have been pointed out in the Old Testament. These would be quite sufficient to prove to him the spuriousness of the Zend, though not of the Pentateuch. The fact is, they both stand exactly upon the same grounds with respect to genuineness. [3]

Much might have been spared which has been said respecting the *fire worshipers* of Persia. It is very probable that, in some degree, the charge of worshiping fire may be substantiated against them, in the same way as the worship of saints, images, and relics, in some parts of Christendom may certainly be proved to have existed; but it is equally as unjust to call the Persians *fire*

---

[1] Prid. Con. Part. I. Book iv. pp. 278, &c., 8vo.   [2] Marsh's Mic. Ch. iv. Sect. ix. p. 161.
[3] Marsh's Mic. Vol. IV. p. 288, Vol. I. p. 433.

worshipers, as it is to call the Christians *idolaters*. The religion of Persia became corrupted, and so did the Christian. Zoroaster reformed one, Luther, &c., the other.

If we are to credit the history, the religion of Abraham's descendants by Sarah, became also corrupted whilst they were in Egypt; and was restored to its original state, at least in all its great and leading features, by Moses. That they were addicted to the idolatry of Egypt is evident from their setting up for themselves *a golden calf*, the image of the God Apis, in less than three months after their escape into the desert of Sinai.

The religion of Abraham was that of the Persians, and whether he were a real or a fictitious personage (a matter of doubt) both the religions must have been derived from the same source. If Abraham really did live, then the evidence both Jewish and Persian shews that he was the founder of both nations. If he were an *allegorical personage*, the similarity of the religions shews them to have had the same origin. Why should not his family by his wife Keturah, as historians affirm they did, have conquered Persia, as his family by Sarah conquered Canaan? Both worshiped the solar fire,[1] as an emblem of their God, of God the Preserver and Saviour—of that God with whom Abraham made a covenant; the same Jehovah or Lord who Jacob (Gen. xxviii. 21) vowed should be his God, if he brought him back to his father's house in peace; the same God worshiped by the brother of Abraham, Nahor, in the land of Ur of the Chaldees, (Gen. xi. 29, xxxi. 53,) and of whom it is written, " My Lord said unto thy Lord, sit thee at my right hand, till I make thine enemies thy footstool." Ps. cx. 1 ; Matt. xxii. 44 ; Mark. xii. 36 ; Luke xx. 42, 43 ; Acts ii. 34, 35.

11. Now perhaps perverseness, bigotry, and ill-temper, will observe, Then you take Abraham and Moses for nothing but Persian magicians and idolaters. I do no such thing. The God of Abraham, of Melchizedek, of the Brahmins, and of the Persians, originally, or about the time of Abraham, was *one*, precisely *the same*—the oriental divine Triad or Trinity, *three* Persons and *one* God. Why Abraham left his country and came into Canaan may be doubtful : but it is not unlikely that he emigrated because the priests had corrupted the religion, as they always corrupt it when they can ; and, that he came into Canaan because he there found his religion in a state of purity, and a priest of the most high God, Melchizedek, at whose altar he could sacrifice, and to whom he could pay his tithes. And it is not unlikely, that he and his family or tribe might have been banished from their country at the time they left it, for endeavouring to oppose the corruption of the priests,—to enlighten or reform their countrymen. Indeed some authors have actually said, and before I conclude this work I shall prove, that this was the case. It is probable, as the Bible says, that the descendants of Abraham, if there were such a man, were induced to take refuge in Egypt for some reason or other ; probably, as stated, by famine ; that after residing in Egypt for some time, two hundred years or upwards, they were beginning to fall into the idolatrous practices of the people among whom they dwelt, and by whom also endeavours were made to enslave them; that to prevent this or to stop its progress, after a severe struggle, they left Egypt, and betook themselves to the desert, under the command of Moses, who was both the restorer or reformer of their religion, and their leader and legislator ; that, after various wars with other Arab tribes, or settled nations, on whose territories they encroached when in search of pasturage, for they had then no country of their own, they at last succeeded in conquering Canaan—where they finally established themselves—though not completely till the time of David. This country they always occupied along with remnants of the ancient Canaanites, till about the

---

[1] Ireneus says, God is *fire*; Origen, *a subtle fire*; Tertullian, *a body*. In the Acts of the council of Elvira it is forbidden to light candles in the cemeteries, for fear of disturbing the souls of the saints. A great dispute took place in Egypt among the monks on the question, whether God was corporeal or incorporeal.

time of Jesus Christ, (in the same way as the Turks have occupied Greece.) when they were finally expelled from it by the Romans, and their tribe dispersed. The country then became partly occupied by Roman colonies, and partly by the remains of the old idolatrous Canaanites, the worshipers of Adonis, Venus, &c., &c. The Jews occupied Canaan, as the Moriscoes occupied Spain. They never completely mixed or amalgamated with the old inhabitans, who continued in slavery or subjection. Every page almost of the Jewish history shews that the Canaanites continued, and had temples. During what is called the time of the Judges it is evident that an almost incessant warfare was carried on between the old inhabitants and the Israelites. The Jebusites possessed, in spite of the latter, the fortress of the city of Jerusalem, until the time of David, who took it by storm ; and the city of Tyre, with its king, set even the power of Solomon at defiance, and never was taken by the Israelites at all.

The difference between the religion of Moses and that of the surrounding nations, consisted merely in this : the latter had become corrupted by the priests, who had set up images in allegorical representation of the heavenly bodies or Zodiacal signs, which in long periods of time the people came to consider as representations of real deities. The true and secret meaning of these emblems, the priests, that is the initiated, took the greatest pains to keep from the people. The king and priest were generally united in the same person : and when it was otherwise, the former was generally the mere tool and slave of the latter. But in either case, the sole object of the initiated was, as it yet is, to keep the people in a state of debasement, that they might be more easily ruled. Thus did the Magi in *ancient* and thus do the chief priests in *modern* times wallow in wealth on the labour of the rest of mankind.

If we may judge of the state of Egypt and Canaan, and the countries in the neighbourhood of Canaan, from the collection of ancient tracts or traditionary histories, called the Jewish canon, we must allow that they had become, in matters of religion, sunk to the very lowest state of debasement. The sacrifices and rites of Baal and Moloch, and the idolatry of Tyre, Sidon, &c., were of the most horrible kind. The priests in almost all ages have found that the more gloomy and horrible a religion is, the better it has suited their purpose. We have this account of the state of the religion, not only from the history of the Jews, but from that of the Gentiles, therefore it can scarcely be disputed. It was to keep his people from falling into this degraded state, that Moses framed many of his laws. To the original religions of these nations, before their degradation, he could have had no objection ; or else he would never have adopted so many of their astronomical and astrological emblems : nay, have even gone so far as to call his God by the same names.

Though the adoption of the astronomical and astrological emblems of the Magi and the Egyptians may be no proof of the wisdom or sagacity of Moses, they are sufficiently clear proofs of the identity of his religion with the religion of the Magi, &c., before their corruption. What are we to make of the brazen serpent set up by Moses in the wilderness, and worshiped by the Israelites till the time of Hezekiah ? What of the Cherubim under the wings of which the God of the Jews dwelt ? These Cherubim had the faces of the beings which were in the four cardinal points of the Zodiac, when the Bull was the equinoctial sign, viz. the ox, the lion, the man, and the eagle. [1] These were clearly astrological.

12. Every ancient religion, without exception, had Cabala or secret doctrines : and the same fate attended them all. In order that they might not be revealed or discovered, they were not written, but only handed down by tradition ; and in the revolutions of centuries and the violent convulsions of empires they were forgotten. Scraps of the old traditions were then collected, and mixed with new inventions of the priests, having the double object in view, of ruling the people and of concealing their own ignorance.

---

[1] See a picture of them in Parkhurst's Hebrew Lexicon in voce, כרב *krb*. See also Jurieu, Rel. Vet. Vol. I. Part. II. Cap. i.

The twelve signs of the Zodiac for the standards of the twelve tribes of Israel, the scorpion or typhon, the devil or the emblem of destruction, being changed for the eagle by the tribe of Dan, to whom it was allotted; the ark, an exact copy of the ark of Osiris, set afloat in the Nile every year, and supposed to sail to Biblos, in Palestine; the pillars Joachim and Boaz; the festival of the Passover at the vernal equinox, an exact copy of the Egyptian festival at the same time; almost all the ornaments of the temple, altar, priest, &c., all these are clearly astrological. The secret meaning of all these emblems, and of most parts of the books of the Pentateuch, of Joshua and Judges, (almost the whole of which was astrological, that is, magical allegory,) was what in old times, in part at least, constituted the Jewish Cabala, and was studiously kept from the knowledge of the vulgar. There is no reason to believe that the Cabala of the modern Jews has any similitude to that of the ancients. The childish nonsense of the modern Cabalists, it would indeed be very absurd to attribute to the sages, who, on Carmel, taught Pythagoras the true system of the planetary bodies—or to Elias, whose knowledge of chemistry, perhaps, taught him to outmanoeuvre the priests of Baal.

On the subject of the reason why Abraham or his tribe left his or its home, I shall have much more to say in the course of this work, when I flatter myself that *that*, and many other things on which I slightly touch here, will be accounted for.

CHAPTER V

Character of the Old Testament——Nature of the Allegory in Genesis

1. The reader will now perhaps ask, What in the result is the truth respecting the Old Testament? It is very difficult to answer this question in a few words. Is it the produce of deep learning and profound wisdom, hidden under the veil of allegory, or is it the mere literal history of transactions of past events, as believed by the Christians and modern Jews? It is probably both : a collection of tracts mixed up with traditions, histories or rumours of events, collected together by the priests of an ignorant, uncivilized race of shepherds, intermixed also with the allegories and fictions in which the ancient philosophers of the eastern nations veiled their learning from the eyes of the vulgar. The Pentateuch is evidently a collection of different mythological histories of the creation, and of the transactions of Moses, the chief of a tribe of wandering Arabs, who was believed to have brought his tribe from the borders of Egypt and to have conquered Palestine : and there is little doubt that it contains a considerable portion of truth. The priests of the hilly part of Judea, after the tribes had united under one government, wanting something whereon to found their system, collected from all quarters the different parts, connecting them together as well as they could, though very unskilfully. And this was probably not all done at once, but by degrees, without any regular preconcerted design. The only part of it which shews any thing like a regular system, is the invariable tendency evident in every page to support the power of the priests or prophets. And this may perhaps be attributed more to a natural effect, arising from the manufacture of the work by priests, than to design.

The treatises in the Pentateuch are put together, or connected with one another, in so very awkward and unskilful a manner, that they would have passed as the work of one person with none but such uncivilized barbarians as the Jews, if they had related to any of the common concerns of life, and *where the reasoning faculty of the human mind could be brought into fair action ;* but in matters connected with religion this has never been done, and never will be done: reason has nothing to do with the religion of the generality of mankind.

To this the priests will reply, The circumstances which mark identity in the religions of the Jews and Gentiles we do not deny ; the Heathens copied almost all their superstitions from Moses and the Prophets ; and probably to multitudes of believers this will be very satisfactory: this satisfaction may naturally be expected to be enjoyed by such persons ; reason does not operate with them. To them it is of no consequence, that those heathenish superstitions which are alleged to have been copied from Moses, were in existence hundreds, perhaps thousands, of years before Moses was born or thought of.

That many parts of the books of the Jews are allegorical, cannot be for a moment doubted, and, as was said before, no doubt the true knowledge of these allegories constituted their first Cabala, and the learning of their priests. But as they are evidently made up of loose, unconnected accounts, very often different accounts of the same history or allegory, it is not possible that any complete and regular system should be made out of them. For instance, Genesis contains two histories of the creation ; Deuteronomy a history of the promulgation of the law by Moses, different from that given in Exodus, which was evidently written by a different author from that of Genesis. This view of the Jewish writings does not militate against parts of them being the produce of the profound wisdom of the oriental philosophers, which was probably the case, as maintained by M. Dupuis. A person may readily believe that the first book of Genesis was written by an ancient philosopher, whose descendants may have taught Pythagoras (perhaps on Carmel) the demonstration, that the square of the hypothenuse is equal to the square of the two sides of a right-angled triangle. From these circumstances it has followed, that in every part of these writings we meet with a strange mixture of oriental learning, and, to outward appearance, nonsensical and degrading puerilities and superstitions, which in all ages have perplexed the understandings of those persons who have endeavoured to use them on these subjects. No *reasoning* being could believe them literally, no ingenuity could make out of them, taken collectively, a consistent allegory.

But as far as concerns the generality or industrious class of the Jews and modern Christians, they are taken literally. In this sense they were and are yet received. Whether the later Jewish collectors of them into one code understood the allegorical meaning of any of them, remains doubtful ; probably they might in part. But it is equally, if not more, probable, that they would care very little whether they understood them or not, so long as they assisted them in establishing their temple, their tithes, and their order. Perhaps after these objects were secured, they would amuse themselves in their leisure hours, like our own priests and bishops, in endeavouring by explanations to make order out of disorder, sense out of nonsense. Hence arose their modern Cabala. And as they were generally men of the meanest capacities, though perhaps men understanding several languages, the modern Cabala is just what might be expected.

The modern and Romish religion being partly founded upon that of the Jews, which was founded upon writings thus connected together, it is not surprising that, like its parent, it should be difficult or impossible to make out a complete system, to fit into or account for every part of it.

2. M. Dupuis, in the first chapter of his third volume, has made many curious observations on the book of Genesis, tending to prove that it was an allegory descriptive of the mythology of the oriental nations in the neighbourhood of Palestine. That it was allegorical was held by the most learned of the ancient fathers of the church, such as Clemens Alexandrinus and Origen, as it had been by the most learned of the Jews, such as Philo, Josephus, &c., so that its allegorical nature may perhaps be safely assumed, notwithstanding the nonsense of modern devotees.

The following extract from the work of Maimonides, called More Nevochim,[1] exhibits a fair example of the policy of the ancient philosophers : " Taken to the letter, this work (Genesis) gives " the most absurd and extravagant ideas of the Divinity. Whoever shall find the true sense of it " ought to take care not to divulge it. This is a maxim which all our sages repeat to us, and " above all respecting the meaning of the work of the six days. If a person should discover the " meaning of it, either by himself or with the aid of another, then he ought to be silent : or if he " speak of it, he ought to speak of it but obscurely, and in an enigmatical manner as I do myself; " leaving the rest to be guessed by those who can understand me."[2]

Although it is clear from the works of Philo and others, that the learned in all ancient times acknowledged an allegorical sense in the accounts of Genesis ; it is equally clear from the works of that learned man, that in his time its meaning was in a great degree lost. The most celebrated of the Christian fathers equally admitted it to be allegorical, but the moderns have a difficulty to contend with, unknown to them and to the Jews. To admit the accounts in Genesis to be literal, would be to admit facts directly contrary to the moral attributes of God. Fanatical as the ancient fathers were, their fanaticism had not blinded them, as it has blinded the moderns, so far as to admit this. But if the story of the garden of Eden, the trees of knowledge and of life, the talking serpent, and the sin of Adam and Eve were allegorical, redemption by the atonement from the consequences of his allegorical fault could not but be equally allegorical. This, it is evident, instantly overthrows the whole of the present orthodox or fashionable scheme of the atonement—a doctrine not known in the early ages of the religion, but picked up in the same quarter whence several other doctrines of modern Christianity will be found to have been derived. If the history of the fall be allegorical, we repeat, that the allegorical nature of the redemption seems to follow as a necessary consequence.

In reasoning from cause to effect, this seems to be a necessary consequence. From this difficulty arose a great mass of contradictions and absurdities. It is impossible to deny, that it has always been a part of the modern corrupt Christian religion, that an evil spirit rebelled against God, and that he having drawn other beings of his own description into the same evil course, was, for this conduct, expelled along with them from heaven, into a place of darkness and intense torment. This nonsense, which is no part of the religion of Jesus the Nazarite, came from the same quarter as the atonement. We shall find them both in India.

It is quite impossible, that the doctrine of the fallen angels can be taken from the Pentateuch ; for not a word of the kind is to be met with there : but it is the identical doctrine of the Brahmins and later Magi. The Devil is the Mahasoor of the Brahmins, and the Ahriman of the Magi ; the fallen angels are the Onderah and Dewtahs of the Brahmins, and the Dowzakh and Dews of the Magi. The vulgar Jews and Christians finding the story of the serpent, did not know how to account for it, and in consequence went to the Persians for an explanation. They could not have gone to a better place, for the second book of Genesis, with its serpent biting the foot of the woman's seed, is nothing but a part of a Hindoo-Persian history, of which the story of the fallen angels, &c., is a continuation.

In several places in this chapter, the reader will have observed that I have used an expression of doubt respecting the existence of Abraham. This I have done because I feel that in inquiries of this kind a person can scarcely ever be too careful. And after reading the works of Sir William Drummond, Mons. Dupuis, &c., suspicion cannot be entirely banished. Besides, I wish not to take any thing for granted ; particularly the questions under examination, and this question will be amply discussed hereafter. I think it is perfectly clear that magical or astrological theories or

---

[1] Pars II. Cap. xxix.   [2] Dupuis, surtous les Cultes, Vol III. p. 9, 4to.

doctrines were connected with every part of the Mosaic system. It is impossible to separate or conceal them; they are connected with the numbers, the names of cities, and of men,—in short, with every thing: but this no more proves that there were not such men as Abraham, Moses, Joshua, &c., than it proves that there were not such cities and places as Damascus, Hobah, Gilgal, Gerizim, Bethel, Jericho, &c. The existence of the cities and places, having astronomical names, is clear. There is nothing in these astrological allusions against the existence of the men, any more than there is against the existence of the cities: and those have gone much too far who, *for no other reason*, have run away with the opinion that there were not such men. Their premises will not warrant their conclusions.

BOOK III

CHAPTER I

Orphic and Mithraitic Trinity similar to that of the Christians—Sir William Jones on the Religion of Persia—Persian Oromasdes, Mithra, Arimanius—Opinions of Herodotus, Porphyry, Strabo, Julian, on the above—Hyde and Beausobre respecting Times of Pythagoras and Zoroaster—Followers of Zoroaster, not yet extinct—Worship Fire—The Vedas describe the Persian Religion to have come come from Upper India—Maurice on the Hindoo Trinity

1. In the former part of this work, in treating of the Trimurti or Trinity, it was found scarcely possible to avoid anticipating part of what was intended to form the subject of the present book, but the author flatters himself, that the apparent repetition will not be found useless or uninteresting.

Having proved the absolute identity of the religions of the family of Abraham and of the Persians, in this book will be shewn a similar identity between several of the dogmas of the Romish and Protestant Christians, generally accounted of the greatest importance, particularly the Trinity and similar dogmas of the religions of Orpheus and Mithra, or the Sun, held by the Persian Magi: of the latter of which Zeradust was either the great prophet or founder, or the reformer. It is very possible that the moral doctrines of two races of people, totally unconnected, may be the same, or nearly so, because the true principles of morals must be the same : there can be only one true morality ; and each, without any connexion, may originally discover the truth. But it is evidently impossible that such artificial regulations and peculiar opinions, as will be pointed out, could have been adopted by two races of people without some very intimate connexion existing between them. Justin Martyr observed the striking similitude, and very easily explained it. He says, the evil spirits, or demons, introduced the Christian ceremonies into the religion of Mithra. Though this explanation of ceremonies and doctrines, existing long anterior to Christianity, might be satisfactory to the ancient and venerable fathers of the church, it will hardly prove so to modern philosophers. It cannot be expected, that the author should go through the whole of the ceremonies of each religion, and shew that in every individual instance they exactly agreed. The unceasing exertions of Christian priests to conceal the truth, and the change, arising from various other causes, which we know always takes place in long periods of time, in every religion, and indeed in every sublunary concern, render such an expectation unreasonable and absurd ; but it is presumed that the circumstances which will now be pointed out, in addition to what has already been stated, will leave no doubt on the mind of any reasonable and unprejudiced person, that the religions under consideration were originally the same.

In contemplating the different, and often contradictory, circumstances of the religion of the ancient Persians, it is impossible not to observe the striking similarity both of its doctrines, and discipline or practices, to those of their Eastern neighbours of India, on one side; and their Western neighbours, the Christians of Europe, on the other. That religion appears to have been a connecting link in the chain, and probably in this point of view it will be regarded by every unprejudiced person, when all the circumstances relating to it are taken into consideration. Like almost all the ancient systems of theology, its origin is lost in the most remote antiquity. Its foundation is generally attributed to a sage of the name of Zoroaster, but in order to reconcile the accounts given of him with any thing like consistency, or with one another, several persons of this name must be supposed to have lived.

2. Treating of the religion of Persia, Sir W. Jones says, " The primeval religion of Iran, if we " may rely on the authorities adduced by Mossani Fáni, was that which Newton calls the oldest " (and it may justly be called the noblest) of all religions; a firm belief that ' one Supreme God " ' made the world by his power, and continually governed it by his providence; a pious fear, " ' love, and adoration of him; and due reverence for parents and aged persons; a fraternal " ' affection for the whole human species; and a compassionate tenderness even for the brute " ' creation.'" [1]

Firdausi, speaking of the prostration of Cyrus and his paternal grandfather before the blazing altar, says, " Think not that they were adorers of fire, for that element was only an exalted object, " on the lustre of which they fixed their eyes; they humbled themselves a whole week before " God; and if thy understanding be ever so little exerted, thou must acknowledge thy dependance " on the Being supremely pure." [2]

However bigoted my Christian reader may be, he will hardly deny that there is here the picture of a beautiful religion. On this subject Mr. Maurice says, " The reader has already been " informed that the first object of the idolatry of the ancient world was the Sun. The beauty, " the lustre, and vivifying warmth of that planet, early enticed the human heart from the adoration " of that Being who formed its glowing sphere and all the host of heaven. The Sun, however, " was not solely adored for its own intrinsic lustre and beauty; it was probably venerated by the " devout ancients as the most magnificent emblem of the Shechinah which the universe afforded. " Hence the Persians, among whom the true religion for a long time flourished uncorrupted, " according to Dr. Hyde, in a passage before referred to, asserted, that the *throne* of God was " seated in the sun. In Egypt, however, under the appellation of Osiris, the sun was not less " venerated, than under the denomination of Mithra, in Persia." [3]

3. The first dogma of the religion of Zoroaster clearly was, the existence of one Supreme, Omnipotent God. In this it not only coincides with the Hindoo and the Christian, but with all other religions; in this, therefore, there is not any thing particular: but on further inquiry it appears that this great First Cause, called Ormusd or Oromasdes, was a being like the Gods of the Hindoos and of the Christians, consisting of *three* persons. The triplicate Deity of the Hindoos of three persons and one God, Bramha the Creator, Vishnu or Cristna, of whom I shall soon treat, the Saviour or Preserver, and Siva the Destroyer; and yet this was all *one* God, in his different capacities. In the same manner the Supreme God of the Persians consisted of three persons, Oromasdes the Creator, Mithra the Saviour, Mediator, or Preserver, and Ahriman the Destroyer. The Christians had also their Gods, consisting of *three* persons and *one* God, the Father, Son, and Holy Ghost. Psellus informs us, Oromasdes and Mithras were frequently used by the Magi for the τὸ Θειον, or *whole Deity* in general, and Plethro adds a *third*, called Arimanius, which is confirmed by Plutarch, who says, " That Zoroaster made a threefold distribution of

---

[1] Sir W. Jones on the Persians, Diss. VI. p. 197.   [2] Ib. p. 201.   [3] Maurice, Ind. Ant. Vol. IV. p. 605.

"things, and that he assigned the first and highest rank of them to Oromasdes, who, in the oracles,
"is called the Father; the lowest to Arimanes; and the middle to Mithras, who, in the same
"oracles, is called the second mind. Whereupon he observes, how great an agreement there
"was betwixt the Zoroastrian and the Platonic Trinity, they differing in a manner only in
"words." [1]

"And, indeed, from that which Plutarch affirms, that the Persians, from their God Mithras,
"called any Mediator, or middle betwixt two, Mithras, it may be more reasonably concluded,
"that Mithras, according to the Persian theology, was properly the middle hypostasis, of that
"triplasian, or triplicated deity of theirs, than that he should be a middle, self-existent God, or
"Mediator, betwixt two adversary Gods, unmade, one good, and the other evil, as Plutarch would
"suppose." [2]   If it were now needful, we might make it still further evident that Zoroaster,
"notwithstanding the multitude of Gods worshiped by him, was an asserter of one Supreme,
"from his own description of God, extant in Eusebius: *God is the first incorruptible, eternal,
"indivisible, most unlike to every thing, the head or leader of all good; unbribable, the best of the
"good, the wisest of the wise; He is also the Father of law and justice, self-taught, perfect, and
"the only inventor of the natural holy.*—Eusebius tells us that the Zoroastrian description of God
"was contained *verbatim* in a book, entitled *A Holy Collection of the Persian Monuments*: as
"also, that Ostanes (himself a famous Magician and admirer of Zoroaster) had recorded the very
"same of him in his Octateuchon." [3]

4. Porphyry, in his treatise, *de Antro Nympharum*, says, "Zoroaster first of all, as Eubolus
"testifieth, in the mountains adjoining to Persia, consecrated a native orbicular cave, adorned
"with flowers and watered with fountains, to the honour of Mithras, the maker and father of all
"things; this cave being an image or symbol to him of the whole world which was made by
"Mithras; which testimony of Eubolus is the more to be valued because, as Porphyrius else-
"where informs us, he wrote the history of Mithras at large in many books,—from whence it may
"be presumed that he had thoroughly furnished himself with the knowledge of what belonged to
"the Persian religion. Wherefore, from the authority of Eubolus, we may well conclude also,
"that notwithstanding the Sun was generally worshiped by the Persians as a God, yet Zoroaster
"and the ancient Magi, who were best initiated in Mithraick mysteries, asserted another Deity,
"superior to the Sun, for the true Mithras, such as was the maker and father of all things, or of
"the whole world, whereof the Sun is a part. However, these also looked upon the Sun as the
"most lively image of the Deity in which it was worshiped by them, as they likewise worshiped
"the same Deity symbolically in fire, as Maximus Tyrius informeth us; agreeable to which is that
"in the Magic oracles; *All things are the offsprings of one fire;* that is, of one Supreme Deity.
"And Julian, the Emperor, was such a devout Sun worshiper as this, who acknowledged, besides
"the Sun, another incorporeal deity, transcendant to it." [4]   The first kind of things (according
"to Zoroaster) is eternal, the Supreme God. In the first place (saith Eusebius) they conceive
"that God the Father and King ought to be ranked. This the Delphian Oracle (cited by Por-
"phyrius) confirms:—Chaldees and Jews wise only, worshiping purely a self-begotten God and
"King.

"This is that principle of which the author of the Chaldaic Summary saith, *They conceive there
"is one principle of all things, and declare that is one and good.*

"God (as Pythagoras learnt of the Magi, who term him Oromasdes) *in his body resembles light;
"in his soul truth.*"

[1] Cudworth, Book i. Ch. iv. p. 289.   [2] Ib. p. 290.   [3] Ib. p. 293.   [4] Ib. p. 287.

In the same sense the Chaldeans likewise termed God a fire; for *Ur*, in Chaldee, signifying both light and fire, they took light and fire promiscuously.[1] " The name and image whereby they " represented the Supreme God was that of Bel, as appears by the prohibition given by God him- " self not to call him so any more. ' Thou shalt call me no longer Baali :' Bel with the Chal- " deans is the same as Baal with the Phenicians, both derived from the Hebrew Baal."[2]

" They who first translated the Eastern learning into Greek for the most part interpret this Bel " by the word $Z\epsilon\nu\varsigma$, Jupiter. So Herodotus, Diodorus, Hesychius, and others : Berosus (saith Eusebius) was priest of Belus, whom they " interpret ($\Delta\iota\alpha$) Jupiter."[3]

From the worship of the one Supreme God, (in Assyria,) they very early fell off to the worship of numbers of gods, dæmons, angels, planets, stars, &c. They had twelve principal Gods for the twelve signs of the Zodiac, to each of which they dedicated a month.[4] The identity of the name Baali among the Chaldeans and the Israelites, as observed by Stanley, raises a strong presump- tion, that all these religions were fundamentally the same, with only such greater or less adventi- tious variations as circumstances produced.

Sir W. Jones informs us that the letters Mihr in the Persian language denote the sun,[5] and he also informs us, that the letters Mihira denote the sun in the Hindoo language.[6] Now it is pretty clear that these two words are precisely the same : and are in fact nothing but the word Mithra *the sun.*

5. Dr. Hyde thought that *Zoroaster* and *Pythagoras* were contemporaries, but Mr. Stanley was of opinion this was not the fact, but that the latter lived several generations after the former. This subject has been well discussed by M. Beausobre,[7] who has undertaken to shew that they might have lived at the same time, and that there *is* nothing in the chronology to render it im- probable.

It appears that the question respecting Pythagoras and Zoroaster was simply, whether they, or either of them, admitted a first moving, uncreated cause, superior to and independent of any other, or whether they admitted two equal, co-eternal beings, the authors of good and evil. The mean- ing of the expressions used by these great philosophers must always remain a subject of very con- siderable doubt. It seems surprising that such men as Stanley and Beausobre should pretend to reduce to a certainty that which, from peculiar circumstances, must always be involved in diffi- culty. In the first place, the line between the *unity* and *duality*, as explained, is so fine, that in our native language, which we understand, it is difficult to distinguish it ; then how much more difficult must it be in a foreign and dead language ! Besides, we have it not in the language of the philosophers themselves, but retailed *to us* in a language foreign to that in which it was deli- vered, and that also by foreigners, living many years after their deaths. After all the ingenuity displayed by M. Beausobre, who has exhausted the subject, considerable doubt must always re- main upon this point, whether the two principles professed by the philosophers were identically the same or not. But yet one thing seems certain, all accounts tending to confirm the fact, that the principles were both derived from the same school, situated on the East of the Euphrates ; and, that they are, in fact, so nearly the same, that no one can tell with absolute certainty wherein they differ. No one can doubt that the doctrines of Pythagoras and those of Zoroaster, as main- tained when the former was at Babylon after its conquest by Cyrus, were, as it has been already remarked, the same or nearly so ; nor can any one doubt that Pythagoras was either the fellow- labourer and assistant of Zoroaster, or a pupil of his school.

[1] Stanley, Hist. Phil. Part xv. Ch. i. p. 765.   [2] Ibid. p. 784.   [3] Ibid.   [4] Ibid. Ch. vii.
[5] Diss. I. on the Gods of Greece, Italy, and India.   [6] Supplement to Ess. on Ind. Chron.
[7] Liv. i. Ch. iii. p. 31.

Manes lived long after both of them ; and if it should be contended that he differed from them in any very abstruse speculative point, this will not be admitted as a proof that he did not draw his doctrine from their fountain, when it is known that it came from the East of the Euphrates, and when it is evidently the same in almost every other particular.

6. The ancient followers of Zoroaster are not yet extinct. There is " a colony of them settled " in Bombay, an island belonging to the English, where they are allowed, without any molesta-" tion, the full freedom and exercise of their religion. They are a poor, harmless sort of people, " zealous in their superstition, rigorous in their morals, and exact in their dealings, professing the " worship of one God only, and the belief of a resurrection and a future judgment, and utterly de-" testing all idolatry, although reckoned by the Mahometans the most guilty of it ; for although " they perform their worship before fire and towards the rising sun, yet they utterly deny that " they worship either of them. They hold that more of God is in these his creatures than in any " other, and that therefore they worship God towards them, as being in their opinion the truest " Shekinah of the Divine presence among us, as darkness is that of the devil's : and as to Zoroas-" tres, they still have him in the same veneration, as the Jews have Moses ; looking on him as " the great prophet of God, by whom he sent his law, and communicated his will unto them." [1] Thus it appears that if the Jews have preserved their religion for the last two thousand years, in order to fulfil a miracle or prophecy, the Persians have preserved the same religion without any miracle or prophecy whatever. And it must not be said, that this is confined to one little spot, for they are, like the Jews, dispersed all over Asia.

Although there is the most indisputable evidence, that the Magi, who were the priests of Persia, acknowledged one Supreme Being, called Oromasdes, yet they certainly worshiped the sun under the name of Mithra, the second person of their Trinity. They are said to have done this as only to an emblem or symbol—the seat and throne—of the Supreme Being. But it probably soon came to pass that the Supreme Being was forgotten, and that his image only was adored by the people. The Persian Magi have always denied that they worshiped *fire* in any other sense than as an emblem of the Supreme Being, but it is extremely difficult to ascertain the exact truth ; and the difficulty is increased by the circumstance that most ancient philosophers, and, in fact, almost all the early Christian fathers, held the opinion that God consisted of a subtile, ethereal, igneous fluid, which pervaded all nature—that God was *fire*. Thus, as I have before remarked, he appeared to Moses in the burning bush, and again upon Sinai.

All the Oriental and Grecian writers agree in ascribing to the Persians the worship of one Supreme God : they only differ as to the time when this first began to take place. Much more attention is due to the ancient Oriental, than to the Grecian, histories of Persia, and they all represent the worship of one Supreme God as having begun very early, and this is confirmed, in a considerable degree, by the rebuilding of the Temple of Jerusalem by Cyrus. There is no doubt that the Persian religion was reformed, or improved by some one, that the capital of the empire of the Magi was at one time at Balch, and that it was from this place their religion spread both into India and the West. It was in the neighbourhood of that city, where the first orbicular caves, of which we have heard so much, were excavated, long before the time of Cyrus.

Mr. Maurice says, " But it is now necessary that we should once more direct our attention " towards Persia. The profound reverence, before noticed, to have been equally entertained by " the Magi of Persia and the Brachmans of India, for the solar orb and for fire, forms a most " striking and prominent feature of resemblance between the religion of Zoroaster and that of " Brahma.

---

[1] Prid. Con. Part i. Book iv. p. 285. 8vo.   [2] Maur. Ind. Ant. V. II. p. 116.

7. The Vedas are supposed by the Brahmins to have existed from the most remote antiquity. The *words* are Sanscrit and the *letters* Nagari.[1] On this subject Sir W. Jones says, "That the "Vedas were actually written before the flood, I shall never believe." Sir William, in his first Dissertation, makes many professions of disinterestedness, of a mind perfectly free from prejudice; but the author must be excused by his friends for observing, that the declaration of his firm resolution not to believe a plain historical fact, "*I shall never* believe," gives us very little reason to hope for a fair and candid examination of any question, which shall in any way concern the truth or falsity of the doctrines he had previously determined to receive or reject. As might be expected, the result of this pious determination may be seen in almost every page of his works. The author finds no fault with the declaration; it is a mark of candour and sincerity, and it has had two good effects : it has secured to Sir William the praise of the priesthood ; and it has put the philosophical inquirer upon his guard. But it would have been a great advantage if so learned a man, and a man possessing so powerful an understanding, as Sir William Jones, could have been induced to examine the subject without prejudice or partiality, or any predetermination to believe either one thing or another. After this declaration of Sir William's, every thing which he admits in opposition to his favourite dogma, must be taken as the evidence of an unwilling witness.

The Vedas are four very voluminous books, which contain the code of laws of Brahma. Mr. Dow supposes them to have been written 4887 years before the year 1769. Sir W. Jones informs us that the principal worship inculcated in them, is that of the solar fire ; and, in the discourse on the Literature of the Hindoos, he acquaints us, that "The author of the Dabistan describes a "race of old Persian sages,[2] who appear, from the whole of his account, to have been Hindoos; "that the book of Menu, said to be written in a celestial dialect, and alluded to by the author, "means the Vedas, written in the Devanagari character, and that as Zeratusht was only a re- "former, in India may be discovered the true source of the Persian religion.[3] This is rendered "extremely probable by the wonderful similarity of the caves, as well as the doctrines, of the two "countries. The principal temple of the Magi in the time of Darius Hystaspes was at Balch, the "capital of Bactria, the most Eastern province of Persia, situated on the North-west frontiers of "India and very near to where the religion of Bramha is yet in its greatest purity, and where the "most ancient and famous temples and caverns of the Hindoos were situate."[4] As we know very well that there are no caves in the Western or Southern part of Persia answering to the description above, we are under the necessity of referring what is said here and in the quotation in Section 4, from Porphyry, to the great caves of the Buddhists and the Brahmins in the Northern parts of India and Northern Thibet. This proves their existence in the reputed time of Zoroaster.

8. Mr. Maurice says, "Of exquisite workmanship, and of stupendous antiquity—antiquity to "which neither the page of history nor human traditions can ascend—that magnificent piece of "sculpture so often alluded to in the cavern of Elephanta decidedly establishes the solemn fact, "that, from the remotest æras, the Indian nations have adored a *Triune Deity*. There the "traveller with awe and astonishment beholds, carved out of the solid rock, in the most conspi- "cuous part of the most ancient and venerable temple of the world, a bust, expanding in breadth "near twenty feet, and no less than eighteen feet in altitude, by which amazing proportion, as "well as its gorgeous decorations, it is known to be the image of the grand presiding Deity of "that hallowed retreat : he beholds, I say, a bust composed of three heads united to one body,

---

[1] Jones, Diss. VI. on the Persians, p. 185.   [2] A Sage is a sagax, or sagacious or wise man, a sophi.

[3] Asiat. Res. Vol. I. p. 349.

[4] Hyde, Hist. Rel. Vet. Pers. Cap. xxiv. p. 320 ; Maurice, Ind. Ant. Vol. II. pp. 120, 126.

" adorned with the oldest symbols of the Indian theology, and thus expressly fabricated, according
" to the unanimous confession of the sacred sacerdotal tribe of India, to indicate the *Creator*, the
" *Preserver*, and the *Regenerator* of mankind." [1]

To destroy, according to the Vedantas of India and the Sufis of Persia, that is, the σοφοι or
wise men of Persia, is only to regenerate and reproduce in another form; and in this doctrine
they are supported by many philosophers of our European schools. We may safely affirm, that
we have *no experience* of the actual destruction,—the *annihilation* of any substance whatever.
On this account it is that Mahadeva of India, the destroyer, is always said to preside over generation, is represented riding upon a bull, the emblem of the sun, when the vernal equinox took place
in that sign, and when he triumphed in his youthful strength over the powers of hell and darkness : and near him generally stands the gigantic Lingham or Phallus, the emblem of the creative
power. From this Indian deity came, through the medium of Egypt and Persia, the Grecian
mythos of Jupiter Genitor, with the Bull of Europa, and his extraordinary title of Lapis—a title
probably given to him on account of the stone pillar with which his statue is mostly accompanied,
and the object of which is generally rendered unquestionable by the peculiar form of its summit or
upper part. In India and Europe this God is represented as holding his court on the top of lofty
mountains. In India they are called mountains of the Moon or Chandrasichara ; in the Western
countries Olympuses. He is called Trilochan and has three eyes. Pausanias tells us that Zeus
was called Triophthalmos, and that, previous to the taking of Troy, he was represented with three
eyes. As Mr. Forbes [2] says, the identity of the two Gods falls little short of being demonstrated.

In the Museum of the Asiatic Society is an Indian painting of a Cristna seated on a lotus with
three eyes—emblems of the Trinity.

CHAPTER II

The word Oм—Omphe. Omphalos—Olympus. Ammon. Delphi—Digression concerning the word Oɴ—Subject of Ammon renewed—Ham the Son of Noah, and
Ammon the Sun in Aries—Niebuhr on the Ombrici of Italy: several remarkable Synonymes—On the Spirit or Ruh, the Dove—Priestley's opinion—Subject of the Persian and Hindoo Trinity resumed

1. Mr. Hastings, one of the most early and liberal patrons of Sanscrit literature in India, in a
letter to Nathaniel Smith, Esq., has remarked how accurately many of the leading principles of the
pure, unadulterated doctrines of Bramha correspond with those of the Christian system. In the
Geeta, (one of the most ancient of the Hindoo books,) indeed, some passages, surprisingly consonant, occur concerning the sublime nature and attributes of God, as well as concerning the properties and functions of the soul. Thus, where the Deity, in the form of Cristna, addresses Arjun :
" I am the Creator of all things, and all things proceed from me,"—" I am the beginning, the
" middle, and the end of all things ; I am time : I am all-grasping death, and I am the resurrec-
" tion : I am the mystic figure OM ! I am generation and dissolution." Arjun in pious ecstacy
" exclaims, " Reverence ! reverence ! be unto thee, a thousand times repeated ! again and again
" reverence ! O thou who art all in all ! infinite in thy power and thy glory ! Thou art the father

---

[1] Maurice, Ind. Ant. Vol. IV. p. 736.   [2] Mem. Orien. Vol. III. Ch. xxxv. p. 444.

" of all things animate and inanimate! there is none like unto thee."[1] In our future investigations we shall find this mystic figure OM of the greatest importance; for which reason I shall now inquire into the meaning of this celebrated, *not-to-be-spoken* word.

" In the Geeta, Arjun is informed by Creeshna, that ' God is in the fire of the altar, and that "' the devout, with offerings, direct their worship unto God in the fire.' ' I am the fire, I am the "' victim.' (P. 80.) The divinity is frequently characterized in that book, as in other Sanscreet "compositions, by the word OM, that mystic emblem of the Deity in India." The ancient Brahmins, as well as the Buddhists, of India, regarded this word with the same kind of veneration as the Jews did the word IEUE, which they never pronounced except on certain very solemn occasions. This is what is meant by the fourth commandment, which we render, " Thou shalt not " take the name of the Lord thy God" (but which ought to be *Ieue thy God)* " in vain." As a pious Jew will not utter the word Ieue, so a pious Hindoo will not utter the word Om. It is the duty of the Jews and Hindoos to meditate on the respective words in silence, and with the most profound veneration.

The word Om is always prefixed in pronouncing the words which represent the seven superior worlds, as if to shew that these seven worlds are manifestations of the power signified by that word. In an old Purana we find the following passage: " All the rites ordained in the Vedas, the " sacrifices to the fire, and all other solemn purifications, shall pass away; but that which shall " never pass away is the word *Om*—for it is the symbol of the Lord of all things." M. Dubois adds, that he thinks it can only mean the true God. (P. 155.)—The sacred monosyllable is generally spelled OM : but, being triliteral, it seems better expressed by A U M or A O M or A W M, it being formed of the three Sanscrit letters that are best so represented. The first letter stands for the Creator, the second for the Preserver, and the third for the Destroyer.[2]

Sir W. Jones informs us that the names of Brahma, Veeshnu, and Seeva, coalesce and form the mystical word Om, which he says signifies neither more nor less than the solar fire.[3] Here I apprehend we have the identical word used by the ancient Egyptians and their neighbours for the Sun, Ammon.

2. The Hindoo word Om, I think, will be found in the celebrated Greek word Ομφη, which I will now examine, before I proceed with the subject of this chapter, as it will often be found to meet us in our investigations.

In the Greek, Ομφη signifies divina vox, responsum à Deo datum consulenti. Φη or φι by itself, according to Scapula, has no meaning, but is merely a paragogic syllable, as is also the word Ομ;[4] but φη is the root of φαω, to speak or pronounce, and of φημι, to say. I therefore go to the parent language, the Hebrew, and I find the word φη or φι, פה *pe* or פי *pi*, to be a noun in regimine, and to mean an opening, a mouth, a measure of capacity. Then the literal meaning will be, the mouth, or the opening, of Om. This is not far from the *divina vox* of the Greek. Hesychius, also Suidas in voce, interprets the word ΟΜΦ to be θεια κληδων, the sacred voice, the holy sound—and hence arose the ομφαλος, or *place of Omphe.* But its real meaning is still further unravelled by explaining it as OM ΦH, the enunciation of the mysterious OM of Hindoo theology, the sacred triliteral AUM, but often written as it is pronounced, OM. The Greeks

---

[1] Maurice, Ind. Ant.   [2] Moore's Pantheon, pp. 413, 414.

[3] Jones, Asiat. Res.

[4] This assertion of Scapula only shews what he had better have confessed, that he knew nothing about it. There are not, I am of opinion, any paragogic syllables, that is, syllables without meaning, in any of the old languages.

often call the oracles, or places where the oracles were delivered, the ομφαλοι, or, as it is interpreted, *the navels* of the earth. These ομφαλοι της γης, (so Euripides, in Medea, calls Delphi,) are by the scholiasts said to be the navels or centres of the earth ; now, as Delphi could not be considered the centre by the Greeks, and as they had many ομφαλοι or centres, it is evident that the true meaning of the word was unknown to them.

The Jews consider Jerusalem to be the navel of the earth.[1]

The above etymon of the word does not quite meet all the circumstances, does not quite satisfy me—unless we consider this MYSTIC WORD to have had more meanings than one. We have seen that ομφαλος meant a navel. It is the name given to Delphi : and Delphi, as Mr. Faber has observed, has the meaning of the female organ of generation, called in India *Yoni*, the Os Minxæ. Jones says, ΟΜΦΗ Oracle, ΔΕΛΦΥΣ—Matrix, womb. In one of the plates in Moore's Hindoo Pantheon, Brahma is seen rising from the navel of Brahme-Maia with the umbilical cord uncut: this justifies the last rendering of Jones, *Matrix*. Closely allied to ομφη seems to be the word ομφαλη, or ομφαλος. I find φαλη or φαλος to mean Phallus or Linga, the *membrum virile*, constantly used for the generative power. Then ομφαλη will mean the generative power Oμ, or the generative power of Om. I find the oracle or Divina vox at Delphi called Omphalos, and the word Delphi or Δελφυς means the female generative power; and in front of the temple at Delphi, in fact constituting a part of the religious edifice, was a large Phallus or Linga, anointed every day with oil. This, all taken together, shews very clearly that Omphale means the oracle of the generative (androgynous) power of Om. But it might also come from the sacred word Oμ and φαλος—BENIGNUS— the benignant Om. In the religious ceremonies at Delphi a boat of immense size was carried about in processions ; it was shaped like a lunar crescent, pointed alike at each end : it was called an Omphalos or Umbilicus, or the ship ARGO. Of this Argo I shall have very much to say hereafter. My reader will please to recollect that the os minxæ or Δελφυς is called by the name of the ship Argo. The Aum of India, as might well be expected, is found in Persia, under the name of Hom, and particularly in the mountains of Persia, amongst the Arii, before they are said to have migrated, under Djemchid, to the South. As usual, we get to the North-east, for the origin of things.[3]

Bacchus was called Omestes, explained *the devourer*. This is in fact the Om-Esta,[3] of Persia. " Ista-char, or Esta-char, is the place or temple of Ista or Esta, who was the Hestia 'Εςια of " the Greeks, and Vesta of the Romans." This Persian ista or esta, is the Latin ista and est, *he or she is ;* it is also Sanscrit, and means the same as the *Jah* of the Hebrews. Bacchus, at Chios and Tenedos, was also called Omadius. This is correctly the God, or the holy Om.

3. Mr. Bryant connects the word Olympus with the Omphe. He observes, that wherever there was an Olympus, of which there were a great number, there was also an Omphi or Ompi, and that the word came from the Hebrew Har-al-ompi, *(Har* means *mount,)* which al-ompi was changed by the Greeks into Ολυμπος Olympus.[4] The word means the mount of the God Omphi, according to Bryant's exposition ; but more correctly, I think, the mount of the Phi, or the prophetic voice or oracle of the God Om : whence *tri-om-phe* chaunted in the mysteries at Rome, the triple Omphe. Mr. Bryant's etymon completely fails in accounting for the syllable Om. He probably did not know of the Hindoo Aum, Om. In his work cited above may be found

---

[1] Basnage, Hist. Jud. B. iii. Ch. xiv. p. 194.   [3] Creuzer, notes, p. 686.
[3] Bryant, Anal. Vol. I. p. 227.   [4] Ibid. p. 239.

many very learned and curious observations respecting the word Om and its connexion with various places. He shews that the meaning of the Ομφι was totally unknown to the Greeks.

From Parkhurst, (in voce שר sr, p. 771,) it is pretty clear that the omphalos had both the meaning of beeve and umbilicus, and that it had also the same meaning as שר sr.

Amon is the *Om* of India, and *On* or אן *an* of the Hebrews. Strabo calls the temple of Jupiter Ammon, Ἱερον Ομανη. Bryant[1] says, המה *eme* is called Hom.[2] Gale says, " In the Persian lan- " guage Hama means the sun."[3] These are all evidently the Om of India, variously translated.

The word Am, Om, or Um, occurs in many languages, but it has generally a meaning some way connected with the idea of a circle or cycle, as ambire, ambages, or circum. This is particularly the case in all the Northern languages. I need not name again the Umbilicus, nor the way in which this seems to be connected with the idea conveyed by the Greek word Δελφυς. Nonnus says, that the Babylonian Bel and the Lybian Hammon were, εν Ἑλλαδι, ΔΕΛΦΟΣ Απολλος.

An attentive perusal of what Jamieson has said, in his *Hermes Scythicus*, (pp. 6, 7,) on the word Am, Om, Um, will satisfy the reader that there is a strong probability that the radical meaning of this word is cycle or circle. The importance of this will be seen hereafter.

It would be going too far to quote Dr. Daniel Clarke as an authority in support of my explanation of the word Ammon, but I will give a note of his in the seventh chapter of his Travels in Egypt, and leave the reader to judge for himself : " Plane ridiculum est, velle *Ammonis* nomen " petere à Græcis : cùm Ægyptii ipsi Αμουν appellent, teste Herodoto.[4] The name of the Su- " preme Being among the Brahmins of India is the first syllable only of this word pronounced " AM." Again,[5] " Sol superus et clarus est AMMON."[6] The ancients had a precious stone called Ombria. It was supposed to have descended from heaven.[7] The place of its nativity seems to connect it with the mysterious Om. The Roman nurses used the letter M, pronounced Mu, as a charm against witchcraft, and from the effects of the evil eye—from being fascinated by the God Fascinus, who had the figure of the membrum virile, and was worn about the necks of women and children, like the Agnus Deis worn by Romish Christians. The latter, I have no doubt, borrowed the custom from the Gentiles.[8]

4. Various derivations are given of the word On, but they are all unsatisfactory. It is written in the Old Testament in two ways, און *aun* and אן *an*. It is usually rendered in English by the word *On*. This word is supposed to mean the sun, and the Greeks translated it by the word Ἡλιος or sol. But I think it only stood for the sun as emblem of the procreative power of nature. Thus, in Genesis xlix. 3, *Reuben, thou art my firstborn, my might, and the beginning of* MY STRENGTH : principium roboris mei :[9] אוני *auni*, וראשית *u-rasit*. It meant the beginning or the first exercise of his pro-creative power. Again, in Deut. xxi. 17, the words אנו ראשית *rasit anu*, refer to the firstborn, and have the same meaning : *For he is the beginning of his strength ; the right of the firstborn is his.* Again, in Psalm lxxviii. 51, we find it having the same meaning : *And smote all the firstborn in Egypt: the* CHIEF OF THEIR STRENGTH *in the tabernacles of Ham :* אונים *aunim* ראשית *rasit :* Primitias omnis laboris eorum, in tabernaculis Cham.[10] In the hundred and fifth Psalm and the thirty-sixth verse, it has the same meaning.

It was from Oenuphis, a priest of On, that Pythagoras is said to have learnt the system of the heavenly bodies moving round the sun in unceasing revolutions. The priests of this temple were esteemed the first in Egypt.[11]

[1] Heathen Myth. p. 3.   [2] Ibid.   [3] Gale's Court of the Gentiles, Vol. I. ch. xi. p. 72.
[4] Vossius de Orig. &c., Idolat. Tom. i. Lib. ii. Cap. ii. p. 362, Amst. 1642.   [5] Ibid. p. 282.
[6] Jablonski, Panth. Ægyp.   [7] Plin. Hist. Nat. Lib. xxxvii. Cap. x.   [8] Vide Ibid. Lib. xxviii. Cap. iv.
[9] Ar. Montanus.   [10] Vulg.   [11] See Plut. de Is. et Osir.

Æuon or עין oinn, where John baptized, was called by a figure of speech only Ænon, or the fountain of the sun. The literal meaning was, The Fountain of the Generative Power.

Mr. Faber, speaking of the calves set up by Jeroboam, says, " that they were, in their use and " application, designed to be images of the two sacred bulls which were the living representations " of Osiris and Isis, is both very naturally asserted by St. Jerome, and may be collected even " from Scripture itself. Hosea styles the idols of Jeroboam *the calves of Beth-Aven :* and imme- " diately afterwards speaks of the high places of the God Aven, whom he denominates *the sin of* " *Israel.* Now we are told, that when Jeroboam instituted the worship of the calves, he likewise " made high places in which their priests might officiate. The high places, therefore, of the " calves are the high places of Aven ; the temple of Aven is the temple of the calves ; and Aven, " the sin of Israel, is the same as at least one of the calves, which are also peculiarly described as " being the sin of Israel. But the God, whose name by the Masoretic punctuation is pronounced " *Aven,* is no other than the Egyptian deity Aun or On : for the very God whose worship Hosea " identifies with that of the calves, is he of whom Potipherah is said to have been the priest : the " two appellations, which our translators variously express, Aven and On, consisting in the He- " brew of the self-same letters. *On,* however, or Aun, was the Egyptian title of the sun, whence " *the city of On* was expressed by the Greeks *Heliopolis;* and the sun was astronomically the " same as the Tauric God Osiris : consequently Ou and Osiris are one deity. Hence it is evident, " that the worship of Jeroboam's calves being substantially the worship of On or Osiris, the calves " themselves must have been venerated, agreeably to the just supposition of Jerome, as the repre- " sentatives of Apis and Nevis." [1]   The calves were probably emblematical of the Sun in his male and female character—Baal and Baaltis.

5. We have seen that Strabo says, the temple of Ammon was called ιερον Ομανε, and we have also seen, that the first syllable of the word אם *am* was no other than the celebrated Hindoo word Aum, which designated the Brahmin Trinity, the Creator, the Preserver, and the Destroyer. These three letters, Sir W. Jones tells us, as stated above, coalesce and form the mystic word OM. In the Geeta, Cristna thus addresses Arjun : " I am generation and DISSOLUTION." It was from the last idea that Heliopolis, or the city of On, was called in some of the old versions of the Bible *the city of destruction.* Here are evidently the Creator and the Destroyer. Mr. Strauss says, that Bethaven means *place of unworthiness.* [2]

The word אם *am* in the Hebrew not only signifies might, strength, power, firmness, solidity, truth, but it means also *mother,* as in Genesis ii. 24, and *love,* whence the Latin Amo, mamma. If the word be taken to mean strength, then Amon will mean (the first syllable *am* being in regi- mine) the temple of *the strength of the generative* or *creative power,* or the temple of the mighty procreative power. If the word *am* mean mother, then a still more recondite idea will be implied, viz. the mother generative power, or the maternal generative power : perhaps the Urania of Persia, or the Venus Aphrodite of Crete and Greece, or the Jupiter Genetrix, of the masculine and femi- nine gender, or the Brahme-Maia of India, or the Alma Venus of Lucretius. And the city of On or Heliopolis will be the *city of the Sun* or *city of the procreative powers of nature,* of which the Sun was always the emblem. [3]

I have proved in my Celtic Druids, Ch. ii. Sect. xxiv. that the old Latin was Sanscrit, and I may affirm, that the Alma of Lucretius is of Oriental, not Grecian, origin. The Greeks knew not the word Alma. This word, I think, means *Al* the preserver, and *ma* mother : it will then mean, the preserving mother Venus. I think in this case no one can doubt that the עלמה *olma* of the

---

[1] Pagan Idol. Vol. I. p. 437.   [2] Hos. x. 5; Amos iv. 4; Helon's Pilgrimage, B. iv. Ch. i.
[3] Drummond, Origines, B. i. Ch. iv. p. 47.

Phœnicians, and the עלמה *olme* of the Hebrews, which both mean *Virgin*, or young woman, were the same as the Latin *Alma*. The Om or Aum of India is evidently the Omh of the Irish Druids, which means *He who is*.[1] It is a very curious circumstance that in almost all etymologies, when probed to the bottom, the Celtic language is found along with the Hebrew.

There was in Syria or Canaan a place called *Ammon*, the natives of which were always at enmity with the Israelites. This was spelt און *omun* in the Hebrew, and by the Greeks was called Heliopolis. This seems to shew that it was dedicated to the same God as the Αμον of Egypt.

This word is used in the writings of the Hindoos precisely as we use the word Amen, which I have no doubt, both in its meaning and use, comes from this word.

6. The name of the son of Noah was חם *Hm*, called Ham. The name of the solar orb was חמה *Hme* the feminine of חם *Hm*. It appears to me that, from misapprehension, the *Ham* of Noah has been confounded with the *Ham*, or *Hm* or *Om* of Egypt—the Jupiter *Ammon* or *Amon*, the God with the Ram's head, adored at the ιεϱον Ομονυ. The word חם *Hm*, the patriarch, and the word חמה *Hme*, the Sun, being the same, were the cause of the mistake. Suppose the LXX. meant to say that Egypt was given to *Ham*, it by no means follows that this was the *Ham* or *Am* of the temples of the Sol Generator. As we have another much more probable way of accounting for the *Om* of the temple than that of supposing the deification of a man living a thousand miles from the temple of the Oasis, I think we are bound to take it. But if the history of the flood was a sacred mythos, the two words might have the same meaning without being copied from one another. I know no reason for believing that the son of Noah was deified—a mere fancy of modern priests; but I have many reasons for believing that Amon was the Sun as the generating power, first in Taurus, then in Aries. " Belus, Kronos, Apis, were solar symbols, and Nonnus " ranks Amon with these :

Βηλος σε' Ευφϱηται, Λιβυς κεκλημενος Αμμων,
Απις αφυς Νειλοος, Αραψ Κϱονος, Ασσυϱιος Ζευς.

" Amon was clearly understood by the mythologists to represent the Sun in Aries."[2] Sir W. Drummond has given many other satisfactory reasons for Amon being the Sun : then how absurd is it to go any farther ! All difficulties are easily explained by attending to the circumstance of the fundamental doctrine, that, in fact, all the Gods resolve themselves into the Sun, either as God or as emblem of the Triune Androgynous Being.

Wilkinson, in his Atlas, has placed on the Eastern shore of Arabia, on a river named Lar, a town called Omanum, which was also called Om. Here a moderately fertile imagination may perhaps find a second or third Ammon—and thus several Ammons, several Heliopolises, several Memmons, &c., &c.[3] Some important words are connected with or derived from the word Om. Mr. Niebuhr says, " The Umbri were a powerful people previous to the Etruscans."[4] He also says, that the Greeks detected in the name of these people, which they pronounced Ombrici, an allusion to *a very remote antiquity*. The reader will not be surprised that I should go to the East for the origin of the Om-brici and of Om-brica, and consequently of our Umber—North-umberland and C-umberland.

7. Mr. Niebuhr does not pretend to explain the meaning of the word Italia, but he informs us that the ancient Greeks referred it to Heracleian traditions, and to a Greek word Ιταλος or Ιτυλος, signifying a BULL. This recalls our attention in a very singular manner to the most ancient superstition. Pliny[5] says, " The people of Umbria are supposed, of all Italy, to be of greatest

---

[1] Maurice, Hist. of Hind. Vol. II. p. 171, ed. 4to.   [a] Drum. Orig. B. iv. p. 330.
[3] Ibid. B. iii. Ch. iii. p. 360.   [4] Ch. vi.   [5] Ch. i. p. 31.   [b] Nat. Hist. Lib. iii. Cap. xiv.

" antiquity, as whom men think to have been of the Greeks named Ombri, for that, in the general
" deluge of the country by rain, they only remained alive." I think it does not require a very
fertile imagination to discover here traces of the flood, the first race of men, and the sacred mysterious Om. Br or Pr, in the Eastern language, means sacred and creative,[1] and Omberland will
mean, The Land of the Sacred Om.

Thus we have several clear and distinct meanings of Ομφαλος. It was mitis, begnignus. It
was the *male* generative power, as Φαλλος. As Omphale, it was the *female* generative power, the
wife of Hercules, and the navel of the Earth or Nabbi. It was also the prophetic voice of the
benignant Om. We shall see by and bye how it came to have all these different meanings. Before we conclude this work, we shall find a similar variety arising from other names connected
with this subject, and in particular it should be recollected that we have found the Indian Creeshna
or Cristna calling himself Om.

I cannot help suspecting that the ancients often adopted an extraordinary play upon words—a
kind of punning. Thus, שר Sr, is the root of Osiris, who changed himself into a bull. He is the
Sun. *Surya* is the Sun, and is the favourite God of Japan, where the celebrated Bull breaks the
mundane egg. שור Sur. is a beeve, as Taurus, at the vernal equinox, the leader of the heavenly
hosts. שרר Srr, means ruler, or absolute director or Lord.

Brahme is the Sun, the same as Surya. *Brahma* sprung from the navel of Brahme. The
Greeks call the oracles ομφαλοι, or navels of the earth. *Srr* has the same meaning as ομφαλος
—and *Sr* means *funis umbilicalis.*

Ομφη means an oracle. The oracle was the spirit of the God, the sanctus spiritus, and came from
the ομφαλος. It founded Delphi in the form of a black Dove. A Dove is always the emblem
the Holy Spirit. יונה *Iune*, is Hebrew for Dove. This is the Yoni of India, the Os Minxæ, the
matrix. At Delphi the response came from a fissure or crack in the mountain, the Yoni of the
earth. This was the emblem of the רוח *ruh* or Holy Ghost, the third person of the Trinity.

8. In Psalm xxxiii. 6, it is said, " By the word of Ieue were the שמים *smim* heavens made;
" and all the host of them by the רוח *ruh* breath of his mouth." Again, ver. 9, " For he *spake,*
" and it was done ; he *commanded,* and it stood fast."

The third person was the Destroyer, or, in his good capacity, the Regenerator. The dove was
the emblem of the Regenerator. When a person was baptized, he was regenerated or born again.
A Dove descended on to the head of Jesus at his baptism. Devotees profess to be born again by
the Holy Ghost—Sanctus Spiritus. We read of an Evil Spirit and of a Holy Spirit ; one is the
third person in his *destroying* capacity, the other in his *regenerating* capacity. We read in the
Acts of the Apostles (ch. xvi. 16) of a spirit of Python or a Pythonic spirit, an evil spirit.
Python, or the spirit of Python, was the destroyer. But at Delphi he was also Apollo, who was
said to be the Sun in Heaven, Bacchus on Earth, and Apollo in Hell.

M. Dubois has observed, (p. 293,) that the Prana or Principle of Life, of the Hindoos, is the
breath of life by which the Creator animated the clay, and man became a living soul." Gen. ii. 7.

The Holy Spirit or Ghost was sometimes *masculine,* sometimes *feminine.* As the third person
of the Trinity, it was as well known to the ancient Gentiles as to the moderns, as it will hereafter
be shewn.

Origen expressly makes the Holy Ghost *female.* He says, παιδισκη δε κυριας τυ αγιυ
Πνευματος ή ψυχη—" The soul is maiden to her mistress the Holy Ghost.[2]

[1] Loubere, Hist. Siam.
[2] Porson against Travis; Class. Jour. No. LXXVI., Dec. 1828, p. 207.

I believe by almost all the ancients, both Jews and Gentiles, the Supreme Being was thought to be material, and to consist of a very refined igneous fluid ; more like the galvanic or electric fire than any thing with which I am acquainted. This was also the opinion of most of the ancient Christian fathers. This was called the anima as feminine, or spiritus as masculine—and was the רוח *ruh* of the second verse of Genesis, which Parkhurst calls breath or air in motion, (Isaiah xi. 4,) an *incorporeal substance*, and the Holy Spirit. From this comes the expression *to inspire*, or *holy inspiration*. The word Ghost means spiritus or anima. This was often confounded with the igneous fluid of which God was supposed to consist ; whence came the baptism by fire and the Holy Ghost. (Matt. iii. 11.) These were absurd refinements of religious metaphysicians, which necessarily arose from their attempts to define *that* of which they had not the means of forming an idea. I should be equally as absurd, if I were to attempt to reconcile their inconsistencies. In the above examples of the different names for the Holy Ghost, a singular mixture of genders is observable. We see the active principle, *fire*, the Creator and the Preserver, and also the Destroyer, identified with the Holy Ghost of the Christians, in the united form of the Dove and of Fire settling on the apostles. Here we have most clearly the Holy Ghost identified with the Destroyer, Fire.

The Dove is the admitted emblem of the female procreative power. It always accompanies Venus. Hence in Sanscrit the female organ of generation is called Yoni. The Hebrew name is יונה *iune*. Evidently the same. The wife of Jove, the Creator, very naturally bears the name of the female procreative power, Juno. It is unnecessary to point out the close relation of the passion of love to the procreative power. There can scarcely be a doubt that the Dove was called after the Yoni, or the Yoni after the Dove, probably from its salacious qualities. And as creation was destruction, and the creative the destructive power, it came to be the emblem of the destructive as well as of the creative power. As the רוח *ruh* or spiritus was the passive cause (brooding on the face of the waters) by which all things sprung into life, the Dove became the emblem of the *ruh* or *Spirit* or Holy Ghost, the third person, and consequently the Destroyer. In the foundation of the Grecian Oracles, the places peculiarly filled with the Holy Spirit or Ghost, or inspiration, the Dove was the principal agent. The intimate relation between all these things, and their dependance on one another, I think, cannot possibly be disputed. We have in the New Testament several notices of the Holy Ghost or the sanctus spiritus, קדש *qdis*, רוח *ruh*, πνευμα άγιον, ψυχη κοσμυ, or anima mundi, or alma Venus. It descended, as before remarked, upon Jesus at his baptism, in the form of a Dove, and according to Justin Martyr, a fire was lighted in the moment of its decent in the river Jordan. It is also said to have come with a sound as of a rushing mighty wind, but to have been visible as a tongue of fire, settling on each apostle, as described Acts ii. 2, 3. Here we have the רוח *ruh* or *air in motion*, according to Parkhurst's explanation, which brooded on the face of the deep, an active agent in the creation ; and we have *fire* the *Destroyer*— the baptism of water, wind, and fire—the baptism of the Etruscans.[1] John says, " I indeed baptize you with water, but one shall come, who shall baptize you with the Holy Ghost and with " fire." (Luke iii. 16.) All this is part of the Romish Esoteric religion of Jesus, which, like other religions, has been lost ; a few fragments only now remaining ; unless it be privately concealed in the recesses of the Vatican.

8. We may see very clearly from the nonsense of Lactantius that my idea is correct. He says, the Son of God is the sermo or ratio (the speech or reason) of God ; also, that the other angels are the breath of God, *spiritus Dei*. But *sermo* (speech) is breath emitted, together with a voice expressive of something.[2] I shall, perhaps, be asked by a disciple of the philosophic Priestley

---

[1] Vide Gorius's Etruscan Monuments.   [2] Priestley, Cor. Christ. Sect. ii.

how I conceive the soul to be connected with or related to the body—to matter. I reply, I know not. I only know that God is good, and that this goodness cannot exist without a state of reward and punishment hereafter to mankind. This makes me certain that, in some way or other, man will exist after death: but *how* the Deity has not given me faculties to comprehend. And if I wanted a proof of this latter proposition, I have only to go for it to the unsatisfactory nature of the Doctor's Disquisitions on Matter and Spirit, from which I think any unprejudiced person must see that he has involved himself in inextricable difficulties, from not attending to Mr. Locke's doctrine, and from attempting that which is beyond the reach of the human understanding.

If my reader will pay a little attention to what passes in his own mind, he will soon see, that when he talks of Spirit or Ghost, he generally has no idea of any thing. This is one of the subjects of which he can acquire no knowledge or idea through the medium of the senses. Therefore, as might be expected, a great confusion of terms prevails. In the foregoing examination, the truth of what I have said will be instantly apparent. The terms betray, in their origin, the grossest materialism. I think the reader must now see that if the *spirit of God* mean any thing, it is a mere figure of speech, and means that God has so modelled his law of creation, that the patient shall have a good disposition, or a good spirit. And if it be said that he has a spirit of prophecy or of foretelling future events, I reply, the expression may as well be, that he has a flesh to foretell as a spirit to foretell. If God have ever given a person a knowledge of what will happen at a future time, this has no more to do with the spirit or the air in motion, than with the flesh Jesus said, the gates of hell should never prevail against his religion. According to your accounts, Christian doctors, they have prevailed and continue to prevail. But I say, No. They have not prevailed, and never will prevail; the pure, unadulterated doctrines of Jesus will stand for ever. They have only prevailed against the corruptions with which you have loaded his religion. The fine morality and the unity of God, which you would have destroyed, can never really be destroyed, though your idols, your relics, your saints, and your mother of God, will all pass away, like yesterday's shadow of a cloud on the mountain.

9. It is now time to return to the Persians.

After enumerating various other instances to prove the existence of an Indian Trinity, Mr. Maurice says, " Degraded infinitely, I must repeat it, beneath the Christian, as are the characters " of the Hindoo Trinity, yet in our whole research throughout Asia there has not hitherto occurred " so direct and unequivocal a designation of a Trinity in Unity as that sculptured in the Ele- " phanta cavern : nor is there any more decided avowal of the doctrine itself any where to be met " with than in the following passages of the Bhagvat Geeta. In that most ancient and authentic " book, the supreme Veeshnu thus speaks concerning himself and his divine properties : ' I am " ' the holy one, worthy to be known.' He immediately adds, ' I am the *mystic (triliteral)* figure " ' Om ; the *Reig*, the *Yagush*, and the *Saman Vedas.'* [1] Here we see that Veeshnu speaks ex- " pressly of his *unity*, and yet in the same sense declares he is the mystic figure A. U. M., which " three letters the reader has been informed, from Sir W. Jones, coalesce and form the Sanscreet " word OM." A little after, in the same page, Mr. Maurice tells us, that the figure which stands for the word OM of the Brahmins, is designated by the combination of three letters, which Dr. Wilkins has shewn to stand, the *first* for the *Creator*, the *second* for the *Preserver*, and the *third* for the *Destroyer*. [2]

M. Sonnerat also states that the Hindoos adore *three* principal deities, Brouma, Chiven, and Vichenou, who are still but one. [3]

---

[1] Geeta, p. 80.   [2] Maurice, Ind. Ant. Vol. IV. pp. 744, 745.   [3] Ibid. p. 747.

M. Sonnerat also gives a passage from a Sanscrit Poornun,[1] in which it is stated that it is God alone who created the universe by his *productive* power, who maintains it by his *all-preserving* power, and who will destroy it by his *destructive* power, and that it is this God who is represented under the name of *three Gods*, who are called *Trimourti*.[2] Mr. Forster[3] says, " One circumstance which forcibly struck my attention was the Hindoo belief of a Trinity; the " persons are *Sree Mun Narrain*, the *Maha Letchimy*, a beautiful woman, and a *Serpent*. These " persons are by the Hindoos supposed to be wholly indivisible; the *one* is *three*, and the *three* " are *one*." Mr. Maurice then states that the Sree Mun Narrain, as Mr. Forster writes it, is Narayen the Supreme God : the beautiful woman is the Imma of the Hebrews, and that the union of the sexes is perfectly consistent with that ancient doctrine maintained in the Geeta, and propagated by Orpheus, that the Deity is both male and female.[4]

Mr. Maurice, in his Indian Antiquities, says, " This notion of three persons in the Deity was " diffused amongst all the nations of the earth, established at once in regions so distant as Japan " and Peru, immemorially acknowledged throughout the whole extent of Egypt and India, and " flourishing with equal vigour amidst the snowy mountains of Thibet, and the vast deserts of " Siberia."

CHAPTER III

Israel Worsley's Account of Ancient Trinities—Opinion of Dr. Pritchard and others on the Trinities—Opinion of Maurice and others on the Trinities—The Christian Trinity—Its Origin—Macrobius on the Trinity—Philo's Trinity of the Jews—Faber's Account of the Universal Belief of the Trinity—Observations on the Doctrine that Destruction is only Regeneration

1. MR. WORSLEY says, " This doctrine was of very great antiquity, and generally received by " all the Gothic and Celtic nations. These philosophers taught, that the Supreme God, Teut or " Woden, was the active principle, the soul of the world, which, uniting itself to matter, had " thereby put it into a condition to produce intelligences or *inferior gods* and men. This the " poets express by saying that Odin espoused Frea, or the Lady, by way of eminence. Yet they " allowed a great difference between these two principles. The Supreme was eternal, whereas " matter was his work, and of course had a beginning. All this was expressed by the phrase, " Earth is the daughter and wife of the universal Father. From this mystical union was born the " God Thor-Asa Thor, the Lord Thor. He was the firstborn of the Supreme, the greatest of " the intelligences, that were born of the union of the two principles. The characters given him " correspond much with those which the Romans gave to their Jupiter. He, too, was the thun- " derer, and to him was devoted the fifth day, Thor's-dag; in German and Dutch, Donder dag,

---

[1] Voyages, Vol. I. p. 259.   [2] Ibid. p. 749.   [3] Sketches of Hindoo Mythology, p. 12.
[4] Maurice, Ind. Ant. Vol. IV. p. 750.

" thunder day. The common oaths of these people mark the same origin. They swear by *donder*
" *and blexen*, thunder and lightning. Friday took its name from Frea, Frea's-dag; as Wednesday
" did from Woden, Woden's-dag. Tuis was the name which the old Saxons gave to the son of
" the Supreme, whence Tuesday. Thor, being the firstborn, was called the eldest of the sons ;
" he is made a middle divinity, a mediator between God and man. Such, too, was the Persians'
" God : for Thor was venerated also as the intelligence that animated the sun and fire. The Per-
" sians declared that the most illustrious of all the intelligences was that which they worshiped
" under the symbol of fire. They called him Mithras, or the mediator God. The Scythians called
" him Goeto-Syrus, the Good Star. All the Celtic nations were accustomed to worship the sun,
" either as distinguished from Thor, or as his symbol. It was their custom to celebrate a feast at
" the winter solstice, when that great luminary began to return again to this part of the Heavens.
" They called it Yuule, from Heoul, Helios, the sun, which to this day signifies the sun in the
" language of Bretagne and Cornwall : whence the French word Noel.

     " How great a resemblance may be seen between the expressions which have been stated above,
" relative to these ancient Trinities, and those of some Christian worshipers, who imagine that
" the Father begat the Son—according to some in time, according to others from eternity—and
" that from these two sprang or proceeded the Holy Ghost !" [1]

     According to Israel Worsley, [2] " It was Justin Martyr, a Christian convert from the Platonic
" school, who, about the middle of the second century, first promulgated the opinion, that the Son
" of God was the second principle in the Deity, and the creator of all material things. He is the
" earliest writer to whom this opinion can be traced. He ascribes his knowledge of it, not to the
" Scriptures, but to the special favour of God." *But Justin is the very earliest admitted genuine
Christian writer whom we have*, not supposed to be inspired, and it seems that he did not attribute
the knowledge of his doctrine to the gospel histories. The reason of this will be explained hereafter.

     Mr. Worsley then proceeds to state that " Modern theologians have defined the three Hypos-
" tases in the Godhead with great precision, though in very different words : but the fathers of
" the Trinitarian Church were neither so positive nor so free from doubt and uncertainty, nor
" were they agreed in their opinions upon it. The very councils were agitated ; nor is that which
" is *now* declared essential to salvation, the ancient Trinity. They who thought the Word an
" attribute of the Father, which assumed a personality at the beginning of the creation, called this
" the generation of the Son ; regarding him still as inferior to the Father, whom they called *the*
" *God* by way of eminence, while, after the example of the old Heathens, they called the Son
" God. This notion of descent implied inferiority, and on that ground was objected to, and the
" Nicene Council, in 325, issued a corrected and improved symbol ; and Christ, instead of only
" Son, was styled God of God, and very God of very God. But even here the equality of the Son
" was not established, the Father by whom he was begotten being regarded as the great fountain
" of life. The investment of wisdom with a personality still implied a time when he was begotten,
" and consequently a time when he was not. From this dilemma an escape was in process of
" time provided by the hypothesis of an eternal generation ; a notion which is self-contradictory.
" The Nicene Fathers, however, did not venture on the term Trinity ; for they had no intention
" of raising their pre-existent Christ to an equality with the Father : and as to the Holy Spirit,
" this was considered as of subordinate rank, and the clauses respecting its procession and being
" worshiped together with the Father and the Son, were not added till the year 381, at the Council
" of Constantinople." [3] I give no opinion on the statement of Mr. Worsley, as it is not my inten-

---

tion to enter into a controversy as to what the Trinity is, but only to give an historical account of it.

2. Dr. Pritchard, in his Analysis of Egyptian Mythology, (p. 271,) describes the Egyptians to have a Trinity consisting of the *generative*, the *destructive*, and the *preserving* power. Isis answers to Seeva. Iswara, or " LORD," is the epithet of Siva, or Seeva. Osiris, or Ysiris, as Hellanicus wrote the Egyptian name, was the God at whose birth a voice was heard to declare, " that the " Lord of all nature sprang forth to light." Dr. Pritchard again says, (p. 262,) " The oldest " doctrine of the Eastern schools is the system of emanations and the metempsychosis." These two were also essentially the doctrine of the Magi, and of the Jews, more particularly of the sect of the Pharisees, or, as they ought to be called, of the Persees.[1] פרס *Prs*,[2] Mr. Maurice[3] observes, that the doctrines of *Original Sin* and that man *is a fallen creature*, are to be found both in the religion of Brahma and Christ, and that it is from this, that the pious austerities and works of supererogation by the Fakirs and Yogees of the former are derived. The doctrine of the Metempsychosis was held by most of the very early fathers, and by all the Gnostic sects, at one time, beyond all doubt, the largest part of the Christian world. Beausobre thought that the transmigration of souls was to be met with in the New Testament. He says,[4] " We find some " traces of this notion even in the New Testament, as in St. Luke xvi. 23, where there is an ac- " count of the abode of departed souls, conformable to the Grecian philosophy; and in St. John " ix. 2, where we find allusion to the pre-existence and transmigration of souls." The works of supererogation and purgatory of the Romish Church both come from this source. A celebrated modern apologist for Christianity believed the metempsychosis.

The God Oromasdes was undoubtedly the Supreme God of the Persians, but yet the religion was generally known by the name of the religion of Mithra, the Mediator or Saviour.

In the same way in India the worship of the *first* person in their Trinity is lost or absorbed in that of the *second*, few or no temples being found dedicated to Brahma; so among the Christians, the worship of the *Father* is lost in that of the *Son*, the Mediator and Saviour. We have abundance of churches dedicated to the second and third persons in the Trinity, and to saints, and to the Mother of God, but none to the Father.[5] We find Jesus constantly called *a Son*, or as (according to the Unitarians) the Trinitarians choose to mistranslate the Greek, *the Son* of God. In the same way, Plato informs us, that Zoroaster was said to be " the son of Oromasdes or Ormis- " das, which was the name the Persians gave to the Supreme God"—therefore he was *the Son of God.*[6]

Jesus Christ is called the Son of God: no doubt very justly, if the Evangelist John be right, for he says, (ch. i. ver. 12,) that every one who receives the gospel, every one, in fact, who believes in God the Creator, has power to become a Son of God. Ormusd, in Boundehesch, says, " My " name is the principle (le principe) and the centre of all things: my name is, He who is, who is " all, and who preserves all."[7]

As the Jews had their sacred writings to which they looked with profound respect, so had the Persians: and so they continue to have them to this day. Mr. Moyle[8] has endeavoured to discredit the genuineness of these writings, by stating " that they contain facts and doctrines mani- " festly taken from the gospels." It is probable that these writings are no more the writings of

[1] The Pharisees were merely Parsees, (the Jews pronounced P like PH or F,) persons who intermingled Magian notions (acquired during the captivity) with the law of Moses: hence a peculiar propriety in *child of fire*, νἱω γεννης, Matt. xxiii. 15; Sup. to Palæromaica, pp. 63, 100.

[2] Parkhurst in Voce, p. 594; Beaus. Int. pp. 16, 132.   [3] Ind. Ant. Vol. V. p. 195.   [4] Int. p. 16.
[5] See Maur. Ind. Ant. Vol. V. p. 87.   [6] Cud. B. i. Ch. iv. p. 287.
[7] Notes to Creuzer's Religions de l'Antiquité, by Guigniault, p. 670.   [8] Works, Vol. II. p. 57.

Zoroaster, or of a man who lived five or six hundred or a thousand years before Cyrus, than that the Jewish Pentateuch is the writing of Moses. Yet they are probably partly his or his compilation, in the same way that the Pentateuch is partly the production or the compilation of Moses. Though these books may not be the writing of Zoroaster, they are the received sacred books of the Magi, the same as the books of the Pentateuch are of the Jews, and their genuineness is entitled to equal respect. It was, perhaps, on account of these matters, that Dr. Hyde's translations of the Persian works never went to press.

3. The doctrine of the Trinity is first to be met with to the North-east of the Indus, and it may be traced Westwards to the Greek and Latin nations; but the two latter seem almost to have lost sight of it as a national or vulgar doctrine; indeed, among the multitude in them, nothing half so rational is to be found. It seems to have been confined to the philosophers, such as Plato —but whether as a secret doctrine or mystery may admit of doubt.

Whether the doctrine of the Trinity formed a part of the Christian religion has been disputed almost from its earliest period, by a great variety of sects, with a degree of bitterness and animosity hardly to be equalled in the history of the world. If the question had been of vital importance to the religion, or, which is of equal consequence in the estimation of too many, had involved the continuance of the hierarchy or tithing system, instead of being merely an idle speculation, its truth or falsity could not have been contested with greater virulence. Several considerable sects affirm, that it was introduced by some of the early fathers from the school of Plato : this others as strongly deny. Mr. Maurice, who being a Churchman is, of course, on the Trinitarian side, candidly allows that it existed in the doctrines of the Jews, and of all the other Asiatic nations from the most remote antiquity. But so far from seeing any difficulty in this, he concludes from it, that it must have been revealed by God to Adam, or to Noah, or to Abraham, or to somebody else, and from thence he most triumphantly concludes that it is true. The antiquity of the doctrine he has clearly proved. His conclusion is another affair. If it be satisfactory to his mind, it is all well; a worthy and good man is made happy at very little expense. In Chapter II. Mr. Maurice has brought together a vast variety of facts to prove that the doctrine of the Trinity was generally held by the Gentiles, but they all at last shew its origin to have been the Egyptian Mithraitic or Hindoo school. From this source the Trinity sprang : a doctrine which it is seen may be traced to very remote periods of time, indeed long prior to the time fixed for the existence of the Jews, or probably of Noah : and it passed to them through the medium of the Persians and Egyptians, as it did also to the Greeks : and from them all it passed to the Christians in a later day. As it might have been supposed, it is found not to be altogether, but yet fundamentally, the same, and in fact to possess much more similarity than might have been expected from the eternal law of change to which it was subject, during the time it was travelling through various climates, nations, and languages, for hundreds, indeed thousands, of years. However, in all the great essential parts it is the same. There are the Father, the Creator—the Son, the Preserver or Saviour—and the evil principle or the devil—in his bad character the destroyer, *in his good one the regenerator*; the same three persons as in the Christian Trinity—except that the ignorant monks of the dark ages, not understanding there fined doctrine of the Eternity of Matter, and, that *destruction* was only *reproduction*, divided the third person into *two*—the Destroyer and Regenerator, and thereby, in fact, formed *four* Gods—the Father, the Son, the Holy Ghost, and the Devil.

4. The immediate origin of the complete and correct Christian Trinity, of that peculiar doctrine on which all orthodox persons seem to think their happiness in this life, as well as in that which is to come, actually depends, will now be exhibited on the unquestionable authority of a most unwilling witness, of one of the most learned and orthodox of its priests—the Rev. Mr. Maurice. Speaking of the Trinity in the oracles of Zoroaster, he says, " Since, exclusive of the error of

" placing PRINCIPLES for HYPOSTASES, [1] which was natural enough to an unenlightened Pagan, it is
" impossible for language to be more explicit upon the subject of a divine Triad, or more confor-
" mable to the language of Christian theologers.

Οτε πατρικη μονας εστι,
Ταυαη εστι μονας η δυο γεννα.

" ' Where the *paternal monad* is, that paternal monad amplifies itself, and generates a duality.'
" The word πατρικη, or paternal, here at once discovers to us the two first hypostases, since it
" is a relative term, and plainly indicates a Son. The paternal monad produces a duality, not by
" an act of creation, but by generation, which is exactly consonant to the language of Christianity.
" After declaring that the duad, thus generated, καθηται, *sits* by the monad, and, shining forth
" with intellectual beams, governs all things, that remarkable and often-cited passage occurs :

Παντι γαρ εν κοσμω λαμπει τριας
Ης μονας αρχει.

" ' For a triad of Deity shines forth throughout the whole world, of which a monad is the head.' " [2]
Thus, after describing the PATERNAL MONAD, as he calls it, he describes a DUALITY, and it is
certainly very remarkable that this DUALITY is not produced by creation or emanation, but by
GENERATION ; and is said to SIT by the side of the MONAD, and to govern all things. It is impossible after reading this, not to recollect the words of our creed, in which this doctrine is clearly
expressed : " Begotten of his Father." " Begotten not made." " He sitteth on the right hand
" of the Father." " And shall come again, to judge both the quick and the dead."

Mr. Maurice then adds, " In the very next section of these oracles, remarkable for its singular
" title of ΠΑΤΗΡ και ΝΟΥΣ, or the Father and the Mind, that Father is expressly said ' to
" ' perfect all things, and deliver them over to Νω δευτερω,' the second Mind ; which, as I have
" observed in the early pages of this dissertation, has been considered as allusive to the character
" of the mediatorial and all-preserving Mithra ; but could only originate in theological conceptions
" of a purer nature, and be descriptive of the office and character of a higher MEDIATOR, even the
" eternal ΛΟΓΟΣ. The whole of the passage runs thus :

Παντα γαρ εξετελεσσε ΠΑΤΗΡ, και ΝΩ παρεδωκε
ΔΕΥΤΕΡΩ, ον πρωτον κληζεται παν γενος ανδρων.

" ' That SECOND MIND,' it is added, ' whom the nations of men commonly take for the first.'
" This is, doubtless, very strongly in favour of the two superior persons in the Trinity."

Mr. Maurice goes on to shew that the term *second mind* is used, and is allusive to the *all-preserving Mithra*. He then adds, " The following passage, cited by Proclus from these oracles, is
" not less indubitably decisive in regard to the *third* sacred hypostasis, than the preceding pas-
" sages in regard to the *second* :

" Μετα δε πατρικας Διανοιας Ψυχη εγω ναιω
" Θερμη, ψυχεσσα τα παντα.

" That is, ' In order next to the paternal Mind I Psyche dwell warm, animating all things.'
" Thus, after observing in the first section, the Triad or το θειον, the whole Godhead collectively
" displayed, we here have each distinct HYPOSTASIS separately and clearly brought before our view."

---

[1] This almost alone proves that these were not copies from the Christian doctrines. According to the authors cited
both by Kircher and Stanley, these oracles were originally written in the Chaldee language, and were translated into
Greek. Maurice, Ind. Ant. Vol. IV. p. 258.
[2] Maur. Ind. Ant. Vol. IV. p. 259.

And thus, by this learned priest,[1] not by me, the whole correct Christian Trinity, with its various HYPOSTASES, is shewn to have existed in the religion of Mithra and the Magi, ages before Christ was born.

There is now no resource left to the priests, but to declare these oracles of Zoroaster spurious, which Bishop Synesius, in the fourth century, called *holy oracles*.[2] But Mr. Maurice provides against this, by informing his reader, that he has only availed himself of such passages in these oracles as have been quoted by such men as Porphyry, Damascius, and other Greek writers unfavourable to Christianity, and such as have a marked similitude to the ancient tenets of India, Persia, and Egypt;[3] and which, therefore, cannot be modern forgeries. The existence in these oracles of such passages as have been cited, is, the author believes, the only circumstance on which the priests have determined that they are spurious. They have said, These passages must have been extracted from the gospel histories, therefore the books containing them must be spurious. It never once occurred to them, that the gospel histories might copy from the oracles, or that they might have both drawn from a common source. And it also never occurred to them, that the fact of their quotation by old authors proves that they must have existed before the gospels. In pointing out this circumstance Mr. Maurice has really great merit for his candour and honesty. I believe there are very few priests who would not have found an excuse to themselves, for omitting to point out the conclusive and damning fact.

Plutarch[4] says, " Zoroaster is said to have made a *threefold* distribution of things : to have " assigned the first and highest rank to Oromasdes, who, *in the oracles*, is called the Father; " the lowest to Ahrimanes; and the middle to Mithras; who, in the *same oracles*, is called " τον δευτερον Νῦν, the second Mind." As Mr. Maurice says,[5] Plutarch, born in the first century, cannot have copied this from a Christian forgery. Besides, he expressly says it is taken from the oracles—herein going very far to confirm the genuineness of the oracles; indeed, he actually does confirm it, in those parts where the quotations are found.

This doctrine of the oracles is substantially the same as that of Plato. It was taken from the Hymns of Orpheus, which we now possess, and which Mr. Parkhurst allows are the very same that were revered by the ancient Greeks as his, and, as such, were used in their solemn ceremonies. He proves this by a passage from Demosthenes.[6] In the Pythagorean and Platonic remains, written long anterior to the Christian æra, all the dogmas of Christianity are to be found. Witness the Δημιεργος or Ζευς Βασιλευς; the δευτερος Θεος, or second God; δευτερος Νυς, or second Mind; the Μιθρας μεσιτης, or mediatorial Mithra; and γεννητος Θεος, or generated God, begotten not made. Again, the ψυχη κοσμε, or soul of the world; i. e. the רוח *ruh* or spiritus, of Osiris and Brahma, *in loto arbore sedentem super aquam*, brooding on the waters of the deep ; the Θειος Λογος, or divine Word, verbum, which Jesus announced to his mother that he was, immediately on his birth, as recorded in the Gospel of his Infancy.[7]

Upon the Logos, Bishop Marsh, in his Michaelis, says, " Since, therefore, St. John has adopted " several other terms which were used by the Gnostics, we must conclude that he derived also " the term Λογος from the same source. If it be further asked, Whence did the Gnostics derive " this use of the expression, ' WORD'? I answer, that they derived it most probably from the " Oriental or Zoroastrian philosophy, from which was borrowed a considerable part of the Mani- " chean doctrines. In the Zendavesta, we meet with a being called ' *the Word*,' who was not

---

[1] Maurice, Ind. Ant. Vol. IV. p. 267.   [2] Ibid. p. 262.   [3] Ibid. p. 291.

[4] De Iside et Osiride, p. 370.   [5] Vol. IV. p. 367.

[6] See his note in voce שם *sm*, XI.   [7] Maur. Ind. Scep. Conf. pp. 53 and 139.

" only prior in existence, but gave birth to Ormuzd, the creator of good; and to Ahriman, the
" creator of evil. It is true, that the work which we have at present under the title of Zendavesta,
" is not the ancient and genuine Zendavesta; yet it certainly contains many ancient and genuine
" Zoroastrian doctrines. It is said, likewise, that the Indian philosophers have their Λογος,
" which, according to their doctrines, is the same as the Μονογενης."

In reply to this, attempts will be made to shew that the Λογος of John is different from the
Oriental Logos : all mere idle, unmeaning verbiage, fit only for those described by Eusebius, who
wish to be deceived : the doctrines as well as the terms are *originally* the same, in defiance of the
ingenuity of well-meaning devotees to hide from themselves the sources whence they are derived.
The variation is not greater than might be expected from change of place, of language, and lapse
of time.

Eusebius acknowledges that the doctrines of the Christians, as described in the first chapter of
John, are perfectly accordant with those of the Platonists, who accede to every thing in it, until
they come to the sentence, *Et verbum caro factum est.* This seems to be almost the only point
in which the two systems differed. The philosophers could not bring themselves to believe that
the Logos, in the gross and literal sense of the Christians, quitted the bosom of God, to undergo
the sorrowful and degrading events attributed to him. This appeared to them to be a degradation
of the Deity. Eusebius allows, what cannot be denied, that this doctrine existed long anterior to
Plato; and that it also made part of the dogmas of Philo and other Hebrew doctors. He might
have added also, had he known it, of the priests of Egypt, and of the philosophers of India.

The origin of the *verbum caro factum est*, we shall presently find in the East. It was not new,
but probably as old as the remainder of the system. Its *grossness well enough suited such men
as Justin, Papias, and Ireneus.[1] For the same reason that it suited them, it was not suitable to
such men as Plato and Porphyry.

In the doctrines of the Hindoos and Persians, as it has already been stated, the third person in
the Trinity is called both the Destroyer and the Regenerator. Although in the Christian Trinity
the *Destroyer* is lost sight of, yet the *Regenerator* is found in the Holy Ghost. The neophite is
said to be regenerate, or born again, by means of this holy spiritus or mind. Plutarch says, that
Mithras or Oromasdes was frequently taken for the το θειον, or whole deity, and that Mithras is
often called the second mind. " Whereupon he observes, how great an agreement there was
" betwixt the Zoroastrian and the Platonic Trinity, they differing in a manner only in words!" [2]
This second mind is evidently the Holy Ghost of the Christians, so accurately described above in
the oracles of Zoroaster, the רוח *ruh* of the second verse of Genesis, which moved, or more correctly brooded, (see Fry's Dictionary,) upon the face of the waters. This, in sacred writ, is often
called יהוה רוח *Ieue ruh*, or אלהים רוח *Aleim ruh*. The words Ieue and Aleim not being in regimine,
which would make it the Spirit of Aleim, or of Jehovah, but being in the nominative case, they
make it the *Ieue ruh* or *Aleim ruh*.

The figure in the Hindoo caves (whose date cannot be denied to be long anterior to the time of
Moses) of the second person, Cristna, having his foot bitten by the serpent, whose head he is
bruising, proves the origin of Genesis.

There can be no longer any reasonable doubt that it came from India, and as the Christian Trinity is to be found in its first chapter, it raises, without further evidence, a strong presumption

---

[1] These, the early fathers of Christianity, believed, that persons were raised from the dead *sæpissime*; that Jesus
would come, before that generation passed away, to reign upon earth for a thousand years; and, that girls were frequently pregnant by demons.

[2] Cudworth, Book i. Ch. iv. p. 289.

that, that also came from India. By the word אלהים *Aleim*, the το Θειον, or whole Deity, or Christian Trinity, is meant. By the word ראשית *rasit*, the *first* Emanation or Æon, Wisdom or the Logos Is meant, and by the word רוח *ruh*, the Spirit of God, the *second* mind, the second emanation, the *third* person in the Trinity is meant—forming altogether the whole Godhead, *three* persons and *one* God.

5. Macrobius, in his Commentary on the Dream of Scipio, (a work of Cicero's,) which he explains by the great principles of the philosophy of the Pythagoreans and Platonists, has given in the clearest manner, in his account of the Trinity of the Gentiles, a description of the Triad or Trinity of the orthodox,—the triple distinction of God the Father, of his Logos, and of the Spiritus, with a filiation similar to that which exists in the theology of the Christians, and an idea of their unity inseparable from that of the Creator. It seems, in reading it, as if we were listening to a Christian Doctor, who was teaching us how the Spiritus proceeds, and the Son is engendered from the Father, and how they both remain eternally attached to the Paternal unity, notwithstanding their action on the intellectual and visible world. The following is in substance what Macrobius says.[1] This learned theologian distinguishes first, after Plato, the God Supreme, the first God, whom he calls with the Greek philosophers τ' Αγαθον, *the Good*, par excellence, the First Cause. He places afterward his *Logos, his intelligence*, which he calls *Mens* in Latin, and Νως in Greek,[2] which contains the original ideas of things, or *the* ideas—intelligence born and produced from the Supreme God. He adds, that they are above the human reason, and cannot be comprehended but by images and similitudes. Thus, above the corporeal being or matter, either celestial or terrestrial, he establishes the divinity, of which he distinguishes three degrees, Deus, Mens, and Spiritus. God, says he, has engendered from himself by the superabundant fecundity of his Majesty, *Mens* or Mind, with the Greeks Νως or Λογος. Macrobius then describes an immense graduated chain of beings, commencing with the First Cause, to be born or produced from itself. He says that the three first links of this immense chain are the Father, his *Logos*, Νως, *Mens*, and *Anima* or *Spiritus Mundi;* or, in the Christian phraseology, the Father, Son, and Holy Spirit, the principles of all things, and placed above all created beings. After this he goes on to explain, in exact Christian style of language, the manner in which the Spirit *proceeds*, and in which the Son is *begotten—engendered* by the Father. If a trifling difference can be discovered between the doctrine of the Pagan Macrobius and that of the orthodox Christian, it is not so great as that which may be met with between the doctrines or opinions of different sects of even orthodox Christians upon this subject. Surely a greater resemblance need not be desired between the Platonic and Christian Trinities.

Upon the Trinity of Plato, M. Dupuis observes, that all these abstract ideas, and these subdivisions of the first *Unity*, are not new; that Plato is not the author of them; that Parmenides before him had described them; that they existed long anterior to Plato; that this philosopher had learned them in Egypt and the schools of the East, as they might be seen in the writings of Mercury Trismegistus and Jamblicus, which contain a summary of the theology of the Egyptians, and a similar theory of abstractions. Marsilius Ficinus has well observed, that the system of three principles of the theology of Zoroaster and the Platonicians, had the greatest similarity with those of the Christians, and that the latter philosophy was founded upon the former. He might have said, that it was not only *similar*, but in reality the same. The curious reader will do well to consult the beautiful and luminous essay of M. Dupuis, *Sur tous les Cultes*, on this subject; he will find himself amply repaid for his trouble.

---

[1] Macrob. Som. Scip. Lib. i. Cap. ii.—vi.   [2] Heb. *Rasit*, Wisdom.

For proofs that the Grecians worshiped a Trinity in Unity, the reader may consult the Classical Journal, Vol. IV. p. 89. It is there shewn that their Trinity was the JUPITER (that is, the Iao) MACHINATOR.

Speaking of the doctrine of the Chaldeans, Thomas Burnet says,[1] " In prima ordine est Su- " prema TRIAS. Sic philosophatur Psellus." Though he gives no account of what this Trias consisted, there is not much room to doubt that it was the Hindoo, Zoroustrian, Platonic Triad.

Mercury was called Triceps; Bacchus Triambus; Diana Triformis; and Hecate Tergemina.

Tergeminamque Hecatem, tria virginis ora Dianæ.[2]

ΣΩΤΕΙΡΑ occurs as a title of Diana on the brass coins of Agathocles.[3]

Plutarch[4] says, διο και Μιθρην Περσαι τον Μεσιτην ονομαζεσι. Orpheus also calls Bacchus Μισης Mediator, the same as Mithra of the Persians.[5] Proserpine had three heads; the Triglaf of the Vandals had also three heads; and Mithras was called Τριπλασιος.

The Trimurti was the Trimighty of the Saxons, the Trimégas of the Greeks, and the Ter-magnus of the Latins.[6] The Trinity is equally found amongst the Druids of Ireland in their Taulac Fen Molloch.[7]

Navarette, in his account of China,[8] says, " This sect (of Foe) has another idol they call " SANPAO. It consists of *three*, equal in all respects. This, which has been represented as an " image of the most blessed Trinity, is exactly the same with that which is on the high altar of " the monastery of the Trinitarians at Madrid. If any Chinese whatsoever saw it, he would say " the SAN PAO of his country was worshiped in these parts."[9]

I must now beg my reader to turn to Book I. Chapter II. Sect. 4, and read what I have there said respecting the material or Pantheistic Trinity, endeavoured to be fixed upon Plato and the Orphic and Oriental philosophers, and I think he must be perfectly satisfied of the improbability that the persons who held the refined and beautiful system which I have developed, could ever have entertained a belief that the Sun, the Moon, and the Earth, were the creators or formers of themselves.

6. As the whole, or nearly the whole, of the ceremonies of the Jews were borrowed from their Gentile neighbours, it would be very extraordinary if their most important doctrine of the Trinity had not been found in the Jewish religion. I shall, therefore, add several more authorities to those already laid before my reader, in Book II. Ch. II. Sect. 5, and particularly that *of the cele-* brated Philo.

Mr. Maurice[10] says, that the first three sephiroth of the Jewish cabala consist of *first* the Omnipotent Father; *second* Divine Wisdom; and *third* the *Binah* or Heavenly Intelligence, whence the Egyptians had their *CNEPH*, and Plato his Νες δημιεργος. But this demiourgos is supposed to be the Creator, as we have before seen that he must necessarily be, if he be the Destroyer. Thus some of the early Christians confounding these fine metaphysical distinctions, and at a loss how to account for the origin of evil, supposed the world to be created by a wicked demiourgos. The confusion arising from the description of *three* in *one*, and *one* in *three*—the community of Persons and unity of Essence—the admitted mysterious nature of the Trinity, and the difficulty, by means of common language, of explaining and of reconciling things apparently irreconcilable, may nevertheless be easily accounted for. On the subject of the Destroyer Mr.

---

[1] Cap. iv. p. 29.   [2] Æneid, iv. 511; Maur. Hind. Ant. Vol. IV. p. 238; Parkhurst, p. 347.

[3] Payne Knight, Essay, Gr. Al. Sect. v. p. 105.   [4] De Iside et Osiride, p. 43.

[5] Stukeley, Palæog. Sac. No. I. p. 54.   [6] D'Ancarville, p. 95.   [7] See Celtic Druids, Ch. v. Sect. xix.

[8] Book ii. Ch. x., and Book vi. Ch. xi.   [9] Parkhurst, p. 348.

[10] Hind. Ant. Vol. IV. pp. 183, 184.

Maurice says, [1] " I must again repeat, that it would be, in the highest degree, absurd to continue
" to affix the name of Destroyer, to their third hypostasis in the triad, [2] when it is notorious, that
" the Brahmins deny that any thing can be destroyed, and insist that a change alone, in the form
" of objects and their mode of existence, takes place. One feature, therefore, in that character,
" hostile to our system, upon strict examination, vanishes." He then shews, from the Sephir
Jetzirah, that the three superior sephiroths of the Jewish cabala were invariably considered by
the *ancient Jews* in a very different light from the other seven; that the first three were regarded
as PERSONALITIES, but the last seven only as *attributes*. [3]

Rabbi Simeon Ben Jochai [4] says, " Come and see the mystery of the word Elohim : there are
" *three degrees*, and each degree by itself alone, and yet, notwithstanding, they are all one, and
" *joined together* in one, and cannot be divided from each other." This completely justifies
what I have formerly said, respecting the words בא *al* and אלהים *aleim*, having a reference to the
Trinity.

Priestley says, " But Philo, the Jew, went before the Christians in the personification of the
" Logos, and in this mode of interpreting what is said of it in the Old Testament. For he calls
" this divine word a second God, and sometimes attributes the creation of the world to this second
" God, thinking it below the majesty of the great God himself. He also calls this personified
" attribute of God his πρωτογονος, or his firstborn, and the image of God. He says that he is
" neither unbegotten, like God, nor begotten, as we are, but the middle between the two extremes.
" We also find that the Chaldee paraphrasts of the Old Testament often render *the word of God*,
" as if it were a being distinct from God, or some angel who bore the name of God, and acted by
" deputation from him." [5]

In reply to this I shall be told that Philo Platonized or was a Platonist. To be sure he was;
because recondite, cabalistic, esoteric Judaism, was the same as Platonism. It would have been
as correct, probably, to have said that Plato Hebraized : for as it is evident that the Israelites
held the doctrine of the Trinity, where was it so likely for him to obtain it as from them ? Philo
was a Jew of elevated rank, great learning, and the highest respectability ; the very man to whom
we have a right to look for the real doctrines, both esoteric and exoteric of the Israelites : and we
find him maintaining all the doctrines of the Platonic and Oriental Trinity—doctrines held by the
nearest neighbours of the Jews, both on the East and West, and from whom Mr. Spencer has
shewn, that they took almost all their rites and ceremonies. I contend, therefore, that the doctrines
taught by Philo afford the strongest presumption that these were also the doctrines of the Jews.

Of Orpheus, who is said to have brought the knowledge of the Trinity into Greece, very little
is known. But Damascius, Περι Αρχων, giving an account of the Orphic theology, among other
things acquaints us, that Orpheus introduced τριμορφον Θεον, a Triform Deity. [6] This was the
Platonic philosophy above described.

Of this person Mr. Payne Knight [7] says, " The history of Orpheus is so confused, and
" obscured by fable, that it is impossible to obtain any certain information concerning him. He
" appears to have been a Thrasian, and to have introduced his philosophy and religion into Greece;
" viz. plurality of worlds, and the true solar system; nor could he have gained this knowledge
" from any people of which history has preserved any memorial : for we know of none among
" whom science had made such a progress, that a truth so remote from common observation, and
" so contradictory to the evidence of unimproved sense, would not have been rejected, as it was

---

[1] Vol. IV. p. 388.   [2] He here alludes to the Hindoos.   [3] Maur. Ind. Ant. Vol. IV. p. 182.
[4] Comment. on the 6th Sec. of Leviticus.   [5] Priestley, Cor. Christ. Sect. ii.
[6] Maur. Ind. Ant. Vol. IV. p. 336.   [7] On Priapus, vide note, p. 33.

" by all the sects of Greek philosophers, except the Pythagoreans, who rather revered it as an
" article of faith, than understood it as a discovery of science.

" Thrace was certainly inhabited by a civilized nation at some remote period; for when Philip
" of Macedon opened the gold mines in that country, he found that they had been worked before
" with great expense and ingenuity, by A PEOPLE WELL VERSED IN MECHANICS, OF WHOM NO
" MEMORIALS WHATEVER ARE EXTANT." I think memorials of these people may be found in
the Pyramids, Stonehenge, the walls of Tyryns, and the Treasury of Messina.

7. The following extract from Mr. Faber's work on the Origin of Heathen Idolatry, exhibits a
pretty fair proof how very general was the ancient doctrine of the Trinity among the Gentiles:—
" Among the Hindoos we have the triad of Brama-Vistnou-Siva, springing from the monad
" Brahm : and it is acknowledged, that these personages appear upon earth at the commencement
" of every new world, in the human form of Menu and his three sons. Among the votaries of
" Buddha we find the self-triplicated Buddha declared to be the same as the Hindoo Trimurti.
" Among the Buddhic sect of the Jainists, we have the triple Jina, in whom the Trimurti is
" similarly declared to be incarnate. Among the Chinese, who worship Buddha under the name of
" Fo, we still find this God mysteriously multiplied into three persons, corresponding with the
" three sons of Fo-hi, who is evidently Noah. Among the Tartars of the house of Japhet, who
" carried off into their Northern settlements the same ancient worship, we find evident traces of a
" similar opinion in the figure of the triple God seated on the Lotos, as exhibited on the famous
" Siberian medal in the imperial collection at Petersburgh : and if such a mode of representation
" required to be elucidated, we should have the exposition furnished us in the doctrine of the
" Jakuthi Tartars, who, according to Strahremberg, are the most numerous people of Siberia :
" for these idolaters worship a triplicated deity under the three denominations of Artugon, and
" Schugo-tangon, and Tangara. This Tartar god is the same even in appellation with the Tanga
" Tanga of the Peruvians : who, like the other tribes of America, seem plainly to have crossed
" over from the North-eastern extremity of Siberia. Agreeably to the mystical notion so familiar
" to the Hindoos, that the self-triplicated great Father yet remained but one in essence, the
" Peruvians supposed their Tanga-tanga to be one in three, and three in one : and in consequence
" of the union of Hero worship with the astronomical and material systems of idolatry, they vene-
" rated the sun and the air, each under three images and three names. The same opinions
" equally prevailed throughout the nations which lie to the West of Hindostan. Thus the
" Persians had their Ormusd, Mithras,[1] and Abriman : or, as the matter was sometimes repre-
" sented, their self-triplicating Mithras. The Syrians had their Monimus, Aziz and Ares. The
" Egyptians had their Emeph, Eicton, and Phtha. The Greeks and Romans had their Jupiter,
" Neptune, and Pluto ; three in number though one in essence, and all springing from Cronus, a
" fourth, yet older God. The Canaanites had their Baal-Spalisha or self-triplicated Baal. The
" Goths had their Odin, Vile, and Ve : who are described as the three sons of Bura, the offspring
" of the mysterious cow. And the Celts had their three bulls, venerated as the living symbols of
" the triple Hu or Menu. To the same class we must ascribe the triads of the Orphic and
" Pythagorean and Platonic schools : each of which must again be identified with the imperial
" triad of the old Chaldaic or Babylonian philosophy. This last, according to the account which is
" given of it by Damascius, was a triad shining throughout the whole world, over which presides a
" Monad."[2]

---

[1] Voss., de Orig. et Prog. Idol. Lib. ii. Cap. ix., says, that the word Mither, in Persian, means Lord, that Mithras
is derived from Mither. A Mediator is called Mithras in Persian. Mithras also means *love, pity.*

[2] Book vi. Ch. ii. p. 470.

Again he says, " To the great Triad of the Gentiles, thus springing from a Monad, was ascribed " the creation of the world, or rather its renovation after each intervening deluge. It was likewise " supposed to be the governing power and the intellectual soul of the universe. In short, all the " attributes of Deity were profanely ascribed to it. This has led many to imagine that the " Pagans did fundamentally worship the true God, and that even from the most remote antiquity " they venerated the Trinity in Unity." [1]

Thus it is evident, from the Rev. Mr. Faber's admission, that a Being called a Trinity, three persons and one God, was worshiped by all the ancient nations of the earth. He very properly says *to the same class we must ascribe the triads of the Orphic, Pythagorean, and Platonic schools.*

The school of Plato has been generally looked to for the origin of the Christian Trinity, but, as we have seen, it would be more correct to look to the oracles of Zoroaster. Christianity may have drawn from Platonism, but there can be no doubt that Plato had drawn from the oracles of the East. The Second Mind, or the Regenerator, correctly the Holy Ghost, was in the oracles of Zoroaster, and will be shewn to have been in the baptismal service of the Magi. And " the many" to whom Mr. Faber alludes, as believing that the Gentiles venerated the Trinity in Unity, believed what was perfectly true. There can be no doubt that the Heathens adored the Trinity before the Christians, and did not copy it from Christianity. *If either copied, the Christians must have copied from their Heathen predecessors.* But all this has a strong tendency to prove, that what Ammonius Saccas said was true, namely, that the religions of the Christians and the Gentiles were the same, when stripped of the meretricious ornaments with which the craft of priests had loaded them.

8. Before I quit the subject of the Persian doctrines it may not be irrelevant again to observe, that the ancient philosophers, meditating upon the nature of the universe, and confining their theories and systems to the knowledge which they derived from experience or through the medium of their senses, the only mode by which knowledge or ideas can be acquired, discovered that they had no experience of the destruction of matter; that when it appears to the superficial observer to be destroyed, it has only changed its mode of existence; that what we call destruction, is only reproduction or regeneration. On this account it is that we always find the *Destroyer* united with the Creator, and also with the Preserver or Saviour, as one person. Upon this curious philosophical and very true principle, an infinite variety of fictions have been invented, by the sportive genius of poets, or the craft of priests. But the simple philosophical principle was at the bottom of them all; and it was that only which philosophers believed. God only knows whither the vanity of the moderns has carried them, or will carry them; but the ancients confined their wisdom or knowledge, in this instance at least, within the compass of their ideas—the limit of real knowledge; and as, in their present state of existence, they could not receive the idea of the annihilation of matter through the medium of the senses, they could not form an idea of it at all; and consequently could not receive as an article of faith that of which they must necessarily remain in profound ignorance. Matter might be created from nothing, or it might not be created; their senses told them it existed; but to them it was unknown whether it had *ever not existed*; and they did not pretend to decide, as an article of faith, the question—for in its very nature it was not possible to decide it by human means. Not so the wise Christian : he and his priest laugh at the ignorance of the ancient philosopher; and at once declare that matter *was* created; and that they have a perfect idea respecting its creation, which they can by no possibility have received from experience, or through the medium of the senses. With the ancient philosopher the Author confesses his ignorance. The Oriental philosopher, who penned the first verse of

Genesis, was too wise to give an opinion upon the subject. He merely says, " God formed (or re-formed) the earth ;" the question of its creation *from nothing,* or *its eternity,* he did not touch.

Thus the reader sees that from the caves of Upper India, Persia, and Egypt, the doctrine of the Christian Trinity was undoubtedly drawn. But though these countries were the places where this doctrine flourished many ages before Christianity ; yet it has been supposed that it was from the Platonists of Greece, who had learned it from these three nations, that the Christians immediately drew their doctrine. And if the keen eye of a modern Thomas Aquinas should discover some minute metaphysical variation between the ancient and modern systems, this will only be what we may expect to arise from the lapse of ages, and the difficulty of conveying ideas, so very abstruse, from one language into another. Nor will it be very surprising if the profound doctrines of philosophers, like Plato and Pythagoras, should happen to have been misunderstood by such philosophers as Papias and Ireneus. And if this should prove to have been the fact, the philosopher of the present day may not think the modern deviation any improvement upon the system.

I shall add no more at present on the subject of the Trinity or Cabala. I shall return to it very often; and it will not be till I come nearly to the end of this volume of my work, that I shall unfold the whole of what I have to disclose on this subject; when several apparent inconsistencies will be reconciled.

BOOK IV

CHAPTER I

Proper mode of Viewing the Religion—Life of Cristna—Subject continued. Maturea—Sir W. Jones's Explanation of the Circumstances, and Mr. Maurice's Admissions—Reflections on the above—Solemn Considerations of Mr. Maurice's in Explanation—Digression on the Black colour of Ancient Gods; of the Etymology of the Nile and Osiris—Subject continued—Christ Black, an Answer to a solemn Consideration—Other solemn Considerations—Observations on Mr. Maurice's solemn Considerations—Mr. Maurice's Pamphlets—Back Reckonings. Maturea—Bryant and Dr. A. Clarke on this Mythos

1. HAVING shewn that the Hindoos and Persians had certain of the leading articles of what is usually called the Christian religion, some thousands of years, probably, before the time assigned to JESUS,—the actual history of the birth and life of the Second Person of the Trinity, or of the Saviour of the Romish or modern Christian religion, will now be given; from which it will be evident to the reader whence most of the corruptions in the histories of the gospel of Jesus have been derived.

When a person takes a view of the whole of what has constituted the Christian system, at any period of the time during which it has existed, if he mean to form a correct idea of it, he must not confine his observation to any one or two of the divisions of which it consists at the time of his survey, but he must take, as it were, a bird's eye view of it. He must bring all its numerous subdivisions within the field of his telescopic vision. No doubt each of them will dispute the propriety of this, because there is not one of them, however small and contemptible it may be, which will not maintain that *it* is the sole and true religion, all the others being merely heresies or corruptions. To this, however, the philosopher, inquiring only for the truth, will pay no attention: each is an integral part, and the union of the whole forms the religion of that day; though it is very possible that it may differ essentially from that taught by Jesus, or from the religion of the present day.

If a person be disposed to dispute the doctrine here laid down, I would beg to ask him what he would do if he undertook to make a survey of the religion of India. Would he consider only the religion of the followers of Vishnu; or of that of the followers of Cali; or of that of the followers of Buddha? No: he would consider each of these as parts of the grand whole; all derived from one common source; and reason upon them accordingly. In the same manner he will consider the sects of Christians, when he takes a philosophical view of the religion. In carrying this intention into effect, I shall, of course, often have occasion to notice the writings of Christians of former times, but which are now little known. Of this kind are what are called the Apocryphal Gospels. This being the correct mode of viewing the religion, it seems evident that if a general corruption have pervaded all its sects, we must not expect to find the cause or origin of this corruption applicable to *one* sect only; but, on the contrary, we shall find it apply in a very considerable degree to the whole of them.

It will not apply alone to the gospel of Paul, or of Montanus, or of Marcion, or of the Egyptians, but it will apply to them all indiscriminately, orthodox and heterodox, without any partiality to any one of them. But it cannot be reasonably expected that the exact place should be pointed out where every one of the facts stated in the whole of the numerous gospels, or histories of the religion, came from. The only question will be, whether sufficient be pointed out to convince the mind of the impartial reader of the identity of the systems, or of the truth of the proposition meant to be established.

It will now be shewn, in the first place, that from the history of the second person of the Indian Trinity, many of the particulars of the gospel histories of the Christians have been compiled.

The book called the Bhagavat Geeta, which contains the life of Cristna, is allowed to be one of the most distinguished of the puranas, for its sublimity and beauty. It lays claim to nearly the highest antiquity that any Indian composition can boast: and the Rev. Mr. Maurice, a very competent judge, allows, that there is ample evidence to prove that it actually existed nearly four thousand years ago. Sir William Jones says, "That the name of Chrishna, and the general outline " of his story, were long anterior to the birth of our Saviour, and probably to the time of Homer, " we know very certainly." In fact, the sculptures on the walls of the most ancient temples,—temples by no one ever doubted to be long anterior to the Christian æra—as well as written works equally old, prove, beyond the possibility of doubt, the superior antiquity of the history of Cristna, to that of Jesus. The authority of the unwilling witness, Sir W. Jones, without attempting any other proof of this fact, is enough. But in the course of this work many other corroborating circumstances will be produced, which, independently of his authority, will put the matter beyond question.

2. These observations being premised respecting the Bhagavat Geeta, we will now consider some of the leading facts which are stated in it relating to the God Cristna, Crisna, or Chrishna.[1] These we shall find are copies of the Christian gospel histories, or the Christian gospel histories are copies from them, or they have both been copied from an older mythos.

In the first place, the Cristna of India is always represented as a Saviour or Preserver of mankind, precisely the same as Jesus Christ. While he is thus described as a Saviour, he is also represented to be really the Supreme Being, taking upon himself the state of man: that is, to have become *incarnate in the flesh*, to save the human race, precisely as Jesus is said to have done, by the professors of the orthodox Christian faith. This is the *Verbum caro factum est* of St. John, to which I alluded in Book III. Chap. III. Sect. 4.

As soon as Cristna was born, he was saluted with a chorus of Deutas or Devatas or Angels, with divine hymns, just as it is related of Jesus in the orthodox Gospel of Luke, ch. ii. 13, 14. He was cradled among shepherds, to whom were first made known the stupendous feats which stamped his character with marks of the divinity. The circumstances here detailed, though not literally the same as those related of Jesus, are so nearly the same, that it is evident the one account has been taken from the other. The reader will remember the verse of the gospel history, *And there were shepherds tending their flocks by night.* Luke ii. 8.

Soon after Cristna's birth, he was carried away by night and concealed in a region remote from his natal place, for fear of *a tyrant* whose destroyer it was foretold he would become; and who had, for that reason, ordered all the male children born at that period to be slain. This story is

---

[1] Sir W. Jones always spells the name of this celebrated person Chrishna.

the subject of an immense sculpture in the cave at Elephanta,[1] where the tyrant is represented destroying the children. The date of this sculpture is lost in the most remote antiquity. It must, at the very *latest* period, be fixed at least many *hundred* years previous to the birth of Jesus Christ, as we shall presently see. But with much greater probability *thousands* instead of *hundreds* of years might be assigned to its existence. Cristna was, by the *male* line, of royal descent, though he was actually born in a state the most abject and humiliating—in a dungeon—as Jesus was descended from King David and was born in a cave, used as a stable. The moment Cristna was born, the whole room was splendidly illuminated, and the countenances of his father and mother emitted rays of glory. According to the *Evangelium Infantiæ* " Spelunca repleta erat luminibus, " lucernarum et candelarum fulgorum excedentibus, et *solari luce* majoribus." Cristna could speak as soon as he was born, and comforted his mother, as did the infant Jesus, according to the same gospel history. As Jesus was preceded and assisted by his kinsman, John, so Cristna was preceded by his elder brother, Ram, who was born a little time before him, and assisted him in purifying the world, polluted with demons and monsters. Ram was nourished and brought up by the same foster parents as Cristna. Thus the Gospel of James[2] states, that the prophecy of Zachariah and the supernatural pregnancy of his wife being notorious, Herod suspected that John might be the expected Messiah, and commanded him to be delivered up, in order that he might murder him; but Elizabeth had sent him into the wilderness to his cousin, by which means he escaped. Cristna descended into Hades or Hell, and returned to Vaicontha, his proper paradise. One of his epithets was that of *a good shepherd*, which we know was that of Jesus. After his death, like Jesus Christ, he ascended into heaven.[3] From the glory described above, in the Evangelium Infantiæ, we see the reason why, in all pictures of the Nativity, the light is made to arise from the body of the infant, and why the father and mother are often depicted with glories round their heads.

3. After the birth of Cristna, the Indian prophet Nared, Σοφος, having heard of his fame, visited his father and mother at Gokul, examined the stars, &c., and declared him to be of celestial descent. As Mr. Maurice observes, here is a close imitation of the Magi guided by his star and visiting the Infant in Bethlehem. Cristna was said to have been born at Mathura, (pronounced Mattra,) on the river Jumna, where many of his miracles were performed, *and in which at this day he is held in higher veneration than in any other place in Hindostan.* Mr. Maurice says, " The " Arabic edition of the Evangelium Infantiæ records Matarea, near Hermopolis, in Egypt, to " have been the place where the Infant Saviour resided during his absence from the land of Judæa, " and until Herod died. At this place Jesus is reported to have wrought many miracles: and, " among others, to have produced in that arid region a fountain of fresh water, the only one in " Egypt. Hinc ad Sycamorum illam urbem digressi sunt, quæ hodie Matarea vocatur; et produxit " Dominus Jesus fontem in Matarea, in quo Diva Maria (*Cristna's mother has also the epithet* " Deva *prefixed to her name*) tunicam ejus lavit. Ex sudore autem, qui à Domino Jesu defluxit, " balsamum in illâ regione provenit."[4]

M. Savary says, that at a little distance from Heliopolis is the small village of Matarea, so called because it has a fresh-water spring, the only one in Egypt. This spring has been rendered famous by tradition, which relates that the holy family fleeing from Herod came hither; that the

---

[1] Maur. Ind. Ant. Vol. II. p. 149.   [2] Protevangelium Jacobi, p. 23, apud Fabric., p. 25.

[3] Maur. Ind. Ant.

[4] Evangelium Infan. Arab. et Lat. p. 71, ed. Syke, 1697; Maur. Hist. Vol. II. p. 318; Jones on the Canon, Vol. II. Part III. Ch. xxii.

Virgin bathed the holy child *Jesus* in this fountain; and that much balsam was formerly produced in the neighbourhood.[1]

Eusebius and Athanasius state, that when Joseph and Mary arrived in Egypt, they took up their abode in a city of the Thebais, in which was a superb temple of Serapis. On their going into the temple, all the statues fell flat on their faces to the Infant Saviour. This story is also told by the Evangelium Infantiæ.[2]

After Cristna came to man's estate, one of his first miracles was the cure of a leper. Matthew (in ch. viii. ver. 3) states an early miracle performed by Jesus to have been exactly similar, viz. the cure of a leper. Upon another occasion a woman poured on the head of Cristna a box of ointment, for which he cured her of her ailment. Thus, in like manner, a woman came and anointed the head of Jesus. Matt. xxi. 7.

At a certain time Cristna taking a walk with the other cowherds with whom he was brought up, they chose him for their king, and every one had a place under him assigned to him. Nearly the same story is related of Jesus and his playfellows. At another time, the Infant Jesus declaring himself to be *the good shepherd*, turned all his young companions into sheep; but afterward, at the solicitation of their parents, restored them to their proper form. This is the counterpart of a story of the creation, by Cristna, of new sheep and new cow-boys, when Brahma, to try his divinity, had stolen those which belonged to Nanda's, his father's, farm.[3] To shew his humility and meekness, he condescended to wash the feet of the Brahmins, as Jesus did those of his disciples. John xiii. 5, &c.

Cristna had a dreadful combat with the serpent Calinaga,[4] which had poisoned all the cowherds. In the Apocryphal Gospel above alluded to, the infant Saviour had a remarkable adventure with a serpent, which had poisoned one of his companions.[5]

Cristna was sent to a tutor to be instructed, and he instantly astonished him by his profound learning. In the Gospel of the Infancy it is related, that Jesus was sent to Zaccheus to be taught, and, in like manner, he astonished *him* with his great learning. This also must remind the reader of the disputation in the temple with the Jewish doctors. (Luke ii. 46, 47.) Cristna desired his mother to look into his mouth and she saw all the nations of the world painted in it. The Virgin saw the same in the mouth of Jesus.[6] Mr. Maurice observes that the Gospel of the Infancy is alluded to by Ireneus,[7] which shews that it was among the earliest of the ancient gospel histories.

Finally, Cristna was put to death by being *crucified*; he descended into hell, and afterward ascended into heaven. For further particulars, see Maurice's Ind. Ant. Vol. II. pp. 149, &c. The descent into hades or hell, and the ascent into paradise or heaven, is stated by Mr. Maurice; the crucifixion is not stated by him; but my authority for the assertion I shall adduce presently.

It is impossible for any one to deny the close connexion between the histories of Jesus and of Cristna. We now come to the most important point—how such connexion is to be rendered consistent with the existence of the whole of the Christian system as at present expounded by our priests,—how the priests are to explain it away,—how those men who are so unfortunate as to feel themselves obliged to yield to such *conclusive* evidence can be proved to be what the Rev. Mr. Maurice, in true orthodox strain, calls *impious infidels*.

---

[1] Savary's Travels in Egypt, Vol. I. p. 126.
[2] Vide Euseb. Demon. Evang. Lib. vi. Cap. xx.; Athan. de Incarnat. Verbi, Vol. I. p. 89.
[3] Maurice, Hist. Hind. Vol. II. p. 322.
[4] *Cali* is now the Goddess of a sect in opposition to that of Cristna, and *Naga* means serpent. It is evidently the same as the old English word for serpent—*Hag*.
[5] Hist. Hind. Vol. II. p. 322.   [6] Maur. Bram. Fraud Exposed, p. 114.
[7] Adv. Heres. Lib. i. Cap. xvii. p. 104, ed. fol. 1596.

4. The mode in which Sir W. Jones gets over the difficulty is very easy. Without pretending that he has any variation of manuscripts, or other authority, to justify him, but merely because he finds the facts to be inconsistent with the existence of the whole of the present Christian system, as he chooses to expound it, he asserts the passages containing them to be interpolations from spurious gospels; but, unfortunately for his credit, this, for many reasons, will not obviate the difficulty. It is evident that much of the history is the same as the *orthodox* gospels, as well as of those called *spurious.*

In reference to the opinion of Sir W. Jones, Mr. Maurice says, " For, however happy and " ingenious, as it certainly is, may be the conjecture of Sir W. Jones concerning the interpolation " of the Bramin records from the Apocryphal Gospels, it still affords but a partial explanation of " the difficulty. Many of the Mythological sculptures of Hindostan that relate to the events in " the history of this Avatar, more immediately interesting to the Christian world, being of an age " undoubtedly anterior to the Christian æra, while those sculptures remain unanswerable testi- " monies of the facts recorded, the assertion, unaided by these collateral proofs, rather strengthens " than obviates the objection of the Sceptic. Thus the sculptured figures, copied by Sonnerat, " from one of the oldest pagodas, and engraved in this volume, the one of which represents " Chreeshna dancing on the crushed head of the serpent; and the other, the same personage en- " tangled in its enormous folds, to mark the arduousness of the contest, while the enraged reptile " is seen biting his foot, together with the history of the fact annexed, could never derive their " origin from any information contained in the Spurious Gospels."

Again, Mr. Maurice says, " To return to the more particular consideration of these parts of the " life of Chreeshna, which are above alluded to by Sir William Jones, which have been paralleled " with some of the leading events in the life of our blessed Saviour, and are, in fact, considered by " him as interpolations from the spurious Gospels; I mean more particularly his miraculous birth " at midnight; the chorus of Devatas that saluted with hymns the divine infant as soon as born ; " his being cradled amongst shepherds, to whom were first made known those stupendous feats " that stamped his character with divinity; his being carried away by night, and concealed in a " region remote from the scene of his birth,[1] from fear of the tyrant Cansa, whose destroyer it " was predicted he would prove, and who, therefore, ordered all the male children born at that " period to be slain: his battle, in his infancy, with the dire, envenomed serpent Calija,[2] and " crushing his head with his foot; his miracles in succeeding years; his raising the dead ; his de- " scending to Hades; and his return to Vaicontha, the proper paradise of Veeshnu," &c., &c., &c.

5. Upon the plea of interpolation, which Sir W. Jones has used to account for the extraordinary similarity in the lives of Jesus and of Cristna, and which Mr. Maurice has allowed, *happy and ingenious as it is !* to be altogether unsatisfactory; it may be asked, what could induce the Brah- mins, the most proud, conceited and bigoted of mankind, to interpolate their ancient books; to insert in them extracts from the gospel histories, or sacred books of people very nearly total strangers to them ; very few in numbers, and looked on by them with such contempt, that they would neither eat, drink, nor associate with them (which, if they had done, they would have been contaminated, and ruined by becoming outcasts from their order) ;—people who came as beggars and wanderers soliciting a place of refuge ? It cannot be pretended that the Brahmins wished to make converts; for this is directly contrary to their faith and practice. The books in which these interpolations are found, were obtained from them with the greatest difficulty;

---

[1] And Mr. Maurice might have added, called Mattra or Maturea, the same name as the place to which Christ was carried, according to Christian tradition, as we have already shewn.

[2] Calija, this is another name for the Calinaga, explained in note p. 131.

they have every appearance of very great antiquity; and are found concealed in the recesses of their temples, evidently built many centuries before the Christian æra. And though the books in which they are found are scarce, yet they are sufficiently numerous, and spread over a sufficient extent of country, to render it impossible to interpolate them all, if they had been so disposed. Upon the impossibility of interpolating the old Hindoo books, I shall treat at large hereafter.

But how is the figure in the cave at Elephanta to be acounted for; that *prominent* and *ferocious* figure, as Mr. Maurice calls it, surrounded by slaughtered infants, and holding a drawn sword? If it were only a representation of the evil principle, how came he only to destroy infants; and, as I learn from Mr. Forbes's Oriental Memoirs,[1] those infants, *boys?* He is surrounded by a crowd of figures of men and women, evidently supplicating for the children. This group of figures has been called the Judgment of Solomon: as Mr. Forbes justly says, very absurdly. But, at the same time he admits, that there are many things in these caves which bear a resemblance to prominent features in the Old Testament. Over the head of the principal figure in this group, are to be seen the mitre, the crosier, and the cross—true Christian emblems.

Again Mr. Maurice says, " All these circumstances of similarity are certainly very surprising, " and, upon any other hypothesis than that offered by Sir W. Jones, at first sight, seem very " difficult to be solved. But should that solution, from the allowed antiquity of the name of " Chrisna, and the general outline of his story, confessedly anterior to the birth of Christ, and " probably as old as Homer, as well as the apparent reluctance of the haughty, self-conceited " Brahmin to borrow any part of his creed, or rituals, or legends, from foreigners visiting India, " not be admitted by some of my readers as satisfactory, I have to request their attention to the " following particulars, which they will peruse with all the solemn consideration due to a question " of such high moment."

We will now attend with SOLEMN CONSIDERATION to these particulars, offering such observa- as occur upon each, as they come in order.

But, gentle reader, if you please, we will, as we go along with the Reverend Gentleman, not forget what Lord Shaftsbury so shrewdly observed, *that solemnity is of the essence of imposture.*

" And first with respect to the name of Christna, (for so it must be written to bear the asserted " analogy to the name of Christ,) Mr. Volney, after two or three pages of unparalleled impiety, in " which he resolves the whole life, death, and resurrection, of the Messiah, into an ingenious " allegory, allusive to the growth, decline, and renovation of the solar heat during its annual " revolution; and after asserting that, by the Virgin, his mother, is meant the celestial sign Virgo, " in the bosom of which, at the summer solstice, the sun anciently appeared to the Persian Magi " to rise, and was thus depicted in their astrological pictures, as well as in the Mithraitic caverns; " after thus impiously attempting to mythologize away the grand fundamental doctrines of the " Christian code, our Infidel author adds, that the sun was sometimes called Chris, or Conservator, " that is, the Saviour; and hence, he observes, the Hindoo god Chris-en or Christna, and the " Christian Chris-tos, the son of Mary. Now, whatever ingenuity there may be displayed in the " former part of this curious investigation, into which I cannot now enter, I can confidently " affirm, there is not a syllable of truth in the orthographical derivation; for Chrisna, nor " Chris-en, nor Christna, (as to serve a worthless cause, subversive of civil society, he artfully " perverts the word,) has not the least approach in signification to the Greek word Christos, " anointed, in allusion to the kingly office of the Hebrew Messiah; since this appellative simply " signifies, as we shall presently demonstrate, *black* or *dark blue*, and was conferred on the Indian " God solely on account of his *black complexion.* It has, therefore, no more connexion with the

---

[1] Vol. III. Ch. xxxv. p. 447.

" name of our blessed Saviour, supposed by this writer to be derived from it, than the humble
" Mary of Bethlehem has with the Isis of Egypt, the original Virgo of the Zodiac : or Joseph, as
" there asserted, has with the obsolete constellation of præsepe Jovis, or stable of Jove, as, in his
" rage for derivation, he ridiculously asserts."

Now, upon the observation of Mr. Maurice, relating to the celestial Virgin, and the Virgin
Mary, the reader is requested to suspend his judgment till he comes to my chapter where she is
expressly treated of. With respect to the remainder of his observation on the *colour* of the
Cristna of India, it is replied, that of all the circumstances connected with this subject, there is not
one so curious and striking as this ; nor one so worthy of the attention of the reader. And
though, at first, he may think the Author, in what he is going to say, respecting the *black* colour,
is deviating from the subject, he will in the end find nothing but what is closely connected with it,
and necessary for its elucidation.

7. On the first view, it seems rather an extraordinary circumstance that the statues of the Gods
of the ancients should be represented of a black colour ; or that they should have been made of a
stone as nearly black as it could be obtained. Where the stone could not be obtained quite black,
a stone was often used similar to our blue slate, of a very dark blue colour ; the drapery of the
statue often being of a different, light-coloured stone. It is evident that the intention was to
represent a black complexion ; of this there can be no doubt. The marble statues of Roman
Emperors are often found with the fleshy part black, and the drapery of white or some other
colour.

Eusebius informs us, on the authority of Porphyry, " That the Egyptians acknowledged one
" intellectual Author or Creator of the world, under the name of Cneph ; and that they worshiped
" him in a statue of human form and *dark blue complexion*." Plutarch informs us, " That Cneph
" was worshiped by the inhabitants of the Thebaid ; who refused to contribute any part towards
" the maintenance of the sacred animals, because they acknowledged no mortal God, and adored
" none but him whom they called Cneph, an uncreated and immortal being." The temple of
" Cneph, or Cnuphis, was in the island of Elephantine, on the confines of Egypt and Ethiopia. [1]

In the Evangelical Preparation of Eusebius,[2] is a passage which pretty well proves that the
worship of Vishnu or Cristna was held in Egypt, under the name of Kneph : Τον Δημιουργον
Κνηφ, οἱ Αιγυπτιοι προσαγορευυσιν, την χροιαν εκ κανν μελανος, εχοντα κρατυντα ζωνην
και σκηπτρον (λεγυσιν). " The Egyptians, it is said, represented the Demiurgos Kneph, as of
a blue colour, bordering on black, with a girdle and a sceptre."[3]

Mr. Maurice[4] has observed that the Cneph of Egypt, and the statue of Narayen, in the great
reservoir of Catmandu, are both formed of black marble. Dr. Buchanan states the statue of Juggernaut to be of wood, painted black, with red lips.

Mr. Maurice says, " That Osiris, too, the black divinity of Egypt, and Chreeshna, the sable
" shepherd-God of Mathura, have the striking similitude of character, intimated by Mr. Wilford,
" cannot be disputed, any more than that Chreeshna, from his rites continuing so universally to
" flourish over India, from such remote periods down to the present day, was the prototype, and
" Osiris the mythological copy. Both are renowned legislators and conquerors, contending
" equally with physical and spiritual foes : both are denominated *the Sun* ; both descend to the
" shades and raise the dead."[5]

Again he says, " Now it is not a little remarkable that a dark blue tint, approaching to black,
" as his name signifies, was the complexion of Chreeshna, who is considered by the Hindoos not

---

[1] Pritchard's Anal. of Egypt, Mythol. p. 171.   [2] Lib. iii. p 115.   [3] Class. Journ. No. XXIX. p. 122.
[4] Ant. Ind. Vol. I. Sect. viii.   [5] Hist. Hind. Vol. II. p. 477.

" so much an avatar, as the person of the great Veeshnu himself, in a human form." [1] That is, he was incarnate, or in the flesh, as Jesus was said to be.

For reasons which the reader will soon see, I am inclined to think that Osiris was not the copy of Cristna, but of the earlier God, Buddha.

That by Osiris was meant the Sun, it is now allowed by every writer who has treated on the antiquities of Egypt. Mr. Maurice, as the reader sees, states him to have been black, and that the Mnevis, or sacred bull, of Heliopolis, the symbol of Osiris, was also black. Osiris is allowed, also, to be the Seeva of India, [2] one of the three persons of the Indian God—Bramha, Vishnu or Cristna, and Seeva, of whom the bull of the Zodiac was the symbol.

It is curious to observe the number of trifling circumstances which constantly occur to prove the identity of the Hindoos and Egyptians, or rather the Ethiopians. The word Nile, in the Indian language, means *black*. Dupuis [3] says, " Nilo in Indian signifies black, and it ought " to signify the same in Egyptian; since, whenever the Arabs, the Hebrews, the Greeks, " and the Latins, have wished to translate the word Nil, they have always made use of a word " which in their language signifies black. The Hebrews call it *Sichor*; the Ethiopians, *Nuchul*; " the ancient Latins, *Melo*; the Greeks, *Melas*—all names signifying *black*. The word or name " *Nilos*, then, in Egyptian, presents the same idea as the word Nilo in Indian." But the name of Nile was a modern one, (comparatively speaking,) a translation of the ancient name of this river, which was Siri. Speaking of the word Nile, Tzetzes says, το δε Νειλος νεον εςι. [4]

Selden [5] says, " Sit Osiris, sit Omphis, Nilus, Siris, sive quodcunque aliud ab Hierophantis " usurpatum nomen, ad unum tandem solem antiquissimum gentium Numen redeunt omnia." He says again, " Osiris certe non solum idem Deus erat cum Nilo, verum ipsa nomina Nili et " Osiridis, sublato primo elemento, sunt synonyma. Nam lingua prophetarum שׁיחר schichor est " Nilus, ut doctissimi interpretum volunt, quod שׁיחרי schichori, lingua Æthiopica (ita monet " illustrissimus Scaliger filius) prolatum—in Σειρις aut Σιρις Græca scriptione, transmigravit." See also Parkhurst's *Lex.* שׁיחר pp. 728, 729.

The word Osiris may be a Greek word, composed by the Greeks from their own emphatic article O, and the Hebrew word שׁיחר *shr*, written with their customary termination Οσιρις. The meaning of the Hebrew word is black. And one meaning of the Greek is evidently *the black*, or *the black God*. This is confirmed by Plutarch, in his treatise de Iside et Osiride.

The Nile was often called יאר *iar*, which is the Hebrew word for river, and was probably the Egyptian one also. It was simply *the river* παΓ εξοχην. It was never called Neilos by the Egyptians, but by the Greeks, and that only from the time of Hesiod, in whose writings *it is first so called*. This pretty nearly proves it a translated name. [6] If the author be right in this conjecture, the reason is evident why this word sets etymological inquiries at defiance. Sir W. Jones says, Nila means *blue*; but this blue is probably derived from the colour of the stone—a dark blue, meant originally to describe *black*. The Nile was called Αιγυπτος *Ægyptus*, before the country had that name. This last name also defies the etymologists. But it was probably an Eastern word mangled by the Greeks, who mangled every thing. It will be explained hereafter.

M. De Lambre tells us, from Censorinus, that the Egytians called the year of 365 days by the word Νειλος, *Neilos*. And he observes that, in the Greek notation, the letters of which this word is composed denote 365. Sir W. Drummond calls this buffoonery, and asks if M. De Lambre has

---

[1] Maurice, Hist. Hind. Vol. I. p. 66, 4to.; also Ant. Ind. Vol. III. p. 375.   [2] Maurice, Ant. Ind.
[3] Vol. III. p. 351.   [4] Drummond, Ess. Zod. pp. 106 and 112.
[5] De Diis Syriis, De Vitulo Aureo, Syntag. i. Cap. iv.   [6] Vide Drummond's Orig. B. iv. Ch. ii.

forgot that the Egyptians did not speak Greek. To which it may be answered, that the polite and learned among them did speak Greek, after the time of Alexander. It is overlooked by Sir William, that this name (as he acknowledges) νεον εστι, is modern. It is probable that the Greeks found the *ancient* Egyptian name to signify *black*, and the letters of it to denote or to signify the year of 365 days. But as they could not in their language give it a term which would signify both, and as they understood why it was called 365 or the year, but did not understand why it was called black, they adopted the former, and called it Νειλος.

The ancient name, as we have said, was Sir, or Siri, the same as O-sir, or Osiris, who was always black; after whom it was called, and by whom was meant the sun. Thus it was called the river of the sun, or the river sun, or the river of Osiris—as we say, the river of the Amazons, or the river Amazon. And this river flowed from the land of the sun and moon. It arose in the mountains of the moon, and flowed through the land of Sir, perhaps the land of Siriad, where Josephus was told that columns had been placed which were built before the flood—κατα την γην Συριαδα. Manetho, 300 years before Josephus, says, these columns stood εν τη γη Συριαδικη, and from them Josephus took his history, which was inscribed on them in the sacred language and in hieroglyphical characters, a language and character evidently both unknown to him. These columns were probably the Egyptian monuments—Pyramids, or *Obelisks*, which had escaped the destruction of Cambyses, perhaps because they were only historical and not religious, or perhaps because they were linghams, to which the Persians might not object—but the knowledge of whose characters was at that time lost amidst the universal destruction of priests and temples, and which has never been really known since, though the new priests would not be willing to confess their ignorance. Query, שור *sur* אי *ia* די *di*, The holy land of Sur?

The river Nile in Sanscreet books is often called Crishna. [1]

שר *sr*, is the origin or root of Osiris, and means a leader, regulator, ruler, or director. The ninth of the meanings given to it by Parkhurst in the form שור *sur*, is that of Beeve.

The modern words Sir, Mon-sieur, Mon-seignor, are all derived from the Hebrew word שר *Sr*, or Lord, as we translate it, which was an epithet of the sun in all the eastern countries. This is the same as the Iswara of India, which means Lord. [2] The Bull of the Zodiac, or the sun, also had a name very similar to this, whence probably it came to be applied to the animal; or at least they had the same names. See Parkhurst in voce שור *sur*.

Mr. Maurice says, [3] Persæ Συρη Deum vocant. Surya is the name of the solar divinity of India. It is also the name of Osiris. Mr. Bryant says, Οσειριν προσαγορευυσι και Συριον. [4] As the God of the Egyptians went by several names, as Apis, Serapis, Cnepb, Osiris, &c., so did the God of the Hindoos. The word *sahle* or *black* was one of their epithets. Thus *Christ* is, in like manner, an epithet of Jesus. He is called Jesus the Christ, *the Anointed.*

8. As the reader has seen above, and also in my Celtic Druids, I have derived Osiris from the word *Sr*, and the Greek emphatic article O. This derivation is justified by Porphyry. But Hellanicus informs us, that it was sometimes written Υσιρις. Now, as Isis was the wife of Osiris, may it not have come from the Hebrew word ישע *iso*, to save, and שר *sr*, or שור *sur*? Osiris was the Sun, so was Surya in India and Persia: for, as we have seen, Persæ Surè Deum vocant. Syria was the land of the Sun. The Sun was called Lord and Saviour; so was Mithra. The Bull was the emblem of the Sun—of Mithra, called Lord, and of the God in the land where Surya or the Sun, with seven heads, was adored, and in Japan, where he breaks the mundane egg with his

---

[1] Maurice, Bram. Fraud Exposed, p. 80.   [4] See Pictet, p. 16.
[2] Ant. Ind. Vol. II. p. 203.   [4] Ibid. p. 221.

horn. The Bull was the body into which Osiris transmigrated after his death; and, lastly, the Hebrew name for bull is שור *sur*. Orpheus has a hymn to the Lord Bull. Iswara of India or Osiris, is the husband of *Isi* or of *Isis*; and Surya is Buddha. Can all these coincidences be the effect of accident?

" Osiris, or Isiris, as Sanchoniathon calls him, is also the same name with Mizraim, when the " servile letter M is left out." [1] The reason of the monogram M being prefixed to this, and to many other words, will be shewn by and by.

I have some suspicion that *O-siris* is a Greek corruption; that the name ought, as already mentioned, to be what it is called by Hellanicus, *Ysiris* or *Isiris*, and that it is derived from, or rather I should say is the same as, *Iswara* of India. Iswara and Isi are the same as Osiris and Isis—the male and female procreative powers of nature.

" Iswara, in Sanscrit, signifies Lord, and in that sense is applied by the Bramans to each of " their three principal deities, or rather to each of the forms in which they teach the people to " adore Brahm, or the GREAT ONE . . . . Brahma, Vishnu, and Mahadeva, say the *Puranics*, " were brothers: and the Egyptian triad, or Osiris, Horus, and Typhon, were brought forth by " the same parent." [2]

Syria was called Suria. Eusebius says the Egyptians called Osiris, Surius, and that, in Persia, *Surē* was the old name of the sun. [3]

In the sol-lunar legends of the Hindoos, the Sun is, as we have seen, sometimes male and sometimes female. The Moon is also of both sexes, and is called *Isu* and *Isi*. [4] Deus Lunus was common to several nations of the ancient world. [5]

The peculiar mode in which the Hindoos identify their three great Gods with the solar orb, is a curious specimen of the physical refinements of ancient mythology. *At night and in the West, the Sun is Vishnu: he is Brama in the East and in the morning: and from noon to evening, he is Siva.* [6]

The adoration of a black stone is a very singular superstition. Like many other superstitions this also came from India. Buddha was adored as a square black stone; so was Mercury; so was the Roman Terminus. The famous Pessinuntian stone, brought to Rome, was square and black. The sacred black stone at Mecca many of my readers are acquainted with, and George the Fourth did very wisely to be crowned on the square stone, nearer black than any other colour, of Scotia and Ireland.

In Montfaucon, a black Isis and Orus are described in the printing, but not in the plate. I suspect many of Montfaucon's figures ought to be black, which are not so described. [7]

Pausanias states the Thespians to have had a temple and statue to Jupiter the Saviour, and a statue to Love, consisting only of a rude stone; and a temple to Venus Melainis, or *the black*. [8]

Ammon was founded by Black doves, Ατρι-Ιωνες. One of them flew from Ammon to Dodona and founded it. [9]

At Corinth there was a black Venus. [10]

In my search into the origin of ancient Druids, I continually found, at last, that my labours terminated with something *black*. Thus the oracles at Dodona, and of Apollo at Delphi, were founded by BLACK doves. Doves are not often, I believe never really, black.

---

[1] Cumberland, Orig. Gen. p. 100.   [3] Asiat. Res. Vol. III. p. 371; Moore's Pantheon, p. 44.

[2] Maur. Ind. Ant. Vol. VI. p. 39.   [4] Moore's Pantheon, pp. 289, 290.   [5] Ibid. p. 291.

[6] Faber, Or. Idol. B. iv. Ch. i.   [7] Montf. Exp. Vol. II. Plate XXXVII. Fig. 5.

[8] Pausanias, Lib. ix. Cap. xxvi. xxvii.   [9] Nimrod, p. 276.   [10] Ibid. p. 400.

Osiris and his Bull were black; all the Gods and Goddesses of Greece were black : at least this was the case with Jupiter, Bacchus, Hercules, Apollo, Ammon.

The Goddesses Venus, Isis, Hecati, Diana, Juno, Metis, Ceres, Cybile, are black. The Multi-mammia is black in the Campidoglio at Rome, and in Montfaucon, Antiquity explained.

The Linghams in India, anointed with oil, are black : a black stone was adored in numbers of places in India.

It has already been observed that, in the galleries, we constantly see busts and statues of the Roman Emperors, made of two kinds of stone ; the human part of the statue of *black* stone, the drapery *white* or *coloured*. When they are thus described, I suppose they are meant to be repre-sented as priests of the sun ; this was probably confined to the celebration of the Isiac or Egyptian ceremonies.

9. On the colour of the Gods of the ancients, and of the identity of them all with the God Sol, and with the Cristna of India, nothing more need be said. The reader has already seen the strik-ing marks of similarity in the history of Cristna and the stories related of Jesus in the Romish and heretical books. He probably will not think that their effect is destroyed, as Mr. Maurice flatters himself, by the word Cristna in the Indian language signifying black, and the God being of that colour, when he is informed, of what Mr. Maurice was probably ignorant, that in all the Romish countries of Europe, in France, Italy, Germany, &c., the God Christ, as well as his mother, are described in their old pictures and statues to be black. The infant God in the arms of his black mother, his eyes and drapery white, is himself perfectly black. If the reader doubt my word, he may go to the cathedral at Moulins—to the famous chapel of the Virgin at Loretto—to the church of the Annunciata—the church of St. Lazaro, or the church of St. Stephen at Genoa—to St. Francisco at Pisa—to the church at Brixen, in the Tyrol, and to that at Padua—to the church of St. Theo-dore, at Munich, in the two last of which the whiteness of the eyes and teeth, and the studied redness of the lips, are very observable ;—to a church and to the cathedral at Augsburg, where are a black virgin and child as large as life :—to Rome, to the Borghese chapel Maria Maggiore—to the Pantheon—to a small chapel of St. Peter's, on the right-hand side on entering, near the door ; and, in fact, to almost innumerable other churches, in countries professing the Romish religion.

There is scarcely an old church in Italy where some remains of the worship of the BLACK VIRGIN and BLACK CHILD are not to be met with. Very often the black figures have given way to white ones, and in these cases the black ones, as being held sacred, were put into retired places in the churches, but were not destroyed, but are yet to be found there. In many cases the images are painted all over and look like bronze, often with coloured aprons or napkins round the loins or other parts ; but pictures in great numbers are to be seen, where the white of the eyes and of the teeth, and the lips a little tinged with red, like the black figures in the Museum of the India Com-pany, shew that there is no imitation of bronze. In many instances these images and pictures are shaded, not all one colour, of very dark brown, so dark as to look like black. They are generally esteemed by the rabble with the most profound veneration. The toes are often white, the brown or black paint being kissed away by the devotees, and the white wood left. No doubt in many places, when the priests have new-painted the images, they have coloured the eyes, teeth, &c., in order that they might not shock the feelings of devotees by a too sudden change from black to white, and in order, at the same time, that they might furnish a decent pretence for their black-ness, viz. that they are an imitation of bronze : but the number that are left with white teeth, &c., let out the secret.

When the circumstance has been named to the Romish priests, they have endeavoured to dis-guise the fact, by pretending that the child had become black by the smoke of the candles ; but it was black where the smoke of a candle never came : and, besides, how came the candles not to blacken the white of the eyes, the teeth, and the shirt, and how came they to redden the lips? The mother is, the author believes, always black, when the child is. Their real blackness is not to be questioned for a moment.

If the author had wished to invent a circumstance to corroborate the assertion, that the Romish Christ of Europe is the Cristna of India, how could he have desired any thing more striking than the fact of the black Virgin and Child being so common in the Romish countries of Europe? A black virgin and child among the white Germans, Swiss, French, and Italians! ! !

The Romish Cristna is black in India, black in Europe, and black he must remain—like the ancient Gods of Greece, as we have just seen. But, after all, what was he but their Jupiter, the second person of their Trimurti or Trinity, the Logos of Parmenides and Plato, an incarnation or emanation of the solar power?

I must now request my reader to turn back to the first chapter, and to reconsider what I have said respecting the two Ethiopias and the existence of a *black* nation in a very remote period. When he has done this, the circumstance of the black God of India being called *Cristna*, and the God of Italy, *Christ*, being also black, must appear worthy of deep consideration. Is it possible, that this coincidence can have been the effect of accident? In our endeavours to recover the lost science of former ages, it is necessary that we should avail ourselves of rays of light scattered in places the most remote, and that we should endeavour to re-collect them into a focus, so that, by this means, we may procure as strong a light as possible: collect as industriously as we may, our light will not be too strong.[1]

I think I need say no more in answer to Mr. Maurice's shouts of triumph over those whom he insultingly calls *impious infidels*, respecting the name of Cristna having the meaning of black. I will now proceed to his other *solemn considerations*.

10. The second particular to which Mr. Maurice desires the attention of his reader, is in the following terms : " 2d, Let it, in the next place, be considered that Chreeshna, so far from being " the son of a virgin, is declared to have had a father and mother in the flesh, and to have been " the *eighth* child of Devaci and Vasudeva. How inconceivably different this from the sanctity " of the immaculate conception of Christ !"

I answer, that respecting their *births* they differ; but what has this to do with the points wherein they agree? No one ever said they agreed in every minute particular. Yet I think, with respect to their humanity, the agreement continues. I always understood that Jesus was held by the Romish and Protestant Churches to have become incarnate; *that the word* was made flesh.[2] That is, that Jesus was of the same kind of flesh, at least as his mother, and also as his brothers, Joses, James, &c.[3] If he were not of the flesh of his mother, what was he before the umbilical cord was cut?

It does not appear from the histories, which we have yet obtained, that the immaculate concep-

---

[1] But though the Bull of *Osiris* was black, the Bull of *Europa* was white. The story states that Jupiter fell in love with a daughter of Agenor, king of Phœnicia, and Telephassa, and in order to obtain the object of his affections he changed himself into a white bull. After he had seduced the nymph to play with him and caress him in his pasture for some time, at last he persuaded her to mount him, when he fled with her to Crete, where he succeeded in his wishes, and by her he had Minos, Sarpedon, and Rhadamanthus. Is it necessary for me to point out to the reader in this pretty allegory the peopling of Europe from Phœnicia, and the allusion in the colour of the Bull, viz. *white*, to the fair complexions of the Europeans? An ingenious explanation of this allegory may be seen in Drummond's Origines, Vol. III. p. 84.

[2] John, ch. i. ver. 14.

[3] I look with perfect contempt on the ridiculous trash which has been put forth to shew that the brothers of Jesus, described in the Gospels, did not mean *brothers*, but *cousins !*

tion has been taken from the history of Cristna.   However, we shall find hereafter, that, in all probability, it came from the same quarter of the world.

Mr. Maurice observes, 3dly, " That it has been, from the earliest periods, the savage custom " of the despots of Asia, for the sake of extirpating one dreaded object, to massacre all the males " born in a particular district, and the history of Moses himself exhibits a glaring proof how " anciently, and how relentlessly it was practised."   The story of Moses, Pharaoh, and the order to murder the boys of the Israelites, will be shewn hereafter to have a certain mystical meaning much closer to the Indian Mythoses, particularly to that of the God Cristna, than Mr. Maurice would have liked, had he known it.

4th. " In his contest with the great serpent, Calija, circumstances occur which, since the story " is, in great part, *mythological*, irresistibly impel me to believe that, in that, as in many other " portions of this surprising legend, there is a reference intended to some traditional accounts, " descended down to the Indians from the patriarchs, and current in Asia, of the *fall of man*, and " the consequent well-known denunciation against the serpentine tempter."   This like the last particular proves nothing.

5th. " In regard to the numerous miracles wrought by Chreeshna, it should be remembered, that " miracles are never wanting to the decoration of an Indian romance ; they are, in fact, the life " and soul of the vast machine ; nor is it at all a subject of wonder that the dead should be raised " to life, in a history expressly intended, like all other sacred fables of Indian fabrication, for the " propagation and support of the whimsical doctrine of the Metempsychosis.   The above is the " most satisfactory reply in my power to give to such determined sceptics as Mr. Volney."

11. The reasons of Mr. Maurice to account for the history of Cristna are so weak, that they evidently do not deserve a moment's consideration ; and, as well as Sir W. Jones's HAPPY AND INGENIOUS theory of interpolation, are only named in order that the Author may not be accused of suppressing them ; that the reader may see how learned divines explain these matters ; and that he may hear both sides.   Mr. Maurice's jeer upon miracles never being wanting to an Indian romance, is rather hard upon such of his friends as believe, or affect to believe, histories or romances where miracles are the very life and soul of the *machine*, to use his own expression ; which, in fact, consist of miracles from one end to the other ; and he seems to have forgotten that most of the early orthodox fathers believed in the Metempsychosis.

The reader will please to recollect that the circumstances related of Cristna come to us very unwillingly from the orthodox *Jones* and *Maurice ;* whether any others of consequence would be found, if we had a translation of the whole Vedas, is as yet uncertain.   Without any reflection on these gentlemen, it may be permitted us to say, that circumstances which did not appear important to them, might on these subjects appear of great consequence to others.

Sir William Jones strives to deceive himself into a belief, that all the cycles or statements of the different astronomical events related in the Hindoo books are the produce of modern back-calculations.   Those books are brought from different nations of India, so remote and numerous, that it is *almost impossible* to suppose them all to be the effect of artifice ; and, when united to the evident extreme antiquity of the Zodiacs, and some of the monuments of both India and Egypt, *quite impossible.*   All this he did for fear his faith in the chronology of the Bible, which he did not know how to reconcile to that of the Indians, should be shaken.   His incredulity is so great as to be absolutely ridiculous credulity.   What a lamentable figure it exhibits of the weakness of mind, and the effect of early prejudice and partial education, in one of the greatest and very best of men !

In the same way that he finds a pretext to disguise to himself the consequences which follow from the great antiquity of the Indian temples, books, and astronomy, he finds an equally satisfactory reason for disguising the evident identity of the history of Cristna, or as he is sometimes called Heri-Cristna, with Christ, (*Heri* means Saviour,) by the idle pretence, as we have seen, that the Brahmins, some way or other, have got copies of part of the Apocryphal Gospels, from which they have taken the history of the birth, life, and adventures, of Cristna—these gospels being written some time, of course, after the birth of Jesus Christ. How wonderfully absurd to suppose that all the ancient emblems and idols of Cristna in the temples and caves, scattered over every part of India, and absolutely identified with them in point of antiquity, can have been copied from the Gospels about the time of Jesus! How wonderfully absurd to suppose that the Brahmins, and people of this widely-extended empire, should condescend to copy from the real or cast-away spurious Gospels, of a sect at that time almost entirely unknown even in their own country, and many thousand miles distant from these Brahmins!

12. After Mr. Maurice discovered that the truths which had been permitted to appear in the Asiatic Researches, and in his History of Hindostan and Antiquities of India, had been observed by the philosophers, he published a couple of pamphlets, the intention of which was to remedy the mischief which he had done. But they contain very little more than what he had said before. When the reader observes that the Brahminical histories not only apply to the New Testament and the Apocryphal Gospel histories, but that the Jewish histories of the creation and fall of man, as translated, not by the Romish Church only, but by Protestants, are also closely interwoven with them, he will not easily be persuaded that they are copies of these Gospels. The battle of the infant Cristna with the serpent is considered as the greatest as well as the first of all his wonderful actions. This is evidently the evil principle, the tempter of *Eve*, described in the sphere: it is evidently the greatest of the victories of the Romish Jesus as well as of Cristna. It is the conquests of Hercules and of Bacchus, when in their cradles. If the Brahmins had been merely interpolating from the Gospels, they would not have troubled themselves with the Old Testament.

When a person considers the vast wealth and power which are put into danger by these Indian manuscripts; the practice by Christian priests of interpolating and erasing, for the last two thousand years; the well-known forgeries practised upon Mr. Wilsford by a Brahmin; and the large export make to India of orthodox and missionary priests; he will not be surprised if some copies of the books should make their appearance wanting certain particulars in the life of Cristna: but this will hardly now be noticed by the philosophical inquirer; particularly as the figures in the temples cannot be *interpolated*, nor very easily erased. No doubt this observation is calculated to give pain to honourable men among the priests; but they cannot be responsible, as they cannot controul their coadjutors, too many of whom have in all ages lost sight of honesty and integrity, in things of this kind.

The Hindoos, far from labouring to make proselytes to their religion, do not admit into it those who have been born in and professed any other faith. They say that, provided men perform their moral duties in abstaining from ill, and in doing good to the utmost of their ability, it is but of little importance under what forms they worship God; that things suitable to one people may be unfit for another; and that to suppose that God prefers any one particular religion to the exclusion of others, and yet leaves numbers of his creatures ignorant of his will, is to accuse him of injustice, or to question his omnipotence.[1] I wish our priests would attend to the sound wisdom and benevolence of these people, called by our missionaries *ignorant and benighted*.

13. In reply to the observation of such persons as have contended that the Hindoos have made use of back-reckoning, Mr. Craufurd pertinently observes, "That to be able to do so, implies a

---

[1] Craufurd's Researches, Ch. ii. p. 158.

" more accurate practice in astronomy than the Hindūs seem to possess ; for it is evident that
" their knowledge in science and learning, instead of being improved, has greatly declined from what
" it appears to have been in the remote ages of their history. And, besides, for what purpose
" should they take such pains ? It may possibly be answered, from the vanity of wishing to
" prove the superior antiquity of their learning to that of other nations. We confess that the
" observation, unsupported by other proofs, appears to us unworthy of men of learning, whom we
" should expect to find resting their arguments on scientific proofs only." [1]

No doubt it is extremely difficult to arrive, on this subject, at mathematical certainty or proof,
but yet it may probably be safely concluded that, if preconceived notions respecting danger to the
literal meaning of the Mosaic text had not stood in the way, no difficulty would have been
found in admitting the sufficiency of the evidence of the Hindoo antiquity. It strongly calls to
recollection the struggle and outcry made against Walton and others for asserting that the
Mazoretic points, in the Hebrew language, were of modern adoption. As long as the discovery
was supposed to endanger the religion, the proofs were pronounced to be altogether insufficient ;
but as soon as it had been shewn that the religion was in no danger, the truth of the new theory
was almost universally admitted. Exactly similar would be the case of the Hindoo astronomical
periods if it could be shewn that religion was not implicated in the question. The author has no
doubt of the side of the question which any unprejudiced person will take, who will carefully read
over the works of Playfair, and the Edinburgh Review, upon this subject, and Craufurd's Researches, and his Sketches. [2]

However, there is a passage in Arrian, which proves that one of the great leading facts, which
forms a point of striking similarity between the Cristna of India and the Christ of Europe, was
not taken from the Gospels after Jesus's death, but was actually a story relating to Cristna, in
existence in the time of Alexander the Great. The reader has seen already all the curious circumstances narrated in the Gospel histories, and by Athanasius and Eusebius, respecting the city of
Matarea in Egypt, to which place Jesus fled from Herod. He has also seen that it was at Mathura
of India, where the holy family of Cristna resided in his infancy. In a future part of this work
I shall shew, that Hercules and Bacchus are both the same, the Sun—one in Taurus, the
other in Aries. Then the following passage from the Edinburgh Review, of the article Asiatic
Researches, Vol. XV. p. 185, will prove most clearly, and beyond all doubt, that the history of
Cristna, his residence at Matarea, &c., cannot have been copied from the histories in the spurious
Gospels ; but must have been older than the time of Alexander the Great.

" Arrian (Ch. viii.) proceeds to relate that Hercules was fifteen centuries later than Bacchus.
" We have already seen that Bacchus was Siva ; and Megasthenes distinctly points out what
" Indian divinity is meant by Hercules. ' He was chiefly adored (says Arrian) by the Suraseni,
" ' who possess two large cities, Methora and Clissobora. The Jobares, a navigable river, flows
" ' through their territories.' Now Herichrisna, the chief of the Suraseni, was born in the metro-
" polis of their country, Mathura : and the river Jamuna flows through the territory of the
" Suraseni, Mathura being situated on its banks, and called by Ptolemy, Matura Deorum ; which
" can only be accounted for by its being the birth-place of Christna ;" in fact, of the triplicate
God Brahma, Cristna, and Seeva, three in one and one in three—the Creator, the Preserver or
Saviour, and the Destroyer or Regenerator. The great city of Mathura or Methora, and the river

[1] Craufurd's Res. Ch. viii. p. 17.
[2] Edinb. Review, Vol. XV. p. 414, Vol. X. p. 469, also Vol. XVI. pp. 390, 391 ; see also Trans. Royal Soc. of
Edinburgh, Vol. II. pp. 155, 160, 169, 185, Vol. IV. pp. 83, 103.

Jobares or Jumna, could not be called after the city or river in Egypt in accommodation to the Christian story.

The statue of Cristna in the temple of Mathura is black, and the temple is built in the form of a cross,[1] and stands due East and West. " It is evident the Hindoos must have known the " use of the Gnomon at a very remote period. Their religion commands that the four sides of " their temples should correspond with the four cardinal points of the Heavens, and they are all " so constructed." [2]

It is to be regretted that Arrian has not given a more detailed account; but in the fact which he gives of Heri-Cristna, Hercules or the Sun, being worshiped at Mathura, called by Ptolemy Maturn Deorum, there is quite enough to satisfy any person who chooses to use his understanding, of the antiquity of the history. [3]

Mr. Bryant says, " It is remarkable that among some Oriental languages Matarea signifies the " sun. This may be proved from the Malayan language, expressed Matahari, and Matta-harri, " and Mattowraye, and Matta'ree, and from that of the Sumatrans at Acheen. It seems to be a " compound of Matta and Ree, the ancient Egyptian word for the Sun, which is still retained in " the Coptic, and, with the aspirate, is rendered Phree." This Phree is, I doubt not, the Coptic ΦPH, explained in my *Celtic Druids*,[4] to mean the number 608, of which I shall have much to say hereafter.

Strabo[5] says, that close to Heliopolis was a city called *Cercesura*. This name and the *Cercasorum* of Herodotus, are, I do not doubt, corruptions of *Clssobora*.

In the Classical Journal will be found an attempt, by Dr. Adam Clarke, to invalidate what Mr. Maurice has said respecting Cristna treading on the serpent's head, and, in return, the serpent biting his heel. He seems to have rendered it doubtful whether there were pictures, or icons, of the serpent biting the heel, but the biting of the foot, I think, is admitted by the learned Doctor. It is of little consequence : but the reader must observe that, since gentlemen of the Doctor's warmth of temper and zeal have considered this to be inimical to their system, the same cause which prevents our finding any icons or pictures of Wittoba, (of which my reader will be informed shortly,) probably prevents our finding exemplars of the biting serpent. It seems perfectly in keeping with the remainder of the system, particularly with the doctrine of Original Sin, which is known to be one of the Hindoo tenets, and for this and other reasons, I confess I believe Mr. Maurice, although I thereby become, according to the Doctor's expression, an Infidel and a viper. The following passage is from Sonnerat, and I think it must be regarded as fully justifying Mr. Maurice : C'est en mémoire de cet évènement que dans les temples de Vichnou, dédiés à cette incarnation, on représente Quichena le corps entortillé d'une *couleuvre capelle*, qui lui mord le pied, tandis qu'il est peint, dans un autre tableau, dansant sur la tête de cette même couleuvre. Ses sectateurs ont ordinairement ces deux tableaux dans leurs maisons.[6]

Dr. Clarke says, " I have proved, and so might any man, that no *serpent, in the common sense* " of the term, can be intended in the third chapter of Genesis; that all the circumstances of the " case, as detailed by the inspired penman, are in total hostility to the common mode of interpre- " tation, and that some other method should be found out."[7] I partly agree with the Doctor; but

---

[1] Maur. Ind. Ant. Vol. II. p. 355.   [2] Craufurd's Res. Vol. II. p. 18.

[3] Many of the Brahmins, declare that there is no need to send missionaries to convert them; that it would better become us to convert ourselves, by throwing off the corruptions of our religion, which is only a branch or sect of theirs; that our Jesus is their Cristna, and that he ought to be black.

[4] Ap. p. 308.   [5] Lib. xvii.   [6] Voyage aux Ind. Vol. I. pp. 168, 169, see plates, fig. 5, 6.

[7] Class. Jour., No. VI. June, 1811, p. 440.

beg leave to add, that without deserving to be called Viper or Infidel, I have as much right to consider the whole as *an allegory*, as he has to consider the serpent to be an *ape*. But here is the Doctor not believing according to the orthodox faith. Then, on his own shewing, he must be both Infidel and Viper. But God forbid that it should be meted to this Protestant heretic, as he metes to others.

The observation which Dr. Clarke has made is extremely valuable, that in the drawings of Sonnerat the serpent is not biting the HEEL of Cristna, but the side of the foot. This clearly shews that they are not servile copies of one another; but records of a mythos substantially the same. Had the Hindoos copied from the Bible, they would have made the serpent bite the heel, whether it were of the mother or of the son. If the author of Genesis copied from the Hindoo, in making the serpent bite the heel, he substantially, and to all intents and purposes, made him bite the foot. But the two accounts are not mutually convertible one for the other. This story of Cristna and the serpent biting his foot, is of itself alone sufficient to prove, that the mythos of Cristna is not taken from the Romish or Greek religion of Jesus Christ, because in it the mother, not the son, bruises the serpent: Ipsa conteret caput tuum, &c.[1]

In a future chapter, I shall take an opportunity of saying much more on the subject of the Indian Hercules.

CHAPTER II

Crucifixion of Cristna, and Wittoba or Baljii—Moore's Observations refuted— More particulars respecting the Temple of Wittoba—Cristna, Bacchus, Hercules, &c., Types of the Real Saviour—Taurus and Aries, and Æra of Cristna— Immaculate Conception, from the History of Pythagoras

1. IN compliance with the rule which I have laid down for the regulation of my conduct, critically to examine every thing relating in any degree to my subject with the most impartial severity, nothing to suppress, and nothing of importance to add, without stating the authority on which I receive it,—I now present my reader with two very extraordinary histories relating to the crucifixion. I say, *fiat veritas ruat cœlum*. Nothing can injure the cause of religious truth, except, indeed, it be the falsities, suppressions, pious frauds, and want of candour of the priests, and of its weak and ill-judging friends. The pious frauds of the priests of all religions, imperiously demand of the philosophizing critic the most severe and suspicious examination. And whether the priests of the modern British church are to form an exception, will be a subject of inquiry in the second part of this work. In the work of Mons. Guigniaut[2] is the following passage:

" On raconte fort diversement la mort de Crichna. Une tradition remarquable et avérée le fait " périr sur un bois fatal (un arbre), ou il fut cloué d'un coup de flèche, et du haut duquel il prédit " les maux qui allaient fondre sur la terre, dans le Cali-youga.[3] En effet, trente ou trente-six ans " après, commença cet age de crimes, et de misères. Une autre tradition ajoute que le corps de

---

[1] Vulgate.   [2] Vol. I. p. 208.
[3] The word Yug or Youga is evidently the same word as the English word *age*, both having the same meaning. Paul, Sist. B. pp. 149, et sq.; vide Sonnerat, I. pp. 169, et sq.; Polier, II. pp. 144, 162, et sq.

l'homme-dieu fut change en un tronc de *tchandana* ou sandal ; et qu'ayant été jeté dans l'Yamou-
na, près de Mathoura, il passa de là dans les eaux saintes du Gange, qui le portèrent sur la côte
d'Orissa : il y est encore adoré à Djagannatha ou Jagrenat, lieu fameux par les pélerinages, comme
le symbole de réproduction et de la vie.[1] Il est certainment fort remarquable, quelques variantes
que l'on puisse découvrir dans les différens récits, de voir Siva et Crichna réunis à Djagannatha,
nom qui signifie *le pays du maître du monde*, en sous-entendant Kchetra ; car, par lui-même, ce
nom est une epithète de Crichna. La Mythologie Egyptienne nous offrira une tradition sur le
corps d'Osiris, toute-à-fait analogue à la dernière que nous *venons de rapporter.*[2]

The first part of the above-cited passage respecting the nailing of Cristna to the fatal tree, and
his prediction of the future evils of the world, is very remarkable, particularly when coupled with
the following recital :

Mr. Moore describes an Avatar called Wittoba, who has his foot pierced. After stating the
reason why he cannot account for it, he says, " A man who was in the habit of bringing me Hin-
" doo deities, pictures, &c., once brought me two images exactly alike : one of them is engraved
" in plate 98, and the subject of it will be at once seen by the most transient glance. Affecting
" indifference, I inquired of my Pundit what Deva it was : he examined it attentively, and, after
" turning it about for some time, returned it to me, professing his ignorance of what Avatar it
" could immediately relate to, but supposed, by the hole in the foot, that it might be Wittoba ;
" adding, that it was impossible to recollect the almost innumerable Avataras described in the
" *Puranas.*

" The subject of plate 98 is evidently the crucifixion ; and, by the style of workmanship, is
" clearly of European origin, as is proved also by its being in duplicate."[3]

This incarnation of Vishnu or CRISTNA is called Wittoba or Ballaji. He has a splendid temple
erected to him at Punderpoor. Little respecting this incarnation is known. A story of him is
detailed by Mr. Moore, which he observes reminds him of the doctrine *of turning the immote
cheek to an assailant.* This God is represented by Moore with a hole on the top of one foot just
above the toes, where the nail of a person crucified might be supposed to be placed. And, in
another print, he is represented exactly in the form of a Romish crucifix, but not fixed to a piece
of wood, though the legs and feet are put together in the usual way, with a nail-hole in the latter.
There appears to be a glory over it coming *from* above. Generally the glory shines from the
figure. It has a pointed Parthian coronet instead of a crown of thorns. I apprehend this is
totally unusual in our crucifixes. When I recollect the crucifix on the fire tower in Scotland,
(Celtic Druids, plate 24,) with the Lamb on one side, and *the Elephant* on the other, and all the
circumstances attending this Avatar, I am induced to suspect I have been too hasty in determining that the fire tower was modern because it had the effigy of a crucified man upon it, and
relating to this we shall find something very curious hereafter.

All the Avatars or incarnations of Vishnu are painted with Ethiopian or Parthian coronets.[4]
Now, in Moore's Pantheon, the Avatar of Wittoba is thus painted ; but Christ on the cross, though
often described with a glory, I believe is never described with the Coronet. This proves that the
figure described in Moore's Pantheon is not a Portuguese crucifix. Vide plates, fig. 7.

2. Mr. Moore endeavours to prove that this crucifix cannot be Hindoo, because there are duplicates of it from the same mould, and he contends that the Hindoos can only make one cast from

[1] Voy. Langlès. Monum., I., p. 186, *conf.* pp. 127, et. sq.

[2] Religions de L'Antiquitié, Du Dr. Fréderic Creuzer, par J. D. Guigniaut. Paris, Treuttel et Wurtz, Rue de
Bourbon, No. 17. 1825.

[3] Moore's Ind. Pantheon, pp. 98, 416, 420.		[4] Jones, Asiatic Res. Vol. I. p. 260. 4to.

one mould, the mould being made of clay. But he ought to have deposited the two specimens where they could have been examined, to ascertain that they were duplicates. Besides, how does he know that the Hindoos, who are so ingenious, had not the very simple art of making casts from the brass figure, as well as clay moulds from the one of wax? Nothing could be more easy. The crucified body without the cross of wood reminds me that some of the ancient sects of heretics held Jesus to have been crucified in the clouds.

Montfaucon says, "What can be the reason that, in the most common medals, some thousands "of which might be got up, we never can find two struck with the same die, though the impres-"sion and inscription be still the same? This is so constantly true, that whenever we find two "medals which appear to be struck with the same die, we always suspect one is a modern piece "coined from the other, and upon strict examination find it always is so." [1]

I very much suspect that it is from some story now unknown, *or kept out of sight*, relating to this Avatar, that the ancient heretics alluded to before obtained their tradition of Jesus having been crucified in the clouds. The temple at Punderpoor deserves to be searched, although the result of this search would give but little satisfaction, unless it were made by a person of a very different character from that of our missionaries. The argument respecting the duplicates on which Mr. Moore places his chief dependence to prove it Christian, at once falls to the ground when it is known that the assertion is not true: duplicates of brass idols, or at least copies so near that it is very difficult to distinguish them, or to say that they are not duplicates from the same mould coarsely and unskilfully made, may be seen at the Museum at the India House; and also in that of the Asiatic Society in Grafton Street, where there are what I believe to be duplicates of figures from the same mould. I therefore think it must remain a Wittoba. But the reader has seen what I have found in Montfaucon, and he must judge for himself.

That nothing more is known respecting this Avatar, I cannot help suspecting may be attributed to the same kind of feeling which induced Mr. Moore's friend to wish him to remove this print from his book. The innumerable pious frauds of which Christian priests stand convicted, and the principle of the expediency of fraud admitted to have existed by Mosheim, are a perfect justification of my suspicions respecting the concealment of the history of this Avatar: especially as I can find no Wittobas in any of the collections. I repeat, I cannot help suspecting, that it is from this Avatar of Cristna that the sect of Christian heretics got their Christ crucified in the *clouds*.

Long after the above was written, I accidentally looked into Moore's Pantheon, at the British Museum, where it appears that the copy is an earlier impression than the former which I had consulted: and I discovered something which Mr. Moore has apparently not dared to tell us, viz. that in several of the icons of Wittoba, there are marks of holes in both feet, and in others, of holes in the hands. In the first copy which I consulted, the marks are very faint, so as to be scarcely visible. In figures 4 and 5 of plate 11, the figures have nail-holes in both feet. Fig. 3 has a hole in one hand. Fig. 6 has on his side the mark of a foot, and a little lower in the side a round hole; to his collar or shirt hangs the ornament or emblem of *a heart*, which we generally see in the Romish pictures of Christ; on his head he has an Yoni-Linga. In plate 12, and in plate 97, he has a round mark in the palm of the hand. Of this last, Mr. Moore says, "This cast is in "five pieces: the back lifts out of sockets in the pedestal, and admits the figures to slide back-"wards out of the grooves in which they are fitted: it is then seen that the seven-headed *Naga* "(cobra), joined to the figure, continues his scaly length down Ballaji's back, and making two "convolutions under him forms his seat: a second shorter snake, also part of the figure, pro-

[1] Ant. Exp. Supplement, Vol. III. B. v. p. 329.

" trudes its head, and makes a seat for Ballaji's right foot, and terminates with the other snake
" behind him. Unless this refer to the same legend as Crishna crushing Kaliya, I know not its
" allusion."[1]

Figure 1, plate 91, of Moore's Pantheon, is a Hanuman, but it is remarkable that it has a hole
in one foot, a nail through the other, a round nail mark in the palm of one hand and on the knuckle
of the other, and is ornamented with doves and a five-headed Cobra snake.

It is unfortunate, perhaps it has been thought prudent, that the originals are not in the Museum
to be examined. But it is pretty clear that the Romish and Protestant crucifixion of Jesus must
have been taken from the Avatar of Ballaji, or the Avatar of Ballaji from it, or both from a common mythos.

In this Avatar the first verse of Genesis appears to be closely connected with the crucifixion
and the doctrine of the Atonement. The seven-headed Cobra, in one instance, and the foot on
the head of the serpent in others, unite him with Surya and Buddha. Some of these figures have
glories at the back of them. In Calmet's Fragments, Cristna has the glory. Some of the marks
on the hands I should not have suspected to be nail-marks, if they had not been accompanied with
the other circumstances : for the reader will see that they are double circles. The nail-holes may
have been ornamented for the sake of doing them honour, from the same feeling which makes the
disgraceful cross itself an emblem of honour. I have seen many Buddhas perfectly naked, with a
small lotus flower in the palms of the hands and on the centre of the soles of the feet. The mark
in the side is worthy of observation and is unexplained. I confess it seems to me to be very suspicious, that the icons of Wittoba are *no where* to be seen in the collections of our societies.

Mr. Moore gives an account of an influence endeavoured to be exercised upon him, to induce
him not to publish the print, for fear of giving offence. If it were nothing but a common crucifix,
why should it give offence ?

3. It cannot and will not be denied, that these circumstances make this Avatar and its temples
at Terputty, in the Carnatic, and Punderpoor near Poonah, the most interesting to the Christian
world of any in India. Pilgrimages are made to the former, particularly from Guzerat. Why have
not some of our numerous missionaries examined them ? Will any person believe that they have
not ? Why is not the account of the search in the published transactions of the Missionary Society ? There is plenty of nonsense in their works about Juggernaut and his temple. Was it
suppressed for the same reason that the father of Ecclesiastical History, Eusebius, admits that he
suppressed matters relating to the Christians, and among the rest, I suppose, the murder of Cris-
pus, by his father Constantine, viz. that it was not of good report ? It would be absurd to deny
that I believe this to be the fact. When Mr. Moore wrote, Terputty was in the possession of the
English, who made a profit of £15,000 a year of the temple. The silence itself of our literati and
missionaries speaks volumes.

Mr. Moore (p. 415) says, " In Sanscrit this Avatara is named Vinkutyeish ; in the Carnatic
" dialect, Terpati ; in the Telinga country and language, Vinkatramna Govinda ; in Guzerat and
" to the westward, Ta'khur, or Thakhur, as well as Ballaji : the latter name obtains in the neigh-
" bourhood of Poona, and generally through the Mahratta country." The name of Terpati, or as
he elsewhere calls him Tripati, identifies him with the ancient Trinity. This word is almost correctly Latin, but this a person who has read Sect. XXV. of Chap. II. and Ap. p. 304, of my CELTIC
DRUIDS, will not be surprised at. Pati or Peti is the Pali[2] word for father. And what does
Wittoba's other name Ballaji look like but Baal-jah, בעל Bol, יה Ie, or יה Iie ? Whenever the
languages of India come to be understood, I am satisfied that Colonel Wilford's opinion will be

---

[1] P. 416.   [2] We shall find in the end that the Pali language was originally the same as the Tamul.

proved well founded, and that they will be discovered at the bottom to be derived from the same root as the sixteen-letter system of the Phœnicians, Hebrews, &c., &c., and their Gods the same.

The circumstance of Ballaji treading on the head of the serpent shews that he is, as the Brahmins say, an Avatar of Cristna. I shall be accused of illiberality in what I am going to say, but I must and will speak the truth. Belief is not (at least with me) a matter of choice, it is a matter of necessity, and suspicion is the same—and I must say, if I speak honestly, that after the circumstances of concealment for so many years stated above, I shall not believe that there is not something more in the Avatar of Wittoba if his temples be not searched by persons well known to be of a sceptical disposition. And even then, who knows that the most important matters may not have already been removed? It is lamentable to think that the lies and frauds of the unprincipled part of the priesthood, and generally the ruling part, have rendered certainty upon these subjects almost unattainable : however, it comes to this, that it is perfectly absurd to look for *certainty*, or to blame any one for an opinion. The fact of the God treading on the head of the serpent is a decisive proof, both in his case and in that of Cristna, that this cannot have been taken from the Romish or Greek writings, or the spurious Gospel histories ; because the sects whose writings they are, ALL make the woman, not the *seed* of the woman, bruise the serpent's head. The modern Protestant churches translate the Hebrew in Genesis by the word *ipse ;* the ancient Romish church, by the word *ipsa ;* the latter, to support the adoration of the Virgin, the Maia ; the former, to support their oriental doctrine of the *Atonement*, which never was held by the latter. I believe the seed of the woman bruising the serpent's head was never heard of in Europe till modern times, notwithstanding some various readings may be quoted. The Brahmins surely must have been deeply read in the modern scholastic divinity, to have understood and to have made the distinction between the Romish and Protestant schools ! They must, indeed, have had a MAGEE on the Atonement. The mode in which all the different particulars relating to the serpent, Osiris, &c., are involved with one another, seems to render it impossible to suppose that the history relating to Cristna can have been copied from the gospel histories. The seed of the woman crushing the serpent's head is intimately connected with the voyage of the God from Muttra to the temple of Jaggernaut,—evidently the same mythos as the voyage of Osiris to Byblos. Of the seed of the woman crushing the serpent's head, or of the descent into hell, similar to that of Cristna, there is not a word in the orthodox gospel histories.

4. I shall presently make some observations on the celebrated Hercules, and I shall shew that he is the same as Cristna, a supposed incarnation of the Sun in Aries. On this God the very celebrated and learned divine Parkhurst makes the following observation :[1] " But the labours of Her-" cules seem to have had a still higher view, and to have been originally designed as emblematic " memorials of what the real Son of God, and Saviour of the world, was to do and suffer for our " sakes,

$$\text{Νοσων ϑελχτηρια παντα κομιζων,—}$$

" *bringing a cure for all our ills*, as the Orphic hymn speaks of Hercules."

Here Mr. Parkhurst proceeds as a Christian priest, who is honest and a believer in his religion, ought to do. This is very different from denying a fact or concealing it. The *design*, of the labours of Hercules here supposed, having nothing to do with the antiquity of nations, does not in any way interfere with my inquiry. For my own part I feel that whether I approve the reason assigned or not, Mr. Parkhurst and other Christians of his school have as much right to their opinion as I have to mine ; and, for entertaining such opinion, ought not to be censured by me or any one. My object is facts—and, if I could avoid it, I would never touch a dogma at all.

---

[1] In voce עז oz, III. p. 520.

I am extremely glad to find such a reason given, because it liberates me from a painful situation; for it is evident, that if Hercules were Cristna or Buddha, they must have been types or symbols of Christ if Hercules were: and if this be the religion which I contend that I am justified in taking from Parkhurst, how absurd is it to suppress the facts respecting Cristna! For, it is evident the nearer and closer they are to the history of Jesus Christ, the more perfect is the type or emblem; and upon this ground the complaint of the philosopher against the religion will be, not that these histories are similar, but that in certain cases they are *not* similar. He will say, this cannot be a type or emblem, because it is not the same. Thus the frauds of the priests in suppressing facts will recoil upon themselves. And when we perceive that the Hindoo Gods were supposed to be crucified, it will be impossible to resist a belief, that the particulars of that crucifixion have been suppressed. To suppose that Buddha and Cristna are said in the Hindoo books to be crucified, and yet that there are no particulars of such crucifixion detailed, is quite incredible. The argument of Mr. Parkhurst is very different from that of Mr. Maurice, and I hail it with delight, because it at once sets my hands at liberty, and shews that in future the defenders of the religion must bring forth, not suppress, ancient histories. This shews the folly of the disingenuous proceedings of our priests with respect to Hindoo learning.

For a long time I endeavoured to find some reason or meaning for the story of the crown of thorns, so unlike any thing in history but itself, but in which the prejudices of our education prevent our seeing any absurdity. I have at last come to an opinion, which I know will be scouted by every one who has not very closely attended to the extreme ignorance of the first professors of Christianity, and it is this, that the idea of the thorns has been taken from the pointed Parthian coronet of Wittoba or Balaji. Not understanding it, and too much blinded by their zeal to allow themselves time to think, as in many other instances, they have run away with the first impression which struck them. If I were not well acquainted with the meanness of understanding of these devotees, I should not certainly harbour this opinion, but it is not more absurd than many other of their superstitions.

5. In many of the most ancient temples of India, the Bull, as an object of adoration, makes a most conspicuous figure. A gigantic image of one protrudes from the front of the temple of the *Great Creator*, called in the language of the country, Juggernaut, in Orissa. This is the Bull of the Zodiac,—the emblem of the sun when the equinox took place in the first degree of the sign of the Zodiac, Taurus. In consequence of the precession of the equinoxes, the sun at the vernal equinox left Taurus, and took place in Aries, which it has left also for a great number of years, and it now takes place in Aquarius. Thus it keeps receding about *one degree* in 72 years, and about a whole *sign* in 2160 years. According to this calculation, it is about 2500 years by the true Zodiac, before the time of Christ, since it was in the first degree of Aries, and about 4660 before the time of Christ, since it was in the same degree of Taurus. M. Dupuis has demonstrated that the labours of Hercules are nothing but a history of the passage of the sun through the signs of the Zodiac;[1] and that Hercules is the sun in Aries or the Ram, Bacchus the sun in Taurus or the Bull. From this it follows that the worship of Jaggeruaut must have been instituted, and his temple probably built, near 6500 years ago, and that the temple and worship of Cristna, or the Indian Hercules, must have taken place at least, but probably about, 2160 years later. This brings the date of Cristna to about 2500 years before Christ. When Arrian says that the Indian Hercules was fifteen hundred years after Bacchus, it appears that he had learnt a part of the truth, probably from the tradition of the country. The great length of time between the two was known by tradition, but the *reason* of it was unknown. But I think we may see the truth

---

[1] In the sphere, Hercules treads on the serpent's head. See Dupuis

through the mist. The adoration of the Bull of the Zodiac is to be met with every where throughout the world, in the most opposite climes. The examples of it are innumerable and incontrovertible; they admit of no dispute.

6. The reader will not fail to recollect that in our observations on the Cristna of India, some difference between him and Jesus Christ, relating to the immaculate conception, was observed by Mr. Maurice, and laid hold of by him as a point on which he could turn into ridicule the idea of the identity of the two histories of Cristna and Jesus. The life of Pythagoras will shew us where the Christians may have got the particulars which differ from the history of Cristna. The early fathers travelling for information, which was the case with Papias, Hegesippus, Justin, &c., mixed the traditions relating to Pythagoras, which they found spread all over the East, with those relating to the Indian Cristna, and from the *two* formed their own system. Pythagoras himself having drawn many of his doctrines, &c., from the Indian school, the commixture could scarcely be avoided. Thus we find the few peculiarities respecting the birth of Jesus, such as the immaculate conception, wherein the history of Jesus differs from that of Cristna, exactly copied from the life of Pythagoras. And the circumstances relating to the immaculate conception by the mother of Pythagoras, I have no doubt were taken from the history of Buddha, as I shall shew in my next chapter, and from the virgin of the celestial sphere—herself of Oriental origin. Thus from a number of loose traditions at last came to be formed, by very ignorant and credulous persons, the complete history of the Jesus Christ of the Romish Church, *as we now have it.* I think no person, however great his credulity may be, will believe that the identity of the immaculate conceptions of Jesus and Pythagoras can be attributed to accident. The circumstances are of so peculiar a nature that it is absolutely impossible. With this system the fact pointed out by the Unitarians is perfectly consistent, that the first two chapters of Matthew and of Luke, which contain the history of the immaculate conception, are of a different school from the remainder of the history.

The first striking circumstance in which the history of Pythagoras agrees with the history of Jesus is, that they were natives of nearly the same country; the former being born at Sidon, the latter at Bethlehem, both in Syria. The father of Pythagoras, as well as the father of Jesus, was prophetically informed that his wife should bring forth a son, who should be a benefactor to mankind. They were both born when their mothers were from home on journeys: Joseph and his wife having gone up to Bethlehem to be taxed, and the father of Pythagoras having travelled from Samos, his residence, to Sidon, about his mercantile concerns. Pythais, the mother of Pythagoras, had a connexion with an Apolloniacal spectre, or ghost, of the God Apollo, or God Sol, (of course this must have been a *holy* ghost, and here we have THE *Holy Ghost,)* which afterward appeared to her husband, and told him that he must have no connexion with his wife during her pregnancy—a story evidently the same as that relating to Joseph and Mary. From these peculiar circumstances; Pythagoras was known by the same identical title as Jesus, namely, *the Son of God;* and was supposed by the multitude to be under the influence of Divine inspiration.

When young, he was of a very grave deportment, and was celebrated for his philosophical appearance and wisdom. He wore his hair long, after the manner of the Nazarites, whence he was called the long-haired Samian. And I have no doubt that he was a Nazarite for the term of his natural life, and the person called his daughter was only a person figuratively so called.

He spent many years of his youth in Egypt, where he was instructed in the secret learning of the priests, as Jesus, in the Apocryphal Gospels, is said to have been, and was carried thence to Babylon by Cambyses, the iconoclast and restorer of the Jewish religion and temple, where he was initiated into the doctrines of the Persian Magi. Thence he went to India, where he learned the doctrines of the Brahmins. Before he went to Egypt he spent some time at Sidon, Tyre, and

Biblos, learning the secret mysteries of all these places. Whilst in this country he chiefly dwelt in a temple on Mount Carmel; probably in the temple of Jove, *in which there was no image.* After his return from India, he is stated to have travelled about the world, to Egypt, Syria, Greece, Italy, &c., preaching reformation of manners to these different nations, and leaving among them numbers of proselytes. He was generally favoured by the people, but as generally persecuted by the governments; which almost always persecute real philanthropists. Here are certainly some circumstances in this history very like those in the histories of Jesus.

The stories told of the mother of Pythagoras having had connexion with an Apolloniacal spectre, is not the only one of the kind: the same story is told of Plato, who was said to be born of Parectonia, without connexion with his father Ariston, but by a connexion with Apollo. On this ground the really very learned Origen defends the immaculate conception, assigning, also, in confirmation of the fact, the example of Vultures, (Vautours,) who propagate without the male. What a striking proof that a person may possess the greatest learning, and yet be in understanding the weakest of mankind!

It seems to be quite impossible for any person of understanding to believe, that the coincidence of these histories of Plato[1] and Pythagoras, with that of Jesus, can be the effect of accident. Then how can they be accounted for otherwise than by supposing that in their respective orders of time they were all copies of one another? How the priests are to explain away these circumstances I cannot imagine, ingenious as they are. They cannot say that Jamblicus, knowing the history of Christ, attributed it to the philosophers, because he quotes for his authorities Epimenides, Xenocrates, and Olimpiodorus, who all lived long previous to the birth of Christ

In my next chapter all these sacred predicted births will be shewn to be supposed renewed incarnations of portions of the Holy Spirit or Ghost. And here I must observe, that these miraculous facts, charged to the account of Plato and Pythagoras, by no means prove that these men did not exist, nor can such facts, charged to Jesus, if disbelieved, justify an Unbeliever in drawing a conclusion that he never existed.

---

[1] Vide Olimpiodorus's Life of Plato

BOOK V

CHAPTER I

Buddha the Sun in Taurus, as Cristna was the Sun in Aries—Names of Buddha—
Meaning of the word Buddha, the same as that of the first word in Genesis—
The Ten Incarnations—Descent of Buddha the same as Cristna's—Buddha and
Cristna the same—Simplicity of Buddhism—Explanation of Plate—Buddha a
Negro—Hierarchy—Maia—Samaneans of Clemens—Incarnation—Cabul—
Buddhism extends over many Countries—Buddha before Cristna

1. THE time is now arrived when it becomes proper to enter upon an examination of the doctrines of the celebrated Buddha of India, which were the foundations of all the mythoses of the
Western nations, as well as of those which we have seen of Cristna; and from these two were
supplied most of the superstitions which became engrafted into the religion of Jesus Christ.

I shall now shew, that Buddha and Cristna were only renewed incarnations of the same Being,
and that Being the Solar power, or a principle symbolized by the Sun—a principle made by the
sun visible to the eyes of mortals : and particularly exhibiting himself in his glory at the vernal
equinox, in the heavenly constellation known by the name of Taurus, as BUDDHA, and subsequently in that of Aries, as CRISTNA.

But I must previously make one observation to guard my reader against mistake.

There is a style of writing or speaking, adopted by our orientalists from inadvertency or inattention to its consequences, which has a great tendency to mislead the reader. They take up a
book in Ceylon or Pegu, perhaps, to learn from it the doctrines of Buddha or of Cristna; they read
this book, and then tell us that these are the doctrines of Buddha, never considering that this book
may contain only the doctrines of an obscure sect of Buddhists. Suppose a Brahmin were to
come to England, and to take up a book of Johanna Southcote's, or of Brothers', or of Calvin's;
how much would he misrepresent the religion of Jesus if he represented it as he found it there!
Except in a few leading particulars, it is as difficult to say what is at present the religion of
Buddha, as it is to decide what is the religion of Christ. Again, if any one would say what the
religion of Christ is at this day, in any particular country, it would be very different from what
the religion of Christ was *four* hundred, or even *two* hundred, years ago. We have no service *now*
in our Liturgy for casting out devils. And it is the same with Buddhism and Vishnuism.
My search is to find the spring-head whence all the minor streams of Buddhism have sprung.
A description of the rivulets flowing from it and which have become muddy in their progress,
however interesting to some persons, is not my object; nor is it to my taste to spend my time upon
such nonsensical matters, which can have no other effect than to disguise the original of the religion, and to gratify evil passions, by depreciating the religion of our neighbour. If his religion
have sunk into the most degraded state, as in Ceylon, the more the pity. It shall not be my task

to expose the foolish puerilities, into which our unfortunate fellow-subjects, now unable to defend themselves, have fallen; but *to shew the truth that, fallen as they are, they once possessed a religion refined and beautiful.*

M. Creuzer[1] says, " There is not in all history and antiquity perhaps a question at the same " time more important and more difficult than that concerning Buddha." He then acknowledges that by his name, his ASTRONOMICAL character, and close connexion, not only with the mythology and philosophy of the Brahmins, but with a great number of other religions, this personage, truly mysterious, seems to lose himself in the night of time, and to attach himself by a secret bond to every thing which is obscure in the East and in the West. I apprehend the reason of the difficulty is to be found, in a great degree, in the fact, that our accounts are taken from the Brahmins who have modelled or corrupted the history to suit their own purposes. I am of opinion that the Buddhists were worshipers of the sun in Taurus, the Bacchus of the Greeks; that they were the builders of the temple of Jaggernaut, in front of which the Bull projects; and that they were expelled from Lower India when the Indian Hercules, Cristna, succeeded to the Indian Bacchus. That is, when the sun no longer rose at the equinox in the sign *Taurus*, but in the sign *Aries*. This is, I believe, the solution of the grand enigma which M. Creuzer says we are not able entirely to solve, and this I will now endeavour to prove.

2. " Buddha is variously pronounced and expressed *Boudh, Bod, Bot, But, Bad, Budd, Bud-* " *dou, Boutta, Bota, Budso, Pot, Pout, Pota, Puti,* and *Pouti.* The Siamese make the final T or " D quiescent, and sound the word *Po;* whence the Chinese still further vary it to Pho or Fo. In " the Talmudic dialect the name is pronounced *Poden* or *Pooden;* whence the city, which once " contained the temple of Sumnaut or Suman-nath, is called *Patten-Sumnaut.* The broad sound " of the *U* or *Ou* or *Oo,* passes in the variation *Patten* into *A,* pronounced *Ah* or *Au;* and in a " similar manner, when the *P* is sounded *B,* we meet with *Bad, Bat,* and *Bhat.* All these are in " fact no more than a ringing of changes on the cognate letters B and P, T and D. Another of " his names is *Saman,* which is varied into *Somon, Somono, Samana, Suman-Nath,* and *Sarmana.* " From this was borrowed the sectarian appellation of *Samaneans,* or *Sarmaneans.* A third is " *Gautama,* which is indifferently expressed *Gautameh, Godama, Godam, Codam, Cadam, Cardam,* " and *Cardama.* This perpetually occurs in composition with the last, as *Somono-Codom* or *Sa-* " *mana-Gautama.* A fourth is *Sacu, Sacya, Siaka, Shaka, Xaca, Xaca-Muni* or *Xaca-Menu,* " and *Kia,* which is the uncompounded form of *Sa-Kia.* A fifth is *Dherma,* or *Dharma,* or " *Dherma-rajah.* A sixth is *Hermias, Her-Moye,* or *Heri-Maya.* A seventh is *Datta, Dat-* " *Atreya, That-Dabia, Date, Tat* or *Tot, Deva-Tat* or *Deva-Twasta.* An eighth is *Jain, Jina,* " *Chin, Jain-Deo, Chin-Deo,* or *Jain-Eswar.* A ninth is *Arhan.* A tenth is *Mahi-Man, Mai-* " *Man,* or (if *Om* be added) *Mai-Man-Om.* An eleventh is *Min-Eswara,* formed by the same " title *Min* or *Man* or *Menu* joined to *Eswara.* A twelfth is *Gomut* or *Gomat-Eswara.* A thir- " teenth, when he is considered as *Eswara* or *Siva,* is *Ma-Esa* or *Har-Esa;* that is to say, the " great *Esa* or the *Lord Esa.* A fourteenth is *Dagon* or *Dagun,* or *Dak-Po.* A fifteenth is " *Tara-Nath.* And a sixteenth is *Arca-Bandhu* or *Kinsman of the Sun.*"[2]

Again. " *Wod* or *Vod* is a mere variation of *Bod;* and *Woden* is simply the Tamulic mode of " pronouncing Buddha: for in that mode of enunciation, *Buddha* is expressed *Pooden* or *Poden;* " and Poden is undoubtedly the same word as *Voden* or *Woden.*"[3] This etymology is assented to by Sir W. Jones, if it were not, as I believe it was, originally proposed by him. Woden was the

[1] Religions de l' Antiquité, Vol. I. p. 285, ed. de Mons. Guigniaut.
[2] Faber, Pag. Idol. B. iv. Chap. v. p. 351.   [3] Ib. p. 355.

God of the Scuths or Goths and Scandinavians, and said to be the inventor of their letters; as Hermes was the supposed inventor of the letters of the Egyptians. This, among other circumstances, tends to prove that the religion of the Celts and Scuths of the West was Buddhism. The Celtic Teutates is the Gothic Teut or Tuisto, Buddhas titles of *Tat, Datta*, or *Twashta*. *Taranis* is *Tara-Nath.* *Hesus* of Gaul is, *Esa, Mu-Hesa,* and *Har-Esa.* But those are by the Latin writers called Mercury.[1]

My reader will observe that I have given from Mr. Faber sixteen different names of Buddha, by which he undertakes to prove that he was known at different times and in different places. Mr. Faber enters at great length into the discussion of each, and proves his case, in almost every instance, in a way which cannot reasonably be disputed. I do not think it necessary to follow him, but shall take those names upon his authority. He makes it evident that Buddhism extended almost to every part of the old world: but we must remember that the British Taranis, and the Gothic Woden, were both names of Buddha. In my Celtic Druids I have shewn that the worship of Buddha is every where to be found—in Wales, Scotland, and Ireland.[2] Hu, the great God of the Welsh, is called Buddwas;[3] and they call their God Budd, the God of victory, the king who rises in light and ascends the sky.[4]

In Scotland, the country people frighten their children by telling them, that *old Bud* or the *old man* will take them. In India, one of the meanings of the word Buddha is *old man.*

3. In this inquiry it seems of the first consequence to ascertain the meaning of the word *Buddha.* From the examination of the accounts of the different authors, this celebrated word appears to have the same meaning as the first word of Genesis, that is, WISDOM, or *extremely wise*, or *wise in a high degree.*[5] M. Creuzer gives it *savant, sage, intelligence, excellente,* et *supérieure.* He says, it allies itself or is closely allied to the understanding, mind, *intelligence* unique, and supreme of God.

This is confirmed by Mr. Ward, the missionary, who tells us, that Buddha is the Deity of WISDOM, as was the Minerva of Greece. When devotees pray for wisdom to their king, they say, May Buddha give thee wisdom.[6]

The etymology of the word Buddha seems to be unknown to the Hindoos, which favours the idea of a date previous to any of the present known languages. In the Pali, of Ceylon, it means *universal knowledge* or *holiness.*[7]

The word Buddha has been thought, by some Hindoo authors, to be a general name for a philosopher; by others it has been supposed to be a generic word, like Deva, but applicable to a sage or philosopher; but still it is allowed to mean, *excellence,* WISDOM, *virtue, sanctity.*

In Sanscrit we have, Sanskrit Root, *Budh,* to know, to be aware; *Budhyati,* he knows, is aware; *Bodhayámi,* I inform, I teach.

Buddhi, wisdom; *Buddha,* sage, wise; *Budha,* WISDOM.[8]

ברא *bda* in the Hebrew means, to devise of himself alone; or I should say, to think or theorise. In Arabic it means, to begin to produce, or to devise something new.

Two facts seem to be universally agreed upon by all persons who have written respecting Buddha. The first is, that at last he is always found to resolve himself into the sun, either as the

[1] Faber, Orig. Pag. Idol.   [2] Celtic Druids, pp. 197, 306, &c.   [3] Davies, Celtic Myth. p. 118.
[4] Ib. p. 116.   [5] Moore's Pantheon, p. 234.   [6] Ward's Hist. of Hind. p. 452.
[7] Asiat. Res. Vol. XVII. p. 33.
[8] Some of our Indian scholars make a distinction between Buddha, and Budd, the Planet Mercury. I can no more admit this, than I can admit that the God Mercury was not the Sun; though I know that Mercury is the name of a Planet, and that the planet is not the Sun. The cases are exactly similar.

sun, or as the higher principle of which the sun is the image or emblem, or of which the sun is the residence. The second is, that the word Buddha means WISDOM. Now, we cannot believe that this WISDOM would be called by so singular a name as Buddha, without a cause.

It has been observed by several philologers that the letters B D, B T, universally convey the idea either of former or of creator. But Genesis says the world was formed by WISDOM. Wisdom was the Buddha or former of the world: thus WISDOM, I conceive, became called Bud. Wisdom was the first emanation, so was Buddha. Wisdom was the Logos by which the world was formed; but Buddha was the Creator: thus the Logos and Budd are identical, the same second person of the Trinity.

Rasit, or WISDOM, was contemporaneous with the commencement of creation—it was the beginning of things, and the beginning was WISDOM, the Logos.

The beginning, as the word *Rasit* is explained by our version, is contradictory to the context, because the existence of space, of time, of created angelic beings, is implied, before the moment which gave birth to the mundane system. This will not be thought to be too refined for the inventors of the Trinity,—the Creator, Preserver and Destroyer. I shall shew that Logos, Bud, and Rasit, were only names in different languages for the same idea.

Mr. Whiter says, " *Through the whole compass of language the element B D denotes Being:* " hence we have the great Deity worshiped all over the East—Budda."[1] Then Buddha will mean the existent or *self-existent wisdom*, self-existent as an integral part of the Trinity. He then informs us that, in Persian, *Bud-en Bud*, signifies *to be*. The same as *Is, est, existo*. Bud is clearly the *I am that I am* of our Bible; or, in the original, which has no present tense, the *I shall be*, or the *I have been*; or what, perhaps, this celebrated text may mean, THAT WHICH I HAVE BEEN, I SHALL BE—Eternity, past and future.

4. Mr. Crawfurd says, oriental scholars have for some time suspected that the religions of Brahma and Buddha are essentially the same, the one being nothing but a modification of the other.[2] This we shall find hereafter confirmed.

The following is the speech of Arjoon respecting Vishnu as Cristna—Thou art all in all. Thou art thyself numerous Avatars. Thy Hyagrive Avatar killed Madhu, the Ditya, on the back of a tortoise. In thy Comma Avatar did the Devites place the solid orb of the earth, while from the water of the milky ocean, by the churning staff of mount Meru, they obtained the immortal Amrita of their desires. Hirinakassah, who had carried the earth down to Patal, did thy Varaha Avatar slay and bring up the earth on the tusks of the boar: and Prahland, whom Hirinakassah tormented for his zeal towards thee, did thy Narasing Avatar place in tranquillity. In thy dwarf or Bahmen Avatar thou didst place Bali in the mighty monarchy of Patal. Thou art that mighty Parasa Rama, who cut down the entire jungle, the residence of the Reeshees:[3] and thou art Ram the Potent slayer of Ravar. O supreme Bhagavat, thou art the Buddha Avatar who shall tranquillize and give ease to Devaties, human creatures, and Dityes.[4]

I think I could scarcely have wished for a more complete proof of the truth of my doctrine of the renewal of the Avatars, than the above. It shews, in fact, that both Buddha and Cristna are nothing but renewed incarnations in each cycle.

The ancient identity of the worship of Buddha and of Cristna, receives a strong confirmation

---

[1] Etymol. Univ. Vol. I. p. 310.   [2] Hist. Ind. Arch. Vol. II. p. 222.

[3] I apprehend the Reeshees, or Rishees, when the word is applied to men, are the Ras-shees—the φιλοσοφοι. They are said to have been seven in number, and the Pleiades were dedicated to them. But I shall return to this subject hereafter.

[4] Camb. Key, Vol. II. p. 294.

from the fact, that the Buddhists have TEN incarnations of Buddha, the same as the followers of Cristna, and, what is remarkable, called by the same names. [1] Mr. Ward says, " Vishnu had ten " incarnations, and Buddha had the same number." [2] These ten incarnations, thus noticed by this missionary, we shall find of the very first importance in our future disquisitions.

The Rev. Mr. Maurice has given a very long and particular account of these ten grand Avatars or incarnations, of the God of the Hindoos. The accounts of the Brahmins consist, to outward appearance, of a great number of idle and absurd fables, not worth repetition. The only fact worthy of notice *here* is, that Buddha was universally allowed to be the first of the incarnations; that Cristna was of later date; and that, at the æra of the birth of Christ, eight of them had appeared on the earth, and that other two were expected to follow before the end of the Cali-Yug, or of the present age. But the Brahmins held that 3101 years of it had expired at the period of the birth of Christ, according to our reckoning.

Between the Brahmins and the Buddhists there exists the greatest conceivable enmity: the former accusing the latter of being Atheists, and schismatics from their sect. They will hold no communication with them, believing themselves to be made unclean, and to require purification, should they step within even the *shadow* of a Buddhist. Much in the same way the Buddhists consider the Brahmins. The ancient histories of the Hindoos are full of accounts of terrible wars between the different sectaries, which probably lasted, with the intermissions usual in such cases, for many generations, and extended their influence over the whole world; and we shall see in the course of this work, that, in their results, they continue to exercise an influence over the destinies of mankind.

Buddha is allowed by his enemies, the Brahmins, to have been an avatar. Then here is *divine wisdom* incarnate, of whom the Bull of the Zodiac was the emblem. *Here* he is the Protogonos or first-begotten, the God or Goddess Μητις of the Greeks, being, perhaps, both male and female. He is at once described as divine wisdom, the Sun, and Taurus. This is the first Buddha or incarnation of wisdom, by many of the Brahmins often confounded with a person of the same name, supposed to have lived at a later day. In fact, Buddha or the wise, if the word were not merely the name of a doctrine, seems to have been an appellation taken by several persons, or one person incarnate at several periods, and from this circumstance much confusion has arisen. But I think we may take every thing which the Brahmins say of the first Buddha to his advantage, as the received doctrine of his followers. They hate all Buddhists too much to say any thing in his favour which they think untrue.

5. The mother of Buddha was MAIA, who was also the mother of Mercury, a fact of the first importance. Of this Maia or Maja the mother of Mercury, Mr. Davies [3] says, " The universal " genius of nature, which discriminated all things, according to their various kinds or species—the " same, perhaps, as the Meth of the Ægyptians, and the Μητις of the Orphic bards, which was of " all kinds, and the author of all things.—Και Μητις πρωτος γενετωρ. Orph. Frag." To this Mr. Whiter adds, " To these terms belong the well-known deities Budda and Amida. The Fo of " the Chinese is acknowledged to be the Fod or Budda of the Eastern world, and the Mercury of " the Greeks." He then gives the following passage from Barrow's Travels: " The Budha of " the Hindûs was the son of Maya, and one of his epithets is Amita. The Fo of China was the " son of Mo-ya, and one of his epithets is Om-e-to; and in Japan, whose natives are of Chinese " origin, the same God Fo is worshiped under the name of Amida. I could neither collect from " any of the Chinese what the literal meaning was of Om-e-to, nor could I decipher the characters " under which it was written."

---

[1] Ward's India, p. 387.   [2] Transac. Asiat. Soc. Vol. I. p. 427.   [3] Apud Whiter, Etymol. Univ. p. 103.

I think there can be no difficulty in finding here the Maia in the Mo-ya, nor the *Om-e-to* in the *Am-i-da* and *Am-i-ta.* Nor, in the first syllable of the three last, the letters A, U, M, coalescing and forming the word OM. The Μητις is well known to mean divine wisdom, and we have seen above, that it is πρωτος γενετωρ or first mother of all.[1] The first of the Æons of all nations was *wisdom.* Is Am-i-da, ־ד *di* ה *e* םy *om?*

The followers of Buddha teach that he descended from a celestial mansion into the womb of Maha-Maya, spouse of Soutadanna, king of Megaddha on the north of Hindostan, and member of the family of Sakya Sa-kia,[2] the most illustrious of the caste of Brahmins.': His mother, who had conceived him, (BY A RAY OF LIGHT, according to *De Guignes,*) sans souillure, without defilement, that is, *the conception was immaculate,* brought him into the world after *ten months* without pain. He was born at the foot of a tree, and he did not touch the earth, Brahma having sought him to receive him in a vase of gold, and Gods, or kings the incarnations of Gods, assisted at his birth. The Mounis[3] and Pundits (prophets and *wise men*) recognized in this marvellous infant all the characters of the divinity, and he had scarcely seen the day before he was hailed Devata-Deva, God of Gods. Buddha, before he was called by the name Buddha or WISDOM, very early made incredible progress in the sciences. His beauty, as well as his *wisdom,* was more than human; and when he went abroad, crowds assembled to admire him. After a certain time he left the palace of his father, and retired into the desert, where he commenced his divine mission. There he ordained himself priest, and shaved his head with his own hands, i. e. adopted the tonsure. He there changed his name to Guatama.

After various trials, he came out of them all triumphant; and after certain *temptations or penitences,* to which he submitted in the desert, were finished, he declared to his disciples that the time was come to announce to the world the light of the true faith, the Gods themselves descending from heaven to invite him to propagate his doctrines. He is described by his followers as a *God of pity,* the *guardian or saviour of mankind,* the *anchor of salvation,* and he was charged to prepare the world for the day of judgment.

Amara thus addresses him : " Thou art the Lord of all things, the Deity who overcomest the " sins of the Cali-Yug, the guardian of the universe, the emblem of mercy towards those who " serve thee—OM : the possessor of all things in vital form. THOU ART BRAHMA, VISHNU, AND " MAHESA : thou art the Lord of the universe : thou art the proper form of all things, moveable " and immoveable, the possessor of the whole, and thus I adore thee. Reverence be unto thee, " the bestower of salvation.— .... I adore thee, who art celebrated by a thousand names, and " under various forms, *in the shape of* BUDDHA *the* GOD *of mercy.* Be propitious, O most high " God."[4]

Buddha was often said not only to have been born of a virgin, but to have been born, as some of the heretics maintained Jesus Christ was born, *from the side of his mother.*[5] He was also said to have had no father. This evidently alludes to his being the son of the androgynous

---

[1] Jupiter took Μητις *Metis,* to wife : and as soon as he found her pregnant, he devoured her : in consequence of which HE became pregnant, and out of his head was born Pallas or Minerva. Now μητις means DIVINE WISDOM. That this is an allegory closely connected with the doctrine of Buddha (wisdom), and of the ראשית *rasit,* or wisdom of Genesis, the first emanation of the Jews, I think no one will doubt, though it may be difficult to explain its details.

[2] If we look back to Section 2, we shall see that Mr. Faber states Sa-kia to be a name of Buddha. This Xaca or Saka is the origin, as I shall shew, of the name of our Saxon ancestors.

[3] Mounis are nothing but Menus or wise men, like the Minoses of Crete, &c., Rashees of India, and Sophis of Persia.

[4] Moore's Pantheon, pp. 23, 33, 39.   [5] And as Mani was said to be born.

Brahme-Maia.[1] This I suppose to be described in the prints in Moore's Pantheon, where Buddha is rising from the navel of Brahme-Maia, with the umbilical cord uncut.

Mons. De Guignes[2] states that Fo, or Buddha, was brought forth not from the matrix, but *from the right side*, of a virgin, *whom a ray of light had impregnated.* The Manichæans held that this was the case with Jesus Christ, and by this single fact, without the necessity for any other, they identify themselves with the Buddhists.

St. Jerom says,[3] Apud Gymnosophistas Indiæ, quasi per manus, hujus opinionis auctoritas traditur, quod Buddam, principem dogmatis eorum, *è latere suo virgo generavit.*

We see here that the followers of Buddha are called Gymnosophists. It has been observed that the Meroe of Ethiopia was a Meru. This is confirmed by an observation of Heliodorus, that the priests of Meroe were of a humane character, and were *called Gymnosophists.*[4]

When we treat of some doctrines held by a gentleman of the name of Bentley, I must beg my reader to recollect that in the account of Jerom, the Mythos of Buddha, the same as that of Cristna, was known to him in the fourth century, and therefore cannot have been invented to oppose Christianity, about the sixth century, or to deceive Mohammed Akbar in the sixteenth.

JAYADEVA thus addresses Buddha: " Thou blamest (O wonderful) the whole *Veda* when thou " seest, O kind-hearted! the slaughter of cattle prescribed for sacrifice—O Kesava! assuming " the body of Buddha. Be victorious, O Heri! lord of the universe."[5] It may be observed that Heri means *Saviour.*

There was a Goddess called JAYADEVI, i. e. the Goddess Jaya.[6]

6. Buddha as well as Cristna means shepherd. Thus, he was the *good shepherd.* M. Guigniaut says, there is a third Guatama, the founder of the philosophy Nyaya. I ask, may not this be the philosophy of a certain sect, which in its ceremonies chaunts in honour of Cristna the word IEYE, in fact, the name of the Hebrew God *Ieue,* or *Jehovah* as we disguise it?[7] We know that names of persons in passing from one language into another, have often been surprisingly changed or disguised; but there is in reality no change here; it is the identical name.

This is one of thousands of instances where the identity of the Eastern and the Western names is not perceptible, unless recourse be had to the sixteen-letter system, which I have exhibited in my CELTIC DRUIDS; and here I must stop to make an observation on the identity of languages. I do not consider the identity of common names, though it is not to be neglected, as of half so much consequence as the identity of proper names. I think no person who has made himself master of my doctrine respecting the ancient system of sixteen original letters, can help seeing here the identity of the IEYE and the *Ieue* of the Hebrews, nor can at the same time help seeing its great importance, in diving to the bottom of the ancient mythologies. The two words are identical; but write the Hebrew word in the common way *Jehovah,* and the truth is instantly lost. It matters not how they are pronounced in modern times; when they were originally written with the same letters, they must have been the same in sound.—Iaya-deva is said to have been a very celebrated poet, but we see he had the name of one of the Hindoo Deities. From the practice of calling their distinguished personages by the names of their Gods and Goddesses, the confusion in their history is irremediable. Iayadevi was the wife of Jina, one of the incarnations of Vishnu.[8]

---

[1] Ratramn. de Nat. Christ. Cap. iii. ap. Fab. Pag. Idol. B. iv. Ch. v. p. 432.
[2] Hist. des Huns, Tome I. Part ii. p. 224.   [3] Hieron. in Jovinianum.
[4] De Paw, Recherches sur les Egyptians, Vol. II.   [5] Moore's Pantheon, p. 234.
[6] Moore's Pantheon, p. 235, and Asiatic Res. Vol. III. art. 13, also Vol. IX.
[7] See Maur. Hist. Hind. Vol. II. p. 339, ed. 4to.   [8] Moore's Panth. p. 235.

One cannot reflect for a moment upon the histories of the different Avatars of India, without being struck with the apparent contradiction of one part to the other. Thus Cristna is the Sun, yet he is Apollo. He is Bala Rama, and yet Bala Cristna. He is also Narayana floating on the waters. Again, he is Vishnu himself, and an incarnation of Vishnu. He is also Parvati, the Indian Venus. In short, he is every incarnation. All this is precisely as it ought to be, if my theory be correct. He is an Avatar or renewed incarnation, in every case, of the sun, or of that higher principle of which the sun is an emblem—of that higher principle which Moses adored when he fell down upon his face to the blazing bush. The adoration of the solar fire, as the emblem of the First Great Cause, is the master-key to nlock every door, to lay open every mystery.

Buddha may be seen in the India House with a glory round his head. This I consider of great consequence. The glory round the head of Jesus Christ is always descriptive of his character, as an incarnation of that Higher Power of which the sun is himself the emblem, or the manifestation.

There were thousands of incarnations, but those were all portions of the divinity. Emanations, perhaps they may be called, in vulgar language, from the Divine Mind, inspired into a human being. But Cristna, as the Brahmins hold, was one of the three persons of their Trinity, Vishnu himself incarnated; he was the second person of their Trinity, become man. Inspired or in-spirated might be said to be the same as *incarnated*; this was exactly the same as the Christian doctrine. We have many inspired persons, but Jesus is held to be God himself incarnated—the *Logos*, one of the three, incarnated.—To return to my subject.

Buddha passed his infancy in innocent sports; and yet he is often described as an artificer. In his manhood he had severe contests with wicked spirits, and finally he was put to death, we shall find, by *crucifixion*,[1] descended into hell, and re-ascended into heaven. The present sect of the Brahmins hold Buddha to have been a wicked impostor; therefore, we need not expect them to say any thing favourable of him; but I can entertain no doubt that he was the same kind of incarnation as Cristna.

In my *Celtic Druids* I have observed, that the word Creeshna, of the old Irish, means the Sun. Now, in the Collectanea of Ouseley,[2] we find Budb, Buth, Both, fire, the sun; *Buide lachd*, the great fire of the Druids. We also find in Vallancey's ancient Irish history, that they brought over from the East the worship of *Budh-dearg*, or king Budh, *who was of the family of* SACA-sa, or *bonus Saca*. In the Hindoo Chronology there is a Buddha Muni, who descended in the family of Sacya: and one of his titles was *Arca-bandu*, or Kinsman of the Sun. If my reader will look back a little, and observe that the Hindoo Budbh was of the family of SAKYA, he will, I think, believe with me that here we have the Hindoo Buddha in Ireland. It is impossible to be denied. How contemptible does it make our learned priests appear, who affect to despise facts of this kind, and to consider the learning wherein they are contained, beneath their notice! But they do *not* despise them; they hate them and fear them. They feel conscious that they prove a state of the world once to have existed, which shakes to their foundations numbers of their non-sensical dogmas, and, with them, their gorgeous hierarchies.

In the above extract General Vallancey calls *Saca-sa*, bonus Saca. I dare say it means bonus,

---

[1] Neither in the sixteen volumes of the Transactions of the Asiatic Society of Calcutta, nor in the works of Sir W. Jones, nor in those of Mr. Maurice, nor of Mr. Faber, is there a single word to be met with respecting the crucifixion of Cristna. *How very extraordinary that all the writers in these works should have been ignorant of so striking a fact!* But it was well known in the Conclave, even as early as the time of Jerom.

[2] Vol. III. No. I.

but it means also, I think, the same as the Greek word Σα, from Σαω *to save*, or the Hebrew word יׁשע *iso*, and means *Saviour*.

The Arca-bandhu, above-mentioned, is the same as the word Nau-banda, and has the same meaning, as well as that of *Kinsman of the Sun*, if Arca-bandu have that meaning; ארק *arg*, in Chaldee, means ship. Of the probability of this, we shall be better able to judge hereafter.

M. Matter has made a very correct observation (as we proceed in our inquiries, every new page will produce some additional proofs of its truth); he says, L'Antiquité vraiment dévoilée, nous offrirait peut-être une unité de vues, et une liaison de croyances, que les temps modernes auraient peine à comprendre.[1] This was the doctrine of the learned Ammonias Saccas, of which I shall treat hereafter.

7. The farther back we go in history the more simple we find the icons of the Gods, until at last, in Italy, Greece, and Egypt, we arrive at a time when there were *no icons* of them. And from this circumstance, which seems to have been applicable to all nations, I draw a conclusion favourable to the superior antiquity of the Buddhist worship. For Buddha is never seen in the *old temples*, where his worship alone prevails, but in one figure, and that of extreme simplicity. And in many temples about Cabul, known to be Buddhist, there are no images at all. In this case they can only be known by tradition.

The stone circles, and the ruins at Dipaldinna,[2] are undoubtedly among the most ancient in India. They are evidently not Brahminical, but Buddhist or Jain. The execution of them may well compete with the works of the most skilful of the Greeks. The drawings which Colonel Mackenzie employed the natives to execute, are very beautifully done, but in many instances a close comparison with the originals at the India House will shew, that they by no means equal them. In these works none of the unnatural monsters, with numerous heads or arms, which we see in the *later* works of the Brahmins or Buddhists, are to be found. These facts seem to shew, that in the most remote periods of Indian history, good taste, as well as skill, prevailed—circumstances which are very worthy of observation.

Though in these drawings, by Col. Mackenzie, of sculptures, at Dipaldinna, near Amrawatty, which are most beautifully executed, no example of a monstrous figure will be found—a figure with three or four heads—yet the Linga and Yoni are every where to be seen as well as the favourite Cobra Capella, shielding or covering its favourite God with its hood.

The images of Buddha can be considered only as figures of incarnations, of a portion of the Supreme Being; in fact, of human beings, filled with divine inspiration; and thus partaking the double quality of God and man. No image of the supreme Brahm himself is ever made; but in place of it, his attributes are arranged, as in the temple of *Gharipuri*, thus:

BRAMA	POWER	CREATION	MATTER	THE PAST	Earth.
WISHNU	WISDOM	PRESERVATION	SPIRIT	THE PRESENT	Water.
SIVA	JUSTICE	DESTRUCTION	TIME	THE FUTURE	Fire.

Thus each *triad* was called the Creator. In the last of these divisions we find the Trinity ascribed to Plato, which I have noticed in B. I. Ch. II. Sect. 4. We see here whence the Greeks have obtained it, and as was very common with them, they misunderstood it,[3] and took a mere figurative, or analogical, expression of the doctrine, for the doctrine itself. Probably the Earth, fire, water, might be given to the canaille, by Plato, to deceive them, as it has done some moderns, to whose superstition its grossness was suitable.

---

[1] Matter sur les Gnostiques, Vol. II. p. 205.   [2] Mackenzie's Collection in the India House.
[3] Moore's Panth. p. 242.

8. The figure in the plates numbered 8, descriptive of Buddha or Cristna, is given by Mons. Creuzer. The following is the account given of this plate by Mons. Guigniaut:[1] Crichna 8e avatar ou incarnation de *Vichnou*, sous la figure d'un enfant, allaité par *Devaki*, sa mère, et recevant des offrandes de fruits; près de là est un groupe d'animaux rassemblés dans une espèce d'arche. La tête de l'enfant-dieu, *noir*, comme indique son nom, est ceinte d'une auréole aussi bien que celle de sa mère. *On peut voir encore, dans cette belle peinture, Buddha sur le sein de Maya.*[2]

M. Creuzer observes that the images of Cristna and Buddha are so similar, that it is difficult to distinguish them; and the groupe pictured above is acknowledged by Moore, in his Hindoo Pantheon, to be applicable to Buddha on the knee of his beautiful mother Maya.[3] But yet there is one circumstance of very great importance which is peculiar to Buddha, and forms a discriminating mark between him and Cristna, which is, that he is continually described as a Negro, not only with a black complexion, in which he agrees with Cristna, but with woolly hair and flat face. M. Creuzer observes, that the black Buddha, with frizzled or curled hair, attaches himself at the same time to the three systems into which the religion of India divides itself.

9. Mr. Moore, on his woolly head, says, "Some statues of Buddha certainly exhibit thick " Ethiopian lips;[4] but all woolly hair: there is something mysterious, and unexplained, connected " with the hair of this, and only of this, Indian deity. The fact of so many different tales having " been invented to account for his crisped, woolly head, is alone sufficient to excite suspicion, that " there is something to conceal—something to be ashamed of; more than meets the eye."[5]

The reason why Buddha is a Negro, at least in the very old icons, I trust I shall be able to explain in a satisfactory manner hereafter. The Brahmins form a species of corporation, a sacerdotal aristocracy, possessing great privileges; but the Buddhists have a regular hierarchy; they form a state within a state, or a spiritual monarchy at the side of a temporal one. "They have their " cloisters, their monastic life, and a religious rule. Their monks form a priesthood numerous and " powerful, and they place their first great founder at their head as the sacred depositary of their " faith, which is transmitted by this spiritual prince, who is supported by the contributions of the " faithful, from generation to generation, similar to that of the Lamas of Thibet." M. Creuzer might have said, not *similar to*, but *identical with* the Lama himself; who, like the Pope of Rome, is God on Earth, at the head of all, a title which the latter formerly assumed. Indeed the close similarity between the two is quite wonderful to those who do not understand it.

The monks and nuns of the Buddhists, here noticed by M. Creuzer, take the three cardinal vows

---

[1] 61, xiii.

[2] Of the two trays which are placed by the figure with the infant, one contains boxes, part of them exactly similar to the frankincense boxes now used in the Romish churches, and others such as might be expected to hold offerings of Myrrh or Gold. The second contains cows, sheep, cattle, and other animals. If my reader has ever seen the exhibition of the nativity in the church of the Ara Cœli at Rome, on Christmas-day, he will recollect the sheep, cows, &c., &c., which stand around the Virgin and Child. It is an exact icon of this picture. Hundreds of pictures of the Mother and Child, almost exact copies of this picture, are to be seen in Italy and many other Romish countries.

[3] Col. Tod says, Dare we attempt to lift the veil from this mystery, and trace from the seat of redemption of lost science its original source? This, I answer my good, learned, and philanthropic friend, I only have done. The allegory of Cristna's Eagle pursuing the Serpent Buddha, and recovering the books of science and religion with which he fled, is an historical fact disguised. True! and its meaning is so clear, it requires no explanation. In the Cave at Gaya, which means the Cave or Gaia or the Earth, it is written—*Heri who is Buddha.* Here the Col. says, that Cristna and Buddha, in characters, are conjoined. This is true, and they mean, Buddha who is Heri, and Heri who is Buddha. —Hist. Rajapoutana, p. 537.

[4] The lips are often tinged with red to shew that the blackness does not arise from the colour of the bronze or stone of which the image is made, but that black is the colour of the God.

[5] Moore's Pantheon, p. 232.

of *poverty, chastity, and obedience,*—the same as the monks and nuns of the European Christians. This singular fact at once proves the identity of the orders in the two communities, and that they must have had a common origin.   I know not any circumstance of consequence in their economy in which they differ.

Maya is called the great mother, the universal mother.   She is called Devi, or the Goddess παρ' εξοχην—the Grand Bhavani, the mother of gods and of men.   She is the mother of the *Trimurti,* or the being called the Creator, Preserver, and Destroyer, whom she conceived by Brahm: and when the Brahmins can get no farther in their mystics, they finish by calling her *Illusion.* Perhaps they had better have said, *Delusion,* which is the very point arrived at by Bishop Berkeley, in his metaphysics.   Plate VI. of Creuzer's work represents Maia receiving the adoration of the other divinities.   On the top of the building appear the Beeve, and, at the side of it, the Yoni and Lingha, in union.   The Burmese make Maria, or Maha-Maria, the mother of their God Somon-Codom, who was Buddha.[1]

10. A certain order of persons called Samaneans are noticed by Porphyry and Clemens Alexandrinus. I do not doubt that these are the Somonokodomites of Siam, and the Buddha called by them their leader—to be the Buddha of Siam, who, as Surya with the seven heads, is the sun and the seven planets.   This Mons. Guigniaut, in his note, by a curious etymological process, has proved.[2]   And that this Buddha was of very remote date is also proved by the fact noticed by Guigniaut, that he is identical with Osiris and the Hermes of Egypt.   " L'Hermes d'Egypte, appelé encore Thoth " ou Thaut, a tous ses charactères, et se retrouve à la fois dans les cieux, sur la terre, et aux enfers : " l'Hermes ou Mercure des Grecs et des Latins *est fils de Maya comme Buddha.*   Nous pourrions " pousser beaucoup plus loin ces rapprochemens."[3]   Learned men have endeavoured to make out several Buddhas as they have done several Herculeses, &c.[4]   They were both very numerous, but at last there was only one of each, and that one the sun.   And from this I account for the striking similarity of many of the facts stated of Buddha and Cristna.   What was suitable to the sun in Taurus, would, for the most part, be suitable to him in Aries, and it was probably about this change that a great war took place between the followers of Buddha and Cristna, when ultimately the Buddists were expelled from Lower India.   This was the war of the Maha-barata.   Maha means *great,* and Barata is the Hebrew ברא *bra* and בראת *brat,* and means Creator or Regenerator. This, I have no doubt, was the meaning of this proper name, in the old language.   What meaning the Brahmins may give to it, in their beautiful, ARTIFICIAL Sanscrit, I do not know.   All the proper names of gods, men, and places, will be found, if we could get to the bottom of them, in the Hebrew.   On this I must request my Sanscrit reader to suspend his judgment till I treat of the Sanscrit language.

Porphyry, in his treatise on *Abstinence,* gives a very good description of the Brahmins and Samaneans,[5] from which it appears that the latter had precisely the same monastic regulations in his time, that they have at this day.

The Hermes of Egypt, or Buddha, was well known to the ancient Canaanites, who had a temple to הרם *erm,* " *The Projector,* by which they seem to have meant the *material spirit,* or rather " *heavens,* considered as *projecting, impelling,* and *pushing forwards,* the planetary bodies in their " courses."[6]   Notwithstanding the nonsense about *material spirit* or *heavens,* the Hermes, or Buddha, is very apparent.

---

[1] La Loubère, P. iii. p. 136.

Hesychius says, that Mau, μαγα, and Maha, had the meaning of great, and Mau has the meaning of *great* in modern Coptic.   Asiat. Res. Vol. III. p. 415.

[2] Vol. I. p. 292.   [3] Ibid.   [4] See the Desatir, published at Bombay, in 1818.
[5] De Abs. Lib. iv. Sect. xvii.   [6] Parkhurst, Lex. in voce הרם *rme.*

The different Buddhas, Cristnas, Ramas, &c., are only different incarnations of the same being. The want of attention to this has caused great and unnecessary confusion. In the Samaneans and Buddha of Porphyry and Clemens, we have a proof that the doctrines of Buddhism were common in their day.

These Samaneaus were great travellers, and makers of proselytes; and by this means we readily account for the way in which the oriental doctrines came to be mixed up with the history of Jesus, by such collectors of traditions as Papias, Irenæus, &c. These writers made prize of every idle superstition they found, provided they could, by any means, mix it up with the history and doctrines of Jesus of Nazareth, as I shall abundantly prove in the second part of this work.

" Both Cyril and Clemens Alexandrinus [1] agree in telling us, that the Samaneans were the sa-" cerdotal order both in Bactria and in Persia. But the Samaneans were the priests of Saman or " Buddha, and it is well known that the sacerdotal class of Bactria and Persia were the Magi : " therefore the Magi and the Samaneans must have been the same, and consequently Buddha, or " Maga, or Saman, must have been venerated in those regions. With this conclusion, the my-" thologic history of the Zend-avesta will be found in perfect accordance. The name of the most " ancient Bull, that was united with the first man Key-Umurth, is said to have been *Aboudad*. " But *Aboudad*, like the *Abbuto* of the Japanese, is plainly nothing more than *Ab-Boud-dat*, or " father *Buddh-Datta*." [2] But this is not the only proof of the Buddhism of the Persians. According to the Desatir of Moshani, Maha-bad, i. e. the great Buddha, was the first king of Persia and of the whole world, and the same as the triplasian Mithras. [3]

Buddha has his three characters, the same as Brahma, which produced three sects, like those of the Brahmins—that of Buddha or Gautama, that of Jana or Jina, and that of Arhan or Mahimau. [4] I think in the last of these titles may be found the Abriman or the Ma-Ahriman, the destroyer, of Persia. But Buddha is allowed by the Brahmins to have been an incarnation of Vishnu, or to be identified with Brahma, Vishnu, and Siva, and like them he was venerated under the name OM.

Colonel Franklin (p. 5) says, " The learned Maurice entertains no doubt that the elder Boodh " of India is no other than the elder Hermes Trismegistus of Egypt, and that that original cha-" racter is of antediluvian race; here then is an analogy amounting almost to positive and irre-" fragable conviction; for Boodh and Jeyne are known throughout Hindostan, with very little " exception, to be one and the same personage." In p. 41, Colonel Franklin remarks, that Bacchus agrees in his attributes with the Indian Boodh. And Mr. Faber observes, " that Thor is " represented as the first-born of the Supreme God, and is styled in the Edda ' the eldest of " Sons.' [5] He was esteemed in Scandinavia as a middle divinity, a *mediator* between God and " man." [6]

Colonel Franklin (p. 99) speaks of " Jeyne Ishura, or Jeyne the preserver and guardian of " mankind." Here is the Indian Osiris as preserver, or saviour, from the same root as the Hebrew יש *iso*, to save.

Buddha in Egypt was called *Hermes Trismegistus*; Lycophron calls him *Tricephalus*. This speaks for itself, as we have seen that *Buddha* is identified with *Brahma, Vishnu, and Siva*.

---

[1] Clemens Alexandrinus in particular states that the Samaneans were the priests of the Bactrians. Strom Lib. i. p. 305; Faber, Pag. Idol. B. iv. Ch. v. p. 235.

[2] Faber, Pag. Idol. B. iv. Ch. v. p. 353.   [3] Ibid.   [4] Ibid. p. 349.

[5] Faber, Horæ Mosaicæ, Vol. I.

[6] Franklin's Res. p. 49. Brahma is generally in the neuter gender. But as Vishnu or Narayen he is masculine, as he is also when he is considered as the Creator. Asiat. Res. Vol. I. pp. 242, 243; Collier, Sect. iv.

Mr. Moore says, " Most, if not all, of the Gods of the Hindoo Pantheon, will, on close investi-
" gation, resolve themselves into the three *powers*, and those powers into one Deity, Brahm, typi-
" fied by the sun."[1]   Again, " In Hindu mythology every thing is indeed the Sun." Nothing
can be more true. Mr. Moore adds, " We may here, as usual with all Hindu deities, trace
" Kama's genealogy upwards to the sun, who is Brahm."[2]

It is admitted that Surya is the Sun, and that he is Buddha : hence Buddha is the sun. He is
described with seven heads. Here he is the sun, attended by five planets and the moon. At
other times, he is described sleeping on a coiled serpent with seven heads, overshadowing and
protecting him, his and the serpent's heads making eight. The first is a mythos probably adopted
before the earth was discovered to be a planet, like the other five, which were only called דוד
smim, or disposers, the angels or messengers of God.

11. About the city of Bamiam, in the kingdom of Cabul, are many caves of immense size without
any sculptures. The formation of these caves is attributed, by tradition, to the Buddhists. They
are in ancient Persia, not far from Balch. The city has been of very great size, and has been
compared to Thebes in Egypt. It is called in Sanscrit Vami-Nagari, or the beautiful city. The
Buddhist caves, *without image* or sculpture, seem to bespeak the most remote period. In the
oldest of the caves in India, those of Ellora, Salcette, Elephanta, the sculptures attest the identity
of Buddha with Cristna. In most of the temples, of which the architecture bespeaks a more recent date, nothing is found relating to Buddha, but he is found in the temple of Jaggernaut, where
there is no distinction of castes or sects. The date of these temples is generally totally unknown.
The colossal Bull in front of that at Jaggernaut evidently betrays Buddhism.

These circumstances confirm the hypothesis that Buddhism was the first religion, and I shall
hereafter prove that the religion of Cristna was engrafted into it, when the festival was changed
from Taurus to Aries.

Colonel Franklin says, " That as the figures in the caves at Cabul all bear the stamp of an
" Indian origin, we may justly ascribe them to the votaries of Boodh, who has already been identi-
" fied with the Mithras of Persia."[3]

M. Creuzer has observed, that the doctrines of Buddha are said to have come to India from the
north. Of this I have no doubt. I think that the place of his birth was in a far higher latitude
than either that of Upper Egypt, or of Lower India—in a latitude where the month of Maia, his
mother, would be the month of flowers and delight. This would be the case in Northern Thibet,
or in a climate very similar to it, but not in a climate where, in the month of May, all verdure was
withering away by the excess of the heat, and the ground fast reducing to a parched desert.

Buddha is stated by Sir W. Jones to be *Woden*, and not a native of India.[4]   But it is remarkable, that *Woden* is his Tamul name, and the Tamulese are now in South India. This will be found
of importance hereafter.

Mons. Guigniaut, in his notes on Creuzer, has very justly observed that the earliest notice we
have of the Persian religion has come from the north, from the ancient Aria or Balch, the ancient
Bactriana. He says, " Nous avons déjà parlé des temples souterrains de Bamiam, à quelque
" distance de Caboul. Ici la Perse et l'Inde, Hom et Brahma, *Bouddha et Zoroaster, semblent se
" donner la main.*"[5]   The doctrine of Buddha extends throughout China and its tributary nations ;
over the great empires and states of Cochin China, Cambodia, Siam, Pegu, Ava, Asam, Tibet,
Budtan ; many of the Tartar tribes, and, except Hindostan perhaps, generally all parts east of
the Ganges, including vast numbers of large and populous islands.[6]

---

[1] Pantheon, pp. 6, 16.   [2] Ibid. p. 447.   [3] P. 113.
[4] Asiat. Res. Vol. II. 4to. p. 9.   [5] Creuzer, Vol. I. p. 677.   [6] Moore's Pantheon, p. 240.

The immense extent of country over which Buddhism prevails surely raises a strong presumption, that it was the root, and Cristnism a branch from it. M. Schegel has remarked, that in the temples of Buddha are to be found *all the Pantheon of the idols of India*; not only their theogony, but their heroical mythology; the same mysticism which teaches man to unite himself by contemplation to the Deity; and, that the chief difference between the Buddhists and Vishnuites consists in the former forbidding the shedding of blood either for sacrifice or food. But as Schegel justly observes, it is also considered to be a great virtue with the devotees of Vichnu to abstain from these practices. The Buddhists are allowed to have been at one time very numerous on this side the Ganges, but it is said they were exterminated or expelled. They are, however, beginning to reappear in the Djainas. M. Schegel says, "I know not in truth what difference one can "establish between the new sectaries and the Buddhists."[1] In the Transactions of the Asiatic Society[2] it is said, "The princes of the country continued Jains till the prince, in the time of "Pratap, turned to Vishnou." It is added, "the Buddists and Jains are the same."

12. The following copy, in Moore's Hindoo Pantheon, of an inscription which was found in Bengal, the very focus of the country of the Brahmins, is of itself, as its genuineness cannot be disputed, almost enough to prove the original identity of Cristna and Buddha. The address is said to be to the Supreme Being: " Reverence be unto thee in the form of Buddha: reverence be "unto thee, Lord of the earth: reverence be unto thee, an incarnation of the Deity, and the "eternal one: reverence be unto thee, O God! in the form of the God of mercy: the dispeller "of pain and trouble: the Lord of all things: the Deity who overcomest the sins of the Kali "Yug: the guardian of the universe; the emblem of mercy toward those who serve thee, om ! "the possessor of all things in vital form. Thou art Brahma, Vishnu, and Mahesa;[3] thou art "the Lord of the universe; thou art the proper form of all things, moveable and immoveable; "the possessor of the whole, and thus I adore thee; reverence be unto thee, the bestower of "salvation: reverence be unto thee, (Kesava,) the destroyer of the evil spirit, Kesi.—O Damor-"dara ! shew me favour. Thou art he who resteth upon the face of the milky ocean, and who "lieth upon the serpent Sesha."[4] Again, Mr. Moore says, " In Ceylon, the Singhalese have "traditions respecting Buddha, that, like the legends of Krishna, identify him with his prototype, "Vishnu." I think with Mr. Moore and Major Mahony, that the identity of Buddha and Vishnu is clearly made out.[5]

I have been asked if they be identical, how are we to account for the wars ? I answer, is not the religion of the Protestant and the Papist identical, that is, alike forms of Christianity ? Then, how are we to account for their wars ? As the wars of the West may be accounted for, so may those of the East.

In my last chapter I said, that the word om was used exactly like our word Amen. In the above prayer is a proof of what I there advanced, with this only difference, that it was not spoken but meditated on, in profound silence, at the end of the distich or the prayer. The worship of Cristna has been proved to have been in existence, at the temple of Mutra or Maturea on the Jumna, in the time of *Alexander the Great.* This accords with what Mr. Franklin[6] has observed, that the Buddhist statues dug up around the ruins of old temples in *every* part of India, prove that the religion of the country was formerly that of Java, which is that of Buddha. He regrets that they have hitherto been treated with neglect. The name of the island Java, is clearly the

---

[1] In the Museum of the Asiatic Society is a Buddha with a Bull on the pedestal of the image. It is a Djain Buddha. No. X.

[2] P. 532.   [3] Is the Ma-hesa of Mr. Moore the Ma or great-*hesus* of Gaul ? I believe so. But, nous verrons.

[4] Pp. 222, 224.   [5] Ib. p. 228.   [6] Researches on Bodhs and Jeynes, Ch. i.

island of Ieua, i. e. יהוה ieue. Mr. Franklin makes an observation which is new to me, that the ancient Etrurians had the countenances of Negroes, the same as the images of Buddha in India.[1] This is very striking, when compared with the proofs which I have given in my CELTIC DRUIDS, Ch. II. Sect. xxv. Ap. p. 304, of the identity of the Sanscrit and the ancient language of Italy. Cristna having been made out to be the sun, the consequence necessarily follows, that Buddha is the Sun; and this easily and satisfactorily accounts for the similarity in the history of Cristna and of Buddha. And all these circumstances are easily accounted for, if Buddha and Cristna were the Sun in Taurus and Aries. In the quotation above, from Mons. Schegel, the second Hermes Trismegistus is alluded to. In the sequel I shall shew that these alleged appearances of second persons of the same name were derived from a system of renewed incarnations, and of unceasing revolving cycles.

The elder Buddha being now admitted by all oriental scholars to have long preceded Cristna, I have no occasion to dwell longer on this subject.

CHAPTER II

Cassini. Lubère. Cycles—Isaiah's Prophecy known to the Egyptians and the Celts of Gaul—Mystical meaning of the Letter M—Explanation of the Oriental Astronomical Systems—Subject continued. Mr. Bentley. Berosus—Mosaic and Hindoo Systems. Various Prophecies—Martianus Capella. Subject continued

1. THE following observations of the very celebrated astronomer Cassini, made more than a hundred years ago, and extracted from La Loubère's History of Siam, will enable me to elicit several conclusions respecting the famous Neros, of the greatest importance. As an astronomer, M. Cassini is in the first rank. No one will deny that his calculations upon *acknowledged* or *admitted facts* are entitled to the highest respect. I think they will enable me to point out the origin of many of the difficulties respecting Buddha and Cristna, and to explain them. They will also enable me to shew the mode which was adopted by the early popes and other priests, in fixing the times of several of the most important Christian epochas; as well as to exhibit the mode in which the Gods Buddha and Cristna have been regenerated. These circumstances have either been unobserved, or they have been concealed from Europeans. After a long discussion on the formation of the Siamese astronomical and civil epochas, in which, with profound learning, Cassini explains the process by which they have been formed, he says,

"The first lunisolar period, composed of whole ages, is that of 600 years, which is also com-
"posed of 31 periods of 19, and one of 11 years. Though the chronologists speak not of this
"period, yet it is one of the ancientest that have been invented.

"Josephus,[2] speaking of the patriarchs that lived before the deluge, says, that ' *God prolonged*
"*their life, as well by reason of their virtue, as to afford them the means to perfect the sciences of*
"*geometry and astronomy, which they had invented: which they could not possibly do, if they had*

---

[1] Researches on Bodhs and Jeynes, p. 149.   [2] Antiq. Jud. Lib. i. Cap. iii.

" *lived less than 600 years, because that it is not till after the revolution of six ages, that the great*
" *year is accomplished.'*

" This great year, which is accomplished after six ages, whereof not any other author makes
" mention, can only be a period of lunisolar years, like to that which the Jews always used, and
" to that which the Indians do still make use of. Wherefore we have thought necessary to
" examine what this great year must be, according to the Indian rules.

" By the rules of the first section it is found, then, that in 600 years there are 7200 solar
" months; 7421 lunar months, and $\frac{47}{71}$. Here this little fraction must be neglected; because
" that the lunisolar years do end with the lunar months, being composed of entire lunar months.

" It is found by the rules of Section II., that 7421 lunar months do comprehend 219,146 days,
" 11 hours, 57 minutes, 52 seconds: if, therefore, we compose this period of whole days, it must
" consist of 219,146 days.

" 600 Gregorian years are alternatively of 219,145 days, and 219,146 days: they agree then to
" half a day with a solilunar period of 600 years, calculated according to the Indian rules.

" The second lunisolar period composed of ages, is that of 2300 years, which being joined to
" one of 600, makes a more exact period of 2900 years: and two periods of 2300 years, joined to
" a period of 600 years, do make a lunisolar period of 5200 years, which is the interval of the time
" which is reckoned, according to Eusebius's chronology, from the creation of the world to the
" vulgar Epocha of the years of Jesus Christ.

" These lunisolar periods, and the two epochas of the Indians, which we have examined, do
" point unto us, as with the finger, the admirable epocha of the years of Jesus Christ, which is
" removed from the first of these two Indian Epochas, a period of 600 years, wanting a period of
" 19 years, and which precedes the second by a period of 600 years, and two of 19 years. Thus
" the year of Jesus Christ (which is that of his incarnation and birth, according to the tradition of
" the church, and as Father Grandamy justifies it in his Christian chronology, and Father Riccio-
" lus in his reformed astronomy) is also an astronomical Epocha, in which, according to the mo-
" dern tables, the middle conjunction of the moon with the sun happened the 24th of March, ac-
" cording to the Julian form re-established a little after by Augustus, at one o'clock and a half in
" the morning, at the meridian of Jerusalem, the very day of the middle Equinox, a wednesday,
" which is the day of the creation of these two planets.

" The day following, March 25th, which, according to the ancient tradition of the church, re-
" ported by St. Augustine,[1] was the day of our Lord's incarnation, was likewise the day of the
" first phasis of the moon ; and, consequently, it was the first day of the month, according to the
" usage of the Hebrews, and the first day of the sacred year, which, by the divine institution, must
" begin with the first month of the spring, and the first day of a great year, the natural epocha of
" which is the concourse of the middle equinox, and of the middle conjunction of the Moon with
" the Sun.

" This concourse terminates, therefore, the lunisolar periods of the preceding ages, and was an
" epocha from whence began a new order of ages, according to the oracle of the Sibyl, related by
" Virgil in these words (Eclog. iv.) :

> Magnus ab integro sæclorum nascitur ordo ;
> Jam nova progenies Cœlo dimittitur alto.

" This oracle seems to answer the prophecy of Isaiah, *Parvulus natus est nobis;* (ch. ix. 6 and 7;)
" where this new-born is called God and father of future ages ; *Deus fortis, pater futuri sæculi.*

" The interpreters do remark in this prophecy, as a thing mysterious, the extraordinary situation

---

[1] De Trin. Lib. iv. Cap. v.

" of a *Mem* final (which is the numerical character of 600) in this word לםרבה *lmrbe, ad multipli-*
" *candum,* where this *Mem* final is in the second place, there being no other example in the whole
" text of the Holy Scripture where-ever a final letter is placed only at the end of the words. This
" numerical character of 600 in this situation might allude to the periods of 600 years of the Pa-
" triarchs, which were to terminate at the accomplishment of the prophecy, which is the epocha,
" from whence we do at present compute the years of Jesus Christ."[1]

On this prophecy Mr. Faber says, " In this extraordinary poem, he (Virgil) celebrates the ex-
" pected birth of a wonderful child, who was destined to put an end to the age of iron, and to in-
" troduce a new age of gold, (precisely the idea of Isaiah).

" *The last period sung by the Sibylline prophetess, is now arrived ; and the grand series of ages,*
" THAT SERIES WHICH RECURS AGAIN AND AGAIN IN THE COURSE OF ONE MUNDANE REVOLUTION,
" *begins afresh.   Now the Virgin Astrea returns from heaven ; and the primæval reign of Saturn*
" *recommences ; now a new race descends from the celestial realms of holiness.   Do thou, Lucina,*
" *smile propitious on the birth of a boy, who will bring to a close the present age of iron, and intro-*
" *duce, throughout the whole world, a new age of gold.   Then shall the herds no longer dread the*
" *fury of the lion, nor shall the poison of the serpent any longer be formidable : every venomous ani-*
" *mal and every deleterious plant shall perish together.   The fields shall be yellow with corn, the*
" *grape shall hang in ruddy clusters from the bramble, and honey shall distil spontaneously from the*
" *rugged oak.   The universal globe shall enjoy the blessings of peace, secure under the mild sway of*
" *its new and divine sovereign.*"[2]

Many of our divines have been much astonished at the coincidence between the prophecy of the
heathen Sibyl and that of Isaiah ; the difficulty I flatter myself I shall now be able to remove, by
shewing that it related to the system of cycles, which Mons. Cassini detected in the Siamese manuscript.

I shall now proceed to prove that the period of 600 years, or the Neros alluded to by Cassini,
which has been well described by the most celebrated astronomers as the finest period that ever
was invented, and which Josephus says was handed down from the patriarchs who lived before
the flood, is the foundation of the astronomical periods of the Indians, and is probably the age or
mundane revolution alluded to by Virgil. On the subject of this fine cycle, and the important
consequences deduced by Mons. Bailly from the knowledge of it by the ancients, my Celtic Druids
may be consulted. There my reader will see proofs that it was probably the invention of a period
long prior to any thing which we have been accustomed to contemplate as founded on historical
records.

In Sect. III. M. Cassini has shewn that there was among the Siamese a very important epocha
in the year 544 before Christ. This is the æra fixed for the second Buddha according to the
Brahmins.   He has also pointed out another epocha, 638 years after the birth of Jesus Christ ;
these my reader will please to retain in recollection.   The æra of Buddha is calculated from his
death, that of Christ from his birth, and this should always be remembered.

The following observations shew Mons. Cassini was of opinion, that these Siamese periods had
some connexion with Pythagoras ; he says,

" This Siamese Epocha (of 543 or 544 B. C.) is in the time of Pythagoras, whose dogmata were
" conformable to those which the Indians have at present, and which these people had already in
" the time of Alexander the Great, as Onesicritus, sent by Alexander himself to treat with the In-
" dian philosophers, testified unto them, according to the report of Strabo, Lib. xv."[3]   Cassini

---

[1] La Loubère, Hist. Siam, Tome II. Sect. xxii. and xxiii.   [2] Pagan Idol. Vol. II. p. 10.
[3] La Loub. Cass. Tome II. p. 203.

has shewn[1] why the above-named epocha ought to be 543 and not 544,[2] (his reasons it is not ne-cessary for me to repeat,) then, if we add 543 to the second period 638, we shall have the space of 1181 years between them; if we add to which the period 19, we shall have exactly 1200, which makes two Neroses. Cassini says, " Between the two Indian epochas there is a period of 1181 " years, which being joined to a period of 19 years, there are two periods of 600 years, which re-" duce the new moons near the equinoxes."[3]

Lalande, in his Astronomie,[4] says, " Si l'on emploie la durée de l'annee que nous connoissons " et le mois Sinodique tel que nous l'avons indiqué ci-devant, c'est-a-dire, des mois de 29 jours " 12 heures 44 min. 3 sec. chacun, on aura 28 heures, 1 min., 42 sec. de trop, dans les sept mille, " quatre cent, vingt-une lunaissons : ainsi la lune retarderoit de plus d'un jour au bout de six " cents ans."

I notice this, here, that a reader learned in astronomy may not suppose me ignorant of it, or that I have overlooked it. In mythological calculations for short periods, small errors like this can be of little consequence. In a *future book of this work*, I shall shew that, at last, a very im-portant consequence arose from this error; and I flatter myself that I shall be able, by its means, to explain a part of the ancient mythology, beyond all question the most curious and important of the whole.

2. The prophecy of Isaiah alluded to by Cassini had reference in the first place to a new cycle, which may be called the cycle of Cyrus, because in Isaiah he is described by name. It probably began about the captivity. The date of it professes to be some time before that cycle of 600 years, which cycle preceded the birth of Christ; which birth ought to be precisely at the end of the cycle above-named, in which the 543 years before Christ are spoken of. It is evident that this prophecy of the cycle of Cyrus would, in a considerable degree, apply to every succeeding cycle of the Neros. In the same manner I shall shew that the prophecies of Cristna and Buddha will be found to apply to their re-appearances.

The prophecy of Isaiah may be said to have been a mystery, an example of judicial astrology. It required no divine inspiration to prove to the initiated, that, at the end of the cycle then run-ning, a new cycle would commence, or that the cycle of the God Cristna, the Sun, would be born again : and this leads us to a discovery which will account for and remove many of the difficulties which our learned men have encountered respecting Buddha and Cristna. It is evident that both of them being the sun, mystically and astrologically speaking, their year was 600 years long, and their birthday on the first year of the 600, on which was a conjunction of sun and moon at the vernal equinox. The day of the first birth of Buddha was at the vernal equinox of that 600 when the sun entered Taurus, of Cristna of that 600 nearest to the time when he entered Aries. The birthdays of both returned every 600 years—when the Phèn or Phenishe or Phœnix was con-sumed on the altar of the temple of the sun at Heliopolis, in Egypt, and rose from its ashes to new life. This, I think, seems to have been purely astrological.

At first many persons will be greatly surprised at the assertion, that the passages of Isaiah, ch. vii. 14, viii. 8, are not prophecies of Christ. In order to force the text of Isaiah to serve this

---

[1] Sect. xix. p. 219.   [2] Vide Asiat. Res. Vol. VI. p. 266. 8vo.

[3] The Brahmins were acquainted with the Cycle of 19 years. Crawfurd says, " It is curious to find at Siam the " knowledge of that Cycle, of which the invention was thought to do so much honour to the Athenian astronomer " Meton, and which makes so great a figure in our modern calendars." Researches, Vol. II. p. 18. The Siamese had the Metonic cycle more correctly than Numa, Meton, or Calippus, and the Epact also more correct than the French in the time of Cassini. Cassini, p. 213. M. Bailli observed that the Chinese, the Indians, the Chaldeans, and the Egyptians, all had the same astronomical formulæ for the calculation of eclipses, though the principles of them were forgotten. Faber, Pag. Idol. Vol. I. p. 37.

[4] Tome II. Art. 1570, ed. 3.

purpose, Clemens of Alexandria, Bishop Kidder, Dr. Nicholls, Bishop Chandler, Dr. Campbel, and many others, have been obliged to suppose that God inspired the author to use a double sense, and that the predictions related both to the prophet's son, born about the time when these were written, and to Christ, born many hundred years afterward. These learned men do not seem ever to have thought either of the unworthiness of the motive which they attribute to the Deity by this deceit, or of the gross absurdity of making the prophecy of Christ, who was to be born so many hundred years afterward, a sign to the people then living. However, the monstrous absurdity of this double sense has been refuted by Dr. Sykes, Dr. Benson, Bishop Marsh, and others; and Dr. Ekerman, and Dr. George S. Clarke, in his Hebrew Criticism and Poetry, Lond. 1810, maintain that the Old Testament contains no prophecy at all which literally relates to the person of Christ.[1]

Again, Dr. Adam Clarke maintains, that the prophecy of Isaiah—*A virgin* [2] *shall conceive and bear a son, and call his name Immanuel*, does not mean Christ.[3]

Dr. Clarke says, "It is humbly apprehended that the young woman usually called the Virgin is "the same with the prophetess,[4] and Immanuel is to be named by his mother, the same with the "prophet's son, whom he was ordered to name Maher-shalal-hash-baz."[5]

I think no one will deny that Dr. Adam Clarke, the annotator on the Bible, is a very learned man, and he is here an unwilling witness, and he comes to this conclusion in the teeth of all the prejudices of his education, after having read all the laboured attempts of our divines to make the prophecy of Isaiah a prophecy relating to Jesus Christ. I maintain then, that this fairly opens the door to the explanation which I shall now give, and which, I think, will be considered probable, when I shew that many other expressions of Isaiah are the same with the Hindoo doctrines and predictions. At all events, with every person whose understanding is not quite dwarfified by superstition, there is an end of the belief in what has been called the prophecy of Isaiah, as a necessary article of faith. The Hebrew for Immanuel is עמנואל *omnual*, which may certainly be rendered *with us God*. But it might also be rendered by OM OUR GOD, the word Om being the first syllable of the name of Ammon, the surname of Jupiter Ammon, of the Ἱερον Ὁμανυ, and of the Ammonites, ch. viii. 8,—"And the stretching out of his wings shall fill the breadth of thy land, O "Immanuel, or *God with us*," or the land of thee, Om our God—the A. U. M. or Om of India.

I can entertain little doubt that this prophecy was well known to the Gauls or Celts and Druids, long before the time of Christ, as is made sufficiently evident by an inscription VIRGINI PARITURÆ, which was found at Chartres upon a *black* image of Isis. This image was made by one of their kings, and the Rev. M. Langevin says it was existing in his day, about 1792.[6] They are almost the words of Isaiah, and Mons. Langevin says, were inscribed one hundred years before the birth of Christ. Along with the statue of Isis was a boat, which M. Langevin says was the symbol under which this Goddess was adored. This was the Argha of India, of which I shall treat hereafter.

---

[1] Class. Journal, Vol. XXXIII. p. 47.

I beg leave to ask the candid reader, if one can be found, how he can expect unlearned persons to pay any attention to these prophecies, as they are called, when some of the most learned divines, much against their inclinations, are obliged to confess that they are no such thing? One fact, however, this clearly proves, that no man can be expected, by a merciful God, under pain of punishment, to believe subjects involved in so much difficulty.

[2] The word *virgin* here is, in the Hebrew, עלמה *alme*, and is preceded by the emphatic article ה *e*, therefore of course it means THE not A virgin. In the Phœnician, Bochart says, עלמה *alme* signifies virgin. This is evidently the same word, the celestial virgin, the Alma Venus of Lucretius, and the Brahme-Maia of India, or the Virgin Astrea, alluded to by Virgil.

[3] Class. Journ. Vol. IV. p. 169, of No. VI. and No. VII.   [4] Chap. viii. 3.

[5] Class. Journ. Vol. I. p. 637. בז *bs* שח *he* ללש *sll* מהר *mer*. I cannot for a moment believe that the REAL, that is, the secret, meaning of these words is, *prædam acceleravit spolium festinando*.

[6] Recherches Hist. sur Falaise, par Langevin, prêtre.

This prophecy, which our divines have been so eager to make apply to Jesus Christ, was known also to the Egyptians and Greeks, as well as to the Hindoos and Jews. This fact strongly supports my rendering, and that it related to their sacred *Om*.[1]

Singular as my reader may imagine it to be that Isaiah should allude to the OM of India, he will not think it so very paradoxical and singular, when he learns, that the history of Cyrus, who is prophesied of by name by Isaiah, is taken from a passage in the life of Cristna, from some history of whom Herodotus must have copied it. For the particulars of this the reader may refer to Mr. Maurice's History of Hindostan.[2] I beg him to reflect on this extraordinary fact before he proceeds. His utter inability to account for it he must confess.

The connexion noticed by Cassini between the prophecy of Isaiah, the oriental cycles, and the prophecy of the Sibyl in Virgil, has a strong tendency to confirm the explanation which I have given above of the word בקומע *omnual* or Immanuel, used by Isaiah.

In addition to all this, in the course of the following work, when I treat of the Sibyls, I shall produce many very striking proofs of identity between the doctrines of Isaiah and those of the Orientalists. And I beg my reader to remember, what I have already proved, that all the learned ancients held that the sacred books had two meanings. He will also remember, that almost every thing is closely connected with judicial astrology.

3. The calculation of the age of the world before Christ, according to Eusebius, ending exactly with the Siamese cycle, is very curious. On the birth of Christ the Eastern astrologers, who, according to the two disputed chapters in Matthew and Luke, had calculated his nativity, came to Bethlehem, or the temple of CERES, where Adonis or Adonai was adored, to make to him the solar offerings, as Isaiah, according to the same disputed chapters, had foretold. All this applies very well to the sun, to Cristna or Buddha, to Jesus of Bethlehem, but has nothing to do with Jesus of Nazareth. When the Irenæuses, Papiases, and early Popes, were intruding the disputed chapters of Matthew and Luke into their canon, they took all the remainder of the story to which these books alluded. The book of Isaiah might probably mislead them.[3]

The book of Isaiah has given much trouble, as already mentioned, to our divines. They have wanted it for a prophecy of Christ, while it *literally expresses* that it alludes to *Cyrus*,[4] and that it was for a sign to the prophet's contemporaries: in consequence, as I have just stated, they have been obliged to have recourse to *a double sense*. No doubt, in one point of view, the double sense is justified, as Isaiah's prediction relating to the cycle next coming would, in a considerable degree, apply to every new revolving cycle, as it arose. As a work of judicial astrology, it is indeed very probable that the prediction had a double sense, for that is strictly in conformity with the spirit of astrology or magic.

Our divines, depending on the very questionable authority of their chronology, will tell me, that Isaiah foretold Cyrus as a Messiah, before he was born. I say nothing of the ease with which these prophecies might be corrupted, a circumstance which we know, either less or more, has happened to every sacred writing in existence: but observe, that the word *Cyrus* is a solar epithet, that in fact it means the sun.[5] Isaiah must have been an unskilful astrologer or Chaldean if he could not

[1] See CELTIC DRUIDS, Ch. v. Sect. viii. p. 163, note.   [3] Vol. II. p. 478. Ed. 4to.

[2] As usual we find them laying their hands on every thing they found. Thus in Luke ii. 25—38, we have a story of Simeon, and of Anna, the daughter of Phanuel, which is a complete interloper. Why it is here no one can tell; but Phanuel is Phan or Phen-our-god, the cycle of the neros; vide Celtic Druids, App. pp. 307, 308; and of Anna, or the year, we shall see more by and by.

[4] Isaiah xlv. 1—4. The circumstance of Cyrus being *called by his name* is different from every other prophecy.

[5] Cyrus was called Cai Coaroe, the primitive of which is, *Coresh*, a Persian name for the Sun. *Maur. Hist. Hind.* Vol. II. p. 478.

foretell the time of a new incarnation of the sun. This solar epithet of honour given to the Persian conqueror, and the events of the incarnation, very well agree with the other part in the same prophecy, where OM *our God*, or the Hero or Messiah of the soli-lunar cycle, is foretold. Of the names of the earliest of the ancients we have scarcely one which has not been given on account of some supposed quality, or something in the life, of the bearers, which could only be known (except by divine inspiration) after their deaths. This must have been the case with the name of Cyrus. It was not till after he lived that he would be known to the world to deserve the solar title. I believe the name Pharaoh, of Egypt, was a similar solar title, meaning, in the Coptic, without vowels, Φ 500, P 100, H 8,=608.

In Usher's Chronology, the famous eclipse of the sun, which caused the battle between the Medes and Lydians to cease, and which was said to have been foretold by Thales, is placed exactly 601 years before Christ. I am well aware that the date of this eclipse has been a subject of much controversy. But the date of it being fixed by Usher, where, according to my theory it ought to be, is striking. In the same year the city of Nineveh is said to have been taken, and the Assyrian empire destroyed, as it was foretold in holy writ, and the Great Cyrus to have been born. These coincidences can scarcely have been the produce of accident. They are all closely connected with the sacred prophecies.

The case of the MEM final in the Hebrew word למרבה *lmrbe*, the sign of 600, noticed by Cassini, leaves little room to doubt of the allusion. Secrets of this kind constitute sacred mysteries, cabala. I am by no means certain that there is not a secret religion in St. Peter's, not known perhaps to any persons but the Pope and Cardinals. I believe I am at this moment letting out their secrets. I beg leave to ask them if they have not in some of the Adyta of St. Peter's Church, a column or lithos of very *peculiar shape*, on which are ascribed the words Σευς Σωτηρ, or some words of nearly similar meaning? I have not seen it, but I have it on authority which I cannot doubt.

This Mem final was understood by Picus of Mirandula, who maintained that the closed ם Mem in Isaiah, taught us the reasons of the Paraclete coming after the Messiah. He[1] evidently understood that there was a secret concealed under this word of Isaiah. He was a man much celebrated for his learning in the antiquities of the Jews, and thus it appears that my idea, taken from M. Cassini, is no modern thought, but that a similar opinion respecting this word was held four hundred years ago, by a man who, of all others in modern times, was the most likely to understand it.[2] This, I hope, will justify me and Cassini against the charge of being fantastical.

In the celebrated history called The Gospel of the Infancy, which, I think it probable, was originally in Arabic, but of which there are some passages remaining in Greek, Jesus is said to have been sent to a school-master, to whom he explained the mystical meaning of the letters. This gospel was peculiarly the gospel of the Nestorians, and of the Christians of *St. Thomas on the coast of Malabar*, of whom I shall have to speak hereafter. This story is repeated in another Gospel, called the Gospel of St. Thomas, which is in Greek, and, for the reasons which the reader will see, was probably translated from Syriac, Hebrew, or Arabic. When the master taught Jesus the word Aleph, (the mystical meaning of which has been proved to be *the Trinity* by Chardin,) he pronounced the second letter, which is written in the Greek letters, but in the Hebrew language, Μπεθ *Mpeth*, after which it is said, that he explained to his master the meaning of the prophets. Here we see the mystical ם *Mem*, or 600 of Isaiah, only written in Greek letters.

---

[1] Basnage, Hist. Jews, B. iii. Ch. xxiv. xxv.

[2] I recommend the perusal of the works of Picus to persons disposed to follow up my inquiries.

This was the explanation of the mystery of Isaiah, of the prophets. If the person translating this work from the Hebrew had given to the letters the Greek names *Alpha, Beta,* &c., the mystery would not have been contained in them; therefore he gave them in the Hebrew. Mr. J. Jones says, these Gospels were published in the beginning of the second century. They were received by the Manichæans, and the Gnostic sects, particularly that of the Marcosians (probably followers of Marcus). The Gnostics existed, as will be proved, not only before St. Paul, who wrote against them, but also before the Christian æra.[1]

It will be objected here, that in the Mpeth, and in several other instances, the Mem or Muin is not the Mem final, but the common Mem or Muin, which stands only for 40. The objection seems reasonable, but I think a great number of circumstances, which I shall produce in the course of this work, will satisfy my reader, that the mystical use of the M final was transferred to the common M, in the languages which had not an M final, and in which another letter was used for the number 600. I suspect that a regard for the sacred character of the M was the reason why the Greeks, in their language, never permitted a word to end with the letter M. Thus the superstition of the Hebrews caused them to use the Teth ט *t* and Vau ו *v* for 15, instead of the Jod י *i* and He ה *e*, the name of their God. This cannot be attributed to a custom with the Greeks of writing the Hebrew B by MP, because, had not the mystery been alluded to, it would have been written Beta. I am not ignorant that the Greeks wrote the double B by M P, as noticed by Georgius[2] and Dr. Clarke, in his Travels in Greece: but I suspect it arose from this sacred mystic practice getting into use among ignorant, uninitiated people.

When the chief priest placed his hands on the candidate for orders or for initiation into the priesthood, he *Samached* him, that is, he made the mark of the cross, or marked the candidate with the number or sign of 600.[3] This letter in the Hebrew means 60 and 600, (the two famous cycles of the Indians,) the Samach being, in fact, nothing but the M final.

And Joshua the son of Nun was full of the spirit of WISDOM ; *for Moses (סמך smk) samached him, laying his hands upon him.* Deut. xxxiv. 9, χειροτονια.

The Mem final—the letter Samach—was adopted for the 600, because the cycles of 60 and 600 are, in reality, the same, or one a part of the other : they would equally serve the purposes of the calendar. If they reckoned by the Neros, there were 10 Neroses in 6000 ; if the reckoning was made by 60, there were 100 times that number in 6000 years. This we shall understand better presently. This explanation of the Samach completes what I have said respecting the X being the mark for 600, in my *Celtic Druids,* Ch. iv. Sect. ix.

In the Coptic language there is a very peculiar use of the letter M. Ptolomeos is there written Mptolomeos : on which Dr. Young says, " The prefix M of the Copts, which CANNOT BE TRANS-" LATED, is frequently found in the inscription, with the same indifference as to the sense."[4] Thus in the quotation above, from the Gospel of the Infancy, it is not written Beth or Peth, but M-Peth. The M is nothing but a sacred Monogram prefixed, and meaning precisely the same, as the + or X, which is found often prefixed to words and sentences in the writings of the dark ages. It is the Samach.

But M is the sign of the *passive* as well as of the *active* principle, that is, of the Maia. Thus it is the symbol of both; that is, of the Brahme-Maia ; and this is the reason why we find this the Monogram of the Virgin upon the pedestal of the Goddess Multimammia, and of the Virgin Mary, with the Bambino, or black Christ, in her arms, as may be seen in many places in Italy.

---

[1] Jones on Canon, Vol. I. pp. 396, 433 ; Vol. II. p. 232.   [4] Alp. Tib. Sect. vi.
[2] See *Celtic Druids,* Ch. iv. Sect. ix.
[4] Mus. Crit. Camb. No. VI. p. 172 ; Rud. of a Dict. of Hieroglyph. Pref.

The Hebrews and the Arabians had the same system of 28 letters for arithmetical figures; but, in order to place this *Mem* or *Muin* in the centre, the former dropped one letter. Thus we have this central letter on the figures of the Virgin, the female generative power; the allusion is plain enough.

The Momphta of Egypt, named by Plutarch, admitted by Kircher to be the passive principle of nature, is evidently nothing but the Om-tha or Om-thas, with the Mem final, the sign of 600, prefixed. The sun was the emblem of the active principle, the moon of the passive principle. Hence she was generally female, often called Isis, to which she was dedicated, and Magna Mater.[1]

The recurrence of the word Om, in the names of places in Egypt, and in Syria,[2] about Mount Sinai, is very remarkable, and raises strong ground for suspicion that it has a relation to the Om of India. We must remember that this Om is the Amen or sacred mystical word of the Bible, of the law given on Sinai.[3] It is also the word Omen—good or bad—which means prophecy.

4. Before I proceed to the following calculation, I must beg to observe, that whether the equinoxes preceded after the rate of 72 years to a degree, or something more or less, was a subject of great debate among the ancient, as it has been among modern, astronomers. But the rate of 72 has been finally determined to be sufficiently near for common mythological purposes, though not correctly true. I must also further premise that our received chronology, that is, Archbishop Usher's, which fixes the creation at 4004 years before Christ, is generally allowed to be in error 4 years, and that it ought to be only 4000. This was done in compliance with a settlement of it by Dionysius Exiguus, who fixed it to the end of the 4713th year of the Julian period. The REAL reason why this is allowed to be too late by our divines is, that it makes Christ to have been born after the death of Herod, who sought to kill him. And the REAL reason why Usher fixed it at 4004, instead of 4000 years, was a wish to avoid the very striking appearance of judicial astrology contained in the latter number.

There was a remarkable eclipse in March 4710 of the Julian period,[4] about the time of Herod's death, and the birth of Christ. This is as it ought to be. The conjunction of the Sun and Moon took place on the birth of Christ. This was exactly 600 years after the birth of Cyrus, who was *the Messiah*, to use the epithet of the Old Testament, who immediately preceded Jesus Christ.

Mr. Fry[5] states, that the year preceding the year 4 B. C., was the year of the nativity. He adds, " We arrive at B. C. 4, the year before which is supposed, by most writers of eminence,

---

[1] Clarke's Travels, Vol. II. p. 318.   [2] Vide Burchardt's Travels.

[3] Some will think this to be paradoxical, and if I did not know that the secret learning of the ancients was in strict keeping with it, I should think so too. But I beg my reader to refer to the history of the Cabala by Basnage, and presuming that he will oblige me in this, I shall push this abstruse speculation a little farther. The 14th, the middle numerical letter in the alphabet is called Muin: this is evidently the *vine*, the Marital tree, sacred to Bacchus, |" *iin*, with the M prefixed. May not this ▭ *m* final be a monogram prefixed to the name, long after it came into use? It is found in all the languages. How came Bacchus to be the God of wine? (Bacchus was the sun in Taurus.) Did it arise from the junction of this Mem, as a Monogram or emblem of the sun in Taurus, mystically given to the name of the tree of wine? I know not. Let it be more probably accounted for; first taking into account the ancient mystic doctrines and practices relating to figures. It was from the mystical emblems carried on the signets of the ancients that our modern coats of arms arose. How can any thing be more recondite and mystical than the figures and monograms on the ancient signets? Any one may see an example in Clarke's Travels, Vol. II. pp. 320, 326, ed. 4to. I shall return to the Om or M in the course of this work.

[4] See Asiat. Res. Vol. X. p. 48; Calmet, Chron.; and Encyclop. Britt. art. Chron., p. 754.

[5] Epocha of Daniel's Proph. p. 5.

" to have been the year of the holy nativity." This is the same as Marsham and Hevelius who fix the Christian æra, calculating from the Hebrew, at exactly 4000 years from the creation.

In calculating periods, a variation of several years has arisen from a very natural cause: one author or translator speaks of the tenth year, another uses the same expression, and, without any ill intention, calls it ten years: this, again, is followed by another, who makes the ten years into the eleventh year, and this again into the twelfth. A similar variation is exhibited in the Indian Cali Yug, which is placed 3000, 3001, 3002 years before Christ.

Dr. Hales has given many very satisfactory reasons why the difference of one or two, in chronological calculations, cannot be admitted to impugn them, chiefly on account of the different methods of speaking of the same number, by different persons. It is not necessary to repeat them.[1]

In addition to what Dr. Hales has said, it may, perhaps, be useful to observe, that a difference of 1 in chronological calculations can seldom be reasonably used as an argument against any conclusion to which there is no other objection, in consequence of authors often neglecting to keep distinct the *last* and *first* numbers of series, whence it happens that one unit is counted *twice over*. Colonel Wilford says, " It is also to be observed, that where we put 0 at the beginning of a " chronological list, the Hindoos put 1, as we used to do formerly: and that year should be " rejected in calculations: but this precaution is often neglected, even in Europe."[2]

The Hindoo astronomical accounts having been found to make a great impression on the public mind, an attempt was made in the sixth volume of the Asiatic Researches to remove it, by a gentleman, before noticed, of the name of Bentley. His essay was attacked in the Edinburgh Review, to which he replied in the eighth volume of the above-mentioned work.

He states that there are only three Hindoo systems of astronomy now known. The first is called *Brahma Calpa*, the second *Padma Calpa*, the third *Varaha Calpa*. I shall not trouble my reader with the details, but merely with certain results. Mr. Bentley states (p. 212) the Cali Yug to have commenced 3101 years before Christ. In the Brahma Calpa, (p. 225,) a Maha or great Yug or Calpa consists of 2400 years, which great Yug was divided into four other Yugs; of course these were 600 years each. The beginning of this 2400 was 3164 years B. C., and it ended 764 years B. C. Here, in the division into four, we have clearly four ages or yugs of 600 years each. I think the Neros cannot be denied here.

In a future page I shall explain how this Brahma Calpa arose, which is unknown to the present Brahmins.

If from 3164 we take 764 and add a Neros 600, we shall have exactly five Neroses between the commencement of the system and the birth of Christ, which commencement we shall afterward see must have been meant, according to this system, for the date of the flood, and of the Cali Yug. I think the four divisions obviously prove, that the sum of 2400 years is only a part of a system consisting of Neroses; and, as we shall soon see, of the ten incarnations, in reality Neroses, spoken of in the first chapter and fourth section of the present book of this work.

In the next system, the Padma Calpa, a Calpa is called 5000 years; but the term called Brahma's life consists of 387,600,000 years. Mr. Bentley says, (p. 220,) " By this table it will " appear, that the Satya, or golden age, as we may call it, of the first system, began on the same " year that the third Manwantara of the second system did; that is, the year before Christ 3164." Here is evidently the same system; and being the same, the Neros must be at the bottom, however carefully hidden: I have, therefore, no occasion to add any thing more at present.

In Usher's Chronology, the death of Shem, when he was exactly the age of a Neros or 600 years old, took place 502 years after the flood: this we shall find of consequence. One of the Hindoo

---

• Chron. Vol. I. p. 121.   † Asiat. Res. Vol. X. p. 161.

systems makes the Cali Yug begin 3098 years B. C.,[1] at which time some Brahmins maintain that the flood happened. This shews the same mythos as that relating to Shem. $98+502=600+3000 =3600-600=3000$ or 5 Neroses.

The third or Varaha Calpa has the famous cycle of 4,320,000,000 years for its duration. This system makes the Cali Yug (Mr. Bentley says) begin 3098 years B. C.[2] In the preliminary discourse, (Sect. 26, p. 6,) we have shewn that a dodecan consisted of 5 days, and 72 dodecans of course formed a natural year of 360 days : 360 solar diurnal revolutions formed a natural year. The Sun, or rather that higher principle of which the Sun was the emblem or the Shekinah, was considered to be incarnated every six hundred years. Whilst the sun was in Taurus, the different incarnations, under whatever names they might go, were all considered but as incarnations of Buddha or Taurus. When he got into Aries, they were in like manner considered but as incarnations of Cristna or Aries. And even Buddha and Cristna, as I have before stated, were originally considered the same, and had a thousand names *in common*, constantly repeated in their litanies—a striking proof of identity of origin. Of these Zodiacal divisions, the Hindoos formed another period, which consisted of ten ages or Calpas or Yugs, which they considered the duration of the world: at the end of which, a general renovation of all things would take place. They also reckoned ten Neroses to form a period, each of them keeping a certain relative location to the other, and together to form a cycle.

5. To effect this, they double the precessional period for one sign, viz. 2160 years, thus making 4320, which was a tenth of 43,200, a year of the sun, analogous to the 360 natural days, and produced in the same manner, by multiplying the day of 600 by the dodecans 72=43,200. They then formed another great year of 432,000, by again multiplying it by 10, which they called a Cali Yug, which was measurable both by the number 2160, the years the equinox preceded in a sign, and by the number 600. They then had the following scheme :

A Cali Yug, or 600 (or a Neros, as I will call it) Age	432,000
[3] A Dwapar, or Duo-par Age	864,000
A Treta, or tres-par Age	1,296,000
A Satya, or Satis Age	1,728,000
Altogether 10 ages, making a Maha Yug, or Great Age..	4,320,000

These were all equimultiples of the Cycle of the Neros 600, and of 2160, the twelfth part of the equinoctial precessional cycle : and in all formed ten ages of 432,000 years each.

This is a most important Cycle, and I think we shall here see the reason for the formation of such very long periods by the Hindoos. The Neros or cycle of 600 was originally invented to enable them to regulate the vernal and autumnal Phallic festivals. After some time they discovered that their cycle of 600 no longer answered, but that their festivals returned at a wrong pe-

---

[1] Asiat. Res. Vol. VIII. p. 237.   [2] Ibid.

[3] It is curious to observe that these Sanscrit names are nothing but Latin, except the first : but this will not surprise a person who has read Ch. II. Sect. XXV. of *The Celtic Druids*, where the close affinity of the Latin and Sanscrit is shewn. The first Cali is a mystical word, a little corrupted by its translation from Sanscrit into English, or by its translation from a primeval language. It may be the Chaldee word composed of the letters כלה *klo*. This word I have shewn, in the Celtic Druids, from General Vallancey, meant כ k=500 ל l=30 ה o=70, total 600. It may also be the same as the Greek word καλος, and mean *benignant, beautiful*, the same as Mundus and κοσμος—*Beauty* arising from order ; peculiarly appropriate to the cycle of the Neros of 600. The Yug means age, and really looks, as before intimated, very like our word *age ;* in fact, it is nothing but our word. One is a corruption of the other, but which *is* the *corruption* I do not say. *Klo* is found in the Greek in the word κυκλος, circle or cycle, and *Herclo* is Hercules, the saviour 600, or the Sun in Aries, when the Cali began. But more of this hereafter.

riod, as the equinox, which once fell on the first of May, now took place on the first of April. This led ultimately to the discovery, that the equinox preceded about 2160 years in each sign, or 25,920 years in the 12 signs ; and this induced them to try if they could not form a cycle of the two. On examination, they found that the 600 would not commensurate the 2160 years in a sign, or any number of sums of 2160 less than 10, but that it would with ten, or, that in ten times 2160, or in 21,600 years, the two cycles would agree : yet this artificial cycle would not be enough to include the cycle of 25,920. They, therefore, took two of the periods of 21,600, or 43,200 ; and, multiplying both by ten, viz. $600 \times 10 = 6000$, and $43,200 \times 10 = 432,000$, they found a period with which the 600 year period, and the 6000 year period, would terminate and form a cycle. Every 432,000 years the three periods would commence anew : thus the three formed a year or cycle, 72 times 6000 making 432,000, and 720 times 600 making 432,000.

Again, to shew this in another way : the year of 360 days, or the circle of 360 degrees, we have seen was divided into dodecans of 5 days, or degrees, each ; consequently the degrees or days in a year or circle being multiplied by 72, that is, 72×360 gives 25,920, the length of the precessional year. In the same way the Hindoos proceeded with the number 600, which was the number contained in a year of the sun ; they multiplied it by 72, and it gave them 43,200 : but as the number 600 will not divide equally in 25,920, and they wanted a year or period which would do so, they took ten signs of the Zodiac, or 10 times 2160, the precessional years in a sign, which made 21,600, thus making their Neros year ten periods, to answer to ten signs ; then multiplying the 43,200 by 10 they got 432,000 : thus, also, they got two years or periods commensurate with each other, and which formed a cycle, viz. 21,600 and 432,000, each divisible—the former by 600, and the latter by 21,600. As the latter gave a quotient of 20, in 20 periods of 21,600 years, or 432,000 years, they would have a cycle which would coincide with the Neros ; and which is the least number of the signs of the Zodiac, viz. 10, which would thus form a cycle with the Neros.

Thus a year of the Clo or Cli or Cali Yug, or age, or 600, is	432,000
Then a year of the double Neros, or 1200, will be	864,000
Of a triple ditto	1,296,000
And of a quadruple	1,728,000

And of a year formed of the ten ages or Neroses altogether, or of the 6000 years,   4,320,000

And this long period they probably supposed would include all the cyclical motions of the Sun and Moon, and, perhaps, of the Planets. Whether this was the result of observations some will hesitate to admit. Persons of narrow minds will be astonished at such monstrous cycles ; but it is very certain that no period could properly be called the *great year* unless it embraced in its circle every periodical movement or apparent aberration. But their vulgar wonder will perhaps cease when they are told that Mons. La Place has proved, that if the periodical aberrations of the Moon be correctly calculated, the great year must be extended to a greater length even than the 4,320,000 years of the Maha Yug of the Hindoos. And certainly no period can be called a year of our planetary system, which does not take in all the periodical motions of the planetary bodies.

As soon as these ancient astronomers had found that the equinoxes had the motion in antecedentia, or preceded, they would, of course, endeavour to discover the rate of the precession in a given time. It is evident that this would be a work of very great difficulty. The quantity of precession in one year was so small, that they must have been obliged to have recourse to observations in long periods, and it is not very surprising that they should at first have been guided, in part, by theory. The orderly arrangement of nature appeared so striking to the Greeks, as to induce them thus to account for the Planets being called *Disposers*, the appellation (as we learn from Herodotus) first given to the Gods,—the םימש *smim* of Genesis. From observations taken during the precession through several degrees, the Hindoos were first induced to suppose that the precession took place after the rate of 60 years in a degree, or 1800 in a zodiacal sign, and of 21,600 in a revolution of the whole circle. And Sir W. Jones informs us, from an examination of their periods, that this was the rate at which they reckoned. But they afterwards discovered, as they thought, that this was not true, and that the precession was at the rate of a degree in 60 years and a fraction of a year ; and that thus the precession for a sign was in 1824 years, and for the circle in 21,888 years. During the time this was going on, they discovered, as they thought, the Soli-Lunar period of 608 years, and they endeavoured to make the two cycles go together. For this purpose they took the periods in a zodiacal circle, viz. $12 \times 1824 = 21,888$, and they found the two cycles of 608 and 21,888 would agree and form a new one, at the end of which both cycles would terminate, and begin anew. Hence came to be formed the sacred 608. But both of them were erroneous.

Among the ancient Romans we find a story of 12 vultures and 12 ages, the meaning of which was certainly unknown ; for the 12 ages of 120 years each will by no means account for all the particulars of the history. But we find among them also the sacred period of 608 years. This arose from the following cause : they came from the East before the supposition that the precession took place a degree in about 60 years, and 1824 years in a sign had been discovered to be erroneous ; and as they supposed the Neros made a correct cycle in 608 years, and believed the precessional cycle to be completed in 21,888 years, they of course made their ages into 12. As both numbers were erroneous, they would not long answer their intended purpose, and their meaning was soon lost, though the sacred periods of twelve ages and of 608 remained.

The equinoxes were believed by Hipparchus and Ptolemy to have preceded after the rate of a degree in 100 years, and of the circle in 36,000 years, thus : 1 deg. : 100 yrs. : : 360 deg. : 36000 yrs., and that then the Ἀποκατάστασις or restitution or regeneration of all things would take place. This, I think, was nothing but a remnant of, probably, the most ancient of the Indian mythoses, when the precessional years in each sign of the Zodiac were supposed to be 3000 in number, and consequently 36,000 in the circle, and 36 seconds in a year.[1] This doctrine of the Greeks is evidently nothing but a theory, and not the result of observation ; for it cannot be believed that erroneous observations should have brought out these peculiar round numbers.

Some time after the arrival of the Sun in Aries, at the Vernal equinox, the Indians probably discovered their mistake, in giving about 60 years to a degree ; that they ought to give 50″ to a year, about 72 years to a degree, and about 2160 years to a sign ; and, that the Luni-Solar cycle, called the Neros, did not require 608 years, but 600 years only, to complete its period. Hence arose the more perfect Neros.

After some time the erroneous Neros of 608 would be lost sight of altogether in the country of its birth, and would be superseded by the more perfect, of 600 years. Hence the old one is only found, as it were, in scraps and detached parts, as in the calculations on chronology, which the reader has seen, and in certain verses of Martianus Capella's, which I shall presently give. But it continued in use among the ignorant devotees in Latium and in Greece, who knew nothing of its meaning, or of the profound astronomy from which it had its origin. As I have just said, I suppose the great Neros of 608 years came to the West before the less and more correct one of 600 was discovered, and, in consequence of the communication between these distant countries being intercepted, the greater one remained, as a sacred number, uncorrected.

Perhaps after some time the Indians found that the equinox did not precede correctly 50″ in a year, or a degree in 72 years ; but 50″ and a fraction, i. e. 50″ 9‴ ¼ in a year, or a degree in 71

---

[1] Costard, Ast. p. 131.

years, eight or nine months, and an entire sign in 2152 or 2153 years.[1]   They, therefore, divided the 43,200 by 71 ; this gave them the number 608 $\frac{32}{71}$, and from this arose the sacred number of their Manwanteras 71.   It is evident that the error is so small a fraction, as to amount in practical effect to *nothing* in these long periods ; for as, in these religious systems, they calculated in whole numbers, the error did not operate unless it was more than a fraction of the 72 years in one degree.

It is necessary to observe, that few of the numbers respecting the precession are *absolutely* correct : for instance, the number of years for a sign is 2153, instead of 2160 ; the difference arises from fractions, as I have stated above, and is so small, that it is not worth notice.   The following observation of M. Volney's will explain it.

" Edward Barnard discovered from ancient monuments that the Egyptian priests calculated,
" as we do, the movement of precession at 50″ 9‴ ¼ in a year : consequently that they knew it
" with as much precision as we do at this day.

" According to these principles, which are those of all astronomers, we see that the annual
" precession being 50″ and a fraction of about a fourth or a fifth, the consequence is, that an entire
" degree is lost, or displaced, in seventy-one years, eight or nine months, and an entire sign in
" 2152 or 2153 years."[2]

Again Volney says, " It is, moreover, worthy of remark, that the Egyptians never admitted or
" recognized, in their chronology, *the deluge* of the Chaldeans, in the sense in which we understand
" it : and this, no doubt, because among the Chaldeans themselves it was only an allegorical
" manner of representing the presence of Aquarius in the winter solstitial point, which presence
" really took place at the epoch when the vernal equinoctial point was in Taurus : this carries us
" back to *the thirty-first* (3100) *or thirty-second* century before our æra, that is, precisely to the
" dates laid down by the Indians and Jews."[3]

The observation respecting the Hindoo period of 3100 years before Christ is striking.   What he means by the Jews, I do not understand.

Besides the Neros of 600 years, and the great Neros of 608 years, which were both sacred numbers, the ancients had also two other remarkable and sacred numbers—650 and 666.   Sir William Jones, I have before observed, has stated that the Hindoos at a very early period must have believed, that the precessional year consisted of 24,000 years.   " They computed this motion
" (the precession of the equinox) to be at the rate of 54″ a year : so that their annus magnus, or
" the times in which the stars complete an entire revolution, was 24,000 years."[4]

I will now try to shew how the above-named sacred numbers arose.

I suppose that at first the Soli-lunar cycle was thought to consist of 666 years, and the great year, caused by the precession of the equinoxes, of 24,000 years.   Nothing can be more awkward and intractable than these numbers.   66 years to a degree give 23,760 to the great year, which are too few ; and 67 years to a degree give 24,120 to the great year, which are too many to complete a period without fractions : thus, $66 \times 30 \times 12 = 23,760$; $67 \times 30 \times 12 = 24,120$.   Nor will 666 divide equally in 24,000, for they leave a remainder of 24.   The Luni-solar period of 666 years was abandoned when its incorrectness was perceived.   About the same time it was thought to be discovered that the equinox did not precede 24,000 in the great year, but 65 years in a degree, and 23,400 in the great year, the Soli-lunar period was thought to be 650 years.   These two periods agree very well, and together form a cycle : $36 \times 650 = 23,400$.   Then 650 became a sacred number, and we have it recorded in the number of the stones at Abury.   Of this cycle M. Basnage has given an account.

[1] Volney, Res. Vol. II. p. 453.   [2] Transl. of Volney on Anc. History, Vol. II. p. 453.   [3] Ibid. p. 455.
[4] Trans. Royal Soc. Edin. Vol. II. p. 141.

If we turn to the *Celtic Druids*, Ch. vi. Sect. xxiii., we shall see the other sacred numbers of the Cycles of India described. Since I wrote that work I have discovered that the sum-total of the pillars discovered by Dr. Stukeley, and confirmed by Sir R. C. Hoare, at Abury, made exactly the sacred Solar number 650. There can therefore be little doubt that they adopted that number of pillars for their temple to record this Cycle.

All these different Neroses form cycles with the then supposed great precessional year, except the number 666. This number, for the reason already assigned, will not form a cycle with 24,000. And it might be on account of this awkwardness that it became a reprobated number—the number of evil, of discord, of the beast in the Revelation. Some persons will probably think these theories fanciful. I should certainly think with them, if I did not bear in mind that all the ancient mythoses were replete with fancies of this kind. Their nonsense respecting sacred numbers is palpable, but the numbers having sacred characters applied to them are not fancies, but historical facts; and, though these fancies are nonsensical in their own nature, they cease to be so when consequences important to the good of mankind depend upon them.

General Vallancey says, " The Saros, according to Berosus, consisted of 6660 days. Syncellus and " Abydenus,[1] tell us, that it was a period of 3600 years; but Suidas, an author contemporary with " Syncellus, says, the Saros was a period of lunar months amounting to 18 years and a half, or " 222 moons. Pliny mentions a period of 223 lunar months, which Dr. Halley thinks is a false " reading, and proposes the amendment by reading 224 months. Sir Isaac Newton makes the " Saros 18 years and 6 intercalary months, which agrees with Suidas; but it is not the simple " Saros, but the tenfold Saros, that makes this number, as will appear from the numerical or celes- " tial alphabet. The word is evidently derived from שור sor, revolutio, mensura. In the old Irish " it is called Siora."[2] We have seen how the 666 arose, and in its multiplication by *ten*, we have the cycle of 6660, which being founded on an erroneous calculation, was itself erroneous, but it was agreeable to the *principle* of the cycle of 6000 years, as I have already explained.

It is impossible to read the above extract with attention and not to see that the meaning of the cycle or Saros of 666 was unknown, because, in order to make the reckoning by months agree, they must use a fraction, and also, *without any reason whatever*, according to their scheme, multiply the number by *ten*. General Vallancey gives the following proof:

	Proof
S—ש—300	360
A—y— 70	18
R—ר—200	6480
V—ו— 6	180 6 months
S—צ— 90	6660
666	222
10	30
6660	6660

The Irish had a festival called *La Saora*, always kept in the night; and many persons have de-rived Serapis, from Sor or Soros Apis, meaning the entombed Apis; Soros being the name of a stone coffin. All this tends to support my idea, that this number of the beast was only an ex-ploded or heretical cycle. The year of the Apocalypse being calculated at only 360 days, I must maintain is a decisive proof of its extreme antiquity.

---

[1] Al. Polyhistor.   [2] Ouseley, Orient. Coll. Vol. II. No. iii. p. 214.

The cycle of 19, a common number of the Irish stone circles, is called, in the Irish language, *Baise-Bhuidin.*[1] I confess I can read this no other way than *Bud-base* or *Buddhist foundation*—it being the foundation, in one sense, of the famous Neros. The temple in Cornwall, called Biscawoon, said to be a corruption of Baise-bhuidin, contains in its circle 19 stones. The meaning of this can scarcely be doubted.[2]

It is curious to observe how often trifling circumstances keep occurring to support the claim of the Etruscans to be placed among the most ancient of the nations. The cycle of 666 is an example of this kind. It is found with them, as the following passage of Niebuhr proves, but its meaning was lost. " In the year of Rome 666 the Haruspices announced, that the mundane day of the " Etruscan nation was drawing to a close." This cycle has a strong tendency to prove, what no one who looks impartially at the apocalypse of John, and the continual recurrence in it of the numbers contained in the ancient cycles, can doubt, that it is an allegorical mythos, and relates chiefly to them; though perhaps only emblematically.

The Etruscan cosmogony is exactly that of one of the earlier Brahmin systems. It supposes that the author of the creation employed 12,000 years in his work. In the first thousand he made the planets and earth; in the second, the firmament; in the third, the sea and waters; in the fourth, the sun and moon, and also the stars ; in the fifth, living creatures : in the sixth, man :— that after they were finished in the six thousand years, they were to last six thousand years, then a new world was to begin, and the same things to go over again.[3] Here is the renewal of the Cycles of Virgil and Juvenal ; but as may be expected of a system, if it can be called a system, which has ripened into form, as circumstances favoured, through thousands of years, the length of the period is unknown, a subject of speculation varying in different nations and different times.

Although Nonnus is perfectly in the dark respecting the length of the great year, making it to be 456 years long, yet he accidentally makes a calculation, from various circumstances, that the Phœnix must have made its appearance in the year 608 before Christ, which evidently produces, to that time, one of the Neroses. This I can attribute to nothing but the fact, that one of the periods had been discovered, though not understood. This is the best kind of evidence to establish facts of this nature.

The Irish expressly state the life of the Phenn or Phennische to have lasted 600 years.[4] In Egyptian, *Pheneh* is cyclus, periodus, ævum. (Scaliger.)

> Phœnix, Egyptiis astrologiæ symbolum.   BOCHART.
>
> Una est quæ reparat seque ipsa reseminat
> Ales, Assyrii Phœnica vocant.   OVID.[5]

If I mistake not, I have pointed out the origin of the Hindoo cycles ; and it is probable, that the principle which I have unfolded will account for the various systems which are found among the learned in different parts of India. One system founded on one series of observations would be adopted by the sect of one nation of that widely-extended country, and another of another. And thus have arisen the different systems which we find. The festivals, forms, and ceremonies, (matters of the VERY FIRST importance to devotees in all nations,) depending on the cycles, we need not be surprised that old, incorrect systems should have been continued in different places. And after the religion was divided into sects, the fortunate detectors of the early mistakes, by which they were enabled to keep their own festivals in order, would probably be very unwilling to

---

[1] Ouseley, Orient. Coll. Vol. II. No. iii. p. 213.
[2] Val. Coll. Hib. Vol. VI. p. 383. Vide ch. ii. Sect. i. of this book for Cassini's opinion on the Metonic Cycle.
[3] Universal Hist. Vol. I. Cosmog p. 64.   [4] Vallancey, Vol. VI. p. 379.   [5] Metam. xv. 392.

communicate information of this kind, to those who were considered by them as heretics. Again, it is not at all unlikely, that the correction of festivals should have actually created sects These are, I think, some of the chief reasons why these systems were concealed, and confined with so much care to a very few persons, and why the knowledge of the principles was forgotten, while the formulæ were continued in use.

I consider that the Hindoo religion was not the produce of premeditation, but like most others of circumstance, of accident—and that it kept pace, in some measure, with the gradual approximation of their astronomy to perfection. And I think it is pretty clear that it must have been fully established some time about the year 3100 B. C., at least not very long after that date. It might, perhaps, be five or six hundred years later, for which time, of course, they must have had recourse to back-reckoning. I think it also probable, that this may, in part, have furnished plausible grounds for much of the nonsense which has been broached on the subject of back-reckonings.

6. Mr. Bentley, notwithstanding he has written so much against the antiquity of Hindoo astronomy, admits (p. 212) that the Cali Yug began 3101 years before Christ; that the Brahma Calpa began 3164 years before Christ; that one of the four ages of the Padma Calpa began precisely at the same time as the Brahma Calpa; and that the third or the Varuha Calpa began 3098 years before Christ. It is very evident that all these systems are the same—and yet the trifling variation shews that they were not contrived for the purpose of deceit or fraud : for, if they had been, they would have been made to agree. They rather seem to shew the result of observations made independently of one another, from some common source. It is very evident from Mr. Bentley's admissions, that the present Brahmins, whatever they may pretend to, do not know much respecting their different systems; and that they have to make them out precisely as they are made out by Europeans—in a considerable degree by conjecture and calculation.

Among other matters, Mr. Bentley, by a long train of reasoning, undertakes to shew the Calpa of 432,000 years to have been invented after the Christian æra. The following table will demonstrate how little his kind of proof can be depended on, because it shews, that this cycle was known long before that æra commenced.

The following is the description of the Chaldean kings given by Berosus, which again proves the system of very great antiquity. I give along with it the system of Moses.

Antediluvian patriarchs according to Genesis			Chaldean Antediluvian Kings according to Berosus		
Names	Ages	In Years	Names	Ages in Sares	In Years
Adam		930	Alor	10	36,000
Seth		912	Alaspar	3	10,800
Enos		905	Amelon	13	46,800
Cainan		910	Amenon	12	43,200
Mahalaleel		862	Matalar	18	64,800
Jared		895	Daon	10	36,000
Enoch		365	Evidorach	18	64,800
Methuselah		969	Amphis	10	36,000
Lamech		777	Otiartes	8	28,800
Noah		950	Xisuthrus	18	64,800
				120	432,000

This proves that one, and the most important, of the immensely-extended cycles of the Hindoos was in existence long before the Christian æra, and of itself entirely overturns Mr. Bentley's doctrine. It also raises a very strong presumption, that the Hindoos and Chaldeans had an intimate connexion in the time of Berosus, for the identity of these large numbers cannot have been the effect of accident.

I will now endeavour to point out the truth of my theory in another way. We will take for granted the truth of the millenary period of 6000 years as an age—the age of iron : the ages are supposed to be in the proportion of 4, 3, 2, 1,—the same as those of the Grecian Hesiod. Now, if we take the last to be 6000 and count backwards, we shall have

Present Iron age or Cali age	6,000	1
Brass	12,000	2
Silver	18,000	3
Gold	24,000	4
Ten periods	60,000	
Multiply this by	72	
	120,000	
	420,000	
as we formerly multiplied the Dodecans by 72 to compose a common solar year, and we shall have a year of Brahma or of the whole system	4,320,000	

The anonymous author of the Cambridge Key to the Mythology of the Hindoos, endeavours to prove this theory of increasing numbers to apply to the period before the deluge of 900 years. Thus 400, 300, 200, and the last, or tenth, to be that now running. But here his theory completely fails ; because the last period instead of being, as it ought to be, only 100 years, has already extended since the flood, according to his own account, to near 4000 years. If the above scheme be right, if the Cali Yug or the last 6000 began 3100 years B. C., there ought to be 1070 yet to run—as 3100+1830=4930+1070=6000. Here we see we have the famous 6000 of the Hindoos, Jews, Greeks, and Romans, for one extreme, and the famous Maha-Yug or great year for the other—the year when all things were to resolve themselves into the Deity. Though this is a second system, yet it is evidently the same in principle, and the two are in perfect accordance.

Mr. Bentley, in a recent work published after his death, states that he has obtained the Janampatri of Cristna, or the positions of the planets at his birth ; that is, if I understand it rightly, the astrological calculation of his nativity. Now, I think this tends strongly to confirm what the reader has seen from La Loubère Cassini has shewn that the birth of Christ, as fixed by Eusebius, exactly agreed with an astronomical epoch of the Buddhists of Siam, which is also connected with the Neros or cycle of 600, as the reader has seen. According to the Janampatri, (the genuineness of which I suppose we must admit,) and the Brahmins' and Mr. Bentley's calculation from the Janampatri, (p. 111,) Cristna was born exactly at the end of 600 years (the termination of a Neros) from the time fixed by Eusebius for the birth of Christ and the Buddhist cycle. Thus the fact comes out, that the birth-days fall at the beginning of the different Neroses ; and, I think, from a consideration of the whole of what Cassini, Loubère, and Bentley say, it is clear that this Luni-solar period of 600 must be considered as the year of both Buddha and Cristna. Mr. Bentley says, (p. 61,) "The[1] epoch of Buddha is generally referred to the year 540 or 542 before "Christ." It is impossible not to see here the epoch of Cassini of 543 years before Christ. From these circumstances we may easily account for many difficulties which have been met with

---

[1] The only difference between the æras of Christ and Buddha is, that one is calculated from the birth, the other from the death of the person from whom the cycle is named.

in the histories of Buddha and Cristna, and which have induced Mr. Bentley and others to imagine them of later dates than they are: for it is evident that very nearly the same relative positions of the Sun and Moon would be renewed every fresh cycle or Luni-solar period as it ran its course. Thus, like the Phœnix, they were eternally renewing themselves.

But though the sun and moon would have the same relative positions, the planets would differ in each of these cycles. Hence Mr. Bentley was induced to believe, that Cristna was first born in this last cycle: whereas he was, in fact, born in each of five preceding ones. His first birth was at the egress of Noah or Menu from the ark, which the Hindoos say took place when they suppose the sun entered Aries at the vernal equinox, and which they fix at 3101 years before Christ.

M. Loubère says that the Siamese date their civil year from the *death of Sommono-Codom*, 544 years before Christ. He, however, adds, " But I am persuaded that this epocha has quite another " foundation, which I shall afterwards explain." (P. 8.) This explanation we have already seen; and it proves that, though he understood the astronomy, he was not aware of the mystery. This epoch, not being like that of Jesus, from his birth or incarnation, but from his death, it seems to me that we shall have another Neros or cycle if we add 56 to the 544, the years of the life of Buddha. This we shall see presently.

M. Bailli professed to have discovered, by calculation, that on the 18th of February, 3102 years before the Christian æra, there was a very remarkable conjunction of the planets and an eclipse of the moon.[1] This is the moment when the Brahmins say their Cali Yug began.

From the epochas and cycles explained by Mons. Cassini we may readily infer the mode which was adopted by Eusebius and the Christian fathers in settling the times of the festivals and of the births, &c., of John and Jesus. It is almost certain that they were indebted to the Sommono Co-domites or Samaneans, noticed by Clemens Alexandrinus, as shewn above. All this dovetails perfectly into the astronomical theories of Mons. Dupuis; into what the learned Spaniard, Alphonso the Great, said,—that the *adventures of Jesus are all depicted in the constellations; into* what Jacob is reported to have said, that the fortunes of his family were read in the stars; and also into what Isaiah said, that the heavens were a book. This was really believed by some of the Ca-balists, who divided the stars into letters.[2]

Itaque hunc in modum intelligi potest, quod in Josephi precatione à Jacobo dicitur; legit in tabulis cœli quæcunque accident vobis et filiis vestris, quia etiam complicabitur quasi *liber*.[3]

I have sometimes entertained a suspicion, that the speech of Alphonso alluded to the Messiah of each Cycle, and that the Zodiacs of Esne and Dendera are of the nature of perpetual calendars, for one of the cycles of 600, or 608 years.

We must recollect that the likeness between the history of Hercules and Jesus Christ is so close that Mr. Parkhurst has been obliged to admit, that Hercules was a type of *what the Saviour was to do and suffer*. Now M. Dupuis has shewn the life of Hercules in the sphere in a manner which admits not of dispute; and Hercules, as it has also been shewn, is the Hericlo, the saviour 600.

The commentary on the Surya Siddhanta says, " The *ayanansa* (equinoctial point) moves east-" ward thirty times twenty (= 600) in each Maha Yug", 600. Again, " By the text, the *ayana* " *bhagana* (revolution) is understood to consist of 600 *bhaganas* (periods) in a *Maha Yug*; but " some persons say the meaning is thirty *bhaganas* only,[4] and accordingly, that there are 30,000 " *bhaganas*." Again, " The *Sacalya Sanhita* states, that the *bhaganas* (revolutions) of the *cranti*

---

[1] Bailli's Astronomie Indienne et Orientale, p. 110, 4to. Ed. 1787.   [2] See Basnage, Hist. Jews, B. iii.

[3] Orig. Comm. in Genes.; Val. Coll. Hib. Vol. VI. p. 345.   [4] Asiat. Res. Vol. II. p. 267.

"*pata* (point of intersection of the Ecliptic and Equator) in a *Maha Yug*[1] are 600 eastward" (4,320,000 years). Again, "The *Bhaganas* (revolutions) of the *ayanansa* (equinoctial points) in " a *Maha Yug* are 600 (4,320,000), the saura[2] years in the same period 4,320,000 : one *bhagana* " of the *ayanansa* therefore contains 7,200 years." Here the Neros and the origin of the famous 432,000 are very clear,[3] where it is shewn that, according to the Hindoos, the equinoxes have a libration.

This La Place is said to have demonstrated, but he makes it very small, while they extend it from the third degree of *Pisces* to the twenty-seventh of *Aries*, and from the third of *Virgo* to the twenty-seventh of *Libra*, and back again, in 7200 years.

It is admitted by all the Brahmins that their Cali Yug, or their *fourth period* (at the beginning of which THEY SAY the vernal equinoctial point was in the first degree of *Aries*) took place or began 3101 years before Christ.[4] The beginning of this fourth period is evidently about the end of the fifth back from the æra of Christ, which is the time assigned by them to the flood of Noah when he came out of the ark. These *five*, and the *three* preceding, make eight ages, or Yugs, or Neroses, which we shall see were known by the initiated in both the Eastern and Western nations. But I must stop my argument to give a specimen of the uncertainty of ancient chronology.

The following statement will shew how little dependance can be placed upon systems of chronology :

Blair and Usher state the period from the creation to Christ, to be in the Hebrew

Version of the Bible	4004 years
The LXX	5872
The Samaritan	4700
Josephus states it to be	4483
And Eusebius	5200

Sir William Drummond, in his treatise on the Zodiacs of Esne and Dendera, gives the following numbers :

Received text		4004
Samaritan text		4245
Septuagint 2262 +3128		5390
Josephus		5688
Seder Olam Sutha		3751
Maimonides	Jewish Authorities	4058
Gersom		3754
Asiatic Jews		4180

Sir William Drummond adopts the LXX., and thus divides it—2262 years to the deluge, and 3128 from the deluge to the birth of Christ.

The following numbers are taken from Dr. Hales :

---

[1] The reader will observe that the Yug, or age as it ought to be translated, is of all lengths—from 5 to 5000 years. Every system, and there is a vast number of systems, has its own yug.

[2] Does the word Saura mean Surya ?

[3] See Asiat. Res. Vol. II. pp. 268—270.

[4] Jones's Asiat. Res. Vol. II. p. 393.

[5] Vide Whiston on Old Testament, p. 214 ; preface to the 21st volume of Universal History ; also Celtic Druids, p. 148.

Alphonsus of Castile	6984 years
—— Hales	5411
Meghasthenes	5369
Other Indians according to Gentil	6204
Arab	6174
LXX.—Abulfaraji	5586
Vatican	5270
Alexandrine	
Abyssinian	5508
Russian	
Josephus	5555
	5481
	5402
	4698

Samaritan computation:

Scaliger	4427
Samaritan text	4305
Hebrew text	4161
Usher	4004
Hevelius	4000
Marsham	

The above is quite enough to shew the utter hopelessness of making out a system of chronology; but in Hales's treatise on this subject there may be seen, in addition to this, a list of more than 100 systems, each proved by its author to be the true and perfect system, and varying in their extremes not less than 3000 years. Each author (as he comes in order, finishing with Dr. Hales, as confident as those who have gone before him) succeeds in nothing but in overthrowing the doctrines of his predecessors; but in this he has no difficulty. Can any thing be devised which shall raise a stronger presumption, that a system of chronology never was the leading object of the books? The whole tends to support the doctrine of *nearly all the learned men of antiquity*, that, like the Mythological histories of the Gentile nations, a secret doctrine was concealed under the garb of history. The same thing is seen in the early history of Rome, in the Iliad,[1] the Æneid, the tragedies of Æschylus, &c., &c.

Mr. Faber says, "There can scarcely be a doubt, I think, that we ought to adopt the longer " scheme of chronology, as it is called, in preference to that curtailed one which appears in the " common Hebrew Pentateuch. I am myself inclined to follow the Seventy in their antediluvian " chronology, and the Samaritan Pentateuch in early postdiluvian chronology."[2] Thus by taking a little of one and a little of another, *ad libitum*, a system is easily to be formed.

It may be considered certain from the above, that no dependance can be placed on any system of Chronology, and that there is no hope whatever of ascertaining the truth, unless some person shall be able to devise a plan of proceeding different in principle from any thing which has hitherto been adopted. Therefore I think it will be allowed, that I am not to be tied down by any of them as authority.

---

[1] Herodotus says, that when Paris ran away with Helen, he was driven by contrary winds to Tarichea, (probably the Heracleum of Strabo,) and that she was detained by the king of the country, and given up to her husband. Here we have a sober fact stated by the historian. Upon this the sacred Mythos might be founded. Vide Rennel on Geog. Syn of Her. Vol. II. p. 155; Herod. Euterpe, 113, et seq. ed. Belœ.

[2] Pag. Idol. Vol. I. p. 234.

Besides, it must be evident, on a moment's consideration, that it cannot be expected that I should make the cycles, which I shall shew existed, agree with any of them. I do not pretend to do it, though it is possible that, in some instances, I may. My object is merely to shew that the Neros *did exist*, and was the foundation of a system, not that it fitted to any of the systems of chronology—systems which not only disagree with one another, but almost every *one of which is totally inconsistent with itself*, as M. Volney, in his researches, has clearly proved.

The extraordinary exaggerations in numbers of years, and in other matters, have been noticed by the Author of the Cambridge Key to the Chronology of the Hindoos, of both the Hindoos and Jews, and he endeavours to shew that they are written in a species of cipher, and how the former ought to be reduced. These statements, taken by the priests in a literal sense, have caused many persons to doubt the whole history, but they no more prove that the Jewish history is in the great leading articles false, than the lengthened cycles of the Indians, before the year 3100, prove that they had no history, or that they did not exist.

7. I will now shew that the Mosaic system is exactly the same as that of the Brahmins and the Western nations; I will unfold one part of the esoretic religion. But first I shall avail myself of the statement of several facts of the highest importance, which cannot be disputed, made by Col. Wilford in the Asiatic Researches. [1]

In consequence of certain prodigies which were reported to have been seen at Rome, about the year 119 before Christ, the sacred College of Hetruria was consulted, which declared that the EIGHTH REVOLUTION OF THE WORLD was nearly at an end, and that another, either for the better or the worse, was about to take place. [2]

Juvenal, who lived in the first century, declared that he was living in the *ninth revolution*, [3] or sæculum. This shews that the cycle above alluded to had ended in Juvenal's time, and that a new one had begun: and this ninth revolution consisted evidently of a revolution of more than 100 or 120 years—of several centuries at least.

"Nona ætas agitur, pejoraque sæcula ferri temporibus: quorum sceleri non invenit ipsa Nomen, "et à nullo posuit natura metallo." On this passage Isaac Vossius says, Octo illas ætates credit appellatas à cœli regionibus, quas octo faciebant Pythagorei: nonam vero, de qua hic, à tellure denominatum opinatur: in libello de Sibyle. Orac. Oxoniæ, nuper edito, Cap. v.

This statement of Juvenal's, which no author has ever yet pretended to understand, will now explain itself, and it completes and proves the truth of my whole system. It is of the greatest importance to my theory, as it is evidence, which cannot be disputed, of the fact on which the whole depends. Virgil lived before Christ, Juvenal after him. This is quite enough for my purpose, as we shall soon see.

About sixty years before Christ the Roman empire had been alarmed by prodigies, and also by ancient prophecies, announcing that an emanation of the Deity was going to be born about that time, and that a renovation of the world was to take place.

Previous to this, in the year 63 B. C., the city had been alarmed by a prophecy of one Figulus, that a king or master to the Romans was about to be born, in consequence of which the Senate passed a decree, that no father should bring up a male child born that year: but those among the Senators, whose wives were pregnant, got the decree suppressed. [4] These prophecies were applied to Augustus, who was born 63 years before Christ according to some persons, but 56 according to several writers in the East, such as the author of the Lebtarikh and others. " Hence

---

[1] Vol. X. p. 33.   [4] Ibid.; Plutarch in Syllam, p. 456.

[3] Satire xiii. v. 28.   [4] See Sup. to Tit. Liv. CII. Decad. Cap. xxxix.

" it is, that Nicolo de Conti, who was in Bengal and other parts of India in the fifteenth century,
" insists that Vicramaditya was the same with Augustus, and that his period was reckoned, from
" the birth of that Emperor, fifty-six years before Christ." Now, it is evident that these fifty-six
years before Christ bring us to the æra of the Buddha of Siam, for the beginning of the new æra,
foretold by the Cumæan Sibyl, as declared by the *Mantuan* or Celtic poet, the Druid of Cisalpine
Gaul, in his fourth eclogue. [1] This, in some old manuscripts seen by Pierius, is entitled *Interpre-
tatio Novi Sæculi.* [2]   This Eclogue was evidently a *carmen Sæculare.*

Virgil says,

> The last great age, foretold by sacred rhymes,
> Renews its finished course: Saturnian times
> Roll round again, and *mighty years*, begun
> From their first orb, in radiant circles run.
> The base degenerate iron offspring, *(or the Cali-yuga,)* ends
> A golden progeny *(of the Crita, or golden age)* [3] from heaven descends:
> O chaste LUCINA, speed the mother's pains:
> And haste the glorious birth: thy own Apollo reigns!
> The lovely boy with his auspicious face!
> The son shall lead the life of Gods, and be
> By Gods and heroes seen, and Gods and heroes see.
> Another Typhis shall new seas explore,
> Another Argo land the chiefs upon the Iberian shore:
> Another Helen other wars create,
> And great Achilles urge the Trojan fate.
> O of celestial seed! O foster son of Jove!
> See, labouring nature calls thee to sustain
> The nodding frame of heaven, and earth, and main:
> See, to their base restored, earth, seas, and air.

Col. Wilford on this passage observes, that these are the very words of Vishnu to the *earth*,
when complaining to it, and begging redress. [4]   Here is the Brahmin periodical regeneration
clearly expressed. And here is an admission by Virgil, that the poem of Homer was a religious
Mythos. All these prophecies, I apprehend, alluded to the renovation of the cycle of the Neros,
then about to take place in its ninth revolution.

I quote these verses here merely to shew that some great personage was expected. The
Ultima Cumæi venit jam carminis Ætas, of Virgil, I shall discuss in a future page, and shew that
it is in accordance with my theory.

Several of the other most celebrated Roman authors have noticed the expectation of the arrival
of some great personage in the first century, so that this could not be a mere *solitary* instance of
Virgil's base adulation in this interesting poem.

Tacitus says, "The generality had a strong persuasion that it was contained in the ancient
" writings of the priests, that AT THAT VERY TIME the East should prevail: and that some one who
" should come out of Judea, should obtain the empire of the world: which ambiguities foretold
" Vespasian and Titus. But the common people, (of the Jews,) according to the usual influence
" of human wishes, appropriated to themselves, by their interpretation, this vast grandeur foretold

---

[1] The æras of the Heroes, or Messiahs, of the cycle, (as the Bible calls Cyrus,) did not always commence on their
births, either in very old or more modern times. Thus Buddha's æra, above-mentioned, was from his death; Jesus
Christ's is four years after his birth. Mohamed was born A. D. 608, his æra begins 625.

[2] Vide Dupuis sur tous les Cultes, Vol. III. p. 156.

[3] We may observe, *and reserve for future consideration,* that Col. Wilford says *the CRITA or Golden age* was about
to return. In his observation of the Cali Yug he is wrong.

[4] Asiat. Res. Vol. X. p. 31.

" by the fates, nor could be brought to change their opinion for the true, by all their adversities.[1]

" Suetonius[2] says, There had been for a long time all over the East a constant persuasion that it
" was (recorded) in the fates (books of the fates, decrees, or fortellings), that AT THAT TIME some
" one who should come out of Judea should obtain universal dominion. It appeared by the event,
" that this prediction referred to the Roman Emperor: but the Jews referring it to themselves,
" rebelled."

Percrebuerat oriente toto constans opinio esse in fatis,[3] ut eo tempore, Judæi profecti rerum
potirentur. Id de imperio Romano, quantum postea eventu patuit, prædictum, Judæi ad se
habentis, rebellarunt.

Josephus says,[4] " That which chiefly excited them (the Jews) to war, was an *ambiguous pro-
" phecy,* which was also found in the *sacred books, that at that time some one,* within their *country,*
" should arise, that should obtain *the empire* of the *whole world* (ὡς κατα τον καιρον εκεινον απο
" της χωρας, της αυτων αρξει την οικυμενην). For this they had received by tradition, (ὡς
" οικειον εξελαβον,) that it was spoken of one of their nation: and many wise men, (σοφοι, or
" *Chachams,*) were deceived with the interpretation. But, in truth, Vespasian's empire was
" designed in this prophecy, who was created Emperor (of Rome) in *Judæa.*",   The Chachams
above are Hakims, from the Hebrew word חכם *hkm,* wisdom. The accompanying word σοφοι
would have proved it, if it required any proof.

Another prophecy has been noticed by Prideaux[6] of one Julius Marathus, in these words:
Regem populo Romano naturam parturire.[7]

Among the Greeks, the same prophecy is found. The Oracle of Delphi was the depository, according to Plato, of an ancient and SECRET prophecy of the birth of a son of Apollo, who was to
restore the reign of justice and virtue on the earth.[8] This, no doubt, was the son alluded to by
the Sibyl.

Du Halde, in his History of China, informs us, that the Chinese had a prophecy that a holy
person was to appear in the West, and in consequence they sent to the West, which I think would
be Upper India, and that they brought thence the worship of Fo, (i. e. Buddha,) whom they call
Fwe, K-yau, and Shek-ya. This is evidently the *Iaw* of Diodorus, and the *Iau* of Genesis, and
the Sa-kia the name of Buddha.[9]

Now, according to my idea, the Sibyl of Virgil would have no difficulty, as, from her skill in judicial astrology, she would know very well when the Neros would end. Isaiah might easily learn
the same (even if he were not initiated, a thing hardly to be believed) from the Sibyl of Judæa,[10]
perhaps called a *Huldah.* Nothing is so likely as that Augustus should permit his flatterers to
tell the populace that his age exactly suited to the prophecy. Few persons would dare to canvas
this matter too closely; it was good policy, to strengthen his title to the throne. But respecting
him I shall have much to say hereafter. The Hindoo works, Colonel Wilford informs us, foretell
the coming of Cristna, in the same manner, at the time he is said to have come. Nothing is more
likely. This has been erroneously supposed to prove them spurious. *Any astronomer might tell*

---

[1] Hist. Cap. xiii.   [2] Frag. apud Calmet, Dict. Vol IV. p. 65; Vespasian, Cap. iv.

[3] I beg my reader to observe the words *fates* and *fatis,* and I think he will see the origin of the unchangeable fates,
i. e. *the true prophets.*

[4] De Bello, Lib. vii. Cap. xxxi.   [6] Apud Calmet, Frag. Vol. IV. p. 65.

[6] Connec. P. ii. B. ix. p. 493, fol.   [7] Suet. in Oct. Cap. xciv.

[8] Plato in Apolog. Socr. et de Repub. Lib. vi.; A. Clarke's Evidences; Chatfield on the Hindoos, p. 245.

[9] Vide B. v. Ch. i. § ii.   [10] Named by Pausanias and Ælian. Vide Asiat. Res. Vol. X. p. 30.

it, for it was what had been told for every new age, before it arrived, that a great personage would appear—in fact the presiding genius, Cyrus, or Messiah, of the Cycle.

In addition to all these prophecies, which are in themselves sufficiently striking, there is yet another very celebrated one respecting Zeradusht, which is noticed by Mr. Faber. He maintains, and I think proves, the genuineness of this famous prophecy of Zeradusht, who declared that in the latter day a virgin should conceive and bear a son, and that a star should appear blazing at noon-day. " You, my sons," exclaimed the seer, " will perceive its rising before any other na-" tion. As soon, therefore, as you shall behold the star, follow it whithersoever it shall lead you : " and adore that mysterious child, offering him your gifts with profound humility. He is the al-" mighty WORD, which created the heavens." [1] This prophecy, Mr. Faber observes, is found among the Celts of Ireland, ascribed to a person of the name of Zeradusht, [2] a daru or Druid of Bock-hara, [3] *the residence of Zeradusht* (whose mother was called Dagdu, one of the names of the mother of the Gods). He shews by many strong and decisive proofs, that this can be no monkish forgery of the dark ages.

Amongst other arguments against its being a forgery, Professor Lee observes, that the very same prophecy, in the same words, is reported by Abulfaragius to have been found by him in the oriental writings of Persia. This prophecy thus found in the East and in Ireland, and in the Virgini parituræ, of Gaul, before noticed, previous to the Christian æra, is of the very first importance. It cannot have been stolen from the Christian books, but they must have been copied from it, *if either be a copy*, (which yet may not be the fact,) for they are absolutely the same. It cannot have been copied from the Jewish prophets, because there is nothing like it, not a word about *a star at noon* in any of them. This prophecy is alluded to in the gospel of the infancy : " Ecce ! magi venerunt ex Oriente Hierosolymas, quemadmodum prædixerat Zoradascht, erantque " cum ipsis munera, aurum, thus, et myrrha." [4]

The star above spoken of, was also known to the Romans. " Chalcidius, a *heathen writer* " who lived not long after Christ, in a commentary upon the Timæus of Plato, discoursing upon " portentous appearances of this kind in the heavens, in different ages, particularly speaks of this " wonderful star, which he observes, presaged neither diseases nor mortality, but the descent of a " God among men : Stellæ, quam à Chaldæis observatam fuisse testantur, que Deum nuper natum " muneribus venerati sunt." [5] Nothing can be more clear than that the Romish Christians got their history of the Star and Magi from these Gentile superstitions.

These prophecies have been equally troublesome to the priests and to the philosophers. The divines would have been very glad of them, but the adoption of them carried with it the shocking consequence, that God must have had such bad taste, as to have preferred even the wicked pagans

---

[1] Vol. II. p. 97.

[2] This Zeradusht is no other than the person generally called *Zoroaster* by our old authors. Now I learn from the learned oriental Professor Lee, of Cambridge, that the latter orthography is a complete mistake, and that in all the old oriental authors it is spelt *Zeradusht.* I think this furnishes a very strong proof of the real antiquity and genuineness of the Irish records : for if they had been merely compiled or formed from the works of the Western nations, they would have had the Western mode of spelling the word, and would not have had the Eastern mode, of which they could know nothing. It proves that they had this word direct from the East, and not through the medium of Western reporters.

If I mistake not, another equally striking proof of the same kind may be found in the word Dagdhu, the mother of the Gods. Circumstantial evidence of this kind excels all written evidence whatever. This is worth the whole of the chronicles of Eri. Dagdhu is איח *eue* or *eve* גדה *dg,* Eve the propagatrix.

[3] Bochara means place of learning.   [4] Jones on the Can. Vol. II. Part iii. Ch. xxii. S. 7.

[5] In Timæum, Platonis, p. 19, apud Hind. Hist. of Maurice, Vol. II. p. 296.

to his own people—his priestly nation—the Pagan prophecies being much clearer than those of the Jews. The philosophers have been annoyed because they clearly foretell a great person to come, and unless they allowed it to be Jesus Christ, they could make nothing of them. The Persians, the Chinese, and the Delphians, could not prophesy of Cæsar, and the close resemblance of the prophecies from all parts of the world, could not be the effect of accident. These matters being premised, we will now compare the calculations made a little time ago, with the periods produced by the precession of the equinoxes. But first it is necessary to recollect, that Julius Cæsar fixed the solstice to the 25th of December, about one in the morning, which brings the Equinox, in the zodiacal circle, to the 25th degree of Pisces.

From the birth of Christ to the beginning of Aries will be—35 degrees, or about   2520 years.
From Aries to the beginning of Taurus   30   2160
            ——
In the whole about   4680

30 degrees in May, *Taurus.* $8 \times 600 = 4800$
30 degrees in April, *Aries.*   4680
 5 degrees in March, *Pisces*   ——
——   120
$65 \times 72 = 4680$

This difference is what we might expect, because the two cycles of the precession, and of the Sun and Moon, the Neros would not coincide till the end of 10 signs. For, $2160 \times 8 = 17280 \div$ by 600, leaves a remainder of 480, to which, if we add the difference of 120, it exactly completes the cycle of 600. Then add 120 to the 4680, and it gives us exactly the time for 8 Neroses, 4800. This shews the reason why, in most of the calculations which I shall presently make, the sum of 2160, the years of the precession in one sign, must first be deducted, to make the sums come right.

These results serve to shew that the system must have been made up, or completed, by the Brahmins, some time after the beginning of their Cali Yug. Their attempts to reconcile facts irreconcileable—the 2160 years of the precession from Taurus to Aries, with the three Neroses, and a wish to begin to count the latter from the beginning of the Cali Yug—in short the whole exhibits a system of expedients, or shifts. The coincidence of numbers in my explanation is so extraordinary as to set at defiance the supposition of accident. The system being originally founded in error, as I will presently shew, when the Brahmins discovered the error, they had recourse to such expedients as offered themselves.

8. In the following verses of Martianus Capella, the celebrated Monogram of Christ ΥΗΣ, 608, is described. These very well apply to the Cristna of India, of the Jews, and also of the father of Ecclesiastical history, Eusebius, by whom the Roman church is followed, and by whom, in fact, it was established; and I beg my reader to pay particular attention to the Sacrum nomen et cognomen, the ΥΗΣ in these verses, which are written in Roman letters on our pulpit cloths, in Greek letters on the inside of the roof of the cathedral of St. Alban's, and in every kind of letters on the churches in Italy.[1]

This period of 608, I have just now shewn, was a celebrated cycle with the Hindoos. I shall call it the Great Neros, to distinguish it from that of 600, the Neros of Josephus.

Solem te Latium vocitat, quòd solus honore
Post Patrem sis lucis apex, radiisque sacratum
Bis senis perhibent caput aurea lumina, *ferre:*

---

[1] For some interesting observations respecting the *crux ansata*, the reader may consult Dr. Daniel Clarke's Travels, Vol. III. ch. iv., and Socrat. Schol. Histor. Eccles., lib. v. cap. xvii.

Quòd totidem menses, totidem quod conficis horas,
Quatuor alipedes dicunt te flectere habenis,
Quòd solus domites, quam dant elementa quadrigam.
Nam tenebras prohibens, retegis quod cerula lucet.[1]
Hinc Phœbum perhibent prodentem occulta futuri ;
Vel quia dissolvis nocturna admissa. *Isæum*
Te Serapim Nilus, Memphis veneratur Osirim :
Dissona sacra Mitram, Ditemque, ferumque Typhonem :
Atys pulcher item, curvi et puer almus aratri,
Ammon et arentis Libyes, ac Biblius Adon.
Sic vario cunctus te nomine convocat orbis.
Salve vera deûm facies, vultûsque paternæ,
OCTO ET SEXCENTIS NUMERIS, CUI LITERA TRINA
CONFORMAT SACRUM NOMEN, COGNOMEN, ET OMEN.
Da, Pater, æthereos mentis conscendere cœtus :
Astrigerumque sacro sub nomine noscere cœlum.
Augeat hæc Pater insignis memorandus ubique.[2]

Latium calls thee, Sol, because thou alone art in honour, AFTER THE FATHER, the centre of light ; and they affirm that thy sacred head bears a golden brightness in twelve rays, because thou formest that number of months and that number of hours. They say that thou guidest four winged steeds, because thou alone rulest the chariot of the elements. For, dispelling the darkness, thou revealest the shining heavens. Hence they esteem thee, Phœbus, the discoverer of the secrets of the future ; or, because thou preventest nocturnal crimes. Egypt worships thee as *Isæan* Serapis—and Memphis as Osiris. Thou art worshiped by different rites as Mithra, Dis, and the cruel Typhon. Thou art also the beautiful Atys, and the fostering son of the bent plough. Thou art the Ammon of arid Libya, and the Adonis of Byblos. Thus under a varied appellation the whole world worships thee. Hail ! thou true image of the Gods, and of thy father's face ! THOU WHOSE SACRED NAME, SIRNAME, AND *Omen*, THREE LETTERS MAKE TO AGREE WITH THE NUMBER 608. Grant us, oh Father, to reach *the ethereal intercourse of mind*, and to know the starry heaven under this sacred name. May the great and universally adorable Father increase these his favours.

For an explanation of the Sacrum Nomen, vide Celtic Druids.[3]

For the reason given above by Colonel Wilford, M. Cassini has shewn that the æra of Buddha ought to be fixed to the year 543, not 544, before Christ. It is said that the Cali Yug took place 3101 years before Christ. The era of Buddha, it has been before stated, is calculated from his death. Now let us count the difference between his death and the beginning of the cycle for his life, and it will be 57. Take this from the time the Cali Yug has run, and it will give 3101—57 = 3044. Take from this the time which Christ is placed too late, accordding to Usher, viz. 4 years, and we shall have from the beginning of the Cali Yug 3040. Divide this by the mystical number of Martianus Capella, the Monogram of Christ, ΥΗΣ, = 608, and we shall have exactly the number of five Yugs, or five great Neroses, between the flood, or the entrance of the Sun into the Hindoo Aries or the beginning of the Cali Yug, and Christ. This and the three in the preceding 2160 years, the time the Sun took to pass through Taurus, make up the eight.

In the 2160 years there is an excess of 360 years over the three Cycles or Neroses. This arises from the system having originally commenced, or at least been in existence, when the precession was supposed to be 1800 years in passing through a sign, treated of before in Section 5. This was probably connected with Enoch's conveyance to heaven, when 360 years of age (not 365), as his age ought to be. I shall return to this presently.

If we take from the period of 5,200 stated by Cassini as Eusebius's, (viz. from the creation to the birth of Christ,) the precession for one sign, viz. 2160, we shall leave exactly 3040, which sum is five sacred Christian periods, or great Neroses of 608 each. Thus : $5 \times 608 = 3040$; which will

---

[1] Quæ cærula lucent?   [2] Martianus Capella, de Nuptiis Philologiæ, Lib. ii. p. 32.   [3] Ch. iv. Sect. viii.

be the time from the Cali Yug, or the entrance of the sun into Aries, to the birth of Christ, according to Eusebius.[1]

Again, add together 4 cycles of 600 each, and we have	2400
Then add the æra of the death of Buddha pointed out by Cassini	543
Then add the difference between the æra of his death and the beginning of a Neros, the duration of his life	57
And it leaves exactly 5 Neroses	3000

The beginning of the Cali Yug is invariable, being 3100 B. C., or 3044 before Vicramaditya.[2] This last 3044+2160=5204, is Eusebius's period, Usher's mistake allowed for.

If in the last calculation we count the æra for the death of Buddha at 544, as uncorrected by Cassini, and take the age of Buddha at 56, exactly the time, according to the Lebtarikh, which Augustus was born before Christ, we shall have 3000 years, or five Neroses from the flood to the birth of Christ.[3]

Wilford says, the Samaritans count 3040 years from the flood to the birth of Christ. From this it appears that they used the Neros of 608 in their calculation.

Again, from the period between the Cali Yug and Christ, 3101 years, take the time between the epoch 543 and Christ, viz. 57, and we have 3044: exactly the time, according to the Samaritan computation, between the birth of Christ and the flood, Usher's error allowed for.

In India there was an æra called the æra of Vicramaditya. Many learned Pundits make him begin to reign 3044 years after the flood, and they add that, after a reign of 56 years, he died in the year 3101, which year 3044 was the first of the Christian æra of the flood, according to the Samaritan computation, Usher's error allowed for; thus completing the cycle, and with three before the flood, make the eight required.[4]

Years of the world to Christ	4000
Years from creation to flood	1656
	2344
Admitted error in Hebrew, or the Samaritan without error	700
	3044
Life of Vicramaditya 56 years	56
	3100

This shews the Indian and Samaritan to be precisely the same.

There was also an æra of Salivahana, of whom I shall have much to say hereafter. He conquered and killed Vicramaditya. His æra commenced at the death of his enemy, that is, at the birth of Christ. The Samaritans, who give 700 years more between the flood and Christ than the Hebrew and Vulgate, appear to have calculated by the precession of the equinoxes, and to have

---

[1] The Cali Yug begins when the Sun enters Aries at the Vernal Equinox. Jones, Asiat. Res. Vol. II. p.393. This is the date of the flood according to the Brahmin doctrines.

[2] Asiat. Res. Vol. IX. p. 86.

[3] According to some calculations, Augustus was born 63 years before Christ. (Asiat. Res. Vol. X. p. 33.) Then 5 Yugs or Neroses=3000+638+63=3701—3101=600. This evidently alludes to the second æra of Buddha, of 638 years after Christ, formerly noticed in Section 1.

[4] Asiat. Res. Vol. X. p. 122.

calculated in such a manner, that 65 degrees, and a part of a degree, had passed at the birth of Christ: $65 \times 72 = 4680$; add for a part of a degree 20 years $= 4700$. The principle on which the Samaritan computation is made is pretty clear.

As the Samaritans count[1] 3044 between the flood and Christ, and as they reckon 4700 from the creation to Christ, they must reckon the same time between the creation and flood as Usher, viz. 1656 years.[2] The Julian period begins, the 4 years' mistake of Usher allowed for, 4709 or 4710 years before Christ. This evidently is meant to coincide with the Samaritan system.

All these periods are correct except the Julian period, which comes sufficiently near to prove very clearly, that what Megasthenes said was true, that the Jews and the Hindoos had the same system of chronology, and we shall see by and by, in a future book, when I come to treat of the Jews, the reason of this.

The Greeks and Romans considered the two numbers 608 and 650 as in a particular manner sacred to Bacchus. Now, when Eusebius was making out his 5200 by deducting from it the years of the precession in the sign Taurus, and then calculating five cycles from the beginning of Aries to Jesus Christ, as the reader has seen, he would naturally inquire, what the other sacred number 650 would do; and he would find, that if multiplied by eight, (the number of cycles stated by Juvenal and Censorinus to have run to Christ,) it would exactly make his number of 5200; so that one made the cycles from Taurus, the other from Aries,—but both coming to the same thing, eight cycles in the whole, and the same number of years. It seems to me to be absolutely impossible, that the coincidence of these numbers can have been the effect of accident.

The cycle of 600 does not appear to have been known as a sacred number to the Greeks and Romans, but only to the Jews and oriental nations. The reason was, because the 608 and 650 came from the East before their error was discovered. I think I need not have desired any thing better to confirm, both my theory of the origin of the sacred solar numbers, and of the eight periods or cycles to the birth of Christ, than that the multiplication of the 650 by eight, should give us the exact number stated by Eusebius to have passed before the birth of Christ.

The following is surely a singular coincidence of numbers :

Usher's age of the world	4004
Usher's time of the flood	1656
	————
Flood before Christ	2348
Add Samaritan correction	700
	————
	3048
Add *real* precession for one sign	2152
	————
	5200

If we suppose, as is the fact, that the sun left the last degree of Aries, and entered Pisces, about the year 380 before Christ, and add the years of the commonly reputed precession for the two signs Aries and Taurus, $2160 + 2160 = 4320$, we shall have exactly the Samaritan computation $4320 + 380 = 4700$. If this be accident, it is surely a wonderful accident, that should bring all those numbers which my theory requires to an exact agreement.

---

[1] Asiat. Res. Vol. V. p. 241.

[2] See Universal History, Vol. I. p. 147, where the Hebrew and Samaritan chronology, before the flood, are reconciled on the hypothesis of Father Tournemine. In this reconciliation, I think, will be found the trifling error or difference before mentioned, of the ten in the Julian period.

I consider this to be very important, because the Samaritan computation not only agrees with the Hindoo in system, but it adopts the error, using its favourite number 72 instead of 71; and again, the Hindoo error of 2160 instead of 2152.

Colouel Wilford says, " The year of the death of Vicramarca and that of the manifestation of " Sal'-ba-han, are acknowledged to be but one and the same, and they are obviously so; according " to the Cumarica-chanda, that remarkable year was the 3101st of the Cali Yuga, and the first of " the Christian æra, thus coinciding also with the Samaritan text, which is a remarkable circum- " stance." [1]

With respect to the time fixed by Eusebius for the age of the world before Christ, we must re- collect that it is very different from all the others, because at the time when he and his master, Constantine, were settling and establishing the Christian religion—destroying by the agency of Theodoret such gospel histories as they thought wrong, and substituting such as they thought right — they may be fairly supposed to have had information on these subjects, which may very easily have been lost in later times. I think no one will believe that it was by accident, that the number of the years of the Sun's precession in a sign, (2160,) the number of Eusebius, (5200,) and the eight cycles, agreed with the doctrines of Juvenal and Censorinus and the eight Avatars of India. [2]

Every part of this curious mythos betrays marks of a system founded originally in error, but at this day lost, and made out by expedients or doubtful calculations : and when we reflect upon the fact stated by Josephus, that the Jews had a knowledge from their ancestors of the beautiful cycle of the Neros, we need not be surprised that their chronology should shew proofs of their know- ledge of the precession of the equinoxes, as the Samaritan, I think, does. When Josephus says that the Jews had the Neros, he of course means the Israelitish nation, the descendants of Abraham.

CHAPTER III

Subject continued—Two Cycles. Joshua stops the Sun and Moon—Jewish Incar- nations—Millenium. Pritchard. Plato—Jewish and Christian authorities from Dr. Mede—Plutarch and other Western Authors on the 600-year Cycle—The Hindoos had different Systems—Observations on Pythagoras, &c.—La Lou- bère on the word Siam

1. As we have the two small cycles 600 and 608, we have in like manner two *systems* of chrono logy depending upon them. The first is Eusebius's. It begins with the egress of Noah from the

---

[1] Asiat. Res. Vol. X. p. 122.

[2] Methodius, Bishop of Tyre, states, that in the year of the world 2100, there was born unto Noah a fourth son, called Ioni-thus. (Nimrod, Vol. I. p. 4.) This has certainly a mythological appearance and looks as if it was meant for the 2160 years, the precessional time between Taurus and Aries. If this 2100 be added to the 3100 years which the Hindoos place between the flood and Christ, it exactly makes up the date fixed on by Eusebius, 5200 years for the age of the world. The word *Ioni*, we know the meaning of, and may not the *Thus* mean *the black?* for it is often written Ioni-chus. Perhaps it may allude in some way to a schism which took place between the followers of Taurus and the Ioni, which I shall treat of presently, and the followers of the Yoni alone. Other chronicles confirm the existence of this Ioni-thus as a son of Noah. He was a famous astrologer and prophet. " He held the region from the entering in " of Etham to the sea, which region is called Heliochora, because the sun riseth there."

ark. Deducting from his statement of the world's age (i. e. 5200) the years of the precession for the sign Taurus, 2160, and it leaves 3040, equal to 608×5, or five Great Neroses to the birth of Christ. This, as we have before noticed, is the correct Samaritan computation, according to Col. Wilford,[1] the mistake of Usher being allowed for, and correct, according to Marsham and Hevelius.

The second system begins at the birth of Shem. The fourth period ends with the death of Shem, who lived exactly 600 years, and who is said[2] to have died in the year of the flood 502. Then, 502+3101 (the duration of the Cali Yug before Christ)=3603; the Neros, that of Shem, being deducted, it leaves 3003, and then Usher's 4 years for the birth of Christ placed too forward, being also deducted, we have 3000, or five correct Neroses of 600 years each, all but an unit, which we have seen is of no material consequence.

It is a circumstance worthy of observation, that Shem is said by Usher to have died at the 2158th which may be called 2160th year of the world's age. These were the years of the precession in one sign. This, like other coincidences, could scarcely have been the effect of accident. If we add to 2160, five great Neroses or 3040, we shall have the calculation of Eusebius, the man of all others, since the time of Christ, the most likely to understand the machinery of the system. And this again shews why, in these calculations, the time which the equinox preceded in one sign, viz. 2160 years, ought to be deducted.

Thus we have two systems of the Neros, one of 600, and the other of 608 years each.

Hesiod, in his Works and Days, makes out that he is *himself* living in the fifth age, that of Iron, the fourth having just passed away. This evidently alludes to the six millenaries, in the fifth of which he lived. A learned and anonymous author of Cambridge (Key to Chronology of the Hindoos) comparing the chronology of the Hindoos and Jews says, speaking of the Works and Days, " The commencement of the fourth age is, if possible, yet more clearly marked. The three first "ages having consumed 1000, 800, and 600 years, the fourth commences with A. M. 2400—and to " this age is assigned 400 years. Hesiod styles it the age of the Demigods, and represents a part of it as a time of great virtue, justice, and piety." We may here observe how the ingenious Cantab,[3] who does not in the least understand or even suspect the nature of my theory, stumbles upon my numbers, only mistaking the end of the fourth age, 2400, for its commencement. He thinks Moses answered to Cristna. This alludes to the period which the Samaritans allotted to the bringing of the ark to Shiloh, by Joshua.

It is stated, Joshua x. 12, 13, that he stopped the sun and moon ABOUT a day : *Sun, stand thou still upon Gibeon; and thou, Moon, in the valley of Ajalon—and the Sun hasted not to go down* ABOUT *a whole day. Is not this written in the book of Jasher ?* [4]

The Bible says, "about *a day.*" I shall endeavour to shew *why* and for *how long a time* Joshua stopped it. This stoppage probably continued during the time between the ending of one of Noah's and one of Shem's cycles, viz. 98 years : i. e. 98 + 502 = 600. By this means he brought the two cycles together. 98 years would be more than equal to one degree, or the 360th part of the circle, but not quite to one degree and a half. At that time each degree, or 72 years, represented a day, of the year of 360 days long. Every festival would fall back a day in about 72 years.

The circumstance of the Moon being stopped as well as the Sun, is allusive to the double cycle, of Sun and Moon. It was a throwing back the Luni-solar period. If this were not so, why should

---

[1] Asiat. Res. Vol. V. p. 241, Map.   [2] Universal History.   [3] Vol. II. p. 289.

[4] As our version says, but as Josephus says, *in the writings laid up in the temple.* (See Parkhurst in voce שור *isr*, and in voce ספר *spr*.) But, as I should say with Parkhurst, *in the emblematical writing* ; and, I should also add, of the Saviour שור *isr*—from the word ישע *ise*, to save.

Joshua make use of the expression to stop the Moon? Surely the Sun gave light enough without the Moon! I suppose nobody is so weak now as to take these texts to the letter.

The system of Shem was that of 608 years to a Neros, and when Joshua is said to have stopped the Sun and Moon, he dropped the use of the 608 and adopted the 600. He corrected the Calendar, as Cæsar did in a later day. In all these calculations I look upon the first books of Genesis as Hindoo works, and, for reasons which will hereafter be given upon the Mosaic and Hindoo systems, in their foundations or principles the same. The Mosaic has been shewn to be the same as the Persian, and Sir William Jones has shewn that the old Persian was the same as the Hindoo, which is also proved, by the Desatir of Moshani.

It is admitted that the Neros could not have been invented without a very great degree of astronomical knowledge, or till after very long and correctly recorded astronomical observations. As I have stated, the great Neros was probably the cycle before their increased knowledge enabled them to bring it to perfection, and was carried very early to the West, and is thus found with the Etruscans.

The cycles would require correcting again after several revolutions, and we find Isaiah making the shadow go back ten degrees on the dial of Ahaz.[1] This would mean nothing but a second correction of the Neros, or a correction of some cycle of a planetary body, to make it agree with some other.

In the annals of China, in fact of the Chinese Buddhists, in the reign of the Emperor YAU, (a very striking name, being the name of the God of the Jews,) it is said, that the sun was stopped ten days, that is, probably, ten degrees of Isaiah,[2] a degree answering to a year, 360 degrees and 360 days.

As might well be expected, when Joshua stopped the sun it was observed in India. Mr. Franklin says, " 1575 years before Christ, after the death of Cristna (Boodh the son of Deirca), the sun " stood still to bear the pious ejaculations of Arjoon. This is the great leader of the Jews— " Moses."[3]

The author of the Cambridge Key says, that in the text of the Bible the sun is said to stand still in A. M. 1451, the year in which Moses died. This is the Cali year 1651, in which the sun stood still to hear the pious ejaculations of Arjoon for the death of Cristna.[4] The learned Jesuit Baldæus observes, that every part of the life of Cristna has a near resemblance to the history of Christ : and he goes on to shew that the time when the miracles are supposed to have been performed was during the Dwaparajug, which he admits to have ended 3100 years before the Christian æra.[5] So that, as the Cantab says, *If there is meaning in words the Christian missionary implies that the history of Christ was founded on that of Crishnu.*

After this, in p. 226, Cantab goes on to shew, that it is almost impossible to doubt that the history of Cristna was written long prior to the time of Christ. The same mythos is evident, in all these widely-separated nations. Its full meaning, I have no doubt, will be some day discovered.

The Cali Yug is fixed to about the year 3100 before Christ, in the middle of the *ninth century*, by Albumasar, a famous Arabian astronomer, who lived at the court of the celebrated Al-Mamun at Balkh.[6] This alone proves that the Hindoo periods are not of modern invention, and is of itself enough to refute all Mr. Bentley's arguments which have been used, and have for their foundation solely his assertion, that the astronomical calculations were forged for the purpose of deceiving Mahmood Akbar in the 16*th century*. George of Trebizond, who died about 1448, says, that the

[1] 2 Kings xx. 11; and Isaiah xxviii. 8.   [*] Pref. to the last Vol. of Univers. Hist. p. xiii.
[3] On Buddhists and Jeynes, p. 174.   [4] Vol. II. p. 224.   [5] Ibid.
[6] Vide Asiat. Res. Vol. IX. p. 142; Vol. X. p. 117.

Persians reckoned from the flood to A. D. 632, the æra of Yesdejird, 3733 years. Thus, 632+3101 =3733. This again shews that the Persians had the same system as the Hindoos,[1] and again clearly proves, that these Hindoo calculations cannot have been made to deceive Mahmood Akbar.

2. Noah began a new world, and thus also did Cristna.

In looking back to the Jewish history, I find the flood ended on the day that Noah finished his 600th year, when a new world began. We have already seen that the year of the saviour Cristna was feigned to be 600 years—the duration of the Neros. He was the saviour of India, expressly predicted in the ancient writings of the Brahmins. The saviour of the Jews and of Europe was the same. The Jewish incarnations were the same as those of the Hindoos, as was indeed almost every part of their system. But from the extremely corrupt state of the details of the Hebrew history in the three old versions of it, there is no probability that the cycles should ever be made out correctly according to either of them.

The first cycle began with the sun in Taurus, the creation of the system, and ended with Enoch, who did not die, but who ascended into heaven. I think this speaks for itself.

Enoch is said to have lived 365 years, but it is probable that his life was only 360, the time which it was necessary to intercalate to make up the difference between the three Neroses, and the precession for one sign, 1800+360=2160, when the system of Noah, the correct system, began. In this theory I am supported by evidence (under the circumstance in which we have it) which I call strong. Dr. Shuckford says, "Now if Enoch was 60 years old at *Methusaleh's* birth, according to " Eusebius himself, from Methusaleh's birth to the 180th year of Noah is but 300 years, and con- " sequently Eusebius, to have been consistent with himself, should have made Enoch's age at his " *translation* 360, but he has made it 365."[2] Dr. Shuckford has some very interesting observations on the different systems of chronology, and professes to have removed or accounted for the difference between the Hebrew and the LXX., with the exception of the very suspicious round sum of 600 years.

As I have just stated, I consider the Mythos of Enoch as an intercalation, to make the periods come right, after the discovery that the precession did not take place in 1800 years, but in 2160; 1800+360=2160. The cyles were like men, and died of old age. The cycle of Enoch not being finished, he was taken up to heaven, but did not die. In every part of this mythos we see proofs that, like most other systems of this kind, it was made up by expedients from time to time, as cir- cumstances called for them. The first errors respecting the true length of the cycles, and their subsequent improvements, rendered this a necessary consequence. The Arabians called Enoch *Edris*, and say that *Edris* was the same as Elijah, who did not die. And the Arabians and the Jews also had a tradition, that Phinehas, the son of Eleazar, revived in Elijah.[3] Thus the Jewish and Arabian traditions unite Enoch and Elijah, and Elijah and Phinehas, by correct renewed incar- nations; and I suppose every one who reads this will recollect, that the Jews are said to have be- lieved Jesus to be Elijah.[4] Jesus declares that John Baptist came in the SPIRIT and power of Elijah.[5] These circumstances have at least a *strong tendency* to prove, if they do not really prove, that the Hindoo doctrine of renewed incarnation was the esoteric religion of the Jews. When Elijah went up to heaven he left his cloak and prophetic office to Elisha, or to *the Lamb of God.*[6]

The Arabians say that Elijah was the same with Enoch and Phinehas, who was the same with a person called by them Al-Choder. But Al-Choder signifies a Palm-tree. In Sanscrit Al Chod is

---

[1] Asiat. Res. Vol. X. p. 119.   [2] Connec. B. i.   [3] See Hottinger de Mohamedis Genealogiâ.
[4] Mark viii. 28.   [5] Matt. xi. 10, 14.
[6] In a future page I shall shew, that this cloak is the Pallium of the Romish church, by the investiture with which the Popes infused a portion of the Holy Ghost into their Bishops. Without the investiture there was no bishop.

God,[1] as it is in English. "Thus, then, according to the Arabian traditions, Henoch was the same
"with Elijah, and Elijah with Phinehas. But all these three were the same with Al-Choder, that is,
"ὁ Φοῖνιξ, palma." This Al-Choder is said to have flourished at the same time with a certain
Aphridun which signified ὁ Φοῖνιξ, avis.[2] We have not inquired respecting the birth-place of this
celebrated bird. Lucian says what we might expect, that it is an Indian bird, Φοῖνιξ το Ινδικον
οργεον. But the Irish have it in Phenn, and Phennische.[3]

The *annus magnus* of the ancients was a subject of very general speculation among the Greeks
and Romans, but not one of them seems to have suspected the sacrum nomen, cognomen, et omen,
of Martianus Capella. Several of them admit that by the Phœnix this period was meant, or at
least that its life was the length of the great year. From this I conclude that, as it was well known
to Martianus Capella, it must have been a secret known only to the initiated. Solinus says, it is a
thing well known to all the world, that the grand year terminates at the same time as the life of the
Phœnix.[4] This is confirmed by Manilius and Pliny.[5]

George Syncellus says, that the Phœnix which appeared in Egypt, in the reign of Claudius, had
been seen in the same country 654 years before. On this Larcher says, "This pretended Phœnix
"appeared the seventh year of the reign of Claudius, the year 800 of Rome, and the 47th year of
"our æra. If we take from 800 the sum of 654, which is the duration of life of this bird, accord-
"ing to this chronographer, we shall have for the time of its *preceding* apparition the year 146 of
"the foundation of Rome, which answers to the year 608 before our æra."[6] It is surely a very
extraordinary *accident* that should make the learned Larcher's calculation exactly agree with the
term of one of the great Neroses, which this bird's name means; and also, that the other term
147 of our æra, should, within one year, be the term of the six last whole Neroses of Shem, from the
flood : 6×608=3648. Deduct one Neros, thus, 3648–608=3040=5 Neroses. We must recollect
that the Neros of Shem, in the time of the flood, was partly before the flood and partly afterward,
so the one spoken of might be said to be either the fifth or the sixth from the flood. Faber says,
"sometimes the Phœnix is said to live 600, sometimes 460, and sometimes 340 years."[7]

We will now return to the cycles. I before stated that I suspected the first ended with the
birth of Enoch. The second ended with the birth of Noah. The third ended with Noah leaving
the ark, when he was 600 years old. The fourth ended about the time of Abraham, and was probably Isaac, whose name may mean *joy, gladness, laughter*, and who was so called because he was
the saviour, not because his mother laughed at God.[8] The word I shall explain in a future page,
when I treat of the Jews. And here it may be observed, that in the conduct of this curious system,
if I correctly develop it, the incarnations ought not to coincide exactly with the beginning of a
cycle; because, though the priests could regulate the dates of long-past events, they could not so

---

[1] Al-Choder is the Syrian and Rajpoot on only aspirated, and with the Arabic emphatic article AL. When the Buddhists address the Supreme Being or Buddha, they use the word AD, which means *the first*. This is exactly one meaning
of the first word of Genesis. Here we have *the first* and Wisdom, (Col. Tod,) as in Genesis.—Buddha, Wisdom, is
called Ad, *the first*.

[2] Sir W. Drummond, Class. Journ., Vol. XV. pp. 12, 13.

[3] In the Irish Trinity called Tauloc PНΣΝΝ Molloch, the Middle, or Saviour, is the Phenn, 600.

[4] Solini Polyhistor. Cap. xxxvi. Ed. Salmas.

[5] Hist. Nat. Lib. x. Cap. ii., and Mem. Acad. Paris, An. 1815, in a treatise by Larcher.   [6] Ibid.

[7] Orig. Pag. Idol. Vol. I. p. 147.

[8] The exoteric reason given to the devotees of Judea, and, as it appears from their being satisfied with it, suitable to
their understandings, as it has hitherto been to the understandings of the devotees of London; but the inhabitants of
the latter are fast outgrowing, when literally understood, such nonsense,—at least they are in St. Giles's, whatever they
may be in Lambeth and St. James's.

easily regulate the births or deaths of individuals, entered most carefully in public registers,—facts which must have been remembered by families,—but events, such as the arrival of the ark at Shiloh, would be easily swelled into importance, and regulated also as to its date, to make it suit. In the course of a very few years the actual date of such an event would be forgotten, and might be advanced or retarded a few years to suit the occasion. It is evident also, that it is only some events of this kind which could be regulated. For example the going out of Abraham must be difficult to reconcile, if it were wished, which it probably was not. This going out I shall by and by explain, and shew its truth. All this is perfectly consistent if there were such persons as Isaac, &c., the supposed incarnations, as I shall shew there were—persons who had those peculiar names given to them, because they were supposed to be incarnations. The meaning of the ages of man in the Jewish books, and the lengths of time which events took in passing, I do not understand; but I have no doubt they had a mythological or figurative meaning, or concealed some doctrines. To suppose that a system of chronology was really meant, is to suppose the writers of the books incapable of adding and subtracting, which any one must be convinced of in a moment by looking into Volney's Researches into Ancient History, where their *arithmetical* inconsistency with one another is shewn.

It was the belief that some great personage would appear in every cycle, as the Sibylline verses prove; but it was evidently impossible to make the birth of great men coincide with the birth of the cycle. But when it was desirable to found power upon the belief that a living person was the hero of the cycle, it is natural to expect that the attempt should have been made, as was the case with the verses of Virgil and others, as I shall hereafter shew. This great person is, according to Mr. Parkhurst, the type of a future saviour.

The fifth Jewish cycle might end when the Samaritans say the prophecy of Jacob was verified, that is, when Osee, expressly called the Messiah or Saviour—Joshua or Jesus—brought the ark to Shiloh. The versions vary more than 200 years respecting the time of Abraham's stay in Canaan and the residence of the Israelites in Egypt; so that the chronology furnishes no objection. The language of the prophecy of Jacob to Judah, that a Lawgiver should not pass from beneath his feet till Shiloh should come, has been a subject of much dispute. Dr. Geddes and others maintain, that it is no prophecy, but Christians in general consider it to be one. The Samaritans insist that it is a prophecy, and that it was fulfilled in the son of *Nun*, Osee, called properly Jesus or the Saviour, and improperly *Joshua*, on his bringing the ark to Shiloh, as remarked above. Sir William Drummond has shewn, in a most ingenious and convincing manner, in his Œdipus Judaicus, how this prophecy is depicted on the sphere.

The sixth incarnation I will not attempt to name. The Jews, like the Hindoos, had many saviours or incarnations, or persons who at different times were thought to be inspired, or to be persons in whom a portion of divine wisdom was incarnate. This makes it difficult to fix upon the right person. Might not Samson be one of them? He was an incarnation, as we shall soon see.

The next cycle must be, I think, that of Elias, ('Hλιος) or Elijah, אל־יהו al-ieu, or God the Lord, according to Calmet and Cruden, but I should say, *God the self-existent;* that is, it means to say, an incarnation or inspiration of 'Hλιος or *the God*, יהו ieu, the Iao of the Greeks, or the solar power.[1] He left his prophetic power to Elisha, which Cruden and Calmet say means *the Lamb of God*.

It seems from the Hebrew words, when they come to be translated into English, that these

---

[1] It is curious to observe numbers of churches in Greece dedicated to St. Elias, which have formerly been temples of the sun.

books must have been esoteric, i. e. *secret* writings, known only to the chief priests, probably first exposed to the public eye by Ptolemy Philadelphus, 246 years before Christ, when he caused the Pentateuch to be translated. The explanation made by Ezra of such parts of the book as he thought proper at the gate of the temple, or the reading of it to the good king Josias, militates nothing against this hypothesis. I feel little doubt that the publication of the Jewish writings was forced, *as the Jews say*, by Ptolemy, and to that publication, I think, we are indebted for them; for, after they were once translated and published, there would be no longer any use in keeping them locked up in the temple, and copies of the original would be multiplied. At the Babylonish captivity they were not destroyed, because the desolation of Palestine happened at two different periods; so that one part of the people preserved the sacred book in their temple, when all was burnt in the temple of the other. When Cambyses sacked Egypt, all was destroyed in a moment, except the obeliscal pillars, which were left, and some of which are standing yet, particularly the finest of them all at Heliopolis.

Of the Hero of the eighth age it is said in our version, *Thus saith the Lord to his anointed,* HIS MESSIAH, *to Cyrus, whose right hand I have holden to subdue nations.* [1] Here I beg it may be observed that if persons doubt the existence of Joshua or Abraham, they cannot well doubt the existence of Cyrus. This observation will be found of importance hereafter. The eighth period began about the Babylonish captivity, about 600 years before Christ. The ninth began, as the Siamese say, with Jesus Christ, making in all eight cycles before Christ.

I do not claim to be the first who has observed the renewal of incarnations among the Jews, nor can I deserve the whole of the ridicule which will be lavished by the priests upon the doctrine, because they cannot refute it. I learn from the Classical Journal, [2] that the Rev. Mr. Faber believed MELCHIZEDEK *to be an incarnation of the Son of God.* Mr. Faber says, " It was con-" tended that every *extraordinary* personage, whose office was to reclaim or to punish mankind, " was an avatar or descent of the Godhead." Again, " Adam, and Enoch, and Noah, might in " outward appearance be *different* men, but they were really the *selfsame* divine person who had " been promised as the seed of the woman, successively animating various human bodies." [3] From the black Cristna bruising the head of the serpent, and the circumstances of the two mythoses being so evidently the same, there seems nothing inconsistent in this. The renewed solar incarnation, every 600 years, seems pretty clear. The fact of a renewed incarnation could not escape Mr. Faber; his mode of accounting for it is a different matter; but I beg leave to add, that I must not be accused by the priests of being fanciful in this instance, since their great oracle, the very learned Mr. Faber, had stated it previously. Although the author of Nimrod does not appear to have the least idea of what I conceive to be the true system, yet the idea of a cycle in the history of Noah forcibly occurred to him. He says the fourth in order from Noah, with whom this present cycle, or system, of the world commenced. [4]

Col. Franklin, in his treatise on the Jeynes and Buddhists, says, " *First* Bood'h, the self-exist-" ing, *Swayam Bhuva,* whose *outar* or period of time commenced 4002 years before Christ, or, " according to the fictitious calculations of the Hindoos, 3,891,102: he ended his mortal career " when the three first ages were complete, or, agreeable to the Hindoo computation, during the " commencement of the fourth age." [5] Here is evidently a proof of the truth of my theory, though concealed under a mythos. Here is the first equinoctial Avatar Buddha, ending when the sun enters Aries, after three Neroses or ages, according to the Brahmins, when Cristna begins.

---

[1] Isaiah xlv. 1.   [2] Vol. XIX. p. 72.   [3] Fab. Orig. Pag. Idol. Vol. III. pp. 612, 613.
[4] Vol. I. p. 7.   [5] P. 172.

Col. Franklin says, the Avatar ended *during the commencement* of the fourth age. He was obliged to use this nonsensical mode of expression, because it would not fit to the end of the third or the beginning of the fourth age. It ended in the middle of the fourth age. This arises from confounding the equinoctial cycle with the Neros, which Col. Franklin did not understand. He had a slight glimpse of the two systems of cycles, but did not see that there were two cycles running, but not exactly *pari passu*.

3. I shall now endeavour to demonstrate the existence of the cycle of 600 or 6000 among the Western nations. Col. Wilford has shewn that the Buddhas and Brahmins were well known and distinguished from each other by Strabo, Philostratus, Pliny, Porphyry, &c.[1]   The alternate destruction of the world by fire and water was taught by Plato. In his Timæus he says, that the story of Phàeton's burning the world has reference to a great dissolution of all things on the earth, by fire. Gale[2] shews that the Jews, as well as Plato, maintained that the world would be destroyed at the end of 6000 years; that then the day of judgment would come : manifestly the Jewish and Christian Millenium.

On this subject Plato says, " When the time of all these things is full, and the change is need-
" ful, and every kind upon the earth is exhausted, each soul having given out all its generations,
" and having shed upon the earth as many seeds as were appointed unto it, then doth the pilot of
" the universe, abandoning the rudder of the helm, return to his seat of circumspection, and the
" world is turned back by fate and its own innate concupiscence. At that time also the Gods,
" who act in particular places as colleagues of the supreme Dæmon, being aware of that which is
" coming to pass, dismiss from their care the several parts of the world. The world itself *being*
" *turned awry*, and falling into collision, and following inversely the course of beginning and end,
" and having a great concussion within itself, makes another destruction of all living things. But
" in due process of time it is set free from tumult, and confusion, and concussion, and obtaineth a
" calm, and then being set in order, returneth into its pristine coùrse, &c."[3]   Nimrod then
adds, " as we farther learn from Virgil, that the next renovation of the world will be followed by
" the Trojan war—I do not think that more words are necessary in order to evince that the Ilion
" of Homer is the Babel of Moses." Cicero says, [4] " Tum efficitur, cum solis et lunæ, et
" quinque errantium ad eundem inter se comparationem confectis omnium spatiis, est facta con-
" versio." And Clavius, Cap. i., says, " Sphæræ quo tempore quidam volunt omnia quæcunque
" in mundo sunt, eodem ordine esse reditura, quo nunc cernuntur."

The doctrine of the renewal of worlds has been well treated by Dr. Pritchard.[5] He shews that the dogma was common to several of the early sects of philosophers in Greece;[6] that traces of it are found in the remains of Orpheus; that it was a favourite Doctrine of the Stoics, and was regarded as one of the peculiar tenets of that school; and that we are indebted chiefly to their writings for what we know of this ancient philosophy. But although the successive catastrophes are shewn to have been most evidently held by them, yet, from the doctor's account, it is very clear that they were not generally understood ; some philosophers describing the catastrophes to have taken place in one way, some in another; some by water, some by fire, and some by both alternately. " Seneca, the tragedian, teaches that all created beings are to be destroyed, or re-
" solved into the uncreated essence of the divinity ;" and " Plutarch makes the Stoic Cleanthes
" declare that the moon, the stars, and the sun will perish, and that the celestial ether, which,

---

[1] Asiat. Res. Vol. IX. p. 298.   [4] Court Gent. Vol. I. B. iii. Ch. vii. Sect. iii. v.
[2] Plat. Polit. p. 37. apud Nimrod, Vol. I. p. 511.   [5] De Nat. Deor.
[3] Anal. of Egypt. Myth. p. 178.   [6] See Lipsius de Physiol. Stoic. Dissert. 2.

" according to the Stoics, was the substance of the Deity, will convert all things into its own
" nature, or assimilate them to itself.[1] And Seneca compares the self-confidence of the phi-
" losopher to the insulated happiness of Jupiter, who, after the world has melted away, and the
" gods are resolved into one essence, when the operations of nature cease, withdraws himself for
" a while into his own thoughts, and reposes in the contemplation of his own perfections."[2] The
Doctor shews that the same thing was affirmed by Chrysippus, Zeno, and Cleanthes; and we find
passages similar to the foregoing cited by Cicero,[3] Numenius,[4] Philo Judæus,[5] and many others.
I think in the account given above of Jupiter from Seneca, we cannot help recognising the Hindoo
doctrine—Brahma reposing on the great abyss. After this, the Doctor goes on to state[6] the
opinions of Numenius, Censorinus, Cassander, &c., as to the alternation from heat to cold, and the
length of the periods, in which they all disagree; but enough comes out, I think, to shew that they
were all connected " with the revolution of the annus magnus, or great year," and must have
originally come from the East, where the doctrine of the change in the angle which the plane of
the ecliptic makes with the plane of the equator was well understood,[7] and whence it probably came
to the Greeks. The words of Plato, cited above, *being turned awry*, are allusive to this. It was
called Λοξιας, unless Λοξιας was applied to the elliptic orbits, of which I have some suspicion. It
is very certain that if it be true that this change in the angle do take place, something very like
the alternations from heat to cold, and cold to heat, in certain long periods, must happen: and
paradoxical as many of my readers may think me, yet I very much suspect that if the angle do
increase and decrease as just mentioned, and the race of man should so long continue, evils very
like those above described must be experienced.

" In the Surya-Sidhanta, Meya, the great astronomer, has stated the obliquity of the ecliptic
" in his time at 24°,[8] from whence Mr. S. Davis computed, that supposing the obliquity of the
" ecliptic to have been accurately observed by the ancient Hindus at 24°, and that its decrease
" had been from that time half a second a year, the age or date of the Surya-Sidhanta (in 1789)
" would be 3840 years; therefore Meya must have lived about the year 1956 of the creation."[9]
It appears from the preceding sentence that Meya's system differs much from the older Puranas.
His begins from the moment the sun enters Aries in the Hindoo sphere, as Mr. Davis says,
" which circumstances alone must form a striking difference between it and the Puranic system."[10]
I am not sufficiently skilled in astronomy to speak POSITIVELY upon the subject, but I should
think that the reduction to nothing of the angle which the ecliptic makes to the equator, that is,
the coincidence of the equator and ecliptic, would necessarily cause some very great changes in the
circumstances of the globe. The decrease of this angle or obliquity we see was certainly known
by the celebrated Brahmin Meya, who fixes it in his time at 24°. The knowledge of this change
gave rise, I think, to the allegory or mythos of the flood. The extraordinary changes which have
taken place at different and remote æras or long intervals, in the crust of our globe, cannot possibly be denied. It was supposed that these were caused by the change in the angle above alluded
to, and the mythos of the flood and ship fastened to the peak of Naubanda was formed to account
for it to the vulgar. This was I think confounded with another flood, of which I shall treat
hereafter.

---

[1] Plut.   [2] Seneca, Epist. ix.   [3] De Nat. Deor. Lib. ii.
[4] Apud Euseb. Prep. Evang. Lib. xv.   [5] De Immortal. Mundi.   [6] P. 183.
[7] Mr. Parkhurst has shewn (in voce נשׁ *ste*, vi. p. 730) that the declination of the plane of the ecliptic to the plane
of the equator was as well known to the ancients of the West as it is to the moderns.
[8] An interesting account of the discovery of this phenomenon may be seen in the preface to Blair's Chronology.
[9] Asiat. Res. Vol. V. 4to, p. 329.   [10] Ibid.

4. The following Jewish and Christian authorities will go far to establish what I have said respecting the above doctrines : Ita enim legitur in Gemara Sanhedrin, Perek CHELEK. Dixit R. Ketina, *Sex annorum millibus stat mundus, et uno vastabitur : de quo dicitur, ET EXALTABITUR DOMINUS SOLUS DIE ILLO.* Sequitur paulo post, *Traditio adstipulatur, R. Ketinæ : sicut e septenis annis septimus quisque annus remissionis est : ita e septem millibus annorum mundi, septimus millenarius remissiones erit : quemadmodum dicitur,* [1] ET EXALTABITUR DOMINUS SOLUS DIE ILLO. Dicitur item [2] PSALMUS CANTICUM DE DIE SABBATI ; id est, *de die quo tota quies est.* Dicitur etiam [3] NAM MILLE ANNI IN OCULIS TUIS VELUT DIES HESTERNUS. *Traditio Domûs Eliæ : Sex mille annos durat mundus ; bis mille annos inanitas, (seu vastitas* תהו *tueu,) bis mille annis lex : denique bis mille annis dies Christi.* [4] None of the Fathers have written more clearly respecting the Millenium than Irenæus, and he expressly declares that, after it, the world shall be destroyed by fire, *and that the earth shall be made new after its conflgration.* [5] Here is the admission of the identical renewal of worlds held by the oriental nations. Irenæus, [6] *Quotquot diebus hic factus est mundus, tot et millenis consummatur. . . . . . Si enim dies Domini quasi mille anni, in sex autem diebus consummata sunt quæ facta sunt : manifestum est, quoniam consummatio isporum sextus millesimus annus est.* Lactantius, [7] *Quoniam sex diebus cuncta Dei opera perfecta sunt : per secula sex, id est, annorum sex millia, manere in hoc statu mundum necesse est. Dies enim magnus Dei mille annorum circulo terminatur. . . . . . Et ut Deus sex illos dies in tantis rebus fabricandis laboravit, ita et religio ejus et veritas in his sex millibus aunorum laborare necesse est, malitiâ prævalente et dominante.* Mede's works, [8] where several other Christian authorities may be found.

St. Augustin had an indistinct view of the true system. He says, that the fifth age is finished, that we are in the sixth, and that the dissolution of all things will happen in the seventh. [9] He evidently alluded to the thousands, not the Neroses ; and that the world should be burnt and renewed. [10] Barnabas says, " In six thousand years the Lord shall bring all things to an end." He makes the seventh thousand the millenium, and the eighth the beginning of the other world. Ovid quotes the expected conflagration :

> " Esse quoque in fatis reminiscitur affore tempus.
> " Quo mare, quo tellus, correptaque regia cœli
> " Ardeat, et mundi moles operosa laboret." [11]

Nothing astonishes me more than the absolute ignorance displayed in the writings of the ancients, of the true nature of their history, their religious mythology, and, in short, of every thing relating to their antiquities. At the same time it is evident that there was a secret science possessed somewhere, which must have been guarded by the most solemn oaths. And though I may be laughed at by those who inquire not deeply into the origin of things for saying it, yet I cannot help suspecting, that there is still a secret doctrine known only in the deep recesses, the crypts, of Thibet, St. Peter's, and the Cremlin. In the following passage the real or affected ignorance of one of the most learned of the Romans is shewn of what was considered as of the first consequence

---

[1] Isai. ii. 11, 17.   [2] Psal. xcii.   [3] Psal. xc.

[4] Capentarius Com. Alcinoum Platonis, p. 322 ; Mede's Works, pp. 535, 894. In the same page of Mede several other Jewish authorities may be seen for the existence of the 6000-year period.

[5] Floyer's Sibyls, p. 244.   [6] Lib. v. Cap. xxviii.   [7] De Divino Præmio, Lib. vii. Cap. xiv.

[8] P. 893.   [9] Civ. Dei, Lib. xxii. Cap. xxx. ; Ouseley, Orient. Coll. Vol. II. No. ii. p. 119.

[10] Floyer's Sibyls, p. 245.

[11] For prophecies of a Millenium, see Isaiah xxvi. 19, lx. 1, 3, 11, 12, 19, 21, lxv. 17, 18, 19, 25, lxvi. 12, 23 ; Ezekiel xlvii. 12 ; Joel iii. 18, 20 ; Isaiah xxiv. 23, xxv. 7 ; 2 Esdras viii. 52, 53, 54.

in their religion—the time of their festivals. Censorinus says,[1] "How many ages are due unto the "city of Rome, it is not mine to say; but what I have read in Varro, that will I not withhold. He "saith in the 18th book of his antiquities, that there was one Vettius, a distinguished Augur at "Rome, of great genius, and equal to any man in learned disputations; and that he heard Vettius "say, that if that was true which historians related, concerning the auguries of Romulus the foun-"der, and concerning the twelve Vultures, then, as the Roman people had safely passed over their "120th year, they would last unto the 1200th."[2] I construe this to mean, that the Vultures had relation to two cycles of 60 years each, or to the two of 600 each; and, as time had shewn that it did not relate to the former, it must relate to the latter. Rome was to finish with the 1200th year, because the world was then to end, as was supposed by the priests, who did not understand their mythology.

But besides the period announced by their twelve Vultures, the Etruscans had also another ill-understood system of ten ages, which was the system common to the Hindoos, the Jews, and the Romans, and this fact adds one more to the numerous proofs of the identity of the two races.

5. Plutarch in Sylla has stated, that on a certain clear and serene day, a trumpet was heard to sound which was so loud and clear, that all the world was struck with fear. On the priests of Etruria being consulted they declared, that a new age was about to commence, and a new race of people to arise,—that there had been EIGHT races of people, different in their lives and manners, —that God has allotted to each race a *fixed period*, which is called the great year,—that when one period is about to end and another to begin, the heaven or the earth marks it by some great pro-digy. The author of Nimrod[3] observes, that Plutarch gives the account loosely and mistakes the age then ending, the eighth, for the ultima ætas; *for the correction of which we are indebted to the invaluable treatise of Censorinus.* This ultima ætas was the same as the Ultima Ætas Cumæi Car-minis of Virgil, which I believe meant, not the last age of the world, but the latter part of the age or cycle sung of by the prophetess of Cuma,—as we should say, the last end of the cycle of the Cumæan Sibyl had arrived. If it be supposed to allude to the periods of 120 years, I ask, how is it possible to believe the Romans could be such idiots as to fancy that new Troys, Argonauts, &c., would arise every 120 years? But I shall return to this again.

Although a certain great year was well known to the Romans, yet the nature of it seems, in the latter times of the commonwealth, to have been lost.[4] The end of one of these great years, and the beginning of another, were celebrated with games called Ludi Sæculares. They were solemnized in the time of Sylla, when the ninth age was said to have commenced by his supporters, probably for the sake of flattering him with being the distinguished person foretold. Nimrod says "Sylla was "born in the year of Rome, 616,[5] but it is uncertain in what year the Sæcular games were cele-"brated, whether in 605, in 608, or in 628. It was a matter of the most occult science and ponti-"fical investigation to pronounce on what year each sæculum ended, and *I am not satisfied whether* "*the Quindecemviri did not publish the games more than once, when they saw reason to doubt which* "*was the true Sibylline year. It was not fixed by law or custom to be an unvarying cycle of* 110 "*years,*

"Certus undenos decies per annos
"Orbis,

"till after the games held by Augustus; if even then."[6]

---

[1] Cap. xvii. *in fine.*   [2] Nimrod, Vol. III. 496.   [3] Vol. III. pp. 459—462.

[4] For proofs that the Etruscans had lost the true length of the Sæculum, vide Niebuhr, Rom. Hist. Vol. I. pp. 93, &c., and p. 164.

[5] Appian, Civil. lib. i. cap. cv.   [6] Sueton. Domit. cap. iv.; Nimrod, Vol. III. p. 462.

The latter part of the above quotation which I have marked with italics, shews that the learned author of Nimrod was not aware that the great year was either the great or little Neros—either 600 or 608 years. His expression respecting the games probably being celebrated in more periods than the 608th year of Rome, in the time of Sylla, seems to shew that they were not then understood, and it seems actually to prove the correctness of the idea also of Nimrod, that all the early Roman history is a Mythos. I consider the fixing of the period by Augustus at 110 years, as a manifest modern contrivance to serve political purposes of the moment. The extreme difficulty and profound pontifical investigation necessary to fix the time of the Ludi Sæculares, admitted by Nimrod, was one of the circumstances which gave weight to the opinion of Figulus, named before, in Chap. II. Sect. 7, because he was considered to be the most learned in dark and mysterious science of any man in Rome.

From a careful consideration of all that has been written on the subject of the Ludi Sæculares, I am quite satisfied that the Romans had no certain knowledge respecting them, which is proved by the circumstance of their having celebrated them at different times, in order that they might hit upon the right time. Another fact, that one of these times was the supposed 608th year from the foundation of Rome, the great Neros, raises a strong presumption that this was originally the religious forgotten period to which they referred. The pretended period of 120 years, as a real period of history, is disposed of by an observation of the only historian of Rome to whom any attention can be paid—Niebuhr—who says,[1] " From the foundation of Rome to the capture, I here find 360 " years, (Rome's fundamental number, twelve times thirty,) and this period as a whole broken into " three parts : one third manifestly occupied by the three first kings, to the year 120 ; the second " by the remaining kings, to the banishment of Tarquin ; the third, the commonwealth. Divisions " so accurate are never afforded by real history. They are a sign which cannot be mistaken, of an " intentional arrangement dependent on the notion of a religious sanctity in numbers." This kind of superstition has every where prevailed and corrupted all history. Mr. Niebuhr's observation, that twelve times thirty make the 360, is true; but why should these numbers have been adopted? I apprehend they, in this case, counted by the cycle of Vrihaspati 60, and they made 6 cycles ; $6 \times 60 = 360$: and this was founded on the Indian dodecan 5, which, with them, was called a Lustrum, and which, equally with the 6, formed a base for the cycle of 60, or of 120, or of 600, or of 1200, or of 6000, or of 432,000. By means of the two sacred numbers, 5 and 6, already described in my preliminary observations, (p. 6,) they would always form cycles, which would be commensurate with one another, so as easily to count their time, in order to regulate their festivals.

The ancient Etruscan sacred period was *ten*—that of the Romans (disguised under a story of twelve vultures) was *twelve*—but to make the two come together the twelve periods were made of 120 years each, $(10 \times 120 = 1200,)$ this makes up just two Neroses. But probably the Indian system of 432,000 was the secret cycle ; for, from the founding of Rome to the building of Constantinople was called 1440 years : $4 \times 360 = 1440$, and $12 \times 360 = 4320$: the same cyclical system. These circumstances, and the evident identity of the Sanscrit and Etruscan written languages, seem to raise a fair presumption, that the sacred cycles were the same in both India and Italy. I repeat that I feel no doubt that the Roman Sæculum of 110 years was, comparatively speaking, a modern invention, when, from the carelessness of the Consuls or Priests, the burning of the sacred books, or some other cause, their ancient measures of time had become lost. Varro states,[2] " In the eighth Sæcu- " lum it was written, that, in the tenth, they were to become extinct." This evidently refers to the 10 Neroses.

The observation of Mons. Niebuhr, respecting the Mythos, is very just, but he might have

---

gone a little farther, and have shewn that the Mythos was a correct imitation of that of Troy and of Egypt.

ROME	EGYPT	TROY
Romulus, Founder	Vulcan	Dardanus
Numa, Legislator	Apollo	Erichton
Hostilius, Warrior	Good Fortune	Tros
Martius	Serapis	Ilus
Tarquin	Pan	Ganymede
Servius Tullius	Osiris, Isis	Laomedon, Hesione
Tarquin the Superb, banished for the rape, by Sextus	Typhon the Superb, destroyed by the Gods	Priam lost the kingdom for the rape of Paris

And even the same system may be found in Kemfer's Japan. The whole may be seen drawn out at length by Gebelin.[1] The seven kings reigned 245 years,[2] thirty-five for each on an average, which is incredible. This shews it to be a Mythos.

When the first 600 years from the supposed foundation of the city arrived, and also when the 1200 arrived, the Roman devotees were much alarmed for fear of some great unknown calamity. This all referred to the lost period either of 600 or 608 years. In the later years of the Republic, or in the early years of the Emperors, the sæculum having become quite uncertain both as to its termination and its meaning, a shorter period was fixed on to gratify the people's love of shows, and the vanity of the ruler of the day in the exhibition of them. It is pretty certain that there were several systems in different nations, all arising from the supposed lengths of the Neros, the real length of which being only found out by degrees, they were obliged to make out their system by expedients as well as they were able.

If we take the period of the Trojan war as settled by Usher at 1194 years before Christ, making it very nearly two Neroses, the period with which these cycles in all different countries end, we shall see that the Mythos of Troy was the same as that of Rome. It is perfectly clear that the Romans knew there ought to be a sacred sæculum or age, that the eighth sæculum from the beginning of the world, was running, but the exact length of it, or when it began or ended, they did not know. The Sibylline verses, foretelling a new Troy and a new Argonautic expedition, cannot be construed to allude to a short period of 110 or 120 years : nor can the expression, *a series of ages which recurs again and again in the course of one mundane revolution,* be construed to refer to it. It may be said that Virgil's prophecy by the Sibyl of the age being about to expire will apply to the eighth century from the supposed building of Rome, as well as to the Neros. But this is not the case, because it will not apply to the renewal of Trojan wars, Argonautic Expeditions, &c.

Among all the ancient nations of the world, the opinion was universal, that the planetary bodies were the disposers of the affairs of men. Christians who believe in Transubstantiation, and that their priests have *an unlimited power to forgive sins,* may affect to despise those who have held that opinion, down to Tycho Brahe, or even to our own times ; but their contempt is not becoming, it is absurd. From this error, however, arose the opinion, that the knowledge of future events might be obtained from a correct understanding of the nature of the planetary motions. This was, perhaps, an improvement on the other. It was thought that the future fortunes of every man might be known, from a proper consideration of the state of the planets at

---

[1] Vol. VIII. p. 428.   [2] Ibid.

the moment of his birth. As, of course, these calculations would continually deceive the calculators, it was very natural that endeavours should be made (overlooking the possibility that the system might be false from the beginning) to ascertain the cause of these failures. This was soon believed to arise from a want of correctness in the calculation of the planetary motions—a fact which would speedily be suspected and then ascertained. This produced the utmost exertion of human ingenuity, to discover the exact length of the periods of the planets: that is, in other words, to perfect the science of astronomy. In the course of these-proceedings it was discovered, or believed to be discovered, that the motions of the planets were liable to certain aberrations, which it was thought would bring on ruin to the whole system, at some future day. Perhaps by reasoning on the character of the Deity they might be induced to believe this to be incorrect, or at least to doubt it, and this would at last be confirmed by the discovery that what appeared, in some instances, to be aberrations, were periodical; and this at last produced the *knowledge*, or the belief, that every aberration was periodical—that the idea of the system containing within itself the seeds of its own destruction was a mistake. Whether they arrived at the point of calculating the exact period of every apparent aberration may be doubtful; but it is very clear they believed that the nearer they got to this point, the nearer to the truth would be the calculation of nativities or of the fortunes of mankind, made from the planetary motions. Experience would teach them that they never could be certain they had discovered all the aberrations, and thus they never could be certain that they had calculated all the periods. They would also perceive that the longer they made their cycles or periods the nearer they came to the truth. For this reason it was, and it was a sensible reason, that they adopted the very long periods: for it was evident that, in every one of the lengthened periods, multiples of 600, the cycle of the Sun and Moon would be included, and with it would make a cycle. When our priests can discover, or suppose, no other reason for these lengthened periods than a wish to appear the most ancient of nations, I fear they estimate the understandings of those who discovered the Neros, by the measure of their own.

I do not pretend to shew how our modern astrologers tell their friends' fortunes, (for, be it observed, these gentlemen never pretend to tell their own, from which defect they sometimes get hanged,) but the ancients proceeded, as Mons. Dupuis[1] has shewn, on a very ingenious plan, and, *if their data had been true*, a very certain one. Believing that all nature was cycloidal, or periodical, as Virgil says—every thing will be renewed—new Iliums, new Argonauts, &c.—they supposed that if they knew in what part of a planet's cycle a thing had formerly happened, they could ascertain when it would happen again. And though this does not prove the truth of judicial astrology, it certainly removes much of its absurdity; for, though the reason is false, it is not foolish. Soon after the discovery of the last of the primary planets, an astrologer called on a friend of the author's who was well known to be a skilful calculator, and requested him to calculate for him the periodical motions of the newly-discovered planet; observing, it was probable that the want of the knowledge and use of its motions was the cause that, in judicial astrology, the predictions so often failed. Here is a beautiful modern exemplification of the ancient reasoning which I have just given above.

I am always rejoiced when I find my theories supported by learned Christian dignitaries. I then flatter myself that they cannot be the produce of a too prurient imagination. Bishop Horsley could not help seeing the truth, that the fourth Eclogue of Virgil referred to the child to whom the kings of the Magi came to offer presents. In the second volume[2] of Sermons, he has undertaken to prove that this Eclogue is founded on old traditions respecting Jesus Christ, and that he

---

[1] Vol. III. p. 158.   [2] Sermon I.

is the child of whom Virgil makes mention. I suspect this learned Bishop had *at least* a slight knowledge of the esoteric doctrine. On this I shall say more when I treat of the Sibyls; I shall then shew that the bishop is perfectly right.

The period of the great Neros, I think, may be perceived in China.[1] La Loubère has observed, that the Chinese date one of their epochas from 2435 years before Christ, when they say there was a great conjunction of the planets; but this seems to be a mistake: for Cassini has shewn that there was no conjunction of the planets, but one of the Sun and Moon, at that time. This mistake arises from the destruction of their books, which was effected by one of their kings, about 200 years before Christ. Their period of 2435 years before Christ has probably been $608 \times 4 = 2432$. They calculated by a cycle of 60 years; this is evidently the same as the 600, Usher's mistake allowed for.

6. I think it is probable that, by Europeans, several allegories of the Hindoos have been confounded together, and it is exceedingly difficult to separate them. They are known to have had various periods called Yogas or Calpas, and it is not unlikely that their allegories alluded to the renewals of different periods : some to the renewal of all visible nature, the fixed stars included ; some to our planetary system, and some only to the renewal of our globe; and to this last, the sæcula or ages of 600 and of 6000 years applied. It has been before observed, that it was anciently thought that the equinoxes preceded only after the rate of 2000, not 2160 years in a sign. This would give 24,000, or 4 times 6000 years, for the length of the great year. Hence might arise their immensely-lengthened cycles, because it would be the same with this great year as with the common year, if intercalations did not take place. It would be more erroneous every common year, till it travelled quite round an immensely-lengthened circle, when it would come to the old point again. Thus there were believed to be regenerations of the starry host, of the planetary host or our solar system, and of this globe. If the angle which the plane of the ecliptic makes with the plane of the equator had decreased gradually and regularly, as it was till very lately believed to do, the two planes would have coincided in about 10 ages, 6000 years; in 10 ages, 6000 years more, the sun would have been situated relatively to the Southern hemisphere, as he is now to the Northern; in 10 ages, 6000 years more, the two planes would coincide again; and, in 10 ages, 6000 more, he would be situated as he is now, after the lapse of about 24,000 or 25,000 years in all. When the Sun arrived at the equator, the 10 ages or 6000 years would end, and the world would be destroyed by fire; when he arrived at the Southern point it would be destroyed by water; and thus alternately, by fire and water, it would be destroyed at the end of every 6000 years or ten Neroses. At first I was surprised that the Indians did not make their Great Year 12 Neroses instead of 10; but a reason, in addition to that which I have formerly given, is here apparent : $12 \times 600 = 7200 \times 4 = 28,800$ instead of 24,000, the first-supposed length of the precessional year. This 6000 years was the age of the world according to the early Christians.

M. La Place professes to have *proved*, that the sum of the variation of the angle made by the plane of the equator with the plane of the ecliptic is only very small, and that the libration, which he admits, is subject to a very short period. Certainly the ruinous state of the strata of the earth might induce a belief that it was not small, but, as the Hindoos believed, very great.

An account is given by Suidas, to which reference has already been made, of the formation of the world as held by the Tuscans, or Etrurians. They supposed that God, the author of the universe, employed twelve thousand years in all his creations, and distributed them into twelve houses : that in the first chiliad, or thousand years, he made the heaven and the earth; in the next the firmament which appears to us, calling it heaven; in the third the sea and all the

---

[1] Hist. Siam. p. 258.

waters that are in the earth; in the fourth the great lights, the sun and the moon, and also the stars; in the fifth every volatile, reptile, and four-footed animal in the air, earth, and water; in the sixth man. It seems, therefore, according to them, that the first six thousand years were passed before the formation of man, and that mankind are to continue for the other six thousand years, the whole time of consummation being twelve thousand years. For they held, that the world was subject to certain revolutions, wherein it became transformed, and a new age and generation began; of such generations there had been in all, according to them, eight, differing from one another in customs and way of life; each having a duration of a certain number of years assigned them by God, and determined by the period which they called *the great year*.[1] If Suidas can be depended on, and I know no reason to dispute his authority, we have here, among these Italian priests, in the six ages of creation, evident proofs of the identity of their doctrines with those of the Hindoos, the ancient Magi of Persia, and the books of Genesis. And what is more, we have, if Mons. Cuvier can be depended on, proofs that these very ancient philosophical priests all taught the true system of the universe, one of the most abstruse and recondite subjects in nature. To what is this to be attributed? Most clearly either to the learning of the primeval nation, or to revelation. Different persons will entertain different opinions on this subject.

There are few readers who have read my abstruse book thus far, who will be surprised that I should look back to an existent state of the Globe in a very remote period. I allude to a time when the angle which the plane of the ecliptic makes with the plane of the equator was much larger than it is at this moment; the effect of which would be to increase the heat in the polar regions, and render them comfortable places of residence for their inhabitants. This easily accounts for the remains of inhabitants of warm climates being found in those regions, which they probably occupied before the creation of man. Every extraordinary appearance of this kind is easily accounted for, as the effect of that periodical motion of the earth which, *if continued*, will bring the planes of the ecliptic and equator to coincide, and, in process of time, to become at right angles to one another. The circumstance of the animals of the torrid zone being found in the high latitudes near the poles, is itself a decisive proof, to an unprejudiced mind, that the time must have been when, by the passage of the Sun in his ecliptic his line of movement was much nearer the poles than it is now, the northern regions must have possessed a temperate climate. This shews, in a marked manner, the sagacity of the observations of Buffon, Baillie, Gesner, &c., though ridiculed by weak people, that the northern climes were probably the birth-place of man. For though in the *cause* which they assigned for this they might be mistaken, in the *effect* they were correct.

7. The date of Pythagoras's birth has been much disputed by learned men. After what the reader has seen, he will not be surprised to find this great philosopher connected, as has been already noticed from the work of La Loubère, like the Jewish worthies, Augustus Cæsar, and others, with one of the Neroses. And the circumstance that the discovery has much of the nature of accident, or, at least, that it is not made out by me or any person holding my system, adds greatly to the probability of its truth. Dr. Lempriere, after stating the great uncertainty of the date of Pythagoras, says, "that 75 or 85 years of the life of Pythagoras fall within the 142 " years that elapsed between B. C. 608, and B. C. 466." Here 608, the boundary of his period, evidently bring out the cycle of the greater Neros. Whether the date of Christ be quite correct or not, there is no doubt that the learned men, who have at different times endeavoured to fix it,

---

[1] Anonym. apud Suid. in voce Tyrrheni, Univers. Hist. Vol I p. 64.—The Universal History adds, that the Druids also taught the alternate dissolution of the world by water and fire, and its successive renovation. Ibid.

have reasoned upon certain principles, and that they have all had access to the same data whereon to ground their calculations. When, therefore, I find this same number 608 constantly occurring as a number in some way or other connected with their periods, I cannot help believing that it has been used by the persons formerly making the ancient calculations. Thus in this I find 608 years to form one boundary, or to come out as one number. Again, in the inquiry into the proper period from the foundation of Rome, on which the Ludi Sæculares ought to be celebrated in the time of Sylla, I find that the result of the very difficult calculations of one or some of the aruspices employed for the purpose of making the calculations, brings out the number 608 as one of the probable periods on which they ought to be celebrated; and, as I find several other such coincidences with this peculiar number, I cannot help thinking that they tend greatly to confirm my doctrines. It shews that this sacred number was in general use, and it justifies me in believing that it was often used in cases where the direct evidence of its use is only weak, but where analogy of reasoning would induce me to expect to find it.

It is impossible to read Stanley's account of the doctrines of Pythagoras and not to see that, as a complete system, they were totally unknown to the persons who have left us the account of them. One says one thing, another says another. But it is evident, that much the greater part of what they say is *opinion* only; or what they had heard, as being the *opinion* of some one else. This state of uncertainty is the inevitable consequence of abstruse doctrines handed down *by tradition*. Then it follows, that evidence in these cases can amount at last only to probability, never to absolute demonstration. But when the probability is sufficiently strong, faith or belief will follow. And I think in reasoning, I have a right to take any asserted fact and reason upon it, depending for its reception by the reader, upon such evidence, positive, or circumstantial, or rational, as I shall be able to produce. Now I will produce an example of what I mean. We have every reason to believe, that Pythagoras travelled far to the East to acquire knowledge. In looking through the great mass of facts or doctrines charged to him, we find much oriental doctrine intermixed with truth and science, the same as we find at this day among the Brahmins: truth and science very much more correct than that which his successors (whose ignorance or uncertainty respecting him is admitted) knew or taught, mixed with an inconceivable mass of nonsense, of that description of nonsense, too, which his followers particularly patronized, and taught as sense and wisdom. Have we not, then, reason to make a selection, and give Pythagoras credit only for such parts as we find of the wise character to which I have alluded, and throw out all the remainder as the nonsense of his successors? What can be more striking than the fact of his teaching that the planets moved in curved orbits, a fact for the statement of which he got laughed at by his ignorant successors, but a fact which we now know to be well-founded!

All his doctrines, we are told by his followers, were founded on numbers, and they pretend to give us what was meant by these numbers, and choice nonsense they give us,—nonsense very unworthy of the man who taught the 47th proposition of Euclid, and the true planetary system. Then are we to believe them? I reply, no; we ought to believe only such parts as are analogous to the oriental systems, and to good sense. All the remainder must remain *sub judice*. I find very nearly the whole of the doctrine of numbers ascribed to him, by his successors, as nonsensical as their story of his golden thigh, so that I can give no credit to them; and, in consequence, I am obliged to have recourse to the East, and to suppose that when they repeat the admitted fact, that his doctrines were founded on numbers, the oriental numbers, on which the astronomical cycles and periods were founded, must chiefly be meant: such as the Zodiacal divisions, the Neros, the precessional year, &c. And this is confirmed when I read what has been extracted respecting Pythagoras from La Loubère, and when I find them stumbling on the cycle of the great Neros. If Pythagoras were not in some way or other connected with it, it seems surprising that this identical number preceding the celebrated epocha of Jesus Christ, as shewn by Cassini, should be found by our modern doctors as a boundary line in the way the reader has seen. There must have been some circumstances closely connected with the great Neros in the ancient data on which our modern divines have founded their calculations, to induce them to pitch upon this number. The effect must have a cause: accident will not account for it. The reader must not forget that all the ancients who give us the account of this philosopher, pretend to what they may, are only possessed of shreds and patches of his system. But I have little doubt that out of the shreds and patches left us by his successors, of the real value of which they were perfectly ignorant, a beautiful oriental garment might be manufactured—bearing a close analogy to the purest of what we find in the East, which, in our eyes, at this day, would be beautiful, but which, by his ancient biographers, would, like his planetary orbits, be treated with contempt. Before I conclude what I have to say, at present, respecting this great man, I will make one more observation. It is said, that the Monad, the Duad, the Triad, and the Tetractys, were numbers held in peculiar respect by him. The last is called the perfection of nature. But Dr. Lempriere says, " Every attempt, however, to " unfold the nature of this last mysterious number has hitherto been unsuccessful." This seems wonderful. Surely Dr. Lempriere cannot have understood the Hebrew language, or he would at once have seen that this can be nothing but the Tetragrammaton of the Hebrews—the sacred name יהוה *ieue* or ieu·e—THE *self-existent*, the *I am*, often called *the name of four letters*, or, in other words, the TETRACTYS. This is confirmed by what, according to Aristotle, Pythagoras said of his Triad. " He affirmed that the whole and all things are terminated by three." Here are the three letters of the sacred word, without the emphatic article,—the three signifying *I am Jah*. Of the Tetractys he says, " Through the superior world is communicated from the Tetractys to the " inferior, LIFE and the being (not accidental, but substantial) of every species." "The Tetractys " is the divine mind communicating." This can be nothing but the Tetragrammaton of the Hebrews. I confess I can entertain no doubt that his Monad, his Duad, his Triad, and his Tetractys, formed the Hindoo Trinity, and the sacred name of four, including the three.

We have already seen that Buddha was born after TEN MONTHS, *sans souillure*, that is, he was the produce of an *immaculate conception*. This was attributed to many persons among the Gentiles; and whenever any man aspired to obtain supreme power, or to tyrannize over his countrymen, he almost always affected to have had a supernatural birth, in some way or other. This was the origin of the pretended connexion of Alexander's mother, Olympias, with Jupiter. Scipio Africanus was also said to be the son of God. There is no doubt that he aimed at the sovereignty of Rome, but the people were too sharp-sighted for him. A. Gellius says, " The wife of Publius " Scipio was barren for so many years as to create a despair of issue, until one night, when her " husband was absent, she discovered a large serpent in his place, and was informed by soothsay- " ers that she would bear a child. In a few days she perceived signs of conception, and after TEN " MONTHS gave birth to the conqueror of Carthage."[1] Arion was a divine incarnation, begotten by the gods, in the citadel Byrsa, and the Magna Mater brought him forth after TEN MONTHS, μετα δεκα μηνας. Hercules was a TEN MONTHS' child, as were also Meleager, Pelias, Neleus, and Typhon.[2] The child foretold in the fourth eclogue of Virgil was also a ten months' child. Augustus also was the produce, after a ten months' pregnancy, of a mysterious connexion of his mother with a serpent in the temple of Apollo.[3] The ten months' pregnancy of all the persons named above, had probably an astrological allusion to the ten ages. The name of Augustus, given to Octavius, was allusive to his sacred character of presiding dæmon of the Munda, κοσμος or cycle. Solomon, according to the Bible, was also a ten months' child.

---

[1] Aul. Gell. lib. vii cap. i.; Nimrod, Vol. III. p. 449   [2] Nimrod, ib.   [3] Ibid. p. 458.

Several of the Hindoo incarnations, particularly that of Salivahana and of Guatama, of whom I shall treat by and by, are said, like Scipio, Augustus, Alexander, &c., to have been born after a ten months' pregnancy of their mothers, and also to have been produced by a serpent entwining itself round the body of the mother. The coincidence is too striking to be the effect of accident.[1]

The author of Nimrod has shewn, at great length, that about the time of Augustus, and a considerable time previously, there had been a very general idea prevalent in the world, that a supernatural child would be born, in consequence of a new age which was then about to arise; but the certain time of which was either unknown or a profound secret. All this was connected with the eighth cycle, which I have explained. To these supernatural births I shall return in a future page.

If my reader have gone along with me in the argument, he must have observed that there is a difficulty arising from the blending of the cycle of 600—the Neros and the cycle—and the distinguished personage who was the hero of it. I find it difficult to explain what I mean. Expressions constantly refer to the cycle of 600 years, and to a person, an incarnation of the divine mind. The age and person are confounded. This, it might plausibly be said, operates against my theory, if I could not shew that it was the custom of the ancient mystics thus to confound them. But we have only to look to the words of Virgil in the prophecy of the Sibyl, B. V. Cb. II. Sect. 7, and the quotation from Mr. Faber, and we have a clear example of what I allude to. The ninth age was to arrive, but a blessed infant also was to arrive with it, to restore the age of gold. The age lasted 600 years, but it did not mean that the child was to live 600 years. The Buddha, the Cristna, the Salivahana of India, each arrived in a period, and they are identified with the period, but they are none of them said to have lived the whole term of 600 years. Cyrus was foretold, and I have shewn that he was born in the eighth age or cycle, but he was not supposed to live to the end of it. I acknowledge this would form a difficulty if it were not obviated by the express words of Virgil, which cannot be disputed. To the objection I reply, that the cycle or age in India and Judæa was used, precisely as it was by the mystics of Virgil. Whatever one meant respecting the child being born, was meant by the other. And this leads to another observation respecting the Messiah of the Jews. We have here express authority from the record itself what a Messiah was— what was meant when a Messiah was foretold. He was a man endowed with a more than usual portion of the divine spirit or nature, and as such was considered to be the presiding genius of the cycle—the αιων των αιωνων—the father of the succeeding ages. We have seen that the word Cyrus meant Sun.

The mother of Cyrus, or of the incarnation of the solar power, had, as we might expect, a very mythological name. She was called MANDA-ne.[2] In the oriental language this would have the same meaning as κοσμος, correctly a cycle. In the same spirit the mother of Constantine was called Helen, her father Coilus. Great mistakes (perhaps intended) have been made in the construing of the word mundus. It has often been construed to mean world, when it meant cycle. It was, I think, one of the words used by the mystics to conceal their doctrine, and to delude the populace.

The results of the calculations made by Cassini are in a very peculiar manner satisfactory. They are totally removed from suspicion of Brahminical forgery, either to please Mohamedan conquerors, or European masters, or sçavans, because they are strictly Buddhist, and have no

[1] Trans. Asiat. Soc. Vol. I. p. 431.
[2] This I take to be a word formed of Mund and Anna.

concern whatever with the followers of Cristna—Siam being far away from the country where the religion of Cristna prevails. The old manuscript which La Loubère sent over to Cassini was not understood by him, but sent to the astronomer for examination. It was not until a hundred years after this manuscript came to Europe, that any of the circumstances relating to Cristna, which the reader has seen from Mr. Maurice, &c., were known: and it is very probable that M. Cassini did not see the consequences which would arise from his calculations.

Mr. Maurice has laboured hard to prove that the Babylonians were the inventors of the Neros. This he does because he fancies it supports the Mosaic system. I shall now shew that it cannot have been invented either by them or by the Egyptians; and I suppose no one will suspect the Greeks of being the inventors of it. And this will compel us to go for it to the ancestors and country of Abraham, if we can only find out who and where they were: this I do not despair of doing in due time.

Respecting the extent of the walls of Babylon we have two histories, one of Herodotus, and the other of Diodorus Siculus, between which there appears at first to be a considerable disagreement. Herodotus states them to be, in his time, 480 furlongs; Diodorus, that they were originally made only 360, *in accordance with the supposed number of days in the year;* that two millions of men were employed to build a furlong a day, by which means they were completed in a year of 360 days.[1] This apparent contradiction Mr. Maurice has reconciled, by shewing from another passage of Berosus, reported by Josephus, that they were lengthened by Nebuchadnezzar, so as to equal those of Nineveh, which were 480 furlongs in extent. From this ignorance of the length of the year I conclude that the builders of Babylon could not be the inventors of the cycle of the Neros; nor could they even have known it. This fact is at once decisive against the whole of Mr. Maurice's theory, that the Babylonians were the inventors of the ancient astronomy. I place my finger on the cycle of the Neros, and unhesitatingly maintain, that the persons acquainted with it could not have believed the year to be only 360 days long.

Mr. Maurice has shewn that the Babylonians were ignorant of the length of the year so late even as the reign of Cyrus, until which time they supposed it to consist of only 360 days. This all tends to confirm Baillie's doctrine, that the Babylonian science is only the débris of an ancient system. The ignorance of the early Egyptians of the true length of the year is as well established as that of the Babylonians. This we learn from Diodorus Siculus, who, among other things, states that the Egyptian priests made 360 libations of milk on the tomb of Osiris, when they bewailed his death, which he says alluded to the days of the *primitive year,* used in the reign of that monarch.[2] I contend also, that the inventors of the Zodiac were in the same state with respect to science as the builders of Babylon, or they would not have divided it into 360 degrees only. Had they known the real length of the year, they would have made some provision for the five days.

Respecting the length of the old year, there is a very curious story in Plutarch, which has been noticed by Sir William Drummond, in his Œdipus Judaicus, p. 103, in the following words: " The number 318 is very remarkable. Plutarch relates, that a connexion having been discovered " between Saturn and Rhea, the Sun threatened that the latter should not be delivered of a child " in any month or year. But Mercury, who was in love with Rhea, having won from the Moon " at dice the 20th part of each of her annual lunations, composed of them the 5 days, which were " added to the year, and by which it was augmented from 360 to 365 days. On these 5 days " Rhea brought forth Osiris, Arueris, Typhon, Isis, and Nephte. Now the old year being com-

---

[1] Berosus, apud Josephus, Antiq. Lib. x. Cap. xi.

[2] Diod. Sic. Lib. xvii. p. 220; Maurice, Observ. on the Ruins of Babylon, p. 39.

" posed of 360 days, the 20th part amounts to 18 days. Let us then take 12 lunations at 28 days
" each, and we shall get a period of 336 days. Deduct a 20th part of the old year of 360 days
" from the 12 lunations at 28 days each, and the remainder will be 318 days. The equation may
" be given as follows : $28 \times 12 - \psi = 318$."

8. In the course of his history, M. La Loubère drops several observations which, when I consider the facts of two islands of Elephanta, two Matureas, the seed of the woman bruising the head
of the serpent in Europe and also in India, &c., &c., seem to me well worthy of notice. I shall
give them in his words and leave them to the reader, but I shall return to them again very often.
Speaking of the name of *Siam*, he says, (p. 6,) " and by the similitude of our language to theirs,
" we ought to say the *Sions*, and not the *Siams:* so when they write in Latin they call them
" *Siones*." Again, (p. 7,) " Nevertheless, Navarete, in his *historical treatises of* the kingdom of
" China, relates, that the name of *Siam*, which he writes *Sian*, comes from these two words *Sien*
" *lo*, without adding their signification or of what language they are." In the same page he says,
" from *Si-yo-thi-ya*,[1] the *Siamese* name of the city of *Siam*, foreigners have made JUDIA."[2] No
doubt at the present moment, my reader will think the facts stated respecting *Sion* and *Judia* of
no consequence, but in a little time, if he read with attention the remainder of this work, he will
find them well worthy of consideration. He will find them, when united to other circumstances,
to be facts to account for which it will be very difficult, upon any of the systems to which we
have been accustomed to give credit. My reader will not forget that we are travelling on mystic
ground; and that the object of our researches, the secret history of the mythoses of antiquity, is
concealed from our view, not only by the sedulous care and the most sacred oaths of our ancestors, in the most remote ages, but by the jealousy of modern priests interested in preventing the
discovery of truth, and also by the natural effect of time, which is itself almost enough to render
of no avail the most industrious researches. It seems to be a law of nature, that the memory of
man should not reach back beyond a certain very confined boundary. We are endeavouring to
break down, to overstep, this boundary.

When we go to India we find that the Brahmins had eight Avatars complete, and were at or in
the ninth at the birth of Christ.[3] The first was Buddha or the Sun in Taurus, and all the Avatars
must have been, properly speaking, his till the flood, or the Sun entered Aries, when the first
cycle of Cristna and that of Joshua began, according to Col. Wilford. Then, after the last cycle
of Cristna, or the cycle of Cyrus, where his history, in part is found, had ended, perhaps such of
the priests as understood the secret doctrines might wish for, and might attempt to introduce, the
ninth Avatar, but to this the populace, and such of them as had perhaps forgotten or did not
know the secret meaning of their Avatars, would not consent.

It is not improbable that the attempt to introduce a new practice at the end of the periods of
six hundred years should have often been attended with religious wars. It seems to be almost a
necessary consequence, that these should take place. The devotees would, of course, be very
averse, as devotees always are, to part with their old superstition, which the initiated would perceive was becoming obsolete and unsuitable to times and circumstances; hence might arise several

---

[1] This is evidently a corruption of the word I-oud-ya, the name of the kingdom of Oude, in Upper India; and this
will be found, when joined to some other matters, to connect the capital of Siam with the city of Oude.

[2] In the city of *Siam* they have a sacred tooth of *Sommona-Codom*, resorted to by many pilgrims. This is the oldest
relic worship which I have met with. They have also a sacred foot of Sommona-Codom, the same as that in Ceylon,
and that named of *Hercules*, in *Scythia*, by *Herodotus*, and that of Jesus in Palestine This is the first sacred foot-
mark I have met with, the last is that of Louis le DÉSIRÉ on the pier at Calais!!!—Printed March, 1831.

[3] " Sree Mun Narrain, since the creation of the world, has at nine different periods assumed incarnated forms, either
for the purpose of eradicating some terrestrial evil, or chastising the sins of mankind. According to the Hindoo tradition a *tenth* is yet expected." Forster's Travels. p. 43.

of the religious wars which otherwise seem inexplicable. On this ground they are easily explained : and this circumstance will satisfactorily explain several other equally inexplicable phænomena, as we shall see hereafter. In some parts of India a *ninth* Avatar was believed to have come, called Salivahana ; in others, Ceylon for instance, he was thought to be another Buddha. Respecting this I shall say more hereafter.

Perhaps I shall be told that the incarnations of the Hindoo Gods are innumerable, and extend through millions of ages. This is true: probably to conceal their real periods from the profane eye.[1] But with these I do not meddle, as they do not militate against the existence of *real* cycles and for periods of *true* time. The ten incarnations were the ten revolutions of the Neros or the sacred Om. At the birth of Christ, *eight* had passed as allowed by the Brahmins, and testified of by Virgil, Zoroaster, and the Sibyls. All the mystics expected the world to end in 6000 years ; that was in ten Avatars, Yugs, Calpas, or ages of 600 years each. The Gentiles were in no fear, as they thought there were yet 1200 years to run, while many Christians, taking their uncertain and doubtful calculations from the LXX. and Josephus, expected the end of the world every day. They saw the calculations in these books could not be brought to any certainty ; and, to make the matter worse, they knew not whether their ages were to begin from the *creation* or the *flood*. But the term of 6000 years, for the duration of the world, was the generally received opinion among the early Christians ; and this continues to be the opinion of many of them. The celebrated mystic, Mr. Irving, who lately preached with great éclat to the rabble of St. James's and St. Giles's, in London, has just announced that the Millenium will commence in a very few years.

The reader may probably have observed that, in my inquiries into the various incarnations of Buddha and Cristna, and into the ancient cycles, &c., I have scarcely ever named any thing later than the supposed æra of Jesus Christ. Since that epoch, however, much very interesting matter and most valuable information respecting the last two cycles, and the origin of the Romish religion, *will be* laid before him ; but, after much consideration, I have determined to defer it until I have shewn whence the various rites and ceremonies of that religion, on which I have not yet touched, were derived. I shall also previously explain many other circumstances relating to the ancient mythoses.

CHAPTER IV

Cross, the meaning of it—Justin and Tertullian on the Cross—Monograms of Christ and Osiris—Cross of Ezekiel and others—Other Monograms of Christ—Chrismon Sancti Ambrogii—Sacred Numbers in the Temples of Britain—Mithra—Josephus and Vallancey on Mystic Numbers—Indian Circles—Lama of Tibet—Indra crucified—Jesuit's Account of Tibet

1. I WILL now shew how the cycle of 600, or the Neros, was concealed in another system and by another kind of mysticism. I scarcely need remind my reader that the cross has been an emblem used by all Christians, from the earliest ages. In my Celtic Druids he may see many proofs that it was used by the most ancient of the Gentiles, the Egyptians, and the Druids. The meaning of it, as an emblem, has been a matter much disputed. It has generally been thought to be

---

[1] Asiat. Res. Vol. II. p. 114.

emblematic of eternal life. It has also been considered, from a fancied similarity to the membrum virile, to be emblematic of the procreative powers of nature. The general opinion, I think, seems to have settled upon an union of the two—that it meant *eternally renovating life*, and this seems to agree very well with the nature of a cycle—with the Neros, which eternally renovated itself, and of which it was probably an emblem. But in my opinion, it is much more probable, that it became the emblem of generation and regeneration, from being the emblem of the cycle, than from any fancied resemblance alluded to above; and that it was the emblem, from being the figure representing the number, of the cycle.

Mr. Payne Knight says, " The male organs of generation are sometimes represented by signs " of the same sort, which might properly be called symbols of symbols. One of the most remark-" able of these is the cross in the form of the letter T, which thus served as the emblem of " creation and generation." [1]

At first I hastily concluded, that the circle which we often see joined to the cross, was meant merely as a handle, but this, on reflection, I cannot believe. It is contrary to the genius and character of the ancient mythologists, to use such a lame and unnecessary contrivance. I am satisfied it was meant, like the cross itself, as an emblem. In some inscriptions, particularly at the end of one of the oldest with which I am acquainted, from Cyprus, that given in Pococke's

description of the East, [2] as a monogram, it is given thus—the cross and ♀ circle of Venus, or Divine Love.

Cyprus was, in former times, a place of great consequence. It must be a delightful island. It is about 130 miles long and 60 broad. In its centre it had its Olympus, now the Mount of the Cross, where, as might be expected, remains to this day a convent of Monks, dedicated to the holy Cross—descended in direct succession, I have no doubt, from the earliest times of Paganism.

The cross was the Egyptian Banner, above which was carried the crest, or device of the Egyptian cities. It was also used in the same manner by the Persians. According to oriental traditions, the cross of Calvary and that supposed to be set up by Moses in the Wilderness were made of the wood of the tree of life, in Paradise. It was carried in the hand of the Horus, the *Mediator* of the Egyptians, the second person in their Trinity, and called *Logos* by the Platonists. Horus was supposed to reign one thousand years. *He was buried for three days*, he was regenerated, and triumphed over the Egyptian evil principle. Among the Alchemists the T with a circle and crescent, is the numerical sign of Mercury. The sign of Venus is a crux ansata, that is, a cross and a circle. [3]

Mr. Maurice describes a statue in Egypt as " bearing a kind of cross in its hand, that is to say, " a PHALLUS, *which, among the Egyptians, was the symbol of fertility*." [4] Fertility, that is in other words, the productive, generative power. On the Egyptian monuments, in the British Museum, may be seen the mystic cross in great numbers of places. And upon the breast of one of the *Mummies in the Museum of the London University*, is a cross exactly in this shape, a cross upon a Calvary.

[1] On Priapus, p. 48.   [2] Vol. I. p. 213, Pl. xxxiii.
[3] Monthly Mag. Vol. LVI.   [4] Ant. Vol. III. p. 113.

The reader may refer to the thirty-ninth number of the Classical Journal, for some curious and profound observations on the Crux ansata.

2. The sign of the cross is well known to all Romish Christians, among whom it is yet used in every respect as is described by Justin, who has this passage in his Apology: " And whereas " Plato, in his Timæus, philosophizing about the Son of God says, He expressed him upon the " universe in the figure of the letter X, he evidently took the hint from Moses ; for in the " Mosaic writings it is related, that after the Israelites went out of Egypt and were in the desert, " they were set upon and destroyed by venomous beasts, vipers, asps, and all sorts of serpents ; " and that Moses thereupon, by particular inspiration from God, took brass and made the sign of " the cross, and placed it by the holy tabernacle, and declared, that if the people would look upon " that cross, and believe, they should be saved ; upon which he writes, that the serpents died, and " by this means the people were saved."

He presently afterward tells us that Plato said, " The *next power* to the Supreme God was " decussated or figured in the shape of a cross on the universe." These opinions of Plato were taken from the doctrine of Pythagoras relating to numbers, which were extremely mystical, and are certainly not understood. Here we have the SON OF GOD typified by the X, hundreds of years before Christ was born, but this is in keeping with the Platonic Trinity.

It is a certain fact that there is no such passage as that quoted by Justin relating to the cross in the Old or the New Testament. This is merely an example of economical reasoning, of pious fraud, in the first Christian father, not said to be inspired, any of whose entire and undisputed works we possess. The evident object of this fraud was to account for the adoration of the cross, which Justin found practised by his followers, but the cause of which he did not understand.

Tertullian says, that " The Devil signed his soldiers in the forehead, in imitation of the Chris- " tians : Mithra signat illic in frontibus milites suos."[1] And St. Austin says, that " the cross " and baptism were never parted : semper enim cruci Baptismus jungitur."[2]

The cross was a sacred emblem with the Egyptians. The Ibis was represented with human hands and feet holding the staff of Isis in one hand, and a globe and cross in the other. It is on most of the Egyptian obelisks, and was used as an amulet. Saturn's astrological character was a cross and a ram's-horn. Jupiter also bore a cross, with a horn.

" We have already observed, that the cabalists left these gross symbols to the people, but the " learned and the initiated piercing through these objects, pretended to aspire to the knowledge and " contemplation of the Deity."[3] Again, " What hideous darkness must involve the Egyptian " history and religion, which were only known by ambiguous signs ! It was impossible but they " must vary in their explication of these signs, and in a long tract of time forget what the ancients " meant by them. And thus every one made his own conjectures : and the priests taking advan- " tage of the obscurity of the signs, and ignorance of the people, made the best of their own " learning and fancies. Hence necessarily happened two things—one, that religion often changed ; " the other, that the cabalists were in great esteem, because necessary men."[4]

From these quotations it is evident the sign of the cross was a religious symbol common both to Heathens and Christians, and that it was used by the former long before the rise of Christi- anity.[5] The two principal pagodas of India, viz. at Benares and Mathura, are built in the form of crosses.[6] The cross was also a symbol of the British Druids.[7] Mr. Maurice says, " We

---

[1] Tertul. de Præscrip.   [3] Aug. Temp. Ser. CI; Reeve's Ap. Vol. I p. 98.

[2] Bas. B. iii. Ch. xix. Sect. xix. xx.   [4] Ibid.

[3] See Justin's Apol. Sect. lxxii. lxxvii.; Tertullian's Apol. Ch. xvi.   [6] Maur. Ind. Ant. Vol. II. p. 359.

[7] See Borlase, Ant. Cornwall, p. 108; Maur. Ind. Ant. Vol. VI. p. 68.

" know that the Druid system of religion, long before the time of Cambyses, had taken deep root
" in the British Isles."[1]   " The cross among the Egyptians was an hieroglyphic, importing the
" life that is to come."[2]

Mr. Ledwick has observed that the presence of Heathen devices and crosses on the same coin
are not unusual, as Christians in those early times were for the most part Semi-pagans. This is
diametrically in opposition to all the doctrines of the Protestants about the early purity of the religion of Christ, and its subsequent corruption by the Romists. It equally militates against the
purity of the Culdees. In fact it is mere nonsense, for there can be no doubt that the cross was
one of the most common of the Gentile symbols, and was adopted by the Christians *like all their
other rites and ceremonies* from the Gentiles—and this assertion I will prove, before I finish this
work.

Nothing in my opinion can more clearly shew the identity of the two systems of the Christian
priests, and of the ancient worshipers of the Sun, than the fact, unquestionably proved, that the
sign or monogram used by both was identically the same. It is absolutely impossible that this
can be the effect of accident.

3. The following are monograms of Christ, ₽₽ ; but it is unquestionable, that they are also
monograms of Jupiter Ammon. The same character is found upon one of the medals of Decius,
the great persecutor of the Christians, with this word upon it, BA₽ATO.[3] This cipher is also
found on the staff of Isis and of Osiris. There is also existing a medal of Ptolomy, king of Cyrene, having an eagle carrying a thunderbolt, with the monogram of Christ, to signify the oracle
of Jupiter Ammon, which was in the neighbourhood of Cyrene, and in the kingdom of Ptolomy.[4]

Basnage says, " Nothing can be more opposite to *Jesus Christ* than the oracle of Jupiter
" Ammom. And yet the same cipher served the false God as well as the true one ; for we see a
" medal of Ptolomy, king of Cyrene, having an eagle carrying a thunder-bolt, with the monogram
" of Christ to signify the Oracle of Jupiter Hammon."[5]

Dr. Clarke has given a drawing of a medal, found in the Ruins of Citium, in Cyprus, which he
shews is Phœnician, and, therefore, of very great antiquity. This medal proves that the Lamb,
the holy cross, and the rosary, were in use in a very remote period, and that they all went together,
long before the time of Jesus of Nazareth.

It is related by Socrates that when the temple of Serapis, at Alexandria, was demolished by one
of the Christian emperors in his pious zeal against the demons who inhabited those places, under
the names of Gods, that beneath the foundation was discovered the monogram of Christ, and that
the Christians made use of the circumstance as an argument in favour of their religion, thereby
making many converts. It is very curious that this unexpected circumstance should have carried
conviction (as we learn that it did) to the minds of the philosophers of the falsity of the religion of
Christ, and to the minds of the Christians of its truth. Unquestionably when the Christians held
that the digging up of this monogram from under the ruins of the temples was a proof that they
should be overthrown by the Cross of Christ, with the Christian Roman Emperor and his legions
at their elbow, they would have the best of the argument. But what was still more to the pur-

---

[1] Ind. Ant. Vol. VI. p. 104; Celtic Druids, by the Author.

[2] Ruffinus, Vol. II. p. 29 ; Sozomen says the same, Hist. Eccl. Vol. VII. p. 15.

[3] I suspect that this word having been inscribed on a coin is circular, and may either begin or end with the O—that
it ought to be OBA₽AT, and that it is a Hebrew word written in Greek letters, meaning *the* Creator, formed from
the word ברא *bra* to create. The X is put in the middle of the word, the same as the Samach or Mem final, in the
passage of Isaiah, and for the same reason.

[4] Bas. B. iii. Ch. xviii. S. iii.   [5] Χρησμον, Scaliger in Euseb. Chron., Hist. Jews, B. iii. Ch xxiii.

pose, the pagan religion was out of fashion. Reason has hitherto had little or nothing to do with religion.

On this subject of the cross Mr. Maurice says, " Let not the piety of the Catholic Christian be " offended at the preceding assertion, that the cross was one of the most usual symbols among the " hieroglyphics of Egypt and India. Equally honoured in the Gentile and the Christian world, " this emblem of universal nature, of that world to whose four quarters its diverging radii pointed, " decorated the hands of most of the sculptured images in the former country ; and in the latter " stamped its form upon the most majestic of the shrines of their deities."[1] I think Mr. Maurice should have said this emblem of the *prolific powers* of nature. In the cave of Elephanta, in India, over the head of the figure who is destroying the infants, whence the story of Herod and the infants at Bethlehem (which was unknown to all the Jewish, Roman, and Grecian historians) took its origin, may be seen the Mitre, the Crozier, and the Cross ; and, a little in the front of the group, a large Lingam, the emblem of generation, the creative power of nature.[2]

4. Mr. Maurice observes, that in Egypt, as well as in India, the letter T, or in other words, the Cross, or the *Crux Hermis*, was very common, in which form many of the temples of India are built, and those in particular dedicated to Cristna : as for example, those at Matterea or Mattra, and at Benares. D'Ancarville and the generality of mythologists explain this symbol to refer to the Deity in his creative capacity, in both ancient Egypt and India. Mr. Bruce frequently met with it in his travels in the higher Egypt and Abyssinia, and it was also very often noticed by Dr. Clarke. It was commonly called the *crux ansata*, in this form and was what was referred to in Ezekiel,[3] in the Vulgate, and the *ancient* Septuagint, according to Lowth, rendered, " I " will mark them in the forehead with the T or Tau." It is also referred to by Tertullian, when he says that the Devil signed his soldiers in the forehead in imitation of the Christians. It is certainly very remarkable that God should select this Mithraitic symbol for the mark to distinguish the elect from those that were to be slain by the sword of the destroyers. This may furnish another reason why Christians should moderate their anger against those who used this symbol of the creative power of God.[4] The Latin Vulgate[5] does in fact read, " You shall mark their forehead " with the letter Thau," i. e. ταυ σημειον, and not as at present in the LXX. το σημειον.[6] In the Mazoretic Hebrew it is תו *tau*, which confirms the Vulgate and shews what it was considered to be by the Mazorites of the middle ages. The cross was much venerated by the cabalists of the early Christians who endeavoured to blend the arcana of Plato and the numerical doctrines of Pythagoras with the mysteries of Christianity. I have no doubt that it is either the origin of the words Taut and Thoth, names of the Egyptian Gods, or, that these words are the originals from which it came ; and perhaps of the Thor of the Celts, who went into Hell and bruised the head of the great snake. The monogram of the Scandinavian Mercury was represented by a cross. The Monogram of the Egyptian Taut is formed by three crosses thus, united at the feet, and forms, to this day, the jewel of the royal arch among free masons. It is the figure and is X=600 H=8=608.

The Samaritans had, in very early times, the Tau of their alphabet in the form of the Greek Tau, as is clearly proved by their ancient Shekels, on which it is so inscribed.[7] St. Jerom and Origen

---

[1] Maurice, Ind. Ant. Vol. I. p. 359.   [2] Forbes's Oriental Memoirs, Vol. III. Ch. xxxv. p. 448.

[3] Ch. ix. ver. 4.   [4] Maurice, Ind. Ant. Vol. VI. p. 67.   [5] Ezekiel Ch. ix. ver. 4.

[6] Maurice, Hist. Hind. Vol. I. p. 245.

[7] The reader may find some curious observations on the Crux Ansata in Monthly Magazine, Vol. LVI. No. III. p. 388.

both assert that it was so in Samaritan copies of the Pentateuch in their day. The Celtic language of Wales has it also in the form of a Tau, though a little changed thus, ᴛ. This tends to prove that the Greeks and Celts had their letters from the Samaritans, or early Chaldeans. Might not the Tat or Taut be TT=600, or TTL=650? This will be explained by and by.

On the decad or the number X, the Pythagoreans say, "That ten is a perfect number, even the " most perfect of all numbers, comprehending in it all difference of numbers, all reasons, species, " and proportions. For, if the nature of the universe be defined according to the reasons and pro- " portions of numbers; and that which is produced, and increased, and perfected, proceed accord- " ing to the reasons of numbers; and the decad comprehends every reason of number, and every " proportion and all species; why should not nature itself be termed by the name of ten, X, the " most perfect number?"[1]

The Hexad or number *six* is considered by the Pythagoreans a perfect and sacred number; among many other reasons, because it divides the universe into equal parts.[2] It is called Venus or the mother. It is also perfect, because it is the only number under X, ten, which is whole and equal in its parts. In Hebrew Vau is *six*. Is *vau* mother Eva or Eve? היא *eua*.

5. The Rabbins say, that when Aaron was made high-priest he was marked on the forehead by Moses with a figure like the Greek χ.[3] This is the Samacbing. This letter X in the Greek language meant 600, the number of the Neros. It answered to the Mem final of the Hebrews, found in so peculiar a manner in the middle of the word למרבה *lmrbe* in Isaiah. We every where meet with X meaning 600, and XH and ΤΗΣ meaning 608, the monograms of Bacchus according to Martianus Capella, in the churches and monuments in Italy dedicated to Jesus Christ; and in this is found a striking proof of what I have said before, in the beginning of this book, respecting the two Neroses; for the use of the X for 600, and the XH and ΤΗΣ for 608, INDISCRIMINATELY AS MONOGRAMS OF CHRIST, connect them altogether, and prove that the two Neroses, the one of 600 and the other 608, had the same origin. This must not be lost sight of, for it is a grand link which connects Christianity with the ancient oriental mythoses, in a manner which cannot be disputed, and most unquestionably proves the truth of the doctrine of Ammonias Saccas, that the two religions are in principle identical. I *do not* know what persons may believe on this subject: but I *do* know that this is evidence, and conclusive evidence.

The T, Tau, was the instrument of death, but it was also (as before mentioned) what Ezekiel ordered the people in Jerusalem to be marked with, who were to be *saved from the destroyer*. It was also the emblem of the Taranis or the Thoth or Teutates or TAT[4] or Hermes or Buddha among the Druids. It was called the *Crux Hermis*. The old Hebrew, the Bastulan, and the Pelasgian, have the letter Tau thus, X; the Etruscan, +X; the Coptic, +; the Punic, XX. It is not unlikely that the Greek priests changed their letters as marks of notation, from the ancient Phœnician or Cadmean, by the introduction of the *episemon bau* or *vau*, to make them suit the mystery contained in the sacred number 608, and the word derived from the Hebrew word *to save* and the sacred cross. Thus the letter X stood for the 600 of the Hebrews, for Ezekiel's sacred mark of salvation, and for the astronomical or astrological cycle.

Nothing can be more common than the letter X in Italy as a monogram of Christ. But we have seen above, from Plato, as quoted by the celebrated Justin Martyr, that it was the emblem

---

[1] Moderatus of Gaza apud Stanley, Hist. Pyth. P. IX. Ch. iv.

[2] In Chapters x. and xiv. of Part IX. of Stanley's History of Philosophy may be seen abundant proofs, that the science of Pythagoras relating to numbers had been then a long time totally lost. For the mystery of letters see Jones on the Canon, Vol. II. p. 425; also Basnage, B. iii. Ch. xxvi. Sect. ii. iii.

[3] Life of Usher, p. 348.   [4] See B. v. Ch. i. Sect. 2.

of the *Son of God*, the Logos, which Son of God is declared over and over again by Justin to be *divine wisdom*, i. e. the same as Buddha. Whenever proselytes were admitted into the religion of the Bull—of Mithra—they were marked in the forehead with this mark of 600, X. The initiated were marked with this sign also, when they were admitted into the mysteries of Eleusis. We constantly see the Tau and the Resh united thus ꓘ These two letters in the old Samaritan, as found on coins, stand the first for 400, the second ꓕ for 200=600. This is the staff of Osiris. It is also the monogram of Osiris, and has been adopted by the Christians, and is to be seen in the churches in Italy in thousands of places. See Basnage, (Lib. iii. Cap. xxiii.,) where several other instances of this kind may be found. In Addison's Travels in Italy there is an account of a medal, at Rome, of Constantius, with this inscription: In hoc signo Victor eris ꓘ. In the Abbey church at Bath, the monogram on the monument of Archdeacon Thomas lately buried is thus: ꓘ. This shews how long a superstition will last, after its meaning is quite lost.

Dr. Daniel Clarke has made several striking observations respecting the Crux Ansata. After repeating the well-known observation of Socrates Scholasticus, that it meant *life to come*, he says, " Kircher's ingenuity had guided him to an explanation of the *crux ansata*, as a *monogram* which " does not militate against the signification thus obtained. He says, it consisted of the letters " ΦΤ, denoting *Ptha*, a name of Mercury, Thoth, Taut, or Ptha." He then observes, that it was often used as a key, and might be the foundation of the numerous allusions in sacred writ, to the keys of Heaven, of Hell, and of Death In a note, he says, " Sed non erat ullum templum, in " quo non figura *crucis ansatæ*, ut eum eruditi vocant: sæpius vixenda occurreret, hodieque in " ruderibus ac ruinis etiamnum occurrat. Ejus hæc est species ꓘ .... Crucem vero istam an- " satam, quæ in omnibus Ægyptiorum templis sæpius ficta et picta extabat, quam signa deorum " Ægyptiorum manu tenere solent, quæ partem facit ornatis Sacerdotalis, nihil aliud esse quam " phallum." [1] " Jamblicus thinks the crux ansata was the name of the Divine Being....Some- " times it is represented by a cross fastened to a *circle* as above: in other instances, with the " letter ꓕ only, fixed in this manner ⚲ to a circle." [2]

I think few persons will doubt, what old Kircher says is true, that it means $+ \text{X} = 600$.

P Thas
$$\left.\begin{cases} \phi &-& 500 \\ \theta &-& 9 \\ \alpha &-& 1 \\ \varsigma &-& 90 \end{cases}\right\} - 600$$

And when accompanied by the circle, it is the Linga and Ioni of India united. The Deity Φθας presided in the kingdom of *Omptha*, *Om-tha*, the cycle *Om*. Here we have the cycle of 600, the *Om* of Isaiah, the cross of Christ, and the *Om-tha* of Egypt all united. The Greek numbers must have been once the same as the Hebrew above, and have been changed, as the reader will be convinced in a moment, by considering the two alphabets in my Table of Alphabets, page 10. The Greek Tau was anciently written $+$. [3]

6. The monogram which constitutes figure 9, I copied from a bad drawing of a stone at the back of the Choir in the Duomo at Milan, lent to me by the Sacristan, who told me that it had been then lately removed, in consequence of a gentleman from Naples having noticed it, and having made a drawing of it. He had come from Naples on purpose. I saw it there myself the first time I went to Milan; when I went again it was gone. (The church is very discreet.) The following is the description of it, taken from Nuova Descrizione Del Duomo di Milano, presso

[1] Vide Jablonski, Panth. Ægyp. I 282.
[2] Clarke's Travels, Vol. III. p. 107.
[3] Vide Parkhurst's Lexicon in voce T.

Ferdinando Artaria, 1820 : " Non lungi da questo monumento si vede incastrata nel muro una
" pietra, la quale, entro a misterioso cerchio contiene scolpito il monogramma ossia l'abbreviatura
" del nome del Salvatore in lettere Greche coll' alfa ed omega dall' una e dall' altra parte, antica-
" mente chiamato il crisma o sia oracolo di S. Ambrogio : Landolfo, scrittore Milanese, assicura
" che questo serviva di primo elemento ai catecumini per iniziarli nei misteri della fide. Sotto
" questa pietra ed agli ornamenti de marmo che vi sono stati posti diutorno, leggesi la iscrizione
" sequente, in parte mascberata da un confessionale :

" Circulus · Hic · summi · continet · nomina · Regis · quem · sine · principio · et · sine
" fine · vides · *principium · cum · fine · Tibi · designat* A · et · Ω nella antica lapida era ag-
" giunto :

" X. · et · P. Christi · Nomina · Sancta · tenet."

In the next page, 30, is a description of the last footstep on Mount Olivet, thus printed :
" Nostro Signore IHV—Cristo." In the Chrismon above are the Etruscan Tau 400 and the Resh
200=600. In my essay on *The Celtic Druids*, (p. 264,) I have shewn an example from Dr.
Clarke of a mixture of the Phœnician and Etruscan letters in a Phœnician inscription in Etruscan
characters.

In this magical device of St. Ambrose, which is a cross with eight points, here are the Alpha
and Omega, the well-known emblems of eternity, united to the cycle of 600, the X and P, pronounced to be emblems of eternal life. See plates, fig. 9.

The learned Spencer says, " Nomen solis mysticum ad numerum octo et sexcentorum pervenie-
" bat, uti nos docet Martianus Capella. Id autem hoc modo notabatur, XH. Cabalisticus ille
" deorum nomina designandi modus eo antiquior habeatur, quod veri Dei (nempe Christi) nomen
" mysticis numeris expressum, in claro illo ænigmate.[1] Sibyllino reperiamus : quamvis haud
" adeo inter doctos conveniat cuinam Christi nomini vel titulo, numerus ille melius congruat."[2]

The Abbé Pluche says that the Egyptians marked their God Canobus indifferently with a T or a
⊥. The Vaishnavas of India have also the same sacred Jar, which they also mark with crosses
thus ⊥, and with triangles thus ✡. The vestment of the priests of Horus is covered with these
crosses +.[3] This is the same as the dress of the Lama of Tibet. These are the sectarian marks
of the Jains, ⊥, ⊥.[4] The distinctive badge of the sect of Xaca Japonicus, is this 卍.[5]
The religion of the Jains, Buddha, or Xaca, and Fo, all having been proved the same, we have
here the sign of Fo, identical with the cross of Christ.

In Montfaucon[6] may be seen several medals of Anubis or Noubis, where he is called X and T,
Noubis or Noumis, or in his fig. 10, Anoubis. Again,

In the same[7] is a medal with the letters ΦPH. Φ=500, P=100, H=8,=608. In the same
plate, No. 36, is a young man crowned ; with a cup in one hand, and the letters X on one side of
him, and Θ on the other ; this last is an Etruscan letter, which stands for 8, X Θ=608. Another,
not numbered, above 33, exhibits a female nursing a child, with ears of corn in her hand, and the
legend ωαι, *Iao*. She is seated on clouds, a star is at her head, and three ears of corn are rising
from an altar before her. The reading of the Greek letters, from right to left, shews this to be no
produce of *modern* Gnosticism, but to be very ancient.

---

[1] Orac. Sibyl. L. i. p. 171, ed. Par. 1599.

[2] Spencer, Lib. ii. Cap. xiv. p. 365.   [3] See Caylus, Vol. VI. Pl. 7 ; Vall. Col. Vol. VI. p. 185.

[4] See Moore's Ind. Pantheon, pp. 401, 451.   [5] Georgius, Alphab. Tib. Ap. III. p. 725.

[6] Ant. Exp. Vol. II. Pl. 49.   [7] Ibid. Vol. II. Pl. 50, Fig. 14.

It is the common and unsatisfactory way of accounting for the mystical character of medals of this kind, to throw them all aside as the idle superstitions of the Gnostic Christians. But here the style of writing from right to left proves the foregoing to be of a date long prior to Christianity. The idle and unfounded plea of Gnostic Christianity has been of inestimable value to the Christian priesthood, by enabling them to conceal many very important facts, which, in consequence of this plea, cannot be adduced as evidence of ancient doctrines. Were it not for this plea I should fill a book with these facts.

In Dr. Daniel Clarke's Travels, at the head of Chapter XI. of Vol II., will be found a print of the medal of the ancient Phœnicians found at Citium or Cyprus, before named, on one side of which are a ram couchant, and on the other the cross, the rosary, and two letters or figures.

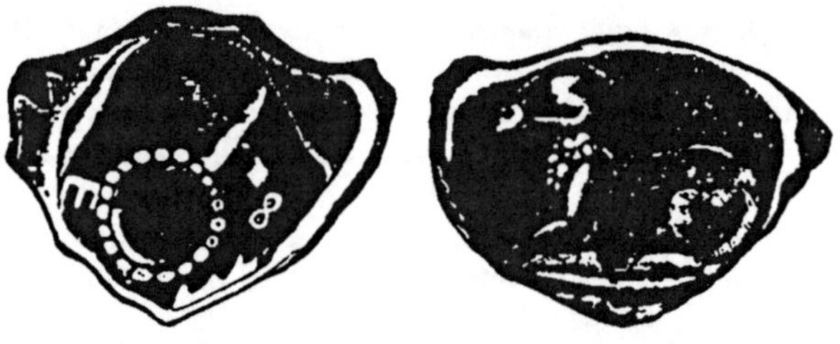

The following are copies, taken most carefully from Mr. Astle's table of the general alphabet of the Etruscans: H ⊟ 8 ⊖ ⊘; M ᗰ ΠΤ. I ask, may not these two letters on the medal, connected here with the lamb, the cross, the circle, and the rosary, (the latter found in the hands of most Hindoo Gods,) signify M. 600, H. 8? The letter M, as described on this medal, differs both from the closed and the open Mem of the Hebrews, in shape, but as there is a variety of ways in which the ancient Etruscans formed this letter, we can never be certain that this may not have been a Mem final standing for 600, like that of the Hebrews. The figure for the H is evidently the origin of our 8. And here, as joined with the Mem and connected with all the other circumstances, raises a very strong presumption that the celebrated 608 is meant.[1] When I consider all the collateral circumstances attending this medal, I cannot help thinking that many things are received in which the imagination is more taxed than in this. I affirm nothing except that I wish some one to give me a more rational explanation of the two letters or figures. I beg my reader to recollect we tread on mystic ground.

The votaries of the Roman Church constantly mark themselves with the cross—the emblem of 600. They will say, they do it in commemoration of the sufferings of their Saviour. When I consider the peculiarity of the cycles and epochs in Siam, that of Mr. Bentley, the *Mem* final of Isaiah, his prophecy, that of Zoradusht, of the Sibyl, and of Virgil, and also that of the Druid of Bochara in Ireland, the magical character of the disputed chapters in Luke and Matthew, and the X and IHΣ XH, the monograms of the black Christ, I cannot help believing that they all refer to the same person—Buddha—or the Christ, the black God of the temple of Bethlehem, but not to Jesus of Nazareth; and, in support of this opinion, a thousand other reasons will be given in the course of this work.

I shall now exhibit, in an extract from my Celtic Druids, another example of the mystical numbers 600 and 608, where few persons would expect to find it, viz. in the ancient Druidical temples of Britain. "The most extraordinary peculiarity which the Druidical circles possess, is

---

[1] Ancient Teutonic M, ᙏ.

" that of their agreement in the number of the stones of which they consist with the ancient
" astronomical cycles. The outer circle of Stonehenge consists of 60 stones, the base of the most
" famous of all the cyles of antiquity. The next circle consists of 40 stones, but one on each side
" of the entrance is advanced out of the line, so as to leave 19 stones, a metonic cycle, on each
" side, and the inner, of one metonic cycle, or 19 stones. At Abury we find all the outward
" circles and the avenues make up exactly the 600, the Neros, which Josephus says was known
" before the flood. The outer circles are exactly the number of degrees in each of the 12 parts,
" into which, in my aerial castle-building, I divided the circle, viz. 30, and into which at first the
" year was divided, and the inner, of the number of the divisions of the circle, viz. 12, and of the
" months in the year. We see the last measurement of Stonehenge, taken by Mr. Waltire, makes
" the second circle 40; but for the sake of marking the two cycles of 19 years, two of the stones,
" one on each side of the entrance, have been placed a little within. I think it very likely that
" the outer circle of the *hackpen* of 40 stones was originally formed in the same manner. Surely
" it is not improbable that what is found in one temple should have been originally in the other.
" I also think that the whole number of stones which Stonehenge consisted of was 144, according
" to Mr. Waltire's model, and including along with it three stones which could not be described in
" Mr. Waltire's model for want of room; thus making the sum-total of stones amount exactly to
" the oriental cycle or vau of 144 years.

Outer circle with its coping stones	60
Inner	40
Outer ellipse	21
Inner parabola	19
Altar	1
Three outer stones	3
	144

" In this temple the outer circle is the oriental cycle of Vrihaspati, 60. Next outer circle, ex-
" clusive of two entrance stones a little removed inside the line, to mark a separation from the
" others, making two metonic cycles, each 19. The trilithons are seven in number, equal to the
" planets. The inner row is a parabolic curve, and the stones a metonic cycle. Now with re-
" spect to Abury we find the same peculiarity.

" Outer circle	100 stones
Northern temple outward circle	30
Inner circle	12
The cove	3
Southern temple, outward circle	30
Inner circle of the same	12
Central obelisk	1
Ring stone	1
Kennet avenue	200
Outer circle of the hackpen or serpent's head	40
Inner circle of ditto	18
Beckhampton avenue	200
Longstone cove	2
Inclosing stone of the serpent's tail	1
Total	650 stones.

" Of these, the whole number of the outside lines of the structure make 600, viz. 100 + 30
" + 30 + 200 + 40 + 200 = 600, the cycle of the Neros, alluded to in Chapter II. Section
" XIII. The whole of the smaller circles make 142; 30 + 12 + 30 + 12 + 40 + 18 = 142.
" When I consider all the other circumstances of the attachment of the Druids to cycles, I cannot
" help suspecting that they have been 144, and that there is some mistake." ...... " If all the
" stones of Abury be taken, except the inner circles, you will have the number 608, a very curious
" number, the sacred number of the God Sol, already described in Chap. IV. Sect. VIII., to which
" I beg to refer my reader. If this be the effect of accident, it is an odd accident."

I confess I cannot help considering the discovery of these cycles in the old temples as confirmatory in an extraordinary manner of my system. My theory respecting the Druids being oriental
Buddhists is confirmed by the oriental Neroses of Siam; and my theory of the origin of the oriental doctrines is confirmed by the temples of the West. Circumstances of this kind surpass all
written testimony: there can be no forged interpolations here. The reader has seen that the total
number of stones in the temple of Abury was six hundred and fifty, as discovered by Stukeley,
and confirmed by Sir R. C. Hoare's later examination. Neither of those gentlemen had any idea
of the importance of the number of the stones, and therefore had no theory to support, which, if
found by me only, might make persons think I was deceived by a prurient imagination. The following is a passage from Basnage's History of the Jews,[1] which I have discovered since I published my Celtic Druids:

" Martianus Capella speaks of two letters, X. and N.; who would not think here was a character
" of Christianity? Χρισος Νικα, Christ victorious: but it was a mystical name of the Sun; and
" these two letters designed a certain number he was used to be signified by;" X = 600, N = 50.
But if it did not mean Χρισος νικα, it meant something very near it, viz. Χρησος νικα, as I
shall shew in the tenth book of this work.

8. The Persian God is often called Mitr. Of course we may expect to find the more perfect Neroses,
or sacred numbers, described by the letters of notation of the later nations, and the ruder Neroses
with the more early, all in fact descriptive of the solar cycle. Thus in Hebrew we have מיתר mitr,
ר 200, ת 400, י 10, מ 40 = 650. This was probably the first way of writing it; the second was Mithras
Μιθρας, written without an E and meaning CCCLX., M 40, I 10, Θ 9, P 100, A 1, Σ 200 = 360;
but afterward, when the length of the year was more perfectly understood, it was as it is commonly found with an e, Meithras.[2] A Mitra Mithridates est, et Mitra quod alii corrupte Misra
scribunt, etiam multi Brahmanes appellantur.[3] Might not the name of the Egyptian Misraim be
a corruption of the word מיתרים mitrim? If this were the case, it would have had the same name
in the oriental, as Italy had in its, language Itala, a bull. Bishop Cumberland thought that Mitz-
raim was the word Isiris or Itziris, with the mystic M prefixed, which seems by no means improbable.

The number 650, sacred to the Sun, and found in the temple at Abury in so remarkable a
manner, again confirms my theory. He must have a prurient imagination indeed who can attribute all these coincidences to accident. Why this number 650 came to be sacred to the Sun I
have explained in Chap. ii. Sect. 5.

The following extract will exhibit the metonic cycle in as remarkable a manner as the Neros:
" At Biscawen'unn, near St. Buriens in Cornwall, there is a circular temple consisting of 19
" stones, and a twentieth stone stands in the centre higher than the rest.—I beg my reader to refer
" to the description of the temple at Classerness in the introduction, plate No. 28. There he will

---

[1] B. iii. Chap. xxiii. p. 236.   [2] See Mont. Ant. Exp. Vol. II. p. 226.   [3] Bartolomeus, Sys. Brach. p 2.

" again find the metonic cycle.—Near Clenenney, in North Wales, is a circle containg 38 stones,
" two metonic cycles.—Near Keswick is an oval of 40 stones. This I have little doubt is in
" number 40, for the same reason as the second circle at Stonehenge, already explained.—Dr.
" Borlase says, ' There are *four* circles in the hundred of Penwith, Cornwall, (the most distant
" two of which are not eight miles asunder,) which have 19 stones each, a surprising uniformity,
" expressing, perhaps, the two principal divisions of the year, the twelve months, and the seven
" days of the week. Their names are Boscawen'unn, Rosmodereny, Tregaseal, and Boskednan.'
" Here the similarity could not escape Dr. Borlase; but the idea of a cycle never occurred to
" him. There is no room to attribute any thing here to imagination."

In the same chapter my reader may see many other examples of astrological numbers in the old
temples of the Druids. Before I quit the temple of Abury, I beg leave to suggest whether it may
not be probable that the number of the stones of the inner circle of the serpent's head may have been
19 instead of 18; that it may have had a centre stone; and that the Longstone Cove which stands
at a little distance may have been considered as part of the temple? This would give, instead of
142 for the number of stones in the inner circles, the number 144, and would not derange any of
the other cyclar sums, as my reader will find on experiment. Amidst the intricacy of the modern
buildings and old stones, Dr. Stukeley and Sir R. C. Hoare might easily be led into so trifling a
mistake. I beg my reader to make this correction, then to take his pencil and try an experiment
or two with the different numbers, and he will find how curiously the sums into which I first supposed the great circle to have been divided come out, viz. 12 signs, 36 decans, 72 dodecans, and
360 degrees. All this may be nonsensical enough, but are not all judicial astrology and the ancient
mystical doctrines of lucky and unlucky, sacred and profane numbers, nonsensical? It is of no
use to say they are nonsensical. Can any one say that even the wisest of the ancients did not
entertain these doctrines?

9. What I have said respecting the division of the great circle into 360 degrees, and into decans
and dodecans, receives a strong confirmation from the description which Josephus gives of the
mystical meaning of the Jewish tabernacle, &c. He says, " And when he ordered twelve loaves
" to be set on the table, he denoted the year as distinguished into so many months. By branching
" out the candlestick into seventy parts he SECRETLY intimated the *Decani*, or seventy divisions of
" the planets; and as to the seven lamps upon the candlesticks, they referred to the course of the
" planets, of which that is the number." Again : " And for the twelve stones, whether we under-
" stand by them the months, or whether we understand the like number of the signs of that circle
" which the Greeks call the Zodiac, we shall not be mistaken in their meaning."[1] The Decani
here mentioned must evidently allude to what Sir William Drummond calls *Dodecans*, each of
which consists of five degrees; and what is here called 70 must mean 72, for $72 \times 5 = 360$; but
70×5 would only equal 350, neither the division of the circle, nor of the year which Moses made
to consist of 360 days. In his account of the flood the year or circle is divided exactly according
to my theory. In his explanation Josephus is confirmed by Philo, another very eminent person,
who states the identical doctrine. The expression used here respecting the *seventy* divisions
of the *planets*, shews that when the word *seventy* is used, seventy-two must be understood,
as it still is, and always was, in some other cases; for example, in that of the version of the seventy, though LXXII. always is meant. It is here evident that though a secret meaning was
known to exist, its nature was only a subject of speculation.

---

[1] Antiq. B. iii. Chap. vii. If this tabernacle was not astrological, I should be happy to be informed what would
make it so.

That 72 constellations were meant, we also know from Pliny, who says (Lib. ii.), that 1600 stars may be counted in the 72 *constellations*, meaning the 72 divisions of the Zodiac. See the Classical Journal, No. XXXI., where the reader may see satisfactory proofs, given by Sir W. Drummond, of what I have said in my Celtic Druids—that the ancients had the use of the telescope. I shall prove the truth of what is said here of the use of the term 70 for 72, more at large hereafter.

The following passage from the Appendix to my Celtic Druids, pp. 307, 308, will exhibit the two Neroses in Ireland.

" Vallancey says, the Irish have the cycle of the Neros by the name of Phennicshe, which in
" Chaldean numerals make the number as given below, No. 1 ; and he says, if you add ח H, which
" alters not the pronunciation, it makes up in the Coptic language the Egyptian period of 608,
" No. 2.

No 1	Ph.	פ	80	No. 2.	Ph.	פ	80
	E.	ה	5		E.	ה	5
	N.	נ	50		N.	נ	50
	N.	נ	50		N.	נ	50
	I.	י	10		I.	י	10
	K.	ק	100		K.	ק	100
	Sh.	ש	300		Sh.	ש	300
	E.	ה	5		H.	ח	8
			——		E.	ה	5
			600				——
							608

" If my reader will refer back to Chapter V. Sect. XIV., he will find Phanes or Fan amongst
" the Irish Gods. He is a God of fire. He is one of the celebrated ancient triad, the Creator,
" the Preserver, and the Destroyer, and the word meant αιων or æternitas. It is in this respect
" particularly applicable to the idea of a cycle.

Φ	Ph.	500
H	E.	8
N	N.	50
N	N.	50
		——
		608

" From this cycle of 600 came the name of the bird Phœnix, called by the Egyptians Phenn,
" with the well-known story of its going to Egypt to burn itself on the altar of the sun (at Helio-
" polis), and rise again from its ashes, at the end of a certain period."   For the word ΦPH *pre*
or *phre*, see Celtic Druids,[1] where the manner in which the mystics concealed various other cycles and objects by means of figures is explained.

In an old Irish Glossary the Phœnix is said to be a bird which lives 600 years or turns of Beal, or the sun, with all the remainder of the history of the burning, &c.[2]

Phanes is called Protogonos, and had the head of a Bull.[3]

In Montfaucon[4] " " is an Isis sitting on the Lotus. She hath a Globe on her head with a radiant
" circle round it, which denotes the Sun. The inscription on the reverse hath some affinity with

---

[1] Chap. IV. Sect. VIII.   [3] Ouseley, Coll. Orient. Vol. II. No. iii. p. 203.

[2] Porphyry on Cave of Nymphs, trans. Taylor, p. 190.

[4] Supplement to the Ant. Exp. Pl. LII. Fig. 7, Vol. II., and in my plates, Fig. 10.

" the figure. It is ΙΕΟΥ ΑΡΣΕΝΟΦΡΗ. Ιευ is for Ιαω, which is the usual way of the ec-
" clesiastic authors reading the Hebrew word Jehovah ; for in these kinds of words the change or
" transposition of vowels is not regarded. The gem here hath Ιευ, and Eusebius hath Ιευω.
" The last syllable in the next word (φϱη which we read phri) signifies, in the Egyptian lan-
" guage, the sun. Therefore the whole word, αϱσενοφϱη, signifies *the sun is male*, if we may be
" allowed to join a Greek word and an Egyptian together. We see here the rays of the sun, but
" they proceed from a woman's head; which particular disagrees with the inscription. Doth
" this signify that Isis, who is taken for the moon, is male?" [1] Here Isis, whose veil no mortal
shall ever draw aside, the celestial virgin of the sphere, is seated on the self-generating sacred Lotus,
and is called Ιευ or יד *ieu*, or Jove, and also the solar cycle φϱη : Φ 500, Ρ 100, Η 8=608.
The breasts shew the female sex, the αϱσενος shews the male, and united, they shew as usual the
Androgynous deity.

In the Greek and Coptic the famous *Io Sabboe* means 360 :

Ι	10
Ο	70
Σ	200
Α	1
Β	2
Β	2
Ο	70
Ε	5
	360 [2]

This shews that the earliest year in Greece was 360 days only. Thus we find the same ignorance in Greece, and in the book of the deluge of Moses, and in the Apocalypse, as well as in
Egypt : but with the Indians, we find the Metonic cycle and the Neros, which evince a more correct knowledge of the length of the year; and it was also shewn by the builders of the Metonic
cycles of pillars in Britain.

Whilst on the subject of Druidical circles, I will take the opportunity of stating, that Dr.
Daniel Clarke found a Druidical circle on the top of mount Gargarus, the ancient Ida, where the
Gods of Homer assembled at the siege of Troy. It may be put down as a parallel to Joshua's
Gilgal, (Joshua viii. 30, 31,) on mount Ebal—the Proseucha discovered by Epiphanius. The
Temples of Greece are constantly said to be surrounded with a τέμενος, the meaning of which has
been doubted. Homer [3] says,

Γαϱγαϱω, ενθα δε οι τεμενος βωμος τε θυηεις

Here I think the temenos was the Gilgal of Dr. Clarke. See CELTIC DRUIDS, *passim*. And from
this we may not unreasonably suspect that the τεμενος meant a stone circle ; or, at all events,
that a stone circle was a τεμενος.

10. In my Celtic Druids I have given an example of two Cromlehs in India, Plates 39 and 40 ;
and I have given a drawing of another in figure 18 of this work. I have since found that stone
circles, similar to our Stonehenge, Abury, &c., are very common in the Northern parts of India.
The natives can give no account of them.

---

[1] P. 243.   [2] Ouseley, Coll. Orient. Vol. II. No. iii. p. 209.   [3] Lib. viii. v. 48.

These circles appear to be a remnant of antiquity of a similar species to those of the Puniha-Pandawars, a great number of which are to be seen scattered on the adjacent heights about a mile west of a place called Durnacotta. The stones composing these circles are of a hard blackish granite, very irregular in shape, measuring in general about 3 feet in height, and of the same dimension in thickness. The country people seem ignorant on the subject of these antiquities, and can give no information for what purposes they were designed. It is reported that circles of a similar description are very numerous among the skirts of the hills of Wudlamaun and others in that neighbourhood, that on some of these being opened by the late Rajah, Vassareddy, they were found to contain human bones of a large size, and that in some there were earthern pots curiously placed together containing ashes or charcoal. Similar to the above at Amravutty, on the river Christna or Kistna, is to be seen a mound called Depaldenna. [1]

Drawings of great numbers of these circles may be seen in Mackenzie's manuscripts abovementioned. I shall give a drawing of only one of them, because, although there is no reason to doubt the general accuracy of the accounts, yet no attempt has been made to ascertain of what numbers of stones these circles originally consisted, which was the only thing that could render them really useful; but which, as was originally the case in England, was thought to be of no consequence. It is, however, remarkable that, in the circle which I have given, fig. 11, as the reader will find on counting them, (allowance being made for one evidently broken,) 19 stones, the number of the Metonic cycle, are found.

11. For the origin of the cross we must go to the Buddhists and to the Lama of Tibet, who takes his name from the cross, called in his language Lamh, which is with his followers an object of profound veneration. [2]

The cross of the Buddhists is represented with leaves and flowers springing from it, and placed upon a mount Calvary, as among the Roman Catholics. They represent it in various ways, but the shaft with the cross bar and the Calvary remain the same. The tree of life and knowledge, or the Jamba tree, in their maps of the world, is always represented in the shape of a cross, eighty-four *Yoganas* (answering to the eighty-four years of the life of him who was exalted upon the cross) or 423[3] miles high, including the three steps of the Calvary. [4]

12. The celebrated Monk Georgius, in his Tibetinum Alphabetum, p. 203, has given plates (in my figures No. 14) of the God Indra nailed to a cross, *with five wounds*. These crosses are to be seen in Nepaul, especially at the corners of roads and on eminences. Indra is said to have been crucified by the keepers of the Hindoo garden of Paradise for having robbed it. The country of Nepaul is evidently the Caucasus where Alexander went to look at the cave of Prometheus, to whom the whole mythos obviously applies. But it is the same as that of Jesus, evidently existing here also, long before the time of Christ. All these crucifixes, &c., &c., must be well known to our Indian travellers. Have the Romish Monks been more honest than our philosophers of Calcutta? It would be absurd to deny that I think *they have*. Ah! old Roger Bacon, how truly hast thou said, " Omnia ad religionem in suspicione habenda" !

Georgius says, " Si ita se res habet, ut existimat Beausobrius, *Indi*, et *Budistæ* quorum religio, " eadem est ac Tibetana, nonnisi a Manichæis nova hæc deliriorum portenta acceperunt. Hæ " namque gentes præsertim in urbe Nepal, Luna XII. *Badr* seu *Bhadon Augusti* mensis, dies

---

[1] See Col. Mackenzie's manuscripts, *India Antiqua Illustrata*, in the Museum in the India-House, No. 9, 1816, 1817, and plates, Fig. 11.

[2] See Celtic Druids, App. pp. 307—312.   [3] This I suppose to be in the original a misprint for 432.

[4] Asiat. Res. Vol. X. p. 123. See my plates, Figures Nos. 12, 13.

" festos auspicaturæ Dei *Indræ*, erigunt ad illius memoriam ubique locorum *cruces* amictas
" *Abrotono.* Earum figuram descriptam habes ad lit. B, Tabula pone sequenti. Nam A effigies
" est ipsius *Indræ crucifixi* signa *Telech* in fronte manibus pedibusque gerentis."[1] See Fig. 14.

Again, he says,[2] " Est Krishna (quod ut mihi pridem indicaverat P. Cassianus Maceratensis,
" sic nunc uberius in Galliis observatum intelligo a vivo litteratissimo De Guignes) nomen ipsum
" corruptum Christi Servatoris."

And again, speaking of Buddha, Georgius says,[3] " Nam Xaca et Christus nomina sunt æquæ
" significationis apud Tibetanos, quemadmodum apud Sinenses, teste et vindice De Guignesio,
" Christus et Fo : apud Indos vero Christus et Bisnu : Christus et Chrisnu." Buddha is often
seen with a glory, and with a tongue of fire on his head.[4]

Gen. Vallancey says, " The Tartars call the cross *Lama* from the Scythian *Lamh*, a band,
" synonymous to the *Jod* of the Chaldeans : and thus it became the *name of a cross*, and of the
" high-priest with the Tartars ; and, with the Irish, *Luam*[5] signifies the head of the church, an
" abbot, &c.

" From this X all nations begin a new reckoning, because it is the number of fingers on both
" hands, which were the original instruments of numbering : hence י *(id) iod* in Hebrew is the
" hand and the number *ten*, as is Lamh with the Tartars."[6]

Though I have noticed this before, I think it right to repeat it here.

This figure X not only stands for ten, but was considered, as it has been already shewn, a perfect number, i. e. the emblem of perfection, and hence stood for 600—the cycle—which, after
many attempts, was erroneously thought to be perfect.

From the abuse of the original incarnation or divine inspiration, for if they were not identical
they were very nearly allied, arose the Lama of Tibet, now become a mere tool of the Monks, by
means of which their order keeps possession of the sovereign sway. If the circumstances of the
Lama and the Pope be carefully examined, the similarity will be found to be very striking. In
each case the Monks and their Pope have the temporal power in the surrounding territory, and in
each case extensive foreign states admit their spiritual authority. And when in former times the
priests gave the Pope of Italy the epithet of Deus, and elevated him as they yet do, ON THE ALTAR
of St. Peter's, and bending the knee to him, offered him, to use their own words, *adoration*—they
in fact very nearly arrived at *Tibetian* perfection. In each case the head of the empire is called
Papa and Holy Father, and in each case the empire is called that of the Lama, the Lamh, or the
Cross—for Lamh means Cross. Lamh looks very like Lamb. I know not the etymology of our
word Lamb ; but each *empire is that of the Lamb of God upon earth, which taketh away the sins of
the world.* I shall hereafter treat on this point.

But the word Ram, ראם *ram*, in Hebrew means both Bull and Ram.[7] This arose, I suspect,
from the Indian incarnation of Rama, who preceded Cristna. In fact he was the incarnation of
the Neros when the Sun left Taurus and entered Aries ; thus he was incarnate in the signs of both
the Bull and the Ram.

" Boodism," Col. Franklin[8] says, " is known very widely in Asia under the appellation of

---

[1] Alph. Tibet, p. 203.   [2] Ibid. pp. 253—263.   [3] Ibid. p. 364.
[4] See Moore's Pantheon, Pl. 71, 72.

[5] This Luam is evidently a corruption of Lamh or Lamh. The High-priest was an incarnation of the Lamb of the
Zodiac.

[6] Celtic Druids, App. p. 312.   [7] Vide Parkhurst in voce.

[8] Treatise on the Tenets of the Jeynes and Buddhists, p. 186.

" Shamanism: the visible head of which religion, the Dalai Lama, resides in a magnificent palace
" called Putala, or the Holy Mountain, near Lassa, the capital of the extensive region of Thibet.
" He is believed to be animated by a Divine Spirit, and is regarded as the vicegerent of the Deity
" on earth, and by some as the Deity incarnate, and death is nothing more, it is pretended, than
" the transmigration of the spirit into another body, like that of the Bull God Apis in Egypt."
Here is the principle which will unravel all the mysteries of antiquity.

In my Celtic Druids I have proved that the first race of man after the flood came from about
the latitude 45, perhaps Balk or Samarkand, not far from Northern Tibet. The following extract
from the work of the Christian Jesuits will shew that some of the Romish doctrines might have
been copied, and probably were copied by the Persian or Pythagorean school, from a source different from that of modern Christianity. The authority of the Jesuits in this case cannot be disputed, and the doctrines, from their being identified with the Buddhism of Tibet, must have an antiquity far higher than that of the doctrines of Cristna.

13. The close coincidence between the religion of Tibet and that of the Christians, can hardly
be disputed, as the knowledge of it comes to us from several persons who do not appear to have
any interest in trying to deceive. " Father Grebillon observes also with astonishment, that the
" Lamas have the use of holy water, singing in the church service, prayers for the dead, mitres
" worn by the bishops ; and that the Dalai Lama holds the same rank among his Lamas, that the
" Pope does in the Church of Rome : and Father Grueber goes farther; he says, that their religion
" agrees, in every essential point, with the Roman religion, without ever having had any connexion
" with Europeans : for, says he, they celebrate a sacrifice with bread and wine; they give extreme
" unction ; they bless marriages; pray for the sick; make processions ; honour the relics of their
" saints, or rather their idols; they have monasteries and convents of young women; they sing in
" their temples like Christian Monks; they observe several fasts, in the course of the year, and
" mortify their bodies, particularly with the discipline, or whips : they consecrate their bishops,
" and send missionaries, who live in extreme poverty, travelling barefoot even to China. Father
" Grueber says he has seen all this : and Horace de la Pona says, that the religion of Tibet is
" like an image of that of Rome. They believe in one God : a Trinity, but filled with errors ; a
" Paradise, Hell, Purgatory; but mingled with fables : they make alms, prayers, and sacrifices
" for the dead ; they have convents, wherein they make vows of chastity and poverty; have con-
" fessors appointed by the grand Lama, and, besides holy water, the cross, chaplets, and other
" practices of Christians." [1] The above is confirmed by Grueber and D'Orville, the missionaries,
in the account of their Voyage to China.

Whatever Protestants may say to the contrary, this is correct Popish, and also Protestant,
Christianity. The Pope, like the Archbishop of Canterbury, is believed by his consecration,
ordination, or installation, that is, by the ceremony of making him pope or bishop, by the imposi-
tion of hands, by the Samach, or by investiture with the Pallium, to have had instilled or inspired
into him a portion of the divine spirit, of the logos, or divine wisdom: thus endowed, as it is
clearly expressed, he has power to remit sins, in the Romish service *on the condition of repentance;*
in the Protestant (as appears in the service for the ordination of priests) *without a condition.*

The accounts of the Jesuits are, in some instances, confirmed by the Journal of a most
respectable gentleman, sent by Mr. Hastings to Tibet. [2] Mr. Turner says, that the mysterious
word Aum or Om, is equally sacred with the Buddhists of Thibet, as with the Brahmins of

---

[1] Remains of Japhet, 4to. p. 201.　　　　[2] Turner's Travels in Tibet.

Bengal, under the form of *Oom maunee primee oom.* The temple at Jaggernaut, and most of the other places in India held sacred by the Brahmins, are equally held sacred by the Buddhists of Tibet.[1] They have monasteries for Monks and Nuns, precisely like those of the Romish Church, in which prayers are chaunted, with music, which never cease night or day for thousands of years, accompanied with occasional processions. They make pilgrimages to the chief holy places in India, the ruined city of Gowr, to Gya, Benares, Mahow, Allahabad, &c., and the rich, like those of the Romish Church, do it by proxy. They say that the Grand Lama has been regenerated at all these places. The principal idol in their temples is called Mahamoonie:[2] the Buddha of Bengal, called Godama or Gautama, in Assam and Ava: Samana in Siam: Amida and Buth in Japan: Fohi in China; Buddha and Shakamuna, in Bengal and Hindostan: Dherma Raja and Mahamoonie, in Bootan and Tibet. From time immemorial they have had the art of printing, *though it has been limited to their religious works;* and it is still more curious, that it has been done upon blocks similar to the stereotype method, and not by moveable letters, which shews that they have not learnt it from the West; for, when Mr. Turner visited them, the art of printing in that manner was not known in Europe. It is much to be lamented that Mr. Turner did not get copies of, or procure more information respecting, their sacred books, of which he states them to have great numbers in their monasteries.

This account of the Buddhists of Upper India, is confirmed by the account given by Mr. Crawford[3] of the same religionists, in the island of Siam, a thousand miles from them. He says, " The " Siamese have as excellent a morality as the Christians. They have their Talapoins or Monks, " who take the vows of chastity and poverty; they have auricular confession; they believe that " the professors of any religion may be saved."

" Agreeably to the prevailing belief in a succession of similar worlds, over each of which pre- " sides a Buddha or Menu, the inhabitants of Ceylon suppose that, towards the end of the present " mundane system, there will be long wars, unheard-of crimes, and a portentous diminution of the " length of human life: that a terrible rain will then sweep from the face of the earth all except a " small number of pious persons, who will receive timely notice of the evil, and thus be enabled to " avoid it; and that the wicked will be changed into beasts, and that ultimately Maitri[4] —Buddha " —will appear and re-establish a new order of things."[5] Here are the metempsychosis and the renewal of worlds; the exact doctrine, which was noticed before, of Irenæus.

I must now beg my reader to pause a little, and to reflect upon the accounts which he has read in this book respecting the prophecies of Cristna, of Isaiah, of Virgil, of the Sibyls, as reported by Figulus and other Romans, of the prophecy of Zoroaster, and of the Druid of Ireland,—and I would then ask him what he thinks of it. Can he for a moment doubt that all this relates to the renewal of the cycles, and to a succession of incarnations? The mysterious child, alluded to in the beginning of this book, was a new incarnation of Divine Wisdom, the πρωτογονος, the first emanation, the logos, the solar fire, the sacred, mysterious, never-to-be-spoken OM, the Trimurti, united in the person of Buddha or Cristna,[6] born to be king of the people of Sion, of the country

---

[1] They have the custom of forming Carns by piling heaps of stones over dead bodies, like those of the Western world, pp. 221, 222. Every traveller passing by adds a stone to the heap.

[2] Pp. 306, 307.   [3] Res. Vol. II. pp. 190, et seq.

[4] I suspect this word *Maitri* is the French *Maître,* the Spanish and Italian *Maistro,* the Dutch *Meester,* and our *Master,*—all probably derived from the Latin *Magister;* and the *last* equally with *Maitri* from a common origin.

[5] Fab. Orig. Pag. Idol. Vol. II. p. 339.   [6] Ibid. p. 43.

of JUDIA, of the tribe of YUDA,[1] whose language was that of the Baali of Siam and Persia—of the people called Palli, or Pallestini or Philistines—of the black nation of Sir William Jones, and whose name was, with the Greeks, X 600, and XH and ΥΗΣ 608; and Jupiter, Ieu-pati, the Saviour, represented in St. Peter's by the stone image to which I have before alluded, having inscribed on it the words Ζευς Σωτηρ.

CHAPTER V

Menu—Sir William Jones on Menu

1. In the Hindoo mythology we meet with a very important personage, called MENU. He is allowed to be identical with Buddha, and with the Sun, and to be surnamed Son of the Self-existent, or, in other words, Son of God. The word Menu signifies *mind* or *understanding*, and is closely connected with the idea of WISDOM. It is, in short, but another epithet for Buddha. This root is closely allied to the root מנר *mnr*, whence comes the Minerva of the Greeks,[2] and the English word man, and the Latin words MENS *mind*, memini *to remember*, and the Sanscrit man or men, *to think*. I am of opinion that the Numa of the Romans, the legislator who had the mystical surname of P-Om-pilius,[3] was a Menu corrupted; read from right to left it is Manu.

Menu, meaning mind, or soul, or spirit, every incarnation was a Menu, or a manifestation of the Divine Mind. This was the same as Divine Wisdom, the πρωτογενος. To this Divine Mind or Wisdom the priests most discreetly attributed their codes of law. Thus Menes in Egypt gave the first laws;[4] and Minos, the son of Jupiter (Iao) and the beautiful Io, was the first legislator of Crete. From the second syllable of the word Menu the Greek word Νοος has been thought to be derived. The heretical Jews worshiped the planetary bodies, under the name of מני *mni*, which means, the disposers or placers in order. In the Hindoo system there are said to have been fourteen Menus, (the last of whom finished with the flood,) or the same person is said to have appeared many times. He is attended by seven companions, who are called Rashees or Rishees, before explained, but evidently the five planets, the earth, and the moon.

2. Menu was maintained by Sir W. Jones to be the נה *nh*, or, as we call him, the Noah of Genesis. This is strongly supported by the fact, that it is said in Genesis viii. 13, " in the six hundred and " first year of Noah's life, in the first month, the first day of the month, the waters were dried " up from the earth." Here is evidently the cycle of the Neros, ending with the drying of the waters, and beginning anew. Here are the ending of one year or life of Menu or Buddha, and the beginning of a new one.

The intimate connexion between Minerva and Buddha, as WISDOM and mind, I need not point out. On this Word or Person Mr. Faber says, " The import of the Greek word *Nous* and of the " Sanscrit Menu is precisely the same: each denotes mind or *intelligence*: and to the latter of

---

[1] Of the tribe of Yuda I shall have much to say hereafter.   [2] See Parkhurst in voce מנר *mnr*.

[3] With *Pi* the Coptic emphatic article, Pi-Om-philius or filius, *the son of Om*.   [4] Maurice, Hist.

" them the Latin *Mens* is evidently very nearly allied: or, to speak more properly, Mens and
" Menu, perhaps also our English Mind, are fundamentally one and the same word."[1]

After the Gods, Diodorus makes the first king of Egypt, Menas, or Menes, to reign at
Thebes, not at Memphis; the latter was a modern city compared with the former. Thus Menes
is found as first king at Thebes and at Memphis; in Crete, by the name of Minos, and in India
as Menu. The Men-des or Pan of Egypt may mean the Divine Mind,[2] in fact, the Holy Mind or
Ghost. Menu is also shewn by various writers to be the Sun, and in this respect the same as
Buddha. All these Hindoo persons, like the different Gods of the Western nations, resolve themselves at last into the Sun.

Of the Theban kings Eratosthenes says, The first who reigned was *Mines* the Thebinite, the
Thebæan, which is by interpretation Dionius: Πρωτος εβασιλευσεν Μινης Θηβινιτης, Θηβαιος,
ὁ ερμηνευεται Διονιος. The second was called by interpretation Ἑρμογενης *Hermogenes*, i. e.
Begotten of Hermes.

Mr. Faber correctly observes, that the Menu of the Hindoos is the Maha-bad or Great Bud of
the Buddhists: he has the same history: what applies to the one, with very little variation, applies to the other.[3] There were fourteen Maha-bads, as there were fourteen Menus. In the Desatir
of Moshani fourteen Mahabads are treated of. These were the imaginary persons of whom Sir
William Jones made a dynasty of kings.

Mr. Faber has very successfully proved that Buddha and Zoroaster,[4] or the star of the Bull,
as he explains the word, are the same person, the same as the Menu of the Chusas of Iran. He
says, " The early worship, therefore, of Iran, according to the Zendavesta, was the worship of
" *Buddha* or *Tat* under the form of a Bull, compounded with the human form."[5]

In Persia they had five Zoroasters: these were but renewed incarnations of the Tauric God.[6]

In short, I believe the word Menu had the same meaning, originally, as Rasit, *Wisdom;* that it
was the same as the mount of Meru, and that Meru and Menu were mere dialectic variations. In
this I am supported by Mons. La Loubère, who states that Maria and Mania are written and used
indiscriminately in the Siamese language: and this fact, when it is considered that the whole
Eastern mythos was removed to the West, justifies a suspicion that along with the others came
the oriental il-avratta, or mount of Meru, and that we have it in the mount now called Baris and
Armenia: that is, *Ar* or *Er-Meni-ia*, the country of mount Meru or Meni. The mount Baris is
the mount of Nau-banda. Dr. Jones[7] says, Βαρις, a structure of any sort, a boat or barge. The
mount of Naubanda, in the Indian language, is said to mean *ship-cabled mount.* To this mount
in the flood of Noah the Ark was said to be fastened. The word *Nau* is the Latin *Navis,* and the
Greek Ναυς: and the word *band* is a common English word for a cord or cable.[8] The
expression mount Meru or Menu, means the mount *of* Meru. In the Hebrew language when a
word is in regimine, in many cases it can only be known by the context whether it be in the
nominative or genitive case. The words for *mount Meru* and *mount of Meru* would be the same.
This, if the Hebrew or any language like the Hebrew were the original language, readily accounts
for the names of many places. If Manes, the son of Budwas, *the son of Thomas, of whom we*

---

[1] Faber, Orig. Pag. Idol. Vol. I. p. 40.

[2] In Egypt there was a city called Mendes. The symbol of Mendes was a Goat: the reason of this I shall explain
hereafter.

[3] Fab. p. 123.   [4] Ch. iii.   [5] Vol. II. p. 83.   [6] Nimrod, 231.   [7] In Lexicon.

[8] This is a good example of the utility of applying to several languages for the meaning of a word, for I am quite
certain no one can doubt the identity of signification in the word *neubands.*

shall hereafter have much that is very extraordinary to offer, were really a man, he had his name from Menu, and when his doctrines were said to be those of Manes, it was meant that they were the doctrines of the INCARNATE WISDOM.

In consequence of the word for moon מן *mn* or Μηνη being the same as the name of the Menu of India, I cannot shew examples of him very clearly in the West, because the two names are so confounded, that it is almost impossible, in most cases, to be certain of *which* the ancient author is treating. But Arrian has observed that the mount Meru was known to the Greeks, and was sacred to Bacchus.[1]

In Genesis v. 29, it is said, that Noah had his name of נח *nh* (ינחמנו *inhmnu*) *because he shall comfort us*; or, *because he shall cause to rest.* Now, I think these explanations of the name of the Man, the grand point of whose life was the ruin of a world by floods and winds, are both ridiculous, and only prove that the meaning of the word, of this half-lost language, is unknown. Under all the circumstances I have a suspicion that there is here a mistake between the letter He ה *e* and the letter Heth ח *h*, and that the word ינח *inh*, followed by the word מן *MNU*, meant, *Menu shall lead or precede.* We have already seen that Noah and Menu were the same. Thus we find that in the Western as well as in the Eastern part of Asia, there was a Menu, and each was saved in an Ark from a flood. The letter ח *h* and the letter ה *e* are often substituted for each other in the Hebrew, as they are in the Greek.

In Gen. ix. 20, Noah is called by Moses איש האדמה *ais eadme*, that is, the husband of the earth. Thus Saturn was the husband of Rhea.[2] I shall have more to say on the meaning of the word *Menu* hereafter.

CHAPTER VI

Hercules and Samson the same—Etymology of Samson—Muttra, Hercules at—
    Drummond on Hercules. The Foxes—Wilfrd on Hercules at Muttra. Mean-
    ing of word Hercules—Hercules Black. Cristna in Egypt

1. I SHALL now proceed to exhibit some other circumstances to prove that the God of Western and Eastern Asia was the same. In the particulars of the God Hercules some striking marks of the identity of the two will be found. In his adventures also a number of facts may be perceived, which identify him with the Samson of the Jews and the Cristna of India.

Samson שמשן *smnsn*, is explained by Calmet and Cruden to mean *his sun*. This explanation I greatly doubt. Samson answers correctly to the Hindoo incarnation Shama, or Shama-Jaya, which is one of the thousand names of Vishnu, which the Hindoos repeat in their litanies, as is

---

[1] Hist. Ind. pp. 318, 321; Diod. Sic. Lib. ii. p. 123; Bryant, Anal. Vol. III. p. 196. Menu in India was the supposed author of a celebrated code of laws called the Institutes of Menu, translated into English by the learned Professor Haughton.

[2] Gale, Court Gent. B. iii. Ch. ii.

done by the Romish Christians. [1]   Bal-iswara was the son of this *Shama*, and the *Sem-i-ramis* of Assur, of Scripture. [2]   Several of the early Christian fathers, and along with them Syncellus, acknowledge the identity of Samson and Hercules, who, they say, was copied by the Gentiles from the Bible. The whole story of Samson, the Philistines, the Lion, Thamnath or Thamnuz, חנמח *tmnte*, is a mythos : it is explained by Dupuis, *sur tous les Cultes*, in his dissertation on the labours of Hercules.

Mr. Faber says, " On the sphere he *(Hercules)* is represented in the act of contending with the " serpent, the head of which is placed under his foot : and this serpent, we are told, is that which " guarded the tree with golden fruit in the midst of the garden of the Hesperides. But the garden " of the Hesperides, as we have already seen, was no other than the garden of Paradise : conse-" quently the serpent of that garden, the head of which is crushed beneath the heel of Hercules, " and which itself is described as encircling with its folds the trunk of the mysterious tree, must " necessarily be a transcript of that serpent whose form was assumed by the tempter of our first " parents. We may observe the same ancient tradition in the Phœnician fable respecting Ophion " or Ophioneus." [3]   The reader will not dispute the authority of the orthodox Faber. Would he wish for a more decisive proof that Genesis is a mythos, as the Rev. Dr. Geddes properly calls it ? If he do, let him consult Mons. Dupuis *sur tous les Cultes*, where Mr. Faber acquired his knowledge, though he wishes to keep M. Dupuis's fine work in the back-ground.

The situation of the foot of the celestial Hercules on the Serpent's head, pretty well identifies him with the Cristna of Genesis and India. Parkhurst admits that the labours of Hercules are nothing but the passage of the sun through the signs of the Zodiac ; and the circumstances relating to him he adopts as " *emblematic memorials of what the real Saviour was to do and to suffer*"—the name of Hercules being, according to him, " A TITLE OF THE FUTURE SAVIOUR." He could not foresee that the origin of Hercules was to be found (viz. at Maturea or Muttra) in India. [4]

2. The etymology of the name of Samson and his adventures are very closely connected with the solar Hercules. Sampsa was the name of the Sun. Among the Arabians Baisampsa was the name of a city of their country, which was the same as Heliopolis or city of the Sun. Isidore, of Seville, says, that the name of Samson signifies the solar force or power ; that is, he defines it as Macrobius defines Hercules. Whatever may be the origin of the name, we know that Samson was of the tribe of Dan, or of that which, in the astrological system of the Rabbins, was placed (casée) under Scorpio, or under the sign with which the celestial Hercules rises. He became amorous of a daughter of Thamnis. חנמח *tmnte*. [5]   In going to seek her, he encountered a furious lion which, like Hercules, he destroyed. Syncellus says of him, " In this time lived " Samson, who was called Hercules, by the Greeks. Some persons maintain, nevertheless," adds he, " that Hercules lived *before* Samson ; but traits of resemblance exist between them, which " cannot be denied." [6]

It is not surprising that Mr. Parkhurst should be obliged to acknowledge the close connexion between Hercules and Jesus—as the fact of Hercules, in the ancient sphere, treading on the head of the serpent leaves no room for doubt on this subject, and also identifies him with

---

[1] The practice of calling the God by many names, and repeating them in their Litanies, is still followed in the Romish Church. I counted forty-three names of the black virgin under her image at Loretto. See plates, fig. 15. Cristna has one thousand names ; as time passed on they probably increased.

[2] See Wilford, Asiat. Res. Vol. V. p. 293.   [3] Faber, Orig. of Pag. Idol. Vol. I. p. 443.

[4] For some interesting observations on this God the reader may consult Parkhurst's Lexicon in voce עז *os*, p. 520.

[5] Judges xiv. 1.   [6] Dupuis, *sur tous les Cultes*, Vol. I. pp. 311, 539.

Cristna of India, who is seldom seen without the head of the Cobra beneath his foot : and these two facts at once locate Cristna *before* the Christian æra.

The identity of Cristna and Hercules has been shewn. Christian priests say that the man treading on the head of the serpent is an emblem of Jesus ; then here we have the same emblem of Cristna, Hercules, and Jesus. Whether this will prove the identity of the three, I leave to the devotees. It surely proves the identity of the doctrine or mythos of the second book of Genesis, of Greece, and of India. I am not surprised that the Rev. and superstitious Parkhurst should state Hercules to be an emblem of the future Saviour. How could any person who had eyes avoid seeing the identity of the history of the two? However, let me not be abused for first seeing this : it was the pious Parkhurst who discovered it, I only repeat his words, and I have no inclination to dispute his explanation of the mythos.

Col. Wilford says, that Megasthenes reckons fifteen generations between Dionysius and Hercules, by the latter of whom, he observes, we are to understand Cristna and Bala-Rama. He adds, " It appears that, like the spiritual rulers of Tibet, Deo-Naush did not, properly speaking, " die, but his soul shifted its habitation, and got into a new body, whenever the old one was worn " out, either through age or sickness." Here we have the true system of incarnations and the metempsychosis. Whether there be in the Hindoo mythos an incarnation called Bala-Rama between Bachus, that is Dionysius, that is Taurus—and Hercules, that is Cristna, that is Aries, or not, is of no consequence. It may have been the fact. It will not affect the general argument. But Bala-Rama is said to be the same as Cristna. The two grand incarnations, whether called Bala-Rama or by whatever other name, were those of Buddha and Cristna. After the equinox began in Taurus, they were all incarnations of Buddha until the sun entered Aries, and after his entrance into Aries, of Cristna ; and both were incarnations of Vishnu, or of the Trimurti.

By the word generation, used above, I apprehend is meant century. Then if we admit that Bala-Rama was the incarnation, as I am inclined to believe he was, of the cycle next before Cristna, and if to the 1500 we add 600, his cycle, this would bring us to the year 2100 from the Sun's entrance into Taurus to his entrance into Aries, for the incarnation of his successor, Cristna. Bala-Rama is constantly held, by the present ignorant Brahmins, to be the same as Cristna. This is because he was the next previous incarnation. The nearness of the two, connected also with the fact, that they were in reality renewed incarnations or regenerations of the same person, prevents the Brahmins from seeing the distinction. Besides, he was the same in another sense ; he was the Sun in the equinoctial sign Aries, and in the cycle of the Neros,—both running at the same time, and crossing each other in their progress. [1]

3. The old statues of the Gods at the famous Muttra or Maturea have been destroyed by the Mohamedans, and the new ones have been erected in modern form, and in consequence have no resemblance to those described by Megasthenes, but at a place called Bala-deva, about thirteen miles from Muttra, there is a very ancient statue, which minutely answers to his description ; it was visited some years ago by the late Lieut. Stewart, who describes it in the following words : " Bala-Rama, or Bala-deva, is respresented *there* with a plough-share in his left hand, with which " he hooked his enemies ; and in his right hand a thick cudgel, with which he cleft their sculls ; " his shoulders are covered with the skin of a tiger." Captain Wilford adds, " Here I shall ob- " serve, that the ploughshare is always represented very small, and sometimes omitted ; and that " it looks exactly like a harpoon with a strong hook or a gaff, as it is usually called by fishermen.

---

[1] The doctrine of regeneration has been actually carried to the letter in India. Mons. D'Ancarville, p. 102, gives an account of a Prince being admitted to the Brahmin caste by being passed through the body of a golden cow. The Brahmins hold that they are the descendants of Brahma, and the Cow or Beeve is the emblem of him.

" My Pundits inform me also, that Bala-Rama is sometimes represented with his shoulders co-
" vered with the skin of a lion." [1]

Our account of Samson and the bone of the Ass is probably some misunderstanding of the text,
or a corruption. I feel little doubt that the gaff and the bone were the same thing, whatever they
were. [2]

On most of the Egyptian monuments a priest is seen with a lituus or crosier of a peculiar shape.
This I take to have been the Hieralpha (described by Kircher) and the ploughshare in the hand of
Bala-Rama, just mentioned. This is confirmed by a passage of Diodorus Siculus respecting the
rites of the priests of Ethiopia and those of the Egyptians : " The several colleges of priests
" (they say) observe one and the same order and discipline in both nations. For, as many as are
" so consecrated for divine service are wholly devoted to purity and religion, and in both countries
" are shaven alike, and are clothed with the like stoles and attire, and carry a sceptre like unto a
" ploughshare, such as their kings likewise bear, with high-crowned caps tufted at the top,
" wreathed round with serpents called asps : by which is seemed to be signified, that those who
" contrive any thing against the life are as sure to die as if they were stung with the deadly bite
" of an asp." Here I think the lituus, which is seen so often and is called a ploughshare, is
meant. [3]

This image of Bala-Deva is probably that of Cristna. The Hindoos know little about the names
of their Gods. Bala-Deva is but one of the names of Cristna and Buddha.

4. Sir William Drummood says, " I have already observed that Gaza signifies a Goat, and was
" the type of the sun in Capricorn. It will be remembered that the gates of the sun were feigned
" by the ancient astronomers to be in Capricorn and Cancer, from which signs the tropics are
" named. Samson carried away the gates from *Gaza* to *Hebron*, the city of conjunction. Now,
" Count Gebelin tells us that at Cadiz, where Hercules was anciently worshiped, there was a re-
" presentation of him, with a gate on his shoulders. [4] The story of Samson and Delilah may re-
" mind us of Hercules and Omphale.

" לחי *Lehi, lhi,* a Jawbone. It will be remembered that in the first decan of *Leo* an Ass's head
" was represented by the Orientalists. רמת לחי *Rmt Lhi, Ramath Lehi,* means the high place of
" the Jawbone.

" Samson had seven locks of hair (the number of the planetary bodies). The yellow hair of
" Apollo was a symbol of the solar rays : and Samson with his shaven head may mean the sun
" shorn of his beams." [5]

Volney says, " Hercules is the emblem of the sun : the name of Samson signifies the sun : [6]
" Hercules was represented naked, [7] carrying on his shoulders two columns called the Gates of
" Cadiz : Samson is said to have borne off and carried on his shoulders the Gates of Gaza. Her-
" cules is made prisoner by the Egyptians, who want to sacrifice him : but while they are pre-
" paring to slay him, he breaks loose and kills them all. Samson, tied with new ropes by the
" armed men of Judah, is given up to the Philistines, who want to kill him : he unties the ropes
" and kills a thousand Philistines with the Jawbone of an Ass. Hercules (the sun) departing for
" the *Indies,* (or rather Ethiopia,) and conducting his army through the deserts of Lybia, feels a
" burning thirst, and conjures *Ihou,* his father, to succour him in his danger : instantly the ce-
" lestial RAM appears : Hercules follows him, and arrives at a place where the ram scrapes with

---

[1] Asiat. Res. Vol. V. p. 294.   [4] Vide Dr. D. Clarke's Travels, Vol. III. Ch. iv.   [5] B. iii. Ch. l.

[2] Drum. Œd. Jud. p. 361.   [3] Ib. p. 360.   [6] In Arabic Shams-on means The Sun.

[7] See Montfaucon, Ant. Exp. Vol. I. p. 127.

" his foot, and there comes forth a spring of water (that of the Hyads or Eridan).[1]   Samson after
" having killed a thousand Philistines with the jawbone of an ass feels a violent thirst : he be-
" seeches the God *Ihou* to take pity on him : God makes a spring of water to issue from the
" jawbone of an ass."[2]   M. Volney then goes on to shew that the story of the foxes is copied
from the Pagan mythology, and was the subject of a festival in Latium.   The labours of Hercules
are all astronomically explained by Mons. Dupuis in a manner which admits of no dispute.   They
are the history of the annual passage of the sun through the signs of the Zodiac, as may be seen
on the globe, it being corrected to the proper æra and latitude.

The story of the Foxes with the fire-brands[3] is vindicated by Ovid[4] —passages which imply,
though the author himself affirms the contrary, more than a solitary instance of mischief, to justify
a general and annual memorial—and is farther explained by Lycophron's Λαμπουρις and Suidas'
voc. γεωρια.   The Roman festival, *Vulpium combustio*, recurred about the middle of April, when,
as Bochart in his Hieroz. remarks, there was no harvest in Italy.   Hence it must have been imported from a warmer climate.[5]

Bochart (in the Pref. to Histor. de Animal.) says, " In memory of Samson's foxes,[6] there were
" let loose *in the circus at Rome* about the middle of April foxes with firebrands.   Whereunto ap-
" pertains that which the Bœotians, who sprang partly from the Phœnicians, boast of themselves,
" that they could kindle any thing by means of a torch affixed to a fox : and that of Lycophron, a
" Cilician, by whom a fox is termed λαμπουρις, from its shining tail : *or from a torch bound to
" its tail.*"   The same Bochart tells us, " that the great fish which swallowed up *Jonah*, although
" it be called a whale,[7] yet it was not a whale properly so called, but a dog-fish, called Carcharias.
" Therefore in the Grecian fable Hercules is said to have been swallowed up of a dog, and to have
" lain three days in his entrails.   Which fable sprang from the sacred history, touching *Jonah*
the Hebrew prophet, as is evident to all."[8]

Hesychius says, that by *Cetus* Κητος, which we translate Whale, was meant a large ship, in
bulk like a whale.   Κητος, ειδος νεως· Κητινη πλοιον μεγα ως Κητος.   Mr. Bryant[9] says, that
when Andromeda is said to have been carried away by a sea-monster, this was probably only a
ship—perhaps by pirates.

Respecting the Hercules of India, Captain Wilford says, " Diodorus Siculus, speaking of
" Palibothra, affirms that it had been built by the Indian Hercules, who, according to Megasthenes,
" as quoted by Arrian, was worshiped by the Surnseni.   Their chief cities were *Methora* and
" Clisobora : the first is now called Mutra, (in Sanscrit it is called *Mat'hura,*) the other *Mugu-
" nagur* by the Musselmans, and Calisa-pura by the Hindus.   The whole country about *Mutra*
" is called *Surasena* to this day, by learned Brahmins.

" The Indian Hercules, according to Cicero, was called Belus.   He is the same as Bala, the
" brother of Crishna, and both are conjointly worshiped at *Mutra ;* indeed, they are considered
" as one Avatar or incarnation of *Vishnu.*   *Bala* is represented as a stout man, with a club in his
" hand.   He is called also *Balarama.*   To decline the word *Bala*, you must begin with *Balas*, which
" I conceive to be an obsolete form, preserved only for the purpose of declension and etymological
" derivation.   The first *a* in *Bala* is pronounced like the first *a* in *America*, in the Eastern parts
" of India : but in the Western parts, and in Benares, it is pronounced exactly like the French *e*

---

[1] Eridan, river of Adonis, from the words ור יר *ir da.*
[2] Judges xv. 4, 5.   [4] Fasti, IV. 681, 707.
[3] Ibid.   [7] Matt. xii. 40, and by LXX. *Jonah* ii. 1.
[9] Anal. Vol. III p. 550.

[5] Volney, Res. Vol. I. p. 35.
[6] Class. Jour. Vol. VI. p. 326.
[8] Gale, Court Gent. B. iii. Ch. ix.

" in the pronouns *je*, *me*, &c.; thus the difference between *Balas* and *Belus* is not very great. " As *Bala* sprung from *Vishnu* or *Heri*, he is certainly *Heri-cula*, *Heri-culas*, and *Hercules*."[1] Here we see the Ball or בעל *Bol*, of Assyria and Ireland, the Bel of Syria and Phœnicia, and the Belinus of Gaul. Cristna is evidently Hercules, and Bala-Rama is the *strong* Bala. Rama is the Greek Ρωμη. To Bel I shall return presently.[2]

It seems here convenient to inquire a little further into the meaning of the word Hercules. This word is admitted to be neither Greek nor Latin; then I think we must look for it to the Barbarians. He is called in the Dionysiacon,[3] 'ΗΡΑΚΛΗΣ astris amictus, Rex Ignis, Princeps Mundi, Sol, &c. He was called (I learn from Vallancey) EREKOELL, that is ה *e*=5+ר *r*=200 +ה *e*=5+כ *k*=20+ע *o* 70+ה *e* 5+ל *l*=30+ל *l*=30=365; or again, E=5+P=100+K=20+E=5 +Λ=30+E=5+Σ=200=365; or, as 'ΕΡΚΛΕΣ=360. In my Celtic Druids[4] I have shewn that this practice of describing persons by letters as numbers was common, (the origin of which I shall endeavour to demonstrate in a future book,) both in writings and in the numbers of pillars in the ancient circular temples, which are equally common in India and Europe.[5] I ask, may not the word Hercules have been derived from *Heri* the *saviour*, and η *k*=500+ל *l*=30+ע *o* =70=600, which was sacred among the Egyptians under the shape of a cat, and which, in their language, had this name? Their cat mummies may be seen in the British Museum. Then he would be the saviour of the Neros or the ם *Mem* final of Isaiah, the X of Plato. By and by we shall find several other examples of Gods whose names had the meaning of more than one cycle.[6]

As *Hercules* was called *Heri-cules* so *Mercury* was called *Mer-coles*, or *Mer-colis*. The *Mer* I do not understand; the *colis* is the *clo* of the *Chaldees*—the *Cali* of India, and the *Coll* or *Cal* of Ireland. Col. Wilford speaks of a God called *Hara-ja or Hara-cula*.[7] Here Heri the saviour and the God *Is* are identified with Hercules or Cristna.[8]

The word *Heri* in Sanscrit means shepherd as well as saviour. Cristna is called Heri, and Jesus is always called Shepherd. He is the leader of the followers of the Lamb. He is the good shepherd, as was also Cristna. In Ireland a shepherd is called *Sheepheri*, or sheep-aire. See Gen.

---

[1] Asiat. Res. Vol V. p. 270.

[2] Bryant says, the most considerable mission in Madura is called Aour (אור *Aur*) at this day. (Travels of Jesuits by Lockman, Vol. I. p. 470.) Near it are a city and the river Balasore. Bal is the Chaldean and Syrian Deity, well known. Anal. Vol. III. p. 207.

[3] Lib. xl. p. 683.   [4] Ch. vi. Sect. xxv p. 245, and Appendix, p. 309.

[5] Vide one of the Metonic cycle plates, fig. 11.

Allowance must be made for *one* stone evidently broken into *two*. A very curious account of a circular temple under a tumulus in the province of Coimbatoor, is given by my particular friend, the learned Physiologist, Sir Anthony Carlisle, in the twenty-first volume of the Transactions of the Society of Antiquaries. He says, " These mounds occur " numerously in the province of Coimbatoor; they are each invariably denoted by a circle of rude stones or masses of " rock, the diameter of the larger areas being often as much as one hundred feet. In one example, the circle was " formed by upright flat obelisks, averaging sixteen feet in height, rude, and without impression of tools. In the " centre of each mound a massive table of unhewn stone forms the roof or cover to four chambers, the sides and septa " being of the same rude, unworked stone, and mortices with tenons apparently ground out by trituration, serve to fix " the roof upon the walls. One of these roofs contained upwards of three hundred cubic feet of Granite, and being " immoveable as a whole, it was divided into four equal divisions by stone-cutters, in order to expose the subjacent " recesses, or chambers." This is, in reality, almost an exact description of the temple and tumulus at New Grange, in Ireland, and its circle of pillars described in my Celtic Druids.

[6] If it be said I have here placed a final *Coph* at the *beginning* of a word, I justify myself by the example of the Mem final in Isaiah, and by the *Mem* in the Gospel of the Infancy.

[7] Asiat. Res. Vol. VI. p. 514.

[8] In an ancient inscription at Delphi Dr. Clarke found the word 'ΗΡΑΚΛΕΙΟΥ. Ib. p. 196. At the foot of Olympus was a town called Heraclea. Ib. 301.

Vallancey, Ouseley's Col. Orien. p. 315, where he proves that the ryots of India were known in Ireland, and were the Ara-Cottii famed for *linen geer* of Dionysius.

In this case there will be two origins for the name of Hercules; and this is certainly mystical enough. But it must be recollected that we are now in the centre of the land of mystery. Cristna is constantly called Heri-Cristna: this is the *black*. But it may be the beneficent or good saviour, or good Heri; for Cristna may come from some old word, whence came the Greek word Χρησος *bonus*. He was called Creechna in Ireland. I have proved that all the very ancient languages are the same, mere dialects, and I will not be fettered in my search after truth either by one language or another. The utility of my endeavour first to prove the identity of the ancient systems of letters and language I hope is obvious. It is no more likely that the *black* Hindoos should call their God the *black* Saviour or Heri, than it is that the *white* French should call Henry Quatre their *white* Henry; but it is as natural for them to call him the *good Saviour*, as for the French to call their king their *good Henry*. It is certain that in Sanscrit *cris* means *black*, and in old Greek χρης means *good*; he may, therefore, have been named from both words. On the subject of the word χρης I shall have much to say hereafter.

Arrian says, on the authority of Megasthenes, that the Indian Hercules had the same habit as the Theban Hercules, and that he had an only daughter called Pandæa.[1] This was precisely the same name as that which was given to the only daughter of Cristna, to whom he left a mighty empire—the Pandæan kingdom.

6. In addition to all the other circumstances of identity between Cristna and Hercules, is the fact that they were both *blacks*. Of Hercules, Homer, in what Nimrod calls his genuine verses, thus speaks:

——— ὁ δ᾽ ἐρεμνῇ νυκτι γεγοικως
Γυμνον τοξον εχων και επι νευρηφιν ὀἴστον.

——— BLACK he stood as night,
His bow uncased, his arrow strung for flight.[2]

In B. iv. ch. i. Sect. 13, I have shewn, from Mr. Bryant, that the last syllable in the word *Maturea*, viz. *re*, meant the sun. The first syllable, I suspect, was the Hebrew מטה *mte*, which meant a resting-place, a couch, a bed, a sofa or sopha, (that is, as the Re was a ray of the sun which was Wisdom,) or soph-ia or place of wisdom,—a resting-place of divine wisdom—a Divan, that is, Deva-ana or holy place, where, in the Asiatic courts, is the Sopha on which the king reposes to administer justice. From the same idea I have no doubt it was, that the kings of the Franks, (or as, in a future page, I shall prove them,) the kings of the Sacæ or Saxons, had their Beds of Justice. In the Maturea of India, Cristna spent his youth, after taking refuge there from the tyrant who strove to destroy him. And in the Maturea of Egypt, Jesus Christ is said, as we have before shewn, to have spent his youth, after he took refuge there from the tyrant Herod.

Mr. Maurice has pointed out a passage of Eusebius from which it seems probable that the Cristna in Egypt was well known in his time. He says, "That at Elephantina they adored an- "other deity in the figure of a man, in a sitting posture, *painted blue*, having the head of a Ram "with the horns of a Goat encircling a disk. The deity thus described is plainly of astronomical

---

[1] Arr. Hist. Ind. ch. viii.; Creuser, Vol. II. ch. v. p. 190.

[2] Nimrod, Vol. I. p. 19, Sup. ed. Nimrod is the name given by a very learned devotee to an anonymous work in three volumes octavo, published by Priestley, Holborn. The first volume was suppressed, and then republished. The work abounds with the most profound Greek learning, but falls short, in many places, in consequence of its ingenious author, most unfortunately, not understanding the Oriental languages.

" origin, denoting the power of the sun in Aries. It is, however, exceedingly remarkable that
" Pococke actually found, and on his 48th plate has engraved, an antique colossal statue of a man,
" sitting in the front of this temple with his arms folded before him, and bearing in his hand a
" very singular kind of Lituus or crosier."[1] I think there can be hardly any doubt that the figure
described by Eusebius was that of Cristna or Buddha. There was a city in Egypt called Hera-
cleopolis.

It does not appear to me to be more surprising that there should be two Matureas, one in India
and one in Egypt, than that there should be two islands of Elephanta in which the statues of
Cristna should be found, one near Bombay, where the famous cavern is seen, and one in Upper
Egypt. Every one knows the fact of our Seapoys discovering their favourite God Cristna, when
they arrived in Egypt, during the last war, and which, very naturally, they immediately fell to
worshiping. This alone at once proves the fallacy of all the deductions which are drawn from the
astronomical calculations and reasonings of Mr. Bentley, on which I will now make some observations, and may serve to shew how little the abstruse and complicated chains of reasoning used by
him can in any case be depended on. The fact of the God Cristna being found in the ruins of the
old temples at Thebes in Egypt of itself settles the question of its antiquity, for it could not be
put there after the birth of Christ.[2]

We have seen above that the striking similarity between the vulgarly-received Jesus of Nazareth and Hercules cannot be denied by the learned and orthodox Parkhurst, and we have also seen
the mode in which he accounts for it. I have fairly stated the facts for the consideration of my
reader, who must see at once that if the explanation of Parkhurst be satisfactory for Hercules, the
same explanation will serve for Cristna. In an honest inquiry into the superstitions of the world,
I could not conceal the circumstances relating to Cristna; and there are many others, which I
shall state. Of course I cannot condemn any one for being satisfied with Mr. Parkhurst's judgment. That it is not satisfactory to me, may be readily accounted for from an opinion which I
entertain, that I *can* and *shall* account for the facts in a very different and more satisfactory manner, when I come to that part of my work where I shall undertake to prove that a person usually
called Jesus Christ did live, and that the doctrines which he taught were true. I must beg my
reader to recollect that in this work I am not writing for the ignorant, nor to gratify the passions
of any class, but that it is the object of my work to develop and unveil the secret history of the
ancient world, which operates influentially upon us; that it is meant for legislators and philosophers, to enable them the better to determine what is the most expedient course for them to pursue for the good of their fellow-creatures.

[1] Ind. Ant. Vol. III. p. 211.

[2] In one of the plates of my Celtic Druids of a round tower in Scotland, the crucified Saviour has a lamb on one
side, and an ELEPHANT on the other. How came an elephant to be thus found in Scotland?

CHAPTER VII

Mr. Bentley—Playfair's Recantation—Vedas—Forgeries—Colebrooke on the Forgeries—Observations on a passage in the Celtic Druids—Mr. Bentley's Recantation to Dr. Marsham

1. Since Bailly, Playfair, and the other learned men have been dead, as might be expected, renewed attempts have been made to shew that the Brahmins' astronomical tables are not the produce of actual observation, but a combination of back reckonings and forgeries. The gentleman of the name of Bentley, of whom I have before spoken, has, by means of the most deeply-learned and profound calculations, published in the Asiatic Researches, endeavoured to shew that the history of Cristna was invented in the year after Christ 600, and that the time of the story was laid about the birth of Christ. The object of this invention he, in his first essays, says, was to prevent the propagation of the Christian religion in India, by a colony which arrived from the West about that time; and in his latter essays he says, the object was to deceive Mohamed Akbar in the 16th century into a belief that they were the oldest of nations.

In these essays, a most inflated and exaggerated account has been given by him, of the forgeries of the Hindoo writings: in answer to which I beg leave to refer to some observations long before written by Mr. Colebrooke, in the Asiatic Researches,[1] where he gives most convincing reasons why the chief part of the Hindoo writings cannot have been forged or materially interpolated. As he justly observes, it would be as fair to conclude that all European books were forged, because there have been forgeries in Europe, as it is, because there have been forgeries in India, to conclude the same thing of them. His argument really shews, that it would be just as easy to forge the gospels *at this day*, as it must have been to forge the Vedas;[2] and the impossibility of the former need not be pointed out.

2. The Vedas of the Brahmins have hitherto been attended with several difficulties. According to the received Brahmin tradition, they were originally, after being revealed by Brahma, transmitted by ORAL TRADITION to the time of Vyasa, who collected them and arranged them into books. And this Vyasa, which word it is said means *compiler*, has been thought to be merely an epoch in the history of the literature of India.[3] The number of the Vedas is also a matter of dispute; some making them in number only three, some four, and some add to them the collection of books called the Pouranas, of which they make a fifth Veda. From these circumstances it seems probable that the Brahmin Vedas were first collected or remodelled, after the great division between the followers of Buddha and Cristna. They are said to contain internal evidence of being composed at different times. The Pouranas are eighteen in number; they are also the work of Vyasa. Each has a particular and characteristic name. For instance, one of the lotus, another of the egg of the world, and the LAST is that of Cristna, called Bhagavad—Baga-veda. Now it has been observed that the Brahmins admit that Buddha was the ninth Avatar; then what is the reason that he has no Pourana? But at the same time that the Brahmins admit him to have been an incarnation or Avatar, they say he was *an impostor*, that he was every thing that is bad, and

---

[1] Vol. VIII. pp. 484—488.

[2] It has been said that Mr. Playfair changed his opinion before he died respecting the antiquity of the Hindoo tables. I have made the most careful inquiry of his friends, and have reason to believe this to be false.

[3] Creuzer, Liv. I. p. 671.

that he lived many ages after Cristna.¹ This appearance of contradiction I shall explain by and by.

In wishing to condemn the whole of the Hindoo writings, because there are, as he says, corruptions in them, Mr. Bentley does not perceive the blow which he is striking at the gospel histories, which contain 30,000 various readings, half of which must be corruptions. He also instances the prophetic style of the Hindoo writings as a mark of corruption. In these cases it is frequently no such thing, not even if a person be designated by name, as the persons, viz. the Buddhas, the Balis, &c., were all the same—re-incarnations, regenerations of the same being, and often called by the same name. I admit that many corruptions and interpolations have taken place; but I maintain that if these are sufficient to condemn the Vedas, the gospels also must be condemned, for they contain various readings or corruptions, some of them of VITAL consequence to the religion. But it is not just to infer of either, that they are not genuine, because the priests have corrupted them.

It is pretty clear that in order to get over the absolute identity of the history of Christ and Cristna, many attempts will be made to shew, that the story of Cristna is an interpolation in the Hindoo books, though they are among the oldest of their records. Mr. Colebrooke observes, that " the former of these (the story of Cristna) is inserted in all the collections of the Upanishads " which" he has " seen."² Dr. Pritchard³ admits, that the history of Cristna, &c., are to be found in all the caves of Ellora, Elephanta, &c., which are known to be the oldest, as he says, by their *flat roofs*, &c. Mr. Colebrooke allows, that the formulas attached to the Vedas for adjusting the periods for celebrating the religious festivals, " were evidently formed in the infancy of astro- " nomical knowledge:" hence he infers that they were written about 200 years after the Penta- teuch. But the fair inference is, that as the Vedas, and the caves, and the astronomical observa- tions, and the formulæ, are all closely interwoven with the history of Cristna—that history is of the same early date, and the formulæ at least equally ancient. However, as Dr. Pritchard allows that the formulæ are much older than Christ, it is evident that they cannot have been written to serve any purpose in any way connected with Christianity.

But the stories related of Cristna are most clearly no interpolation; they are intimately blended with, they are, in fact, the ground-work, of the whole system. The system of the Brahmins can- not exist without them. Besides, what is to be said of the sculptures in the caves? Are they interpolations too? What, of the tremendous figure destroying the infant *boys*? What, of the cross-shaped temple in the city of Mathura, allowed by Mr. Maurice to have been once the capital of a great empire?⁴ This is most certainly proved by Arrian to have been in existence in the time of Alexander. Was this built to support the apocryphal gospel history? The April festival, in Britain and India, was it founded for the same purpose; or the statue of Hercules and Samson still remaining at Rama-deva? Mr. Maurice acknowledges that the Evangelists must have copied from the Puranas, or the Brahmins from the Evangelists.⁵ The reader has seen the reply of Mr. Maurice given in his Antiquities, and must judge for himself. There is nothing in Mr. Maurice's pamphlets but a mere repetition. But in his pamphlets I do not perceive that he makes a single observation on the subject of the figures in the caves. This is prudent; but it settles the question.

¹ Dr. Collier observes, that the genuineness of the Vedas is proved by Mr. Ward beyond dispute. (Ward's Account of Hindoos, 4to. edit. Serampore.) By this the Doctor does not mean proved to be free from modern interpolation, but that they are the real Vedas.

⁴ Vide Asiat. Res. Vol. VIII. p. 494.   ³ Anal. Egypt. Mythol. p. 261.
⁴ Maur. Bram. Fraud Exp.   ⁵ Ibid. p. 31.

When the small number of the Christians, in comparison with the immense number of Hindoos spread over all India, and using a great variety of dialects, is considered, it seems perfectly incredible, that the system of fraud supposed by Mr. Bentley can have taken place; that for this object the figures in the temples should have been cut out of the rock, or the caves excavated, or the temples themselves erected. Mr. Bentley's effect is out of all proportion to its cause. Cristna, his statues, temples, and books, &c., respecting him, are to be found where a Christian never came. Is it not absurd to suppose that all at once the Brahmins could invent the story of Cristna, and make it dovetail into all their other superstitions—make him form an integral part of their curious Trinity, the actual Trinity of ancient Persia and of Plato—make him also exactly fit into the theological inferences of the modern Christians respecting the meaning of the first chapters of Genesis—make his story exactly agree with the orthodox massacre of the innocents— and, finally, make all this be received as an ancient doctrine and article of faith, by millions of people who must have known very well that it was all perfectly new to them, and that they had never heard of it before!¹ Besides, it is not only the immaculate conception and crucifixion of Cristna which must have been invented to serve Mr. Bentley's purpose; the crucifixion of the God Indra in Nepaul; in fact, the immaculate conception, crucifixion, and resurrection of Buddha, in Nepaul and Tibet, equally with the religion of the Samanæans of Clemens Alexandrinus, ² and of the Buddha of Porphyry and Jerom, born from the side of his mother, must have been invented. Yes, *all these things* must have been forged.

3. The forgeries of the early Christians are so numerous as to be almost incredible; but they bear no proportion to what, if we are to believe Mr. Bentley, has been taking place in India in modern times. In the history of Buddha, as well as of Cristna, are to be found many of the stories which are supposed to be forged; so that two sects hating one another, and not holding the least communication, must have conspired over all the immense territories east of the Indus, to destroy and to rewrite every old work, to the amount almost of millions; and so completely have they succeeded, that all our missionaries have not, in any of the countries where the Brahmins are to be found, or in which there are only Buddhists, been able to discover a single copy of any of the works uncorrupted with the history of Cristna. Buddha is allowed by Mr. Bentley to have been long previous to Cristna, and he is evidently the same as Cristna, which can only arise from his being the sun in an earlier period. This identity with Mercury and Woden, the Budvar day, the *Maia* mother of Mercury and Buddha, the Maturea in India and Egypt, the two Elephantas with their Cristnas, and the destroying tyrant of the gospel history in that of the Eastern, the Samaneans of Clemens Alexandrinus, and many other circumstances, unite to prove that something must be wrong in the principle of Mr. Bentley's very learned and abstruse calculations. As I have said before, the fact of Cristna being found in Egypt by the seapoys of itself decides the question. It is of importance to observe, that by far the greatest part of the writings stated by Mr. Bentley to be forgeries, have little or no relation to religion. Those that have, are filled with stories of immensely elongated cycles and complication, for the sake, perhaps, of secrecy; or, perhaps, as our priests say, to produce astonishment in the minds of weak and ignorant persons, and for the gratification of the silly vanity of being thought the most ancient of nations. That this has caused the adoption of their old cycles, which is done by merely adding a few ciphers,

---

¹ See Buckingham's Oriental Herald.

² Clemens (Lib. i. p. 305) says, that the Indian Gymnosophists consisted of two sects, the Sarmanæ and the Brachmanes; that there are also some in India who followed the doctrines of Buttæ. He says Hellenicus writes, that there are Hyperboreans beyond the Riphæan mountains, who eat no flesh, but live on fruits, &c. Again, (p. 451,) he says, that the Brackmens neither eat flesh nor drink wine.

may, however unlikely, be true. But this will not account for the destruction of the old works in all the dialects spoken by various sects over all the countries east of the Indus, which existed before a certain period, and the manufacture of almost innumerable new works, *for the use of all these different and hostile sects.*

4. It has been observed by Mr. Colebrooke that the observations of Hindoo astronomers were ever extremely coarse and imperfect, and their practice very inferior to their theory of astronomy. An improved theory, or the hint of it, was borrowed from the West: but they did not learn to make correct observations. They were content, in practice, with a rude approximation.. ... Again Mr. C. says, " We are not to try their rules by the test of their agreement with accurate observations " at any assignable moment, and thence conclude that the rule and its correct application are " contemporaneous. This has always been the point at issue between Mr. Bentley and me. He " mentioned, in his first essay, that the age of a Hindu astronomical treatise can be so determined " with precision : I have always contended that their practical astronomy has been too loose and " imperfect for the application of that test, except as an *approximation.* In one instance, by the " rigorous use of his test he would have had to pronounce that the work under examination is of " *an age yet to come* (1454 years after A. D. 1799).[1] To avoid so monstrous an absurdity he " rejected this case, and deduced a mean from the other results, varying from 340 to 1105 years"[2] But I think the example of the fallacies to which Mr. Bentley's mode of argument is liable, which the deduction of Mr. Colebrooke in this case has shewn, is quite sufficient to prove that Mr. Bentley's conclusions cannot on any account be permitted to weigh against all the facts and powerful reasons which have been given. Indeed, Mr. Colebrooke's observation seems to me at once to *prove* the fallacy of his rule, notwithstanding that it has been admitted by some very eminent astronomers.

Respecting the manuscripts of India, the missionary Dr. Buchanan says,[3] " The greater part " of *Bengal* manuscripts, owing to the badness of the paper, require to be copied at least once in " ten years, as they will in that climate preserve no longer: and every copiest, it is to be sus- " pected, adds to old books whatever discoveries he makes, relinquishing his immediate reputation " for learning, in order to promote the grand and profitable employment of his sect, the delusion " of the multitude." Or as he probably would say, (in fact as *all priests* would say,) the enlight- ening of the multitude. I know no reason why the Doctor should be guilty of any deceit here : but if he state the fact fairly we see how completely he justifies what Mr. Colebrooke has said respecting the corrections of the ancient astronomical works by the moderns ; and thus entirely overthrows Mr. Bentley's specious reasonings, from the correctness of the astronomical observa- tions. The fact here stated at once accounts for no old manuscripts being found uncorrected. No man would renew a copy except from the last version.

Mr. Colebrooke seems to consider the adoration of Cristna as Hero-worship ; the same of Menu. This is a great mistake. They are both personifications or incarnations, like Buddha, of Divine Wisdom—from the latter of which came the Hebrew חֵ nh, the Greek Νοος, and the Latin *Mens,* as I have before shewn. I have no doubt that the Buddhists and Brahmins constituted one sect, followers of Brahma, till the Sun entered Aries ; then they divided ; and the Buddhists were driven out of India. But the Buddhists had the renewed incarnations, precisely the same in number as the Brahmins—for the systems were the same ; and this accounts for the younger Buddha, after Christ, whom the Brahmins call an impostor. That there were to be ten incarna- tions in all, was a doctrine admitted by both.

---

[1] See Asiat. Res. Vol. VI. p. 570.   [2] Asiatic Journal, March 1826, p. 365.   [3] Asiat. Res. Vol. VI. p. 174.

When it is considered that the Vyasa, of whom so much has been said, is an imaginary character, that the word means merely a compiler, and that when we say *Vyasa* compiled the Vedas, we ought to say, the compiler compiled them at such or such a time, and, that it is admitted that they were compiled from oral traditions—it does not seem to me probable, that the Brahmins had any fraudulent or dishonest intention in correcting the astronomical parts of them. They contained astronomical facts, in which, in their old books, they discovered errors, and they corrected them. The astronomical tables had no connexion with religion: nor was it possible the Brahmins could foresee that these tables could ever, in London or any where else, at a future day, have any connexion with it. After the Mythos was established about the year B. C. 3101 on the Cycle of the Neros, it stood still; but the astronomy constantly advanced. The same thing takes place with our astronomical tables, tables of Logarithms, &c., &c. In every new edition errors are corrected.

Mr. Colebrooke[1] after a very careful examination of the credit due to the genuineness of the Vedas, inclines to think the worship of Cristna may have been introduced at or after the time that the persecution took place of the Buddhists and Jains.[2] This I think is the truth, and as far as the fact goes agrees perfectly with my theory, that Cristna is only the Indian Hercules, the Sun in Aries. And this obviates entirely another opinion of Mr. Colebrooke's, and proves that the Hindoos did not deify heroes.[3] The precise time when the struggle took place between the followers of the Sun in Taurus, and those of the Sun in Aries, is doubtful. It *must*, however, have taken place at some time—it may have been a long time—and if they did not then perfectly understand the precession of the equinox, it probably was *a long time after* the Sun entered Aries.

The argument relied on by Mr. Bentley is of an extremely abstruse and difficult nature: and I should say, in opposition to the numerous facts, and the mass of circumstantial evidence in favour of the antiquity of the Hindoo works, will itself serve as an example of the fallacy of the system recommended by him. I know not better how to describe it, than by giving an extract from a paper of Mr. Colebrooke's in the Asiatic Researches.[4] The practice of modernizing books, alluded to by Mr. Colebrooke, seems to harmonize the facts, which cannot be questioned, with the plausible hypothesis of Mr. Bentley, and thus to remove a very great difficulty:

" Without entering at length into any disquisition on this subject, or discussing the accuracy
" of the premises, but acceding generally to the position, that the date of a set of astronomical
" tables, or of a system for the computation of the places of planets, is deducible from the ascer
" tainment of a time when that system or set of tables gave results nearest to the truth; and
" granting that the date above-mentioned approximates within certain limits to such an ascertain-
" ment; I shall merely observe that, supposing the dates otherwise irreconcilable, still the book
" which we now have under the name of Súrya, or Saura, Sidd'hanta, may have been, and
" probably was, modernized from a more ancient treatise of the same name, the later work borrow-
" ing its title from an earlier performance of a different author. We have an instance of this
" practice in the kindred case of the Brahme-sidd'hanta: for we are acquainted with no less than
" three astronomical treatises bearing this title: and an equal number of tracts, entitled Vasisht'ha-
" sidd'hánta, may be traced in the quotations of authors. This solution of the objection also is
" entirely compatible with the tenour of the references to the Saura, which have been yet remarked
" in the works of Brahmegupta and Várahamira; none of them being relative to points that furnish
" arguments for concluding the age of the book from internal evidence."

---

[1] Asiat. Res. Vol. VIII. 8vo. pp. 377, 480, 497.   [4] Vide p. 495, ed. Lond. 1808.

[2] Ibid.   [4] Vol. XII. p. 228.

This passage is of the very first importance; because, as all the arguments against the antiquity of the Hindoo learning have been refuted, so as to leave no question except this of Mr. Bentley's, it shews that this last hold, even if not removed by other arguments and presumptive evidence, is not any longer tenable. And it shews this in the best manner; for it does not shew that Mr. Bentley has been wrong, either in his reasoning or his fact: but it harmonizes both to the assumed assertions of the Hindoos and the other circumstances. This also harmonizes perfectly with the system of renewed incarnations which I have exhibited to the view of the reader; and thus the minute examination, consequent on the controversy, in the end, as it always does conduce, has conduced to the cause of truth. All this also harmonizes perfectly with what has been said in the preliminary observations respecting the great antiquity and the identity of the Tauric festivals in India and Britain.

The undisputed fact noticed above by Mr. Colebrooke of the practice of the Brahmins in modernizing their ancient treatises, at once renders Mr. Bentley's arguments *inconclusive*, and leaves in full force all that Mr. Colebrooke has said respecting the impossibility of forging books to the extent contemplated by Mr. Bentley, though that would be absolutely necessary to support his system. The quantity of fraud and forgery necessary for deceiving the single despot Mohamed Akbar about the year 1556,[1] according to the theory of Mr. Bentley, unsupported by any authorities, constitutes an effect so out of all proportion to its supposed cause, that it is, I believe, by almost all scientific Europeans of the Hindoo school, looked upon with the most perfect contempt. The observation of Mr. Colebrooke in the last sentence of the quotation above, that the references are to works unconnected with the internal evidence seems conclusive, and I cannot find in Mr. Bentley's answer any thing to afford a satisfactory reply to this. I therefore feel obliged to adopt Mr. Colebrooke's mode of accounting for the apparent difficulties which Mr. Bentley has pointed out. But I apprehend, independently of the other argument, that the circumstance of the old æra of the Cali-yug exactly agreeing with its present date, having been observed by Al Mansor at the court of Balk, as noticed before by me, tends strongly to overthrow all the nonsensical speculations of modern forgery to please Mohamed Akbar.

5. In my Celtic Druids I have said that the renovation of the cycles would account for the appearance of Cristna in one of those of late date. As I have observed before, it may be replied to this, that although the sun and moon would hold the same relative situation to one another in consequence of the precession of the equinoxes, they would not hold the same situations in relation to the planets and fixed stars. It is very clear that this must have been observed by the Hindoo astronomers, in a very little time, if they made any actual observations, and in each cycle, when they renewed their books they would endeavour, as they thought, to correct them. This perfectly agrees with what Mr. Colebrooke has informed us above respecting the Brahma Sidhantha, &c. These tracts, which he notices, have evidently escaped the correction, and serve in a different and distant clime to confirm the profound argument of Michaelis and Bishop Marsh respecting the difficulty of corrupting the gospel histories *in later times*. It is evident that the Brahmins who made the corrections, have not had possession of all the old copies, which, in some retired temple of some of the numerous sects, have probably been copied by a person ignorant of what was done at Benares or Ougein. The Janampatri of Cristna, given by Mr. Bentley for about the year 600 after Christ, was not long before the time when the Mohamedans overran India, and destroyed all the temples and colleges: and from this time probably may be dated the ignorance of the Brahmins, and the cessation of the general correspondence among them, which

---

[1] Vide Bentley on Hindoo Astr. p. 164.

would be a consequence of the overthrow of their *universal* power, and hence they could no longer attempt to correct astronomical errors. Thus we find their tables most correct, at the time of their conquest, the destruction of their power, and the pollution of their temples and colleges.

These considerations also account for the correction without the imputation of intentional fraud in the Brahmins, to whom (though I do not consider them better than other priests, for all priests, as bodies, will deceive, if they have the power) I do not like to impute fraud, if I can avoid it. These considerations also leave Mr. Bentley's astronomical arguments all their force, and to him all the credit which is justly due for his ingenuity. The greatly exaggerated accounts of Mr. Bentley betray a consciousness of weakness in argument. The doctrine that a renewed incarnation was expected every 600 years, is supported by a great number of facts which cannot be disputed, totally independent of each other, and found in widely-separated countries. For example—the *ten* ages in India and in Europe, *eight* of them nearly finished, and a ninth expected to arrive, when a new saviour was to appear—a new incarnation of the Supreme Being. This supplies a clue to all the difficulties respecting the date of the God with a thousand names. He was born in the time of Joshua, and in the time of Cæsar; but though he had different names, yet he had the same name. This is similar to the mistake of the Jewish rabble in taking Jesus Christ for an incarnation of Elias, Eλιος, or the God יהו *ieu*, אליהו *alieu*, al-Ieu.

Mr. Bentley has admitted several facts of consequence, which, as he is an opponent to my doctrines, the reader will know how to estimate.

Mr. Bentley has observed, that Hermes was the son of Osiris and Maia, and that Mercury was the son of *Jupiter* and Maia; that Buddha was also the son of Maia, and was the same as Mercury, and that his name meant Wise or Wisdom.[1] He allows[2] that the image of Siva, is generally accompanied with a Bull *to indicate the commencement of the year from the sign Taurus, or first of May.* He says that *Sura* in Sanscrit means light, and *Asura* means darkness. This is evidently the Surya, and שר *sr*, Osiris. Mr. Bentley also shews that the Hindoo mansions of the moon were *originally* 28 not 27 in number.[3] Coming from Mr. Bentley, my opponent, these are all important admissions—strongly supporting my system.

6. Long after I had written the above respecting Mr. Bentley, I found what at once settles the question; but as I think it extremely desirable, in a case of such importance, that my reader should see the steps by which I have gradually arrived at my conclusions, I shall not expunge what I had previously written.

If any dependence can be placed on Mr. Bentley's own words, he was at last satisfied that the story of Cristna having been copied from that of Jesus Christ, of which I have treated in my Celtic Druids, and also before in this work, was not to be supported. In a letter from him, published by the Rev. J. Marsham, D. D., in his Elements of the Chinese Grammar, is the following passage: " July 4th, 1813, *Krishna was contemporary with Yoodhisht'hira (see the Geeta), and the epoch of Yoodhist'hira's birth was the year 2526 of the Cali Yug of the present astronomers, or about* 575 *years before the Christian æra.*" The fact of Cristna's living more than 500 years before Christ at once disposes of all the nonsense, both oral and written, about the history of Cristna being copied from that of Christ. The admission also removes the only plausible objection to the whole of my theory, and at once shews that my explanation of the nature of the Janampatri of Cristna is correct. Mr. Bentley's admission opens the door to my theory, that renewed incarnations of the same persons were believed to have taken place, and indeed nearly proves the truth of it respecting them: for we have here one Cristna about 600 years before Christ, and another Cristna about 600 years after him. Here are three persons of the same name in the world, at three very pecu-

---

[1] Pp. 55, 56, 60.   [2] P. 58.   [3] P. 5.

liar epochas—Cristna about 600 B. C., Christ himself at the end of this 600, and Cristna 600 years afterward.

After this, in another letter, (Ib.) Mr. Bentley goes on to shew, by ASTRONOMICAL CALCULATIONS AND PROOFS, that he is correct, and that Cristna was certainly, as he had before said, more than 500 years before Christ.

The date of the æra of Yudist'hira is the only fact which materially concerns my argument, this being allowed by Mr. Bentley to be the date of the birth of Cristna. This date, *in his posthumous work*, I find fixed, to use his own words, *decidedly beyond the possibility of doubt*, to the year 575 before Christ. (See pp. 67, 72.) Then the history of Cristna cannot have been copied from that of Christ. I shall return to Mr. Bentley several times in the course of the work.

No doubt the difficulty of coming at the truth in questions of this nature is exceedingly great and almost insuperable. It is very evident that written evidence can scarcely ever be made free from objection, as the controversy between Mr. Colebrooke and Mr. Bentley proves; and I conceive that it can be discovered which side is in the right, only from collateral circumstances, over which neither party engaged can have any controul, and which we learn from persons or writings that cannot by any possibility have any interest in the question. I allude to such evidence respecting the Heri-Cristna at Mutra as is afforded by Arrian, and to such facts as the existence of two Mutras or Matureas. All this goes to prove the great absurdity of believing that God would give a system to his creatures to be believed under pain of damnation, depending on written evidence of this kind. In this case I cannot forget that passion, religious bigotry, and interest, are on one side, and *dis*interested philosophy, and nothing that I can perceive but a love of truth, on the other. When I consider the letters to Dr. Marsham, with the ultra pietism of Mr. Bentley, and all the circumstances relating to his last work, partly written, as I am told, on his death-bed, I confess I feel rather inclined to adopt, of his two opinions, that entertained when he was sound both in body and mind. It is very unwise and generally very unkind, in surviving relatives to publish the death-bed works of their friends. Nothing can be more unsatisfactory than the opinions of persons in this situation.

There can be no doubt now, I think, that the history of Cristna is the history of the equinoctial sun in Aries, and that Buddha was the equinoctial sun in Taurus. Buddha was Bacchus, Cristna was Hercules, in reality, one 2160 years after the other: this nearly agrees with what is said by Arrian, that Hercules was many generations—1500 years—after Bacchus; and that, as Plutarch says, Bacchus and Hercules were modern Gods,[1] that is, they were not so old as the Gods which gave names to the planets. After the sun, I suppose the five planets, the *disposers*, as Moses and the Pelasgi[2] called them, were the objects of adoration, and the foundation of astrology. The signs of the Zodiac, and the festivals at the vernal equinox, followed in due course.

---

[1] Plutarch says, De Iside et Osiride, (Squire, p. 35,) " Osiris and Isis were translated as some say to the rank of " Gods, as Bacchus and Hercules were in after ages"—thus confirming my idea, that the latter were not the oldest Gods.

[2] Pelasgi, Phœnician Sailors. See Celtic Druids, pp. 258 et seq.

CHAPTER VIII

Maturea—Objections—Mr. Seeley's Observations on the Serpent—Atonement, Original Sin—Black Nation of Buddhists in Asia

1. When the identity of the doctrines of Genesis with the story of Cristna is considered, the circumstances of the Egyptian city of Heliopolis or Maturea, the city of the Sun, as I have formerly shewn, are very striking. It was the capital of Goshen, (Goshen means *house of the sun,*) where the Israelites settled under Jacob. It was here the priest Potiphar lived and officiated, to whose daughter Joseph was married. It was here, where a Jewish temple was built by Onias, who was at the head of a sect of schismatical or heretical Jews, whose doctrines we *cannot* know, or on what grounds they maintained that this was the proper place for the temple of Jehovah. But we *do* know that they were hated by the orthodox, as almost always happen to heretics.

Jerusalem, ACCORDING TO THE PENTATEUCH, had no more right to call itself the place chosen *by Jehovah to place his temple there,* than Heliopolis or any other city. This same Heliopolis was the place to which, as has been already shewn, Joseph and Mary fled from Herod, and where Jesus performed great miracles—and, in his time, was called Maturea—the name of the birthplace of Cristna, the Maturea Deorum of Ptolemy. It may be said these things do not *prove* the identity of Jesus and Cristna, and that the story of the former was copied from the latter. This I admit. But though they do not prove the identity of Jesus and Cristna, they prove that the corruptions of the religion of Jesus have been collected from the mythoses of India, which is the object for which they are produced. Before I conclude this work, I shall produce evidence that the man Christ Jesus, to use the words of the gospel histories, was not a man living in India. [1]

I feel a perfect conviction that I have proved that Buddha preceded Cristna, and I am equally convinced that no unprejudiced person can doubt the existence of the worship of Cristna in the reign of Alexander the Great. We have seen that Buddha was the son of Maia, a virgin, in whose womb he was incarnate *sans souillure,* [2] and whose birth was foretold many centuries before it took place. This is the identical history of the immaculate conception of Pythagoras, and in like manner of Jesus, foretold before Jesus was born. Almost immediately afterward we have Buddha and the Samaneans, his priests, noticed by Clemens Alexandrinus, who states Buddha to have been the founder of the sect of the Gymnosophists, in the same manner as the Brahmins were used to attribute their institution to Brahma. [3] Reland says, " *Vehar,* templum Dei primarii " Buddæ βουττα quem Indos ut Deum venerari jam olim notavit Clemens Alexandrinus." [4]

---

[1] " The Antonine Itinerary gives 24 MP. between Heliopolis and Memphis; of which 12 are taken up between Heli- " opolis and Babylon. The former of these places is universally allowed by travellers to have been at Matarea, where, " amongst other remains, an obelisk is still standing. Besides the remains at Matarea which are by no means equivocal, " in respect of the fact which they indicate, there are other circumstances which must be allowed in proof of the posi- " tion. The fountain at Matarea is named Ain Schams, or the fountain of the sun. A modern town, situated so near to " the site of the remains at Matarea, as that the skirts of the two are within a mile and half of each other, is named " Keliub: which is no doubt the same with Heliopolis, a little changed. The province is also called Keliubie; and an- " swers to the ancient prefecturate of Heliopolis. The mound of Heliopolis, according to Dr. Pococke, is about a mile " in length, by half that breadth. The obelisk, now standing, occupies nearly the centre of it." Rennel, Her. p. 496.

[2] An immaculate conception.   [3] Asiat. Res. Vol. I. p. 168.

[4] Strom. Lib. I. p. 223, Dissert. xi. pars tertia, p. 85.

2. Our inquirers into the history of the mythology of the natives of India generally take their accounts from the writings of the followers of Cristna, never recollecting that they are all denied any authority by the greatest part of the immense population of those countries in which Buddhism prevails—a population covering a country ten times as large as that of the Brahmins. In consequence of this, as might be expected, they are merely echoes of the misrepresentations of the Brahmins. But at last enough escapes from their own writings, notwithstanding all the attempts of the Brahmins at concealment, to shew that there was a Buddhism before the time of Cristna; and I never can forget the unexceptionable testimony of Arrian to the Indian Bacchus having long preceded the Indian Hercules.

In the various accounts which different authors have given us respecting Buddha, I perceive but one plausible objection to the theory which I have proposed of his being the Sun in Taurus, as all allow that he *was* the Sun; and that is, the difficulty of accounting for the Cristna of the Brahmins having come to Egypt. That a colony did pass from India to Egypt no one can doubt, and that, too, after the rise of the name and mythos of Cristna. At first to account for this, when the prejudices of the Brahmins against leaving their country or making proselytes is considered, seems difficult. Yet I think there are certain facts, now well known, which will justify us in supposing, that the Brahmins had not always the same objection to leaving their country which they have had for many centuries past. It is very certain that the Sanscrit language, in its present state, is an artificial one, and that it is not the oldest of India. Now, it is equally certain that the mythos did come to Italy; then it must have come previous to the Sanscrit being perfected. The examples of the personal verb, the formation of the degrees of comparison of the adjective, and the identity of the names of numbers, &c., with those of the Latin, which I have given in my *Celtic Druids*, decidedly and incontrovertibly prove the identity of the two languages. I suppose it will not be held that Italy has colonized India. Will any one be absurd enough any longer to maintain that Egypt colonized India, making *two* islands of Elephanta—*two* Matureas, carrying also thither an astronomical mythology, suitable to no part of its own territory, or of that to India, and that India sent back in return a language to Italy and the ΟΜ ΠΑΞ ΚΟΓΞ,[1] in language not *Greek* but *Indian*, to Eleusis?

The fact of the black God Cristna being found in Italy, Germany, Switzerland, and France, is of itself, independent of all other circumstances, sufficient to decide the question. How came the French and Italians to dye their own God *Cristna* black, before they sent icons of him to India? How came his mother to be black?—the black Venus, or Isis the mother, the virgin mother of divine love, of Aur or Horus, the Lux of St. John, the Regina Cœli, treading, in the sphere, on the head of the serpent—all marks of the Jesus of Bethlehem—of the temple of the sun, or of Ceres, but *not of Jesus of Nazareth*.

3. The following observation of Mr. Seely, is alone quite sufficient to determine the question as to which of the two countries, Egypt or India, colonized the other.

Mr. Seely says, " The Cobra capella, or hooded Snake, being unknown in Africa, except as " hieroglyphic, it may be concluded (as also from other arguments), that the Egyptians were the " depositaries, not the inventors, of their mythological attainments."[2] If it be true that there are *no snakes of this kind* in Africa, though they are very commonly found among the hieroglyphics, I

[1] Celtic Druids, Ch. II. Sect. XXVII.

By a *pretended emendation* of the text of Hesychius, a learned German of the orthodox school, of the name of Lobeck, has attempted to overthrow the argument of Col. Wilford respecting these curious words, but he is obliged first to emend the text. I prefer the opinions of Creuzer, Schelling, Munter, and Uwarrow, upon this passage, to that of Mr. Lobeck. Vide Foreign Quarterly Review, Jan. 1831, p. 51.

[2] On the Caves of Ellora, p. 216.

can scarcely conceive a more decisive proof, that the Egyptian mythology came from India. From the union of these considerations and *indisputable facts* I conclude, that, in very early times, soon after the sun entered Aries, the Brahmins did not, as at this day, object to travel from their own country; and I think we may find a probable reason for their present dissocial system being adopted. We know that the Buddhists, under the name of Sekhs or Jaines, have been for many centuries endeavouring to convert the Vishnuites, and it was probably to prevent this that their followers were forbidden by the Brahmins to hold any commerce with strangers, or to quit their own country: and that it was thus their rule of seclusion became established. There seems in this to be nothing very improbable. There is no miracle, nothing contrary to the order of nature, required here. Of course, I suppose this to have taken place some time after the change of the equinoctial festival from May to April,—from Taurus to Aries. This change, there is reason to believe, was not made without considerable bloodshed and confusion. But I think wherever it took place, there is now no Buddism, properly so called. I think there is evidence enough to prove that it took place in Egypt, and that Moses adopted it. We read in ancient times of several Brahmins having come into the West. But, according to Mr. Wilford, the difficulty really does not exist; for *he* says, " The Hindoos are not prohibited from visiting foreign countries,— " they are only forbidden to pass certain rivers; but there is no objection to their *ascending round* " *their heads*, so they only do not cross them." [1]   This interpretation has evidently been adopted to evade the law.

4. As we find that most of the other absurd doctrines with which fanatics and priests have loaded the religion of Jesus have come from India, so we also find that, from the same source, has come *original sin*. Mr. Maurice says, " It is the invariable belief of the Brahmins that man is a " fallen creature. Upon this very belief is built the doctrine of the migration of the souls through " various animal bodies, and revolving Bobuns or planetary spheres." Hence arose all the austerities of the Yogees, Fakirs, and other fanatics, which were carried to an excess that is scarcely credible.

The Rev. Dr. Claudius Buchanan has the following passage: [2] " The chief and distinguishing " doctrines of Scripture may be considered the four following—the Trinity in Unity: the incarna- " tion of the Deity: a vicarious atonement for sin: and the influence of the Divine Spirit on the " mind of man. Now, if we should be able to prove that all these are represented in the systems " of the East, will any man venture to affirm that it happens by chance?" No, indeed, no man, who is not a fool, will venture to say any such thing. The Doctor then goes on to admit, that the Brahmins must have known of the plural nature of the Aleim, which he calls the ELOHIM, the " Let us make man," of the first chapter of Genesis, the incarnation, the atonement, and the influence of the Holy Spirit,—the doctrine of regeneration or *man twice born*. Thus in having shewn that all these Jewish and Christian doctrines are to be found among the ancient Brahmins, I am supported in the fact by divines of the first eminence. The fact that the doctrines are common to the East and West of the Indus, cannot be disputed, and the only question will be, whether the East copied the doctrines of Christianity from the West, BEFORE the birth of Christ, for they were there BEFORE his birth, or the West copied from the East its ancient doctrines, to the corruption and almost ruin of the beautiful and simple system of their Founder and Saviour.

Original Sin, the foundation of the doctrine of the atonement, was not known to the early Christians, [3] and therefore it is perfectly clear that it cannot have been copied from them. Original

---

[1] Asiat. Res. Vol. VI. p. 533.   [2] Christian Researches in Asia, p. 266.
[3] See Jones on the Canon, Vol. II. p. 348.

Sin entirely depends on the story of the fruit-tree of Genesis being taken in a literal sense. But the ancient fathers of the church understood that it was an allegory; therefore, in their writings, there could be nothing about original sin. The doctrine is not known to the Romish or Greek Churches, and the reason of this is, in addition to what I have stated respecting allegory, that *these churches* make the text say, the woman, not the seed of the woman, shall bruise the serpent's head: " Inimicitias ponam inter te et mulierem, et semen tuum et semen illius: IPSA conteret caput tuum, et tu insidiaberis calcaneo ejus." [1] This decisively proves, when joined with the other circumstances, as I have said before, that the Hindoo doctrines have not been copied from the Christian. It seems probable that the doctrine of the Metempsychosis was gradually superseded by that of the Atonement in the Christian religion. The former was held by most or all the early Christians, to whom the latter seems to have been unknown. The two appear to me to be totally incompatible. Perhaps we do not find in history any doctrine which has been more pernicious than that of Original Sin. It is now demoralizing Britain. It caused all the human sacrifices in ancient times,[2] and actually converted the Jews into a nation of Cannibals, as Lord Kingsborough, in his splendid work on Mexican Antiquities, has proved that they were.

5. The reader will recollect what was said in the first chapter respecting the two Ethiopias—the opinion of Sir W. Jones and Mr. Maurice, that a nation of *blacks* formerly ruled over all Asia, and the other circumstances where the black colour occurred in various ways: and now I think he will be prepared for a few questions, for which I have been from the beginning paving the way: May not this nation have been a nation of *black* Buddhists? May not the peaceable religion of the curly-headed Buddha have pervaded and kept in peace for many generations, of which we have no history, the whole of Asia? May not the people professing it, have been the Palli or Pallestini of Mr. Maurice and Sir William Jones, or the shepherd kings or Cushites, of whom so much has been said? Sir W. Jones thought the seat of this empire may have been Sidon. The Grand Lama, or the sovereign priest of this empire, might as easily reside in the neighbourhood of Sidon, as in any other place. And in favour of this opinion, there are many trifling circumstances which may induce a person to think, that Mount Gerizim, the favourite place of Joshua, was, in very remote times, like the capital of the Lama of Thibet, a place of great sanctity. Who was Melchizedek? Was he a Grand Lama? That Gerizim, not Jerusalem, was his residence, we are told by the disinterested witness Eupolemus, whose evidence also is confirmed by various circumstances. Why should not a nation have ruled all Asia in peace, as the Chinese have done their empire, for several thousand years? If these were Jain Buddhists, their propensity to propagate their doctrine, so different from the practice of the Brahmins, easily shews why it was carried to the extremest West, and why it was found in Britain. But if they were the first people, the Celts, for instance, as I believe they were, and their religion the first, it would of course go with them.

" Buddha, the son of Máyá, is considered as the God of Justice; and the Ox, which is sacred " to him, is termed Dherma. So that this epithet, like that of Buddha, is not confined to any in- " dividual or any race."[3] " On the contrary, we learn from the Institutes of Menu, that the very " birth of Brahmins is a constant incarnation of Dherma, God of Justice." Here I think we have a Melchizedek. In the interior of the great temple of Bali, at Maha-bali-pore, is a couch called the bed of Dherma-rajah.[4] This compound word translated, is *Bed of the king of justice* or *Bed of Melchizedek.*

Against a nation, as Sir W. Jones thought, having ruled over all Asia, I see no objection; and

[1] Vulg.   [2] See Celtic Druids, last chapter.   [3] Camb. Key, Vol. I. p. 216.
[4] Chambers' Asiat. Researches.

if they were Cushite Buddhists attached to their religion in the way we see many oriental nations attached to their religion at this day, I know no reason why their royal high-priests should not have ruled them with justice, and in peace, for many generations, till they were disturbed, perhaps, by the inroads of some northern tribes. During this golden age a most intimate correspoudence among the priests of different and remote countries may have been kept up; and this may account for the transfer of the festival of Taurus to that of Aries, in some countries, in Britain perhaps, without any struggle. When I contemplate what the character of a Buddhist must have been before corruption crept into the religion, I can readily believe any thing which is good of a people professing it. The real, true, conscientious Buddhist, must have been an exact prototype of Jesus Christ, as I shall prove, both in doctrine and practice. It is pretty evident from the Pascal feast, the sacrifice of the Lamb, the change of the beginning of the year to the first of Aries, the anger at Aaron's Bull or Bulls, the going back of the Israelites to the Bulls of Bethavon, אן בית און *bit œi*, &c., &c., a great part of Moses's object was the change of the festival of the equinox from Taurus to Aries. I cannot help suspecting that in very ancient times a human being was sacrificed at the Pascal festival by some devotees, and that the story of Abraham's sacrifice of Isaac was the mythologic mode of describing the change, either from this worship, or from the offering of the bull or calf, to that of the Lamb, perhaps of both.

The simultaneous existence of the worship of the sun in Taurus with the sun in Aries, is, in most cases, easily accounted for. In general it was not an abolition of an old worship so much as the addition of a new one, which was required to keep the festivals in order. So that in most cases the two would go on amicably together, the prejudices of the followers of the old religion being indulged. Thus we find the festival of Taurus continued along with that of Aries in Britain. In the peninsula of India there appears to have been a severe struggle, and the old religionists were expelled; but even here some remains of the old or Tauric religion are found: for instance, in the temple at Jaggernaut, and at Mavalipuram or Mahabalipore, the city of the Great Bali, the ruins of which on the coast of Coromandel, near Sadrass, prove it to have been of vast size. In Egypt they appear to have gone on amicably. And we have Osiris, Apis, Serapis, and Jupiter Ammon—Osiris, after his death, regenerated, transmigrated into the body of Apis. Plutarch says that the Bull Apis was an image of the spirit of Osiris. [1]

CHAPTER IX

Baal—Sir Wm. Jones and the Desatir—Etymology of the world Bal—Dr. Hager on Apollo—Cufa Grass, Sacrifice of

1. BALA or Bal was one of the names of Buddha. [2] It cannot be modern; in most ancient times it is every where to be found—in Carthage, Sidon, Tyre, Syria, Assyria—the Baal of the Hebrews. It is impossible to modernize him. The temples with the Bull remaining, and the ruins of the most magnificent city of Maha-bali-pore not quite buried beneath the waves, and the

---

[1] De Is. et Osir.   [2] Wilford, Asiat. Res. Vol. X. p. 134.

figures in the temples prove the antiquity of this crucified God. Captain Wilford has pointed out some very striking traits of resemblance in the temples of Bal or Buddha, in Assyria, India, and Egypt: but this is not surprising, for they were all temples of Apis, the Bull of the Zodiac.

From a great variety of observations it appears to me that the earliest remains of antiquity may be expected to be found in the most remote situations—on the extreme bounds of continents, or in islands, or in places the most distant from the centre of migration. Thus, Syria from upper India; again, the Ionians on the West of Asia Minor, the British, and still more the Irish. In these situations the migrators from the first hive settled, and removed no more; and here, in consequence, the earliest habits, customs, and Gods, are found.

In the Indian Archipelago there are an island of Madura, and an island of Bali. In the first, where the Brahmin religion prevails, it is difficult not to recognize a duplicate of the Muttra or Maturea of Cristna, on the Jumna. In the second, Bali, we have the same name as the temples of Maha-Bali-pore, a little to the south of Madras—of the Bali so often connected in upper India with Cristna, of the Baal of Syria, of Han-ni-bal and Asdru-bal of Carthage, of Belinus of Bretagne, and of Baal or Bal-timore, Bal-linaaloe, and of the fires of the Baal of Ireland, through which the people yet pass their children, as they did of old time in Asia. The identity of these respective Bals does not depend on identity of names only, but is confirmed by historical and present existing facts and local customs, like that last named. [1]

Of the islands here alluded to Crawford[2] says,

" There are two islands near the east-end of the island of Java called Balli, or Baly, and Ma-
" dura. They have an acient language of their own, which differs entirely from their neighbours':
" the latter is the grand emporium of the Brahmin religion in the Indian Archipelago. It is now
" almost confined to these two islands."

When all the other circumstances are considered, it will not have surprised the reader to find the Hebrew God *Baal*, the bull-headed, among the Hindoo Gods. He is called *Bala-Rama* or *Bala-hadra*. He is the elder brother of Cristna, that is, probably, he preceded Cristna. M. Guigniaut says, Bala is evidently an incarnation of the sun; and Mr. Muller remarks, that he is a modification of *Sri-Rama*, and forms the transition or connecting link between *Sri-Rama* and Cristna. This *Sri* is evidently the שר *sr* or Osiris, with the bull of Egypt. This *Sri* is found in the Surya of India, which is no other than Buddha; as we have seen, it is the oriental word for Bull, שור *sur*, from which perhaps Syria, where the worship of Baal prevailed, had its name. Bali is allowed by the Brahmins to have been an incarnation or Avatar, but he is also said to have been a great tyrant and conquered by Cristna. In the history of this Avatar the rise of Cristnism is described. Vishnu or Cristna at first pretends to be very small, but by degrees increases to a great size, till at last he expels the giant, but leaves him the sovereignty of a gloomy kingdom. [3]

2. Sir W. Jones, in his Sixth Annual Discourse, gives an account of a celebrated Persian work, called the Desatir, written by a person named Moshani Fani, in which is described a dynasty of Persian kings descending from a certain Mahabad who reigned over the whole earth, by whom, he says, the castes were invented; that fourteen Mahabads or Great Buddhas had appeared or would appear; and that the first of them left a work called the Desatir, or Regulations,[4] and which was

---

[1] The word Baal or Bal was in fact a title of honour. Dr. Russell observes, " that this same title was conferred by
" the Phœnicians, the Persians, the Syrians, the Phrygians, and even by the remote people of India, on all their sove-
" reigns " The Jews, who passed their children through the fire to Baal, were called pupils of Buddha or Bauddhers.
2 Kings xvii. 17; Cambridge Key, Vol. II. p 220.

[2] Hist. Ind. Archipel. Vol. II. p. 97.   [3] Creuzer, Vol. I. p. 187.

[4] Of which we now have a translation, published by Mulla Firuz Bin Kaus, from the Courier press, Bombay, 1818.

received by Mahabad from the Creator. This Maha-Bad is evidently the great Buddha;[1] and the *Maha-Bul* or *Maha-Beli* the great Baal or Bol of Syria, with the head of a bull, in fact the sun—the whole most clearly an astrological or astronomical mythos or allegory. The Desatir, the work here alluded to, is written in a very *ancient language*, which, it is said, would have been unintelligible without the Persian translation. As a mythos the Mahabadian history of Moshani Fani is very interesting; as the true account of a dynasty of kings it is nothing. But I think there is great reason to believe that the Desatir is one of the oldest religious works existing, though probably much corrupted by the Mohamedan Moshani. This work confirms what I have said in B. V. Ch. V. S. 2, that Menu and Buddha were identical.

Sir William Jones maintains that Mahabad is the same as the Indian Menu; that the fourteen Mahabads are the fourteen manifestations of Menu; that the celestial book of Mahabad is the celestial book of Menu; and that the four castes of Mahabad are the four castes of Menu.[2] Mahabad and Menu were the same, because both were the sun. But they were probably not the same incarnation. This, however, is of little consequence.[3]

3. To return to the word Baal. The word בעל *bol*, called by us Baal, seems to be an original root. It makes בעלים *Bolim* in its plural. Schleusner says, Βααλ ὁ et ἡ Baal. Nomen Hebraicum indeclinabile; בעל *bol* quod significat *dominum*. Like the word אל *al* it seems to make both its masculine and feminine in ים *im*. בעל *bol* is also called אלהים *aleim*. It is said by Parkhurst to be equivalent to the Greek Ὁ ἔχων, one having authority. It is also said by him to mean the solar fire. Baal is also called *Lord of heaven*, which may be the meaning of בעל שמין *Bol smin*, translated Lord of heaven. But שמים *smim* or שמין *smin* meant the planets or the disposers. Its most remarkable meaning was that of a Beeve of either gender. It was an idol of the Syrians or Assyrians, often represented as a man with the head of a bull.[4]

In the Hebrew or Chaldee language, we see the word Baal is written בעל *Bol*. The Syrians had constantly the habit of changing the y *o* in the ה *e*, and the *e* into *o*; thus, with them, on the sea-coast, it was called בהל *Bel*. These sea-coast people were the Pelasgi, who went to Greece, and, from their changing the B into P, probably came the Greek Homeric verb Πελω *I am*. From these Pelasgic sailors of Syria, came the Bel or Belinus into the West. All this confirms Parkhurst's idea of its meaning ὁ ἔχων, or *one having authority*. From this comes the word Pelorus: Pel-aour, or Bel-aour—Self-existent fire—the son of Isis, the Maia or Great Mother. The true

---

[1] Vide Faber, Pag. Idol. Vol. II. pp. 74—83.   [2] Disc. on Pers. Asiat. Res. Vol. II. p. 59.

[3] Faber, Pag. Idol Vol III. p. 441.

It is clear to me that the Desatir is a work of Sabean Buddhists, or Buddhists who worshiped, as a kind of mediators, the Planets. With them Hurmusd is Jupiter, or Iao-piter. (P. 74.) The planets are all named and are supposed to have intelligent souls, and are called angels. The stars also are supposed to have intelligent souls. I shall hereafter say more respecting the fourteen Mahabads.

[4] For Bull-worship, see D'Ancarville, Vol. I.

My explanation of the word Pelasgi, in the Celtic Druids, Ch. VI. Sect. XXIX., is of considerable importance, as it removes many obscurities which are caused by these people in ancient history. I am happy to find myself supported in a conclusive manner by Bishop Cumberland, (Origen Gent. p. 295,) who says, " My opinion is, that their name " comes from πελαγος, by inserting the letter s, which was usually done in ancient times : and such were the times " when this name was first given. For one example of this, he is called *Mames* in *Dionysius Halicarnassensis*, who is " *Munes* in *Herodotus*. Again, Casmienæ for Camænæ : Casmillus for Camillus: and Dusmus for Dumus, &c., &c. " For I believe it only signifies that they were strangers that came by sea (πελαγος) to settle more commodiously than " they were before : so they might be adventurers of any tribe, family, or nation : or mixt of many that would agree to " seek their fortune by shipping into another country." Myrsilus, the Lesbian, says, the Tyrrhenians obtained the name of Storks or Pelasgi because they depart and return again. This shews them to be sailors. Niebuhr, Vol. I. p. 69.

God was originally called בעל *Bol*,[1] *Thou shalt no more call me Baali.* He was afterward called יה *ie* or יהוה *ieue*, which meant the Self-existent, and was the root of the word I*au*, or Iao-pater, Jupiter, and in Egypt, with the head of a ram, was called Jupiter Ammon. The followers of Baal were the worshipers of the sun in Taurus : those of Iao of Ammon—of the sun in Aries. From the word בעל *Bol* probably came our word Bull. Here the struggle betwixt the two sects of Taurus and Aries shews itself.

4. The Apollo of the Greeks was nothing but the name of the Israelitish and Syrian Bol בעל *bol*, with the Chaldee emphatic article prefixed and the usual Greek termination.

Dr. Hager says, " Heliopolis, (of Egypt,) or the city of the sun, where the first *obelisks* were " erected, and where the sun was first worshiped. It (Jablonski's Proleg.) seems that the name " of Apollo, or the sun among the Greeks, was likewise derived from *Bel*, otherwise Baal, with an " ain." Then, after some reasoning in which I cannot agree with him, he says, " Thus in the " Greek alphabet, which is derived from the Phœnician, the *o micron* stands exactly in the same " place where the ain (as he miscalls the oin) of the Phœnician stood, whose shape it also has re- " tained. Besides, what in Chaldæa was pronounced like an *a*, in Syria sounded like *o*—as *oluph* " instead of *aleph*, *dolath* instead of *daleth*, &c. If we then join a Greek termination, and prefix " the Phœnician article *Ha*, we have the Apollo of the Greeks and Romans, who had no aspirate " letters, like the modern Greeks and Italians, their descendants, or did not pronounce them. The " same *Bel* was also called *Pul :* which we ought not to wonder at, the ain being a guttural sound, " sometimes approaching to *a*, sometimes to *o*, and sometimes to *u*. Thence we find the different " pronunciations of *Bal*, *Bol*, *Pul*, just as *But*, *Pot*, *Fo*, in more Eastern countries."[2]

On le voit (Baal or Bel) comme nom du Soleil, says Count de Gebelin, sur des médailles Phé- niciennes de Cadiz et de plusieurs autres villes d' Espagne.[3] Hence Baalbek in Syria was called by the Greeks *Heliopolis*, and according to Macrobius Assyrii Heliopoli solem magnâ pompâ coluere sub Jovis Heliopolitani nomine.[4]

The most remarkable of the remains of the Indian Bal or Bala-Rama yet to be found in the West, is the temple of Heliopolis or Balbec in Syria. Jablonski informs us, that Bec and Beth are synonymous. Then this will be the בית *bit* or temple or house of Bal. The remains of the modern temple are very large and magnificent ; but I learn from an intelligent young friend and traveller, that this building is evidently of two dates—that it is a Grecian building, erected upon Cyclopæan foundations. There is one stone upwards of 60 feet long, and 12 feet thick, which is placed in a wall, at least 20 feet from the ground. The Cyclopæan remains prove that this temple was erected in the most remote æra. It is remarkable that, like Stonehenge and Abury, no Roman or Greek writer has noticed it before the time of Augustus. Antoninus is said to have rebuilt the temple, but it must have been on the old foundations. The Greek name Heliopolis proves, if proof were wanting, the meaning of the word Bal.[5]

---

[1] Hosea ii. 16.

[2] Diss. on Babyl. Ant. p. 35. That Bel was the Sun, see Voss. de Idol. ; Vitringa, Comment in Isa xlvi. ap. Brucker; Hist. Crit. Philos.; de Philos. Chaldæor. Lib. ii. Cap. ii. ; Hist. Babyl. ; Univers. Hist. Vol. III. Sect. ii.

[3] Monde Primitif, Vol. IV.   [4] Saturn. Lib. i. ; Hager, Dissert. on Bab. Ant.

[5] In my Celtic Druids, (p. 198,) I have derived Jupiter from Iao-pater. Mr. Sharon Turner (Trans. Soc. Lit.) en- ables me to go to a more distant fountain, perhaps the fountain-head of the same stream. He says, p. 49, Sanscrit *Matri* mother; p. 60, Sanscrit *Ipatri* father. Here are most clearly the *Mater* and *Pater* of Italy. But how came the *I* to precede the *Patri?* I think it was the same *I* which I have noticed in my Celtic Druids, Chap. V. Sect. XLII., as the sacred name of the Island of Iona, called II in the annals of Ulster, and by which the God Jehovah or יהוה *Ieue* is always called by the Chaldee paraphrases, which confirms what I there said respecting Iona. It is almost impossible to read a page of Sir William Jones's works and not to observe the elements of the word יהוה *ieue* recurring continually

5. The Hindoos have a sacrifice held in very high esteem which, their traditions state, goes back to the most remote æra : this is the sacrifice of a certain species of grass, called Cufa grass. This ancient sacrifice was also in use among the Egyptians. It is noticed by Porphyry *de abstinentid*,[1] in these words : " It seems that the period is of immense antiquity, from which a nation, " the most learned of all others, as Theophrastus says, and who inhabit the most sacred region " made by the Nile, began first, from the Vestal hearth, to sacrifice to the celestial Gods, not " myrrh, or cassia, or the first-fruits of things, mingled with the crocus of frankincense : for " these were assumed many generations afterward, in consequence of error gradually increasing, " when men wanting the necessaries of life offered, with great labour and many tears, some drops " of these, as first-fruits to the Gods. Hence they did not at first sacrifice these, BUT GRASS, " which, as a certain soft wool of prolific nature, they plucked with their hands."

The identity of the two sacrifices of grass assimilates very well with the veneration of the Egyptians and PHŒNICIANS for the cow.[2]

CHAPTER X

Yajna or Passover—Eight Vasus

1. IF the religions of Moses and the Hindoos were the same, it was reasonable to expect that we should find the celebrated Egyptian festival of the Passover in both countries, and it is found accordingly. We have it in the most solemn of the religious rites of the Brahmins, the sacrifice of the Yajna or the Lamb.

I have no doubt that, with the Hebrews, this succeeded to the Mithraitic sacrifice of the Bull ; and that it was in celebration of the passage or passover of the equinoctial sun from the Bull to the Ram. This history of the passage of the sun and of the passage of the Israelites from Egypt, affords a very remarkable example of the double meaning of the Hebrew books. The story of the ten plagues of Egypt might be very suitable for the rabble[3] of Jerusalem and London, but the higher classes in the former had, and I should hope in the latter now have, too much sense to believe such degrading accounts of the Deity as the LITERAL meaning of this history exhibits.

---

in the names of Indian Gods. It is, in fact, the יה *ie* Jah of the Chaldees. Father is also, in the Sancrit and Bali languages, *Pita.* The planet Jupiter is called *Vrihaspati* in Sanscrit. From the attributes of this God, Sir W. Jones has shewn him to be the Jupiter of the Latins. This is probably the *Patri* with some other word prefixed, perhaps as a title of honour : and it is probably the way in which *Ie* and *Ye* are used in the names of the Sanscrit Gods. But in the old Bali or Pali, a language much older than the improved Sanscrit, Mr. Turner gives Pati for father.

[1] Taylor, B. ii. p. 47.

[2] Ibid. p. 51. For want of a system, Mr. Maurice falls into great mistakes. In page 40 of his Modern History, ed. 4to., he calls Cristna *Bacchus* ; in p. 129, he makes him to be *Hercules* ; and in page 135, he makes him Bali. In one sense he is right, for they are all the sun, but the sun at different epochs. M. Guigniaut has observed, that all the Gods and Goddesses of India return or run into one another. This exactly accords with what the reader has already seen—that all the Gods and Goddesses of the Western world centre in the Sun.

[3] See Bryant on the Plagues of Egypt.

Rabbi Bechai, in commenting on the twelfth chapter of Exodus, speaks to the following purport : *Scripsit Maimonides, in ratione hujus præcepti, quod propterea quod sidus Aries in mense Nisan maxime valeret, et hoc sidus fructus germinare faceret, ideo jussit Deus mactare arietem.* Here is a pretty clear avowal on the part of Maimonides, the most learned of the Rabbins, that the paschal lamb was a type of the astronomical Lamb.[1]

Before the time of Moses, the Egyptians fixed the commencement of the year at the vernal equinox. R. A. Seba says, *Incipiebant autem Ægyptii numerare menses ab eo tempore, quo sol ingressus est in initium sideris Arietis,* &c. In the Oriental Chronicle it is said, that the day when the sun entered into Aries, was *solennis ac celeberrimus apud Ægyptios.* But this Ægyptian festival commenced on the very day when the Paschal lamb was separated. *Insuper die mensis decimo,* says R. A. Seba, *ipso illo die quo Ægyptii incipiebant celebrare cultum Arietis, &c., placuit Deo ut sumerent agnum, &c.*[2] In this festival the Israelites marked their door-posts, &c., with blood, the Ægyptians marked their goods with red.[3] The Hebrew name was פסח *psh* pesach, which means *transit.* The Lamb itself is also often called Pesech, or the Passover.

In India, the devotees throw red powder on one another at the festival of the Huli or vernal equinox. This red powder, the Hindoos say, is in imitation of the pollen of plants, the principle of fructification, the flower of the plant. Here we arrive at the import of this mystery. A plant which has not this powder, this flower or flour, is useless ; it does not produce seed. I could carry this farther, *sed sat* for the present.[4] This Huli festival is the festival of the vernal equinox ; it is the Yulé ; it is the origin of our word *holy ;* it is Julius, Yulius.

The followers of Vishnu observed the custom, on grand occasions, of sacrificing a ram. This sacrifice was called Yajna ; and the fire of the Yajna was called *Yajneswara,* or the God fire. The word " Yajna, M. Dubois says, (p. 316,) is derived from Agni *fire,* as if it were to this God " that the sacrifice was really offered. I need not point out the resemblance between the word " *Agni* and the Latin *Ignis.*" And I suppose *I* need not point out the resemblance of the word Agni to the Latin Agnus, to those who have seen the numerous extraordinary coincidences in the languages of Italy and India, which I have shewn in this work and in my Celtic Druids. Mr. Bentley says, (p. 45,) " Aries or the Ram is to be found in the sign of Agni, who, according to " the fictions of the Hindus, was feigned to ride that animal." It seems to me that the Rev. M. Dubois did not choose to see the *Agnus,* though he could clearly see the *Ignis.*

Agnus is not so properly the Latin word for a lamb as for an animal peculiarly dedicated to God, hostia pura ; therefore similar to the Greek αγνὸς purus. The lamb being the animal peculiarly sacred, thus became called Agnus. This the reader will see confirmed at once by turning to Moore's Hindoo Pantheon, (Plate 80,) where there are three examples of the Agni Avatar ; one is riding on a Ram, the other two have flags in their hands, on which are inscribed the Ram. He may also see the same repeated several times in the plates of M. Creuzer.

In this ceremony of sacrificing the lamb the devotees of India chaunt with a loud voice, *When will it be that the Saviour will be born ! When will it be that the Redeemer will appear !* The Brahmins, though they eat no flesh on any other occasion, at this sacrifice taste the flesh of the animal : and the person offering the sacrifice makes a verbal confession of his sins[5] and receives absolution.[6] On this I need make no observation. Mr. Parkhurst's doctrine of types explains

---

[1] Drum. Œd. Jud. p. 376.   [2] Ibid. p. 378.   [3] Ibid. p. 380.

[4] See a beautiful note, No. 66, in Professor Haughton's Laws of Menu, to which I shall return.

[5] Loubère says, auricular confession is practised by the Siamese.

[6] Travels and Letters of the Jesuits, translated from the French, 1713 ; London, 1714, pp. 14—23, signed Bouchet.

it to those who admit the doctrine of types. The Hindoos have a sacred fire which never dies, and a sacrifice connected with it, called Oman.[1] They have also the custom of casting out devils from people possessed, by prayers and ceremonies,[2] which is also practised by the people of Siam. All this is very important.

The first sentence of the Reg-Veda is said to be Agnim-ile, *I sing praise to fire.* Here we are told that Agnim means fire. When we reflect upon the slain lamb, and the call for the Saviour, we must be struck with the scene in the fifth chapter of the Apocalypse, from verse five to ten, where praise is given to the slain Lamb. The identity of the Mythoses cannot be denied.

That the word *agnus* means *lamb* every one knows; but it will, perhaps, be said, that though it may have this meaning in Latin or Etruscan, it has it not in Sanscrit. To this I reply, if it have not this meaning in the Sanscrit, it must have had it in the old language on which the Sanscrit was built, because it is impossible to consider the way in which we find the Indian language mixed with Latin, and to see the Agni always mounted on a lamb, or in some way or other accompanied by the lamb, and the lamb slain and burnt, without believing that, however it may have changed, it must once have had this meaning. But it probably had both the meaning of the Lamb and of fire—of the *Sun* in Aries. The whole seems to raise a presumption that this Lamb worship was in existence before the artificial Sanscrit was composed, and that the Brahmins have lost the meaning of their mythology as well as of their astronomy. I only wish my reader to cast his eye over the plates of the Agni in Moore and Creuzer, to be convinced of what I say. It is the same with the word Iaya, and several others, which I have pointed out in the course of this work.

It seems to me to be quite impossible for any person who has studied this subject, and considered the Zodiacal Agnus, the Yajna sacrifice, the worship of the lamb in the East and in the West, and the icons of Agni with the Lamb on them, to doubt that the Agnus means lamb: then, to such a person, the proof that the Agnus meant lamb, must carry the conviction, that the original language of the early mythology is lost. This is of great consequence, as it removes the only impediment to my interpretation of the name of the God מיה *ieue*, which, as I have shewn, is found in all the names of the Gods. I am told that, in the Sanscrit, Massib means alike Aries, fire, and Saviour. This is correctly the משיח *msih* of the Hebrew, the anointed, or Saviour. Thus the Lamb is the Messiah.

I know that my method of rendering many Indian names will be contested by Hindoo scholars, who will *poh, poh* me down,—as we are told by the traveller, *I have seen, Sir, and sure must know!* But I am not to be put down in this way. I tell them that their authority, in many cases, is exactly similar to that which was proffered to me in the case of the sacrifice of the Yajni. I said in a large party of learned Orientalists, that this sacrifice of the God Agni was not that of the God of Fire merely, but that also of the Lamb; the Aries of the Zodiac. I was *poh, pohed* down, put down with authority: these learned gentlemen said, it had not that meaning in Sanscrit; but as I persisted, and shewed them that the thing offered in the sacrifice was a Lamb, tasted by Brahmins on that occasion, though *they* never eat flesh at any other time;—that this God of fire, though always surrounded by a glory, was at the same time *invariably* accompanied by a Lamb, he mostly riding a lamb, they were silenced. The truth was, they had never looked so far. But the fact itself of this meaning of the word being lost in the Sanscrit, tends to prove the modern date of that language. I cannot believe that the Brahmins do not know the meaning of the word Agnus. Their wish for secrecy can be the only reason that I can imagine for the signification of it not being found in

---

[1] ON the generative power of OM.

[2] Travels and Letters of the Jesuits, pp. 14—23.   [3] Ibid. p. 29.

their dictionaries. Another example of *lost* signification is in the word Ya, Ya, chaunted in their ceremonies. I shall be told it means only *victory ;* but is not the God Jah, יהוה *ieue* and יה *iеiе*, always called the God of victory? It has, therefore, both these meanings. What can be more striking than the invocation in both cases of the slain lamb and of the Saviour?

There is in India a sect or tribe called Agniculas. These I suppose to be followers of the Cycle of the Agni or Igni. It is observed by Ainsworth, that the word Agniculus is not Latin. I think my readers will be satisfied, before I have finished, that the Sanscrit must have been formed upon a great number of other languages.

Yajn-eswara is Janus-osiris, or Lord Janus. Eswara is found united to numbers of words, and seems now to be used as an epithet of honour, like *Lord* with us. The sacrifice of the Ram is the Ram of the Zodiac at the vernal equinox. Thus the adoration of the Ram succeeded to the Bull, (but it did not entirely abolish it,) as in the case of Asteroth of the Sidonians, which had first the head of a Bull, and afterward that of a Ram.

2. I beg my reader to recollect that, in the ancient languages, the V and the l are perpetually confounded and written for one another, and that the Brahmins had eight Vasus,[1] or Gods of the winds, or of air in motion, and that Agni was the NINTH ; Agni, the Lord of fire, carried on the back of a Ram and sacrificed at the vernal equinox. Thus there were eight Vasus, the number of the Cycles B. C., and of the Salivahanas, of whom I shall treat by and by. This Wind was also called Vayu—query יהוה *ieie ?* I cannot help believing that Yasu-vati (query *Jesu-vates ?*) and Ya-du, the tribe of Cristna's ancestors, and Vasus and Vayu and Agni and the Lamb were all closely connected. Cristna is identified with *Vasu-deva* by the orthodox Vaishnavas.[2] Having first considered all the circumstances relating to Cristna, the extraordinary transformations which names undergo in passing from one country to another, and the interchanges of the letters V and I, I beg my reader to consider and compare the two syllables of the name *Vasu* with the word *Jesus*, and I think he will be obliged, with me, to entertain a strong suspicion that there has been some connexion between them. The word *deva* is evidently *deus*, and thus, with *Vasus*, making the God Vasus.

Jadu was the ancestor of Cristna,[3] that is, יה *ie*, ד *di, holy Ie*.

Moore says, " Agni is the Hindu regent or personification of fire." Again, " I will here observe, " that although all the Hindu deities partake more or less remotely of the nature and character of " Surya, or the Sun, and all more or less directly radiate from, or merge in, him, yet no one is, I " think, so intimately identified with him as Vishnu ; whether considered in his own person, or in " the character of his most glorious Avatara of Krishna."[4]

It is evident from a careful perusal of Moore, from pp. 265—272, that the Brahmins did not know what to make of the Vasus or holy air in motion. When Jesus was baptized in the Jordan, (a river having the same name as Padus and the Ganges,) he was filled with the Holy Ghost or air in motion, which descended in the form of a dove, and the Agni, or Lord of fire, appeared in the water.[5]

From the following passage of Porphyry, *de abstinentiâ,* I cannot help thinking the Yajna sacrifice is probably alluded to, which receives considerable confirmation from its connexion with Pythagoras, whose æra was the same as that of Buddha, B. v. Ch. ii. S. i. The *tasting,* but not *eating,* is the identical practice of the Brahmins. " The truth of this may also be perceived from the altar " which is even now preserved about *Delos,* which, because no animal is brought to, *or is sacrificed* " *upon it, is called the altar of the pious.* So that the inhabitants not only abstain from sacrificing

---

[1] Moore's Ind. Panth. p. 268.   [2] Colebrooke, Trans. Asiat. Soc. Vol. I. p. 576.   [3] Ibid. p. 538.

[4] Moore's Ind. Panth. pp. 294, 295.   [5] Justin Martyr.

" animals, but they likewise conceive, that those who established are similarly pious with those
" who use the altar. Hence the Pythagoreans, having adopted this mode of sacrifice, abstained
" from animal food through the whole of life. But when they distributed to the Gods A CERTAIN
" ANIMAL instead of themselves, *they merely tasted of it*, living in reality without touching other
" animals."[1] This is the very picture of the Brahmin practice at this day; it tends strongly to
satisfy me of the identity of the Brahmin and Pythagorean systems. In Book iv. p. 152, of the
same work, Porphyry informs us that in very old times, the sacrificing or indeed the using of the
flesh of animals was not practised either by the Athenians or by the Syrians—the Syrians, that
is the natives of the ancient city of Iona and the Pallistini, the Ionians, of whom I shall speak
presently. Advancing still eastwards, we find Porphyry giving an account of the Magi from Eubolus, who wrote their history, in which he states that " the first and most learned class of the Magi
" neither eat nor slay any thing animated, but adhere to the *ancient abstinence* from animals."
After this he goes to the Gymnosophists called Samaneans and Brahmins of India, of whom he
gives an account, and from which it appears that they have varied very little from what they were
in his time. But all these accounts seem to shew signs of the first black Buddhist people, as
eating no animal food—of the Black Pelasgi or Ionians, as coming to Italy and bringing the black
God and his mother along with them. And they not only brought the black God and his mother,
but they brought his house, the house at Loretto, as I shall shew in its proper place.

CHAPTER XI

Rasit, or Wisdom, resumed—Secret Doctrines—Bull-headed and Ram-headed Gods—Date of the System. Names of Buddha, &c.—Ignorance of the Brahmins and Ancients—Creuzer, Hammer, Guigniaut, &c.—Tree of Genesis at Ipsambul, and the same in Montfaucon

1. THAT the tribe of Israelites did go out from Egypt and conquer Canaan I feel no doubt; but
it is very clear to me that the priests, in their books, have wrapped up the whole in allegory;
that, in fact, as the learned philosophers of the Jews say, these writings had two meanings—one
for the priests, and one for the people. The former meaning, as might be expected, has been
nearly lost; the latter is still received by *most* Jews and Christians. What evils have been produced by the system of endeavouring to keep the mass of mankind in ignorance! The words
בראשית *b-rasit* no doubt had two meanings, one for the priests, and one for the people—*wisdom*
for the former, *beginning* for the latter. This is strengthened by the fact, that the Jews divided
their Cabala into two parts. T. Burnet says, Barischith et Merkavah, illic philosophiam naturalem,
hic Metaphysicam intelligi.—In the distribution and system of nomenclature adopted by Joshua
for the land of Canaan, an astrological, or, if my reader like it better, an astronomical system was
adopted of the same kind as that which the Israelites had left in Egypt. Sir William Drummond
has proved this in his Œdipus Judaicus. This was in compliance with an order in Deuteronomy

---

[1] Taylor's Trans. B. II. p. 65.

to pull down the altars of the nations they subdued, to cut down their groves, burn their graven images, and to destroy and blot out their names from under heaven. [1]

If divines deny that the word רִאשִׁית *rasit* means *wisdom*, and affirm that it only means *beginning*, they forget that they are *moderns* expounding a language which has been dead more than a thousand years, a great part of which the best judges have allowed to be lost, or no longer understood; and that they are deciding against the collected opinion of the divines or priests of the people whose vernacular language it was; in short, against the opinion of their church, held by that church when the language was yet a living one, and therefore must have been well understood. These reasons joined to those which I have before given, and by which I have shewn that the meaning *beginning* as applied to the creation is actually nonsense, fully justify me in maintaining that the word has two meanings, and that it means both *beginning* and *wisdom*. Besides, the reader will not fail to observe, that the meaning *wisdom* is in good keeping with all the cabalistic doctrines which must have been founded upon this verse. The Jewish Sephiroth consisted, as I have already shewn, of ten existences, which answered to the trinity, and to the spirits or emanations of the seven planetary bodies. By some later Jews the first three were said to be Hypostases, the other seven Emanations. Here we have the beginning of our Hypostatical Trinity. The first of the Sephiroth was *corona*, and answered to the Father, or *Brahma*; the second was *wisdom*, Σοφια, the Πρωτογονος and Λογος, and answered to *Vishnu*, the Preserver; the third was *prudentia* or Πνευμα, and answered to *Siva* in his regenerating capacity. I confess it appears to me to be somewhat presumptuous for a modern divine to assert, that a word in an ancient *dead* language, a religious epithet, *has not* the meaning which was given to it by the priests of that people whose language it was, when it was a *living* language, merely because it does not support a modern religion. Like many other words, it had two meanings. In this case the translation of the word רִאשִׁית *rasit* will rule the word Αρχη.

2. The pretended genealogy of the tenth chapter of Genesis is attended with much difficulty. It reads like a genealogy: it is notoriously a chart of geography. It is exoterically *genealogical*, esoterically *geographical*. I have no doubt that the allotment of the lands by Joshua was astronomical. It was exactly on the same principle as the nomes of Egypt, which every one knows were named astronomically, or rather, perhaps, I should say, astrologically. The double meaning is clear; but probably the exact solution of the whole riddle will never be made out. Most of the names which are given in the tenth chapter of Genesis are found in the mystic work of Ezekiel. The works of all the prophets are mystical. This chapter divides the world into 72 nations. Much ingenuity must have been used to make them agree with the exact number of dodecans into which the great circle was divided. But who, after observing this fact, can help seeing the mystical character of the chapter? Many of the works of the Greeks were equally mystical.

I request any person to read the travels of Pausanias in Greece, and he must be astonished at the puerile nonsense which that good man appears to have believed. But did he believe it? Was not the book written merely for the amusement of devotees, like the *novels* of our evangelical ladies or gentlemen?—like the Paradise Lost of Milton? It is evident he knew that there was a *secret* doctrine, for in several passages he admits it in distinct terms.[2] "*But the particulars respecting the pomegranate*, as they belong to a secret discourse, I shall pass by in silence." Again,[3] "that such of the Greeks as were formerly reckoned wise, designedly concealed their wisdom in enigmas: and I conjecture, that what I have just now related concerning Saturn contains some-

[1] Ch. vii. 5, 24, ix. 14.   [2] B. i. Ch. xiv., B. i. Ch. xxxvii., B. ii. Ch. xvii.
[3] For the mystical nature of the pomegranate, see Cumberland's Origines Gentium.

"thing of the wisdom of the Greeks. And we should consider things relative to divine concerns "after this manner." Plutarch undertakes to prove that Osiris and Bacchus are the same, without recourse to the secret rites, which are not to be divulged.

Speaking of the statements respecting the Gods in Homer, Maximus Tyrius says, "For every "one on hearing such things as these concerning Jupiter and Apollo, Thetis and Vulcan, will im- "mediately consider them as oracular assertions, in which the apparent is different from the latent "meaning." This is confirmed by Herodotus, who constantly says, when describing things in Egypt, there is a sacred reason (ἱερος λογος) for this, which I shall not give. I suspect that Cicero, Pausanias, &c., were like Gibbon and Warburton, and many other of our authors, who, for the sake of the peace of society, pretend to be what they are not, a mischievous device of the priests, which has done more to retard the improvement of mankind than all other causes put together.

3. The Greeks have been supposed by some persons to have learnt their mythologies from the Egyptians. But I have shewn, on the authority of their own writers, that all their OLD oracles came from the Hyperboreans by way of Thrace. Their Eleusinian mysteries I have also shewn to have come by the same route, probably from India. I consider Osiris, Bacchus, Astarte with the Bull's head, Bol or Baal, Mithra, Adonis, Apis, and Buddha, to have been contemporary, or to have constituted one class. In the same manner I consider Hercules, Cristna, and (Jupiter) Ammon, and Astarte with the Ram's head, to have been contemporary, or to have formed a second class. My theory is strikingly confirmed by the fact, which, I believe, has not been noticed before, that the first class are all ταυροκιφαλοι, or Bull-headed. Buddha is closely allied or connected with the Siamese or Japanese bull, breaking the Mundane egg with his horn, and was partly man, partly bull, in Persia, as Mr. Faber has proved; and therefore I conclude from this, exclusive of the other reasons given above, that these Gods are nothing but the Sun in the sign of Taurus, at the vernal equinox: and the other class are all κριοπροσωποι, or Ram-headed, and are in like manner, for similar reasons, the sun in the sign of Aries, at the vernal equinox. Several of those which were first bull-headed became ram-headed in later times. Ammon, for instance. In the histories of the births, deaths, funerals, and resurrections, of all these Gods, a striking similiarity prevails, as I shall shew in a future page; but yet there are between the two classes some trifling discrepancies. These discrepancies probably arose from the circumstance that one class refers to the adventures of the God Sol in the sign of the Bull, the other to those of the God Sol in the sign of the Ram. It is evident that almost every where civil war arose on the change of the worship from Taurus to Aries. But though this may account for the trifling differences which we find, yet we may readily suppose that the great points of resemblance, being equally applicable to the sun in both cases, might remain unaltered.

The adoration of the Bull still continued in most countries after the equinox had receded to Aries. This was the case in Egypt, where Apis still continued, though Ammon with his sheep's-head arose—if he did not, as I believe he did, change his beeve's head for that of a ram. I have shewn that Ammon meant the generative power of Am, or Aum, or Om: but Am was the Bull

---

¹ B. viii. Ch. viii.　　　　　² De Iside et Osir. Sect. xxxv. Squire.
³ Max. Tyr. Ed. Taylor, p. 87, and Dissertation xvi.
⁴ In Fig. 3, Plate 36, Vol. II. of the Montf. (Ant. Exp.) is exhibited an Isis sitting, nursing the infant Orus. She has the head of a cow, but the body of a woman. Plutarch (de Iside et Osir. Ed. Squire, Sect. xxxv. p. 46) says, that to Bacchus the Greeks gave the face and neck of an Ox. The women of Elis called Bacchus Ox-footed; the people of Argos called him Ox-begotten. Porphyry (de Abstin. Sect. xvi.) says, the Greeks united the Ram to Jupiter, but the horns of a Bull to Bacchus.

Mithra, Buddha—therefore it must have changed. The prayers to the God Bull, of Persia, given by Mr. Faber, are very curious. Asteroth, or Astarte, in Syria, was first represented with the horns and head of a beeve, and in later times with those of a sheep.[1] Thus in India the Bull, the emblem of Buddha, continued to be adored long after Cristna arose, and along with him at some few places.

From Waddington and Hanbury's voyage up the Nile, I think it appears that in Egypt, as in Syria, the emblems of the conjoined Sun and Moon, the Cycle, the Crescent, and the Disk, which are found on the oldest Tauric Monuments, were taken from the Bull, and removed to the Ram.[2] I think the lunette and circle on the head of the Bull, and in later times on the head of the Ram alluded both to the compound cycle of the Neros, and to the precession, or to the male and female generative powers.

In the temple cave at Ellora, the Bull Nundi, or Nandi, is placed opposite to the Yoni and Liugham, as an emblem of the prolific power. In this temple, on each side of the entrance is a Sphinx, similar to those in Egypt, placed on the outside of the entrance exactly in the same manner.[3]

I have already remarked on the alleged disinclination of the Brahmins to leaving India for the purpose of colonization. I do not think Egypt was first colonized by them as the priests of Cristna, but by Buddhists, the worshipers of the Sun in Taurus. The story and effigies of Buddha are so similar to those of Cristna, that the Seapoys of India, when in Egypt, might very readily mistake one for the other. But the theory of religion, as time advanced, would cause the Ram-headed God to arise in both places, without copying one another; and supposing the icons not exactly the same, they might be near enough to exhibit the same mythos to our seapoy officers and men, who would not be very careful inquirers. Yet every thing tends to confirm what I have before said, that there is reason to believe the first Brahmins were not so averse to communicate with, or to visit foreigners, as are those of a later day : and thus the worship of Cristna may have been brought at a later period to Egypt.

M. Dubois confirms my opinion that the Brahmins came from the north, and that they established their religion on the ruins of that of Buddha. He adds, that he lived in the midst of the Jainas or followers of Buddha, and that they far surpassed the Brahmins in probity and good faith.[4] Herodotus[5] says the Pelasgians learnt the *names* of their Gods from the barbarians; "that at first they " distinguished them by no name or surname, for they were hitherto unacquainted with either; but " they called them Gods, which by its etymology means disposers, from observing the orderly dis- " position and distribution of the various parts of the universe." It is easy here, I think, to recognize the planets, the disposers, the שמים *smim*, of the first book of Genesis.

4. In all our speculations hitherto, we have reasoned that the facts under consideration must have taken place *before* such or such a time. I think we shall now be able to deduce a very important consequence in an opposite direction. We have seen that the days of the week are, in the most remote corners of the world, called by the names of the same planets, and in the same order, and these planets after the same Gods. The universality of this shews its extreme antiquity— that in all probability it must have been adopted before the human race became divided into nations. But the fact that all these Gods were identified with the Bull of the Zodiac in some way or other, proves that they must have been adopted later than the time when the sun, at the vernal

---

[1] Drummond, Orig., Vol. III. p. 229.   [2] Landseer, Sabæan Res. p. 228.
[3] Seeley's Wonders of Ellora, p. 138. The cave temples in Cabul are 12,000 in number, all dedicated to Buddha. Ibid. p. 139.
[4] Pp. 42, 305, 324, 326, 327, 549, &c.   [5] Euterpe, LII. p. 377.

equinox, entered Taurus by the true Zodiac, which would be about 4700 years before Christ. (A very great French philosopher, Mons. Dupuis, for some other reasons, has thought this time so much too short, that he has been induced to suppose the period ought to be thrown back, to where Taurus would be at the autumnal equinox, about 11,000 years; but, though this might be correct, yet I think sufficient proof of its correctness is not produced.) This consideration seems to offer something like a boundary to our researches; something like a distant view of our journey's end, which I greet with pleasure; for I think we can find no traces of any thing before the Tauric worship commenced. And this brings our chronology to agree, as near as can be expected, with the various systems. The *eight* ages, about the time of Augustus, cannot be doubted. If these were 600 years each—4800, and we add a thousand before the Tauric worship commenced for mankind to arrive at their then state of civilization, we shall not be very much out of the way in our calculations.

The *Disposers*, as Herodotus says the Pelasgi first called their Gods, that is, the שמים *Smim* of Genesis, or the Planets, were in later times all called by names appropriated to the days of the week which were dedicated, by astrologers, to the Gods who were typified by the Bull: Monday to the horned *Isis*; Tuesday to Mercury, the same as Hermes and Osiris; Wednesday to Woden; Fo, Buddha, and Surya; Thursday or Thor-day, or תור *Tur*, (written both Tur and Sur,) or Taurus, or Bull-day, to Jove or Jupiter, who, as a Bull, stole Europa, which shews what he was at first; (the manner in which he is called not merely *Jupiter*, but *Jupiter* with the word *Ammon* added, seems to shew that the two words were not always joined. In Montfaucon's Antiquities [1] may be seen an account of various Jupiters connected with the Tauric worship, which proves that, although he had latterly the head of a Ram, he had originally that of a Bull.) Friday was dedicated to Venus, Ashteroth, or beeve-horned Astarte; Saturday to Saturn, identified by Mr. Faber [2] with Moloch and the *Centaur Cronus* or Taschter; Sunday to the Sun, every where typified by Taurus. All these, I think, must have taken their names after the entrance of the Sun into Taurus; and before this date all history and even mythology fails us. Each of the days and the planets had a monogram, consisting of a *cross* with some form annexed to it; another proof of the great antiquity of the adoration of the cross.

But yet it seems fair to infer, that man must have existed a great number of years before he could have divided the heavens into signs, degrees, &c., &c. How long a time may have been required for this I pretend not to say. It must have depended upon that which we can never know, the exact state in which he was turned out of the hand of his Creator. But I think many generations must have passed before the May-day festivals were established in Britain and India.

Some of the cave-temples of India which are *arched*, are, on that account, supposed to be more modern than those with *flat* roofs; but I think this is a hasty inference. If, indeed, the arch were formed of wedge-shaped stones, like modern arches, this would be probable; but when the curve is merely cut out of the solid granite without any of the architectural knowledge necessary in throwing an arch, I do not think the inference warranted. Mr. Seely says, " Karli and Canarah " are evidently the production of the followers of Buddha." He states, that the arched temple of Vishvacarma at Ellora is also Buddhist; and he adds, " Their whole history is involved in such a " labyrinth of mystery from beginning to end, that there is not the most remote chance, by the " deepest research, of arriving at any satisfactory data." [3] I hope Mr. Seely is mistaken. But in the assertion of the unsatisfactory nature of all the theories hitherto proposed, he is certainly correct.

What I have said respecting the temple of Jaggernaut in Orissa being *Buddhist*, is confirmed by

---

[1] Fig. 8, Plate 11, p. 31.   [2] Pag. Idol. Vol. II. p. 86.   [3] Pp. 186, 194.

one of the flat-roofed cave temples at Ellora being dedicated to him by the name of Jaggernaut, i. e. Creator.[1] The Brahmins not being able to conceal the Buddhist doctrines in some of their temples, without their entire destruction, are obliged to admit a ninth Buddhist Avatar, at the same time that they most absurdly maintain that this Buddha, this ninth Avatar, was an impostor. It is singular enough that the Buddha in the cave at Ellora is called the Lord paramount, the Maha-Maha-Deo,[2] the great great God. At this temple the Brahmin uttered the name BUDDHA without any hesitation, which is what a Brahmin will seldom do.[3] Their ninth Avatar was a Buddha, because he was an incarnation of *divine wisdom*, perhaps not understood by modern Brahmins. The Brahmins and Buddhists have, as already stated, each the same number of Avatars, and, at the time of Jesus Christ, they both say that eight were gone, and that a ninth then came. The Buddhists say he came among them, and was called Buddha. The Brahmins affirm that he came among them, and was called Salivan, of whom I shall treat hereafter. This is the reason why they allege that the ninth Buddha was an impostor.

It is no small confirmation of the superior antiquity of Buddha, that over *all* India, whether among Bauddhas, Saivas, or Vaishnavahs, the day of Woden, or Wednesday, is called BUDHVAR.[4] In Sanscrit it is Bou-ta vâr, and in the Balic, Van Pout; in the northern nations, Woden's day; the latter having no B, write W,[5] where the reader may also find additional proofs that Mercury or Hermes, Sommonacodom and Buddha, are all the same—with Maia for their Mother.

As I have formerly said, the fact of Buddha giving name to one of the days of the week, Wednesday, fixes him to the very earliest period of which we have any record or probable tradition. He is acknowledged to be the Sun or the Surya, with seven heads, of Siam and Japan and Ceylon; and to be the son of Maia. Thoth and Teutates and Hermes are allowed to be identical, and Hermes is allowed to be Mercury; and Mercury is the God to whom Wednesday is dedicated, and the mother of Mercury is Maia. Sir William Jones clearly proved that the first Buddha was Woden, Mercury, and Fo, and I think, however he may have alarmed himself and his prejudices when he came to see the consequences of his proofs, he never was able to overthrow them.[6] Mr. Faber says, " The Egyptian cosmogony, like the Phœnician, is professedly of the Buddhic school: for the " fullest account which we have of it is contained in a book ascribed to Hermes or Thoth: but " Hermes or Thoth is the same person as Taut, who is said to have drawn up the Phœnician sys- " tem: and Taut again is the same as the Oriental Tat or Buddha."[7]

The Tau, T, is the emblem of Mercury, of Hermes. It is the *crux ansata*, and the *crux Hermis*. It was the last letter of the ancient alphabets, the end or boundary, whence it came to be used as a terminus to districts; but the crux Tau was also the emblem of the *generative power*, of eternal transmigrating life, and thus was used indiscriminately with the Phallus. It was, in fact, *the phallus*. The Tau is the Thoth, the Teut, the Teutates of the Druids;[8] and Teutates was Mercury, in the Sanscrit called Cod or Somona-cod-om; and in German God. In old German Mercury was called Got. The remains of the crosses are to be found in the highways at the boundaries of the parishes, and every where at cross-road ends in this country. They have precisely the same meaning as the Roman Terminuses, and had the same origin. It is the same with the crosses which have now the crucified Saviour on them, all over the continent, and, being engrafted into Christianity, were thus preserved. Many of them are thousands of years old.

---

[1] Seely, Wond. of Ellora, p. 218.
[2] Here, in the repetition of the word Maha, we may perceive the Hebrew practice of expressing the superlative degree by a repetition of the adjective.
[3] Seely, Wond. of Ellora, 220.   [4] Moore's Pantheon, p. 240.   [5] See Asiat. Res. Vol. I. pp. 161, 162.
[6] Asiat. Res. Vol. VIII. 8vo. p. 531; also Diss. on Chron. of Hind. Asiat. Res. Vol. II.
[7] Pag. Idol. Vol. I. p. 223.   [8] See Herod. Euterpe, LI. p. 375.

M. Sonnerat thinks Rama is Buddha; "Sir W. Jones is of a very different opinion, and thinks " that Dionysos and Rama were the same person."[1] They are both right, they all were the Sun: and it is very surprising to me that those gentlemen did not perceive that what applied to one, applied to all three; with this only exception, perhaps, that one might be the Sun in Taurus, the other the Sun in Aries. And into the Sun, in his male or female character, all the great Deities of India and the Western world resolve themselves. I think it not improbable that many images ascribed to Cristna may belong to Buddha—their histories being so very similar.

5. The uncertainty of the real names of the Gods of India has been pointed out by Mr. Seely, who, after stating that he has detected the Brahmins in forgetting names which they had bestowed a day or two before on the same figure, says, "On making inquiries the Brahmins rather confound " than assist in your researches. Each has his favourite deity and peculiar local name, generally " accompanied with some fanciful theory of his own. My Brahmin was a native of Poonah; he " was fond of his Wittoba, Ballajee, Lakshmi, and others, and wished them to be paramount in all " the temples. A different list would have been preferred by a Benares Brahmin; while a coast " (Coromandel) Brahmin would probably have been for the Buddhist heroes. If to this discrepancy " we add the numberless host of minor or secondary deities, all with their consorts, giants, sages, " and holy men, the whole wrapped up in impenetrable and mysterious fable, some faint idea may " be entertained of the difficult and abstruse subject of Hindoo mythology." The description is, I do not doubt, just. The accounts of the present Brahmins can be little depended on. Of the minor details of their mythology they are totally ignorant. After a careful consideration of the work of the father of history, Herodotus, I have no doubt that the generality of priests in his day were as ignorant as the Brahmins in ours. The Priests, whenever they were ignorant of a fact, coined a fable, which the credulous Greek believed and recorded; and which the still more absurdly credulous modern Christians continue to believe. Witness, as one out of many examples, the history of Jupiter and Europa,[2] believed by classical scholars to have been actually a king and queen, to have reigned, had children, &c., &c.

I cannot help thinking that even the oldest of both the Greek and Roman writers, unless I except Homer, were absolutely and perfectly ignorant of the nature of their Gods—whence they came, and of what they consisted. As the people by degrees emerging from barbarism began to open their eyes, they found them. They received the Gods from their ancestors, who, having no writers, transmitted their superstitions, but not the histories of their Gods. Whether the initiated into the mysteries were any wiser seems very doubtful. But I think it is possible that the only secrets were, the admission of their own ignorance and the maintenance of a doctrine respecting the nature of God (of which I shall treat hereafter) and in substance of the unity of God. We can hardly suppose that such men as Phornutus, Lucian, and Cicero, were not initiated in the higher mysteries. Then, if the nature of the Gods had been known in these mysteries, I think we should not have those men writing about them: and, in every sentence, proving that of their real nature they were perfectly ignorant. If they were not ignorant, they were dishonest. But this I can scarcely believe. If they *were* ignorant I cannot entertain a doubt that Messrs. Dupuis and D'Ancarville were much more likely to discover the secret nature of the Gods than Cicero or Phornutus, Porphyry or Plutarch. The mistaken vanity which prevented these latter philosophers from looking to the Barbarians for their Gods, tended to keep them in a state of ignorance, in a bondage from which we are free, and, in consequence, are much more likely to discover the truth.

I shall be told *I* have a theory. This is very true: but how is it possible to make any sense out of the mass of confusion without one? And are not facts sufficient collected to found a

---

[1] Seely, p. 176.   [2] Drum. Orig. Vol. III. p. 82.

theory upon? My theory has arisen from a close attention to the facts which transpire from the writings of a vast variety of authors, and is, I think, a theory which will be found to be established by them. I have not first adopted my theory, and then invented my facts to confirm it. The facts have come first, and the theory is the consequence. Whether they be sufficient to support the theory, is the only question. This must be left to the reader. I feel confident that I can explain every thing which appears inconsistent with the theory, unless it be a very few of the histories of the inferiors Gods, which may very well be supposed to have been mistaken or mistated, by the Priests, whose ignorance or deceit is acknowledged.

6. After studying with great attention the very learned and able review of the German authors Creuzer, Hammer, Rhode, Goërres, &c., by Mons. Guigniaut, my opinions founded on the works of Maurice, Bryant, Cudworth, Stanley, &c., are nothing shaken. I am more than ever confirmed in my opinion, that all the Gods of the ancients resolve themselves into one—the Sun, or into the refined or spiritual fire seated in the Sun: and that the Trinity, contended for by Mr. Maurice and Mr. Faber, cannot be disputed. The hypothesis of Mr. Maurice, respecting the great antiquity of the worship of the Bull of the Zodiac, can never be overthrown, until it can be shewn that all our Indian travellers, who tell us of the celebration of our May-day games and April-fool festivals, have deceived us. I place my foot upon the identity and ubiquity of these Tauric, Phallic Games, as upon a rock, from which I feel nothing can remove me. They set at defiance all books and all systems of chronology. Next to them is the reasoning of Mons. Bailly on the septennial cycle, and on that of the Neros. Collectively they form a mass of evidence of the existence of a state of the world in a most remote period, very different from what any of our historians contemplate. In searching into the records of antiquity it is impossible to move a step without meeting with circumstances confirmatory of the Tauric worship, the date of which the known precession of the equinoxes puts out of all dispute. My excellent and learned old acquaintance Mr. Frend would make the cycles Antediluvian, but how are the bull on the front of the temple of Jaggernaut, and hundreds of other similar circumstances, to be accounted for? Was the temple built before the flood? I am very far from wishing to depreciate the learned and meritorious labours of the German scholars to whom I have just alluded, but I feel confident if they had paid a little more attention to the FACTS pointed out in the writings which contain the whimsical theories [1] of our Bryants, Fabers, &c., they would have been more successful in discovering the secret meaning of the ancient Mythoses. Had they attended to what is indisputable —that all the Gods of antiquity resolve themselves into one—the Sun—either as an original object of worship or as the type, or the Epiphania, or Shekinah of the triune male and female Deity, they would have found themselves in their researches relieved from many difficulties.

Protestant priests for some years past have endeavoured to shew that the Mosaic accounts are to be found in India, and generally among the Gentiles. What good this can do them I cannot understand. However, they have certainly succeeded. The labours of the learned Spencer have shewn that there is no rite or ceremony directed in the Pentateuch, of which there is not an exact copy [2] in the rites of Paganism. The Rev. Mr. Faber has proved that the Mythoses, as the Romish Dr. Geddes properly calls them, of the creation and the flood have their exact counter-

---

[1] Though I call them whimsical I mean no disrespect to their authors. The world is much obliged to these gentlemen for their labours.

[2] From this must be excepted some few laws adopted by the Jewish law-giver to make a line of demarcation between his people and the Gentiles—such, for instance, as the Sabbath on the *last* instead of the *first* day of the week, and a few others that are very apparent. The object of Moses was to restrict his law to the Jews as much as possible, to the exclusion of all other nations. The object of the law of Jesus was to restore the worship of Jehovah to all nations,

parts among the wild mythologies of the followers of Buddha and Cristna ; and the history of the serpent and tree of life have been lately discovered by Mr. Wilson to be most correctly described on the ruins of the magnificent temple of Ipsambul in Nubia.[1]   So that it is now certain, that all the first three books of Genesis must have come from India : the temple at Ipsambul, as well as the famous Memnon, being the work of the ancient Buddhists—the latter proved most satisfactorily by Mr. Faber.

After what the reader has seen he will not be surprised that I should have been struck most forcibly by an observation which seems casually given by M. Denon in his account of the Temples in Upper Egypt. He does not appear to have been aware of its importance, or, indeed, in a theological point of view, that it had any importance at all. In[2] speaking of a very beautiful small temple of the ancient Egyptians at Philoe, he says, " I found within it some remains of a " domestic scene, which seemed to be that of Joseph and Mary, and it suggested to me the sub- " ject of the flight into Egypt, in a style of the UTMOST TRUTH and interest."

It is said, by late travellers, that the Christians converted the ancient temples of Upper Egypt into churches, and they thus account for the Christian Mythos. But in this case, at Ipsambul, the pretence is totally destitute of foundation, because the figures were in that part of the temple which was buried in sand, and were excavated by Belzoni. No person will believe that the sand was brought here since the Christian æra. But I shall discuss this matter at length presently.

7. In the supplement to Vol. I. of Montfaucon,[3] is exhibited a tree, on the two sides of which are Jupiter and Minerva. He says, " It was preserved for several centuries in one of the most " ancient churches of France, and passed for an image of terrestrial paradise, to represent the fall " of Adam. The tree bearing fruit, in the middle, passed for that from whence the forbidden fruit " was gathered. The robe on Jupiter's shoulders, the thunderbolt which he has in his hand, the " helmet on Minerva's head, and her habit covering her all over : these particulars might easily " have undeceived persons moderately versed, I will not say in mythology, but even in the history " of the Bible, that it was a mere conceit. But in those times of simplicity, people did not con- " sider some things very closely. Jupiter holds the thunderbolt raised in his right hand ; he has " a robe on, which does not cover his nakedness. Minerva is armed with a helmet and dressed " as usual : the serpent at her feet is the peculiar symbol of Minerva polias of Athens, which " seems to support the opinion of the gentlemen of our academy, that this agate relates to the " worship of Jupiter and Minerva at Athens. The tree, and the vine curling round the tree, the " goat beneath Jupiter's foot, and all the animals pictured about—the horse, the lion, the ox, and " others, seem to denote nature, of which Jupiter is the father. An Hebrew inscription graved " round the gem, appears to be modern ; it is in Rabbinical characters, scarcely to be deciphered : " the sense of it is this : *The woman saw that the tree was good for food, and that it was pleasant* " *to the eyes, and a tree to be desired to make one wise.*"[4]

Who can help seeing here a refined allegory ? Here is the God Ieo, Jove, יהוה ieu. Here is Minerva, divine wisdom, which sprung from the head of Jove—the πρωτογονος, the first-begotten, Buddha. Here is the tree of the knowledge of good and evil. Here is the vine with its fruit

---

pure and undefiled as held by Melchizedek. Moses made his Sabbath on the day of Saturn, in opposition to the festival of all other nations, which was on the *dies solis.* The doctrine of the Nazarite of Samaria being intended for the whole world, his followers acted very properly in restoring the festival to the dies solis, on which no doubt it was in the time of Melchizedek, of which religion Jesus was declared to be a priest.

[1] Wilson's Travels ; Franklin's Researches on the Jeynes, p. 127.

[2] The English Trans. by Arthur Aikin, 1803, Vol. II. Chap. xiv. p. 169.

[3] Ant. Exp. Plate 5, Fig. 17.   [4] P. 35. See my plates, fig. 16.

united to the elm, which Virgil met with at the side of the road to hell, loaded with science—as the Mem, the 600, was united to the *vin* in the name of the word Muin, the name of the letter which denoted the most sacred of the cycles. The elm is commonly planted in Gaul and Italy for the vine to ascend, and selected as the tree of knowledge, because it was the name of the first letter of the alphabet, or the Aleph of the Hebrews, which meant the trunk of a tree, which was the tree of Virgil, and bore all the remainder. The circumstance of this gem having a Hebrew legend round it is exceedingly curious, and is not to be got quit of by the observation of Montfaucon, the innocent produce of his prejudice and ignorance, that it appears to be *modern*. It was of the same school with the Virgo Paritura, the Bacchus's Wine-cask and Tiger-hunt of St. Denis,[1] the Isis of Notre Dame, and several other matters which I shall adduce in their proper time and place.

In fig. 9 of the 52nd plate of the Supplement to Montfaucon's *Antiquité Expliquée*, there is a representation of Abraham sacrificing Isaac: but Abraham has not a sword or a knife, but a thunderbolt, in his hand. Can any thing be more clear than that the makers of these very ancient gems considered that the story of Abraham covered a mythos? Vishnu or Cristna is often represented with thunder and lightning in his hand—as in the act of giving the benediction with *three* fingers, and as wearing a triple crown.

CHAPTER XII

The Eagle Garuda—Spencer, Faber, Burnet, Calmet, &c., on Genesis and its Allegory—Faber's Trinity of the Indians and the Hebrews

1. THE following example of an Eastern mythos, in the West, will be thought not only curious, but will be found, in a future page, to involve some important consequences.

Mr. Moore says, " Sonnerat notices two basso-relievos placed at the entrance of the choir of " Bourdeaux Cathedral : one represents the ascension of our Saviour to heaven on an Eagle : the " other his descent, where he is stopped by Cerberus at the gates of hell, and Pluto is seen at a " distance armed with a trident. In *Hindu* pictures, VICHNU, who is identified with Krishna, is " often seen mounted on the Eagle GARUDA, sometimes with as well as without his consort " Lakshmi.[2] And were a *Hindoo* artist to handle the subject of Krishna's descent to hell, which " I never saw, he would most likely introduce Cerbura, the infernal three-headed dog of their " legends, and Yama, their Pluto, with the *trisula*, or trident : a farther presumption of early in- " tercommunication between the Pagans of the Eastern and Western hemispheres."[3] An account

---

[1] In the church of St. Denis near Paris. See Prel. Obs. Ch I. Sect. 115.

[2] Whence comes the name of Cristna's consort Lakshmi? We will write it as it may be pronounced, and we shall have no farther trouble—L'Akmè. It is not surprising that Wisdom, חכמה *Akme*, should be the wife of Cristna, the incarnation of Vishnu, the second person or the Logos of the Indian trinity; but it is very curious, indeed, that we should find it here in Greek and modern French. If this stood alone, it might be taken for accident, but with its concomitant circumstances, this cannot be admitted. I believe the Lamed of the Hebrew is often used as an emphatic article, as it is in the Arabic, Italian, and French. It is an abbreviation of the Arabic *Al*. Thus we find it in the word Aceldama—*Ac* place of, *el* the, *dama* blood.

[3] Pantheon, p. 214.

is given by Arrian of a visit of Alexander the Great to the cave of Prometheus [1] on the borders of India.

In addition to what Mr. Moore and M. Sonnerat have said, I beg to observe that Bourdeaux, in whose cathedral this Garuda was discovered by them, is watered by the river Garumna, evidently the Latinised Garuda or the Frenchised Garonne. It is situated in the department of the Gironde. Messrs. Sonnerat and Moore seem to have overlooked the striking names of the river and the department. Respecting Garuda and Prometheus, Colonel Wilford says, " I inquired after Garuda-" sthan and was perfectly understood. They soon pointed it out to me in the Puranas and other " sacred books, and I immediately perceived that it was situated in the vicinity of Cabul, where " the historians of Alexander have placed it, and declare that this hero had the curiosity to go and " see it." [2] He then states how he inquired for the legend relating to Prometheus and the eagle in the books of the Buddhists, where he found it, and from which inquiry he discovered, that the Buddhists and Vedas had many valuable books of their own, different from those of the Brahmins, by which he was induced to retract an opinion hastily given against the Buddhists. [3] The eagle Garuda, as appears from Moore's Pantheon, is intimately blended with the history of Cristna in a variety of ways: and, if I mistake not, forms in the three facts of the Garuda at Bourdeaux on the Garumna, in the Gironde—of Alexander's visit—and of its connexion with the Cristna of India and the Cristna of Europe—a chain of evidence in proof of the intimate connexion between the East and the West; and equally so of the existence of Cristna and his mythos in India long previous to the birth of Jesus of Nazareth; though perhaps not of Jesus of Bethlehem. And this again overthrows all Mr. Bentley's doctrines, except recourse be had, as I believe it ought to be had, to renewed cycles. Admit the cycles, and Mr. Bentley's alleged proofs are all in my favour.

Prometheus formed the first woman, for the formation of whom he stole fire from heaven, &c., &c. The word Prometheus is the Sanscrit word PRAMATHAH or PRAMATHAS, which comes from PRA-MAT'HA-ISA, which coalescing, according to the rules of Sanscrit grammar, [4] form PRAMATHESA. Now, *Bra* is the Siamese *Pra*, creator or former; Matha is Mati, in the Bali language *Mother*, and esa is Isa or Iscah or Eve or Isis—the whole meaning, maker of mother Eve or Isis. It is no small confirmation of what I have said, that Prometheus, the name of the *Greek* God, is *Sanscrit;* [5] as is also Deucalion, his son. The latter is Deo-cala-yun or Deo-Cala-Yavana. There is an account of his contest with Cristna, who was driven from Mathura by him, but by whom he was at last, with his Ya-vanas, finally expelled from India. On this I shall say more presently. I am well aware of the forgery practised on Colonel Wilford, but the knavish priest could not forge the image in Bourdeaux Cathedral, nor the passage in Arrian respecting Alexander the Great. I am also well aware, that an elegant, flowery style of writing would have the effect of convincing many readers better than dry facts. People of this description are not worth converting to any opinion, and no opinion of theirs can be worth having. But to persons of critical judgment, who know the value of evidence, a fact of the kind here stated is worth volumes of declamation. The authority of the ancient historians of Alexander, in a case circumstanced like this, cannot be doubted; nor, in consequence, can the fact that there was a cave of Prometheus in the time of

---

[1] In my account of the cave of Prometheus, I have carefully omitted the parts where Colonel Wilford was deceived by his Pundit.

[2] Asiat. Res. Vol. VI. p. 512.   [3] Ibid.   [4] Ibid. p. 515.

[5] The absolute identity of the Indian mythos at Bourdeaux and the Indian mythos of Prometheus and his Eagle, of whom I shall have much more to say hereafter, will prepare us for the reception of another and a similar mythos at Baieux, in a future page of this work.

Alexander, in Upper India, some one of the numerous cave temples yet remaining, similar to those at Ellora, Elephanta, or Cabul—hereby decidedly proving that the Greek mythology was not brought *into* India in the time of the Seleucidæ, as a learned and ingenious author has, as a last resource, alleged. This is of the same nature as that of the Hercules at Matures, as described by Arrian, and noticed before. These are *proofs* not *probabilities*. Trifling as they appear to be at first sight, they are worth volumes of fine reasoning. They are like the Maypole, and April festival in India and in England, and must carry conviction to the mind of every person who knows the value of evidence. Many facts of this kind cannot be expected, but very few, *one* indeed, if it be clear, is enough to prove the truth of the suspected history. It has also been said, that if the books of the Hindoos, the Vedas, &c., had been in existence in the time of the Seleucidæ, the Greek authors would have noticed them. I do not admit that the argument has any weight, when the contempt of the Greeks for the Barbari is considered; and when it is also considered with what difficulty we have obtained the Brahmin books. It is as inconclusive as the argument of those who maintain that Stonehenge is modern, because the Romans do not notice it.[1]

2. How the proof of the histories in Genesis being intermixed with the mythoses of the Gentiles can be of any service to the defenders of the literal construction of these books, I cannot conceive. It seems to me that if the plagues of Egypt and the history of the flood were found in every parish throughout the world in the most ancient of times, they would not be rendered in their literal meaning in the least degree more credible, not even though supported by the Oracles, the Sibyls, and the affirmations of the priests. Throughout all the world the same system prevailed, nor could any country be properly said to have copied its system from others. It travelled with the aborigines; with them it flourished, and with them decayed: at first as the religion of Buddha, that is of Brahma or divine wisdom, afterward as the religion of Cristna, another incarnation of the same being or hypostasis.

Mr. Faber[2] says, " The close resemblance of the whole Levitical ceremonial to the ceremonial " in use among the Gentiles has often been observed, and has differently been accounted for. This " resemblance is so close and so perfect, that it is alike absurd to deny its existence, and to as- " cribe it to mere accident. The thing itself is an incontrovertible matter of fact: and it is a fact " which might at first seem to be of so extraordinary a nature, that we are imperiously called on " to account for it." Again, he says,[3] " Spencer has shewn at full length, that there is scarcely " a single outward ordinance of the Mosaical law, which does not minutely correspond with a " parallel outward ordinance of Gentilism."

If persons will only reflect a little they will perceive that, if every ordinance of the Jews is the same as the ordinances of the Gentiles, the Mythoses must necessarily be the same: that is, that the religions in their chief part must be the same.

Mr. Maurice says,[4] " After all, we must own, with Calmet, that the temple of the great " Jehovah had many decorations similar to those in the hallowed temples of Asia. He was served " there, says the last cited author, with all the pomp and splendour of an Eastern monarch. He " had his table, his perfumes, his throne, his bed-chamber, his offices, his singing-men and his " singing-women."

Mr. Faber states three ways of accounting for these facts. The first is, that the Gentiles copied

---

[1] Since I published my CELTIC DRUIDS, it has been observed to me, that of all the numerous tumuli which surround Stonehenge and which have been opened, though a variety of articles have been found, there has not been the least appearance of any thing Roman or of later people's. Can a more decisive proof be desired, that the bodies were buried before the time of the Romans, and that the tumuli ceased to be cemeteries on their conquest of the island?

[2] *Orig. Pag. Idol.* Vol. III. p. 624.   [3] Ibid. p. 629.   [4] Ind. Ant. Vol. V. p. 174.

from the Jews. This he easily refutes. The second is, that the Jews copied from the Gentiles. Of this he says, " The second theory, which is precisely the reverse of the first, and which sup-
" poses the Levitical ark to be a copy of the ark of Osiris, is wholly unincumbered, indeed, with
" chronological difficulties : but it is attended by others, which, perhaps, are scarcely less formi-
" dable. Its orignal author was, I believe, the Jew Maimonides : the learned Spencer has drawn
" it out, at full length, and has discussed it with wonderful ingenuity : and the mighty Warburton,
" without descending to particulars, has given it the honourable sanction of his entire approba-
" tion." [1]   He then satisfactorily shews that neither of these schemes is defensible, and undertakes to prove, that all the ceremonial and ritual in principle originated from an old patriarchal
religion. And in this I quite concur with him; though I cannot allow that religion to have consisted in the adoration of Noah, his ark, and his family ; the idea of which is to me altogether ridiculous, too ridiculous to deserve a serious refutation. But by and by I shall shew from what
patriarchal religion these Mosaic rites were derived. [2]

Had not Mr. Faber been bound by the prejudices of his education, and by the sacerdotal oaths
which he took, whilst almost a boy, and by which he in fact solemnly engaged never to abandon
the former, I have no doubt that my present labours would have been unnecessary. No man
before him ever came so near the truth. The following is nearly his account of the ancient
philosophy, taught in the mysteries, with the exception of a few sentences which I have omitted,
and which are inserted by him to make it apply to his ship and old women—to make his ship and
old women appear the originals, and the heavenly bodies and the recondite philosophy, the
mythological representations under which they were disguised ; instead of the heavenly bodies
and the philosophy being the originals, and the ship and old women the mythological representations under which the latter were concealed from the vulgar eye. He has certainly proved the
second and third books of Genesis to be Hindoo Mythoses.

As we have seen, it is acknowledged that the Jewish and the Gentile ceremonies are the
same. It is also admitted that neither can have been borrowed from the other. We have
seen also, that the doctrines are the same. Then is it not reasonable to look for the origin of the one,
where you look for the origin of the other? At first, the same system must have pervaded
the whole world. I think I have already proved, that all ancient nations, almost within even the
reach of history, had a form of worship without idols. The ancient Latins, the ancient Greeks,
the Egyptians, the Pelasgi, the Syrians, who made treaties with Abraham and Isaac, had no
names for their Gods. What can this universal religion have been, but that of Buddha or
Brahma ?

If it be true that the Pentateuchian system is a mythos, or more properly several detached
parts of a mythos, in principle the same as the mythoses of the neighbouring nations, it is no ways
surprising that it should have many traits of similarity to them. The reader has seen what I

---

[1] Orig. Pag. Idol. Vol. III. p. 628.

[2] Although our great men can swallow the literal meaning of the first chapter of Genesis now, and find no difficulty
in it ; yet the stomachs of the ancients were not quite so capacious. Siracides says, the world was not created day
after day, but all at once—*simul* in the Latin Vulgate ; χοινῆ in the LXX. (Eccles. xvi. 1.) Philo calls it silly, to think
that the world was made in the compass of six days. Lib. Alleg. St. Augustin also says, it was produced at one time.
(De Civ. Dei, Lib. xi. Cap. xxxi.; Morer. Dial. on the Sabbath, II. p. 107.) The absurdity of the history those
men could not get over, therefore they had recourse to explanations. And although the SAINT, Augustin, could not
believe such things, he was canonized ; but if a man doubt *now* he is damned. But the fact was, that all these apparent
absurdities had an allegorical meaning, and do not prove, as some persons have imagined, the falsity of the religion ;
they only prove that the esoteric religion has not been thrown open to the vulgar. The esoteric religion was a masonic
mystery ; I am under no tie, and I will explain to the world what it really was.

have said to have been the foundation, or nearly the foundation, of all the mythoses of antiquity; but he has yet a great deal more to see. It is natural to suppose that in long periods of time, and in different nations and languages, great changes would take place, and that a vast variety of minor systems or mythoses would arise. It is equally natural to expect that a general similarity should nevertheless prevail, *or*, that in all the different superstructions some traces of the original should be found. As with the systems of *writing*, though they became very different, yet enough (indeed super-abundant) relics of the old first language are apparent in all of the sixteen-letter system, to shew that they are all from one source. From the above-named mythoses, Mr. Faber and Nimrod have selected a great number of similar matters, which have given to their systems a certain degree of plausibility. The ingenuity of Mr. Faber is shewn in annexing the word *Helio* to the word ark, by which means he succeeds in attributing to his imaginary worship of the ship, the real worship of the sun. Divide the words, and what will apply to the sun, is, in general, ridiculous as applied to his ship or to an old man, the exalted father its sailor: and, on the contrary, what will apply to the ship is ridiculous as applied to the sun. But it is impossible to deny, from the facts, the etymologies, and the analogies, pointed out by these learned and ingenious devotees, that it is apparent an universal mythos has prevailed—that the Pentateuch and the Iliad (of which I shall say more hereafter) have originally had the same mythological doctrines for their foundations. These gentlemen taking the allegorical or mythological accounts of the Bible to the letter, have made the mythoses of the Gentiles bend to them. Had they possessed understandings a little more enlarged, their learning and ingenuity would probably have organized the chaos. But what can be expected from persons, however learned, who believe like Nimrod that the old Gentile oracles *really* prophesied,[1] or that the possession of human beings by dæmons once prevailed.[2] Persons who can believe in dæmonology, second sight, witchcraft, and similar nonsense,[3] although very learned and skilful in writing novels, or making pictures, are weak men, undeserving the name of philosophers. They may amuse a few of their sect to-day; posterity will only smile to-morrow.

The philosophy in question taught that matter itself was eternal, but that it was liable to endless changes and modifications; that over it a demiurgic INTELLIGENCE presided, who, when a world was produced out of chaos, manifested himself at the commencement of that world as the great universal father both of men and animals: that, during the existence of the world, every thing in it was undergoing a perpetual change: no real destruction of any substance taking place, but only a transmutation of it: that, at the end of a certain appointed great period, the world was destined to be reduced to its primeval material chaos: that the agent of its dissolution was a flood either of water or of fire: that at this time all its inhabitants perished; and the great father, the Brahme-Mai, from whose soul the soul of every man was excerpted, (i. e. emanated,) and into whose soul the soul of every man must finally be resolved, was left in the solitary majesty of abstracted meditation: that, during the prevalence of the deluge and the reign of chaos, he floated upon the surface of the mighty deep, the being on which he reposed being represented by a ship, a lotus, an egg, the sea-serpent, the navicular leaf, or the lunar crescent: that the two generative powers of nature, the male and female, were then reduced to their simplest principles, and were in a state of mystic conjunction brooding on the surface of the deep. The Brahme-Maia or Great Father was but mystically alone: for he comprehended within his own essence three filial emanations, and was himself conspicuous in eight distinct forms:[4] that at the close of a divine year, the deluge abating,

---

[1] P. 488, of Supp. Edition.   [2] Also Dolphin, p. 405, *ib.*

[3] Vide story of the Ghost seen by the Rev. Mr. Ruddle, &c., &c.! in Nimrod, p. 588, *ib.*

[4] Wonderful to tell, Mr. Faber can see nothing here but Adam, Cain, Abel, and Seth—or Noah, his wife, and Shem,

the Great Father awaked to the reforming of the world out of the chaotic mass; and that he appeared with his three emanations,[1] and in his eight forms,[2] as he had appeared at the commencement of former worlds: that this new world was destined to run the same course as former worlds: that this alternation of destruction and reproduction, was eternal both retrospectively and prospectively: that to destroy was, consequently, nothing more than to create under a new form.[3] This is the doctrine which Mr. Faber supposes was taught in the ancient mysteries, except my leaving out and altering some trifling parts forced in to suit it to his peculiar theory. But it will not be denied to be on the whole a sublime system. It has the merit, too, of being, when thus corrected, nearly the true system of the first sages of antiquity.

3. The following account of the Hebrew and Indian Trinities, according to Mr. Faber, is very striking:

" In the preceding citations from the Geeta, we may observe that Vishnou or Crishna is identi-
" fied with Brahm, although one of his three emanations; and we may also observe, that in the
" single character of Brahm, all the three offices of Brahma, Vishnou, and Siva, are united. He is
" at once the creator, the preserver, and the destroyer. He is the primeval Hermaphrodite, or
" the great father and the great mother blended together in one person. Consequently he is the
" same as the hermaphroditic Siva, in the form which the Hindoos call *Ardha-Nari;* the same
" also as Brahma and Vishnou, for each of these is similarly an hermaphrodite by an union with
" his proper Sacti or heavenly consort;[4] the same moreover as the Orphic Jupiter and the Egyp-
" tian Osiris; the same as Adonis, Dionusus, and Atys; the same, in short, as the compound
" great father in every part of the pagan world."—" Yet this compound great father, as the whole
" of his history shews, is not the true God; but a being, who has been made to usurp his attri-
" butes. He is primarily Adam and the Earth, and secondarily Noah and the Ark. In the former
" case, his three emanations of children, who partake of his nature, and who discharge his pre-
" tended functions, are Cain, Abel, and Seth; in the latter, they are Shem, Ham, and Japhet.
" Accordingly, Brahm himself is declared to be the same as Menu; and Brahma, Vishnou, and
" Siva, are identified with those three sons of Menu, who appear at the commencement of every
" Manwantara, whose proper human names are said by the Hindoos to be *Sama* and *Cama* and
" *Pra-Jupati,* and who transmit to their descendants the sceptre of sovereignty throughout the
" whole duration of their allotted period.

" On this point the Hindoo writers are sufficiently explicit; though by their wild system of
" personal multiplication and repeated Avatarism, they have superinduced a certain degree of con-
" fusion. The evidence may be summed up in the following manner:

" We are taught on the one hand, that Brahma, Vishnou, and Siva, are essentially but a single
" person; and this single person is Brahm, who unites in himself the divided attributes of the

---

Ham, and Japhet, and their three wives—in all eight. He either conceals, or his prejudice has blinded him to the Brahme-Maia, the Supreme Being and his three emanations—Brahma, Vishnu, and Siva—the creator, the preserver, and the destroyer; and the eight planetary bodies, the Sun, the Earth, the Moon, and the five Planets. I really can hardly bring myself to the belief that he can be so blind. But he pretty well proves where the mythos of Genesis came from, or on what it was founded.

[1] Powers. The forming power, the preserving power, and the destroying power; attributes of omnipotence.

[2] The planetary substances having form, his Angels or Messengers, the שמים *amin.*

[3] Orig. Pag. Idol. Vol. III. p. 117.

[4] From this hermaphrodite described by Mr. Faber, probably came the construction of the verse in Genesis, (*so God created man in his own image, in the image of God created he* HIM; *male and female created he* THEM,) that the first male and female human beings were joined in one body, or were, in some way, Hermaphroditic. This was the belief of many Jews and Christians in former times. Here, as usual, we go to India, both for the book and its meaning.

" three; and that the triplicated Brahm is materially the World, astronomically the Sun, and mys-
" tically the great Hermaphrodite, who is equally the father and the mother of the universe. But
" we are told, on the other hand, that Menu-Swayambhuva is conjointly and individually Brahma,
" Vishnou, and Siva; that he had three sons, who sprang in a mortal shape from his body, and
" who named his three daughters; and that these three sons were severally Brahma, Vishnou, and
" Siva.

    " Such are the declarations of the Hindoo theologists; and the inference to be drawn from them
" is abundantly obvious. Since Brahma, Vishnou, and Siva, are conjointly Menu-Swayambhuva;
" and since they are also conjointly the imagined supreme God Brahm; it is evident, that Brahm
" and Menu-Swayambhuva must really be the same person. And again, since Brahma, Vishnou,
" and Siva, are severally the three sons of Menu-Swayambhuva; and since they are also three
" supposed emanations from Brahm; it must plainly follow, that the famous triad of Hindoo theo-
" logy, which some have incautiously deemed a corrupt imitation of the Trinity, is really composed
" of the three sons of a mere mortal, who, under the name of Menu, is described as the general
" ancestor of mankind. Brahm then at the head of the Indian triad, is Menu at the head of his
" three sons. But that by the first Menu we are to understand Adam is evident, both from the
" remarkable circumstance of himself and his consort bearing the titles of *Adima* and *Iva*, and from
" the no less remarkable tradition that one of his three sons was murdered by his brother at a sa-
" crifice. Hence it will follow that Brahm, at the head of the Indian triad, is Adam at the head of
" his three sons, Cain, Abel, and Seth." [1]

    This may be true, unless the reader should think with me that the profound Hindoo doctrine
does not arise from the history of the men, but that the doctrine is disguised under the allegory of
men to conceal it from the vulgar eye, after the manner of all the other Mythoses of Antiquity.

    Again, Mr. Faber says, " Each Menu, however, with his triple offspring, is only the reappearance
" of a former Menu with *his* triple offspring; for, in every such manifestation at the commence-
" ment of each Manwantara, the Hindoo Trimurti or Triad becomes incarnate, by transmigrating
" from the human bodies occupied during a prior incarnation; Brahm or the Unity appearing as
" the paternal Menu of a new age, while the triad of Brahma, Vishnou, and Siva, is exhibited in
" the persons of his three sons. The first Menu, therefore, with his three sons, must be viewed
" as reappearing in the characters of Menu-Satyavrata and his triple offspring—Sama, Cama,
" and Pra-Japati. But the ark-preserved Menu-Satyavrata and his three sons, are certainly
" Noah and his three sons, Shem, Ham, and Japhet. Hence again it will follow, since Menu-
" Satyavrata is only a reappearance of Menu-Adima, and since the triplicated Menu-Adima is the
" same as the triplicated Brahm, that Brahm at the head of the Indian triad is likewise Noah at the
" head of his three sons." [2]

    Notwithstanding the nonsense in the above extracts about Brahm being the world, &c., and the
ingenious misrepresentation that Brahm is not the true God, enough transpires to shew that the
mythoses of the Israelites and of the Brahmins are essentially the same. When this is added to
the general character of the history, of the serpent, of the tree of knowledge, &c., &c., and to the
proof which has been given by Sir W. Drummond, in his Œdipus Judaicus, that the names of
the persons and places in Genesis have astronomical meanings, I think no one can hesitate to
agree with the ANCIENT JEWS AND FATHERS OF THE CHRISTIAN CHURCH, that the whole is
allegory. In this I believe few people would differ from me, if a literal interpretation were
not wanted to bolster up those pernicious heresies, Original Sin and the Atonement—the wild
chimeras of insane fanatics, of former times, and held by the moderns through the prejudices of

---

[1] Faber, Orig. Pag. Idol. pp. 117, 118.   [2] Ibid. p. 119.

education. How surprising that a man of learning and talent like Mr. Faber should succeed in persuading himself that the Platos and Ciceros of antiquity, were contemptible enough to adore three or four old women and a rotten ship!

It seems never to have occurred to Mr. Faber, in his attempt to prove that all the profound theories and learning of the Platos, Pythagorases, and Hindoo philosophers, were nothing but figurative representations of his ship and old women, that he might prove the ship and its crew were nothing but an allegorical representation or an incarnation of the theories of the philosophers. However, with great learning and talent, he has certainly rendered this extremely probable, if he have not actually proved it—which, indeed, I think most unprejudiced people will allow that he has done. In this he has shewn that the priests of the Israelites were like those of all other nations, who dressed up or disguised their recondite philosophical doctrines under the representation of human adventures of different kinds, in order the better to secure to themselves dominion over the vulgar—that vulgar who will be in a fury with me for endeavouring to undeceive them.

The similarity of the numbers, in the Mosaic history, with the numbers constantly recurring in the Hindoo systems, seems very striking. Here are Adam and his three sons, and Noah and his three sons, each class answering to Brahm and his three emanations—Brahma, Vishnou, and Siva. There are eight persons in the ark, answering to the sun and seven planetary bodies. But whether the histories of Adam and Noah and their families were taken from the metaphysical and profound theory of the hermaphroditic creator, preserver, and destroyer—the sun presiding over the planetary system; or, the recondite system was formed, and the sun and planets numbered after him and his family, I leave to every person to judge of as he thinks proper. The pious devotee, to the literal meaning, will, no doubt, take the former. I incline to the latter, which will enable me by and by to prove the truth of Christianity to the philosophers. But I do not mean by Christianity, that of the Pope, putting up the picture of the massacre of St. Bartholomew in his chapel; or that of Calvin, burning Servetus; or that of Cranmer, burning Joan Bocher.

The book of Genesis was considered by *most*, if *not all*, of the ancient Jewish philosophers and *Christian fathers* as an allegory. For persons using their understandings, to receive it in a *literal* sense, was impossible: and when we find modern Christians so receiving it, we only find a proof that, with the mass of mankind, reason has nothing to do with religion, and that the power of education is so great, as in most cases to render the understanding useless. In the Jewish religion, as in all other religions, there was an esoteric and an exoteric meaning of its dogmas. One great object of Moses evidently was to destroy idolatry; he was of the Iconoclastic sect—that was all. He was, in fact, of the Linga sect of the Indians, and of the Persee sect, or of the religion of the Persians. He adored the sacred fire as the emblem of the Supreme Being, precisely after the manner of the Oriental nations, and he reprobated the worship of Adonis, the name equally of the Israelitish and Heathen God, and Astarte, in the shape of a Golden Calf,[1] at Sinai. This was the chief object of his system; but something more will be pointed out hereafter.

---

[1] In the annunciation of the festival of the golden calf Aaron expresses himself in the following words: Festum Adonai cras. (Selden de Diis Syriis Synt. I. Cap. iv.) In Arabia, where Aaron then was, Bacchus, the Saviour, was adored under the name of Urotalt, and under the title of Adonai or of Adoneus. (Auson. Epig. 29.) Urotalt is evidently the two Latin words *Urus* and *Altus*—the lofty Bull or Beeve. Probably the title of Urania, given to Venus, came from the Urus. The junction of the two, the Venus and the Urus produced God the generator. D'Ancarville, Vol. I. p. 47.

In Jer. xlvi. 15, the LXX render the passage, ὁ Ἄπις, ὁ μοσχος ὁ εκλεκτος σε—Apis thy chosen Calf. This is justified by forty-six of Dr. Kennicot's manuscripts, which read אבירך *abirk* in the singular, and not אבירך *abirik* in the plural. Now, as I look upon the LXX as a most valuable gloss, and as being unprejudiced wherever it gives a meaning against the doctrines of the Jews of its own or of later times, I pay much attention to it, particularly when, as here, I find it supported by the various readings.

There is one fact which must, I should think, have been observed by every person conversant with inquiries of the nature of those on which I have been employed, and it is this: all those works, without exception, which we call early histories, are deeply tainted with mythology; so that we have not, in fact, one early real history. Whatever may have been the cause, the effect is, that the early history of every state, like that of Rome, has been made use of as a kind of peg to hang a system of priestcraft or mythos on. The mythos, not the history, is the object of the writer: as might be expected, the *history* bends, not the *mythos*, if they do not fit. Of this the early Roman history is an example. The historians not understanding it have recorded as history the most palpable nonsense. Herodotus is an example of this. His story is the first in Greece which was told for the purposes of history. All former stories were for the purpose of a secret doctrine, desired to be perpetuated in secrecy: first verbally told in verse or rhythm for the assistance of the memory, next written. Such were the works of Hesiod and Homer.

Mr. Faber has clearly proved, as the reader has seen, that the Mosaic accounts of the creation, and of the flood of which I shall treat in my next book, are to be found in the works of the Hindoos; the outlines or great points being evidently the same. Yet the particulars differ sufficiently to induce a suspicion, that they are not copies of each other, but were probably drawn from a common source. The material parts of the history may be true. I believe it, as I believe the history of Tacitus. I believe that Vespasian lived; but Vespasian's miracles, as related by him, I cannot believe. I believe in a creation; but I do not believe that God walked in the Garden. I believe in a flood; but I cannot believe that all the animals of the old, as well as those of the New World,[1] were put into one ship. Many other things I believe, and many other things I do not believe; but it is always a pleasure to me to find (if the doctrines of Jesus alone be the religion of my country) that my faith, though differing from it, in a few trifling and unimportant points, is nevertheless *the same* in its great foundations. If the reader will consult the Transactions of the Asiatic Society of Calcutta, particularly Volume IV., he will find innumerable proofs that the Grecian histories, equally with the Mosaic and Hindoo mythologies, are most of them drawn from the same common fountain, in Upper India, about Balk, Cabul, and Samarkand. The same universal system pervaded the whole, and, no doubt, had its origin in ancient Buddhism.

Many facts stated by Mr. Faber having been taken from the works of Mr. Wilford, before the frauds which one of the Brahmins practised upon him were discovered, it is necessary to read with caution, and exclude the parts in which he might be deceived; but there is quite enough to satisfy any unprejudiced person, that the books of Genesis are mythoses or parables, the same as those of the Hindoos, and, in short, of all the other nations of antiquity.

That the Mosaic ceremonies were the same as those of the Gentiles, has been proved by Spencer, Faber, and other learned divines, beyond dispute. This being the fact, it does not seem surprising that the doctrines of the two should also partake of the same character, when stripped of the corruptions which the priests and the infirmities of humanity have introduced into them. We see not only the same fundamental Trinity, but we see the same system of concealment under apparently absurd mythoses or allegorical representations,—absurd, indeed, to outward appearance, but probably, if perfectly understood, covering a system of wisdom and truth. But enough escapes to prove that, for our good, as much is known as is necessary. I am of opinion that the object of Jesus was the reform of the Jewish polity, and the restoration of the religion of the Gentiles to that of Abraham and Melchizedek, that is, Buddha; for I am persuaded they were originally the same—the religion of the first Persians, or something very near to it, described by

---

[1] None of which were ever found in the old world.

Sir W. Jones as being so beautiful. But the discussion of this point belongs to the latter part of my work.

Let the reader look at the print of Cristna bruising the serpent's head, and that also of his brooding on the waters, and then doubt, if he can, that the system of Genesis and that of India were the same. This proves the doctrine, as well as the ritual, to be identical. They are prints of statues cut out of rocks long before the Christian æra. Let him consider the histories of Samson, Hercules, and Bala-Rama, of Buddha and Osiris, Budvar, Hermes, and Fo, and doubt the identity if he can. Then, how is it possible to doubt, that the original mythoses on which these are founded were the same?

On this subject Maimonides says, " Non omnia secundum litteram intelligenda et accipienda " esse quæ dicuntur in opere Bereschet, (Genesis,) sicut vulgus hominum existimat......sensus " enim illorum pravas vel gignunt cogitationes, imaginationes, et opiniones, de natura Dei, vel " certe fundamenta legis evertunt, hæresimque aliquatenus introducunt." [1]

The learned Spencer says, E superioribus evidens esse censeo, *omnis generis* arcana sub rituum " Mosaicorum tegmine latuisse. Quod itaque Plutarchus, credulâ temeritate, de religiosis Egyp- " tiorum institutis dixit, de Judæorum sacris et ceremoniis usurpemus. Nihil à ratione dissonum, " fabulosum nihil, nihil superstitionem olens, in eorum sacris constitutum est: sed quædam ethicas " et utiles doctrinas in recessu continentia, alia vero non expertia elegantiæ cujusdam historicæ vel " philosophicæ." [2]

The fact that the books of Moses do cover a secret doctrine being here broadly admitted by Spencer, one of the most learned divines of the British Protestant Church, I hope and trust I may stand excused, if I find myself under the necessity of adopting his principle—which, under the words *omnis generis*, is pretty extensive. This has nothing to do with the question whether the esoteric doctrine, admitted to exist, be or be not rightly understood by me. I only *here* contend that there *was* a secret doctrine. What that secret doctrine was, is not the subject of this section.

The following is the opinion of the learned Thomas Burnet, one of the first of Christian philo- sophers : " Sed quid tandem, inquies, omnibus perpensis, de Hebræorum Cabala statuendum erit ? " Nil habet arcani sensûs, nil sapientiæ reconditæ; neque olim habuit ? Rabbinorum cordatissi- " mus, Moses Maimonides, ait, olim fuisse apud Hebræos de rebus divinis multa mysteria, sed " periisse : vel injuria temporis, et repetitis gentis istius calamitatibus; vel ex eo quod prohibitum " fuit, mysteria divina scriptis consignare. Sed audiamus, si placet, ipsius verba Latinè. Scito " multas egregias sententias, quæ in gente nostra olim fuerunt, de veritate istarum rerum, partim " longinquitate temporis, partim infidelium et stultorum populorum in nos dominatione: partim " etiam quod non cuivis (sicut exposuimus) concessa erant mysteria, periisse, et in oblivionem " devenisse. Nihil enim permissum erat litteris mandare, nisi ea quæ in libros sacros digesta et " relata erant. Nosti enim Talmud ipsum inter nos receptum, olim non fuisse in certum librum " digestum, propter rationem istam, quæ tum passim obtinebat in gente nostra: VERBA QUÆ " DIXI TIBI ORE, NON LICET TIBI SCRIPTO DIVULGARE." Hæc est sententia Maimonidis " de " occultâ veterique Judæorum sapientiâ." [3] Again he says, " Si veniam damus conjecturis, in illam " opinionem facile descenderem, Antiquam Cabalam *Realem* (nam *verbalis* est figmentum huma- " num) tractasse potissimum *de rerum originatione*, et gradationibus. Sive de modo productionis " aut profluxus rerum a primo ente, et earundem rerum gradibus et descensu a summis ad ima." [4]

---

[1] Maim. More Neroc. Pars ii. Cap. xxix. p. 273; Beaus. Hist. Manich. Vol. II. p. 451.
[2] Lib. i. Cap. xi Sect. 3.   [3] Burnet, Archæol. Cap. vii. p. 84.   [4] Ib. p. 85.

Again, " Hæc est rerum et temporum ratio, in historia primi hominis et Paradisi. Quæ cum sin-
" gula mecum revolvo, æquo animo, et in omnem partem flexili, qua ducit ratio et veritatis amor:
" succensere non possum, ex patribus, et authoribus antiquis, illis, qui in symbola, aut PARABOLAS
" aut sermones populares, hæc convertere studuerunt." [1]   After this Burnet goes on to exhibit the
opinion of Cicero, Seneca, Zeno, and others, from which it appears that many of the learned Greeks
and Latins held the identical doctrine respecting the absorption of all things into the Deity, and
their periodical renovation and regeneration, with those of the oriental philosophers.   I shall say
nothing more at present respecting the esoteric religion of the Jews, or the secret meaning of their
Pentateuch, except, if the modern priests will persist in discarding the opinions of the learned
ancients, both before and after Christ, that these books had an allegorical meaning, and will still
persist in taking them *to the letter*, that the time is rapidly coming, when they will not be received
at all, except by a few persons of very mean understandings—persons who remind me of the very
appropriate speech of the Egyptian priest to Solon : *Vos Græci semper pueri estis : Senes Græcorum est nullus.*   And I should say, *Vos* religiosi semper pueri estis : Senex ultra-piorum est
nullus.

CHAPTER XIII

Disputed Chapters of Matthew and Luke—Cause of the Black Curly-head of Buddha—General Observations on the Moral Doctrines of different Religions

1. EVERY one knows the violent altercations which have taken place among learned Christians,
almost from the beginning of Christianity, respecting the last eight verses of the *first* and the whole
of the *second* chapter of Matthew—and the whole of the *second*, and all the *first* chapter, except the
first four verses, of Luke.   Great numbers of men, of first-rate character for learning and talent,
have declared them and proved them spurious, men who have shewn their sincerity by the resig-
nation of rich livings rather than appear to tolerate them against their consciences. [2]   Some interesting questions here naturally suggest themselves.   What are those chapters?   Are they mere
forgeries of the orthodox?   Why should the orthodox wish for *an immaculate conception* or *a
divine incarnation?*   They would have been just as rich and powerful without these doctrines.   I
cannot think they were mere forgeries.   They have no appearance of any such thing.   Then what
are they?

I think they are evidently the effects of the same cause as that which produced the oracles of
Zeradust, the different prophecies which alarmed the Romans, [3] the Sibylline oracles, the
prophecies of Virgil, &c., in the West; and as that which produced the same species of prophecy
among the Brahmins, named above, of expected saviours—the saviours expected and prayed for in
the Yajna sacrifice, " *When will it be that the Saviour will be born ! when will it be that the Re-
" deemer will appear !*"   To deny these heathen prophecies is impossible.   I know not how to

---

[1] Burnet, Archæol. p. 400.   [2] Amongst whom were Lindsey, Disney, Jebb, and Frend.
[3] Cited in Chap. II. Sect. 7.

account for them, except by supposing that they alluded to the renovating cycles demonstrated above. With this, the whole Jewish history and the disputed chapters are in perfect keeping. We have seen that all the ceremonies and much of the doctrine of the Jews, indeed the most important part, their Trinity, were exactly the same as those of the Gentiles. And I think if a person will pay but a very little attention, he must see that the incarnation described in these chapters was but the counterpart or repetition of former incarnations, or extraordinary conceptions, such for instance as that of Isaac or Samuel, or Buddha, or Cristna, or Pythagoras—the arrival of the three Magi, with the gifts sacred to the God Sol, or Mithra—the episode of Anna or the year, and Phanuel, or Phan, our God—of John having the power of the God Ieu (Elijah) אליהו *alieu.* All this dovetails very well into the remainder of the Gentile history, and proves these chapters to have a secret meaning, and to refer to the prophecies alluded to above. It all tends to prove the truth, a truth of which I have no doubt, that an identical secret system pervaded the whole world; singular as it may appear, in its universal extension, perhaps, unknown to the world. We have most unquestionably the same prophecy in Ireland, in Greece, in Persia, in Judæa, in Italy, and in India. But we have no reason to believe that any nation had merely copied the prophecy of the other nations. We read in Roman and Greek authors of the eighth age, and the ninth age, but scarcely another word do we meet with about them. So that it seems as if the meaning of these ages had become lost; and this I really believe was the truth. I should set it down as part of the secret mysteries, without any difficulty; but I cannot help believing that the mysteries, the real meaning of the Gods, &c., was actually lost. Cicero, Phornutus, Macrobius, &c., would not have written as they have done had they been understood. A general traditionary opinion had descended from the Buddhists, that the world would be renovated at the close of every ten ages, or ten Neroses, or six thousand years. These were the ages the knowledge of which was almost, but not entirely, lost. The priests and prophets had some slight perception of them, but it was, as through a glass, *darkly.*

2. I must now once more bring back the attention of my reader to the curly-headed, flat-faced, thick-lipped, black-skinned Buddha, almost forgotten. For these singularities we have not yet attempted to give any reasons. This Negro God cannot have been the only *Negro* East of the Indus, without some cause. On this subject credible history is silent. Let us try if we can form a theory.

It will not be denied that the animal, man, is in many respects like most other animals with which we are acquainted, and the philosophers Buffon and Lawrence have proved, that he partakes of the animal character in a much greater degree than was generally admitted in former times. And I think it will scarcely be denied that, like most other animals, he is capable of being improved, as well in person as in mind. I suppose that no one will deny the latter, how much soever the bigots may turn into ridicule the march of intellect, or improvement of the human understanding. Now I suppose, that man was originally a Negro, and that he improved as years advanced and he travelled Westwards, gradually changing, from the jet black of India, through all the intermediate shades of Syria, Italy, France, to the fair white and red of the maid of Holland and Britain. On the burning sands and under the scorching sun of Africa, he would probably stand still, if he did not retrograde. But the latter is most likely to have happened; and, accordingly, we find him an unimproved Negro, mean in understanding, black in colour. We know from experience that by coupling animals of beautiful forms, our animals constantly increase in beauty; indeed, our breeders of sheep, horses, and other domestic animals, know how to give them almost any colour or character they choose. They breed the high-mettled racer, the bold and warlike game-cock, or the sluggish, fattening Leicestershire sheep. The same effect has arisen in the form of man. In the rich soils of India, unfit for pasturage or hunting, but well calculated for the operations of agriculture, distinctions of rich and poor would much sooner arise than among the nomade or wandering tribes ; and as soon as a class became rich, the natural propensity would operate in causing the most handsome of the males, which would be the rich, those who were well fed and lived without labour, to couple with the most handsome of the females. This cause, in long periods of time, constantly acting, produced a great improvement in the human form. The scorching climate kept man black ; but, by degrees, the curly hair, flat face, and thick lips, yielded to the improved appearance of the present race.

Mr. Crawford has observed, that no country has produced a great or civilized race, but a country which, by its fertility, is capable of yielding a supply of *farinaceous* grain of the first quality. This he ingeniously supports by a great many examples.

When the Equinoctial Sun entered Taurus, he found man in India, like the first Buddha, a Negro ; when he entered Aries, he found him black, it is true, but with the aquiline nose and long hair of the handsome Cristna. The God of wood, of stone, of gold, stood still : the man in the space of 2160 years, perhaps of peace and prosperity, had materially improved. Not so the curly-haired man of Africa. Every thing tended to the improvement of the former, every thing to stop the improvement of the latter. In the African Ethiopia he remains a curly-headed black. In Egypt he formerly was so ; as the Memnon, Sphinxes, &c., prove. But in Egypt, where he became rich and civilized, and where good farinaceous food was grown, the same effects, in a great measure, took place as in India : and if he be not quite so black, the mixture of white Europeans, and, comparatively speaking, *white Turks*, will account for the difference. It has been observed, that the figures in the old caves of India are representations of a very different race from the present inhabitants ; that, although the figures possess a graceful elegance of form, yet a remarkable difference may be observed in the countenance, *which is broad and full : the nose flat : the lips, particularly the under lip, remarkably thick*, and the whole very unlike the present natives of Hindostan.[1] All these circumstances are easily accounted for, by the reasons alleged to account for the singular appearance of the curly-headed Buddha.

I request my reader to reflect with me upon the present state of different parts of the world ;— go to Lower Egypt and look at the tinted natives, and ascend to the torrid zone, and we shall find them to grow darker as we approach the Sun, always, when humanized, described as black. The straight hair grows woolly as we approach the scorched, steril regions of Nubia, and generally the parched sands of Africa, *where no corn grows*, where the tree of the Sun, the *everlasting*[2] Phœnix or Palm tree, is perhaps the only plant on which man depends for the certain production of a scanty subsistence ; the only fruit-bearing tree which raises its head, a majestic head, around the few solitary springs of the parched desert. Let us go to India, and we find the same effect, with this only difference, that in this grain-growing country, this land of ease and luxury, the persons are more handsome, and the hair straight and long. And, above all, let us contemplate the Jewish character, the jet-black hair, and peculiar complexion, verging to the oriental, among the white European followers of Abraham. Let us reflect on all these circumstances ; when my reader has done this, I trust he will think that the solution of the enigma, which I have attempted, is the most probable which has been devised.

The opinion which I have here given, is supported by the ingenious Dr. Pritchard, in his Researches into the Physical History of Man, p. 41. He says, " The perception of beauty is the " chief principle, in every country, which directs men in their marriages. It is very obvious that " this peculiarity in the constitution of man, must have considerable effects on the physical

---

[1] Maur. Ant. Hind. Vol. II. p. 376.   [2] To be explained by and by.

" character of the race, and that it must act as a constant principle of improvement."........
Again, (p 43,) " The noble families of modern Persia were originally descended from a tribe of
" ugly and bald-headed Mongoles. They have constantly selected for their harams the most
" beautiful females of Circassia. The race has been thus gradually ameliorated, and is said now to
" exhibit fine and comely persons."

I believe that all the Black bambinos of Italy are negroes—not merely blacks; this admitted,
it would prove the very early date of their entrance into Italy.

Dr. Pritchard has successfully proved that the blackness of the skin is not caused by heat alone;
that the Negro is to be found in cold as well as hot climates, and that the change which, in
various instances, has taken place in his complexion, is to be ascribed more to civilization than to
climate. This perfectly agrees with the observation of Mr. Crawford, that man is found improved
in rich and farinaceous, but stationary in *desert* districts. Civilization was the effect of the former
—barbarism of the latter.

Dr. Pritchard[1] has observed, that the Brahmins are, as might be expected, the finest formed
race in India. He has also shewn, in a very satisfactory manner,[2] that the ancient Egyptians,
the masters of Thebes, were Negroes—or, that they were black, with curly heads.

Col. Wilford says, " It cannot reasonably be doubted that a race of Negroes had formerly
" pre-eminence in India."[3] These were the inhabitants of India in the time of the curly-headed
Buddha, who was succeeded, after 2160 years, by the long-haired Cristna—one an incaruation of
the solar God in Taurus, the other in Aries.

Thus I account for the Negro Buddha, and for the handsome, though black, Cristna.[4]

In aid of this theory, a reconsideration of the foregoing pages will shew, that we have found the
black complexion or something relating to it whenever we have approached to the origin of the
nations. The Alma Mater, the Goddess Multimammia, the founders of the oracles, the Memnons
or first idols, were always black. Venus, Juno, Jupiter, Apollo, Bacchus, Hercules, Asteroth,
Adonis, Horus, Apis, Osiris, Ammon,—in short, all the wood and stone Deities were black. The
images remained as they were first made in very remote times. They were not susceptible of any
improvement; and when for any reason they required renewal they were generally made exactly
after the former sacred pattern. I once saw a man repainting a black God on a house-side in Italy.

3. The shocking state of degradation into which the religion of the Brahmins has sunk, gives a
plausible appearance of truth to the rantings of our Missionaries; but, nevertheless, the religion
of Brahma is no more idolatrous than the religion of the Romish Church. Abul Fazil, a Mahometan author, in the Ayeen Akbery, states, that the opinion that the Hindoos are Polytheists has
no foundation in truth, but that they are worshipers of God, and only of one God. They maintain (with all enlightened followers of the Romish Church), that images are only representations of
the great Being, to which they turn whilst at prayer, in order to prevent their thoughts from
wandering. They hold that " the Being of beings is the only God, eternal, and every where
" present, who comprises every thing; there is no God but He."[5] The religions of Brahma and
of Buddha have both become corrupted, but a third has arisen—that of the Sikhs, a reformed
Buddhism, more pure than either of them, and which may perhaps be destined to possess the
sovereignty of India. Certainly nothing but the British can prevent it.[6]

---

[1] P. 390.   [2] Sect. v. p. 376.   [3] Asiat. Res. Vol. III.

[4] It is remarkable that the Abyssinian or Ethiopian has always continued the Indian Sanscrit custom of writing his
letters from left to right, in the syllabic form retaining the vowels. This appears to have been a remnant of the first
Buddhism of India. Much will be said upon this subject by and by, and the reason of the change in the custom of other
nations shewn.

[5] Crawford's Researches, Vol. I. pp. 200—220.   [6] Ibid. Ch. vii. of the Sikhs.

The following is the most celebrated verse of the Vedas, called the Gayatri: " Let us adore the " supremacy of that divine Sun, the Godhead who illuminates all, from whom all proceed, to whom " all must return, whom we invoke to direct our understandings aright in our progress towards " his holy seat." [1]   On this Sir William Jones says, " The many panegyrics on the Gayatri, the " Mother, as it is called, of the Vedas, prove the author to have adored, not the visible material " sun, but that *divine and incomparably greater light which illumines all, delights all, from which* " *all proceed, to which all must return, and which alone can irradiate* (not our visual organs merely, " but our souls and) *our intellects.*   These may be considered as the words of the most venerable " text in the Indian Scripture." [2]   The words in italics mark the words of the Veda text.

If we are to believe our priests, at the same time that nothing can be more pure than our religion, or more charitable than themselves, nothing can be more horrible than the religion or practices of the wicked Heathens.   Yet it is worthy of observation, that we curse *sinners* on Ash Wednesday, and our *enemies* whenever we are at war: but when the Athenians in a moment of fury ordered the priestess to curse Alcibiades for having insulted the mysteries, she REFUSED— saying, *she was the priestess of prayers, not of curses.*[3]   The passage in Martianus Capella, cited Chap. II. Sect. 8, shews that the Pagans were no more Idolaters than the modern Romans.

One of the most common and triumphant boasts of the Christian priests has been, that no morality could be put in competition with theirs.   The following extract, from the eleventh discourse of Sir William Jones to the Asiatic Society, will abundantly prove how slender are the foundations upon which these arrogant pretensions are built.   These are the words of the pious president; though they be rather long, their importance will plead their excuse:—" Our divine " religion, the truth of which (if any history be true) is abundantly proved by historical evidence, " has no heed of such aids, as many are willing to give it, by asserting that the wisest men of " this world were ignorant of the two great maxims, that *we must act in respect of others, as we* " *would wish them to act in respect of ourselves;* and that, *instead of returning evil for evil, we* " *should confer benefits even on those who injure us:* but the first rule is implied in a speech of " Lysias, and expressed in distinct phrases by Thales and Pittacus; and I have even seen it word " for word in the original of Confucius, which I carefully compared with the Latin translation.   It " has been usual with zealous men, to ridicule and abuse all those who dare on this point to quote " the Chinese philosopher; but instead of supporting their cause, they would shake it, if it could " be shaken by their uncandid asperity,—for they ought to remember, that one great end of reve- " lation, as it is most expressly declared, was not to instruct the wise and few, but the many " and unenlightened.   If the conversion, therefore, of the Pandits and Maulavis in this country " shall ever be attempted by Protestant Missionaries, they must beware of asserting, while they " teach the gospel of truth, what those Pandits and Maulavis would know to be false : the former " would cite the beautiful A'ry'a couplet, which was written at least three centuries before our æra, " and which pronounces the duty of a good man, even in the moment of his distraction to consist " *not only in forgiving, but even in a desire of benefiting, his destroyer, as the Sandal tree, in the* " *instant of its overthrow, sheds perfume on the axe which fells it ;* and the latter would triumph in " repeating the verse of Sadi, who represents *a return of good for good as a slight reciprocity,* but " says, the virtuous man *confers benefits on him who has injured him ;* using an Arabic sentence, " and a maxim apparently of the ancient Arabs."   Thus we see the essence of the Christian moral doctrine was known at least three hundred years before Jesus was born.

And the following extract will shew that the Mohamedans were as enlightened upon this subject

---

[1] Moore, Panth p. 410.   [2] Ibid.   [3] Plutarch, apud Payne Knight on Sym. S. lvii. n.

as any of them :—" Nor would the Mussulmans fail to recite four distichs of Hafiz, who has
" illustrated that maxim with fanciful but elegant allusions :

> " Learn from yon orient shell to love thy foe,
> " And store with pearls the hand that brings thee woe :
> " Free like yon rock, from base vindictive pride,
> " Imblaze with gems the wrist that rends thy side :
> " Mark, where yon tree rewards the stony show'r,
> " With fruit nectareous, or the balmy flow'r :
> " All nature calls aloud ; *shall man do less,*
> " Than heal the smiter, and the railer bless ?"

" Now there is not a shadow of reason for believing that the poet of Shiraz had borrowed this
" doctrine from the Christians." [1]

In Mr. Maurice's History [2] may be found many moral sentiments identically the same as those
of the Christians.

In order to exalt the credit of the Christian religion, nothing which talent and ingenuity could
contrive has been left untried by divines to depreciate the philosophy of the ancients, and to
blacken the characters of its professors. No doubt among the followers of Socrates, Pythagoras,
Aristotle, Plato, &c., as well as among the followers of Jesus and Mohamed, brawls and squabbles
the most disgraceful have taken place. But it does not appear that better men have been produced by the latter, than by the former. The Antonines and Epictetus are not to be placed below
any men whom modern history can produce : and although we cannot now give a catalogue of illustrious ancient names equal in number to that of the moderns, this by no means proves that such
individuals did not formerly exist. The peculiar circumstances of the case prevent our knowledge
of them, and that principally in consequence of the destruction of their works—an effect arising
from various causes.

The oldest and wisest of the Grecian philosophers taught the very best parts of the Christian
morality, many hundred years before Jesus was born. Pythagoras said, that the best way for a
man to revenge himself of his enemies was to make them friends : and Socrates, whose character
has been vindicated from reproach by Dean Prideaux, [3] says in the Crito, that it is not permitted
to a man who has received an injury to return it by doing another. An able defence of Socrates
may be found in the Travels of Mr. Buckingham to India, published in 1829.

Our treatises on the Christian religion are sufficiently numerous ; but it may be doubted very
much whether they exceed in number those of the ancient philosophers, or even of the modern
Mohamedans. On the philosophy of Plato eight thousand commentaries were said to have been
written. The greatest fault of the ancient philosophers consisted in the affected obscurity with
which they strove to conceal their real doctrines from the public eye. Into this error they all
seem to have fallen ; though in different ways. Many of them concealed their principles under
fables and figurative expressions,—by the literal interpretation of which Christian divines, overlooking the corruptions into which religion had fallen, have very unjustly succeeded in persuading
mankind that their doctrines were both pernicious and contemptible in the highest degree.

The liberal and benign doctrine of the followers of Brahma, in its original purity, can never be
too much praised, and must fill every one with admiration. No doubt in succeeding ages its corrupt and mercenary priests engrafted into it, as we see daily to take place in all religions, and
wherever priests are concerned, doctrines and practices utterly repugnant to the mild spirit of its

[1] Jones, 11th Dis. to Asiat. Soc.   [2] Vol. II. Ch. iii.   [3] Vide Moyle's Works, Vol. II. p. 77.

founders. Those founders maintained that all religions come from God, and that all modes of adoring him, when springing from an upright heart, are acceptable to him. Their enlightened followers still affirm that " the Deity is present with the Mahometan in the mosque counting his " beads, and equally in the temple at the adoration of the idols; the intimate of the Musselman " and the friend of the Hindoo; the companion of the Christian, and the confidant of the Jew." They are of opinion that he has many times appeared and been incarnate in the flesh, not only in this world, but in others, for the salvation of his creatures; and that both Christians and Hindoos adore the same God, under different forms. [1]

The fine sentiment here given from the ancient religion of the Brahmins, and on which I fear they did not always act, has been copied by the Christian historians of the gospel; but, either from its mixture with other doctrines of a pernicious nature, or from some other cause, it has unfortunately scarcely ever been acted on: *Then Peter opened his mouth, and said, Of a truth I perceive that GOD is no respecter of persons: but in every nation he that feareth him, and worketh righteousness, is accepted with him.* [2] (Acts x. 34, 35.) Beautiful as is this sentiment, clear as is the language, and beneficial to mankind as is its tendency, I have found divines who, with a narrowness of mind almost inconceivable, have endeavoured to explain away its plain and obvious sense, and to limit its meaning to countries in which a man may dwell. But how little can such men know of the Divine paternity who need to be told that God will not damn a man because he was a Frenchman, a Dutchman, a Turk, or a Hindoo!

Much fault has been found with the Decalogue, and justly, as a *code* for the whole world. But not justly when it is confined, as it ought to be, to the country of Judæa. By its language, when properly translated, it is strictly confined to the Israelites. And as a code, in its totality, it was never adopted by Jesus Christ. The whole of it is as impossible to be obeyed by the remainder of mankind, as it is to make a circle triangular, or a triangle, the angles of which shall not be equal to two right-angles. Jesus Christ never inculcated it, though part of the moral doctrines which he taught are to be found in it. In this instance, by not understanding or attending to the letter of the old language, priests have mistaken the doctrine both of Moses and of Jesus. They are both correct when properly understood. The Decalogue may be easily defended—but not on the mistaken grounds taken by our priests. I should like to meet a disciple of M. Voltaire on the subject of the *jealous God.*

There is in the Geeta, (p. 81,) a sentiment which is peculiar to the religion of Brahma, and which (at least if the happiness of mankind in this world is to be considered as one object or end of religion) places it above all others. Happy, indeed, would it have been for the world had the Mohamedan and Christian religions contained this most admirable and benevolent doctrine. The Deity speaks—" *They, who serve even other Gods with a firm belief, in doing so, involuntarily " worship me. I am he who partaketh of all worship, and I am their reward.*" [3] How admirable is this sentiment! How superior to the Jewish doctrine of a *jealous* God, improperly adopted by Christians! and how true! True, at least, if benevolence, justice, and mercy, are the attributes of the Creator. For the peace and happiness of mankind in this world, it may safely be affirmed that, in all the Jewish, Christian, and Mohamedan religions, there is no dogma of half so much importance, or which has been of the twentieth part of the utility, as *this* would have been, had it been taught in those religions. Yet there is a very fine and nearly similar sentiment in the Koran:

[1] Maurice, Hist. Ind. 4to. Vol. II. p. 301; see Anathema, 1 Cor. xvi. 22!!!
[2] This is, indeed, the genuine doctrine of the philosophical Nazarite, Carmelite, or Essenian of Samaria.
[3] Maurice, Ind. Ant. Vol. V. p. 1052.

" If God had pleased, he surely had made you one people : but he hath thought fit to give you
" different laws, that he might try you in that which he hath given you respectively. Therefore
" strive to excel each other in good works ; unto God shall ye all return, and then will he declare
" unto you that concerning which ye have disagreed."[1]   How superior is this to the *faith without works* of our modern and fashionable fanatics ![2]

Mr. Maurice[3] pours out a torrent of abuse upon M. Volney for having endeavoured to rob him
of his immortality, and to destroy the best interests of society by violating the truth of history,
&c. It seems difficult to conceive why M. Volney should wish any one to be robbed of his immortality, or why he should not be very glad to have the hope of it, if he could entertain it on
what appeared to him reasonable grounds. But he, no doubt, felt an utter repugnance to admit
such doctrines, or any doctrine, on the mere assertion of priests, paid to support their systems,
right or wrong; who find Cristna a God in Asia, and Jesus in Europe; who are the regular
paid appendages to every arbitrary government, and are as naturally found to belong to it as an
exciseman or a soldier. When Mr. M. rails at Volney for violating the truth of history, he
should have shewn distinctly how he violated it : empty railing will not answer any longer : men
begin to use their understandings. And when Mr. Maurice says Volney violated the truth of
history in order to destroy the best interests of society, he ought to have said, the best interests
of a hired priesthood, whose interests have always been opposed to the best interests, and to the
liberty and happiness, of mankind. But there is no reason to believe that M. Volney ever intentionally violated the truth of history.

If the work which is now presented to the world be executed with any tolerable degree of talent,
no doubt the author will be honoured like M. Volney with the abuse of the priests. It will be
said that he has violated the truth of history ; that he hates the religion of Jesus, &c., &c. That
he has violated the truth of history *intentionally* he utterly denies. He equally denies that he
hates the religion of Jesus. He does hate the hypocrisy of its priests, and the intolerance of
their, not *its,* principles—as, on the contrary, he loves the liberality and tolerating spirit of the
ancient, uncorrupted religion of the Buddist or Brahmin ; which teaches that God is equally the
Father of the devout and sincere Chinese, Brahmin, Christian, and Deist ; which contains no creed
inculcating that *except a man believe this or that he cannot be saved ;* a creed whose tendency is to
fill the world with war and bloodshed, and to sacrifice, indeed, the best interests of society to those
of a corrupt and pernicious order or corporation.

---

[1] Koran, Ch. v. p. 131.

[2] On the subject of the Koran, the *Apology for the Life and Character of Mohamed,* by the author of this work, may
be consulted.

[3] Hist. Ind. Vol. II. pp. 499, 501.

BOOK VI

CHAPTER I

Flood of Noah—Learning of Genesis—Text of Genesis—Inland Seas of Asia—
Theory of a learned Cantab—Theory of Mr. Gab—Rennel on Egypt—Origin of
the Delta of Egypt—Caspian Sea—Plato's Atlantis—Geological Fact in Yorkshire

1. I now propose to fulfil the promise which I gave in my last book—to make some observations
on the flood or floods which have taken place upon our globe. To treat this subject fully would
require a volume. I must confine myself to one or two observations, upon a few well-known
facts.—I suppose it will not be denied that the history of the flood is an integral part of the
Mosaic system; that whether it be allegory or a literal history, the whole book or collection of
books called Genesis must go together, and be considered on the same principle: if the first and
second tracts be allegory, so likewise must the third.

In almost every part of the world the fossil remains of animals are found,—animals which the
researches of Mons. Cuvier have proved must have been deposited at long intervals of time,
between which depositions great floods or catastrophes must have taken place.[1] He has shewn the
order in which the different classes of living creatures have been formed; and it has been observed,
that they have taken place exactly in that order in which they are said to have been formed, in
the first book of Genesis, which figuratively describes them as being created in successive days.
The observation strikingly illustrates the allegorical principle: for, though it absolutely proves
the falsity of the *letter* of the record, it, at the same time, proves the truth of the allegory, as far
as we clearly understand it. Now, if man had been formed before the flood, at the same time
with the Elks, Elephants, &c., found fossilized, it is not possible to believe that some remains of
him would not have been found among them in some part of the earth. " Human bones have
" been found indurated and preserved by vitriolic, sparry, and ferruginous incrustation : these are
" modern operations of daily process, but have no relation to the petrefaction incident to the bones
" of elephants and other animals confined in the bowels of the earth: in earth undisturbed since
" its original formation of consistency, and which bones (in some cases) are indurated to the
" hardest agate."[2]   The whole world has been ransacked for a specimen; but it has not been
found: for the priests have seen that the want of such specimen strikes a death-blow, at their
literal interpretation of the text, and at what I must call their modern, mischievous, demoralizing
doctrines, depending upon it. This failure alone has brought the matter to this point—either
Genesis is *false*, or, it is an allegory or parable; and to the latter conclusion every enlightened
Christian must now come. The creation of the world in six successive days and nights, and the
creation of man before the floods which embedded the animals in the strata above alluded to, are
assertions, the falsity of which, if taken to the letter, is as well proved as the nature of the case

---

[1] Vide Celtic Druids.   [2] Gent. Mag. Vol. LVIII. A. D. 1788, p. 384.

will admit. Therefore the doctrine of allegory must now be revived—the doctrine of the ancient Jews, and the earliest and most learned fathers of the Christian Church—a doctrine lost in the darkness and debasement of intellect during the middle ages. It is said that the proof of the allegorical signification is only *negative* proof; but it is a very peculiar kind of negative proof; for the fossil elephant is *found*—but in the same strata the positive *absence of the remains of man* is palpable. The history of Noah and the Deluge being the same in India and Western Syria, [1] whatever may be the meaning of the one must be the meaning of the other.

M. Cuvier, after shewing *that there are no human bones in a fossil state*—that is, in a *fossil state properly so called*, [2] goes on to prove that the bones of men and birds, or of very small animals, are as indestructible in their nature as those of Elephants, &c. He concludes, " How-" ever this may have been, the establishment of mankind in those countries in which the fossil " bones of land animals have been found, that is to say, in the greatest part of Europe, Asia, and " America, must necessarily have been posterior not only to the revolutions which covered up " these bones, but also to those other revolutions by which the strata containing the bones have " been laid bare. Hence it clearly appears, that no argument for the antiquity of the human " race in those countries can be founded either upon these fossil bones, or upon the more or less " considerable collections of rocks or earthy materials, by which they are covered." [3]

The way in which M. Cuvier's fear of the priests shews itself here, is very marked. It is true, as he says, that no argument for the antiquity of the human race can be formed from the fossil bones, or collections of rocks by which they are covered; but it is clear that an argument which he keeps back can be formed, and must be formed, *for the contrary*—for its *modern* creation— that is, that it must have been created since the great catastrophe here alluded to took place : [4] and thus, that the third book of Genesis or Mosaic book of the Flood, contains a figurative account like the other two.

2. The history of Genesis conceals, under its allegory, the most profound knowledge of natural philosophy, and the general formation of the world, as proved by the most learned researches of Mons. Cuvier and other Geologists : and this has a strong tendency to support the opinion of the great Bailly, that a profoundly learned race of people existed previous to the formation of any of our systems. In this investigation we must recollect, that M. Cuvier's doctrines are not founded on what are called theories, but on experimental philosophy.

On the existence of living animals M. Cuvier states, that when the Spaniards first penetrated into South America, they did not find it to contain a single quadruped exactly the same with those of Europe, Asia, and Africa. The Puma, the Jaguar, the Tapir, the Capybara, the Lama or Glama, and Vicugua, and the whole tribe of Sapajous, were to them entirely new animals, of which they had not the smallest idea. [5]

Dr. Pritchard says, [6] " The Count de Buffon observed that the animals which inhabit the old

---

[1] In a future page I shall shew that there were two Syrias.

[2] Cuvier, ap. Jameson, pp. 62, 63, 128.   [3] Ibid. p. 134.

[4] Thus away goes the learned Mr. Faber's Helio-archite hypothesis, that is, his *Sunned-ship* or his *shipped-Sun* worship. It is often very useful when you treat with superficial persons, to use an unintelligible word, like Helio-archite. Similar to this is our word *Heavens* in the first verse of Genesis.

[5] Cuvier ap. Jameson, pp. 62, 63. My reader will often find the expression *before the flood* used. He will recollect I formerly warned him, that he must consider this to mean merely *the earliest known period*. He must not consider it as the giving of an opinion as to the occurrence or non-occurrence of that event, before the creation of the present race of man.

[6] Sect. iii. p. 101.

" world are in general different from those of the new, and that whatever species are found to be
" common to both are such as are able to endure the extreme cold of the Arctic regions, and may
" therefore be supposed to have found a way from one continent to the other, where they approach
" very near together, and may probably have been formerly joined." After a careful examination
of this opinion of the Count's, Dr. Pritchard concludes thus : " But as far as accurate knowledge
" extends, the opinion of Buffon and his followers seems to be well founded. It does not appear
" that any one animal was originally common to the warm parts of the old and new world." [1]
Here, again, I think is an end of the universal deluge, taken with all its details, except in the
sense in which most of the other parts of Genesis must be taken ; namely, as an allegory, under
which some secret doctrine is concealed : like the expression of God's walking in the garden,
&c., &c., it must be construed figuratively. And I think, for hundreds of reasons given in Mr.
Faber's learned work on Pagan Idolatry, it is evident, that the story of the ark of Noah is the
same as that of the Argha of the oriental Menu, in which the germ of animated nature is supposed
to have floated on the ocean, and to have been thus preserved.

The deductions of Dr. Pritchard and M. Buffon, as stated above, are perfectly legitimate, and
are decisive against the *literal* meaning of the text taken as a whole. I cannot bring myself to
believe that the Doctor can be in earnest, in the sophistry which he uses in page 138, to assuage
the anger of the priests, by pretending to reconcile the deduction to the literal meaning. But he
probably was aware that, if it did not pacify them, the same fate would befal his work which
afterward happened to Mr. Lawrence's. The Doctor's argument is, that God, by a great miracle,
brought every animal to the ark, and carried it back again,—great Elephants, and, of course, the
little mite of the Cheshire-cheese. But, unfortunately for the learned and ingenious Doctor's
scheme, the text does not warrant any such inference. Besides, how came God not to have
completed his work, and to have carried all the animals back again ?—for example, the Horse, the
Cow, the Elephant, and the Camel; and how came he not to leave us some of the animals which
they have, but which we have not ? [2]

That several floods have taken place cannot be doubted; ocular demonstration as well as
tradition prove this. Like what has been called *early history*, the fact was seized on by the priests,
and made subservient to the secret religion which every where prevailed. Thus we have a story
in India, or Eastern, Syria, Mesopotamia or Chaldea, of the germ or seed of all nature preserved
in a ship fastened to the mount of *Nau-band-a,* or the *ship-banded* or *cabled* mount; [3] in Western, [4]
Syria or Mesopotamia or Chaldea, the story of the ark of Noah and his eight sailors. But because
the fact was thus converted into a parable, and used for the purpose of preserving a mythos, and
the same mythos in both countries, it does not therefore follow that there was not a flood.

3. The account of the flood, taken from our common version, is plain and unaffected ; and
has probably been misunderstood from its too great simplicity. It is as follows : *And the waters
prevailed exceedingly upon the earth ; and all the high hills that were under the whole heaven were
covered. Fifteen cubits upward did the waters prevail ; and the mountains were covered.* (Gen.
vii. 19, 20.) Now I take the liberty of asking, of what earth, and of what mountains or hills, does
the author speak ? I answer, most clearly not of those of the new, but of those of the old world,
of the height of which we know nothing. All that we know of them is, that there were hills, or

---

[1] Sect. iii. p. 133.

[2] The Ark was a correct parallelogram, square at the ends, 300 cubits long, 50 cubits broad, and 30 cubits deep.
It had no pretensions to the name of a *ship*. As it was like nothing else, perhaps its most appropriate name is Ark.
Origen calculated that it was about *thirty* miles long.

[3] See B. V. Ch. V. Sect. 2.   [4] There were two countries of each of these names.

mounts, or mountains; but we have many reasons for believing that they were not at that time very high: besides, the text certainly implies that they were not *more* than fifteen cubits high, for the water, having risen fifteen cubits, covered them. Now, if we consider the history in this simple point of view, which is the only way the words will fairly bear to be considered, because the whole context relates to the old world, it is by no means improbable that the same convulsion which covered the highest land of the old world with water only fifteen cubits or less than thirty feet deep, might also throw up Mont Blanc and Chimborazo.

But I must make another observation. The text does not say, that the surface of the whole globe was covered. The word צרֶאָה *e-arz* does not necessarily include the whole surface of the globe: for this observation I am indebted to my friend Cooper, the learned Professor of Columbia College, in America. It may mean nothing more than the surface of the old land, and have nothing to do with the Americas, for it often means countries as well as the earth.[1] When a word has clearly two meanings, it is a most unwarrantable proceeding to adopt that which gives an impossible sense, instead of that which is consistent with reason and probability. Professor Cooper observes, "If the acknowledged facts cannot be explained without a miracle, we must "admit the miracle: if they can, we ought not to resort to supernatural interposition, when the "known action of secondary causes will suffice." If this reasoning be adopted, we have nothing in sacred writ respecting the deluge merely, at variance with possibility. For, if the hills of the old world were not very high, there is ten times as much water in the ocean as would cover the land to thirty feet deep; and no one can say, that the cause which forced up Mont Blanc was not powerful enough to cause a proportionate concussion of the waters.

Now, if we consider the history of the flood in this point of view, there is nothing improbable in the destruction having been so great over the world as to have left only a very few persons of one or two nations (the Indians and Chinese perhaps) in such a state as to retain possession of their books and records—whence they might be called the inhabitants of the city of Sephora, that is, the city of letters; Sephor, in Hebrew, meaning a letter, or a cipher or figure of notation. No person has ever pretended to find this city, but it has been thought to be Babylon. At all events, I think I have shewn that when the prejudices of philosophers against the nonsense of devoteeism, and the prejudice of devotees for nonsense, are disposed of, and the text fairly understood and explained, there is nothing implied in the *flood* of Noah impossible or incredible, or that may not rationally be accounted for from natural causes. When I look at Ætna and count the volcanoes burning and worn out, I have no difficulty in believing that what has caused them, may have split the globe in pieces, as we see it has been. So far as this, I think geologists will go with me. I am well aware that there are many phenomena which my theory *will not reach*, but which I think are not in opposition to it, or which do not impugn it, and which must be accounted for from other and additional causes, probably previous deluges. These are not in my province; I leave them to the Geologists, and come to this conclusion merely,—that there was a convulsion or flood, which raised the highest mountains: and, that there may have been other convulsions which destroyed the people of Greece, &c., of which Plato gives us an account. But none of these can have been the flood which buried the Elks, &c., before treated of.

4. When the first of the great convulsions spoken of above had ceased, I suppose that the world was left with the Mediterranean a great lake, overflowing a head or bank at the straits of Gibraltar; covering with water the Delta, or Lower Egypt, if it then existed, the Pontine Marshes of Italy, and many islands and shores of the Mediterranean now dry. The Aral, the Caspian Sea, the Sea of Asoph or Maietis or Mæotis, and the Euxine, were probably one sea, or a series of

---

[1] Gen. x. 5, 20, 31, ii. 11, 12; Deut. vi. 1, 3, 10; Psa. cvi. 27, cv. 44, et al.

lakes, exactly like the series of lakes in North America, flowing over the head at Niagara. After a long course of years, the breaking down of the banks which held up these eastern or higher lakes might cause very great local floods, probably those alluded to by Plato,—might cause first the low lands on the banks of the Mediterranean to be flooded, and, at last, by breaking through the barrier at Gibraltar, cause them to be again left dry. All this is within the bounds of possibility, and probability too, if what the traveller Pallas says be true, that the appearance of the surface of the countries between the Aral, the Caspian, and the Sea of Asoph, shews that they have formerly all been connected. In all this we have nothing more than natural effects succeeding to natural causes. [1]

In some author, whose name I have forgotten, I have met with an assertion, that the plain of Troy has certain appearances which indicate that a great flood has formerly swept over it, which may have destroyed the city of Ilion. This may readily account for the general character which the rivers, &c., bear to the account in the poem of Homer, and for the difficulty in minute particulars of making them agree. Although the poem is evidently a sacred mythos, there was probably a true basement on which it was erected, as was the case with the Roman mythos, treated of by Niebuhr.

5. A learned orientalist of Cambridge, in a work called the Cambridge Key to the Chronology of the Hindoos, has made some pertinent observations on the subject of a flood. The work of this gentleman is the best defence of the flood of Noah that I have seen. He shews that an immense flood was believed by all nations to have taken place, and he produces proofs, I think satisfactory, that in all of them certain traditions were nearly the same as to date, and that these traditions place it at or about A. M. 1656, [2] of Usher's Chronology. His great object is to prove that the Mosaic history of the Patriarchs before the flood is real history and not a mythos, and he considers the proof of the existence of a general tradition of a flood, a proof of the truth of Noah's flood with all its details. But there may be a demur to this conclusion, even by persons who may admit most of the premises. Assuredly the circumstances and traditions, so generally found, furnish strong grounds for belief that some great flood did take place since the formation of the world and of man. But the reasons which I have given to prove that man has been created since the universal flood, which buried the last race of fossilized animals, seem to be satisfactory; therefore, the flood of which I now speak must have been of later date, and this later flood is what the priests of all religions have exaggerated into an universal deluge, burying the highest of our present mountains fifteen cubits deep. This flood may have taken place in the period of from about two to three thousand years before Christ. At this time the celebrated city of the great Bali, or Maha-Balipore, near Sadrass, in India, may have been destroyed. Of this city the Cambridge Key [3] says, " The stately palaces, august temples, and stupendous edifices, of this once magnifi-
" cent city, are universally believed by every Hindoo, whether learned or unlearned, to have been
" destroyed by ' *a general deluge brought upon the earth by the immediate mandate of the Supreme*
" *God.*' They still shew the chasm in the rock, that forms one of the largest choultrys ; and
" the divided sculpture but too plainly shews that nothing less than such a convulsion of nature

---

[1] *From the relations of Pallas* and other travellers in the neighbourhood of the Caspian, there are distinct traces of the Aral, the Caspian, the Mæotis or Sea of Asoph, the Euxine, all having been once united. Quarterly Review, No. LXXXVI. p. 447.

[2] We have formerly seen that Hercules succeeded Bacchus about fifteen generations (meaning centuries) or 1500 years. This tradition alludes to the three Neroses before the flood. The Indians fixed the flood at the Cali Yug, and this was the mistaken time between Taurus and Aries.

[3] Vol. I. p. 313.

" could have rent so large a mass of solid stone, leaving the divided sculpture on each side the
" chasm,—evidently denoting that it was carved before the convulsion took place. This is a truth
" too apparent to be denied."

Here we have an argument worthy the consideration of a philosopher, and not far from being
conclusive as to a very great convulsion, if the account given by the Key be not exaggerated. I
wish this Indian scholar had been a little more full, and had told us that he had seen it himself:
for I have a high opinion of his sincerity. It seems to me to be a place more worthy of careful
examination than perhaps any other in the world.

The account given by this gentleman is, in general, confirmed by William Chambers, Esq., in
the first volume of the Asiatic Transactions.[1]

As I have just said, all this tends to prove that there really has been a very great convulsion
since the creation of man, and the foolish exaggerations of priests are not enough to invalidate it,
any more than the mythos spliced on to the history of ancient Rome, as satisfactorily shewn by
Niebuhr, is enough to prove that Rome did not exist. Few persons, except priests of very confined education, now believe the account of the flood literally, as expounded by devotees, but
consider it, as they consider the texts which say that God wrestled with Jacob, and strove to kill
Moses at an inn, *but failed*. The case is very difficult—but I am inclined to look upon the history
of the flood, as Mr. Niebuhr shews that the early history of Rome ought to be considered; and
that it is not a mere fable, but, on the contrary, that it has real history for its foundation—though
disguised by the contrivance of priests to excite astonishment in the minds of their votaries, or
perhaps merely to conceal their secret doctrines.

We are told by Plato, that before the race of people who occupied Greece in his time lived, a
previous race had been destroyed by a great flood. Now, I think it may be possible to find a
probable cause for this effect : but I will previously make a few observations on the Pyramids and
Delta of Egypt, from which I think we may, in our search, gain some assistance.

6. I shall, in the first place, give an extract from the work of a learned priest of the name of
Gab, of the Romish Church, which contains a statement of several curious and unobserved facts.
He says, " But before I draw any further inferences from the discoveries, or perhaps I should say
" revival of facts, (sunk, through the inattention of the learned, into a temporary oblivion,) now
" submitted to their consideration, by one who has little to boast of beyond taste and diligence in
" such a pursuit ; I will hazard the experiment, and see what progress I can make in the investi-
" gation of the antiquity of this interesting monument, this paragon so replete with principles of
" science, the great Pyramid of Giza, or ancient Memphis.

" There appears no convincing reason to conclude the other pyramids to be coeval with this,
" as may be gathered from the sequel of the present discussion. I have before observed, that
" were I to hazard a conjecture of this Pyramid being erected by the Antediluvians, I should
" not want for arguments to bear me out. But if I have deceived myself, and should fail in this
" attempt, still the Pyramid will neither fail, nor suffer any diminution of its beneficent utility in
" assisting in further discoveries.

" It has been a very prevailing, not to say a general, opinion, that the sands which environ the
" Pyramid, and hide a great part of its reclining sides, next to the foundation, have been drifted by
" the winds from other parts of those regions, and lodged in the circuitous strata now seen on
" every side of it. A strange property, surely, must be imagined in those winds, thus invariably
" to combine their efforts to bury this stupendous monument of art, without ever taking back

---

[1] Page 152, Ed. 8vo.

" any part of their deposite. Strange, however, as it appears to me, it has been received by most
" writers and visiters of the Pyramid, which opinion I now shall venture to combat.—At the time
" Herodotus reported the length of the side of the base to be 800 feet, (proved above to be of the
" standard chest, and equal to 583 feet 8 inches of ours,) all will agree that he dug not, like the
" French of late, through the sands, in search of the exact length of the foundations of a pile,
" which he was led to believe to be a sepulchral monument, but only measured on the adventitious
" surface, and that probably to no great exactness, but thought a few feet of no such consequence
" as to spoil the round number of 800, by inserting them.

" Now, if the surface had continued to rise by the incessant arrival of sand; as, about 2000
" years after Herodotus, Mr. Greaves, Professor of Astronomy, most accurately measured the side
" of the base also on the adventitious surface, he must have necessarily found, from 2000 years'
" accumulation of sand against the declining sides, a much less length of side than Herodotus
" records : whereas he made the length 693 feet English, which exceeds it by 110 feet. And
" the learned admit that we may depend on the veracity of Herodotus in such matters as fell
" under his cognizance : and who can deny Mr. Greaves an equal character? This inference,
" then, may fairly be drawn, that the winds in those regions have been imperceptibly stripping
" the sand-covered sides of this Pyramid, for at least 2000 years, instead of increasing the accu-
" mulation. This conclusion, however, rests not entirely on the accuracy of these stated dimen-
" sions. The argument is supported by these further considerations.

" All who have written on the Pyramids, agree in one point, though scarce any two in many
" others, that the sands which cover the surface of the rock, and are accumulated about the sides
" of the Pyramids, are adventitious. But by what agency, is the question? Most have taken it
" for granted, without further investigation, they have been brought by the winds : and indeed we
" read of wonderful effects thus produced in those regions of the earth : as tremendous columns
" of sand, raised by the impetuous whirlwinds, to the great terror of the alarmed travellers : but
" where do we read of these phenomena becoming stationary even for a day ? Common obser-
" vation teaches us, that fine sands and pulverized earth are invariably driven by the wind from
" higher grounds and summits, and lodged in vales. All readers and travellers know the surface
" whereon the Pyramid stands, is the summit of an extensive rising ground or covered rock, at
" a sufficient distance from the mountains of Lybia to give the wind free access to the site
" whereon the Pyramid is built. And it is directly contrary to common experience to attribute
" that deposite of sand to the agency of the wind, since the removal of it is rather the natural and
" invariable effect of that agitated element. And that this has been the case with the sands
" deposited about the Pyramid, the greater altitude of them at the time of Herodotus, and the
" less altitude when Mr. Greaves visited the Pyramid, seems to be a proof, wanting nothing but
" accuracy in their statements to be a demonstration : and though no man is infallible, can it be
" reasonable to argue two such reputable characters, as Greaves and Herodotus, could either of
" them, in so short a length, as at most one stadium or furlong, have deviated from the other and
" from truth, by 110 feet ?

" But if this deposite of sand is not the effect of the winds, by what agency came it there ?
" Not by any extraordinary overflowing of the Nile, from which a sediment might be left : for it
" is known, that river never rose to near the height of that plain of rock, nor are there any kind
" of shell-fish in the Nile : whereas shells and petrified oysters are found in the sands about the
" Pyramids.

" And it must be allowed, when this Pyramid of Giza was built, there were no such depths either
" of sands or of earth upon the rock, as in the time of Herodotus, from the absurdities that would
" follow such a supposition : since the builders must first have dug out their depth of sand equal

" in extent to twelve English acres : and when their work was completed, must be argued to have
" filled in, against the declining sides, to the level of the former surface, and thus have buried a
" considerable part of their own work.

" From these positions, it evidently appears, this Pyramid must have been erected by the
" Antediluvians before the universal deluge, called Noah's flood, and the description given of it in
" Holy Writ will account in a satisfactory manner for the lodgment of sands on the surface of
" that extensive rock.

" It is natural to conclude the heavier particles of sand, when the waters became tranquil,
" would sink first, and the lighter particles, of course, both on account of their texture as well as
" their more exposed situation, would easily pulverize, and be sooner conveyed by the winds to
" distant places, than the ponderous, compressed layers, intermixed with shells and portions of
" loam, which more immediately covered the sides of the Pyramid nearer the rock. Of course
" the reduction of this consolidated mass has been by slow degrees, and its dispersion by the
" winds so imperceptible as to defeat observation." [1]

Herodotus stated the length of the side to be about 600 feet, of our measure about 583 feet ;
Mr. Greaves states it to be 693 feet English, or 110 feet more. The French found the base of
the Pyramid 31 feet below the surface : now, taking the area at eight acres, the builders must
have removed 611,177 cubic yards to lay the foundation. And if Herodotus's account be taken,
of the less height of the Pyramid and increased depth of sand, it would be 3,745,928 yards. The
French found Mr. Greaves's measurement correct.

In addition to the argument of Mr. Gab, upon the excavation to acquire a foundation for the
Pyramids, it may be asked, If they were built on the rock before it was covered with sand from
the desert, how *came* the rock itself not to be covered ? Did the winds only begin to blow sand
when the Pyramid began to be built ? During the thousands of years before, was no sand blown ?
This appears to me to form a very strong argument in favour of Mr. Gab's hypothesis, though it
seems to have been overlooked by him.

7. The oases in the deserts are much more exposed than the Pyramids to the drifting of the
sands by the winds, and they are not covered, nor are likely to be so. The ruins of the old
temple of Jupiter Ammon are yet remaining, and the groves of palm trees, and the ruins of temples
around it, would form as effectual obstructions to the free passage of the sands as the Pyramids.
But between the sandy deserts of Lybia and the Pyramids, is a ridge of mountains placed, as if on
purpose to form a barrier against the sands ; and so completely have they answered this purpose,
that, as Major Rennel says, [2] " So little have the sands of Lybia raised the country, that they
" have not even filled up the old bed of the Nile, which runs past the Pyramids, and which is
" easily distinguishable by a hollow and series of lakes, and an old canal. And it appears that
" Giza is several miles from the present Giza, where the Pyramids are." Authors speak of the
Etesian winds as causing this effect. I believe these winds do not blow from West to East, but,
on the contrary, blow mostly up the river from North and North-east to South and South-west. [3]

From the best information which I have been able to acquire, it does not appear that the sand
ever continues for any great length of time higher on one side of the Pyramid than on the other,
but, in fact, as we might expect, it varies with the winds—sometimes higher on one side, sometimes on another.

Ancient Giza was, I think, the sea-port before the Nile changed its bed ; and the change was
probably effected by the inundation of which I shall speak, which at the same time buried the

[1] Gab's Finis Pyramidis.   [2] Geog. Syst. of Herod. Vol. II.   [3] Univers. Hist. Vol. I. p. 419.

Pyramids in sand, changed the bed of the river, and, in great part, if not entirely, formed the Delta. The flood which, I shall shew, flowed up Egypt, probably covered a considerable part of Lybia, and carried thither shells similar to those found at the foot of the great Pyramid, and on the surface of the sand around the temple of Seva or Jupiter Ammon,[1] to which it is not impossible the flood extended. The phenomena noticed by Mr. Gab, I think may be accounted for in the following manner:

I suppose that when the Pyramids at Giza were built, Memphis was the capital, and Giza the sea-port, placed at the end of a gulf or bay. By the breaking of the mounds which formed banks to the Euxine, the Palus Mæotis, the Caspian and Aral Seas, when they were all in contiguous lakes or in one sea, as I have expressed my persuasion that they formerly were, before the opening of the Darnanelles took place—a sudden, mighty rush of water would be made on to the shores of Athos and Greece, which being stopped directly in front, would be divided, and half of it turned into the bay of Egypt, and over the land of Upper Egypt; and the other half of it into Thrace,—causing the flood, recorded by Plato, drowning the first race of people on the East shores of Greece, and carrying along with it, in each case, the mass of sand and sea-shells now found around the Pyramids.[2] However this may have been, the petrified oysters and other sea-shells never can have been brought thither by the winds of Libya, nor by the downward annual flowings of the Nile. The former supposition is, upon the face of it, impossible, and the oyster shells are never found except in salt water, and therefore cannot be supposed to have come down the river, but must have gone up it. In the assertion that there are no oysters in the Nile, I have ascertained that Mr. Gab has fallen into a great mistake. There are oysters in the lower part of it, some of which, of course, would be carried up by any great body of water suddenly rushing into the country above Memphis.

If it be not thought possible that a great rush of water coming from the Euxine, against Greece and Negropont, might flow up Egypt, I know of no resource we have, except, perhaps, *the more probable theory* of Mr. Gab, that in the universal deluge, which raised up Mont Blanc and Chimborazo, and which happened since the building of the Pyramids, *and left them perfect and uninjured*, the oyster shells may have been brought down from the mountains of the Moon, for I know no where else that they can have come from.

If we suppose that the strait of Gibraltar was originally closed like the Isthmus of Suez, and that the water flowed over the neck of land, we may readily conceive how Lower Egypt, the Isthmus of Suez, the Pontine Marshes, and many islands, would be left dry, on its breaking down the neck into the Atlantic. Whether the opening increased gradually for a great number of years after its first disruption, or it happened at once, it will readily account for the Pharos of Alexandria having once stood a considerable distance from the land, and for the city of Hadria and the sea-port of Padua, in Italy, being left far inland, where they are now found.

8. Pretty nearly as numerous as the theories of the origin of the Nile and its floods, and as nonsensical, have been the theories of the origin of the Delta of Egypt. Herodotus, Diodorus Siculus, Strabo, and Ptolemy, assert that the Delta of Egypt was once overflowed by the sea.[3] This is perfectly consistent with reason and probability, and with the experience which we have of the formation of deltas at the mouths of other rivers; and I cannot see why, for its mere formation, we are to seek for any other cause: but this argument does not apply to the question of the *slow* or *speedy* formation of the Delta.

In a discourse recently delivered at Paris, Cuvier declared, that *" we come by a very simple*

---

[1] Vide Rennel, ib. pp. 238, 257.   [2] See Asiat. Journal, Jan. 1828.   [3] Ency. Britt. art. Phil.

" calculation to the result, that 2000 *years before Christ the whole of Lower Egypt had no exist-*
" *ence.* We presume that the learned philosopher does not mean to bind us to the strict letter, or
" we shall find some difficulty, even on the lowest system of chronology, in constructing that
" kingdom of Egypt which Abraham visited, and the city of Zoan (Tanis), where in all probability
" its king resided." [1]

I apprehend there can be no doubt that the flood of the Nile is the effect of the periodical rains,
or the melting of snow in the mountains of Africa, or of both these causes united. For many
generations the river has not deposited annually much sediment, but, for obvious reasons, this can
raise no objection to the supposed formation of the Delta by the deposite from the river, aided by
the North winds blowing into the mouth of it. For though, as appears from Mr. Bruce's account,
all the rivulets by which the Abyssinian Nile is fed, now have stony beds, free from mud;
yet what Herodotus has said may probably be perfectly true, that the Delta was raised by the
gradual deposition of *mud* brought from the high countries,—because this may have taken place
before the mud was exhausted; before the hill-sides and the beds of the rivers of the high
country were washed almost clean: since that time no very considerable deposite may have taken
place. The same process is now going on in the lake of Geneva. The Rhone deposits its mud,
and forms islands or lagunes at the top of the lake, and runs out at the bottom as clear as crystal.
At first the sediment would be invisible, until at last it would come near the surface, and the whole
bay would become very shallow, with the exception of one or perhaps two deep gullies: and when
the disruption, to which I have before alluded, took place, and the great mass of water escaped at
Gibraltar, the land which had been gradually forming under the water would be left dry, and the
Delta would shew itself.

When I look at a map, and contemplate the little progress made by the Euphrates and Tigris,
by the Indus, Ganges, and Burrampoutra, in filling up the gulfs at their mouths, and in converting
their bays into promontories; and again at the promontory of the Nile, and the recession of
the sea from the shores of the Mediterranean in various parts, and reflect on what the ingenious
geologist, Mr. Lyal, has said respecting the rate of the formation of Deltas generally, I cannot help thinking that there must have been some *peculiar* cause for the more rapid formation,
or at least exaltation above the sea, of the Delta of Egypt, than mere subsidence of alluvial matter.
And this I attribute to the breaking down of the bank at the straits of Gibraltar, or the widening
of an ancient opening at those straits, or to the lowering, from some other cause, of the waters of
the Mediterranean. For the elevation of the Pontine marshes and other shores and islands of this
sea must be accounted for, which cannot be done by the subsidence of the sediment of any rivers,
because in many cases there are no rivers to deposit sediment. No doubt a strong surface current
sets into the Mediterranean at present from the Atlantic, which makes against my system, but
this may not always have been so, and a deep counter current is generally believed at present to
take place. The ingenious author of the review of Mr. Lyal's fine work on Geology, says, the
latter is an unwarranted hypothesis. I have been told, on the contrary, that it has been ascertained, from actual experiment, by some of our naval officers, to be true. [2]

But, whatever may be the fact with respect to the current at Gibraltar, the truth of which is not
yet, I think, ascertained, I cannot doubt that the water of the Mediterranean, fed by the Danube,
Nile, Rhone, Tiber, Tanais, Dnieper, &c., &c., must have some way of escaping. Evaporation is
not enough to account for the effect. Evaporation must take place in the great Atlantic as well as
the small Mediterranean. If it do not go by the straits of Gibraltar, it must have a subterraneous

---

[1] Quarterly Review, No. LXXXV., May 1830, p. 131 n.   [2] Ibid. No. LXXXVI. p. 446.

passage, like the Dead sea and the Caspian. Some time ago I was told by an Indian traveller, that the surface of the Caspian was forty feet below the surface of the Indus at its mouth, and that he supposed the water of this sea escaped by an immense whirlpool which was not far from its South end. On naming this circumstance to another Indian traveller, to Captain E—, whose public duty it is to inquire into matters of this kind, he told me my friend, Col. W—,[1] was mistaken; that he had made a mistake from having a defective barometer; that he had tried it himself with a good instrument made by Troughton, and he found it not forty, but one hundred and forty feet below the Indus. Now this is an extremely interesting fact, and raises the questions, What becomes of the water? Does the water circulate when heated by an equatorial sun, and flow up to the poles and back again, as it flows out and back again in the newly-discovered apparatus for warming buildings?

10. We learn from Plato, and other Greek authors, that, in a very remote æra, a large island in the Atlantic ocean was swallowed up by the sea, and with it numerous nations, at one moment, drowned. This history does not seem improbable, and will, if admitted, account for many coincidences between the natives of the old and new worlds.

Of the size of this Atlantis we know really nothing. It may have been three times as large as Australia, for any thing which we know to the contrary. If we look at the map of the globe, and consider the relative space of its surface which is occupied by land and water, we must at once see, that if there be only an equal quantity of each, there is infinitely more than enough water to cover the land fifteen cubits high, above even the hills of the old world, which might be low. But in addition to this, the space of sea is not merely equal, but is much greater than the space of land.

The first convulsion of which I have spoken is that which made Britain an island, and threw up Mount Blanc and Chimborazo. After that convulsion another might have been caused by the sinking of Atlantis. This may have been caused by that which occasioned the destruction of Mahabali-pore. Another great change in all the islands and shores of the Mediterranean may have taken place when the opening was made at the straits of Gibraltar, and another great change may have taken place when the lakes Aral, Asoph, and Euxine, broke their banks, by which the flood described by Plato may have been first effected, and the Delta of Egypt and the shores of Italy left dry, after it had escaped at the straits. All those different catastrophes probably happened. Of their order, except with respect to the first, I give no opinion.

I think it not at all unlikely that when the Atlantis sunk, the level of the water of the Mediterranean may have been changed, in some way or other, which we cannot discover, though the sinking of the island would have a tendency to raise it. But since the building of Adria, Padua, &c., it seems certainly to have been changed. This is an indisputable fact, which it is of no use to deny. At the time that this happened, the passage which connected the Dead sea with the Red sea, shewn by Burchardt formerly to have existed, and the isthmus of Suez formerly covered with water, may have been both left dry. I shall in a future page give some reasons to prove, that Egypt was not peopled by tribes passing over the isthmus of Suez, but across the Red sea from some place near Mecca.

If ever the rock over which the water rushes at Niagara should suddenly give way, no doubt a very sensible flood would be experienced in Ireland. In consequence of having a vastly greater space to expand its waters over, this flood, when compared with those in the Mediterranean, would be trifling. On the order of the floods of which I have spoken we must always remain ignorant; but it is probable, I think, that one of them, and perhaps the second spoken of by me, 2500 or 3000

---

[1] Both gentlemen are now in India, and I have not permission to give their names.

years before Christ, caused the destruction of almost the whole of mankind; a few might be saved in ships, and it might happen that among these few might be the possessors of our system of letters. The distressing state in which they may have been left will account, without difficulty, for the loss of the learning which their fathers, as Bailly supposed, possessed. But all these matters are mere theories; of their truth we cannot be certain.

11. I have lately discovered a geological fact of a nature which bears strongly upon this subject. There is in Yorkshire, near the confluence of the rivers Ouse and Trent, within the angle which they make before they unite and form the river Humber, a tract of alluvial country of great riches and fertility, which has formerly been covered with oak and fir timber, the lower parts of which yet remain in the ground fixed as they grew. Sometimes whole trees are found lying on their sides. The firs are mostly a little bent by the weight of the superincumbent soil, but they yet retain their white colour. The oak is generally perfectly black. This country is now defended from the tides by banks maintained at a very great expense; but the fact to which I have alluded is this—the tides now rise at least six feet above the surface of the soil where the remains of these trees are yet found. From the appearance of the trees, it is probable, that after being long covered with water they have rotted off a little above ground, the tops have fallen, and most of them been floated away by the tides and floods, and the bottoms have been by degrees covered with alluvial soil as they are now found.

From this it is quite certain that a great change must have taken place in the relative levels of the land and ocean, because these trees could never have grown in a soil where they were daily flooded with the salt water. What I have stated with respect to the tides and the remains of the trees which I have seen, are facts which cannot be disputed, and I think they shew that a very *great* but *unsuspected* change has taken place, or is taking place, in the relative situations of the land and the sea. Every thing tends to shew, that the surface of the Mediterranean sea, with respect to its shores, has been lowered. The facts stated respecting the trees in Yorkshire PROVE that the Atlantic, with relation to the land of Britain, has been raised, or vice versâ, the land lowered. The district where these trees are found was drained, in the time of Charles II., by one Sir Cornelius Vermuyden, and there does not appear any reason to believe that the relative altitudes of the land and ocean have undergone any perceptible change since that time. Of course, in a country like this, the natives watch every thing relating to those altitudes with great anxiety. The relative levels of the land and tides have lately been ascertained by experienced engineers with very great care.

The bold shores on the east and south-east coast of Britain keep constantly yielding to the washing of the bases of their cliffs by the tides; but the rising within the last century of the large and valuable tract of land called Sunk island, at the mouth of the Humber, proves, that if any change be taking place in the relative altitude of the island and the ocean, the former is now rising, not sinking; but I do not think there is reason to believe that any change is taking place. The whole subject is one of very great curiosity and interest: I shall now leave it to the consideration of my reader, but I shall return to it again in the course of the following pages. For more information on subjects connected with the series of lakes, or the inland seas of Asia, the reader may consult, among the ancients, Strabo, Lib. i.; Pliny, Hist. Nat. Lib. ii. Cap. 90; and *Diodorus Siculus*: among the moderns, Pallas, Reise, durch Siberien, Book v.; Klaproth's Survey of the Country North of Caucasus; Mons. Choiseul Gouffier, Memoire de Institut. Royal de France, 1815; Dr. Clarke's Travels; and Muller's Univers. Hist. Eng. Trans. Vol. I. p. 33.

CHAPTER II

Adoration of the Virgin and Child—Carmelites attached to the Virgin—Virgin of
the Sphere—Festival of the Virgin—German and Italian Virgin—Mansions of
the Moon—Montfaucon—Multimammia—Isis and the Moon—Celestial Virgin
of Dupuis—Kircher—Jesus Ben Panther—Lunar Mansions

1. In the two following chapters I shall repeat, with some important additions, or shall collect into
one view, what has been said in a variety of places in the foregoing work, respecting the Queen of
Heaven, the Virgin Mary, and her son Iaw; to which I shall also add some observations respecting the famous God Bacchus.

In very ancient as well as modern times, the worship of a female, supposed to be a virgin, with
an infant in her arms, has prevailed. This worship has not been confined to one particular place
or country, but has spread to nearly every part of the habitable world. In all Romish countries to
this day, the Virgin, with the infant Jesus Christ in her arms, is the favourite object of adoration;
and it is, as it has been observed before, a decisive proof that the Christ, the good shepherd, the
Saviour of the Romish church of Italy, is the same as the person of the same name in India; that
he is, like him, described to be black, to be an Ethiopian. It seems that if a person wanted a fact
to complete the proof of the identity of the person of Cristna and the Romish Jesus, he could not
have invented any thing more striking than this, when all the other circumstances are considered.
But though they were both black, I think they had both the name of Crish, or Christ, or Χρησος,
from a word in a very ancient language, (the parent both of the Greek and the Sanscrit,) having
the meaning of *Benignus*, of which I shall say more hereafter. We will now try to find out who
the celebrated virgin, the mother of this person, was.

The Virgin Mary, in most countries where the Roman faith prevails, is called the Queen of
Heaven: this is the very epithet given by the ancients to the mother of Bacchus, who was said to
be a virgin. The Rev. Dr. Stukeley writes, "Diodorus says Bacchus was born of Jupiter (mean-
"ing the Supreme) and Ceres, or as others think, Proserpine."—"Both Ceres and Proserpine
"were called Κορη, which is analogous to the Hebrew עלמה *virgo*, παρθενος, LXX., Isaiah vii. 14:
"Behold a virgin shall conceive. It signifies eminently *the* virgin. Αθηναιοι Διονυσον τ Διος
"και Κορης σεβωσιν. Arrian, Alex. II. The Egyptians called this same person Bacchus, or the
"sun-deity, by the name of *Orus*, which is the same as the Greek word Κορος aspirated. The
"heathen fables as oft confound Bacchus's mother and wife."

"Ovid, Fasti iii., makes Libera, the name of Ariadne, Bacchus's pretended wife, whom Cicero,
"de Nat. Deor., makes to be Proserpina, Bacchus's mother. The story of this woman being
"deserted by a man, and espoused by a God, has somewhat so exceedingly like that passage,
"Matt. i. 19, 20, of the blessed virgin's history, that we should wonder at it, did we not see the
"parallelism infinite between the sacred and the profane history before us.

" — Ariadne was translated into heaven, as is said of the Virgin, and her nuptial garland was
"turned into an heavenly crown: she was made queen of heaven."

Testis siderea torta corona Dea. Propert. iii. 17.

" — There are many similitudes between the Virgin and the mother of Bacchus in all the old

" fables; as for instance, Hyginus (Fab. 164) makes Adonens or Adonis the son of Myrrha.
" Adonis is Bacchus beyond controversy."

> Ogygia me Bacchum vocat
> Osirin Egyptus putat
> Arabica gens Adoneum.   AUSON.

" Adonis is the Hebrew אדני *(Adni)* Adonai, which the Heathens learned from the Arabians—
" one of the sacred names of the Deity. Mary or Miriam, St. Jerome interprets *Myrrha* MARIS:
" Mariamne is the same appellation of which Ariadne seems a corruption. Orpheus calls the mo-
" ther[1] of Bacchus, Leucothea, a *sea Goddess*.

" — Nonnus in Dyonys. calls Sirius star Mœra, Μαιρης. Hesychius says, Μαιρα κυον το
" αςρον. Our Sanford hence infers this star to mean Miriam, Moses's sister. Vossius de Idolal.
" approves of it. Μαιρα by metathesis is Μαρια."[2]

Thus we see that the Rev. and learned Gentleman, Dr. Stukeley, has clearly made out, that the
story of Mary, the queen of heaven, the mother of אדני *(Adni)* Adonis, *or the Lord*, as our book
always renders this word, with her translation to heaven, &c., was an *old story* long before Jesus
of Nazareth was born. After this, Stukeley observes, that Ariadne, the queen of heaven, has upon
her head a crown of twelve stars. This is the case of the queen of heaven in almost every church
on the continent.

2. In the service or liturgy of the Carmelites, which I bought in Dublin at the Carmelite monastery, the Virgin is called STELLA MARIS; that is, in fact, the star of the sea—" Leucothea"—
Venus rising from the sea.

All monks were Carmelites till the fifth century.[3] After that time, from different religious mo-
tives, new orders branched off from the old one, and became attached to new superstitions: but
the Carmelites always remained, and yet remain, attached in a peculiar manner to the Virgin Mary,
the Regina Stellarum.[4] The Carmelites were the original monks, Ναζωραιοι, translated from

---

[1] Nurse.   [2] Stukeley, Pal. Sac. No. I. p. 34.   [3] Priestley, Hist. Cor. Vol. II. p. 403.

[4] I am of opinion that a certain class of persons, initiated into the higher mysteries of the ancients, were what are
called *Carmelites Therapeutæ* and *Esseniens*, or that they constituted a part of, or were formed out of, these sects, and
were what we now call *Freemasons*. They were also called Chaldæi and Mathematici. I think that the rite of circumcision was originally instituted for the characteristic mark of the fraternity or society. I doubt its being a religious
community solely. Abraham brought circumcision from Urr of the Chaldees. When the Jewish tribe was declared a
priestly tribe it was circumcised, part of the secret rites were thrown open to all, probably the tribe refused any longer
to be excluded from them, and the rite no longer continued the secret symbol. We read of three hundred and eighteen
servants trained in Abraham's own house. On these persons, the Apostle, St. Barnabas, the companion of St. Paul, has
the following passage:

" For the Scripture says, that Abraham circumcised three hundred and eighteen men of his house. But what, there-
" fore, was the mystery that was made known to him? Mark the eighteen and next the three hundred. For the
" numeral letters of *ten* and *eight* are I H, and these denote Jesus; and because the cross was that by which we were
" to find grace, therefore he adds, *Three hundred*: the note of which is T *(the figure of his cross)*. Wherefore by two
" letters he signified Jesus, and by the third his cross. He who has put the engrafted gift of his doctrine within us
" knows that I never taught to any one a more certain truth: but I trust ye are worthy of it."—Epist. Barnabas, Sect.
ix. ed. Wake.

This epistle of St. Barnabas was formerly read in the Romish churches; but the Protestants do not allow it to be
genuine. One reason why Jones contends that it is spurious is, because it says that Abraham circumcised 318 men of
his family, which is not now in the text. But the Hebrew word which Jones renders circumcised חניכיו *Anikiu*, in one
sense means initiated, and this justifies Barnabas. In fact, this word *Anikiu* is our initiate. (Jones on Canon, Pt. III.
ch. xli. p. 449.) If what I suspect be true, viz. that circumcision was the mark or test of initiation, Barnabas the Apostle
might not understand the full import of the *Greek*; but he cannot be supposed to have been ignorant of the *Hebrew*,

Meru and Tibet to Mount Carmel, or the mount of *the garden of God*, or *of the sun*, at the foot of Lebanon, or of the mountain of the moon. They were the original monks of Maia or Maria; the others were all offsets from the parent tree, or perhaps they were a species of heretics who arose from the original monkish religious system. This accounts for the Carmelites being, in a peculiar manner, attached to the adoration of the Virgin.

Isidore of Seville says, that the meaning of the word Mary is, One who begins to illuminate—*Maria illuminatrix*. He gives to this virgin, as her mother, a person called Anna, an allegorical name, by which the Romans meant the annual revolution of the sun, which they personified, and for whom they had a festival, under the name of *Anna Perenna*, at the beginning of the year. [1] The Hindoos have the same person as a Goddess under the name of Anna, or Unnu Poorna. [2] Poorna is evidently Perenna, or Porana. There is extant, in Jones on the Canon, a gospel history called that of *James* or of *Mary*, in which her mother is called Anna, of whom I shall say more presently.

Dr. Pritchard says, " The beneficent form of Bhavani, termed Devi or Anna Purna, is doubtless, " as Sir W. Jones remarked, the Anna Perenna of the Romans." Again, " Anna Purna is, how- " ever, also the counterpart of the Egyptian Isis. She is figured as bent by the weight of her full " breasts, and reminds us of the statues of Isis Multimammia." Again, " Bhavani is invoked by " the name of Ma, as was Demeter among the Greeks by that of Maia." [3] In the passages where the Hebrew word מרים *nrim* of the Old Testament is translated by the Vulgate, it is rendered Maria, and the LXX. render it Μαριαμ. All this clearly proves that they are the same name. [4]

3. Though there can be no doubt, that the celestial virgin of the sphere was one original source whence the Madonna, Regina Cœli, Θεοτοκος—and Mater Dei, were derived, yet the Goddess Cybele was another. She was equally called the Queen of Heaven and the Mother of the Gods. As devotees now collect alms in the name of the Virgin, so did they in ancient times in the name of Cybele, in which they were protected by a law when begging was not otherwise allowed. The Galli now used in the churches of Italy were anciently used in the worship of Cybele. Our Lady-day, or the day of the blessed Virgin of the Roman Church, was heretofore dedicated to Cybele. " It was called Hilaria," says Macrobius, " on account of the joy occasioned by the arrival of " the equinox." Lampridius also says, that it was a festival dedicated to the Mother of the Gods. A Greek commentator on Dionysius cited by Demster, in his Antiquities, also states, that the Hilaria was a festival in honour of the Mother of the Gods. In the fourth century there existed a sect of Christians called Collyridians, who made offerings of cakes to the Virgin Mary as a Goddess and Queen of Heaven. [5]

The Collyridians are said, by Mr. Sayle, [6] to have come from Arabia. They worshiped the Virgin Mary for God, offering her a sort of twisted cake called collyris, whence the sect had its name. This notion of the divinity of the Virgin Mary was also believed by some persons at the Council of Nice, who said there were two Gods besides the Father, viz. Christ and the Virgin

---

because he was a Jew, and therefore must be supposed to understand the common powers of notation of the letters of his own language. He here makes the Hebrew T stand for 300, which, in my table, appears to stand for 400. The canons of criticism by which Jones pretends to try the genuineness of ancient books, can on no account be admitted.

[1] Dupuis, Vol. III. p. 47, 4to.

A very learned dissertation on the Anna of the Romans, with much very curious information, may be found in Nimrod, Vol. III. p. 47. See also Taylor's Calmet, Vol. IV. p. 68. For the history of *Anna*, the mother of Mary, and of *Joachim*, that is חנה *hhm*, Jah the wise, Jones on the Canon, Vol. II. p. 145, may be consulted.

[2] Vide Ward's India.   [3] Anal. Egyp. Mythos. p 280.   [4] Exod. xv. 20.

[5] Jortin, Eccles. Rem. Vol. I. 332.   [6] Prem. Dis. to Koran, Sect. ii. p. 45.

Mary; and they were thence named Mariamites.[1]   Others imagined her to be exempt from humanity, and deified; which goes but little beyond the Popish superstition in calling her the Complement of the Trinity, as if it were imperfect without her.

It is very evident that the idea of Mary being the mother of God, and also God himself, in some way or other, arose from the Maia of India, the spouse of Brahme. Maia was the female generative power, and, as such, the Deity, and the mother of Buddha, or Divine Wisdom or the Logos. Thus she was the mother of Iao or of IHΣ or of Jesus, and still a part of the Deity. She was also the חרי *ruh*, and thus it was that this word was feminine in the Hebrew or the Buddist book of Genesis.

4. Samuel and John the Baptist had the same person for their mothers as the Virgin Mary, viz. Anna, or at least persons of the same name, who all produced their sons in their extreme old age. Samson's mother was delivered of her son in the same way, but her name is not given : but from the similarity in other respects it was probably the same. All these ladies might very properly be called what, I have no doubt that they were called, PERENNAS or PER-ANNAS; having the same meaning as Per-vetustas. But this Per-anna, or old year, seems nonsense. I believe it secretly or mystically alluded to the MIGHTY year celebrated by Virgil, (see B. v. Ch. ii. Sect. 7,) and that it was the period of 608 years, to which it alluded.[2]

The 25th of March was a day of general festivity throughout the ancient Grecian and Roman world, and was called Hilaria. The Phrygians kept the same holiday and worshiped Atys, the mother of the Gods, with similar rites. Hence the appointment of this day, Lady-day, to the honour of the mother of Jesus, called by the Catholics, the mother of God.[3] Here Atys is made a female. Atys in the Persian means *fire*. This must be Vesta. Is it anagrammatically *ysta*, Latin ista ?

In the 15th verse of the third chapter of Genesis God says to the serpent, which had tempted Eve, " I will put enmity between thee and the woman, and between thy seed and her seed : IT " shall bruise thy head, and thou shalt bruise HIS heel." Here the seed is called IT, and afterward HIS in the masculine gender. But the Roman Church (as I have before shewn) translates this in the Vulgate IPSA *conteret caput tuum*, by which they cause the woman to bruise the serpent's head, and not, as the Protestants do, the seed of the woman to bruise it. The Hebrew language having no neuter gender, therefore a *literal* translation must have either *he* or *she*. Availing themselves of this equivocal or double meaning, they have made this passage serve as a justification of their adoration of the celestial virgin, which they found in Italy and other countries ; and which, of course, in compliance with their much abused traditionary practice, they adopted.

When I first examined this subject, I was of opinion that the adoption of the *ipsa* instead of the *ipse* was the effect of ignorance; but since I considered the matter more deeply, I have been induced to believe that this rendering was the effect of profound learning, not of ignorance ; and that it was done in order to adopt secretly the adoration of the double principle. The adoption of the word *ipsa* instead of *ipse* is of very great importance ; as, when combined with the reasoning which the reader has seen respecting the serpent's biting of the foot, and not the heel, of Cristna, it shews most clearly that the Mythos of the East cannot have been copied from that of the West.

In Dr. Geddes's Critical Remarks on this passage may be seen every thing of any consequence which has been said upon the question, whether the Hebrew ought to be rendered by *he* or *she* ; but I am quite certain that the result of unprejudiced examination must be, that it may be ren-

---

[1] Vide Beausobre, Hist. Manich., Vol. I p. 532.   [3] Magnus ab integro sæclorum nascitur ordo.

[2] Israel Worsley's Enq. p. 13.

dered either way. The two words אֵיָּה *eia* and אֵּוּה *eua* Mr. Parkhurst[1] has very correctly shewn are convertible, and both of them have a masculine and also a feminine meaning.

5. In many churches as well as in many places in the streets of Mayence on the Rhine, the Virgin is seen having the child on one arm, and a branch of lilies, the lotus, in the hand of the other arm, standing with one foot upon the head of a serpent, which has a sprig of an apple-tree with an apple on it in its mouth, and its tail twisted about a globe partly enveloped in clouds; therefore evidently a celestial globe. Her other foot is placed in the inside of a crescent. Her head is surrounded with a glory of stars. Can any one doubt that this is the Regina Stellarum of the sphere? The branch of the apple-tree in the mouth of the serpent with the Virgin's foot upon its head, shews pretty clearly who this Virgin of the sphere was—*Ipsa conteret caput tuum.* The circumstance of the Virgin almost always having the lotus or lily, the sacred plant both of Egypt and India, in her hand (or an angel has it and presents it to her) is very striking. It is found, Sir R. Ker Porter observes,[2] " in Egypt, Palestine, Persia, India, all over the East, and was of old in " the tabernacle and temple of the Israelites. It is also represented in all pictures of the saluta- " tion of Gabriel to the Virgin Mary; and, in fact, has been held in mysterious veneration by " people of all nations and times."

The worship of the *black* Virgin and Child probably came from the East. The *white* one is the Goddess Nurtia or Nortia of the Etruscans.[3] I saw in the palazzo Manfreni, at Venice, in a collection of Etruscan antiquities, some small figures of the Virgin and Child in Bronze, evidently originally from Egypt. In the Museum F. Gorii will be found a print of an Etruscan Virgin and Child; the Goddess Nurtia or Nortia, as he calls her.[4]

There can be no doubt, that the Virgin of the sphere, who treads on the head of the serpent, is the Virgin of the first book of Genesis. This is all explained by Mons. Dupuis.[5] In some of the spheres we see the Virgin with the lotus or lily, in others with ears of ripe corn in her hand. I apprehend the Virgin with the ripe corn was the Virgin of Taurus: and that the birth-place of this mythos will be found in a latitude where corn will be ripe in August or the beginning of September, and this will fix it to a latitude very far from Lower India or Upper Egypt; to about that latitude where May, or the month of Maia, the mother of the God Buddha, would be the leading spring month, in which all nature would be in its most beautiful attire, and this would be at least as high as latitude 45, or North of Samarkand.

The Abbé Pluche admits, what indeed is evident, that Virgo symbolizes the harvest season. But in the plains of Sennaar the harvest season is over several months before the sun passes into that sign.[6]

---

[1] Vide his Hebrew Grammar.   [2] Travels in Persia, VI. p. 628, 4to.

[3] The present church of St. Stephen at Bologna is formed from several Heathen temples which have stood together like those at Tivoli and Ancona. The centre one, of a circular form, has been a temple of Isis. On the side of the church is to be seen an ancient inscription in these words: Dominae victrici Isidi.

[4] Tab. 4, Ant. Fran. Gorii, Nortia Tuscorum Dea. Summa religione à Volsiniensibus et Volaterranis culta. A statue of a female much covered with drapery, with a child in swaddling clothes in her arms. The head of the mother is broken off, and the complexion of the figures cannot be judged of from the print. She was called the Magna Dea by the Etruscans: on the arm of the mother is an inscription in Etruscan letters. See plates, fig. 17; also Pliny, Lib. xxxvi. Cap. vii.; Livy, Lib. vii.; etiam Festum Pompeium: Juvenalem, Sat. x. v. 74; and the treatise Donianas inscriptiones antiquas Francisci Gorii. Class. I. Num. 149, 150; Tertullian, Apologet. Cap. xxiv. Reinesius states, Class. I. Num. cxxxi., that an inscription was found in the foundation of the Church of S. Reparata at Florence in these words—*To the great Goddess Nortia.* See also Cicero, Lib. ii. de Officiis; Martianus Capella, Lib. de Nuptiis Philolog. Cap. ix.

[5] Tome III. p. 90, and his plate, No. 19. In this plate is described the whole horoscope of the birth of Jesus, &c.

[6] Drum. Zod. p. 95.

The Virgin's having generally the *lotus*, but sometimes an *ear of wheat* in her hand, arose from a very profound and mysterious doctrine—connected with the pollen of plants—of which I shall treat hereafter, as already intimated.

6. The signs of the Zodiac are not any of them remarkable for being connected with objects of an Indian nature. The twenty-eight Hindoo lunar mansions and the asterisms are almost all named after objects peculiarly Hindoo. This raises a strong presumption against the solar Zodiac being of Hindoo invention. If the solar Zodiac had been of Hindoo or African growth, the elephant and camel would have been found there. [1]

Mr. Maurice has observed, that the signs of the Zodiac cannot be of Egyptian origin because they are not adapted to the order in which the seasons succeed each other in Egypt. For instance, Virgo with ears of ripened corn in her hand evidently points to the season of harvest—such, in fact, it is when the sun enters into September; but the corn harvest in Egypt is in March. The same argument applies to Aquarius, which denotes the chilling cold rains of winter, when, in reality, the depth of winter is the season of pleasure in Egypt. [2] All the arguments of Mr. Maurice against Egypt being the birthplace of the Zodiacal signs apply with equal force against India. They must, in fact, have all come from a latitude far higher than Egypt, India, or even Chaldæa. Samarkand is the lowest that can be admitted. There being in these Zodiacs no sign of the elephant, the pride of the animal creation both in Africa and India, is a fact alone sufficient to shew that the Zodiac is not an invention of these countries.

Maia, the mother of Mercury, Mr. Davies says, [3] is the universal genius of nature, which discriminated all things, according to their various kinds or species: the same, perhaps, as the Meth of the Egyptians and the Μητις of the Orphic bards, which was of all kinds, and the author of all things—και Μητις πρωτος γενετωρ.

" Sir William Jones was told by a Cashmirian, that Maya herself is the mother of universal " nature, and of all the inferior gods. This exactly agrees with the import of the word among the " Geeks. Maia properly denotes a *grandmother* or *a great mother*." Hesychius (Lex.) says, Μαια, πατρος και μητρος μητηρ. [4]

We have seen, I think, that it is beyond the possibility of doubt that Buddha and Mercury, sons of Maia, were the same person. This receives a very remarkable confirmation from the fact, that Mercury was always called by the Gentiles the Logos—" The *word* that in the beginning was " God, and that also was a God." [5] But this Logos we have also shewn to be the *Divine Wisdom*, and he was, according to the Pagan Amelius, the Creator. He says, " And this plainly was " the Λογος by whom all things were made, [6] he being himself eternal, as Heraclitus would say: " and by Jove the same whom the barbarian affirms to have been in the place and dignity of a " principal, and to be with God, and to be God, by whom all things were made, and in whom " every thing that was made has its life and being: who, descending into body, and putting on " flesh, took the appearance of a man, though even then he gave proof of the majesty of his na- " ture: nay, after his dissolution, he was deified again." If this do not prove the identity of Buddha and the Romish Jesus nothing can do it.

Sommona Codom I consider to be admitted as one of the names of Buddha. M. La Loubère says, " His mother, whose name is found in some of their Balie books, was called, as they say, " Maha Maria, which seems to signify the *great Mary*, for *Maha* signifies *great*. But it is found

---

[1] Maur. Ant. Hind. Vol. VII. p 604.

[2] Apud Whiter, Etym. Univ. p. 103.

[3] R. Taylor, Dieg. pp. 183—185.

[4] Ind. Ant. Vol. I. p. 29.

[5] Fab. Pag. Idol. B. iv. Ch. v. p. 333.

[6] Ibid.

" written *Mania*, as often as *Maria*. ...... This ceases not to give attention to the missionaries,
" and has, perhaps, given occasion to the Siamese to believe that Jesus being the Son of Mary was
" brother to Sommono-Codom, AND THAT HAVING BEEN CRUCIFIED, he was that wicked brother
" whom they give to Sommono-Codom, under the name of *Thevetat*, and whom they report to be
" punished in hell, with a punishment which PARTICIPATES SOMETHING OF THE CROSS. The
" father of Sommona-Codom was, according to this same Balie book, a king of *Teve-Lanca*, that
" is to say, a king of the famous Ceylon."[1] Cyril of Alexandria calls the Egyptian Mercury
Teutat.[2] Now *Tat* has been shewn to be one of the names of Buddha; and Teve-Lanca is evidently the same as Deve-Lanca, which has been called island Lanca—in the same manner as the
island in the West was called *I* or *Ii*, which it is said means island; but it means also *holy*, or is
the name of God. From all this it follows pretty clearly, that Deve-Lanca, or Teve-Lanca, means
holy Lanca, or *Seren-*DIVE, and that *Teve-Tat* means *holy*, or God or Divus Tat : but *Tat* is
Buddha ; and, of course, as Tat is the son of Mary, Buddha is the son of Mary. But *Tat*, or
Deve-Tat, or *Theve-Tat*, was crucified !!

The Mercury of Egypt, Teut-tat, is the same as the Gothic Thiod-tat, or, query, Thiod-ad?[3]
Here we come, perhaps, at the origin of Θεος. Jayadeva describes Buddha as bathing in blood,
or sacrificing his life to wash away the offences of mankind, and thereby to make them partakers
of the kingdom of heaven. On this the author of the Cambridge Key[4] says, " Can a Christian
" doubt that this Buddha was the type of the Saviour of the world?" This Buddha the Cantab.
supposes to have been Enoch.

The circumstance of Maria being called Mania is worthy of observation. In the old language,
without vowels, MN means moon. Is this one of the reasons why Mary is always represented
with a moon in some way or other—generally standing on it ? If Maria be the same as Maia, and
is the female generative power, we see wny she is always connected with the moon. This Mary
is found in the kingdom of *Sion* or Siam in the city of Judia.[5] The mother of the gods was
called Ma in the Phrygian dialect.[6] In the Hebrew and Arabic languages we have the word
Maria מריא *mria*, which means a female beeve, and also a wild dove.[7] The word in the Hebrew
is attended with much difficulty. I suspect it is in some way mystical, and not understood.

Maia the the mother of Mercury was the daughter of Atlas. Virgil calls her Maia or Maja.[8]
Hesiod calls her Μαιη.

Ζηνι δ' αρ Ατλαντις Μαιη τικε κυδιμον Ἑρμην.

But Pausanias calls her Maera.

Μαιρας γυναικας το Τηγεατ· θυγατερα δε Ατλαντις φασιν ειναι την Μαιραν.[9]

Wen is acknowledged to belong to the Celtic terms for a woman, from which the Latin *Venus* is
derived.[10] Then Alma Venus might mean *the mother*, the mother Venus, the Deity-mother woman,
or the female great Deity. This Alma might mean virgin, because the mother Goddess, though a
mother, was always held to be a virgin. From these abstruse, misunderstood doctrines, might
arise the idea of some of the Christian heretics, that Jesus was taken from the side of his mother.

---

[1] Part iii. p. 136. [2] In Julian. Vide Anc. Univer. Hist. VI. p. 50; Jameson's Herm. Scyth. p. 130.
[3] Hermes Scythicus, Origin of Greeks, p. 131; Univers Hist. Vol. VI. p. 33.   [4] Vol. I. p. 118.
[5] La Loubère, pp. 6, 7.   [6] Sir William Jones, Asiat. Res. Vol. III. p. 14. 4to.
[7] Vide Bochart's Opera, Vol. II. p. 283.   [8] Æn. VIII. v. 138.
[9] Arcadic. Cap. xlviii. p. 698; Jameson's Hermes Scyth. p. 130.
[10] Whiter, Etymol. Univ. p. 757; Davies on the Druids, p. 445.

7. In the fourth plate of the first volume of Montfaucon's Antiquity Explained may be seen several exemplars of the Mother of the Gods. She is called Cybele, and she is on the same monument often joined with Atys. But her most remarkable name is that of Suria. She is loaded in some figures with paps, and on the base of one statue[1] is the word *Suriæ.* On another, *Mater Deor. Mater Suriæ.* This figure is sitting, and is crowned with a mitre of the Romish church, and in appearance is altogether the very picture of the Pope, when seated in his chair, giving his benediction; with the exception that he has not the caduceus, the sistrum, and the emblematic animals with which she is covered. She is evidently the same as Diana or the Multimammia, many figures of which may be seen in Montfaucon's 46th plate.' But the most remarkable figure is in plate 47, where the text describes her as black, but with long hair, therefore not a Negress. On one of the other figures are the words ΦΥCΙC ΠΑΝΑΙΟΛΟC ΠΑΝΤ ΜΗΤ, and on another, Φυcιc παναιολοc. None of these figures seem to be of very great antiquity. I have seen many of them in Rome, but it has happened that all which I recollect to have seen have had white drapery, —although the face, hands, and feet, were black. I suspect that this Syrian goddess, or Dea Suriæ, or Syriæ, is of a far more *eastern* origin; that she is closely connected with the Buddhist Syria; that she is a native of Syra-stra, or Syra-strene.[2] In Fig. 11 of the thirtieth plate to the Supplement to Montfaucon's Antiquity Explained, is a tablet, on which are described *three* females. It was found at Metz. The inscription is, *In honorem Domûs Divinæ* DIS MAIRABUS *Vicani Vici Pacis: In honour of the divine house, to the Goddesses Mairæ, they of the street of peace.* Montfaucon thinks them deities of the country. These are the three Marys of the Christians, before Christ was born; of course one of them must have been the Gallic *Virgo paritura.* A plate of this and of several other German triads may be seen in the preface to Maurice's Ind. Ant.[3] All the three women who attended Jesus at his death were called Marys,—Mary, the mother of Jesus, Mary, the mother of James, and Mary Salome.[4] In Sanval's History of the Antiquities of Paris, the virgin is called *étoile éclatante de la mer.* He says that St. Denis was the first bishop of Paris: he came thither in the time of the emperor Decius.

8. On a first examination the Goddess Isis will be generallly taken to be the moon, and as such *it* will appear to receive the adoration of its votaries. Osiris, the sun, is said to be her spouse, and also her brother: and Horus, called the πρωτογονος θεος, or first-born, is said to be their son. The name Horus is derived from the Hebrew or Phœnician word אור *aur,* lux, or light: but yet there are some circumstances unaccountable upon this supposition, except the moon was merely adored as an emblem of the Supreme Being. On the front of the temple of Isis at Sais, under the synonyme of Minerva, according to Plutarch, was the following description of her:

Ισις εγω ειμι παντο γεγονος, και ον και
εσομενον, και το εμον πεπλον
 αδεις των θνη
θων απι
καλυ
ψε
ν.

---

[1] Fig. 3.

[2] Vide my plates, fig. 19, taken from a figure of the Goddess Multimammia, in Montfaucon's 47th plate, cited above.

[3] Vol. V., ed. 8vo.   [4] Calmet, Dict. in voce Salome.

I *Isis* am all that has
been, that is or shall
be; no mortal Man
hath ever
me un-
vei-
le-
d. [1]

This cannot apply to the moon. The Indian deity is described to be, All that is, everywhere, always. On many words closely connected with this topic, almost every page of Sir William Drummond's Essay on a Punic Inscription may be consulted.

I am persuaded that there is no subject on which more mistakes have been made than on that of the Goddess Isis, both by ancients and moderns. She has constantly been taken for the moon, which in many countries was masculine. But she is constantly declared to be the same as Ceres, Proserpine, Juno, Venus, and all the other Goddesses; therefore they must all be the moon. This is out of the question. The case I believe to be this;—the planet called the *moon* was dedicated to her in judicial astrology, the same as a planet was dedicated to Venus or Mars. But Venus and Mars were not those planets themselves, though those planets were sacred to them. The inscription in front of her temple at Sais at once proves that she cannot be the moon; it is totally inapplicable to that planet. The mistake of the ancients is only one proof among hundreds, that they had lost the knowledge of the principles of their mythology, or that we do not understand it. I am of opinion that much of the confusion in the ancient systems arose from the neglect, or the ignorance, of the distinction between religion and judicial astrology.

Apuleius makes Isis say, I am nature, the parent of all things, the sovereign of the elements, the primary progeny of time, the most exalted of the deities, the first of the heavenly Gods and Goddesses; whose single deity the whole world venerates in many forms, with various rites, and various names. The Egyptians worship me with proper ceremonies, and call me by my true name, Queen Isis.[2] Isis is called Myrionymus, or Goddess with 10,000 names.[3] Herodotus[4] says, that the Persian Mithra was Venus.

No person who has considered well the character of the temples in India and Egypt, can help being convinced of the identity of their character, and of their being the production of the same race of people; and this race evidently Ethiopian. The Sphinxes have all Ethiopian faces. The bust of Memnon in the British museum is evidently Ethiopian. The worship of the Mother and Child is seen in all parts of the Egyptian religion. It prevails everywhere. It is the worship of Isis and the infant Orus or Osiris. It is the religious rite which was so often prohibited at Rome, but which prevailed in spite of all opposition, as we find from the remaining ruins of its temples. It was perhaps from this country, Egypt, that the worship of the black virgin and child came into Italy, where it still prevails. It was the worship of the mother of the God Ιαω, the Saviour; Bacchus in Greece, Adonis in Syria, Cristna in India; coming into Italy through the medium of the two Ethiopias, she was, as the Ethiopians were, *black*, and such she still remains.

Dr. Shuckford[5] has the following curious passage: " We have several representations in the " draughts of the same learned antiquary *(Montfaucon)*, which are said to be Isis, holding or

---

[1] Basnage, p. 217; Maurice, Ind. Ant. Vol. IV. pp. 682—684.   [2] Metamorph. Lib. xi., Payne Knight, p. 67.
[3] Squire's Plutarch, de Iside et Osir. cap. liii. p. 74.   [4] Clio. Sect. cxxxi.
[5] Con. Book viii. p. 311.

" giving suck to the boy Orus; but it should be remarked, that Orus was not represented by the
" figure of a new-born child: for Plutarch expressly tells us, that a new-born child was the
" Egyptian picture of the sun's rising."[1] Plutarch and Montfaucon were both right. Orus
was the sun, and the infant child was the picture of the sun, in his infancy or birth, immediately after the winter solstice—when he began to increase. Orus, I repeat, is nothing but the
Hebrew word אור *aur*, lux, light — the very light so often spoken of by St. John, in the first
chapter of his gospel. Plutarch[2] says, that Osiris means a benevolent and beneficent power, as
does likewise his other name OMPHIS. In a former book I have taken much pains to discover the
meaning of Omphi. After all, is it any thing but the OM, with the Coptic emphatic article *Pi*?

There is no more reason for calling Isis the moon, than the earth. She was called by all the
following names: Minerva, Venus, Juno, Proserpina, Ceres, Diana, Rhea seu Tellus, Pessinuncia,
Rhamnusia, Bellona, Hecate, Luna, PolymorphusDæmon.[3] But most of these have been shewn to be
in fact all one—the Sun. Isis, therefore, can be nothing but the sun, or the being whose residence
was the sun. This being we have seen was both masculine and feminine: I therefore conclude that Isis was no other than the first cause in its feminine character, as Osiris was the first
cause in the masculine. The inscriptions cited above, upon the temples of Isis, completely
negative the idea of her being the moon. From Pausanias[4] we learn that the most ancient statue
of Ceres amongst the Phigalenses was black; and in chap. vi. that at a place called Melangea, in
Arcadia, was a Venus who was black, the reason for which, as given by him, evidently shews that
it was unknown. At Athens, Minerva Aglaurus, daughter of Cecrops, was *black*, according to
Ovid, in his Metamorphoses.[5] Jerom observed, that " Juno has her priestesses devoted to one
" husband, Vesta her perpetual virgins, and other idols their priests, also under the vows of
" chastity."[6] The Latin *Diana* is the contract of *Diva Jana.*[7] Gale says they styled the moon
" Urania, Juno, Jana, Diana, Venus, &c.; and as the sun was called Jupiter, from יה *(ie,) ja,*
" πατηρ, and Janus from יה *(ie) Jah, the proper name of God;*[8] so Juno is referred to the moon,
" and comes from יה *(ie) Jah, the proper name of God, as Jacchus from יה (ie) ja-chus.* Amongst
" the ancient Romans Jana and Juno were the same."[9] That the moon was the emblem of the
passive generative power cannot be denied, but this was merely astrological, not religious. She
was not considered the passive power itself, as the sun was himself considered the active power,—
but merely as the planets were considered: for though the planet was called Jupiter, as I have
before observed, that *planet* was not considered Lord of heaven, the Great Creator.

Some years ago I was informed, by a friend, since deceased, that he had seen a church (I think)
in the Netherlands, dedicated to the Black Virgin, à la Vierge Noire. I have no doubt of the fact,
though I have forgotten the place. Here we have the black Venus and Ceres. To make the
thing complete, we want nothing but a church dedicated to the Black Saviour; and if we cannot
shew this, there is scarcely a church in Italy where a black bambino may not be seen, which
comes very near it. If Pausanias had told us that the *infant* Jupiter[10] which he found in Arcadia
had been *black*, we should have had all we required; for he had before told us,[11] that Jupiter had
the title of Saviour, and Statius tells us he was black.[12]

Heres signifies the sun, but in the Arabic the meaning of the radical word is *to preserve*, and of

---

[1] Lib. de Iside et Osiride, p. 355.   [2] De Iside et Osiride, Sect. xlii., Squire

[3] Kircher, Œd. Egypt. Tom. I. p. 188.   [4] Book viii. ch. v. and ch. xlii.   [5] Nimrod, Vol. III. p. 151.

[6] Priestley, Hist. Cor. Vol. II. p. 336.   [7] Voss. de Idolat. Lib. ii. cap. xxv.   [8] Ib. xxvi.

[9] Clarke's Travels, Vol. II. p. 317. ed. 4to.   [10] Book viii. ch. xxxi.   [11] Book ii. ch. xx.

[12] Asiat. Res. Vol. V. p. 299, ed. 4to. Vide my plates, fig. 20, from Montfaucon.

haris, guardian, *preserver.*[1] This is the name of the Messiah Cyrus, and also of Ceres, for it is only a different way of pronouncing the same word, aspirated or not, *and this makes out a Ceres or Heres of both the masculine and feminine genders.* All this is easily accounted for, on the androgynous principle. Hara-Hara is a name of Maha-Deva, which is *Great God;* Heri means Saviour. When people are in great distress they call on Maha-Deva by the name of Hara-Hara.[2] In Greek, Αμμα *Amma* means at once Mother and Great Mother of all the Earth. Ceres is called Alma Ceres, and among the Trœzenians, *Amæa.*[3] The generative principle is considered to have existed before light, and to be the mother of both gods and men, as the generative source of all things. In this character she is the black Venus of Orpheus,[4] and the black Maia or Maria of Italy, the Regina Cœli, Regina Stellarum, &c. "From the God Maius of the Etruscans, and " his wife Maia, the month of May received its denomination : and at its commencement, when the " sun entered into Taurus, were celebrated in their honour those phallic mysteries, of which the " now almost obsolete May-games are a transcript and a relic."[5] Jupiter, Bacchus, Hercules, Apollo, Æsculapius, had each the appellation of Saviour. They are all indeed the same person— Jehovah. Stukeley[6] allows that the thyrsus of Bacchus is only the rod of Aaron and Moses, called הרה pinus.[7]

9. M. Dupuis says, the celestial sign of the Virgin and Child was in existence several thousand years before the birth of Christ. The constellation of the celestial Virgin by its ascension above the horizon presided at the birth of the God Sol, or light, and seemed to produce him from her side. Here is the origin of Jesus born from the side of his mother. The Magi, as well as the priests of Egypt, celebrated the birth of the God Sol, or Light, or Day, incarnate in the womb of a virgin, which had produced him without ceasing to be a virgin, and without connexion with man. This was he of whom all the prophets and mystagogues prophesied, saying, "A virgin shall " conceive, and bear a son" (and his name shall be Om-nu-al, Om our God). One may see in the sphere the image of the infant god Day, in the arms of the constellation under which he was born, and all the images of the virgin offered to the veneration of the people represent her, as in the sphere, nursing a mystical infant, who would destroy evil, confound the prince of darkness, regenerate nature, and rule over the universe. On the front of the temple of Isis at Sais was this inscription, below that which I have given above : "The fruit which I have brought forth is the " sun." This Isis, Plutarch says, is the chaste Minerva, who, without fearing to lose her title of virgin, says she is the mother of the sun.[8] This is the same virgin of the constellations whom, Eratosthenes says, the learned of Alexandria call Ceres or Isis, who opened the year and presided at the birth of the god Day. It was in honour of this same virgin, (from whom the Sun emanated, and by whom the god Day or Light was nursed,) that, at Sais, the famous feast of lights was celebrated, and from which our Candlemas, or our feast of the lights of the purification, was taken. Ceres was always called the Holy Virgin.[9]

The Christians have a feast called the Assumption of the Blessed Virgin. In one of the ancient Gospel histories an account is given of the assumption of Mary into heaven, in memory of which event this feast was kept. On this feast M. Dupuis says, "About the eighth month, when the " sun is in his greatest strength, and enters into the eighth sign, the celestial virgin appears to " be absorbed in his fires, and she disappears in the midst of the rays and glory of her son." The Roman calendar of Columella marks at this epoch the death or disappearance of the virgin. The

[1] Trans. Asiat. Soc. Vol II. p. 313.   [2] Asiat. Res. Vol. V. p 137.   [3] Whiter, Etym Univ. p. 107.
[4] Orph Hymn. lxxxiii. 5, ii. 1, 2; Faber, Pag. Idol. Vol. III. p. 49.   [5] Fab. Pag. Idol. Book iv. ch. v. p. 397.
[6] Pul. Sac. I. p. 27.   [7] Ib. p. 28.   [8] Plutarch, de Iside, p. 354; Procl. in Tim. p. 30.
[9] Dupuis, Vol. III. pp. 40, &c , 4to.

sun, it says, passes into the Virgin the 13th before the kalends of September. The Christians
place here the assumption, or reunion of the Virgin to her Son. This used to be called the feast
of the passage of the Virgin. At the end of three weeks, the birth of the Virgin Mary is fixed.
In the ancient Roman Calendar the assumption of the virgin Astrea, or her reunion to her son,
took place at the same time as the assumption of the Virgin Mary, and her birth or her disengagement
from the solar rays at the same time with the birth of Mary.[1] How is it possible to believe that
these extraordinary coincidences are the effect of accident?[2] Every particular necessary to constitute actual identity is found in the two systems, which the reader will find explained at much
greater length by M. Dupuis. As the Christians celebrated the decease or assumption of the
celestial virgin into heaven, called by them the Virgin Mary, so also they did her impregnation or
annunciation; that is, the information communicated to her that she should become pregnant by
the holy ghost. "The Pamylia were on the 25th of the month Phamenoth, and on the new moon
" of that month the ancient Egyptians celebrated the entrance of Osiris into the moon," or Isis.
This, " Plutarch says,[3] is the beginning of the spring......'The moon is impregnated by the
" sun.' Nine months after, at the winter solstice, Harpocrates is born. It is no wonder, there-
"fore, that Dupuis[4] compares the Pamylia, a word which in Coptic, according to Jablonski,[5]
" means ' annunciation,' to the annunciation of the Blessed Virgin, which is marked in our
" calendars on the 25th of March, four days after the vernal equinox, and nine months before the
birth of Christ."[6]

The identity of the Holy Virgin of the Christians and of that of the Gentiles had been observed
before M. Dupuis's time. Albert the Great says,[7] that the sign of the celestial virgin rises
above the horizon at the moment in which we fix the birth of the Lord Jesus Christ.—All the
mysteries of his divine incarnation, and all the secrets of his miraculous life, from his conception
even to his ascension, are traced in the constellations, and figured in the stars which announced
them. For a more detailed proof of the assertion of Albert, the reader may consult Dupuis.[8]
Bochart[9] says, that Leo X. gave the Virgin Mary the title of Goddess. Pelloutier,[10] as noticed
before,[11] has observed, that more than a hundred years before the Christian æra, in the territory of
Chartres, among the Gauls, honours were paid to the virgin (VIRGINI PARITURÆ) who was about
to give birth to the God of Light. That this was really the Buddhist worship, I have no doubt.
The Virgin was the beautiful Maya, the mother of Buddha—the Budwas found in Wales, as
noticed in my Celtic Druids.[12]

Adonis, the Syrian God, was the son of Myrrha.[13] This Myrrha was feigned to be changed into
a tree of the same name with it, consecrated by the Eastern nations to the sun.[14] This was what
was offered by the Magi to Christ at his birth. The trifling, but still striking, coincidences
between the worship of the god Sol and the stories of Jesus are innumerable.[15]

Kircher the Jesuit gives an astrological[16] account of the seven planets, of the twelve signs of

---

[1] On the 8th of September in our calendars What can have induced our priests to retain this figment of Heathenism I do not know, and do not think it worth the trouble of inquiring.
[2] Dupuis, Vol. III. p. 48, 4to.   [3] De Iside, cap. xliii.   [4] Tom. I. pp. 375—409, ed. 4to.
[5] Lib. v. cap. vii. sect. v.   [6] Mr. Carlile's Republican, Vol. XII. No. xii. p. 371.   [7] Lib. de Univers.
[8] Vol. III. p. 47, and notes, p. 318, ed. 4to.   [9] Against Veron. p. 815.
[10] Hist. des Celtes, liv. v. p. 15; Dupuis, Vol. III. p. 51.   [11] In Book v. ch. ii. sect. 2.
[12] Ch. v. sect. viii. and xxxvii.   [13] Dupuis, Vol. II p. 157, ed. 4to.
[14] Vide Kircher, Œd. Tom. II. Part ii. p. 206.   [15] Dupuis, Vol. II. p. 272, notes, ed. 4to.
[16] The whole of this part of Kircher's work is a development of the judicial astrology of the Egyptians, the Arabians,
and the Hebrews, which he shews to have been common to them all.

the Zodiac, of the thirty six decans into which the twelve signs were divided, and *De* 48 *Asterismis, sive mansionibus Deorum αντιτεχνων*: in the latter of which he has the words, *In medio autem horum numinum, Mithram, quem et* Μεσιτην, *hoc est Mediatorem, ponebant, id est, Solem.* He afterwards has the following heading to a chapter, p. 200: *Dispositio Iconismorum, quâ Egyptii ex mente Avenaris, singulorum signorum dodecutemoria, in tres facies subdiviserunt, singulisque faciebus appropriatas imagines attribuerunt ;* in which is this passage :

" 5. Intra Virginis et Libræ mansiones ascendit aspis magna, quæ et Agathodæmon Ophionius
" dicitur, una cum cratere vini, teste Avenar.   Tametsi Indorum astrologi hoc loco arborem
" ponant magnam, in cujus ramis Canis et Ibis existant.   Sed audiamus verba authoris : *Ascendit-*
" *que* [1] *ibi arbor magna, in cujus ramis Cœnis et Ciconia, quæ et Ibis dicitur, et à Philostorgid ap-*
" *pellatur Hebræis Rachama* רחכמה *rhkme.* Nihilque hoc aliud, quam stationem Mercurialium
" Numinum indigitabant.   Dicunt præterea Ægyptii apud Avenarem, hoc loco poni virginem pul-
" chram, capillorum longitudine spectabilem, duas in manu spicas habentem ; sedet autem in throno,
" et puerum lactat parvulum, nutritque ipsum summâ diligentiâ.   Verum cum verba Avenar con-
" sideratione dignissima sint, ea hic adduco : [2] *In prima, inquit facie virginis, ascendit virgo pul-*
" *chra, longis capillis et duas in manu spicas continet, sedetque supra sedem, et nutrit puerum adhuc*
" *parvulum, et lactat eum, et cibat eum.* Expressiùs multò Albumazar ea in suo in astrologiam
" introductorio describit, quæ verba allegat Stefflerus in Sphæra Procli ; ita autem disserit : *Oritur*
" *in primo virginis decano puella, Arabicè dicta* [3] *Aderenosa, id est, virgo munda, virgo immaculata,*
" *corpore decora, vultu venusta, habitu modesta, crine prolixo, manu duas aristas tenens, supra*
" *solium aulæatum residens, puerum nutriens, ac jure pascens, in loco, cui nomen Hebræa, puerum*
" *dico à quibusdam nationibus nominatum Iesum, significantibus Issa, quem et Græcè Christum*
" *dicunt.* Hæc Albumazar. Ex his manifestè patet, Salvatorem nostrum ex illibata Virgine
" natum indigitari. Oritur ergo hæc virgo Iesum pascens. Pudeat hic protervos Hebræos, dum
" virginem matrem renuunt, cum tantis ætatibus, tot ante secula Gentiles ista præviderint. Quod
" si Verpus dicat : *Non dicunt hi ipsam virginem pueri illius matrem, sed tantum jure ipsum pas-*
" *centem :* erubescat infelix, quia quæ jure ipsum pascet, non nisi mater est. Simile quid legitur
" apud Sybillam Europæam : *Veniet montes et colles transiliens, et in paupertate regnans cum silentio*
" *dominandi è Virginis vase exiliet.* Ponitur quoque hoc eodem loco ab Ægyptiis figura hominis
" Ταυρομορφε, id est, figuræ Taurinæ. Ita Avenar." [4]

11. Mr. Faber says, Jesus was not called originally Jesus Christ, but Jescua Hammassiah. Jescua is the same as Joshua and Jesus, and means Saviour ; and Ham is evidently the Om of India, (the Ammon,) and Messiah is the *anointed.* It will then be, *The Saviour Om the anointed ;* precisely as Isaiah had literally foretold : or, reading in the Hebrew mode, *The anointed Om the Saviour.* This was the name of Jesus of Bethlehem. The name of Jesus also was Jesus ben Panther. Jesus was a very common name with the Jews. Stukeley observes, that the patronymic of Jesus Christ was Panther ; and that Panthers were the nurses and bringers up of Bacchus ; and adds, " 'Tis remarkable that Panther was the sirname of Joseph's family, our Lord's " foster-father. Thus the Midrashkoheleth, or gloss, upon Ecclesiastes : 'It happened that a

---

[1] Hebrew text omitted.   [2] Hebrew omitted.   [3] Corrupt.
   [4] Kircher, Œdip. Ægypt. Tom. III. cap. v. p. 203. For more particulars upon this subject my reader may consult
Drummond's Œdip Jud. p. 277 ; also p. 318 of Dupuis' notes, Vol. III. ed. 4to. The Jesuit Riccioli calls this virgin
of the Sphere *Virgo Dei para.* Dupuis, Vol. III. pp. 2, 52, ed. 4to. She had the name of Ceres, whom Hesychius
calls the Holy Virgin. Ibid. Avecenna calls her Isis, the mother of the young Horus, who died and rose from the
dead Ibid.

" ' serpent bit R. Eleasar ben Damah, and James, a man of the village Secania, came to heal him
" 'in the name of Jesus ben Panther.' This is likewise in the book called Abodazara, where the
" comment upon it says, *This James was a disciple of Jesus the Nazarene.*"

Here, in this accidental notice of Jesus, by these two Jewish works, is a direct and unexceptionable proof of his existence; it is unexceptionable, because, if it be not the evidence of unwilling
witnesses, it is the evidence of disinterested ones. On this I shall have occasion to say more
hereafter. No one will dispute the piety of Dr. Stukeley. The similarity of the circumstances
related of Jesus and Bacchus could not be denied, and therefore he accounts for it by supposing
that God had revealed to the Heathen part of what was to happen in future. This may be satisfactory to some persons, as it was no doubt to the Doctor. The accidental manner in which the
assertion is made, that the father of Jesus was called Panther, removes the possibility of accounting for it by attributing it to the malice of the Jews. In a former chapter it has been proved that
Bacchus was mistaken by the Romish priests for Jesus. Here the reader sees that the pious Dr.
Stukeley has proved, as might be expected, that the mother of Bacchus is the same person as the
mother of Jesus, viz. Mary. And as the persons who brought up Jesus were called Panthers, the
name of an animal, so Bacchus was brought up by the same kind of animal, a panther. When
the reader reflects that the whole Roman Christian doctrine is founded, as the Roman Church
admits, on tradition, he will have no difficulty in accounting for the similarity of the systems.
The circumstance of Joseph's family name being supposed to be Panther, is remarkably confirmed
by Epiphanius,[1] who says, that Joseph was the brother of Cleophas, the son of James, sirnamed
Panther. Thus we have the fact both from Jewish and Christian authorities.[2] It is very clear
that Bacchus's Panther must have been copied from that of Jesus or IHΣ, or that of Jesus from
Bacchus's. I leave the matter with my reader.

The worship of the Virgin was in no sense applicable to Mary the wife of Joseph. If this
worship had been originally derived from her, or instituted in her honour, she would not have
been called a virgin as a distinguishing mark of honour; for she was no more a virgin than any
other woman who had a large family: for such a family, after the birth of Jesus, It cannot be denied
that, according to the Gospel accounts, she had. Therefore why, more than other women, should
she be called a virgin? The truth is, that the worship of the virgin and child, which we find in
all Romish countries, was nothing more than a remnant of the worship of Isis and the god Horus
—the Virgin of the celestial sphere, to whom the epithet virgin, though a mother, was without
absurdity applied.

I know very well what the devotees have said to conceal the fact of the Virgin's family, but it
is all answered at once by the observation, that if James, &c., were the children of Joseph by a
former wife, they were not brothers of Jesus, but half-brothers. They are totally different things.
But what folly there is in all this! Is there any thing wrong in a married woman having a family?

12. It is well known that almost all the oriental nations, the Hindoos, the Persians, the Syrians,
the Arabians, the Egyptians, the Copts, and, I believe, the Jews in their astrology, had a Lunar
Zodiac divided into 28 parts, allusive to the days in the moon's period—called the mansions of the
moon. Over each of these divisions a genius or dæmon presided. There can be no doubt that it
was the same system in all these nations, and probably the doctrines held respecting it may have
been originally the same in each of them, although it may not be possible to demonstrate this
by a rigorous proof: but for the sake of argument I shall consider them the same. The access to

---

[1] Hæres. 78, Antidic. S. vii.   [2] See Jones on the Canon, Vol. II. p. 137.

these mansions was supposed to be by the milky way, as it was called by the Greeks and Romans, who, not understanding it, as usual, invented a story of their own to account for it.[1]

But the original oriental name was the *strawey way*—via straminis seu paleæ—and was thus called from an astronomical allegory of the celestial virgin, who, fleeing from the evil principle Typhon, let fall some of the ears of corn, or corn in the straw, which she carried in one of her hands. This celestial virgin was feigned to be a mother: she is represented in the Indian Zodiac of Sir William Jones with ears of corn in one hand, and the lotus in the other: in Kircher's Zodiac of Hermes, she has corn in both hands. In other planispheres of the Egyptian priests she carries ears of corn in one hand, and the infant Horus in the other. In Roman Catholic countries, she is generally represented with the child in one hand, and the lotus or lily in the other. This milky way is placed immediately under that degree of North latitude, which is called the tropic of Cancer, and the two tropics of Cancer and Capricorn have been called by the astrologers the Gates of Heaven or the Sun;[2] at each of which the sun arrives in his annual progress. The reason why these two lines were called the *gates* was this : they were the boundaries to the North and South, beyond which the sun never extended his course. The space between them might be called the dominion of the sun, and when you passed into the space between them you might be said to pass into his kingdom. The Southern gate is called the tropic of Capricorn, an amphibious animal, half *goat* half *fish*, in our present Zodiacs, but in the most ancient Zodiacs of India, it is described as two entire beings, a goat and a fish.

The Brahmins also call the tropics of Cancer and Capricorn the Gates of the Sun. Kircher, in his Œdipus Egyptiacus,[3] has undertaken to give the names of the dæmons or genii who presided over each of the Lunar mansions, and the meanings of these names. The sincerity of the learned old Jesuit cannot be doubted, though some of his etymologies may. He states that the first is called the gate of the *fish*. This evidently alludes to the Indian sign of Capricorn, and is very satisfactory. The thirteenth is called the station of *love* by the Egyptians or Copts ; by the Arabs, the *alzarphet*, or that which takes away cold ; and by the Greeks and Romans the *ear of corn*. Of this Cicero says, Spicam illustrem tenens splendenti corpore Virgo. Kircher says, Incipit hæc statio a quarto virginis, et terminatur in decimo octavo gradu ejusdem dodecatemorii Virginis. Genius est Masaiel ; statio pacis et unionis conjugalis.

The following passage is from p. 278 of Sir William Drummond's Œdipus Judaicus : " חשמן " *(hsmun)* Heshmon. It is clear that the letters in this name have been transposed, and probably " for a mysterious purpose. In the Onomasticon, the word Heshmon is brought from " משח *(msh)* unxit, and even the English reader will easily see that this is only a transposition " of the radicals in חשמ-ן *(hsm-un)*. The Jews, in fact, pretend that one Messiah משיח *(msih)* " was to be born of the tribe of Judah, and another of the tribe of Ephraim.[4] This *Heshmon* " seems to indicate him who was the anointed of Judah, and who indeed is called Ben-Jehudah, " Judah's son." Let us inquire if there be any astronomical allusion here. " Again," he says, " Immediately on leaving the sign of Leo, the emblem of Judah, the sun passes into the sign " where, as we have already seen, the ancient Persians, Arabians, and Syrians, depicted *Virgo* " with a male infant in her arms. Now I observe, that the Arabians make Messaiel, the pro-

---

[1] It was said to have the name of milky, from its whiteness, which was caused by the accidental spilling on the ground of some of the milk of Juno.

[2] Porphyry, Cave of the Nymphs, Taylor, p. 193.   [3] Vol. III. Cap. x. p. 241.

[4] We see here that one Messiah was to come from the tribe of Judah under the tropic of Capricorn, the other from the tribe of Ephraim, the exactly opposite in the camps of the Hebrews. See Drummond, plate 15, which would place him in the tropic of Cancer. (Can the reader doubt the astrological meaning of all this?)

" tecting genius in the sign of Virgo.[1]   This Messaiel seems a manifest corruption from Messiah-
" El.   It is vain to talk of the Shin being dageshed by the Masorites,.....................
" or of the aspirate being suppressed.   We ourselves suppress the sound of the aspirate in Eve,
" Messiah, and many other words.   Besides, the Syrians certainly often softened the harsh
" aspirate ; and the Arabians may have caught the sound from them.   Mesai-El, then appears to
" be a corruption for יאל-חשמ (msih-al) Messiah-El—the anointed of El, the male infant, who
" rises in the arms of Virgo, who was called Jesus by the Hebrews, that is, ישע (iuso) the Saviour,
" and was hailed the anointed king or Messiah."

When it is considered that this Heshmon, and the whole of the towns specified in this passage
of Joshua, are part of the allotment given to the tribe of Judah, it can scarcely be doubted that a
close connexion with the Christian Messiah will be found here.   Sir W. Drummond has shewn,
that all the names of the other places which are certainly understood have an allegorical meaning
allusive to the heavenly bodies.   It must also be recollected that these astrological circumstances
preceded the birth of Jesus Christ.

CHAPTER III

Bacchus an Imaginary Personage—Opinions of Different Authors—Subject continued—Bacchus in India. Mount Meru—Adventures similar to those of Cristna

1. We will now make a few inquiries respecting the celebrated God Bacchus, the son of the
Goddess of whom we have been treating.

Diodorus Siculus acknowledges that some historians maintained that Bacchus never appeared
on earth in a human shape.[2]   Had we but the works of these authors, probably at that time despised, we should see the truth, which their narrow-minded contemporaries were not able to
appreciate.   Diodorus Siculus also says,[3] that the Libyans claim Bacchus, and say that he was
the son of Ammon, a king of Libya, who reigned in a city called Ammon ; that, after various
adventures, he returned to Libya, and built a temple to his father Ammon.   The account of
Diodorus is full of contradiction, but the result is, that Bacchus built the temple of Ammon, and
was succeeded by Jupiter ; consequently that the Bull worship preceded the Ram-headed Jupiter.
Plutarch[4] says, that Bacchus was the same deity as Osiris, and that he was also the same as the
Ερως πρωτογονος of Orpheus and Hesiod.   The word Ammon in Greek is often written Αμυν :
this is, when written from right to left, Numa.[5]   It is also written Ομανος.   In Hebrew the word
is written עמן omun, which, if read from left to right, is Numo.   In the last chapter it was noticed
that Osiris was called Om-phi, and that Om-phi might be merely Pi-Om—The Om : Pi being
the Coptic emphatic article.   Plutarch[6] says, Phylarchus taught that Bacchus first brought into

---

[1] See Kircher's Œdipus, Vol. III. p. 245.   [2] Lib. iii. p. 137.   [3] Ibid. iii.   [4] De Iside et Osirida.
[5] Nothing was more common with the ancients than to transpose the letters of names, or to write in anagrams for
the sake of secrecy.
[6] De Iside et Osiride.

Egypt from India the worship of Apis and Osiris. Eusebius has stated that Bacchus came to Egypt from the Indus. In the temples of Diana a festival of Bacchus was celebrated, called *Sacaæ*.[1] Of this Saca I shall treat at large hereafter. Bacchus had generally the horns of a bull, though often hidden beneath a crown of ivy or grapes.[2] The Pope is always accompanied by one or two large fans made of feathers. The Buddhist priests of Ceylon always have the same,—as Mr. Robinson says, *the mystic fan of Bacchus*.[3] Bacchus and Hercules were both Saviours, they were both put to death, and rose again the third day, at our time of Easter, or the vernal equinox: so were Osiris and Adonis.

Porphyry[4] says, " Hence, a place near to the equinoctial circle was assigned to Mithra as an " appropriate seat. And on this account he bears the sword of Aries, which is a martial sign. " He is likewise carried in the Bull, which is the sign of Venus; for Mithra, as well as the Bull, " is the demiurgus and Lord of Generation." Again,[5] he says, " Thus also the Greeks united a " ram to the statue of Jupiter: *but the horns of a bull to that of Bacchus*." Again,[6] " Homer " calls the period and revolution of regeneration in a circle Circe, the daughter of the Sun, who " perpetually connects and combines all corruption with generation, and generation with corrup- " tion." Again,[7] " Nymphs, says Hermias,[8] are Goddesses who preside over generation, and are " the attendants of Bacchus, the son of Semele. On this account they are present with water, " that is, they ascend, as it were, and rule over generation. But this Dionysus, or Bacchus, " supplies the regeneration of every sensible nature."

2. Bacchus and Osiris are the same person, and that person has been shewn to be the sun; and they were both black. But Bacchus was also the Baghis of India, as Sir W. Jones has shewn. Baghi-stan in Persia was the town of Bacchus. Bacchus was called Dionusos or Dionissus: this is simply Dios-nusos, or the God of the city spoken of by Arrian, on the confines of India—Nysa, the capital of Nysea. He is also the Dios Nysa, a city of Arabia, and Nysa, on the top of a moun-tain in Greece. He is also Seeva, one of the three persons of the Hindoo Trinity. But Seeva is called Om.[9] Plutarch witnesses that Osiris and Isis were Bacchus and Ceres, and there can be no doubt that they were the Eswara and Isa of India. He is found in the Old Testament under the name IEUE *Nissi* יהוה נסי which, translated from the Greek, would be Dios Nyssos or Dionusos, a name of Bacchus.[10] Indeed, being the Sun, he is naturally enough found every where.

> Ogygia me Bacchum vocant,
> Osirim Ægyptus putat,
> Mysi Phanacem nominant,
> Dionyson Indi existimant,
> Romana Sacra Liberum,
> Arabica gens Adoneum,
> Lucaniacus Pantheum.

He was also Deo-Naush, or Deva-Nahusha, and Ram or Rama-Deva. He was three times born in India; and the Greeks call Osiris πρωτογονον, διφυη, and τρίγονον.[11]

Strabo[12] says, " It is for this reason that they give to this God (Bacchus) the name of Μηρο-" τραφης, *Merotraphes*." This means One nourished in Meru, the propriety of which is evident

---

[1] Strabo, Geog. Lib. xi.; Pausan., Lib. iii. cap. xvi.; Hoffman, voc. Anaitis; Jameson, Herm. Scyth. p. 136.

[2] See Spence, Polymetis, p. 129, folio ed.   [3] Last Days of Heber, p. 43.

[4] In his Cave of the Nymphs, Sect. ii. p. 190, ed. Taylor.   [5] De Abstin., Sect. xv. p. 110.   [6] Ibid. 247.

[7] Ibid. 248.   [8] In Plat. Phædrum.   [9] Malcolm's India, p. 505.   [10] Stukeley, Paleog. Sac. No. I. p. 10

[11] Maurice, Hist. Vol. II. 133, 4to; Moore's Pantheon, p. 272.   [12] Lib. xv.

enough to us, since we have acquired the Indian learning. Casaubon proposed to change the word to Μηροῤῥαφης, Merorrhaphes. This shews the danger, in these old authors, of changing a word because we do not understand it. Had the suggestion of the learned Casaubon been adopted, we should have lost the most important fact, that Bacchus was nourished in the celebrated Mount of the Indians.

According to Herodotus,[1] Bacchus was called Iacchus, in the mysteries. Και προκα τε φωνῆς αχυειν, και οἱ φαινεσθαι την φωνην ειναι τον μυςικον Ιακχον·—και την φωνην τῆς αχυεις, εν ταυτη τη ὁϱτη Ιακχαζυσι. Selden and Vossius allow this to be the same as the Jah, or Iaω of Diodorus. Now, from Hamilton[2] I learn that the people of Pegu, in a district called Syrian, give their God the name of Kıacκ, also of Kıacкıacк, *God of Gods*. This is nothing, I think, but the corrupted, or perhaps only aspirated, *Iack* of the mysteries. It answers to the Βαχχεβαχχος. Casaubon[3] says, " Sed nomen Βαχχεχορος, ut alia item quam plurima, alibi " quam apud Orpheum non legas. Imitatus est eleganter in novanda ea dictione vetustissimam " Bacchi appellationem Βαχχεβαχχος, quam heroici metri lex non admittebat: ita Liberum " patrem in ipsis orgiis et mysteriis vocant." Βαχχεβαχχος, Ὁ Διονυσος ουτως εχαλειτο εν ταις θυσιαις.[4] I ask if Bacchus, in the Æolic dialect, proved above by Herodotus to be Iacchus, be anything but Iacchus? Pococke[5] says,

> Baccнa, grandem, magnum, præclarum, esse denotare.

I have a strong suspicion that the K in the above word Kiack is only the aspirate; and that the final ck is only the barbarous mode of writing the Hebrew ח h, adopted by most of our grammarians ח ch. This would make the word יה *ie*, called in the Psalms Jaн, into the word *Kiach.*

Mr. Taylor, in his Diegesis, has called the word Jah, Jack. Those who will persist in miscalling the Hebrew ח h by the letters *ch*, have no right to complain. According to their practice he is right: but they are wrong, as I have proved in the table of Alphabets, p. 11

Bacchus is said by Orpheus[6] to have slept three years.

> Ὁς παρα Περσεφονης ιεροισι δομοισιν ιαυων
> Κωμιζει ΤΡΙΕΤΗΡΑ χρονον Βαχχιον αγνον.

This is exactly met by a fact which the natives of Pegu named of their god Kiack, that he was then asleep, and was to sleep 6000 years. This God in Pegu was of immense size, and lay in a temple in a sleeping posture, evidently the Buddha whom we see sleeping in the India House. When, in their ceremonies, the Hindoos call out IEΥE, IEΥE, what is this but the EΥOE, EΥOE of the Bacchantes?

3. Diodorus Siculus in his second book says, that, after Bacchus had conquered India, his army becoming unhealthy, he retreated to a mount in the north, called Meros, (Μηρον in the accusative case,) where he refreshed them, and that this word Μηρῳ meaning *thigh* in Greek, the Greeks feigned the story of his being nourished *in a thigh*. Pomponius Mela[7] says, " Urbium " quas incolunt, Nysa est clarissima et maxima: Montium Meros, Jovi sacer: famam hinc præ- " cipuam habent, in illa genitum, in hujus specu Liberum arbitrantur esse nutritum: unde " Græcia autoribus, ut femori Jovis incitum dicerent, aut materia ingessit aut error." Here we have the connexion, or, in fact, identification of Bacchus with the resident of Meru, and here

---

[1] Lib. viii. cap. lxv.   [2] New Account of East Indies, ch. xxxvi. p. 43.   [3] De Poēsi Satyr. Græcorum.
[4] Hesychius.   [5] Spec. Hist. Arab. p. 107.   [6] Hymn in Bacchum, No. 52.   [7] Lib. ii. cap. xi.

we have also a very pretty example of the way in which the minor details of the Greek mythologies were made up. The ignorance of the Greeks in their own concerns is inconceivably ridiculous, as well as their absurd credulity. In addition to the above, Philostratus[1] says, "The
" inhabitants of India had a tradition that Bacchus was born at *Nysa*, and was brought up in a
" cave on Mount *Meros*." And Diodorus Siculus says, that " when Semiramis marched into India,
" she stopped and formed fine gardens at a place in Media called Βαγιϛανον, Baghistan," that is,
place of Bacchus.[2] The story of Pythagoras' shewing his golden thigh to the people in the public
assembly in Greece, is well known. When the other accounts of Pythagoras, and his profound
philosophy, are considered, this seems a most unaccountable story, and can be regarded only as a
fable, or an allusion to something which we do not understand. We have seen that Mount Meru
was a type or symbol of the Linga and Ioni. Now I suspect that what Pythagoras shewed to the
people was one of the models of Meru, or of the united Linga and Ioni, which we see in such a
variety of ways in the museum at the India-house. Of this the rabble made a golden thigh. If
impartial philosophers could be found to search for it in India, I doubt not that all, or nearly all,
the ancient mythology would be explained; and no small part of that of the Greeks would be
found to have arisen from their mistakes. Herodotus says that Jupiter carried Bacchus in his
thigh to Nyssa. This confirms what I have said, that, in his story, there is some unknown
meaning.[3]

We have seen above, that Bacchus was identified with Mount Meru, the residence of Brahm,
where he held his court in the sides of the North. But the reader will not forget that Bacchus
was called Broumios. This was the Bruma of the Etruscans. In Ovid's *Fasti*, Janus announces
that he is the same with Bruma, and that the year began of old with Bruma, and not with the
Spring, because Bruma had the first honour. Bruma meant also the winter or the north. All the
ancients looked to the north for the seat of the Deity, and I believe in all nations the letters B. R.
and P. R. conveyed the idea of Former or Creator. Ovid says,

> Bacchumque vocant, Bromiumque, Dyœumque,
> Ignigenam, Satumque iterum, solumque Bimatrem.
>
> Ovid's Met. Lib. iv.

Here I beg my reader to observe that Bacchus is both *Igni-genam* and *Bi-matrem*. The igni-
genam I suppose I need not explain. The poetical expression of Bi-matrem, which I suppose
means twice born, alludes to Bacchus in his character of Menu or Noah, and to the mythological
fact of his having lived in two worlds, or the life of Noah having continued into the fourth cycle.
Noah or Menu lived in two cycles—in the third, and in part of the fourth. He lived also in two
worlds—*before* the flood, and *after* the flood; in two ages—in the Cali-yug, and in the age before
it. He lived when the sun at the equinox was in two constellations—in Taurus and in Aries : so
that on many accounts he might be called twice born, as Bacchus was, according to Ovid.

Diodorus Siculus also reports that, according to some authors, he was twice born. Here the
renewed incarnation creeps out, as well as the striking similitude to Noah. Bacchus is said, like
Noah, to have planted the vine, to have made wine, and to have been the victim of its inebriating
quality. M. D'Ancarville[4] shews that the name of Brouma given to Bacchus was Brama, and that
Diodorus calls this name indigenous (εγχωριον διαλεκτον). He also shews, in the most satisfactory
manner, that Bacchus was brought from India ; that the object of his religion was God the Creator
of all things, the generative power of which was represented under the form of the Bull.[5]

---

[1] In Vita Apol. Lib. ii. cap. ix.   [4] Lib. ii.   [3] Herod. Euterp. cap. cxlvi.   [4] P. 98.
[5] Ibid. p. 127.

Strabo says, that Bacchus reigned over all the oriental nations, but that Hercules reigned over only those of the western parts: Περι δε Ἡρακλεης οἱ μεν επι τ᾿ αναντια μονον μεχρι των ἱσπεριων περατων ἱςορυσιν, οἱ δε εφ᾿ εκατερα. [1] This alludes to the fact, of the truth of which I have no doubt, that the religion of Buddha or Bacchus once extended throughout Ava, China, Tibet, and the islands as well as the peninsula of Hindostan. But the religion of Cristna or Hercules extended only over the peninsula.

4. Bacchus was called ΕΥΟΙ. This is the ΙΕΥΩ, ΙΑΩ, ΙΑΟΥ, or Yahouh, the same as the ΙΕ on the temple of the Delphian Apollo. [2] Bacchus was also called a Bull, and a Son of God. When the Prince of Thebes forbade his mysteries, neglected his miracles, and denied his divinity, he put on the appearance of man, and submitted to be bound and led to prison. He was exposed by his grandfather king Cadmus, was preserved in an ark, and nursed in a cavern by Rhea, the mother of God. [3] Bacchus was twice born, was represented at the winter solstice as a little child, born five days before the end of the year. On his birth a blaze of light shone round his cradle. [4] The Romans had a god called *Quirinus;* he was said to be the brother of Bacchus. His soul emanated from the sun, and was restored to it. He was begotten by the God of armies upon a *virgin* of the blood royal, and exposed by order of the jealous tyrant *Amulius,* and was preserved and educated among shepherds. [5] He was torn to pieces at his death, when he ascended into heaven; upon which the sun was eclipsed or darkened. [6] Bacchus's death and return to life were annually celebrated by the women of Delphi; his return was expected by his followers, when he was to be the sovereign of the universe. [7] He was said to sit on the same throne as Apollo. He was three nights in hell, whence he ascended with his mother to heaven, where he made her a goddess. [8] He killed an amphisbæna which bit his leg; and he, with several other gods, drove down the giants with serpents' feet, who had made war against heaven. [9] The same general character is visible in the mythoses of Hercules and Bacchus. Hercules was called a Saviour: he was the son of Jove by the virgin Prudence. [10] He was called the UNIVERSAL WORD. [11] He was reabsorbed into God. [12] He was said by Orpheus to be self-produced, the generator and ruler of all things, and the father of time. [13]

---

[1] Strabo, Lib. xv. p. 687.

[2] Vide a Dialogue, the taste of which I cannot admire, supplied by a literary friend of mine to Mr. Carlile, for the first number of Vol. XI. of the Republican. I am not at liberty to give his name, but I shall quote his Dialogue by his initials, J. H. As I know him to be a man of deep learning, and have a perfect confidence in his honour, I shall depend upon him for his references, which are almost innumerable, to which the learned may apply for proofs of the assertions.

[3] J. H., Dial. in Rep.   [4] Ibid; see also the Gospel of the Infancy.   [5] J. H. in Rep.   [6] Ibid.
[7] Ibid.   [8] Ibid.   [9] Ibid.   [10] Julian, Orat. vii. p. 427.
[11] Cornut. de N. D. p. 89; Lucian, Hercul. cap. iv. and v.   [12] Ibid. p. 409.   [13] J. H. in Rep.

CHAPTER IV

Names of Jesus and Iao—Chifflet and others on these Names—Kircher on the
Name Iao—Name Iao—Name Iao known to the Gentiles—YHS, derivation of
it—Observations

1. I will now submit to my reader some observations on the origin of the word *Jesus*, and the
opinions of different learned men both on the word itself, and on various points connected with it.
Here will be found several facts repeated in a similar manner to what has taken place with the
Queen of heaven, his mother; but I hope the importance of the subject will excuse their being all
brought together under one view.

In the ancient books of the Jews we constantly find mention made of the god Jehovah, who
ought to be called JAH, or IEUE. This God answered to the person whom the Hindoos designate
by the name of Cristna, the second person in their trinity, or their God the saviour or preserver;
and was he whom the Persians designated by the name of Mithra, the second person in *their* trinity,
and also *their* preserver or saviour; and was he whom the Romish Christians designate by the name
of *Jesus*, also the second person in *their* trinity, and *their* saviour or preserver. He is called by the
Jews the Lord of hosts, God of Sabaoth: which means God of the stars and constellations. This
name with the Greeks, Romans, and Gentiles in general, was understood and meant to designate both the Supreme Being and the Sun, Dominus Sol, the Lord of heaven and the heavenly
host.

The God Iaω, יהוה *ieue*, IHS, Jehovah, was the son of the celestial virgin, which she carries in
her arms; the ואו *aur*, Horus, Lux, of the Egyptians;[1] the Lux of St. John. It is from this
infant that Jesus took his origin; or at least it is from the ceremonies and worship of this infant,
that his religion came to be corrupted into what we have it. This infant is the seed of the
woman who, according to Genesis, was to bruise the head of the serpent, which, in return, was to
bite his foot or heel, or the foot or heel of her seed, as the figure of the Hindoo Cristna proves.[2]
From the traditionary stories of this god Iao, which was feigned annually to be born at the winter
solstice, and to be put to death and raised to life on the third day at the vernal equinox, the
Romish searchers after the evangelion or gospel, made out their Jesus. The total destruction of
every thing at Jerusalem and in Judæa,—buildings, records, every thing—prevented them from
coming to any absolute certainty respecting the person who, they were told by tradition, had come
to preach the gospel of peace, to be their saviour, in fulfilment of the prophecy which their sect of
Israelites found in their writings, and who had been put to death by the Jews. From all these
circumstances he came to have applied to him the monogram of IHS, and the name of IHΣους,
and to him at last all the legendary stories related of the god Iao were attributed. Jesus was
commonly called Christ.

" The ineffable name also, which, according to the Masoretic punctuation, is pronounced Jehovah, was anciently pronounced Jaho, Iaω, or Ieuω,[3] as was also Sabazius or Sabadius,[4] which
" is the same word as Sabaoth, one of the scriptural titles of the true God, only adapted to the

---

[1] See Plate 19 of Dupuis, the Celestial Sphere.   [2] Plates, No. II. and V.

[3] Hieron. Comm. in Psalm viii.; Diod. Sic., Lib. i.; Philo-Bybl. apud Euseb. Prep. Evang. Lib. i. cap. ix.

[4] Macrob. Sat. Lib. i. cap. xviii.

" pronunciation of a more polished language. The Latin name for the Supreme God belongs also
" to the same root; Ιυ-πατηρ, Jupiter, signifying father Ιευ, though written after the ancient
" manner, without the dipthong, which was not in use for many ages after the Greek colonies
" settled in Latium, and introduced the Arcadian alphabet. We find St. Paul likewise acknow-
" ledging that the Jupiter of the poet Aratus was the God whom he adored;[1] and Clemens
" Alexandrinus explains St. Peter's prohibition of worshiping after the manner of the Greeks not
" to mean a prohibition of worshiping the same God, but merely of the corrupt mode in which he
" was then worshiped."[2]

Diodorus Siculus says, that Moses pretended to receive his laws from the God called ΙΑΩ.
This shews that the Greeks considered the name of the Jewish God to be, not Jehovah, but, as I
have stated it, ץץ ieu, or Ieo. Ιηιος[3] is one of the names of Apollo: and Nimrod[4] says, ΙΑΩ
means *I heal, I make sound.* It was probably from this the Essenian monks, his followers, in
Egypt and Syria were called Therapeutæ, or physicians of the soul. In the first volume of Asiatic
Researches Sir W. Jones names a female deity called Hygeia, or *health*, and another called Iaso,
whom he calls *remedy*, daughters of Æsculapius. May not this *remedy* mean Preserver? Perhaps
the reader may think that the use of any correct etymology is not to be expected from such
grammarians as Justin, Papias, and Irenæus. The last gives the following derivation of the name
Jesus: " Jesus nomen secundum propriam Hebræorum linguam litterarum est duarum et dimi-
diæ......et secundum antiquam Hebraicam linguam cœlum est.[5] Is it possible to believe that
Irenæus had ever seen the gospel history by Matthew?

2. Chifflet, speaking of Iao in his treatise on coins, says, that except the Christians no other
sect or religion has given this name to the divinity. This is unquestionably a very great mistake.
M. Beausobre says,[6] " Supposing that to be true, it does not follow that these figures belonged to
" the Basilidians; they might be from some I know not what Gnostic sect, which pretended that
" Iao is the name of an angel. One *must* allow that it is that of Jehovah, which the ancients have
" written and pronounced sometimes Jaho,[7] sometimes Jevo,[8] and sometimes Iaou.[9] But it is
" necessary also to allow, that Iao is one of the names that the Pagans give to the sun. I have
" noticed the oracle of Apollo at Claros, in which Pluto, Jupiter, the sun, and Iao, divide the
" seasons amongst them. These four divinities are at bottom the same.

Εις Ζευς, εις Αδης, εις Ηλιος, εις Διονυσος,

" that is to say, Jupiter, Pluto, the Sun, and Bacchus, are the same. That which is called
" Dyonusus in the last verse is the same which is called Iao in the oracle. It is Bacchus who
" presides over the autumn. Macrobius reports another oracle of Apollo which is couched in
" these terms :

Φραζυ τον παντων υπατον θεον εμμεν Ιαω·

" ' I declare to you that Iao is the greatest of the Gods.' It would be doing too much honour to
" the Demon, if one believed that the god called Iao is the Jehovah of Scripture, or the true God.
" This is no other than the sun. Iao, which was a barbarous name, has been changed by the
" Greeks into Ιηιος (Ieios). Macrobius, well instructed in the Pagan theology, affirms, that Iao

[1] Acts xvii.   [2] Stromat. Lib. v.; P. Knight, p. 195.   [3] Scapula.   [4] P. 617.
[5] Iren. contra Hær. lib. ii. cap. xli.; Dalleus, De Usu Pat. p 243.
[6] Beaus. Hist. Manich. Vol. II. liv. iv. chap. iv. p. 59.   [7] Euseb. Dem. Ev. lib. iv. p. 129.
[8] Euseb. Præp. Evan. lib. i. x.   [9] Clem. Alex. Strom. lib. v. p. 562.

" is the sun, and that Cornelius Labeo had shewn this in a book entitled, ' *Concerning the Oracle*
" ' *of Apollo at Claros.*' " Speaking of the oracle of Apollo above-named by Macrobius, Dr. Cudworth says,[1] "And the oracle applied this to the sun as the supreme God." Porphyry says, that
Sanchoniathon received information from Hierombalus, a priest of Ιαω. The Ευοι Βαχχε λεγον-
τες is nothing but the IEUE of the tribe of Judah, in the country of Palestine, miswritten
by the Greeks, who miswrote every thing. "Athenæus IX. gives Bacchus the name of Ιηιος.
" I doubt not but it is the great name of Jehovah, which they learnt from among the Jews : and that
" Evòhe Sabòhe is the Jehovah Sabaoth, Lord of Hosts, in the Scripture ; whence Bacchus was
" called Sabazius likewise. Diodorus Siculus says expressly, the Jews call God Iao ; and the
" learned universally agree *that* is Jehovah. Evòhe is but another awkward way of pronouncing
" it."[2]

In almost innumerable places in Italy *very old* paintings may be seen of Christ in various situations, labelled with the words in the middle of the painting, *Deo Soli.* These words it is evident
have two meanings—To God alone, and To the God Sol. In most of them there are seen the
attributes of the latter, such as the glory, &c. The former sense is in no way applicable to Christ,
because as one person of the Trinity he cannot be called *solus.* These pictures, with their two
meanings, shew an example like the first verse of Genesis, one for the priests, and one for the
people—the *esoteric* and the *exoteric* religion.

I think we may now assume that we have found the origin of the word Jesus. M. Beausobre
may talk as much as he pleases about honour to the Dæmon, but all his ingenuity will never be
able to overthrow the fair and legitimate consequence which arises from his argument. He has
clearly proved that the Sun, Iao, and Jesus, were all taken for the same being by the ancients, and
it will require more than the skill of the whole priesthood to disprove it. But there is another
way of deriving the name of Ιησυς more probable than the explanation of M. Beausobre ; though
they both come so nearly to the same thing that they are in fact and substance evidently the same.
On this subject Sir W. Drummond says,

" That the sun rising from the lower to the upper hemisphere should be hailed the Preserver or
" Saviour appears extremely natural : and that by such titles he was known to idolaters can-
" not be doubted.[3] Joshua literally signifies the preserver or deliverer ; and that this preserver
" or deliverer was no other than the sun in the sign of the ram, or lamb, may be inferred from
" many circumstances. It will be observed that the LXX. write Ιησους for Joshua, and the lamb
" has always been the type of Ιησους."[4]

Matthew[5] says, that the son of Mary was called Jesus, *because he would save* (i. e. preserve)
his people from their sins.[6] The Jews say in their Talmud, that the name of Jesus was Bar
Panther, but that it was changed into Jesus. The word Jesus, as was before remarked, is the

---

[1] Book i. chap. iv. p. 285.   [2] Stukeley, Pal. Sac. No. I. p 21.
[3] " The Sun, according to Pausanias, was worshiped under the name of Saviour, at Eleusis."
[4] Drummond, Œdip. Jud. p. 195.   [5] Chap. i. verse 21.
[6] We are told in Numbers, (xiii. 16,) that Moses changed the name of Osee to Joshua.
ויקרא משה להושע בן-נון יהושע *And Moses called Leuso, son of Nun, Ieuso.* I believe there is in this passage a
correct example of the word לה *le,* being used as the emphatic article, and the correct translation would be, And
Moses called the saviour or guardian or protector, (*who was* understood) the son of Nun, ה *is* יוו *uso :* as we should
say, He entitled the protector (who was) the son of Nun, *the Lord Protector.* It is exactly our practice, our idiom,
and even the very word Lord, according to our translation. At this time the Hebrew nation was a federative republic
of twelve tribes, under leaders elected by the people, or often by the prophet or priest. I believe that *ie* became a title
of honour, like Bal and Lord, and, for several reasons which I shall give hereafter, that the word לה *le* or the letter ל *l,*
the *el* or *al* of Arabic, the *le* of France, and the *il* of Italy, was a Hebrew emphatic article.

same as the word Joshua in the Hebrew, and has the same signification. It may be correctly derived either from the Hebrew word יֹשׁע *iso*, or from the Greek word σωω or σωζω *to save;* σοος, *safe.* It may be correctly derived from the Greek as well as the Hebrew, because the Greek is itself derived from the Hebrew.[1] It may be derived also from הי *ie*,[2] the name of the Hebrew God, often rendered Jah, and יֹשׁע *iso*, saviour; or Jehovah or Iao saviour.[3] In the old Irish and Etruscan languages the word Aesar means God. In Sanscrit the word Isa, Iswara, means Lord and Saviour. Probably the Greeks understanding that the Hebrew word יֹ *ie* meant God the Saviour, added a significant termination according to the genius of their language, taken from the word σαω *to save*, and so made of it Iη-συς, or Iao the Saviour.

3. Kircher informs us, that "the ancient Jews absolutely applied the three first letters of this "name (יהוה) to denote the three superior Sephiroth, and he remarks that, in fact, there are but "three distinct letters in the word, which are Jod, He, and Vau; the last letter being only a repe- "tition of the second."[4] "This name (says Buxtorf) signifies ENS, EXISTENS A SEIPSO, *ab* "*æterno et in æternum, omnibusque aliis extra se essentiam et existentiam communicans:* the being "existing of necessity from all eternity and to eternity." Again, "Nam, litera JOD ab initio, "characteristica est *futuri:* VAU in medio, participii, temporis *presentis:* HE, in fine, cum "Kametz subscripto, *præteriti.*"[5]

In my Celtic Druids[6] I have said, that the יהוה *ieue* of the Israelites was but Iao with the em- phatic article, making it *the Iao:* and that it was originally Ieu, not Ieo; the first three letters of of the word *ieu-e.* In the Bible we constantly meet with the expression *the Aleim,* but in no instance with the expression THE Jehovah. This arises from the expression *ieue* meaning *the ieu.* I have in the Celtic Druids also shewn that the word Abraxas meant 365, the solar period or the sun. This Abraxas is constantly identified on the coins of Chifflet and Kircher with the names of God, Adonai, Sabaoth, &c. Kircher[7] says, "Gnostici natione Ægyptii, religione primum He- "bræi, dum virtutem nominis Dei tetragrammati ex veterum relatione cognoscerent, ad impietatis "suæ complementum, superstitiosa sua nomina passim nomine IAω et CEBAω, quod idem est "ac יהוה *(ieue)* Jehova et צבאות *(sbout)* Sabaoth, summa tamen nominum corruptela indigitarunt." But the name of Jesus was sometimes written Ieu. I have observed before, that in the Duomo at Milan, the first time I went to Italy, I found it written thus, IEV—Cristo. In the above passage we see the identity of the Jesus of the Roman Church and the Iao of the ancients proved, not by implication, but by documents produced by the learned Jesuit Kircher. In a few pages later,[8] the learned father adds, "Hujus farinæ fecit quoque quæ lib. ii. cap. xiii. Irenæus de Gnosticorum "impietatibus refert, ubi nomen absconditum Redemptoris sic profantur. *Messian fromagno in* "*scenchaldin mosumeda ecacha saronhepseha Jesu Nazarene:* quorum interpretationem hanc esse "dicunt: *Christi non divido spiritum, cor et supra cælestem virtutem misericordem fruar nomine* "*tuo Salvator veritatis:* confirmatus autem et redemptus respondet: *Ego redimo animam meam* "*ab hoc æone et omnium quæ ab eo sunt in nomine IAO, qui redimit animam meam.* Hujus quo- "que impietatis censenda sunt pleraque lapidibus, gemmis, laminisque metallicis insculpta sine "numero nomina."

Cedrenus says that the Chaldeans adored the light: that they called it intellectual light, and that they described it, or symbolized it, by the two letters α and ω, or αω, by which he meant the extreme terms of the diffusion of matter in the seven planetary bodies, of which the first or the

---

[1] Parkhurst, p. 299, ed. 7.   [2] הי *Ie,* self-existing—existing by his own power.   [3] See Pictet, pp. 6—16.
[4] Maur. Hind. Ant. Vol. IV. p. 196.   [5] Ibid. p. 198.   [6] Chap. v. sect. xxxviii.   [7] Vol. III. p. 416.
[8] P. 469.

moon, answered to the vowel α, and the last, or Saturn, to the vowel ω; and that the letter I described the Sun; and this altogether formed the word Iαω—the *Panaugria* of the Gnostics, otherwise the universal light distributed in the planets. All this is evidently judicial astrology. St. John says, "and the life was light, and the light was life, and the light was the word: Vita erat lux, et lux erat vita, et·lux erat verbum, in Greek *Logos*,[1] where Christ is described in the midst of seven candlesticks, and seven stars in his band. The Guebres, the Magi, and the Manicheans, all describe God to be an eternal, intelligent, and perfectly pure light. The Manicheans call this, Christ, the son of The Light Eternal, which Plato calls the Sun. The Scriptures and the fathers of the church all call God a sublime light.[2]

4. On the word יהוה *Ieue*, or Jehovah, Mr. Parkhurst, p. 155, has the following observations, which confirm what Beausobre has said upon it. His authority will not be disputed. That this divine name " יהוה *ieue* was well known to the heathen, there can be no doubt. Diodorus Siculus, " lib. i., speaking of those who attributed the framing of their laws to the Gods, says Παρα τοις " Ιουδαιοις Μωσην ιςορουσι τον ΙΑΩ επικαλουμενον Θεον. Among the Jews they report that " Moses did this to the God called Iao. *Varro*, cited by St. Austin, says, Deum Judæorum esse " Jovem, that Jove was the God of the Jews; and from יהוה the Etruscans seem plainly to have " had their *Juve* or *Jove*, and the Romans their Jovis or Jovis-Pater, that is, Father Jove, after- " wards corrupted into Jupiter. And, that the idolaters of several nations, Phœnicians, Greeks, " Etruscans, Latins, and Romans, gave the incommunicable name יהוה, with some dialectical varia- " tion to their false Gods, may be seen in an excellent note in the Ancient Universal History."[3] It is rather whimsical that Mr. Parkhurst should state this name of God to be incommunicable, when, in the same sentence, he informs us that it was common to almost all nations. Here seems a manifest and gross contradiction, which, in a note, I will now try to account for.[4]

The truth will sometimes escape from learned sectaries when they very little intend it. The pious Dr. Parkhurst, as we have just seen in his Hebrew Lexicon, proves, from the authority of Diodorus Siculus, Varro, St. Augustin, &c., that the Iao, Jehovah, or יהוה *ieue*, or יה *ie* of the Jews, was the Jove of the Latins and Etruscans. In the next page, and in p. 160, under the word הלל *ell*, he allows that this יה *ie* was the name of Apollo, over the door of the Temple of Delphi. He then admits that this יהוה *ieue* Jehovah is Jesus Christ in the following sentences: " It would be " almost endless to quote all the passages of scripture wherein the name יהוה (*ieue*) is applied to " Christ: let those, therefore, who own the scriptures as the rule of faith, and yet doubt his essen- " tial deity, only compare in the original scriptures (the passages too numerous to insert), and " I think they cannot miss of a scriptural demonstration that Jesus is Jehovah." But we have seen it is admitted that Jehovah is Jove, Apollo, Sol, whence it follows that Jesus is Jove, &c.

---

[1] See Apocalypse, Ch. i.   [2] Dupuis, Vol. III. p. 105, ed 4to.   [3] "Vol. XVII. pp. 274, &c."

[4] The Jews maintain that the fourth command in the decalogue, not to mention the name of God, means not to mention the word *Ieue*. But from considering that it is so often named in their writings, and the manner in which it is named, and ordered to be named in them; as for instance, in Exodus, ch. vi.,—in the decalogue,—and also to Moses by God in the bush, &c., &c.,—that it is directed to be used in such a manner as to carry with it the necessity of constantly repeating it in the performance of the service in their synagogues, and also considering other parts of their Cabala, the prophecy of Isaiah, the names of places, and the identity of Jewish and Heathen doctrines, (of Heathens both East and West of them,) I have been induced to suspect that their secret word was the Indian Om, and not really Ieue. It seems to be nonsense to tell them the word *Ieue* is not to be repeated when it is ordered to be repeated continually. If I be right, the verse of the decalogue might be paraphrased thus: " *Thou shalt not repeat the secret name of thy God Ieue.* This exoteric and esoteric meaning of the passage is in perfect keeping with what we know of the remainder of the Jewish Cabala; but upon this subject I must entreat my reader to suspend his judgment till he has travelled with me over countries the most distant, and times the most remote, in search of this celebrated cabala.

5. The three letters I H S, from the very earliest age of the Romish Christians, have been adopted for the insignia of their religion. We now very commonly see them embroidered in golden letters upon the velvet pulpit cloths of the churches in England, and the clergy say they mean *Jesus Hominum Salvator.* But it is very remarkable, as I have observed in B. v. Ch. ii. S. 8, that these three letters, in the Greek language, are the insignia of Bacchus or the Sun, and stand for the mystical number 608, which is sacred to him; a pretty striking proof of the identity of the two. Of the signs or monograms to express in a short way the names of their gods, used by the Gentiles, perhaps there is no one of them more striking than their celebrated YHS. These letters were anciently placed upon the temples or other buildings sacred to Bacchus or Sol; as they are now by Christians in their churches: and as the Christians, in the very dark ages, when temples, churches, towns, every thing indeed was *destroyed,* by the unceasing anarchy and civil war which for many ages prevailed, supposed the ruins upon which they were found to have belonged to their religion, they construed them to mean Jesus Hominum Salvator. Thus the ruins proved the truth of the monogram, the monogram the truth of the Christian ruins. *Of course every stone or inscription where this is found, is at once,* by all Christian antiquarians, settled to be of Christian origin; and this happy accident has converted to Christianity, old stones, temples, and statues innumerable, in almost all nations.

We find the word rendered *Jehovah* in English, for several words which are differently spelt in the Chaldaic Hebrew. In most places it is spelt יוה *Ieue,* particularly in Exod. vi. 3, where God says, *I appeared unto Abraham, unto Isaac, and unto Jacob, by the name of Al Sadi* אל שדי, *but by my name of* יהוה *Ieue was I not known unto them.* But in other places it is spelt יהיה *Ieie.* In the Hebrew, words are often met with repeated in a peculiar manner, as שבת שבת *sbt, sbt,* sabat, sabat. This has been considered by grammarians merely as an intensitive, or to do honour, to give emphasis to a word, for various purposes, as we write a word in italics. This may have been the case with the word יהיה *Ieie.* No word is more likely to be so distinguished. Whether it were meant as at present written for one word, or two, cannot be known; in the old manuscripts there were no divisions between the words. יה *ie* is often translated by the word Jah:[1] *My strength and my song is Jah. Praise him by his name Jah.* Psalm lxviii. 4. This יה *ie* in the Syriac dialect was יו *io,* and was the Androgynous *Io* whom the Bull Jupiter ran away with.

Mr. Parkhurst has very properly observed, that, from one of those divine names, the Greeks had their Iη Iη in their invocations of the Gods, particularly of Apollo. " And hence ƎI (written after " the oriental manner from right to left), afterward IE, was inscribed over the great door of the " Temple of Apollo at Delphi."[2] No doubt what Mr. Parkhurst says is true, and from this source came also the Greek *Io triumphe* of Bacchus. The reason why the word ƎI was written to be read from right to left was, because it had been adopted in a very early time, when the Greek language was read βεϛροφηδον, or from right to left, and back again.

The " Devatas of India sing out in transport in honour of Cristna the words JEYE! JEYE!"[3] Here we have the identical name Jehovah.—IEVE יהוה ƎIƎI or IEIE. That the word יה[4] translated *Jah* is correctly the word of the Greeks over their temple at Delphi, *My strength and song is Jah, Praise him by his name Jah,* is still more clearly proved from the circumstance that, in the Hebrew and Greek, they are the same letters in order and in numerical power, I standing for *ten,* and η E for *five,* in each language. They would not, however, be in exactly the same order, if a letter were not inserted in the Greek for the number *six,* which makes them agree.

---

[1] Exod. xv. 2.   [2] Parkhurst, voce היה, p. 157.   [3] Maurice Hind. Hist. Vol. II. p. 339, ed. 4to
[4] Exod. xv. 2, and Psalm lxviii. 5.

The followers of Iao, יהוה *ieus*, constantly sung the word *Hallelujah* in his praise. This they did in the temple of Solomon, in the temple of Delphi, and they still continue the same hallelujahs in the temple at Rome. Dr. Parkhurst says, "הלולים *elulim* praises, [1] הללויה *(elluie) Praise ye Jah—* " Eng. Marg. *Hallelujah :* and so the LXX. throughout, leaving it untranslated, Αλληλυϊα. It " occurs very frequently at the beginning and end of the Psalms. And from this solemn form of " *praise to God*, which, no doubt, was far prior to the time of David, the ancient Greeks plainly " had their similar acclamation Ελελυ Ιη *(eleleu ie)*, with which they both began and ended their " Pæans or Hymns in honour of Apollo, i. e. *The light*."[2]

Jesus in the gospels is always called Lord, or in the Greek Κυριος. This is the word by which the Hellenistic Jews, in translating Hebrew into Greek LXX, constantly rendered the word יהוה *ieus*. The word Κυριος is derived from the word Κυρω, *to be, exist, subsist ;*[3] and is a very excellent word to use for the Hebrew word יה *ie*, which has precisely the same meaning. But this word יה *ie*, as it has been before observed, was the name given to Apollo or the sun at Delphi, who is always called Κυριος, and the day dedicated to him κυριακη, *dies dominica*, or the Lord's-day. From some, or from a combination, of these circumstances, Jesus took the name of Lord, the etymological meaning of which will be explained hereafter. Eupolemus states, that there was a temple of Iao or Jupiter on Carmel, without image, which is confirmed by Tacitus.[4] This was evidently the temple of Melchizedek, of Joshua, and the proseucha discovered by Epiphanius. This, probably, was also the temple where Pythagoras, who sacrificed to the bloodless Apollo at Delos, went to acquire learning, or to be initiated. Numa autem rex Romanorum erat quidem Pythagoreus, ex iis autem quæ à Mose tradita sunt adiutus, prohibuit Romanis ne homini aut animali similem Dei facerent imaginem. Cum itaque centum et septuaginta priuis annis templa ædificarent, nullam imaginem, nec affictam, nec depictum fecere. Occulte enim eis indicaret Numa, quod est optimum, non alia ratione quam sola mente ulli, licet attingere.[5]

Alexander autem in libro de symbolis Pythagoreis, refert Pythagoram fuisse discipulum Nazarati Assyrii. Quidum eum existimant Ezechielem, sed non est, ut ostendetur postea: et vult præterea Pythagoram Gallos audiisse et Brachmanas.[6] I have very little doubt that a considerable part of the ancient idolatry arose from a cause apparently trifling, but yet quite proportionate to the effect. This was the necessary personification of objects by the primeval language which had no neuter gender, as we know was and yet is the case with the synagogue Hebrew; and I doubt not all its cognate dialects, in early times, were the same. "None dare to enter the temple of Serapis, who " did not bear on his breast or forehead the name Jao or J-ha-ho, a name almost equivalent in " sound to that of the Hebrew Jehovah, and probably of identical import; and no name was " uttered in Egypt with more reverence than this of Iao. In the hymn which the hierophant or " guardian of the sanctuary sang to the initiated, this was the first explanation given of the " nature of the Deity: *He is one, and by himself, and to him alone do all things owe their existence.*" Translation from the German of Schiller.[7]

Voltaire, in his commentary on Exodus, tells us, that some critics say the name Jehovah signi- fies destroyer.[8] The Egyptians pronounced it Jaou, and when they entered into the temple of the Sun they carried a phylactery, on which the name Iaou was written. Sanchoniathon wrote it Jevo.

---

[1] Lev. xix. 24.   [2] Parkhurst's Lexicon, voc. הלל, p. 160, ed. 7.   [3] Ibid. voc. הוה, p. 155, ed. 7.
[4] Vide Diss. III. in Preface to Whiston's Josephus and Tacitus.   [5] Clem. Alex. Strom. Lib. i. p. 304.   [6] Ibid.
[7] Monthly Repository, Vol. XX. pp. 198, 199.
[8] Where Voltaire got his authority for Jehovah meaning *destroyer* the author does not know, but it is probably true, as it is in perfect keeping with the remainder of the picture, and arose from the mistake between the Creator and Destroyer.

Origen and Jerom think it ought to be pronounced Jao. The Samaritans called it Jave. From this name comes the ancient Jovis, (ancient nom. case, see Parkhurst,) Jovispiter—Jupiter with the ancient Tuscans and Latins. The Greeks made from Jehova their Zeus.

The god *Horus* is stated by Dodwell to have the meaning of *destroyer*.

Shuckford says, " The name Jehovah was, I believe, known to be the name of the Supreme " God, in the early ages, in all nations." Again, " Ficinus remarked, that all the several nations " of the world had a name for the Supreme Deity, consisting of four letters only.[1] This I think " was true at first in a different sense from that in which Ficinus took it: for I question not but " they used the very same word, until the languages of different nations came to have a " more entire disagreement than the confusion at Babel at first caused."[2] He goes on in the same page to observe, that it is said by Philo-Biblius in Eusebius, that the God of the Phœnicians was called *Jevo* or *Jao*. How can any one doubt that this is the Jove, who, according to the report of the Greeks, had a temple in Carmel, where no image was adored? To this temple, as I have before remarked, Plato and Pythagoras probably withdrew for study.

Adrian Reland, De Nomine Jehovah, says, " It is plain that the Latins formed the name of " their god Jupiter, whom they called Jovis, from the name Jehovah."[3] Mr. Maurice says, " From this word יהוה *Ieue*, the Pagan title of Jao and *Jove* is, with the greatest probability, formed."[4] " In the Indra or Diveaspiter of India, and his symbol, the vaira or forked bolt, we im- " mediately recognize the *Jupiter Tonans* of the Greeks and Latins. Jupiter conquered the " Titans, Indra the Assoors, with their bolts."[5] Deva, or Deo, was a sacred title.[6] It was pro- phesied that Cristna was to become incarnate in the house of YADU at Mathura, of his mother *Devaci*.[7] The elements of the words *Ie* and *Deus* or *Diva* are evident in these names. Cristna was born in the eighth month, on a Wednesday at midnight, in the house of *Vasudeva*, his father, of *Devaci*, his mother.[8] The same is here again to be found in the word Vasudeva. I cannot entertain a doubt that the Indra of the Brahmins is the Jupiter of the Etruscans and Latins. He is called Dyupeti and Dyupetir.[9] Although various specious derivations of the word Jupiter may be given, yet I think the most probable is, that it is nothing but Peti or Pater יהו *ieu*, or Jupiter: the Ieu shortened into Ju. Mr. Whiston, in a note on Book ii. chap. xii. of Josephus, has ob- served, that the way I write Jehovah by Jao is correct. Even amongst the Chinese *the God* is to be found. In ascending to their fabulous history, they say their first legislator was Yao.[10] In short, it is evident that *all* these derivations are, at the bottom, essentially the same.

6. It is thus proved by fair deduction and logical reasoning on unquestionable authority, that the God יהוה IEUE Jehovah, יה IE or Jah of the Jews, the God 31, the Apollo of Delphos, the Deus, the Jupiter, Jovis, Jovispiter of the Latins, the god Mithra of the Persians, and all the gods of the Heathens, are identically the same person or being; not merely derivatives from one another, but that they are, with only such trifling apparent differences as may reasonably be expected to arise from the lapse of many ages, and from the inevitable uncertainty of names translated without any definite rule out of one language into another, one and the same; and this same being, *the sun*, or shekinah of the self-existent Being. In short, that Jehovah was the sun; for if Jehovah was Iao, and Iao was the sun, Jehovah must be the sun. Dr. Parkhurst admits that Jesus was Jehovah; but if Jesus was Jehovah, and Jehovah the sun, it follows that Jesus, that is, the Romish Jesus,

[1] The Hebrew word for the God of Abraham consisted merely of vowels, but we have put three consonants into our translation of it, *Jehovah*.
[2] Book ix. pp. 388, 391.   [3] Val. Col. Lib. ii. p. 296.   [4] Hind. Ant. Vol. IV. p. 73.
[5] Hist. Hind. Vol. I. pp. 461, 462.   [6] Asiat. Res. Vol. V. p. 238.   [7] Maurice, Hind. Sceptic Refuted, p. 56.
[8] Maurice, Bram. Frauds exp.   [9] Moore's Pantheon, p. 259.   [10] Muller's Hist., Vol. I. p. 320.

but not the Jesus of Nazareth, must be the sun. Perhaps the reverend, pious, and learned doctor would not have been so ready to make this admission, if he had foreseen the consequences to which it would lead. But he was perfectly right; the Jehovah of the Jews is the Jesus of corrupted Christianity, and multitudes of passages in the gospels prove it, or allude to it, as the Doctor truly says—passages which are *really genuine parts* of these works, as well as many which are misrepresented by accident, many by design, and also many which are forged. The philosophical Unitarians may continue their toils to overturn this doctrine of Dr. Parkhurst, by exposing the false or misunderstood passages in the text; but when they have done their utmost, enough will remain for its support.

The author will not attempt an argument with them; he leaves them to the doughty champions of the church—the Burgesses and the Wranghams, who are never backward to take the field in defence of the favourite doctrine of the Trinity, which is evidently involved in this question. It cannot be said that these doctrines are merely a chimera, an invention of the author's own imagination; almost every assertion which he has made is supported by the authority of some one or other of learned *Christian* divines who have studied the subject most carefully. Jesus being mistaken, by the founders of the Roman church, for the god Sol or the sun, it follows that the rites, ceremonies, and doctrines of the devotees of the god Sol or the sun may be expected to be found in their religion. In the following part of this work it will be shewn that that which may be expected to be found, is really found; and that most of the rites and doctrines of modern Christianity are nothing more than the rites and doctrines of the old religion, collected by devotees of very weak and mean understandings, and applied either to a real, or to an imaginary personage. Which of these two is the truth, it will be the final object of this work to determine.

BOOK VII

CHAPTER I

Ionians, Origin of—Derivation of Ionian—Argonauts—Linga and Yoni—The Argha

1. It has been a general, but a very erroneous opinion, that there were no religious wars among the ancients. But we read of them in Egypt, and from the inquiries of our countrymen into the habits and manners of the oriental nations of very remote times, we learn that traces yet exist, which cannot be mistaken, of religious wars in India of the very worst description—wars not exceeded in duration or atrocity by any of those in modern Europe, bad as they have been. It also appears that the religions of India became, in very early times, divided into an almost inconceivable number of sects, some of which, after bloody wars, were expelled to the West, under different names. In one of these sects, either driven out or emigrating from India, I think will be found the ancient Ionians. These people are chiefly found in Attica, and on the most Western coast of Asia Minor. The story of the latter being a colony from Athens is not worth a moment's consideration. The vain Athenians found traces of them in Greece and in Asia; then, of course, their national vanity suggested that the Ionians must have come from Athens. It probably never occurred to them that the two remnants might have a common origin. As usual, the Greeks being perfectly ignorant of their origin, in order to account for it they invented a story; and in this case, it was of a king called Ion, from whom it was said that they took their name. It is not improbable that they might have arrived at Athens from the North-east by way of Thrace. But it may be a doubt whether part of them may not have come by sea at a more early period to Argos, and the Argolis, where they are found to have been settled. They were also said to have once dwelt in Achaia, whence the adjoining sea and islands had the name of Ionian. But their principal settlement was in Asia Minor, on the western coast of which they had a very fine country, and twelve states or tribes in a confederacy, which all assembled at stated times to worship at a temple built by them in common, like that of the Jews, a circumstance worthy of attention; it was called Pan-Ionium. We have here a very close resemblance to the Israelitish system. I suspect that the district was called by this name, but that the national temple was at Ephesus, a town which was said to have been built by Amazons, and was certainly *one* of the principal Ionian cities, if not the chief of them. Here was the famous image of the BLACK Di-ana, or Di-jana, or Dia-jana, which was supposed to have descended from heaven.

2. On the derivation of the word Ionian, Dr. Lempriere says, " It is generally thought *to* come " from the Hebrew *Iavan*, or (if pronounced with the quiescent *vau) Ion ;* and in like manner " the Hellenes are thought to be the same with *Elisa*, in the sacred writings, more especially " their country Hellas. Hence Bochart makes *Iavan*, the son of *Japhet*, the ancestor of the " Iones." He had just before observed that Greece was anciently divided between the Hellenes and the Ionians, and that Hellen has the same meaning as Ioni, and both that of the female generative power. They are said by Conon to have descended from a king called Hellen, the son

of Deucalion, one of whose grandsons settled in the Peloponnesus, then called Apia. Thus we find them to descend from a man saved at the flood of Noah, Japeti; and also from Deucalion, said by the Greeks to have been saved from the flood, whose son was called *Hellen.* They are also said to have built a town called Argos, and to have dwelt in a country called Apia, the name of the Egyptian Apis. In their city of Argos the goddess Juno was particularly worshiped; and here Io, the daughter of Jasus, or Ιασος, or Ιησος, was born, with whom Jupiter or the God Iao fell in love; to prevent whose intrigues the bull-eyed[1] Juno set Argus, with a hundred eyes, to watch. Jupiter turned Io into a beautiful heifer; she wandered into Egypt, and, as they say, became the goddess Isis, the wife of the bull-headed Osiris or Apis. Another story says, she was the daughter of Jordanus, a king in Phœnicia; that Jupiter turned himself into a bull; and after persuading her to mount him, swam over the sea with her to Crete, where she brought forth a most celebrated lawgiver, called Minos, who is the same as the lawgiver of India, called Menu, and as the first king and lawgiver of Egypt, Menes. Respecting king Jordanus, that is, the king named after the river Jordan, I shall say more hereafter. I think the reader will agree with me, that all this is sufficiently mystical.

The Hindoo books are full of accounts of the expulsion from India of a class of persons called Yavanas. Now who were these Yavanas; and when expelled, what became of them? To this I think I can produce an unanswerable reply,—the evidence of, *in this case,* an unimpeachable witness. The person in the Pentateuch called *Juvan* is thought to have planted Greece; the LXX. were of this opinion, and constantly translate the Hebrew word Javan into Ἑλλας, the country of Hellen, or Greece.[2] When I consider the circumstance of the Yavanas being Greeks, and the fact, that many Greek towns, as I shall presently shew, were called after those in India, I cannot doubt that some at least of the Greek states were colonies from that country. " Javan was called by Moses יון *iun.* Between this name and that of Janus there is thought to be " a great similitude."[3]

Respecting the word Helen, Proclus[4] says, that all the beauty subsisting about generation from the fabrication of things, is signified by Helen: about which there is a perpetual battle of souls, till, the more intellectual having vanquished the more irrational forms of life, they return to the place from whence they originally came. Mr. Taylor, the Platonist, says, that the word Helen signifies *intelligible beauty,* being a certain *vessel* (ἑλενη τις ουσα) attracting to itself intellect.[5]

3. The elegant, polite, and enlightened Greeks, a nation celebrated for wise men, had a history of a voyage called the Argonautic expedition, of a company of heroes, who sailed from Greece in a ship called the Argo, to the kingdom of Colchis, in search of the golden fleece of a Ram. Although the history literally taken is full of the most puerile nonsense and absurd contradictions, it was in substance generally believed; the ancient wise men, as in some similar cases modern ones do, endeavouring to explain the difficulties away. The story is very long and is really so foolish, if understood literally, that I cannot bring myself to repeat it, but it may be found in Dr. Lempriere's Classical Dictionary, gravely told, not disputed, but countenanced, for the instruction of our youth—and a very beautiful thing it is for the purpose. He finishes, instead of expressing any doubt about its having taken place, by observing, that many persons, *the learned no doubt,* consider it as a commercial enterprise, that Dr. Gillies considers it partly as a voyage of instruction for young Greeks, and partly for retaliation for injuries sustained by Greece from strangers; and

---

[1] Homer.   [2] Shuckford, Lib. iii.   [3] Bryant, Anal. Vol. II. p. 251.   [4] In Plat. Polit. p. 393.
[5] Class. Journal, No. XLV. p. 39.

the Leviathan of wise men, the Aleim or God of modern Britain, Sir Isaac Newton, considered it
to be an embassy: and so firmly was this talented and silly, wise and foolish,[1] though very
good man, convinced of its truth, that he founded upon it a system of chronology. It is probably
an astronomical allegory: and from various terms used and incidental circumstances, it is evidently
not of Grecian invention, though accommodated by them to their traditions and localities. On
this part of the subject Mr. Maurice says,[2]

" Now the mythological history of Canopus is, that he was the pilot of that sacred vessel,
" (meaning the ship Argo,) and was adored as the God of mariners among the Egyptians, who,
" therefore placed him on the rudder, calling him Canobus, from *Cnoub*, the Coptic term for gold—
" in reference to the singular colour and lustre of a star, one of the most brilliant in the southern
" hemisphere. The circumstance of this star not being visible in any of the celebrated cities of
" Greece has already been noticed from the same author, and Dr. Rutherford, in proof that the
" Greeks were not the original inventors of that asterism."

Again, Mr. Maurice says, " Dr. Rutherford, in one of the most ingenious productions on the
" subject of natural philosophy that ever was published, has in the clearest manner evinced that
" the constellations delineated on the sphere, though apparently allusive to the Argonautic expe-
" dition, could not possibly be the fabrication of Chiron, or any other Grecian for that purpose ;
" since the greatest part of the stars in the constellation Argo, and, in particular, Canopus, the
" brightest of them, were not visible in any part of Greece; and no astronomer would be so absurd
" as to delineate constellations to direct the course of a vessel, the principal stars in which ' could
" ' not be seen by the mariners either when they set out or when they came to the end of the
" ' voyage.' "[3]

Here is an end of the Argonautic expedition as a Grecian story ; we will try if we can find it
elsewhere.

Of the Argonautic expedition Sir W. Jones says, " That it neither was according to Herodotus,
" nor indeed could have been originally, Grecian, appears even when stripped of its poetical and
" fabulous ornaments, extremely disputable: and I am disposed to believe it was an emigration
" from Africa and Asia, of that adventurous race who had first been established in Chaldæa."[4]

In a little treatise of Mr. Maurice's, called Sanscreet Fragments, published in 1798, is an account of a sage called Agastya, whom he shews to be the star Canopus, the famous steersman or
pilot of the Argo of Greece. The circumstance that this star was not visible in Greece, and that
it was in this particular manner noticed and said to be a hero, placed in the heavens by the Sanscreet historians, is very remarkable, and pretty well shews that the mythos of the Argonauts is,
as we might expect, of Hindoo origin. When we consider how intimately this Argonautic story
is blended with all the Greek mythoses—what multitudes of their towns and districts are called
from it—the accounts of it in the poems of Homer—and that its stars are not visible in Greece,
how can we doubt that all their systems came from the same place whence it came, viz. India ?

Sir W. Jones has observed, that the asterisms of the Greek and Indian hemispheres are so similar, that it is plain the systems are the same, yet that there are such variations as to make it
evident they were not copied from one another ; whence it follows, that they must have come from
a common source.[5]

When the almost infinite variety of ways in which the Argonauts are connected with the
mythoses of Greece is considered, it of itself affords a strong probability, amounting very near to a

---

[1] Witness his Essays on the Revelation of St. John. He was the greatest of natural, and the least of moral, philosophers.
[2] Hist. Hind. Vol. II. p. 38.   [3] Ind. Ant.   [4] Supplement to Ind. Chron.
[5] Asiat. Res. Vol. IV. p. 10.

demonstration, that the Grecian mythology came from India. Indeed, I think a probable opinion might be very safely founded upon it alone.[1] Babylon must have been the great connecting link between India and Europe.

4. It now becomes necessary to make a few observations on the Indian Linga and the I, or Yoni, as connected with the celebrated boat of the Hindoos, called *Argha*, which I propose to shew gave rise, among the Greeks, to the fables of the above-named Argo, Argonauts, &c., &c. In the old philosophy of the Hindoos I have shewn that the world was supposed to be destroyed and renewed at the end of certain periods, and this process was supposed to be of immense, if not of eternal, duration. This was a very recondite and philosophical idea, and was partly founded upon the principle that God was perfectly wise, and that he would form or create nothing that was bad, and that as he was not changeable, he would not really finally destroy that which he had made, which was necessarily good: and that consequently what appears to us to be changed must be only periodical, and therefore that a periodical renovation of every thing would take place. At the end of every period the world was supposed to be destroyed. At this moment Brahme or Brahme-Maia, the Creator, was believed to be in a state of repose or inaction in the profundity of the great abyss or firmament: and the male and female generative powers of nature, in conjunction, were said to float or brood on the surface of the firmament or abyss, and in themselves to preserve the germ of animated nature,—of all plants and animated beings. This operation of the two powers is described by the Linga, in the shape of a mast, fixed in the Yoni, in the shape of a boat, floating in the firmament. After this operation has proceeded a certain time, the female generative power begins to act, by feeling the passion of love, the ερως of the Greeks, which is described by the sending forth of a dove, and this is the beginning of a new age. Of this Col. Wilford says,[2]

" Satyavrata having built the ark, and the flood increasing, it was made fast to the peak of " Naubandha with a long cable.[3]

5. The mystic Ocean in which the ship Argha floated, is the ethereal space or fluid, the רקיע rqio,[4] called firmament in Gen. i. 7, in which the bodies of the planetary system revolve. The Ark or Argha, the ship, with its mount Meru in the centre by way of mast, may be seen in every temple of India, and requires no explanation. It is the Omphale of Delphi. See the Yoni and Linga, plates, fig. 21.

The Earth was often called the Arga: this was imitated by the mystic Meru. The north pole was the Linga, surrounded by seven dwips or zones rising one above another, and seven seas, or rivers, or waters, and an outward one called Oceanus. In this Oceanus the whole floated. Thus the earth, mother Eartha, became the Argha or Ione, and Meru the pole, the Linga.

---

[1] I ought to have explained to my reader before, that a probable opinion is such a one as a man may entertain, whether it be true or false, without being damned for it. It is the scientific term for a doctrine of the Jesuits, discussed and misrepresented by Pascal in the Provincial Letters. The Jesuits, making allowance for the infirmities of human nature, maintained, that if a person by inquiry of those who were likely to be informed, or by the best means in his power, came to an erroneous conclusion, he would not be subject to condemnation for it. The Calvinists, and those who adopt the Athanasian creed, are of a different opinion; but then they are a more enlightened race than the benighted Jesuits!

[2] Asiat. Res. Vol. VI. p. 524.

[3] Nau-band-a I have explained before (in B. v. chap. v. sect. 2). Sati-avrata is composed of the word Sati, meaning Saturn, (which I shall explain hereafter,) and a-vrat, which is the Hebrew emphatic article, and ברא brat, and means former or creator, from ברא bra, to form or create: and jointly it means mount of Sati the Creator. Thus Il-avrata is the mount of God (Il) the Creator. In the Sanscrit the b and v are used indifferently for each other.

[4] From this word rqio came the *rack* of Shakspeare. "Shall leave not a *rack* behind." See title-page of the Celtic Druids.

It is quite clear that this mythos must have been formed in the infancy of astronomical science, when the plane of the ecliptic was believed to coincide with the plane of the equator.

" During the flood, Brahma,[1] or the creating power, was asleep at the bottom of the abyss: the " generative powers of nature, both male and female, were reduced to their simplest elements— " the Linga and the Yoni. The latter assumed the shape of the hull of a ship, since typified by " the Argha, whilst the Linga became the mast. (Maha-deva is sometimes represented stand- " ing erect in the middle of the Argha, in the room of the mast. Maha-deva means *magnus-deus.)* " In this manner they were wafted over the deep, under the care and protection of Vishnu." (The three in *one*, and one in *three.*) " When the waters had retired, the female power of nature ap- " peared immediately in the character of *Capoteswari,* or the DOVE, and she was soon joined by " her consort *Capoteswara.*"[2] I think *he* must be very blind who does not see here the duplicate of the Mosaic allegory of a ship and a deluge. The animated world in each case preserved in a boat, or Argha, or Theba, תבה *tbe,* Θιϐη, but in the latter, instead of putting all the live animals into one ship, the germ or principle of generation is substituted.[3]

The Argha is represented by a vessel of copper, by the Brahmins in their sacred rites.[4] It is intended to be a symbol or hieroglyphic of the universal mother. It is very often in the form of an elliptic boat or canoe, having both ends similarly pointed, or biprora, as its name was.[5] In the centre of it is an oval rising, embossed, which represents the Linga. But it is to be seen in the shape described in the plate, repeated in every variety of way, in every temple of India. By this union of the Linga and Yoni, or Ioni, it is intended mystically to represent the two principles of generation—to represent them as one. This boat, as I have already intimated, was the Argo of Greece, the name of the mystic ship in which the Ionians, who lived at Argos, sailed to seek the golden fleece of the Ram. It was also the name of a man, Argos, who is said to have lived at Amphilochium, in the bay of Am-brasius, and it was the invention of *divine wisdom* or Minerva. This Argha was also the cup in which Hercules sailed over the ocean.[6]

In my plates, fig. 21, is an example of the Argha and Linga and Ioni, from a great number in Moore's Hindoo Pantheon, and from Creuzer's plates. The Argha of India was the same as the

---

[1] Brahma is ברא *bra, creator,* and ma, or maha, *great*—that is, great Creator. Vide Book v. chap. i. sect. 10, n.

[2] Asiat. Res. Vol. VI. p. 523.

[3] This leads me to digress a moment to make an observation upon the ιλυς or mud of Sanchoniathon, into which the mass of our globe was supposed, not unphilosophically, to have been reduced ; a state into which M. Cuvier's researches shew that it has been at least nearly reduced many times. This substance, Genesis says, was תהו *tâu,* ובהו *u-bâu,* incapable of generation or of producing any of those beautiful animal or vegetable forms which we see around us. God communicated to it this faculty, and we know not, and probably never shall know, how far it extended. For any thing we know, he might subject it to certain rules, or endow it with certain properties, which should give it the power, under certain limited circumstances, of what we call self-generation, or self-production. I contend that, if we admit a God, we cannot doubt his possession of this power; and, as we cannot know that he has not exercised it, we cannot, I think, from equivocal generation, conclude that he does *not exist.* When certain particles of matter, under certain circumstances, come together, they shoot into certain regularly-shaped crystals, always having the same forms, but not animated. Where is the improbability in the Creator having subjected matter to such other rule or law, that when other particles of it come together, under certain peculiar circumstances, certain other forms having the faculty or capability of vivification, the property of animation, to a certain limited extent, should be produced? For instance, the animalculæ observed to appear in vinegar, in which any vegetable matter is steeped. We are totally ignorant of the means by which the principle of vitality acts upon matter. Then shall we draw positive conclusions merely from our ignorance? Heat applied to an inanimate egg produces what we call life. This egg is matter under a certain modification, fitted, when heat is applied, to produce the effect, *life.* In the same manner, the matter in the vinegar is under such circumstances as are fitted to produce the effect which we see.

[4] Asiat. Res. Vol. VIII. pp. 52, 275.   [5] This was the shape of the ship of the Argonauts.

[6] Asiat. Res. Vol. III. pp. 363, 365.

Patera of the Greeks and Romans, so sacred in the mysteries of Delphi, and every where in those of Apollo. It is called among the Hindoos sometimes Argha, and sometimes Patera, and sometimes Argha-patera. It is also called Pan-patera or Pan-patra. Among the numerous plates in Moore's Pantheon, there is scarcely one in which the Linga and Ioni or Argha are not to be seen, varied in different ways.[1] In the ceremonies of the Hindoos there is no emblem in more universal use. For a full account of it, I must refer my reader to the book itself.

The meaning of the word Argo as applied to the ship Argo, is generally acknowledged to be unknown, and not to be intelligible in the Greek language. Argölis is Argo-polis. Argia, the other name of the same place, is Argo-ia; written in Hebrew letters it would be ארגיא *argia*, or ארגאי *argai*, and would mean the place of Argo. This was in Arcadia, which was called the cradle of the Greeks, where also was Delphi. Arcadia is Arca or Arga-dia, the Sacred Arga. The Greeks were called Argives. The mariners of this ship were called Argonautæ. The ship carried a beam on her prow cut in the forest of Dodona, by Minerva, which gave out oracles, and which falling on Jason, the captain of the ship, killed him. Of course it must have been carried upright as a mast, or it could not have fallen down upon him. The ship was built by seven Cyclops, who came from Syria or the country of the Sun, שר *sr*. It conveyed many passengers[2] who at one time carried the ship 150 miles, from the Danube to the Adriatic, on their shoulders. They passed from Greece by way of the river *Tanais* or *the Don* to the ocean. Some authors have said the ship was built by Hercules; Dr. Lempriere *solemnly assures us* this is false. I therefore place no dependence on it. He seems really to have believed that there once was such a ship.

There was also a town of Acarnania, called Argos Amphilochium,[3] in the bay of Ambracius. It was founded by Amphilochus of Argos, son of Amphiareus son of Apollo. It is at present called Filoquia. Here again we find the words Argo and Amphe or Omphe or Om closely connected. There was also a city in Macedonia called Amphipolis, of which Thucydides gives an explanation, but which was not satisfactory to D'Anville. It had the name of Crysopolis. Its Turkish name is Iamboli or Emboli. It was anciently also called Eion, out of which the Greeks made Iampolis. It is at the mouth of the Strymon, near Palæo-Orphano, and not far from the tomb of *Orpheus*, near which Dr. Clarke[4] found a medal with a Boustrophedon inscription thus : AM

IΦ.

These names may be considered to be translations of one another. Crysopolis is πολις, Χρησος *benignus, mitis*.[5] Iam-boli is polis-om, or om-polis, with the monogram *I* prefixed, as was very common. The Eïon is the ON of Egypt and the Delphic ει. But of the meaning of these words we shall see more presently. Col. Leake found an inscription at a village near the Strymon in Macedonia, called at this time Yenikeni, the remains of the ancient Amphipolis.[6] Mr.

---

[1] Panth. p. 388.   [2] Onomacritus makes the passengers by the Argo amount to fifty-two.

[3] I suspect that this is Om-pi-lbkm or Omphi-l'-hkm—town of the wise Omphi, or of the wisdom of Om, or Omphi. If my suspicion be correct, the mystic Om ought to be found wherever the mythos is found. I much suspect that in all these words, even in the word Omphi, the phi, as I have before intimated, is the Coptic emphatic article *Pi*, and that we have sought too deeply for the meaning of this word. I shall be told that Pi is not Greek; but is it not evident that the Greek and Coptic were originally one? Can any thing, therefore, be more likely than that the names given to places should be similar in both of the languages ? The Egyptian, however, must have been the oldest : but I shall discuss the question of this language presently.

[4] Travels, Vol. IV. p. 401. 4to.

[5] Why not Χρωτος will be explained hereafter.

[6] Walpole's Travels, Vol. II. p. 512. In the same work, p. 516, I find Apollo called ΑΠΛΟΤΝ, in Thessaly. This is, I think, Apollyon.

Bryant has observed that the Greeks new-named many places. For example, Palmyra, for Tad-mor; but that among the natives the ancient names are yet to be found in use, the Greek name being forgotten. I suspect this is the case with Amphipolis and Yeni-keni, and that the former part of this word was a corruption of Yoni. The country about Amphipolis was peculiarly sacred. The river Strymon was anciently called Ioneus.

The Greeks considered Delphi to be the navel of the earth, as the Jews, and even the first Christians, thought that the true navel was Jerusalem; and the Mohamedans still consider Mecca as the mother and navel, or nabbi. All these notions appear to have arisen from the worship of which we have been treating. The Yoni and Nabhi or navel, are both denominated *Amba* or mother: but Wilford says, the words *Amba*, *Nabhi*, and *Argha*, have gradually become synony-mous; and as αμϐη and *umbo* seem to be derived from *amba* or the circular *argha*, with a boss like a target, so ομφαλος and *umbilicus* apparently spring from the same root: and even the word navel, though originally Gothic, was the same anciently with *Nabhi* in Sanscrit and *Naf* in Persian.[1] This is also the same with the *Nau* in Sanscrit for ship, and *Navis* in Latin. A great umbilicus, carried in the processions both at Delphi and in Egypt, had the form of a boat or Nau. From this Nau the centre part of our churches was called Nave, and built in their present oblong, inconvenient form.

The Protogenos or first Emanation from the divine power—from the head of Jupiter, was Mi-nerva or Divine Wisdom, or the female generative power, of which the Ioni or Argha of India was an emblem. See plates, fig. 22. This was the Rasit of Genesis, the Wisdom or the FIRST prin-ciple (or *principe* in French) by which God formed the world. It was the Argo of Greece: it was the Αρχη of the feminine gender, which meant *the first cause, the ruler, the beginning.*[2] Its verb was Αρχω, *to command, to set in order.*[3] The Ionian Pelasgi or Ionian sailors called their gods *disposers* or *placers in order.* Here is the Argha or Argo or Αρχη, the *first* or pre-eminent placer in order, both in time and dignity. The way in which these profound doctrines emanate from one another is striking and beautiful. This shews how the Exoteric meaning of Genesis is *beginning*, and its Esoteric *wisdom*. As I have before observed, if the Greek had merely meant *in the first place*, or *in the beginning*, it would have said πρωτως. The Argha or Ark is called κιϐωτος by the LXX. When a Buddha or new Incarnation of *divine wisdom* appeared in Japan he was called Cobotos.[4] Can any one doubt that this was the Argha or κιϐωτος of the LXX.? This shews that the κιϐωτος could not mean a ship, but, as I have said before, it had the same meaning as Argha, the female generative power, in opposition to the Linga. As a boat was also the emblem of the female generative power, the two came at length to be confounded.

---

[1] Asiat. Res. Vol. III. p. 367.   [2] See Jones's Lex.

[3] The Hebrew ערך *ord* and the English *order* are the same Saxon words.   [4] Kæmpfer, Japan.

CHAPTER II

The Lotus—Maurice on the Lotus—Payne Knight on the Same—Moore on the Same—Nimrod on the Same

1. The double sex typified by the Argha and its contents is also by the Hindoos represented by the " Nymphæa or Lotus, floating like a boat on the boundless ocean, where the whole plant " signifies both the earth and the two principles of its fecundation. The germ is both Meru and " the Linga : the petals and filaments are the mountains which encircle Meru, and are also a type " of the Yoni : the leaves of the Calyx are the four vast regions to the cardinal points of Meru : " and the leaves of the plant are the Dwipas or isles round the land of Jambu."[1] As this plant, or the lily, was probably the most celebrated of all the vegetable creation among the mystics of the ancient world, and is to be found in thousands of the most beautiful and sacred paintings of the Christians at this day, I must detain my reader with a few observations respecting it. This is the more necessary, as it appears that the priests of the Romish Church have lost the meaning of it : at least this is the case with every one of whom I have made inquiry. But it is like many other very odd things, probably understood in the Vatican, or the crypt of St. Peter's.

2. Maurice says, " Among the different plants which ornament our globe, there is no one which " has received so much honour from man as the Lotos or Lily, in whose consecrated bosom " Brahma was born, and Osiris delighted to float. This is the sublime, the hallowed, symbol that " eternally occurs in oriental mythology : and in truth not without reason ; for it is itself a lovely " prodigy. Throughout all the Northern hemisphere it was every where held in profound venera- " tion, and from Savary we learn that that veneration is yet continued among the modern Egyp- " tians." And we shall find in the sequel, that it still continues to receive the respect, if not the adoration of a great part of the Christian world, unconscious, perhaps, of the original reason of their conduct.

3. The following is the account given of it by Mr. Payne Knight, in his very curious disserta- tion on the Phallic worship :[2]

" The Lotos is the Nelumbo of Linnæus. This plant grows in the water, and amongst its " broad leaves puts forth a flower, in the centre of which is formed the seed vessel, shaped like a " bell or inverted cone, and punctuated on the top with little cavities or cells, in which the seeds " grow. The orifices of these cells being too small to let the seeds drop out when ripe they shoot " forth into new plants, in the places where they were formed : the bulb of the vessel serving as " a matrix to nourish them, until they acquire such a degree of magnitude as to burst it open, and " release themselves, after which, like other aquatic weeds, they take root wherever the current " deposits them. This plant, therefore, being thus productive of itself, and vegetating from its " own matrix, without being fostered in the earth, was naturally adopted as the symbol of the " productive power of the waters, upon which the active spirit of the Creator operated in giving " life and vegetation to matter. We accordingly find it employed in every part of the northern " hemisphere, where the symbolical religion, *improperly called idolatry*, does or ever did prevail. " The sacred images of the Tartars, Japanese, and Indians, are almost all placed upon it, of which

---

[1] Asiat. Res. Vol. III. p. 364.

[2] Pp. 84—86. This book was never sold, but only given away. A copy is kept in the British Museum, but it is *not in the catalogue*. The care displayed by the trustees in keeping it out of the catalogue, to prevent the minds of the studious gentlemen who frequent that institution from being corrupted is above all praise!!! I have read it in the Museum.

" numerous instances occur in the publication of Kæmpfer, Sonnerat, &c.. The Brahma of India
" is represented sitting upon his Lotos throne, and the figures upon the Isiac table hold the stem
" of this plant surmounted by the seed vessel in one hand, and the cross representing the male
" organs of generation in the other : thus signifying the universal power, both active and passive,
" attributed to that Goddess."

Creuzer says,[1] from the peculiar mode in which the sacred Lotus propagates itself by its bean,
came the religious veneration for this seed ; on which Mr. Muller observes, that it was from this
that Pythagoras, who was of the school of the Buddhists, ordered his disciples to hold in veneration and to abstain from beans. See my plates, fig. 23. The Nelumbo Nymphæa is not a
native of Egypt, though seen upon almost all its ancient monuments, but of the North-eastern
parts of Asia.[2] This is the correct and proper plant of the sacred mysteries, but after the original meaning of it had become lost, in modern times, any lily was indiscriminately used, as may
be observed in the Romish pictures of the Virgin, particularly of the annunciation or impregnation, where the ministering angel is always seen to carry in his hand a branch of some kind of
lily.

4. Of the Lotos, Mr. Moore says, " The Nymphæa or Lotos floating on the water, is an emblem
" of the world : the whole plant signifies both the earth, and its two principles of fecundation.
" The stalk originates from the navel of Vishnu, sleeping at the bottom of the ocean,[3] and the
" flower is the cradle of Brahma or mankind. The germ is both Meru and the Linga : the plants
" and filaments are the mountains which encircle Meru, and are also the type of the Yoni : the
" four leaves of the calyx are the four vast *dwipas*, or countries, toward the four cardinal points.
" Eight external leaves, placed two by two in the intervals, are eight subordinate *dwipas* or coun-
" tries."[4]

5. Concerning the Lotus of the Hindoos, Nimrod[5] says, " The Lotus is a well-known allegory,
" of which the expanse calyx represents the ship of the Gods floating on the surface of the water,
" and the erect flower arising out of it, the mast thereof : the one was the Galley or Cockboat,
" and the other the mast of Cockayne : but as the ship was Isis or Magna Mater, the female
" principle, and the mast in it the male deity, these parts of the flower came to have certain other
" significations, which seem to have been as well known at Samosata[6] as at Benares." This
plant was also used in the sacred offices of the Jewish religion. In the ornaments of the temple
of Solomon the Lotus or lily is often seen.[7]

Athenæus says that Suson was a Greek word for a Lily, and that the name of the city Susa
meant the city of Lilies.[8] This is very remarkable, as it was the capital of the Cushites or Ethiopians. But the Lotus of the Nile and Ganges was, I believe, dark blue, which sometimes was
the colour of Cristna : but he was as often black as blue. He is perfectly black in the India
House. John Crawford says, " I suppose the Lotos to be here an emblem of *Parvati*, who, as
" well as *Sri*, I find has the epithet of Padmi in the nomenclature of the Gods." Again, " A
" Lotos is frequently substituted for the Yoni."[9] This may be seen in thousands of places in
Egypt and India. We will now return to our Ionians and their Argo.

---

[1] Liv. prem. Ch. ii. note, p. 160; Maurice, Ant. Hind. Vol. III. p. 245.

[2] Payne Knight's Inquiry, Sect. 146.   [3] See plates 7 and 8 of Moore's Pantheon.

[4] Asiat. Res. Vol. VIII. p. 308 ; Moore, Hind. Panth. p. 270.   [5] Vol. I. p. 127, Sup. Ed.

[6] Vide Luc. Ver. Hist. Lib. ii. Cap. xlv.

[7] In the North of England children make boats of Walnut shells which they call *cock*-boats, a remnant of the same
superstition. See Nimrod, Vol. I. p. 441, note.

[8] Nimrod, Vol. I. p. 44.   [9] Asiat. Res. Vol. XIII. p. 359.

CHAPTER III

The Loadstone—Helen Athena—Yavanas—Division of the Followers of the Male and Female Principles, and their Reunion

1. In my CELTIC DRUIDS I have proved that the loadstone was known to the ancients; and I think it was used by the priests for the purposes of superstition, for which it was evidently peculiarly calculated.[1] " The Temple of Jupiter Ammon was esteemed of the highest antiquity, and " we are informed that there was an Omphalus here : and that the Deity was worshiped under " the form of a navel."[2] Quintus Curtius says, " Id quod pro Deo colitur, non eandem effigiem " habebat, quam vulgo Diis artifices accommodarunt. *Umbilico* maxime similis est habitus, " smaragdo, et gemmis, coagmentatus. Hunc cum responsum petitur, navigio aurato gestant " sacerdotes, multis argenteis *pateris* ab utroque navigii latere pendentibus." I think with Scotus and Hyde that this relates to the compass.[3] I have little doubt that here was the sacred Argha concealing in it a loadstone or magnet, or carrying it perhaps upright as the mast, by which the credulous devotees were duped. The Pateræ ab utroque latere pendentes were votive offerings.[4]

2. The name of the chief Grecian city of the Ionians, Athena, was the name of the female generative principle, as was also Helena, called by Lycophron *the Dove*, which is a translation of the word Pleias, and also of the word Semiramis,[5] and Ion or Ione. The Ionian Athenians claimed to be called Athenians from Athena, which was the name of Minerva, who was both the female generative principle and divine wisdom. The Greeks were called Hellenes, which has precisely the same meaning as Ionians. And they are called Argives from the ship Argo, which was invented by Minerva, who fixed in the prow of it the pole or phallus cut at Dodona, as before

---

[1] Aristotle describes the Mariner's Compass. See Niebuhr, Vol. I. p. 28.

[2] Bryant, Anal. Vol. I. p. 246.   [3] Hyde de Relig. Vet. Pers. App. p. 496.

[4] For what I have said in my Celtic Druids on the subject of the Telescope, Gunpowder, the Mariner's Compass, and other examples of the learning of the ancients, as might well be expected, I have been turned into ridicule by ignorant, narrow-minded persons, whose understandings permit them to see no further either behind or before them than the length of their noses. However, the doctrine I advocate has been placed above the reach of cavil by Sir W. Drummond, in the 19th volume of the Classical Journal, p. 297. Among other matters, he there observes, that we are not to laugh at the powers which the ancients claimed to possess, because we do not possess them ourselves; and he instances the burning of the Roman ships by the Mirror of Archimedes, which was not believed to be possible till it was successfully imitated by Buffon : and the hatching of eggs in an oven in Egypt, which was laughed at till imitated by Reaumur : and which I have been told is now commonly practised in breeding poultry for the London market. Roger Bacon believed in the possible transmutation of the baser metals into gold, and his reasoning amounted to this— Since *carriages have been moved without the aid of animals*—since *boats have been impelled through the water* without oars or sails—since men have been *transported through the air*—since very distant and very minute objects may be made perfectly clear to vision by means of *glasses*—and since the effects of thunder have been produced by a few grains of powder—how can it be contended that the transmutation of metals is impossible? Class. Journ. Vol. XIX. p. 303. From this most extraordinary exhibition of the words of this most celebrated natural philosopher or alchemist, or magician, or judicial astrologer, I feel very little doubt that among the ancient priests or astrologers, all these secrets were known; and that from his books of the occult sciences he came by the information, that these important secrets were formerly known, though perhaps only known to a very few of the heads of a secret order, guarded as Masonic secrets, and consequently in later times lost.

[5] Nimrod, Vol. I. p. 451.

noticed. All these names have a direct reference to the female generative power, and had their origin in India. Minerva was both the female generative power and divine wisdom, because wisdom was the first emanation of the Divine Power, and man can conceive no way in which it can become active except by producing ; thus the mystics united the two.

Mr. Bryant says, " The Grecians were, among other titles, styled Hellenes, being the reputed " descendants of Hellen. The name of this personage is of great antiquity : and THE ETYMOLOGY " FOREIGN." Again, " The Hellenes were the same as the Iönim, or Ιωνης, whence Hesychius " very properly mentions Ιωνας, Ἑλληνας. *The Ionians and Hellenes are the same family.* " The same is to be said of the Æolians and Dorians : they were all from one source, being de- " scended from the same ancestors, the *Ionim* of Babylonia and Syria : as the Phœnician women " in Euripides acknowledge :

$$\text{Κοινον}^1 \text{ αιμα, κοινα τεκνα}$$
$$\text{Τας κερασφορε τεφυκεν Ιες.}$$

" The term Hellen was originally a sacred title."[2]

Many states of Asia Minor and other countries were said to have been colonized by Greeks. This, in most instances, arose from mistakes respecting the word Helen. Sometimes they were Hellenes, sometimes Argives, and sometimes Ionians ; but neither ancients nor moderns have suspected the real meaning of these words, and therefore have applied them all to the Greeks—in doing which they have fallen into innumerable inconsistencies. Mr. Bryant has shewn that Jason was as well known in the East as in Greece ;[3] that he was styled Argos, and gave name to a mountain near Ecbatana in Media. All this tends to strengthen the proofs that the Argive, Hellenian, or Ionian doctrines came from the East. Mr. Bryant says,[4] " The city Antioch, upon the " Orontes, was called Iönah.[5] Ιωνη οντως εκαλειτο ἡ Αντιοχεια, ἡ επι Δαφνη, ἡν ωκισαν Αργειοι. " *Who these Argeans were that founded this city, Iöna, needs not, I believe, any explanation.*" I think not. And I trust my reader will soon think with me, if he do not think so already.

Jeremiah says,[6] " Arise, and let us go again to our own people and to the land of our nativity, " from the face of the sword of the *Ionim.*" The LXX. translate the last words, Απο προσωπυ μαχαιρας Ἑλληνικῆς : and in chap. l. ver. 16, it is translated in the same way. Johannes Antiochenus calls the Midianites Hellenes. He calls Jethro, father-in-law of Moses, Αρχιερευς των Ἑλληνων. I think, though it is a difficult etymon, that the word must have come from the Hebrew אל *al* the sun, and עין *oin* a fountain or an eye.[7]

3. Among the Hindoos, the natives of the Western world are called Yavanas. The word Yavana is a regular participial form of the Sanscrit root *Yu,*[8] from which root the word Yóni or the female nature is derived. Thus the Yavanas are the same as Yónijas or the Yoni-ans. And here we find the origin of the Ionians, as we might expect, in a religious principle—a principle which, though now almost lost and forgotten, I do not doubt formerly placed one half of mankind in arms against the other, the feuds of the two covering the world, for many generations, with carnage and blood : a feud about the most ridiculous and trifling of nonsense. " The Yavanas " were so named from their obstinate assertion of a superior influence in the Yoni or female, over " the Linga or male nature, in producing perfect offspring."[9] And from this nonsense, almost as

---

[1] Phœniss. V. 256.   [2] Anal. Vol. III. p. 383.   [3] Ibid. Vol. II. p. 513.

[4] Anal. Vol. III. p. 370.   [5] Steph. Byzant. Ιωνη.   [6] Chap. xlvi. ver. 16.

[7] Vide Trans. Roy. Soc. Edinb. Vol. III. p. 140.   [8] In Syriac Yo or Io both male and female.

[9] Asiat. Res. Vol. III. p. 358.

absurd as most of the sectarian doctrines of the Christians, the whole world was involved in war and misery.

In the earliest times of which we have any records, the Brahme-Maia, that is the male and female generative principles in union, or the Linga and the Ioni, were the objects of adoration. After some time the division, which I have just noticed, took place, and a terrible war arose between the followers of the Linga and those of the Ioni, and the latter were at last expelled, with great slaughter, to the West. This war was between the followers of Iswara the *active* generative principle, and the Yónijas the followers of the *passive* generative principle. It was probably the origin of the Greek fable of the war between the Gods and the Giants, or sons of the earth,[1] which we know, from Nonnus, had its origin in India.[2] For a more particular account of this war I refer to the Asiatic Researches.[3] This was the famous war of the Maha-barat, in which the Buddhists were expelled from South India. The Buddhists were particularly attached to the male principle.

4. In this manner the ancient religion became divided into two: the sect which adored the sacred Yoni or female generative principle alone, were called Yavanas,[4] and were expelled from India, and are to be found almost all over the Western world. But we are informed that after some time a reconciliation took place, and the two parties united, and once more returned to the worship of the double principle. This is very important. We shall find traces of it in our researches almost every moment, which will enable us to account for many seemingly inconsistent circumstances. Although various sects went out from India, as one party or other prevailed, the natives of that country now make no distinction, but call them all Yavanas.

From the reunion of the two principles it is that we have the Ioni and Linga united in almost every temple in India, as well as at Delphi, &c., in Greece; in the former, described by the two objects in union, in the latter, by the stone pillar and orifice in the earth called Omphe, and by the boat, the Argha, with a man in it, carried in procession in their ceremonies. The meaning of the united two, the *self-existent* being, at once both male and female—the *Aleim*, called *Jah* in Genesis, and the IE on the temple at Delphi, the Ieo of Greece, the Iu-piter Genetrix of Latium.

Of the reality of the great wars here noticed, I think there can be no doubt, and if the habits of life of the ancient Indians were in any degree similar to those of the present Afghans, they must in a very remarkable manner have been calculated for easy emigration. The existence of nations in the form of tribes yet continues in North India, and when we look back in Europe to the most remote periods, we every where find traces of it—many indeed yet remaining. In the earliest periods, the population of the world consisted of many tribes, with a few cities, the slow produce of commerce. In modern times, the latter have prevailed; there are *few* tribes, and *many* cities, and the land has become divided and appropriated.

In these doctrines respecting the Ioni I am not singular, for, according to Theodoret, Arnobius, and Clemens Alexandrinus, the Youi of the Hindoos was the sole object of veneration in the mysteries of Eleusis.[5] In this temple was the celebrated OM ΠΑΞ ΚΟΓΞ. When my friend, Colonel Tod, author of the beautiful history of Rajah Poutana, was at Pæstum in the neighbourhood of the temple of Ceres, he saw at that place several little images of the Goddess holding in her hand the Linga and Ioni, or mysterious Argha; and he observed the same on the porch of the temple of Isis at Pompeii. It is probable that in early times the Yoni alone may have been adored

---

[1] Asiat. Res. Vol. III. p. 360.   [2] Dionys. L. 34, v. 241, ab. Asiat. Res. ibid.   [3] Vol. III. p. 361.
[4] Asiat. Res. Vol. VI. p. 510.   [5] Asiat. Res. Vol. III. p. 365.

at Eleusis; but here, as elsewhere, I have no doubt the two sects united. At Eleusis there was a famous vessel called the Mundus Cereris, used in the mysteries. It was probably the Argha of India; it was supposed to contain the male and female organs of generation.

5. Another sect which was expelled from India was called by the name of *Iadavas*. They were said to be descendants of one Yadu,[1] the father of *Cristna, to have been persecuted by an enemy of Cristna's, and to have emigrated during his minority.*[2] But it is said that after Cristna came of age, he conquered and punished their persecutors. As Cristna certainly was not the female generative power, though the emblem of the two united principles is seen now in all his temples, this story serves to shew that the Iadus were probably in enmity to it also, and this by and by will be found of consequence, for we shall find they continued in this religion in the West. The word Ia-du is evidently the Deus or the Divus *Ia* or *Ie*, the God *Ie*. Of course the descendants of Ya-du are his votaries or followers. Of Ia-du and his descendants, or tribe, I shall treat very much at large presently.

Mount Meru, the Moriah of India, is the primeval emblem of the Linga and the earth, Mother Eartha, is the mysterious Yóni expanded, and open like the Padma or Lotos, which is, as we have seen, with its seed in the centre, an emblem of the same thing. Iswara is called Argha-nát'h'a or the Lord of the broad-shaped vessel; and Osiris or Ysiris, as Hellanicus calls him, was, according to Plutarch, the commander of the Argo, and was represented by the Egyptians, in their processions, in a boat carried on the shoulders of 72 men, and at Delphi in an umbilicus of white marble. I have some suspicion, that the history of the Argonautic expedition is an allegorical description of the war of the two principles, and of their reunion.

CHAPTER IV

Ship of Egypt and Greece—Dupuis on the Argonauts—Arks and Area—Thebes, Tibet

1. In the mysteries of Egypt and Greece a ship was commonly used—this was the Argha. But it has been remarked by Mr. Bryant that this ship was not a common ship, but was of a peculiar construction; was, in fact, a mystic ship.[3] It had both ends alike, was a correct, very much elongated, ellipse, and was called Αμφιπρυμναῖς Amphiprumnaus. Hesychius says, Αμφιπρυμνα, τα επι σωτηρια πεμπομενα πλοια. That is, *Amphiprumna are used in voyages of salvation.* This alludes to the processions in which these ships were carried about, in the middle of which was placed the phallus. They were sometimes of immense size. "Ælian[4] informs us, that a "Lion was the emblem of this God in Egypt (i. e. Hephaistos): and in the curious description "which Capella has given us of the mystic ship navigated by seven sailors, we find that a Lion

---

[1] Cristna, called Yadava, was the descendant of Yadu, the son of Yayáti. Asiat. Res. The Iadu of Mr. Maurice ought probably to be written Idv—it would then mean the God *I*.

[2] Asiat. Res. Vol. III. pp. 326, 327.   [3] Bryant, Anal. Vol. II. p. 224.   [4] Lib. xii.

" was figured on the mast in the midst of the effulgence which shone around. This ship was a
" symbol of the Universe—the seven planets were represented by the seven sailors—and the Lion
" was the emblem of Phtha, the principle of light and life." [1] The Hindoos have a stone called
Shalgramu, which they worship. Mr. Ward saw one which had fallen down and broken, by which
it appeared to be a shell petrefaction. The shell in the inside of this stone is that which is
called the Argonauta Argo, [2] or the Nautilus, which sets its pretty sail before the wind. Every
Hindoo God almost has one of them in his hand. How this shell-fish came to have the name of
Argo-Argonauta in the West, I know not; but I have no doubt it has a connexion in some way
with the Indian superstition, and that it relates to the Argha. In the cabinet of the Baptist Missionaries at Bristol, is an Indian one in copper. I think in the ship Argo, or Nautilus, with its
mast supplied by Minerva or divine wisdom, I can perceive a beautiful mythos. It is really a
ship, not of human, but of divine, invention and manufacture. From a careful consideration of the
Argonautic story, I can entertain little doubt that it is a mistaken and misrepresented Indian
mythos. The arguments of Dr. Rutherford, given in Chapter I. Section 3, clearly prove, that it
must have had its origin very many degrees to the South of Greece; and this must have been, I
think, where, as I shall presently shew, the Bay of Argo, and the Golden or Holy Chersonesus,
that is, South India and Siam, are to be found. It is probable that the solution of this enigma
will be found in the Vedas or Puranas.

I believe, fantastical as my opinion may be thought, that, as I have before stated, our churches
were built in the inconvenient oblong form, instead of square or round, in imitation of these ships,
and that hence the centres of the churches are called naves. [3] This was exactly the case of many
of the ancient temples from which we have copied ours—if indeed our mysticism and theirs be not
the same. This ship was very often described as a lunar crescent ☽, and was mistaken for the
moon, and thus she often became an object of adoration, when in fact she was not meant to be so.
The meaning of the Argo or Argha, or the origin of the Argives, was all entirely unknown to the
Greeks. If the moon were intended, why should her infant state have been always chosen ? Why
is she never worshiped when at full or in the quarters, by her figure in the latter of which on monuments she would be much the best described ? I suspect she never was an object of adoration
till the meaning of the Amphiprumna or Argo was lost. Besides the moon was very often a male.

There was an order of priests in Greece called Argeiphontes—that is, priests of Argha or Argus.
Their origin or meaning was probably unknown to the Greeks. The chief of them, at Athens, had
the second rank to the Archontes, that is, the second rank of the magistracy. He wore a crown
and had the title of king. [4]

2. Mons. Dupuis thought the Argonautic story merely astronomical. I must say I cannot *entirely* agree with him. I believe it was both astronomical and astrological, or magical or alche-
mical. It was, in fact, all four, for they were so closely united, and folly and nonsense were so
completely mixed up with real science, that it is impossible to separate them. Sir W. Jones calls
it a mixed story. He says, " This is a mixed fable, which is astronomical in one sense, and che-
" mical in another ; but this fable is of Egyptian, not of Grecian, invention. The position of the
" ship Argo in the heavens would render this assertion evident, were we even without the autho-

---

[1] Drummond, Class. Journ. No. XXXIX.

[2] Ward's India, Table of Contents, p. 5; Asiat. Res. Vol. VII. p. 240.

[3] These amphiprumna or naves were all prophetic. I have no doubt that the Hebrew word for prophet, *Nabi*, and
these naves, had the same origin.

[4] Montfaucon, Vol. II. p. 6.

" rity of Plutarch for saying, that this constellation is of Egyptian origin. *Canopus*, the great
" star at the helm, is not visible beyond 35 deg. N. lat. Now the chemical sense of the fable, say
" the alchemists, is so clear, that some ancient Greek author, of whom Suidas, according to his
" custom, probably borrowed the language, thus expresses himself: ' *Golden fleece—this is not*
" ' *what it is poetically said to be, but it was a book written on skins, containing the mode of making*
" ' *gold by the aid of chemistry.*' The alchemists have explained what was meant by the dragon,
" and the oxen with brazen feet, which guarded the golden fleece : nor is their explanation with-
" out some show of plausibility : but I wonder that they have neglected to cite a passage in Hesiod
" about Medea, and another passage in Apollonius Rhodius, in which it is said that the ram which
" carried Phrixus was converted into gold by Mercury."[1]

I believe that whatever was meant by the Μηλον of the Argonauts, was also meant by the
Μηλον of the Hesperides. The same mythos is concealed—that the Ionian heresy of the Magna
Mater, and the tree of the knowledge of good and evil, of Paradise, and the allegories of the tree
bearing twelve fruits, &c., &c., are all implicated. In one case, the book or written skin conveyed
the knowledge ; in the other the tree, of which the leaves were letters ; the fruits, the books conveying knowledge, &c.

The doctrine of regeneration is closely connected with the Yoni and its emblem the Dove. In
India are various clefts in the ground or in rocks, (these are all nabi or navels,) into which devotees
go, and from which when they come out they are regenerated or born again. There is a large
stone in Nepaul called Gubya-sthan used for this purpose. Here is a curious mixture of Greek
and English found in India[2] —the stan or stone of Γαια, *Gaia* the earth. There is a similar
opening in several of the Celtic monuments of the British Isles, and particularly in the rocks at
Brimham, near Harrowgate in Yorkshire, a place formerly much used by the Druids. See Celtic
Druids. If the hole in the stone were too small for the body, as Col. Wilford says, they put a
hand or a leg in, and WITH FAITH *it did as well.*[3] The early Christians called those things *Cunni
Diaboli*, and from the former of these words came the vulgar appellation for the membrum fœmineum in England.

The country of Greece, the Peloponnesus where the Ionians dwelt, was called Apia or the country of Bees, and Archaia. The Athenians had a story, that when they sent out their pretended
colony to Asia Minor, it was preceded by the nine Muses in the form of Melissæ or Bees ; and
the emblem of the generative principle in Egypt, the Bull, was called Apis. That this has some
meaning connected with this subject cannot be doubted. Porphyry *de Abstinentia*[4] says, it was
reported that Apis gave the first laws to the Greeks.

3. Great confusion seems to have taken place respecting the different Arks. The Ark of Noe
or of נח *nh* is called תבה *tbe* (Gen. vi. 14) in the Hebrew ; Κιβωτος by the LXX ; and *Arca* by
the Vulgate. The Ark of the covenant (Exod. xxv. 10) is called ארון *arun* or ארן *arn*, in the Hebrew ; and by the LXX. and the Vulgate as above. It is very remarkable that the Ark of Noah
should not be called in any one of the three versions by any name which answers to our word
ship—in Hebrew אניה *anie* or אני *ani* ; in Greek ναυς ; in Latin Navis. The Latin word Arca
may be old Etruscan, therefore it cannot be objected to, as an original name of the ark. But
still, I repeat, it is very remarkable, that not one of the three versions should have called it by any

[1] Class. Journ. Vol. XIX. p. 301.

[2] In England we have Penis-stone, and Girdle-stone, and Gods-stone, &c., &c., &c. ; in India Garga-stan, and Gher-
ghis-stan, and Aitni-stan, &c., &c. all having the same meaning.

[3] Asiat. Res. Vol. VI. p. 502.   [4] Bk. iii. p. 110, Taylor.

name answering to our word *ship*; for Arca means *box* and not *ship*. This has certainly a mystical appearance. From the profound secrecy observed respecting the Hebrew Arca, I suspect came the word arcanus. All the ancient nations appear to have had an ark or Argha, in which to conceal something sacred; and in all of them (unless I except that of the Jews) the Yoni and Linga were inclosed.

Now, from the studied avoidance of every thing like a ship, either in the name of the article or in its shape, for it was not shaped at all like any boat that ever was built, being a solid parallelogram, with rectangular ends, (cubits 300 by 50 by 30,) I contend that I am justified in supposing, that it was meant expressly to exclude the idea of a ship. The Argha of the Hindoos is of various shapes,[1] oval, like a boat, having *both ends alike*, that is crescent-shaped, as well as round and square. The name Argha does not mean a boat, but merely the proper name of that variously-shaped structure. The boat Ark of Moses is called תבה *tbe* in the Hebrew; but in the LXX generally κιϐωτος; but where the infant Moses is preserved on the river, it is called Θιϐη in the LXX. This word Θιϐη is the name of the city of Thebes; Theba, and both Nimrod and Faber admit that it has the meaning of the female generative power; the Argha and the Ioni. All this tends to shew that the ark and all the other vessels had one mystical meaning, which meaning is plain.[2]

The famous Argha of India, I believe, never means an inclosed box, therefore it is rather forced to fetch the Latin Arca from it; but, in our necessity, we must be obliged to do so, for we have no where else to fetch it from. On this very questionable word *Arca* all Mr. Bryant's and Mr. Faber's etymology turns. The word Argha in India does not answer to our word ship, but is the proper name given to a certain ship or boat, as we name our ships. From the name of a mount, *Naubanda*, I conclude that *Nau* is their name for ship: then it would be the *nau* called *Argu*. In the Chaldee, ארג *arg* meant a ship. In Greece many places are called by words something similar, but not the same, (which Mr. Bryant constantly refers to the Ark—for instance, Αρχυαιοι he calls Arkites,) because there is no such word as αρχος for ship or box in the language; and the letter Χ being one of the new letters shews that it is a new word, and must be a corruption of some old word. There is no word known to us to which it can apply but the word Αργος. It will then mean Argives, or followers of the Argha. Thus when we read in Macrobius[3] of the Arkitæ or Architæ, in Syria, we ought to read Αργιιοι. These considerations render almost all Mr. Bryant's reasoning respecting these words inconclusive.

If my reader will turn to the table of alphabets, *Prel. Obs.* Sect. 47, he will observe, that the Latin C answers to the Greek Gamma and the Hebrew Gimel, each being the third letter in the respective alphabets; and it is the same in the Arabic and Ethiopian. Then, the identity of all these alphabets being allowed, it seems to follow that the powers of notation in each of them must originally have been the same; and that the third letters must consequently have been the same, that is, that the C in Latin answered to the G in the other cognate languages. This admitted, the Latin Arca, and the Greek Αρχη, and Hebrew Arga, ארגא *arga*, must have been all the same. Every Greek scholar will allow that the word Αρχη is a most obscure word, in fact a word not understood—like many of the Greek names of the Gods. In early periods, if written at all, it

[1] Asiat. Res. Vol. II. p. 364.

[2] The Egyptians had two Gods called Apis and Nevis, Beeves. The first was the male, the second the female, and from this called Neve or Nave—that is, the Argo.

[3] Sat. Lib. i. Cap. xxi.

could not have been written with the X but with some other letter, (because the X, as already remarked, was a *new* letter,) and this letter would, I think, be the gamma or gimel or c.

4. It is a striking circumstance that the two cities of Thebes should be called by the Hebrew word for this ship or box—the word תבה *Tbe* or Θιϐη or Thibe, which answers to the names of several Greek towns—Argos. It is also the name of Tibet, whence came all the sacred concerns of the Hindoos, the cradle, in fact, of the human race. One name of Tibet is also Baltistan, i. e. place of Baltis. In or near Tibet is the mount called Naubanda, or mount of the *ship's cable*, called so, as the Brahmins say, from this ship Argha being simulatively fastened to it when it floated in the ocean, carrying within it the two principles of generation or the germ of animal life, in a state of quiescence and union—before the *ϵρος*[1] or divine love began to act upon the Brahme-Maia who was reposing at the bottom of the profound abyss. After a time divine love began to act, and the creator, Brahm, divided himself into three, *the creating, the preserving, and the destroying powers,* described in our books by Adam and Eve and their three sons, and by Noah and his three sons. This all alludes, I think, to the origin of the sects which became dispersed about the world.[2]

In all ancient towns, we find an elevated place of the nature of a mount called by different names. All these mounts were imitations of the Meru of India. In Greece this was called the Acropolis—place of the Arca, Arca-polis; in Rome, the capitol. In this place the moveable Arca was always kept, and it was itself an Arca. The Capitolium of Rome will be said to have been so called from an imaginary likeness to the head of a man, it being the highest part. This may be true; but it was called *caput* for another reason: it was an icon or model of the Meru, which was itself an icon of the sun and planetary bodies—the sun, the visible sign or icon of the protogonos or Rasit of Moses, Rachid of the Arabians, Αρχη of Greece, Caput-olium of Latium, and the Arca of Jerusalem. The Arabic and Ethiopic Rachid means head, the same as the Roman Caput the Greek αϱχη, and the Hebrew ראשית *rasit,* and they have all the same mystic allusion. At last, they are all allusions to the protogonos, to divine love—recondite and mystical enough I do not deny; but, I am persuaded, not more mystical than many doctrines, both of the ancients and of modern Christians. I need not remind my reader of the allegorical allusions in our own language to *head* and *wisdom.* A wise man has a good head; he is a long-headed fellow; his mind always resides in the head. Tibe or תבה *tbe* or Θιϐη or Thebes or the Beeve of the Zodiac, is Tibet, a noun in the feminine form. Georgius has shewn that Ti-bet is Di-bud—Holy Bud; the generative power, divine wisdom, of which the Arga and Ioni were symbols. We have before observed in Book V. Ch. I. Sect. 1, 2, and 3, that the letters B D, B T, are found in almost every country to mean Creator, but we have not seen clearly why. I think we have the reason in the Hebrew טוב *tub* good, the same as Καλος or Cali. This is nothing but the name of Budda, Butta, But, read in the Hebrew, instead of the Indian, fashion—בוט-די *but-di.* The origin of the word Di or Ti, I shall explain in a future page: but it is די *di,* Δις, dius, divus.

---

[1] Cupid, called in some mythoses the oldest of the Gods.

[2] To Noah a fourth son was said to be born, called Inachus, the father of the Ionians.

CHAPTER V

Janus—Aphrodite and Diana. Ganesa—Thales, and meaning of Proper Names—
Two Syrias; Two Merus; Two Moriahs—The Greeks new-named their Conquests. Om

1. THE Romans and Etruscans had a God called *Janus:* of his origin they were perfectly ignorant. He was absolutely unknown in Greece. Of the different circumstances connected with
these recondite subjects, there is none more surprising and unaccountable than the complete state
of ignorance in which the best-informed persons were of the meaning and origin of their Gods.
Janus was not one of what they called their twelve *great* Gods, but he was said to be the father
of them all. He had twelve altars erected to him. He held in one hand letters denoting 365, and
in the other the keys of heaven, which he opened to the *good* and shut to the *wicked.* The first
month of the year, Januarius, was dedicated to him. He was represented sometimes with two,
and sometimes with four faces; the reason of which is unknown. He was called Junonius from
the Goddess Juno, whose name Mr. Bryant resolves into Juneh, which signifies *a dove,* and is in
the Hebrew language יונה *iune,* and is the same as the Yoni or Yuni, the female principle, as observed by Col. Wilford. On his coins are often seen a boat and dove, with a chaplet of olive
leaves, or an olive branch. Gale, after observing that Juno was the same as Jana, and that Janus
came from יה Jah of the Hebrews, and that Diana was Di-va Jana, or Dea Jana, says also, that
she was the same as Astarte or Asteroth of the Sidonians, and had the head of a Bull. He also
says; that she was the Belisama of the Hebrews. [1] In Sanscrit Di-Jana is the Goddess Jana.

Macrobius tells us, that the *introitus* and *exitus,* the *front* and *back*-door entrances of buildings,
were sacred to Janus: on this account he had two faces, he was *bifrons.* Zeno says that Janus
was the first who built temples and offered sacred rites in Italy to the Gods, that, therefore, he
deserved to be the first to be sacrificed to. [2] He was supposed to open and shut the gates of heaven
in the morning and evening, and thus the prayers of men were admitted by his means to the Gods.
C. Bassus says, he was represented (bifrons) double-faced, because he was the porter (janitor) of
heaven and hell. January was called after him, because it was the gate of the year—the opening
of the year. Twelve altars were erected to him, because he presided over the first days of the
twelve months. The doors of his temple were shut in time of peace, and open in time of war.

Gale, [3] who wrote more than 150 years ago, and therefore could have no prejudice arising from
Hindoo learning, likens Janus to Noah, on account of the "cognation of his name with the He-
"brew יין *jain* wine, whereof Noah was the inventor;" and he says the entrance of a house called
janua, and the month *January,* were sacred to him, because he was, after the flood, the beginner
of all things. Again, he says, "others refer the origination (both of name and person) of Janus
"to Javan the son of Japhet, the parent of Europeans. For, 1st, יון (*iun*) Javan is much the
"same with Janus; 2nd, Thence that of *Horat.* Lib. i. 3, *Japeti Genus.* So Voss. Idol. Lib. ii.
"Cap. xvi. Janus's name taken historically is the contract of *Javan.*"

Bochart [4] asserts, that from *Japhet,* mentioned Gen. x. 2, the Grecians refer their first genealogies to *Japetus,* whom they make to be the most ancient man. Thus from *Javan, Japhet's* son,

[1] Court Gent. Vol. II. pp. 120, 121.
[2] Court Gent. Book ii. Chap. vi. Seq.
[3] Mac. Sat. Cap. ix.
[4] Phaleg. Lib. iii. Cap. i.

the Grecians derived their *Ionians*. Also from אלישה *Alise*, (Elishah,) Javan's son, Gen. x. 4, they had their Hellas.

Jana was the same as Diana, (i. e. Di-iana,) or Venus, or Juno, or Lucina, the goddess of parturition, in which capacity she was called Diana, Di-iana, or the divine *Jana*. Mr. Faber[1] observed, that the Italians had a Goddess called Maia. This was evidently the Maia of India, and answered to the Di-jana; they had also a God called Maius, who answered to the Janus. There was also a God called Aius, and a Goddess called Aia; evidently the same. One with the monogram M prefixed, the other without it.[2] I think in the Jain or Janus and Jana, we have the reunion of the two principles. Some persons have thought that the word *annus* came from the word Janus; and certainly the holding of the number 365 in his hand seems to shew a close connexion between them. And the same may be said of his wife (or mother as I suppose) Annaperenna, and Di-ana or Diva-Iana. From Bryant I learn that the name of this God was often written Jannus, or I-anuus. In this latter case the *I* was prefixed as a monogram, as the *M* was above.[3] Mr. Faber says, " Juno herself, indeed, was the same character as Isis or Parvati, in " her varied capacity of the ship Argha, the Yoni and the sacred Dove.[4]

2. In Cyprus, Venus, I believe, was particularly called Αφροδιτη. But Dr. Clarke[5] has observed from Tacitus, that *simulacrum Deæ non effigie humana*. From what he says, and from the paterns with the cone in the centre of them, it seems probable that she was here represented by the Linga and Ioni in conjunction—the Meru in the Argha. Juno was called Hera, which is probably the same as Heri in Sanscrit, and means Saviour: she was also called Argiva. A certain Deïone was feigned to be beloved by Apollo. This is the Indian De and Ione.[6] " Diana is " a compound of De lùna, and signifies the Goddess Jana. That her name was a feminine from " Janus, we may learn from Macrobius, who quotes Nigidius for his authority. Pronunciavit " Nigidius Apollinem Janum esse, Dianamque Janam. From this lùna, with the prefix, was " formed Diana, which I imagine was the same as Dione:" that is, Di-Ione[7] in the Sanscrit. The God Janus was the unknown God of the Romans, whose first legislator was Numa, which, as I have already intimated, I take to be a corruption of the word Menu. According to Cornificius,[8] the name of Janus was probably *Eanus*. But Eanus was undoubtedly the same as the Οιvας of the Greeks, and the Iōnas of the Eastern nations.[9]

" One of the names of Buddha is Jain or Jain-Esa: and it has been clearly shewn by Sir W. " Jones, that the mythology of Italy was substantially the same as that of Hindostan," and I have proved their ancient languages the same. " Such being the case, it seems highly probable that " the oriental Jain ought to be identified with the Western Janus, whose worship, like that of " Suman, the Romans apparently borrowed from the Etruscans or ancient Latins. To this opi- " nion I am equally led by similarity of appellation, and by unity of character. Janus, when the

---

[1] Vol. II. p. 397.

[2] See B. V. Ch. II. S. 3. The M, which is found in a very unaccountable manner in the beginning of Egyptian words, Drummond (Orig. Vol. III. p. 456) calls the *nominal* prefix. He so called it because he did not know what to make of it.

[3] The letters I, M, and X, were constantly prefixed to words as monograms, the reason for which will be explained by and by. The practice is still kept up with the X. See signature to a letter from Bishop Doyle, Morning Chronicle, August 2, 1831.

[4] Pag. Idol. Vol. I. p. 389.   [6] Travels, Vol. II. p. 334, Ed. 4to.

[5] Bryant, Anal. Vol. II. p. 339.   [7] Bryant, Anal. p. 340.

[8] Etymorum libro tertio, Cicero, inquit, non Janum, sed Eanum nominat. Macrob. Sat. Lib. i. Cap. ix. p. 158.

[9] Bryant, Anal. Vol. II. p. 258.

" Latin termination is omitted, is the same as Jain."[1]   Mr. Faber then observes, that, like Buddha, he stands insulated as it were from the reigning superstition : and his worship appears rather to have been super-added to it, than to have formed an originally constituent part of it.   Of this Ovid seems to have been fully conscious when he asks, not unnaturally, in what light he ought to consider the God Janus, since the theology of the Greeks, which was radically that of the Romans, acknowledged no such divinity.   Mr. Faber proceeds to observe, that precisely the same actions are attributed to Janus, which are attributed by the Greeks to Dionusus, and by the Egyptians to Osiris.   But the Dionusus or Bacchus of the Greeks, Wilford and Jones have shewn to be the god Deo-naush of India.   Lucian says, Bacchus was born of Semele and also out of Jupiter's thigh ; that, after he was born, he was taken to Nysa, whence he was called Dionysius.[2]

Having proved that the Jains were Buddhists, I think it cannot well be doubted that the Etruscans, with their four-faced god, Janus, were anciently descended from that stock.   The extraordinary circumstance that the god Janus was unknown to the Greeks, shews that the first settlers of Italy did not come from Greece, but confirms, in a remarkable manner, the hypothesis laid down in my CELTIC DRUIDS, that these countries were peopled by tribes from the North-east.

3. Sir W. Jones has endeavoured to prove, that the Ganesa of the Hindoos is the Italian Janus. This seems not unlikely.[3]   Ganesa is called Pollear : this is evidently the polis[4] in the sense of gate.

Ganesa has almost all the attributes of the Roman or Etruscan Janus.   He opens the year ; he is the chief and preceptor of the heavenly host.   He has often two heads.   He is the leader of all enterprises, and his name is inscribed in the beginning of books and on the doors.[5]   I think no one can doubt that this is the Janus of the Romans, of whom it appears that Cicero knew little or nothing, except that he was the *oldest of their Gods.*   No doubt he was the Ganesa brought to Italy by the persons who brought the Indian words given in Ch. II. Sect. XXV. of my Celtic Druids ; and as there were no historical records, those things not being then invented—nothing but mere traditions—and our Indian knowledge not being possessed by them, it is not surprising that they should be ignorant of every thing relating to their origin.[6]

The Heliopolitæ, or inhabitants of On, in Egypt, worshiped the god Gennæus in the form of a Lion : so Damascius in Photius, in the life of Damascius, τον δε Γεννειον Ἡλιουπολιται τιμωσιν εν Διος ὑδρυσαμενοι μορφην τινα Λεοντες.[7]   Now is this Gennæus the god Janus or not ?   It is true the gamma answers not to the Iota of Janus, but the Greeks and Latins made such sad havock in their rendering of the proper names of one country into those of another, that there is no answering for any thing.

In general, the meaning of the names of the old hero Gods (as they are called) of Greece, was unknown to the Greeks *and cannot be ascertained from their language ;* in it, they have no meaning : but many of them are to be found in, and explained by, the oriental languages, in which they have significant meanings.   This is at once a proof that the mythologies travelled from India to Greece and not from Greece, or from any country West of the Indus, to India.   It is to me surprising that this decisive argument should have been overlooked.   Of this Prometheus is one ex-

---

[1] Fab. Pag. Idol. Vol. II. p. 369.
[2] See Asiat. Res. Vol. I. p. 226.
[3] Creuzer, Liv. prem. Ch. ii. pp. 166, 167.
[4] Like Janus, Mithra held in his hand two keys.   Vide Montfaucon, Vol. I. p. 232 ; Monthly Mag. Vol. LVI. p. 22.
[7] Mr. Beverley's unpublished book, called Religion Critical, xxxiv.

[5] Dial. between Neptune and Mercury.
[6] Asiat. Res. Vol. VII. p. 343.

ample : Deucalion and Saba,[1] the latter of which means *host* or *congregation*, are others. Semi-ramis, whose history, except as a mythos, has always been attended with insuperable difficulties, is another. She was Sami-Rama. Col. Wilford says, " Sami-Rama is obviously the Semiramis " of the Western mythologists, whose appellation is derived from the Sanscrit Sami-Râmèsi, or " Isi (Isis)."[2]   They are also further identified by the fact that *Capotesi*, or the Dove, was consi-dered a manifestation of Sami-Rama, in India.   And in Assyria, Semiramis was born of a dove, and disappeared at last in the form of a dove.   Besides these, there are many other circumstances which make the identity of the two unquestionable, of which I shall observe more hereafter.

4. The natural philosophy of Sanchoniathon and Mochus *(Query* Moses ?) is said to have been brought into Greece from Phœnicia, by Thales, the founder of the Ionic school of philosophy.   I have a strong suspicion that Thales, who was most certainly a mythological person, was a corrup-tion of the Φθας of the Egyptians.   But I state this as a suspicion only.

I have said that there never were such men as Hercules and Bacchus, but that they are merely mythological persons, their histories being, in fact, astronomical allegories. This I think Mons. Dupuis has most satisfactorily proved. But I do not mean this rule respecting the mythological personages to be entirely without exception ; because it is very difficult to point out the boundary-line where mythology ends, and history begins ; and on this account it is possible, that some per-sons having a suspicious appearance may have been real persons. For the cause of truth, how-ever, we had better mistake in believing too little than too much. This observation I apply to Thales. What he was, it is very difficult to make out, as the various fables about his genealogy prove. I have no doubt that, *generally*, ancient names had a meaning, particularly technical terms or terms of art. But from this I must except such names as are taken, that is transferred, from one language into another. As this was done by the ancients, as indeed it is yet constantly done by the moderns, without any rule or system, this great class of names will *of course form an* ex-ception. As a consequence, whenever, in ancient history, I meet with a word, a rational or pro-bable meaning of which I cannot find, either in its own or any other language, I set it down as unknown, and by no means accept what appears an absurd meaning. On the subject of language, Nimrod[3] has some very pertinent observations. " We now make a difference between a name " which is positive and insignificant, like Mr. White and Mr. Brown, (for these names are insig- " nificant *quoad* the individuals,) and a title which has relation and significancy, as William " Rufus. But in those early times, when language was analogical and nearly perfect, all appella- " tions were significant, and represented some quality, or some religious symbol, or something of " good omen : and men gave as many names to famous characters, as their fancy, guided by " various circumstances, might chance to dictate : and oftentimes the very same sense, essentially, " was given in different phraseology. If any one of those could be called the name rather than " the others, it must have been when a name was imposed by divine authority, with a prophetic " import. Many of the great men recorded in scripture had several appellations, as Solomon, " Lemuel, Jedidiah. Achilles had two other titles, Liguron and Pyrissous. We must not there- " fore wonder at finding him called Bellerophon in Glaucus's pedigree, who in some others is " called Memnon, or Theseus or Romulus."

5. That the Ionic philosophy should come from the coast of Phœnicia, from the natives, per-haps, of Antioch, anciently called Iona, or from the Palli or Philistines, the natives of Gaza, (also anciently called Iona,) who were the great enemies of the tribe of Abraham, seems natural enough,

---

[1] Nimrod, Vol. I. p. 393.   [2] Asiat. Res. Vol. IV. p. 368 ; Nimrod, Vol. II. pp. 249—253.
[3] Vol. I. p. 91, Sup. Ed.

and not inconsistent with my theory. For the Pelasgi or sailors may, I think, without any great violence, be supposed to have extended the whole length of the sea-coast of Syria, or Assyria, as it has been said that it was most anciently called, the whole being the country, no doubt, of the same priests, the Culdees or Chaldees of the Ionas, and of Babylon. Now, when I reflect on the singular repetition of names of places in the Eastern part of Asia, and in the Western part of it, the Sions, the Moriahs or Merus, the Rama, near Jerusalem and near Gaza, the Semi-rama-is of Babylon, of India, and of Ascalon, the Hercules of Matures, and the Hercules or Samson of Gaza, (Iona,) I cannot help suspecting that Syria or Suria is the Western country of the Soors of India, and that Assuria is the Western country of the Assoors, two celebrated and opposed sects of India, the first meaning devotees of Sur, the sun or light; and the other a name of reproach given them by their enemies, meaning a-soor or a-sur, *without light*, darkness, the meaning of the names of the two sects in India, but which we may be well assured the latter never gave to themselves, but only received it from their enemies, their real name being not told to us, or being Suri or Soors. The Assoors of India were a very bad race of people; so were the Carthaginians; and both for the same reason, probably, because we only hear the account from their enemies, who may have destroyed all their records and books, if they had any. It is thought by Gale, that the Assuri were only Suri, with the emphatic article prefixed: this I would readily admit if they were Assuri only in the Greek books, as we English talk about the Arabic Al-koran, which is *The The* Koran; but they are called אשורים *asurim* by the authors of the country, who would never make such a mistake. The poets Dionysius and Apollonius observe, that there were more countries than one called Assyria. Mr. Bryant[1] has shewn, that the word *our* was often written *sour*. Syncellus[2] says, Abraham was born εν τη χωρα των Χαλδαιων εν Σουρ τη πολει.

A treatise, *De Dea Suriæ*, was published by Lucian, which has been much celebrated. It appears that this was meant to convey the idea of a treatise relating to the Goddess of Syria. This is only one of the numerous mistakes of the Greeks. This Goddess was the Goddess Suria, from which Syria took its name, not the Goddess of Syria: though she certainly was the Goddess of that country. My idea that Syria and Assyria were rather *sectarian* than *proper* names of these countries, is confirmed by a passage of Strabo noticed by Mr. Bryant: "Those whom we Gre-"cians name Syrians, are by the Syrians themselves named Armenians and Aramæans."[3]

As we have seen that there were two Elephantas, two Matureas, and two Sions, the reader will not be surprised to find two Moriahs. The *Moriah* of Isaiah and of Abraham, is the *Meru* of the Hindoos, and the *Olympus* of the Greeks.[4] Cruden expounds it *the mount of doctrine*. This is so unsatisfactory as at once to prove that the word is not understood; and the reason of this is, because it is a word of some far more Eastern clime. Of the mountain Moriah, Mr. Faber[5] says, " I greatly doubt whether the name of this hill be Hebrew: with Mr. Wilford, I am much inclined " to believe, that it was a local Meru or imitative Paradisiacal Ararat." In this I quite agree with Mr. Faber. It was nothing but a Meru.[6]

6. It is a well-known fact, that the Greeks gave new names to almost all the towns and countries which they conquered or acquired. If the place had a name whose meaning was known to them, the new title was often a mere translation. But this had all the effect of new names. It might arise from the same superstition as that noticed by me in B. V. Ch. XI. Sect. 1. It is pro-

---

[1] Anal. Anc. Myth. Vol. III. pp. 147, 446, 463, 465.   [2] P. 95.   [3] Bryant, Anal. Vol. III. p. 90.

[4] Al-om-pi.   [5] Orig. Pag. Idol. Vol. III. p. 620.

[6] The Hindoos had in the North of upper India a mountain of the moon. In imitation of this when the Palli or Palestini took possession of Syria, they called the most northern of its mountains Lebanon, which means Moon. See Celtic Druids, App. p. 310.

bable that the ancient names always continued among the natives, and Dr. Clarke has observed, that after the conquest of the countries by the Saracens and Turks, they appear to have retaken their old appellations. This is similar to the observation which I quoted in Chap. I. Sect. V. from Mr. Bryant: and it is a very interesting observation, and will be found to lead to some very important consequences. I shall return to it very often. In the following names of places, the Om of India I think is very apparent. I cannot help suspecting that this Om is, at last, nothing but the monogram M, the numerical symbol of the God of the cycle of 600. Generally speaking, a person will look in vain into the Greek geographers for these Oms, and nobody will doubt that they are ancient and not modern names.[1] " Homs-Emesa; Om Keis-Gadara; Om el Djemal; " Om-Ezzertoun; Om-Haretein; Om-el-Kebour; Om-Waled; Om-'Eddjemal; Om-ba, where " resides the Sheikh or El HAKEM; Om-el-Sheratyth; Tel-Houm, Capernaum; Om-el-Taybe; " Ammon or Philadelphia; Om Djouze; Om-el-Reszasz; Om-Aamed; Om-teda; Biar Om- " shash; Om-megheylan; Omran tribe of; Hom-mar river of; Om-Hash; Om-haye; Om-Had- " jydjein; Omyle; Om-Kheysyr; Om-Shomar; Om-Dhad, places near Sinai," &c., &c.[2]

In or near the island of Meroe, Burckhardt calls a place Senaar, (which I consider a corruption of Shinar,) and he mentions Tuklawi and an island of Argo, and below Assouan, two temples called Hierosyeaminon. In many places, particularly near Mount Sinai, he notices *mountains* called Om; as Om Thoman. Animals also are called Om. And from one passage it appears as if this word had the meaning of Mother. But it is also applied to a village called Om Daoud, evidently *David*. And near Mount Sinai he met with a tribe of Arabs, who paid adoration to a saint called *El Khoudher* (St. George). This is evidently the name of Al Choder, of the ancient Arabs. But how Burckhardt came to know that he was St. George does not appear. Burckhardt says, that, at the period of the Mohamedan conquest, the peninsula of Mount Sinai was inhabited exclusively by the tribe of Oulad Soleiman, or Beni Selman. It is clear that this tribe of sons (Beni) of Solomon, cannot have come, or had their name, from the Mohamedans.

CHAPTER VI

Id-Avratta, Meru and Meroe—Eden and its Rivers—Whiston and Josephus on ditto—Delos—Plan of the Mystic City—Hanging Gardens and Seven Hills— Seleucus of Antioch—Greek Mythologies—Homer—Troy, Ilion—Ulysses and St. Patrick

1. To the work of the learned person under the name of *Nimrod*, I am chiefly indebted for the following observations: they appear to me to confirm the doctrines advanced by me, in a very remarkable manner.

Ilavratta, Id-avratta, or Ararat, or Mount Meru, of the Indians, was surrounded with seven belts of land, and seven seas, and, beyond them, by one much greater, called *the Ocean*. This was exactly in imitation of the earth and the seven planets. The Mount, with its seven belts in the

---

form of an ellipse, was a type of the planets in their elliptic orbits—with the sun, the seat of the generative principle in their centre, all floating in the ocean or firmament. The whole was represented by the Lotus, swimming in the water; by the ship of Noah and its eight sailors; by the Argha and its mast; and (as we shall soon see) by a tower in each city, or an Argha-polis, or Arco-polis, or acropolis, and seven other hills, and surrounded with seven districts, and one larger than the others, called oceanus, at the outside. On the top of the Mount Meru, called the Mount of Saba, or of the congregation or heavenly host, was the city of Brahmapore; the place of assembly of the Gods, and it was square, not round or elliptical. There the Gods were said to assemble in consultation, *on the side of the Mount of the North.*

Here we find the seat of God with its seven earths, emblematical of the sun and seven planets. And the Hindoo Sabha, called congregation, meaning the same as Sabaoth, " *Lord God of Sabaoth,*" Lord God of the heavenly host, the starry host. We always end with the sun and heavenly host. And here is also Il-avratta, Id-avratta, *holy* Avratta, or Ararat. The Saba is what we call in the Bible Sabaoth, but in the Hebrew it is the same as the Sanscrit צבא *zba;* and generally means Lord of the planetary bodies—צבא ה שמים *zba-e-smim*, though, perhaps, the stars may sometimes be included by uninitiated persons. Here is the origin of the Sabæans, which has been much sought for. See Parkhurst in voce. [1]

The learned Dr. Hager says, [2] The number *seven* seems to have been sacred among the *Chaldeans*, in the same way as it was afterward among other nations, in honour of the *seven planets*, over which they believed that *seven angels* or *Cabirian deities*, presided; and therefore they may have built *seven* towers. In the eighth, says Herodotus, was the temple of Belus. Belus's tower consists of eight stories, a perfect square circuit, 2250 feet. [3] Τον δε Βηλον, ον και Δια μεθερμηνευουσιν—" Belus whom they interpret Jupiter." That is, the Babylonians interpret. [4] Sanchoniathon says, that Jupiter Belus was the son of Saturn. In Syria is a river Belus, near which is a tomb of Memnon; and here Hercules was cured of his wounds. [5]

If my reader wish for a short and very clear account of the great learning of the ancient Chaldeans and Egyptians, he may consult a treatise on this subject, published by Sir W. Drummond, in the thirty-first number of the Classical Journal.

The striking similarity between the Meru of India and of Babylon, could not escape Mr. Faber, and, to prove the identity of their designs and objects, he has [6] given a very ingenious paper, which he concludes with the following sentence: " Agreeably to the just opinion of the Hindoo " Theologians, the Pyramid on the banks of the Euphrates, an artificial mountain raised in a flat " country where there are no natural mountains, was *the first erected copy of the holy mount Meru* " *or Ararat.*" I refer my reader to Mr. Faber's essay, which will much please him, if he will make only a reasonable allowance for Mr. Faber's *official* superstition.

Meru, as I have already intimated, is the Ararat of the Hindoos. There has been a considerable difference of opinion respecting the precise situation of Ararat. Most persons have placed it in the high land of Armenia, near the fountains of the Euphrates: but some have supposed that it lay in the mountainous country of Cashgar, to the North of India, and that it was a part of that lofty chain of hills which the Greeks called the Indian Caucasus. The latter of these opinions was

---

[1] Faber, Orig. of Pag. Idol. There was an obelisk in Babylon, according to Diodorus Siculus, (Lib. ii.) erected by Semiramis, 130 feet high. The name of Ἑρμαικ Λιθοι (Hesychius) or Hermæ given to the places of the obelisks, shew that they were Buddhist, Hermes being Buddha.

[2] Diss. Babyl. Bricks, p. 27.   [4] Bombay Transactions, Vol. I. p. 137.

[3] Berosus, ap. Scal. Græc. Euseb. p. 6.   [5] Clarke's Travels, Vol. II. p. 395, ed. 4to.

[6] In the Classical Journal, No. XLI.

held by Heylin and Shuckford:[1] and it has lately been revived, with much ingenuity and with the advantage of great local knowledge, by Mr. Wilford.[2] I cannot help thinking that there were two Ararats. The hypothesis of the oriental site of Ararat, as maintained in my *Celtic Druids*, but ridiculed by some pragmatical individuals, is supported both by Heylin and Shuckford. "Ila-" vratta or Ida-vratta signifies the circle of Ila, the earth, which is called Ida. The Jews and "Greeks soon forgot the original Meru, and gave that name to some favourite mountain of their "own country: the first to Sion or Moriah. The Greeks had their Olympus and Mount Ida, "near which was the city of Ilium, Aileyam in Sanscrit, from Ida, whose inhabitants were "Meropes, from Merupa: being of divine origin, or descended from Meru."[3] Meru is Olympus, or Olympus is Meru. There are several Olympuses, but only one Meru, though several less sacred mounts, called *Splinters of Meru*. This raises a strong presumption that Meru was the original, and, when joined to the consideration that almost all the Greek proper names are Indian, is conclusive as to which is the original and which is the copy. It is very likely that *vratta* may mean circle, for the divine mind was constantly represented by a circle ; but I believe the deriva-tion of it is בראת *brat*, from ברא *bra, to form*. Ida is the Hebrew ירי *ido*, idea or mind, and the whole is the mount of the creative or *formative mind.*

In most countries, there was a sacred mount, an Olympus, an Athos, or Atlas, or Ida, in short, a Meru—and a sacred city. In Egypt, Thebes was the city ; and as they could not conveniently have a mount, without, in fact, going out of the valley of the Nile, they had a sacred island, and this was Phylæ or Meroe. The most sacred oath of the Egyptians was, by the bones of Osiris, buried at Phylæ. And Diodorus Siculus says, that when the priests of Phylæ thought proper, they sent a command to the king to put *himself to death*, with which command he was obliged to comply. The first rulers of nations were Priests, Kings *their* generals.

It appears from Diodorus Siculus,[4] that the Babylon of Egypt was built on a hill, which was selected for the purpose—Meru, I can scarcely doubt. That Meroe was a Meru receives strong confirmation from the fact, that its priests had the same name, Gymnosophists, as the Indian priests of Buddha.[5] This has been observed before,[6] and is the name given to the Buddhists by Jerome ; and also by Clemens Alexandrinus, who says that Butta was the institutor of them ;[7] and in this my idea or suspicion that the Meroe of Egypt was an imitation of the Hindoo Meru is strongly supported. Here is evidently an establishment of the oriental priests or sectaries, in imitation of that which had been left. This adds probability to all the other examples of the same kind already produced in the course of this work, and of which we shall yet see several others.

In the map to Waddington's Travels, at a considerable distance above Assouan will be found an Argo and a Merawe,[8] and the author says, "As far as we could judge, from the granite and "other sculptures remaining at Argo and Djebel el Berkel, that art (sculpture) seems to have "been as well understood, and carried to as high perfection by the sculptors of Meroë, as it was "afterward by their scholars at Thebes and at Memphis."[9] Now I ask any incredulous reader, whether he do not perceive something worthy of notice in a Meru and an Argo being found

---

[1] Connect, Book II. p. 98.   [2] Faber, Pag. Idol. Vol. I. p. 307.   [3] Wilford, Asiat. Res. Vol. VIII. p. 316.

[4] Lib. i.   [5] De Paw, Recherches sur les Egyptiens, Vol. II.

[6] Book I. Ch. IV. Sect. 6 ; also, Book V. Ch. I. Sect. 5.   [7] Hager, p. 9.

[8] Mr. Waddington has justly observed, that the accounts of the building of Meroe by Cambyses, as given by Strabo and Diodorus, are not worth notice.

[9] P. 185.

together in Nubia or Ethiopia? I desire him to recollect my observation, that in many instances after the conquerors of a country, the Greeks for instance, had given new names to it, the old inhabitants or their descendants restored the original ones.

2. The Hindoo religion states Mount Merou to be the Garden of Eden or Paradise, out of which went four rivers. These rivers are the Burramputer, or Brahmapouter, the son of Brahma; 2dly, the Ganges, Ganga or river καῖ ἐξοχην, female or Goddess Ganges, in fact, a generic name for sacred rivers; 3dly, the Indus, Sind, the river *blue* or *black*; and, 4thly, the Oxus, Gihon, or Djihhoun.

These rivers were also called Chaishu, Bhadra, Sita, and Ganga, in the Hindoo language: and the country between two of the rivers was called a douab from duo-aub, like Mesopotamia, from μεσος ποταμος-ια. In like manner, the rivers Euphrates and Tigris were supposed to flow from Ararat and Paradise; but still one of them was thought to be the river Ganges, which flowed underground from India, and appeared at the foot of the Armenian mountains: and they formed, likewise, a Mesopotamia. The Nile also was supposed to be the Euphrates, which, by an underground channel, was conveyed into Africa. In this way is accounted for the apparent absurdity of the Nile being one of the rivers of Paradise. The Ganges was called Padus, one of the names of Buddha, and the same as the Eridanus of Italy. Whether the Euphrates, or the Tigris, or the Nile, was ever called Padus I do not know; but I do know, that Buddha was the sun, and that two of those rivers, the Ganges and the Nile, were called rivers of the sun, as I shall shortly prove to have been the meaning of Eridanus.

Volney, in treating on the four rivers of Paradise, and the fact that Josephus makes one of them to be the Ganges, observes, that the Buddhists' and Brahmins' seven chains of mountains with their seven seas which surround Mount Meru, or the sacred mount of the Gods—the seven planetary bodies with their seven ethereal spaces around them in which they float, are, with the Buddhists, circular; but, with the Brahmins, elliptical. From this he infers the superior antiquity of the Buddhists. The inference is curious and interesting.

3. Mr. Whiston, on the passage where Josephus states the Ganges to be one of the rivers, observes, that upon the face of it an allegorical or esoteric meaning is intended by him—but adds, that what it is he fears it is now impossible to be determined. The record of Josephus, that one of the rivers was the Ganges, can scarcely be supposed to have been made without some traditionary or doctrinal connexion with India. But the passage of Josephus deserves much attention; indeed, more, I believe, than it has hitherto received. Mr. Whiston observes, on the work of creation, that Moses speaks of it *philosophically*, which must mean, according to the words of his preface, ænigmatically or allegorically;[1] and the whole of the work of this *ancient priest* shews the absurdity of the moderns, in construing these allegories or parables to the letter. It is evident that his account of the rivers flowing from Paradise has a secret meaning. Whiston observes, " Moses says farther, that God planted a paradise IN THE EAST, flourishing," &c........." Now " the Garden was watered by one river which ran *round about the whole* earth, and was parted " into four parts. And Phison, which denotes a multitude, running into India, makes its exit " into the sea, and is by the Greeks called Ganges. Euphrates also, as well as Tigris, goes down " into the Red Sea.[2] Now the name Euphrates, or Phrath, denotes either a dispersion or a " flower: by Tigris or Diglath, is signified what is swift, with narrowness: and Geon runs through " Egypt, and denotes *what arises from the East*, which the Greeks call *Nile*."

---

[1] See Whiston's note on Ch. i. Book i.

[2] Mr. Whiston shews that all the Eastern Sea had the same name, which we call Red Sea.

Josephus knew that the Ganges was the sacred river of the original Ararat or Paradise, and to account for the fact of its being in India, it was feigned to run under ground; but can any circumstance tend more to confirm my hypothesis that the mythos is of oriental birth? If the whole had not originally sprung from the Ganges, how could the Ganges have ever been thought of as one of the rivers? and had not Josephus known this, he would have made the Ganges, if he had noticed it at all, run from Armenia to India. If my reader will turn for a minute to the map, he must either admit an allegory or a secret meaning, or take Josephus for an idiot. But if he will for a moment consider the Hindoo accounts of the river *Oceanus* (the name of the Nile) running round the earth, and again of some of the rivers running under ground, he will see that the account is in reality nothing but a confused copy of the mythos of the Hindoos. It is, in fact, an ænigmatical explanation of an ænigma; and it is evidently a version of the Hindoo history, so couched as to be now evident to us who have the Hindoo mythos as a key, but must have been unintelligible to the Greeks or Romans, who never heard of, or had access to, the books of the Brahmins. That they never heard of these books, will surprise no one who pays the least attention to the vanity which made them despise the learning of the Barbarians, and to the difficulty which we, the *possessors* of India, have had to get the better of the excessive repugnance of the Brahmins to let them be seen by persons not of their own caste or religion.

4. Gale says, " דחל *dhbi*, is often used in the Chaldee paraphrases for the Gentile gods; so Exod. " xx. 23; wherefore the Phœnicians called Delos דחל *Dhl* Deel; that is, the island of the god " Apollo;[1] or, in the plural, דחלן *dhbi* of the gods Diana and Apollo, for the birth of whom this " place was famous. Thence Inopus was called by the Phœnicians און *aub* עין *oin* the fountain of " Python, being a river in the same island, *derived by secret passages* under the earth from Nilus, " as supposed, and Cynthus, the mountain of Delos, where Latona brought forth Apollo, from חנט " *hnt, to bring forth*; whence the Phœnician חנתא *hnta*, and the Greek Κυνθος, ט being put for θ, " as in Cadmus's alphabet."[2] The circumstance of the Nile having a subterraneous passage to this famous mountain and temple, is exactly parallel to the Ganges and Nile coming to the Ararat of Armenia; but still more curious and striking is the name of the mountain *Cyn* or *Cunthus*, being exactly the same as the Hindoo name of the goddess of the generative power, *Cunti*, and the name of the membrum fœmineum in Britain. The name of the membrum virile, god of generation, in Hebrew, is אלתולד *altuld, al tolad*.[3] In the north of England, by boys at school, it is called sometimes Tally, at other times Tolly. Is there any one so blind as not to see here the identity of the ancient languages of India, Syria, and Britain?

5. The following description of the city on Meru is given by the author of Nimrod, with a copy of his plan:—" In the sides of the north," that is, at the North Pole, " according to the fictions of " Indian mythology, is the pure and holy land of Ilavratta, and in the centre of that land stands " Brahma-puri, the city of the gods, and in the centre of Brahma-puri rises Mount Meru, their " Olympus. The forms which have been the subject of our discussion have been curiously com- " bined on this occasion. The land of Ilavratta is a perfect circle, but the city Brahma-puri is a " perfect square; and instead of right concentric lines fencing in the central sanctuary, eight cir- " cular towers are placed round the wall."[4] See my plates, fig. 23.

The author of Nimrod has shewn that Babylon was built with the tower in the middle of it, *square*, in imitation of Meru, or the Indian city or their Ararat, surrounded by streets, making seven concentric squares of houses, and seven spaces, and twenty-eight principal streets, (like the

[1] Or in Hebrew דיאל *dial*.   [2] Boch. Can. Lib. i. Cap. xxiv.; Gale, Court Gent., p. 43.
[3] Drummond Œd. Jud. 285.   [4] Wilford, Asiat. Res. VIII. 285, 376, No. 4, X. 129; Nimrod, Vol. I. p. 257.

seven lands and seas of Meru,) and the eighth, the outward fosse or Oceanus.[1] He has shewn that the tower was formed upon seven towers, one above another, exactly as the Indian priests taught or imagined that the world was formed of belts of land and sea, step above step to the Meru or North pole, in the centre and at the top. Here appears to be a complete jumble of astronomy and mythology. The seven seas and mount of the North, Isaiah's seat of the gods, were theological, the seven planets astrological, and concealed from the vulgar.

Nimrod has shewn, I think pretty clearly, that Meru was surrounded with its paradise. Now we have seen how closely Bacchus was connected with Meru, or this place of Paradise. Diodorus says, that Semiramis made a Garden or a Παραδεισον, at a place in the mountains of Media called Baghistan, or the place of Baghis. Sir W. Jones had no doubt that Bagbis was Bacchus.

Ecbatana or Egbatana, in like manner, was built in seven inclosures, one rising above the other; it was in the mountains of Media, and was the summer residence of the kings of Persia, who resided in the winter at Susa, the city of Memnon who was supposed to have built it. Susa means Lotus or Lily—the city of the Lotus.[2]

On the island of Bali, a small appendage to Java, are the ruins of an ancient temple, in which the mount Meru is exactly copied. It is a square stone building, consisting of seven ranges of wall, each range decreasing as you ascend, till the building terminates in a kind of dome. It occupies the whole of a small hill which is shaped to receive the walls and to accommodate itself to the figure of the whole structure. It contains 310 images of Buddha yet entire. This temple is in the district of Kodu. This Kodu is a corruption of Iodu or Ioud. Of this more hereafter.[3] The Pagoda of Vilnour has seven stories : il y a un huitième étage, says Gentil, qui soutient le faite de la pyramide, mais l'escalier ne mène qu' au septième étage.

6. From the supposition that Meru or Ararat stood in the middle of the garden of paradise, came the attachment of all religious to groves or gardens. In imitation of this, the hanging gardens were built at Babylon : rising like the seats of the Amphitheatre at Verona one above another, but oblong in imitation of the elliptic Meru.[4] These raised-up or hanging gardens round the temple of Belus, no doubt were in analogical imitation of the seven belts of land rising above one another around mount Meru, and of the mystic garden of Paradise. In imitation also of Babylon and Meru, the city of Iona,[5] or the Syrian Antioch, was built on seven hills, and was likewise supplied with its sacred groves, called the gardens of Daphne, which were very famous. The gardens of Adonis, at Byblos, in this country, were also very celebrated. Daphne was the name of the bay tree, (sacred to Apollo the Hellenistic deity,) and of the tree of knowledge of the Sibyl.[6] In or near most cities where the adoration of the Magna Mater prevailed, these gardens are to be found. The celebrated garden of delight or Paradise of Daphne, planted by Seleucus at Iona or Antioch, was placed on the site of a former one, which was said to have been planted by Hercules.

7. If, as I think cannot be denied, I have proved or shall prove that one universal religion— that of Buddha or Cristna—pervaded the whole of the old world, the conduct of Seleucus, as I shall presently shew, in the building of his city of Antioch on the ruins of the ancient Iona, in imitation of Babylon, Egbatana, Aia-aia, Mount Meru, &c., &c., will sufficiently demonstrate the reason why we meet with the several Babylons, Troys, Sions, &c.; namely, that it proceeded from a superstitious imitation of the first sacred city. In the old Greek authors a city called Aia-aia is often named. This means *Earth of Earth*, or *Land of Lands*. It is celebrated as the

---

[1] Vol. I. p. 279.   [2] Nimrod, Vol. I. pp. 248, 239.   [3] Asiat. Res. Vol. XIII. p. 161, 4to. ed.

[4] Vide Nimrod, Vol. I. p. 279.   [5] Ibid. Vol. III. p. 382.   [6] Ibid. Vol. I. pp. 249, 287.

residence of king Æetes, of the Orphic Argonauts, and was also the island of Circe and Aurora. It had its central tower, its seven or eight precincts, its garden or τεμενος or grove : but I suppose it is merely mythological, and in reality never did exist. Its remains are no where to be found.[1]

Thebes in Bœotia was called Heptapylos, as Nimrod supposes, from its seven gates in succession, one within the other, which formed it into districts like Babylon ; and, in the centre like all other Greek cities, of course had its acropolis. And though we have no absolute authority for saying so, it is probable that Thebes in Egypt, that is the city of Theba, of the Heifer or of the Argha, was the same ; for the French scavans clearly made out five of the seven circuits among the ruins. It was one of the oldest cities of Egypt or of the world.[2]

M. Volney has observed that, in the language of the first observers, the great circle was called *mundus* and *orbis*, the world. Consequently, to describe the solar year, they said that the world began ; that the world was born in the sign of Taurus or of Aries ; that the world ended in such another sign. If this explanation be justified by the oriental languages, of which M. Volney was, I believe, a very competent judge, it will remove several difficulties.

Of Troy not much is known, except that it was placed on seven hills. Near it was the famous Mount Ida or Gargarus, with its Buddhist Gilgal, or stone circle, or τεμενος of Homer, seen and described by Dr. Clarke, where the gods were accustomed *to assemble on the sides of the North.* In my Essay on the *Celtic Druids*, (Ch. VI. Sect. XXI.,) I have given a quotation, with a translation, from Homer, where the chiefs are represented as assembling in counsel, on seats, each at his stone pillar, in a circle. It is only fair to suppose that the circle of stones found on Gargarus, by Dr. Clarke, were the very stones alluded to by Homer, for they exactly suit to the description ; and, by this fact, afford a remarkable piece of circumstantial evidence, that the poem is not entirely destitute of foundation.

Rome was built upon *seven* hills, with a capitol or acropolis, which was square, and in other respects was an exact imitation of Babylon. It is worthy of observation that Constantinople also was built, by the Christian Constantine, upon *seven* hills. These circumstances tend to shew that one secret system was at the bottom of them all. The oriental trinity is found in each of the cities in different ways ; but, after the observations on the universal prevalence of the trinity which the reader has already seen, it is unnecessary to add more here. The word Troia or Troy, the district [3] in which the city of Ilion was placed, I have before observed means in Greek and Hebrew *the three places :* or, in English, Tripoly, of which name we have several towns now remaining.

8. We can with certainty trace back the history of the Greeks till we are lost in absolute barbarism ; and in that state we find them in possession of gods, of whose origin they know nothing, except that the priests in their temples tell them they have learned from their predecessors that they are foreigners, and that they came from the East or the North-east—some say by land, others by sea. In the earliest periods there were no idols attached to these temples, but in lieu thereof a plain upright obelisk or stone pillar, which was daily anointed with oil. The God or Gods had then no names. By degrees they got idols, and gave them names which are universally acknowledged to have come from the East or Egypt. We examine these temples and Gods now, and we find the earliest ceremonies in a language unknown to the Greeks—the names of the Gods unintelligible, in fact, also in an unknown tongue. But we find these ceremonies and these names intelligible in the Sanscrit, and the same ceremonies and Gods now in existence in India, the his-

---

[1] Nimrod, Vol. I. pp. 300, 311, 322.   [2] Volney, Res. Anc. Hist. Vol. II. p. 403.
[3] Nimrod, Vol. I. p. 438.

tories of which all agree in saying, that they were sent in remote times to the West. We find as soon as the Greeks became civilized, that their learned men travelled to the East for knowledge, and that they brought back with them the identical philosophical doctrines taught in India from the most remote antiquity: the Metempsychosis and the Trinity for instance. We are, however, desired to believe, that the whole or the most important of these facts, gods, and doctrines, were learned by the people of the East from those of the West, among whom it is asserted they arose hundreds of years after we know that they were taught by the travelling philosophers. Surely persons who tell us to believe this, must think us very credulous. Nimrod says, " The word " Syrian is oftentimes confounded by the Greeks with Assyrian, but it doth nevertheless denote a " very different country, that between Euphrates and the Mediterranean, famous or infamous for " the Ionian or Hellenic worship, for the lewd groves of Daphne, the mysteries of Hermaphroditus, " and the Dove temples of Hierapolis and Ascalon, at which last Semiramis was fabled to have " been born. This was mere fable, for it only means that that was the country of the Dove. The " Syrians at large bore the appellation of IONIANS and IONITES."[1]

Again, Nimrod says,[2] " From the Semiramis or Dove, the heretical people got the denomina-" tion of Ionic, which, as a sectarian name, may apply to them all: but, as a Gentile name, was " particularly affected by certain of the Pelasgi or Graïcs. The name Ione was borne by the " Syrian city which afterwards took the title of Antiochia, and which, with its Daphne, was a " great type of Babylon: and also by other places. When Alexander of Abonos Teichos sought " to reanimate Paganism BY A SHAM AVATAR OF APOLLO PYTHON, in the form of a serpent which " he called Γλυκ-Ων, he requested of the Emperor that the town might change its name to Iōno-" Polis. The name was evidently applicable, and καT εξοχην, to Babylon, which city was the " Iona vetus of Propertius."

After this, Nimrod endeavours to shew that the Ionians were emigrants from Babylon; that Ionia, in Greece, was founded by one *Caunus*, son of Miletus, son of the second Minos; that the capital of Attica was a type of Babylon, and that it adopted, to an unusual extent, the legends as well of the Diluvian as of the Tauric age; that the Acropolis, with its olive, was the Ark-tower, which, he says, is the meaning of Acro-polis or Acra: to which purpose may be noticed the Smyrnean coin inscribed Ζευς ΑΚΡΑΙΟΣ Σμυρναιων Πανιωνιος. All this evidently alludes to the celebrated Yoni or Argha. The Acropolis was the high-place or the Meru. Again; that not less than seven cities had the name of Athena, who was no other than the female principle in her warlike form, springing from the head of Jupiter Ammon, and supporting her own party with *wisdom* and *power*; that one city was the Minyeian Archomenus, whose citizens manned the Argo; that the emigration of these colonies was the celebrated η Ιωνικη αποικια, and the age in which it happened the Χρονος Ιωνικος—and that Homer was one of these αποικοι, and thence called an Ionian : that there were other colonies besides the Ionians, one of which " bore the " name of Aiol or the whole earth;" (the Æolians;) and others again that of D'Ore, or D'Aour (the Dorians); that the Bacchic pomp,[3] in the Eleusinian mysteries or singing the Iacchus, which he explains as the mysteries of *the son shall come*, (but which I think were the mysteries of *the son of Sul, ινις* Ἡλιος, Eleus-in,) was in commemoration of these emigrations; that the Iacchus was named Τρι-Ομφ and Τρι-Αμβ—and that " now when the causes of their connexion have been

---

[1] Tz Exeg. in Iliad, p. 135; Nimrod, p. 121, Sup. Ed.   [2] Vol. I. Sup. Ed. p. 163.

[3] Bryant explains our word *pomp* from P'umpha. I have before said that the second name of Numa, that of Pompilius comes from the same source.

" long forgotten, the name Iacch is identified with John or Joban, and is said to be a diminutive
" thereof, although exactly of the same length." [1]

It seems probable that Babylon was a great emporium of Ionism, as it advanced to the West. If
the reader cast his eye on the map, he will see that it could scarcely be otherwise. It must have
come, I think, from the North of India, as Persia does not seem to have been much tainted with it,
if at all, for any great length of time. Greece was chiefly divided between the Æolians, Aiolians
or Aiol-Iones and the Ionians, [2] and in this I think may be seen an example of the subdivision of
the religion : the name of Aiol-ians, I believe, means a mixed race or sect—perhaps a mixture of
the male and female, the Linga and Ioni in opposition to the Ioni alone. The emigrations are
called αποικοι or *the going out* or *leaving the house.* (This is the very expression applied to
Abraham : he is said to have left his father's house.) The Aiolians were the larger sect in Greece,
occupying Bœotia, Thessaly, Eubœa, Locris, &c. [3]

9. The opinion which I entertain, in common with such of the ancients as were most likely to
be *well-informed,* that the Iliad is a *sacred mythos,* by no means carries the consequence that
there was *not* such a city as Ilion, or a war and siege of it. I am strongly inclined to believe that
its neighbourhood was a holy place, in a very remote æra. The Druidical circle or Gilgal, found
by Dr. Clarke on the summit of mount Gargarus, in a very striking manner reminds me of the
Proseucha, probably a similar circle, found by Epiphanius on Gerizim. I suspect Olympus, Parnassus, Athos, Ida, Gerizim, and Moriah, were each a Meru or high-place ; a sacred place of the
same universal primary religion, that of Buddha, of which the same distinctive marks in its stone
circles, tumuli, carns, lingas, and Cyclopean buildings, are every where to be found, from India to
Stonehenge and Iona. It is very remarkable that on these mountains, either numbers of monks
or numerous remains of them are always found. Are these remains of the colleges of the prophets, named in the Old Testament, remains of Buddhist monks of Thibet, with the tria vota substantialia ? These three vows completely identify them with Christian Monks — Carmelites.
Lycurgus is said to have found the poems of Homer, being, as the Rev. G. Townsend describes
them, [4] merely a collection of ballads, with their appropriate titles. In the 5th, 6th, and 7th volumes of the Asiatic Researches, the story of the Trojan war is given from Sanscrit authors : its
episodes, like those of Homer, are placed in Egypt : and the traditions of Laius, Labdacus,
Œdipus, and Jason, are all found among the same ancient compositions. When, in addition to
all this, the fact is considered, that the works of Homer are discovered to contain more than 300
Sanscrit words, the true character of the Iliad will be seen ; namely, that it is a *sacred poem,* made
up by Pisistratus, and after him by Aristotle, out of a number of ballads relating to the religion of
the Indians and Greeks. Many of them have been thought to have a reference to events described
in Holy Writ, and this is natural enough if *holy writ* itself be indebted to the East for its events
and doctrines.

The resemblance between the Cristna of Valmic and the Achilles of Homer, proves the identity
of the origin of the two mythoses. Each of them, in mythology, is supposed invulnerable, except
in the right heel : each was killed by an arrow piercing that part : each was the son of the mother
of the God of Love : and the presence of each was indispensable for the overthrow of the enemy. [5]
I can scarcely believe that this identity is accidental.

I should suppose no man was more likely to understand the nature of the poems of Homer than

---

[1] Nimrod, Vol. I. p. 170, Sup. Ed.   [2] Strabo, Lib. xiii. p. 841 ; Steph. Byzant.
[3] Nimrod, Vol. I. p. 167, Sup. Ed.   [5] Class. Journ. No. XLVII. p. 9.
[4] Key to Chron. Camb. p. 221.

Plato, and the question whether they were to be construed literally or allegorically, and he banished them from his imaginary republic, because youth would not be able to distinguish *what is, from what is not, allegorical.*[1]   And Porphyry· says, we ought not to doubt that Homer has secretly represented the images of divine things under the concealments of fable.[2]   The very name of the Iliad, viz. Rhapsodies, precludes all reasonable expectation of discovering the meaning of the whole of the minute parts of it, for they were known originally to have been loose detached songs, very much in the style of what Ossian's poems are said to have been.   Besides, it is evident from Mr. Payne Knight's observation, that it is full of very large interpolations, as he calls them, or at least parts inserted, perhaps by different authors, which are unconnected or awkwardly interwoven with the poem, but which are still necessary to unite the songs.   But if the reader consider the history of its collection by Pisistratus, and its revisal by Aristotle and his friends, for the use of Alexander, he must see at once that the expectation of shewing or making a regular system out of it is hopeless.   I have no doubt that poetry or rhythm was originally invented for the purpose of assisting the memory to retain the sacred and secret doctrines; that when used in the mysteries, it was set to music, and repeated in the manner of chaunting or recitative.

I think it will not be denied, that the observations of Nimrod respecting the war of Troy are marked with much good sense; but yet there is a difficulty to be found in Greece and many other countries, in the gigantic Cyclopean buildings every where scattered about them.   Who were they that built the stone circles, the walls of Tyrins, the cave at Mycenæ, &c., &c. ? Great and powerful people must have lived who executed these works, and that before even the fabulous periods of Grecian history.   Were they the people who formed the Trojan Mythos ? But if they were, they must have lived long before the time assigned for the date of the Trojan war.   They were the Cyclopes, as I shall shew; but they had not each only *one* eye.

The opinion which I have expressed respecting the Western names of Gods being found in India is strongly confirmed by Dr. Vincent.   On Indian names he says, " Most, if not all, of the " Indian names which occur in classical authors, are capable of being traced to native appellations, " existing at this day among the Hindoos, at least, if not the Moguls."[3]

Col. Franklin[4] has observed the connexion between the Mythoses of the East and West.   He says, " The Gods are *Merupa* (Meropes of Homer) and signify in Sanscrit *Lords of Mount Meru,* " the North-pole of the Hindoos, which is a circular spot, and the strong hold of the Gods: it is " called Ila: or, in a derivative form, Ileyam or Ilium.   There is a Triad (Troiam) of towers " dedicated to the three Gods.   The Trojans are styled divine, and αθανατοι, athanatoi, immor- " tals; they are Meropes and came from the place where the *sun stables his horses.*   The Gods " and giants at each renovation of the world fight for the *Amrit* or beverage of immortality (Nec- " tar), and also for the beautiful *Laeshmi* (or Helen): she is called Helena.   In Sanscrit all these " derivations, Meropes, for Merupa, Ileyam or Ilium, Troiam or Troia (Troja), Helena or " Helene, are the same, and point to the same thing.   The story is told with some variations: " and the Trojan war happened soon after the flood of Deucalion, called in Sanscrit *Deva Cala* " *Yavana,* but to be pronounced *Deo Calyun.*"   " All the expressions in the mysteries of Bac- " chus are Erse, according to General Vallancey : Sanscrit, according to Col. Wilford in the 5th " volume of the Asiatic Researches : and Hebrew, according to Parkhurst in his Lexicon : three " singular opinions, which only persuade the unprejudiced reader of their immense antiquity and " their Eastern origin."[5]   It is then noticed that Homer refers to a language different from the

---

[1] Taylor on the Myth. of the Greeks, Class. Journ. No. XLV.   [2] Ibid. p. 41.

[3] Voyage of Nearchus, 129.   [4] Researches into the Jains, p. 43.   [5] Class. Journ. Vol. III. p. 179.

Greek, called *the speech of the Gods.* Mr. Van Kennedy's 300 Sanscrit words, in Homer, I take to be part of the speech of the Gods.

Diodorus, in his preface to his fourth book, says, that many authors, for instance, Ephorus, Callisthenes, and Theopompus, passed over the ancient mythology on account of its difficulty. This proves it unknown.

It is recorded in old traditions, that Homer, in a temple in Egypt, found a poem relative to a war against a city called Troy, near Memphis. The town, I believe, is admitted to have existed.[1] Tatian, in his oration ad Græcos,[2] says, that Metrodorus, of Lampsacus, in his treatise on Homer, made not only the Gods and Goddesses, but the heroes, of the poem, allegorical persons.

It may be a matter of doubt, whether the whole story of the Iliad may not be found in the histories of Joseph and Uriah, the gallantry of David, his marriage with Michal, his banishment, &c.[3]

Maximus Tyrius, as I have noticed in a former chapter, expressly asserts, that the stories of the Gods and Goddesses in Homer are oracular, and have a meaning different from what is apparent at first sight.

It has been said that the celebrated Dr. Bentley wrote a treatise to prove that the Iliad and Odyssey were written by Solomon, king of Israel. But to guard himself from persecution for so singular an opinion, he added, that they were written after the apostacy of this WISE MAN. Lempriere says,[4] that the Bentley manuscript (the treatise was never published) is in the British Museum. A writer in the Times newspaper of April 30th, 1829, p. 5, says the MS. is not there. Its contents were wicked, and have been probably destroyed by the priests in whose hand that establishment is. But it proves one fact,—that Bentley thought he could prove the Mythos of the tribe of Judah and of Homer were the same; and we have just now seen, that there was an Ileyam or Ilium in India; that, in fact, Meru was Ilium. Ilavratta, or the Indian Ararat, was often written *Idavratta.* This is evidently mount Ida.

The system of renewed incarnations is not strongly marked with the Greeks and Romans, but it may occasionally be found: the prophecy of a renewed Trojan war by the Sibyl cannot be mistaken, particularly when we find there were formerly many Troys and Trojan wars, with their ten years' sieges and cities taken. And this leads to the question, who was Homer? He was born at or in Cyprus, Egypt, Lydia, Italy, Lucania, Rome, and Troy. His college or place of education was Chios, Smyrna of Æolis, Colophon, Argos, Athens, Ithaca, Teos, Tenedos, Grynium, and Crete. The Sibyl of Babylon said he stole from her. Lucian of Samosata says he was a Babylonian, called Tigranes:[5] and Proclus,[6] that he was a cosmopolite—καθολυ πασα πολις αντιποιειται του ανδρος, οθεν εικοτως κοσμοπολιτης λεγοιτο. The name consists of two syllables, *Hom* and *er*, or *eer*, which word, Nimrod says, " is indicative of early or beginning time, whether it be THE OPENING " OF A MUNDANE CYCLE, the spring of a year, or the morning of a day."[7] In one word, I know nothing about him; but yet I believe I know as much as any body else. I believe with Bentley or Barnes, it matters not which, that the Iliad is a sacred oriental mythos, accommodated to Grecian circumstances, written, perhaps, by a Solomon, though not the Solomon of Jerusalem, and that *Homer* or *Om-eer* was a Solomon—if the epithet given to the poem do not mean the poems of *Om-heri* the saviour OM. Near Ajemere, in India, is a place called *Ummerghur,* that is, the walled city of *Ummer* or *Omer.* The *Ipthi-genia* of Homer is literally Jeptha's daughter.[8] It

[1] Class. Journ. Vol. V. p. 18. [2] Sect. 37. [3] See Pope's note on the Iliad, Bk. vi.
[4] Class. Dict. Barker's Ed. [5] Luc. Ver. Hist. Lib. ii. Cap. xx. Vol. IV. p. 279, ap. Nimrod, p. 545.
[6] De Genere Homeri, Ed. Barnes, ap. Nimrod, Vol. II. p. 544. [7] Ibid. pp. 514, &c. [8] R. Taylor, Dieg. p. 21.

is impossible for this identity of name, joined to almost identity of history, to be the effect of accident.

10. It seems desirable to know what was the meaning of the name Troy, and the learned Nimrod explains it as follows : " Tr'oia is the triple oia, and oia means *one* or *unique*, so that Tr'oia " is three in one, the tripolitan and triunal kingdom. Oia was the chief of a Tripolis or of three " cities, belonging together in Libya, near the fertile banks of the Cinyps, which was reported to " flow from the *High-place of the three Graces* : and the said Oia, having survived her two sisters, " still keeps to herself the name of Tripoly. [1] But Troia was the land of the universal *Omphè* or " of all the *Omphès*, according as you will take the word *Pan* distributively or collectively, for in " that country from its first beginnings

Ara pan-omphæo vetus est sacrata Tonanti.—Ovid.

" Omphè is a word for voice or speech, but, like ossa, it is confined to such as proceeds from a " deity, or otherwise in a præternatural way. Ομφη θεια κληδων......Ol-ymp, properly Hol- " ymp, is the *universal voice*, and equivalent to Pan-omphæus......Iphis, in Greek, is a woman " with a familiar spirit. Hence we often find the word *Am-phi* in the name of soothsayers, as " Amphiareus, Amphilochus, Amphion." [2] Troy meant the country of which Ilium or Ηλιον was the capital. There was a Troy in Egypt built by Semiramis. [3]

I have said that there may have been an Ilion. Nimrod has observed, that it would be considered blasphemy to doubt it ; yet with him I must be guilty and doubt. That the wars of Troy related to the Phrygian Troas is certain ; but that the remains of this city should be invisible to the scrutiny of the oldest of those who sought for its foundations is almost incredible. The existence of a mighty monarchy in Greece, and an organized system, ages before the dawn of civilization in that country, he maintains, is utterly fabulous ; and that no means are apparent which could have thrown back into barbarism a country so far advanced, as to give birth to the league of so many nations, to a decennial siege by more than one hundred thousand men, and above all to the artful writings of Homer. Barbarous, by their own accounts, the Greeks were before this war—barbarous for ages after. What then shall we make of this gleam of glory, dividing, as it were, the upper from the lower darkness ? It is very extraordinary, that this paltry town should have interested all mankind. Every nation desired it to be believed, that they came from conquered Troy. There was a Troy or Ilion in Phrygia in Asia Minor, one in Epirus, one in Latium, one in Egypt, and one near Venice. Every state almost was founded by its conquered and dispersed refugees. They are found in Epirus, Threspotia, Cyprus, Crete, Venice, Rome, Daunia, Calabria, Sicily, Lisbon, Asturia, Scotland, Wales, Cornwall, Holland, Auvergne, Paris, Sardinia, Cilicia, Pamphylia, Arabia, Macedonia, and Libya. Every people descended from unfortunate Troy. It was a mythos, a sacred history. It was like the ancient history of all nations, a mythos—*tons* of fable mixed up with some *grains* of truth. All nations were alike. There were two Moriahs, two Sions, two Ararats, an African and an European Thebes ; an Asiatic and Egyptian Babylon ; multitudes of Memnoniums, seven cities of Athena, the name of the Goddess, the Magna Mater, the female principle in her warlike form. The Titans fought the Gods ten years ; the Sabeans besieged Babylon ten years ; Rome besieged Veii, the site of which nobody can find,

---

[1] There was a Tripoly in Africa and one in Western Asia, and a Tripetti and Trichinopoly in India—a Tanjore in India, and one in Africa.

[2] Nimrod, Vol. II. p. 443.   [3] Asiat. Res. Vol. III. p. 454.

ten years; Eira in Messenia, and Eiran in Æolia had ten years' wars; and Thebes was besieged by the Epigons for ten years. And all this, grave and wise men call history and believe it true.

How can any one consider these striking circumstances and not see that almost all ancient history and epic poetry are mythological,—the secret doctrines of the priests, disguised in parables, in a thousand forms? Mr. Faber, Mr. Bryant, and Nimrod, have proved this past doubt. Whether they have found the key to the parable or mythos is another matter. The talents and learning of these gentlemen cannot be doubted. If they had not brought minds to the subject bound by a predetermined dogma, which was to be supported, there is very little doubt but that they would have solved the ænigma. But they have failed. Weak and credulous as man has been, he did not mistake a rotten ship and a few old women for his God and Creator. Under the guise of the ship and old women a system is emblematically described. Our priests have taken the emblems for the reality. The lower orders of our priests are as much the dupes as their votaries. The high-priests are wiser. Our priests will be very angry and deny all this. In all nations, in all times, there has been a secret religion: in all nations and in all times, the fact has been denied.

"There is nothing new under the sun," said the wise Solomon, who never uttered a wiser speech; and in its utterance proved that he understood the doctrines of the eternal renewal of worlds; that new Troys, new Argonauts, would arise, as the Sibyl of Virgil subsequently foretold.

11. In the CELTIC DRUIDS, Chap. V. Sect. XLIV., I have said, "Thus there is an end of St. Patrick." I shall not repeat the reasons which I have given for that opinion, which are quite sufficient for its justification. A learned and ingenious gentleman has written a life of St. Patrick, and Nimrod says, "Firstly, and most obviously, the express tradition that St. Patrick's fosse and "purgatory were the fosse and *necyia* of Ulysses. Ogygia (moreover) was the isle of Calypso, in "which Ulysses sojourned: and Plutarch informs us that it was situated five days' sail to the "West of Britannia, and that there were three other islands near it. From the South-east of "Britain, where the Romans used to land, it would have been a five days' journey to Ireland for "ancient navigators. The first name of Ulysses, before he came to be styled Ho-dys-cus, was "*Nanus*, and the first name of St. Patrick was *Nannus*. In Temora, the bardic capital of Ireland, "*Nani* tumulum lapis obtegit, and it is one of Ireland's thirteen mirabilia. Ulysses, during his "detention in Aiaia, was king of a host of Swine: and Patrick, during a six years' captivity in "the hands of King Milcho or Malcho, was employed to keep swine. Ulysses flourished in Babel, "and St. Patrick was born at Nem-Turris or the *Cælestial Tower*; the type of Babel in Irish "mythology is *Tory* island or the isle of *the Tower*. At the time of its expugnation Sru emigrated "from the East. Rege *Tutane* gestum est prælium campi Turris et expugnata est Troja Tro-"janorum: but Tutanes is the Teutames, King of Assyria, whose armies Memnon commanded. "Ulysses the κλωψ δελφινοσημος was the Koiranus (or king) whom a dolphin saved, and whom "all the Dolphins accompanied from Miletus: his son Telemachus, whom a dolphin saved, was "the bard Arion; but Arion was King of Miletus in the days of Priam, King of Troy: and as "Miletus was a considerable haven of Asia Minor in Homer's time, it is the most probable place "of Ulysses's departure. But a great consent of tradition brings the colonists of Ireland from "Miletus. Miletus, father of *Ire*, came to Ireland in obedience to a prophecy."[1] The above is a very small part of the similitudes between Ulysses and St. Patrick; but it is enough to confirm what I have said in the *Celtic Druids*, and to blow the whole story of the saint into thin air. I believe that the whole is a Romish fable.

---

[1] Nimrod, Vol. II. p. 638.

Nimrod[1] afterward goes on at great length to shew how the story of St. Patrick is accommodated to the ancient Homeric Mythos, and Patricius and the Pateræ to the saint; and he particularly notices a famous ship temple, described by General Vallencey in the Archæologia. Now I think it is quite impossible to date this great stone ship after the rise of Christianity. This at once raises the strongest probability, indeed almost *proves*, that the stories of Ulysses King Brute, &c., &c., detailed in the old monkish historians, are not their invention in the dark ages, as they are now considered by all our historians, and as such treated with contempt, but are parts of an universally extended Mythos, brought to the British isles in much earlier times, and as such in a high degree worthy of careful examination. The proof of any part of this Mythos having existed in Ireland or Britain before the time of Christ opens the door for the consideration of all the remainder, and is a point of the greatest importance.

Jeoffrey of Monmouth gives an account of King Brutus, grandson of Æneas, who having killed his father Sylvius in Italy, after many adventures arrived in Britain, which he conquered. He had three sons, LOGRIN, to whom he gave England;[2] CAMBER, to whom he gave Wales, Cambria; and ALBANACT, to whom he gave Scotland, Albania, or Callidonia—Callidei-ania.

CHAPTER VII

Cassandra——Babylonian Mythos——Constantine and Helena. Astrology——Bryant on Early History——Native Country of the Olive and Ararat

1. There is existing, in the Greek language, a very dark and obscure poem called Cassandra; purporting to be written by a person named Lycophron, in the time of Ptolomy Philadelphus. It pretends to be chiefly poetical and prophetic effusions delivered by Cassandra, during the Trojan war. For its profound learning it was in the highest estimation with the Greek philosophers. It has been called το σκοτεινον ποιημα, *the dark poem.* This may excuse my inability to explain it. But if the reader be satisfied with me that the Iliad is a sacred poem relating in part to the renewal of the Sacrum Sæculum, he will probably think, that the following lines prove that the prophecies of Cassandra relate to the same subject.

> But when athwart the empty, vaulted heaven
> Six TIMES of years have roll'd, War shall repose
> His lance, obedient to my kinsman's voice,
> Who, rich in spoils of monarchs, shall return
> With friendly looks, and carolings of love,—
> While Peace sits brooding upon seas and land.

It speaks of the Healing or Saviour God *who thus ordained and poured the voice divine* (l. 1607); of the impious railers *who taunt the God of light, scorning his word, and scoffing at his truth.* It calls the different ages Woes.

> *One Woe is past! another woe succeeds.*

The distribution of these woes seems impenetrably dark, but the last, I think, clearly alludes to the wars of Alexander. As the Sæculum or Neros was confounded by the early Christians

---

[1] Vol. II. p. 637.　　　[2] Query, Ingli-aria? or, Angli-aria—Onglir—L'Ongir

and Jews with the sæculum of one thousand, and with that of six thousand years; so I think the ages were confused by Lycophron, which arose probably from his having only an obscure and indistinct view of his subject. Like all the other mythologies and mysteries, they were in the West, after the time of Cambyses, only partly understood. Thus, though the Mellenium was the established doctrine of the early Christians, the date of its commencement, though expressly foretold, was yet unknown. I shall shew, in the second part of this work, what was the opinion of the authors of the Gospels and Canonical Epistles. The renewal of the Argonautic Expedition is foretold by Lycophron's Cassandra, exactly as it was afterwards made to be foretold in Virgil by his Sibyl.

— Again rush forth the famished wolves, and seize
The fateful fleece, and charm the dragon guard
To sleep; so bids the single-sandall'd king,
Who, to Libystian Colchis, won his way, &c.

In the course of the work she says that the Egyptian Sphynx was black; and, what is very extraordinary, she says the same thing of the *White* Sow of Alba Longa, calling her Κελαινή. Jupiter is called Ethiopian or black. I have no doubt that whatever was meant by the prophecy of Virgil's Sibyl, was meant by Cassandra. Nothing can be more dark and mystical than this poem. But I think its general tendency may perhaps be discovered from detached passages like the above. It speaks of a Budean Queen, and compares her to a dove: *dragged like a dove unto the vulture's bed.* This is an evident allusion to Semiramis, the Dove, and to the Promethean cave.

2. The author of Nimrod has bestowed almost incredible labour to prove, that the Mythos of the Trojan war, the early history of Rome, &c., &c.; in short, almost all ancient mythology, came from Babylon, and *were close copies of the Babylonian history* (say, Babylonian *mythos*). The close similarity between the Gods of India and those of Greece, has been proved over and over by Sir William Jones and others. Then, did they come direct from India? It is difficult to conceive how that could be effected. Nimrod has untied the knot: for Colonel Wilford has shewn,[1] that all the Babylonian Mythoses came from India, its Semi-ramis or Sami-Rama-isi, &c., &c. It is evident, therefore, that from India they came to Babylon or Assyria, thence to Syria and Sidon; thence brought by Cadmus or the Orientals to Greece: hence the duplicates and triplicates of the cities, the ten years' wars, &c. And thus at last the grand truth will be established, that they are all mythoses from the East or North-east of the Indus.

3. I have said, that Mr. Faber, Nimrod, and Niebuhr, have proved that all ancient history is little better than fable. This is true. It is all mythological. By this I do not mean to say that there is not some truth in it; but I mean to say, that there is scarcely one history, perhaps not one, which does not contain more religious fable than truth. They do not appear to have been written for the same purpose as our grave and serious histories; or they were mythoses made up of old traditions. They seem to have been a species of *religious novels.* Even so late as Constantine, Nimrod has pointed out something very suspicious. He says, " It is to me a matter of " grave suspicion whether the woman, his mother, was really and by her true name *Helena;* or " whether her name was not purely fictitious, as her parentage from *Coil* or *Uranus,* King of " Britannia. In the church legend, when she dug and found the true cross, she also found a " statue of *Venus.* A most suspicious legend. Venus was daughter of Coilus, (*how,* I need not " say,) and Helena was Venus."[2] This, no doubt, is suspicious enough. Alas! what is to be

---

[1] Asiat. Res. Vol. IV. pp. 378, &c.   [2] Nimrod, Vol. III. p. 150.

believed? Concerning this Lady, I beg my reader to peruse the eighth chapter of Usher's Anti-
quitates, headed thus: De patria Constantini Magni, et Matris ejus HELENÆ, variæ et discre-
pantes Authorum Sententiæ, quam alii Britanniam, alii Galliam, alii Bithyniam, Nonnulli etiam
Daciam fuisse volunt. She was said to have produced Constantine at York.[1]

I am quite certain that no one possessing the least candour can deny the mystical character of
the story of Helen. Then, what are we to make of it? Are we to disbelieve the story of the
churches built by Helena and Constantine? If we are to throw this out, what are we to believe?
Where is our incredulity to stop? But can the existence of the suspicious circumstance be denied? It surely cannot.

The explanation of the Helena probably is this: it was desired to make out that her son was a
renewed incarnation, and therefore he and she adopted the sacred mythical names. He wished
to be thought, and perhaps thought himself, the Paraclete prophesied of by Jesus Christ. This
will easily account for his hitherto unaccountable mixture of Heathenism and Christianity.

Sir W. Drummond pointed out the mythological character of the history of Jacob. This was
finely ridiculed by a gentleman of the name of Townsend, who undertook, by the same means, to
prove the twelve Cæsars to be the twelve signs of the Zodiac, and his success is wonderful; but
it all raises the most unpleasant state of uncertainty in my mind, and makes me, after very long
consideration, almost to doubt whether we really have one history uncontaminated with judicial
astrology. I ask, why have we twelve Cæsars? Why do the learned historians labour to make
out twelve? Twelve emperors called after the Celtic God of war, Æsar?

I feel a great difficulty, indeed I may say an impossibility, to bring my mind to believe, that the
story of Helena and the twelve Cæsars are not true histories. But I recollect, that only as yesterday, I should have had the same feeling with respect to the early history of Rome. By degrees
I began to doubt of Remus, Antius, Camillus, &c., &c., and at last Mr. Niebuhr has dissipated
all this trash, and has converted my doubts into conviction. Then am I to doubt the existence
of the Cæsars? This is impossible. Then what am I to do? I am obliged to believe, that all
true history has been debased and corrupted by judicial astrology and mythology; that all histories are like the Acta sincera of the Christian martyrs, very far from SINCERE. I think no one
can deny, that the desire to make out the twelve Cæsars to be *twelve*, and not *eleven* or *thirteen*, is
astrological, and I believe that the names given to them, or assumed by them, had astrological
meanings; and that it is from this circumstance that Mr. Townsend has been enabled to support
his ingenious raillery in apparently a plausible manner. Without its professors intending to do
so perhaps, I believe judicial astrology has corrupted almost every ancient history which we
possess.

It has been observed that Cæsar was an astrological name. It was in fact the Celtic Æsar, or
God of war, taken, as the Hindoo princes take their names, from a favourite God—the God of the
country which Cæsar conquered. Gen. Vallancey has observed, that Cæsar did not give the
name to the solstitial month, but that he took his name from it. In the old Irish, half June and
half July was called *Mi-Jul:* thence Cæsar's name of Julius.

---

[1] On the ancient Roman road, at the ford over the river Wharf, between Tadcaster and Wetherby, a mile from
Thorparch, is a place called St. Helen's Ford, and near it St. Helen's Spring, not far from which, on a mount, formerly
stood a curious stone cross. A few years ago this cross, after standing perhaps 1500 years, was carried away, in my
Lord Elgin's style, by an Antiquarian Lady of the name of Richardson, who took it to her garden at Gargrave. She is
now dead, and it has probably become useful *to mend the roads*. The spring used to perform miracles, and if we may
judge from the votive rags which I have seen hanging on the bushes adjoining, suspended by the persons who have experienced the efficacy of its water, its power still continues.

—— " Venerisque ab origine proles
" Julia descendit cœlo, cœlumque replevit,
" Quod regit Augustus socio per signa Tonante,
" Cernit in cœtu Divum, magnumque Quirinum,
" Ille etiam cœlo genitus, cœloque receptus."

MANILIUS.[1]

Augustus was also a mystical name given to their princes by the Egyptians. I suspect Julius was Cæsar's family sacred name, what we call *Christian* name. Cæsar was a name he assumed as conqueror of Gaul, and Augustus was assumed by his successor as prince of Egypt; but we shall understand this better hereafter.

Sir William Drummond has shewn, that the names of most of the places in Joshua are astrological; and General Vallancey has shewn, that Jacob's prophecy is astrological also, and has a direct reference to the Constellations. The particulars may be seen in Ouseley's Orient. Coll.[2] To this, probably, Jacob referred when he bade his children *read in the book of heaven what must be the fate of you and your children.*[3] The meaning of all this is explained by the passage of Virgil, that new wars of Troy and new Argonauts would arise.

It is evident that where we meet with such names as Heliogabalus, connected with such numbers as twelve, or with other numbers which we know are astrological, we may be certain some superstition, probably astrological, is alluded to; thus we may be perfectly assured that both Sir W. Drummond and Mr. Townsend are right, that the names noticed by the latter, such as Lucius, Augustus, Julius, and the number 12, have all astrological allusions. I beg Mr. Townsend to recollect that there is scarcely a name in *very ancient* history, either sacred or profane, which was not an adopted or second name, or a name given with a reference to the supposed quality or office of its owner. I beg him to begin with Abram, and he may end, if he please, with the Saviour and his cousin, John; the latter formed from the oriental word for *dove*, the holy messenger, and the former called Jesus, *because he should save his people.* Matters such as these have made some persons hastily disbelieve, and treat with contempt, all early sacred history. Although Niebuhr has shewn that almost all early Roman history is fable, this does not prove that during the three or four hundred years of Rome's fabulous period, that there was no Rome, that there were no Consuls, no Senates, or no people. It is equally rash to maintain, that there were no wars of Joshua or Judges, because we find the walls of Jericho falling to the sound of Rams' horns, or the mythological history of Hercules as Samson, or of Iphigenia as Jeptha's daughter. At the same time that Mr. Faber and Nimrod have proved the early Jewish history to be in great part the same as the mythology of the nations, they have shewn us, from the history of this mythology, that it is the height of rashness hence to conclude that it is ALL FALSE. It in *no way* differed from the history of other nations; like them it had much fable; like them it had much truth. The very ancient, curious, and interesting records of the Israelites, have never had fair play. One class of readers swallows every thing—the Frogs of Egypt, the Bulls of Basban, the Giants, and all; the others will swallow nothing; and I am rather surprised that they admit the inhabitants of Duke's Place ever to have had any fathers. Why cannot the Jewish books be examined like the history of Herodotus, by the rules of common sense and reason? But this, I fear, is not likely very soon to happen.

Thucydides, in the beginning of his history, allows, that before the Peloponnesian war, which was waged in the time of Arta-Xerxes and Nehemiah, he could find nothing in which he

---

[1] Ouseley Orient. Coll. Vol. II. No. III. p. 221.   [2] Vol. II. No. IV. pp. 336, &c.   [3] Ibid. p. 103.

could place any confidence. This is confirmed by Bochart, in the preface to his Phaleg, and also by Stillingfleet,[1] and again by Gale.[2]

4. The following is the state of ancient history given by Mr. Bryant, and nothing can be more true:—" Besides, it is evident that most of the deified personages never existed : but were mere " titles of the Deity, the Sun ; as has been in a great measure proved by Macrobius. Nor was " there ever any thing such detriment to ancient history, as the supposing that the Gods of the " Gentile world had been natives of the countries where they were worshiped. They have been " by these means admitted into the annals of times: and it has been the chief study of the " learned to register the legendary stories concerning them : to conciliate absurdities, and to " arrange the whole into a chronological series—a fruitless labour, and inexplicable: for there " are in these fables such inconsistencies and contradictions as no art, nor industry, can remedy. " ....This misled Bishop Cumberland, Usher, Pearson, Petavius, Scaliger, with numberless " other learned men, and among the foremost the great Newton. This extraordinary genius has " greatly impaired the excellent system upon which he proceeded, by admitting these fancied " beings into chronology. We are so imbued in our childhood with notions of Mars, Hercules, " and the rest of the celestial outlaws, that we scarce ever can lay them aside.........It gives " one pain to see men of learning and principle, debating which was the Jupiter who lay with " Semele, and whether it was the same that outwitted Amphitryon. This is not, says a critic, " the Hermes that cut off Argus's head ; but one of later date, who turned Battus into a stone. " I fancy, says another, that this was done when Io was turned into a cow. I am of opinion, " says Abbé Banier, that there was no foundation for the fable of Jupiter's having made the night " on which he lay with Alcmena, longer than others: at least this event put nothing in nature " out of order ; since the day which followed was proportionably shorter, as Plautus remarks. " Were it not invidious, I could subjoin names to every article which I have alleged, and produce " numberless instances to the same purpose." Mr. Bryant, after this, goes on to shew that the early fathers believed these Gods to have been men, and then turns the numerous Gods into ridicule ; observing, that a God was always ready on every occasion—five Mercuries, four Vulcans, three Dianas, five Dionususes, forty Herculeses, and three hundred Jupiters. He then asks why Sir Isaac Newton, in his chronological[3] interpretations, chooses to be determined by the story of Jupiter and Europa, rather than by that of Jupiter and Leda.[4] Thus he goes on to shew that the whole, if literally understood, was a mass of falsity and nonsense.

On the account given by Mr. Bryant these questions naturally arise—Has he mended the matter ? Has he satisfactorily removed the difficulty ? I believe nine-tenths of mankind will say No ; though he has certainly great merit in clearing the way for others. He was followed by Mr. Faber, and he by Nimrod, who have given as little satisfaction ; and the reason is, because these gentlemen have all set out with begging the question under discussion: then making every thing bend to it—bend to a certain dogma, because they happen to have been born in England, where it was held. It may be reasonably asked of me, What right have you to think that you will succeed any better ? I answer, I have no predetermined dogma ; but the chief and most important of my opinions have arisen during my examination, and from it. And in addition I have the assistance of the learning of Mr. Bryant, Mr. Faber, Nimrod, and several others, which gives me, without any merit of my own, a great advantage over them. I have the advantage also of their errors as well as of their learning.

---

[1] Orig. Sac. Book i. Ch. iv.

[2] Newton's Chronology, p. 151.

[3] Court. of Gent. Book iii. Ch. ii.

[4] Bryant, Anal. Vol. I. p. 460.

The idea of a reduction of the Western nations to the situation of Tibet, will be turned into ridicule by the priests, who would wish the rest of mankind to believe them to be the most industrious and useful of bees, only working and storing up truths for the good of mankind; but experience shews that they can never be watched too carefully; and if they do not anew establish their empire of the tenth century, to the printing-press alone their failure must be attributed. However amiable in private life many priests may be, there is scarcely one of them who ever loses sight of the aggrandisement of his order. Look at them in Portugal, Spain, and France; look at the wicked and unhallowed exertions of the priests of the Protestant sect in Ireland to oppress the followers of the Romish Church, and to rivet and continue their own usurped power. And however we, the *philosourists*, may flatter ourselves with the effects of the press, it is yet to be proved that it cannot be rendered subservient to the designs of the order. Though the Protestant and Romish sects are at present in opposition, there is no doubt in my mind, that if government were to hold a just and equal hand to both, they would speedily unite. *Then* it is much to be feared, that the liberties of Europe would speedily be destroyed.

5. No doubt the question of the originality of the ancient mythoses is, to the present generation, of the greatest possible importance; as it, in fact, involves the existence of a most terrific system of priest-craft and priest-rule—a system most dangerous to the well-being of all mankind, except the favoured caste—a system which cannot stand still, but which must either soon fall or go on increasing in power till it reduce the remainder of the world to the situation of its parent in Tibet. To resist successfully the artful sophistry of the able men among the priests is a task of the greatest difficulty. The reader must have observed that written evidence can scarcely, in any case, be made conclusive, but fortunately circumstances may; and I consider that of the olive as an example of these fortunate circumstances. It cannot have been forged, and the recourse which the very able priest, or the priest-ite Nimrod, is obliged to have, as we shall see, to the stale plea of miracle, shews that it is conclusive and incapable of being explained away.

The observation of Nimrod is confirmed in a remarkable manner by Col. Wilford, when treating of the Oriental Ararat, which at once proves where the *third* book of Genesis, or the book of the Flood, came from: " The region about Tuct-Suleiman is the native country of the olive-tree, " and I believe the only one in the world. There are immense forests of it on the high grounds, " for it does not grow in plains. From the saplings, the inhabitants make walking-sticks, and " its wood is used for fuel all over the country; and as Pliny justly observes, the olive-tree in " the Western parts of India is sterile, at least its fruit is useless, like that of the Oleaster. " According to Tenestalla, an ancient author cited by Pliny, there were no olive-trees in Spain, " Italy, or Africa, in the time of Tarquin the Elder. Before the time of Hesiod, it had been " introduced into Greece: but it took a long time before it was reconciled to the climate, and " its cultivation properly understood: for Hesiod says, that, whoever planted, never lived to eat " of its fruit. The olive-tree was never a native of Armenia; and the passage of Strabo cited " in support of this opinion, implies only that it was cultivated with success in that country."[1] Of the two Ararats this pretty well proves which is the original, and which the copy.

The argument drawn from the olive is like that of Mr. Seely's respecting the Cobra Capella not being found in Egypt, but which will be soon brought thither, if it should be thought decisive. The Missionaries will not be long in bringing them; this will be easily effected.

The author of Nimrod is as unwilling a witness as can be imagined to any circumstance that shall remove Ararat from the country between the two seas, and place it to the East of the

---

[1] Asiat. Res. Vol. VI. p. 525.

Caspian: for it at once upsets the whole of his ingenious system, and scatters the fruits of his immense labour into thin air. The observation respecting the olive has not escaped him. The following extract will shew how he surmounts the difficulty : " The olive is ΝΟΤ an Armenian " tree : nor, if it had been so, could it have been τανυφυλλος (as Homer supposed) by any " natural means. The transaction is a miracle, (that is, a thing in which the divine power is not " only exercised unaccountably, as it is in all things, but conspicuously, and for a *particular* " purpose, and that purpose an *apparent* one,)[1] and I surmise that it may have been a miracle " of creation, producing a new thing such as the rainbow was,[2] and which had not existed " before. It was a tree of peace and reconciliation, and a pledge that the tree of life should one " day be restored. It was probably removed to Babel, and thence propagated over the world. " Whether plants sprung up, after the flood, from seeds that were preserved in the mud, or by " an original creation, is unknown. The Ambrosia of the Gods, or elixir of immortality, was, " according to one ancient opinion, the oil of olives. Thetis anointed Achilles every day with " Ambrosia, and exposed his body to the action of fire by night, that he might become immortal " and exempt from old age, which the scholiast Apollonius explains by these words, θειοτατῳ " ελαιῳ περιεχρει. If this does not mean the oil of olives, it at least alludes to the sanctity of " that ointment."[3]

CHAPTER VIII

Rome—Images not anciently used. Origin of the name Roma—Labyrinth—Observations on Proper Names—Hero Gods accounted for—Seleucus Nicator Antichrist—General Observations—Yavanas expelled from the Towns they built

1. A GREAT number of curious circumstances are known respecting the city of Rome—the *eternal city,* which convince me that it was a place of very great consequence, and closely connected with the universal mythos which I am endeavouring to develope, long before the time usually allotted to Romulus and the wolf. The following particulars extracted from the work of Nimrod are very striking : " I cannot help suspecting that Roma was, when occupied by the " predecessors of the Tusci and the Ombri, called Rama. Rome herself was supposed by many

---

[1] Though, for a purpose not connected with the question of miracle, and that I may not be accused of unfair quotation, I insert this definition, I by no means admit any thing so unphilosophical and confused.

[2] Here Nimrod supposes, as a matter of course, that there was no rainbow before the flood, and that it was the effect of an instant miracle. If there had been rain there must have been a bow. From a former expression it seems he believes that the obliquity of the ecliptic to the equator did not exist, but that it was the effect of miracle, contrary to the doctrine that it is the effect of the periodical revolution of the pole of the equator round the pole of the ecliptic, as the Hindoo philosophers hold. But even if this were so, it ought not to be spoken of as he speaks of it : for it is in that case a natural effect arising from a natural cause. The miracle was the disturbance of the direction of the pole of the earth, not the appearance of the bow.

[3] Nimrod, Vol. I. p. 272.

" authors[1] to have been a city of the Etrurians, during the time anterior to its foundation in the
" year B. C. 752, and subsequent to its abandonment by the ancient aborigines : and the site of
" Rome had been excavated by certain subterraneous passages of extraordinary size and solidity,
" the cloacæ, or rather cluacæ maximæ: operum omnium dictu maximum suffosis montibus
" atque urbe pensili,[2] subterque navigatâ. This work is ascribed by some to the imaginary
" king, Tarquin the ancient : but so inconsistent is Roman mythology, that we find them existing
" as buildings of indefinite antiquity in *Romulus's* time, when the image of Venus Cluacina (the
" expurgatrix, the warrioress, or the illustrious, for the sense is doubtful) was discovered in
" these gloomy canals. They were not adapted to the shape[3] and ground-plan of Rome, but
" probably were conformable to that of some older city. Fabretti observes,[4] that there are
" several very ancient watercourses at Rome, entirely subterranean, one of which is situated
" between the church of St. Anastasia and that of St. George, and leads directly into the caverns
" of Cloaca Maxima. They were large enough for a waggon loaded with hay[5] to pass, and
" upon one occasion, *after they had been neglected*, the cleansing of them was contracted for at
" 3000 talents.[6] It has been justly and sagaciously observed, by Dr. Ferguson, that works of
" convenience or cleanliness were rarely undertaken in times of remote antiquity, and if these
" were made with such an intent, they stand alone among those *wonderful monuments*, whose
" having existed is only credible because they still exist and are visible, and which were all sub-
" servient to the uses of ambition or fanaticism. And we may infer in a more particular manner,
" that the works in question were directed to one or both of these objects from the example of
" the Egyptian Theba Hecatompylos,[7] which was excavated with navigable canals, through
" which the kings used to lead forth their armies, under the city, and unobserved by the inhabi-
" tants. M. Vipsanius Agrippa,[8] in like manner went into the cloacæ with his barge and sailed
" through them into the Tybur."[9]

On the subject of these *Cloacinæ* Dr. Ferguson[10] says, " These works were, in the midst of
" Roman greatness, and still are, reckoned among the wonders of the world. And yet they are
" said to have been works of the elder Tarquin, a prince whose territory did not extend in any
" direction above sixteen miles : and on this supposition they must have been made to accom-
" modate a city that was calculated chiefly for the reception of cattle, herdsmen, and banditti.
" Rude nations sometimes execute works of great magnitude, as fortresses and temples, for the
" purposes of war and superstition : but seldom palaces : and still more seldom works of *mere*
" convenience or cleanliness, in which for the most part they are long defective. It is not there-
" fore unreasonable to question the authority of tradition in respect to this singular work of anti-
" quity, which so greatly exceeds what the best-accommodated city of Europe could undertake
" for its own conveniency. And as these works are still entire, and may continue so for thou-
" sands of years, it may be suspected that they were even prior to the settlement of Romulus,
" and may have been the remains of a more ancient city, on the ruins of which the followers of
" Romulus settled, as the Arabs now but or encamp on the ruins of Palmyra or Balbec. Livy
" owns that the common sewers were not accommodated to the plan of Rome as laid out in his
" time: they were carried across the streets, and past under buildings of the greatest antiquity.
" This derangement he imputes to the hasty rebuilding of the city after its destruction by the

---

[1] Dion. Hal. Arch. Rom. I. Cap. xxix.   [2] Plin. Lib. xxxvi. Cap. xxiv. Sect. 2, p. 698, Franz.

[3] Lib. v Cap. lv.   [4] De aquis Romæ, Dis. III. p. 190, Rom. 1680.   [5] Strabo, v. p. 336.

[6] Dion. Hal Lib. iii. Cap. lxxxvii.   [7] Plin. xxxvi. Cap. xx. (or xiv.) p. 688, Franz.

[8] Dion. Cassius, xlix. Cap. xliii.   [9] Nimrod, Vol. I. p. 321.

[10] Hist. Rom. Rep. Vol. I. note, p. 13, 4to.; Liv. Lib. i. Cap. xxxviii.

" Gauls. But haste it is probable would have determined the people to build on their old foun-
" dations: or at least not to change them so much as to cross the directions of former streets."
Nimrod observes upon this,[1] " Dr. Ferguson has omitted to notice one remarkable passage of
" Lactantius, which shews that the sewers were in existence before the time of Romulus, and an
" object of ignorant veneration to that founder and his colleague. Cloacinæ simulacrum in cloacâ
" maximâ repertum Tatius[2] consecravit, et quia cujus effigies esset ignorabat, ex loco illi nomen
" imposuit. Yet we are to believe, that they were made by the fourth king after Romulus."
After this Nimrod goes on to shew what is extremely probable, that the first Roma, which
would probably be the Roma or Rama of the Ombri, or Osci, was destroyed by a natural convulsion, a volcano.

It is very certain the old traditions agreed that Rome was built on the site of a former city.
The chronicle of Cuma (which Niebuhr calls modern and worthless, but, query ?) says, that the
name of the first city was Valentia, and that this name was synonymous with Roma. Now, there
was a Valentia in Italy, and one in Britain; there is one in Ireland, and one in Spain. There
was also a Brigantia in England, and there is one yet in Spain. There was Umbri in England,
(North-umberland and river Umber,) and Umbri in Italy. The Hindoo Gods by the same names
are all found in Ireland, as well as the Etruscan. Now, I ask, have these singular names of
people descended from a people from Upper India, speaking the Sancrit language before it was
brought to its present perfection ? How can the singularity be otherwise accounted for ? The
early history of Rome is most certainly a mythos, its real history is absolutely unknown. The
Greeks also, namely Lycophron and Aristotle, state, that there was a city in old time before that
of Romulus, called Roma or Ῥώμη.[3]

I suspect with Nimrod, that Rama, so common both in India and in Syria, was the same as
Roma; that it was a noun adjective appellative, and meant, in one sense, *strong*. Thus Bala-
rama, the *powerful* or *potent Bal*. He says, " I believe that Roma is radically the same word as
" Rama, the Romans being Pelasgi, and here we have the vowel E concurrent with A and O, for
" Remus is always in Greek Ῥῶμος, and the name Romulus, ón the contrary, was sometimes
" expressed Remulus. Livy gives me further confirmation by deriving Ram-nenses à Romulo."
Nimrod says, " For the flatterer of Octavius, the pretended Ænead prince, freely owns that
" when Æneas landed, Evander the Arcad,

Evandrus Romanæ conditor arcis,

" was already established at mount Palatine: nay, even he displayed to Æneas the ruins of yet
" an older city. And Antiochus, an authority far elder and graver than Virgil, makes Rome an
" established city in the time of Morges." Nimrod then compares the Cloacæ to the Labyrinths
of Egypt, &c., and the Caves of Ellora, and observes, that these things are inconceivable and
mark an astonishing state of society. This is, indeed, very true, and the history and date of it,
is that of which we are in search.

2. In the course of this work the reader must have observed, that it has been shewn that the
Romans, the Greeks, and the Egyptians, had none of them originally the use of images. This I
believe was when the Buddhist doctrine prevailed, or rather I should say the Buddhist Jaines:
and probably for some time also after that of Cristna had succeeded to it. I think there can be
no doubt that images were used by the Etruscans. This seems to be fairly implied in the order
of Numa, that in the Roman service they should not be used; for, if they had not been used by

---

[1] Vol. III. p. 76.   [2] Lactant. Lib. i. Cap. xx.   [3] Niebuhr's Rom. Hist. Vol. I. p. 151.

some persons, he would never have thought of prohibiting them. I have said that I suspect Numa of being a Menu or a Noah, as it is written in the Hebrew a *Nuh* נוח. The tribe of Juda were strictly followers of the doctrines of Noah or Nub, and in this respect were correctly followers of the same doctrine as Numa. It was from this cause that his city was called by the Brahmin name of Rama or Roma, or Ρωμη, the name of several cities in Syria and India. The words in India, in Greece, and in Latium, having the same meaning, shew them to be the same. [1]

Mr. Heyne in his work entitled *Veteris Italiæ Origines Populi et Fabulæ ac Religiones*, in the following passage, has suggested another origin for the name of Rome. He says, " Quid quod " satis probabile mihi sit, etsi aliquid pro liquido et explorato in his, quorum nulla fides historica " est, tradere velle ineptum sit, ipsam fabulam de Romulo et Remo a lupa lactatis a-nominis in- " terpretatione esse profectam : nam a ruma, seu rumi, quod vetus mammæ nomen est, Romæ " nomen deduxisse nonnullos videmus ; ut alios a virtute ac robore ad Græcum vocem ρώμην. " Ignoratio originis, a qua nomen urbis ductum esset, hominum animos ad conjecturas convertit, " quæ postea in narrationes abierant. Quod si verum est et ex antiquioribus sumptum, quod " Servius ad lib. 8, 90, et alibi habet, ut Tiberis priscum nomen Rumon fuerit (neque illud " adeo abhorrens ab antiquissimo aquarum et omnium nomine per Celtas et Græcos vulgato : " Rha, Rho, Rhu, Rhin, Rhiu, Rhei, (ρέω, ρόος,) non improbabile sit, urbis nomen A FLUMINE " esse DUCTUM, ET *omnia alia, quæ narrantur, pro commentes seriorum ætatum esse habenda.*" On this my learned friend who pointed out to me the passage of Heyne observes, that the epithet of *Roma* or *strength* given to Rome, must have been given after it grew strong. Of course the observation falls to the ground when it is known that it was a mystical name, *given from an ancient mythos or city in the East,* and was itself built on the foundation of an ancient city. The following assertion of Atteius settles this question : Atteius asserit Romam ante adventum Evandri diu Valentiam vocitatam. [2]

I cannot answer for the opinions of others, but the fact of these names having the same meaning, and the numerous other circumstances connected with them, compel me to believe that the Numa was a Menu, and that the Roman religion was from India. But we all know that it was also from Ilium or Troy; that is, that it was closely connected with the Trojan mythos in some way or other. This raises a strong presumption that that of Troy must have been from the East. Every thing increases the probability that the Hindoo system once universally pre-vailed. All this tends also to add probability to what the reader has seen respecting a city of Valentia having formerly occupied the site of the present Roma. If I prove that the early Roman history is a mythos, I open the door to very latitudinarian researches to discover its origin. And for the proof that it is so, I am quite satisfied to depend upon what Niebuhr has said, supported by the numerous facts pointed out by Nimrod. Taking Valentia and Roma to be the same, we find them in England, in Ireland, in Spain, in Italy, in Phrygia, in Syria, (as Rama,) and in India. Then, when can these synonymous cities have been built but when or before the Hindoo Gods Samanaut, Bood, Om, Eswara, &c., &c., [3] came to Ireland, and the God Jain or Janus to Italy ? I beg my reader to recollect that however different the Cristnuvites may be at this day, the Jains and Buddhists are, and always were, great makers of proselytes.

Numa expressly forbade the Romans to have any representation of God in the form of a man or beast, nor was there any such thing among them for the first 170 years. And Plutarch adds to this, that they were Pythagoreans, and shed no blood in their sacrifices, but confined them

[1] Hesychius says, Ραμας 'Ο υψιστος Θεος.
[3] Celtic Druids, Ch. V. Sect. XXVI.
[2] Serv. in Æn. I. 277; Nimrod, Vol. III. p. 110.

to flour and wine. Here is the sacrifice of Melchizedek again; the Buddhist or Mithraitic sacrifice, which I have no doubt extended over the whole world.[1] In the rites of Numa we have also the sacred fire of the Irish St. Bridget, of Moses, of Mithra, and of India, accompanied with an establishment of Nuns or Vestal virgins. Plutarch also informs us, that May was called from the mother of Mercury, and that in the time of Numa the year consisted of 360 days.[2] " Numa ordered fire to be worshiped as the principle of all things: for fire is the most active " thing in nature, and all generation is motion, or at least with motion: all other parts of matter " without warmth lie sluggish and dead, and crave the influence of heat as their life; and when " that comes upon them they immediately acquire some active or passive qualities. And there- " fore Numa consecrated fire, and kept it ever burning, in resemblance of that eternal power " which actuates all things."[3] Again, in the Life of Numa, he says, " Numa built the temple " of Vesta, which was intended as a repository of the holy fire, in an orbicular form, not with a " design to represent the figure of the earth, as if that were Vesta, but the frame of the universe, " in the centre of which the Pythagoreans place the element of fire, and give it the name of " Vesta and Unity: but they do not hold that the earth is immoveable, or that it is situated in " the middle of the world, but that it has a circular motion about the central fire. Nor do they " account the earth among the chief or primary elements. And this they say was the opinion " of Plato, who, in his old age, held that the earth was placed at a distance from the centre, for " that being the principal place was reserved for some more noble and refined body."

The Phliasians had a very holy temple in which there was no image, either openly to be seen or kept in secret.[4]

The Abbé Dubois states, that the Hindoos in the earliest times had no images. As we have found that this was the case in most other nations it was to be expected that it would be the same in India.

3. The ancients had a very curious kind of building, generally subterraneous, called a laby- rinth. The remains of this are found in Wales, where the boys yet amuse themselves with cutting out SEVEN inclosures in the sward, which they call the city Troy. There is a copy of it taken from Nimrod's work,[5] in my plates, figure 25. Pliny names it,[6] and his de- scription agrees with the Welsh plan.[7] This, at first sight, apparently trifling thing, is of the very first importance; because it proves that the traditions respecting Troy, &c., found in the British isles, were not the produce of monkery in the middle ages, but existed in them long before.

The Roman boys were also taught a mazy or complicated dance, called both the Pyrrhic war- dance, and the dance of *the city Troy*. Pliny says that Porsenna built a labyrinth under the city of Clusium, in Etruria, and over it a monument of enormous and incredible dimensions.[8] The Cloacæ Maximæ, under the city of Rome, have by some been thought to be a labyrinth. These labyrinths were sometimes square and sometimes elliptical. The sacred mazy dance was to imitate the complicated motions of the planets,—was in honour of the Gods—that is, of *the dis- posers:* in short, it had the same object as the labyrinths.

The Roman circus was an allegory corresponding to the labyrinth, as the author of Nimrod supposes. The circuits were seven, saith Laurentius Lydus, because the planets are so many. In the centre was *a pyramid on which stood three altars to Saturn, Jove, and Mars,* and below it

---

[1] Vide Plut. Life of Numa.   [2] Ibid.   [3] Plut. Life of Camillus.
[4] Cumb. Orig. Gent. p. 264.   [5] Vol. I. p. 241.   [6] XXXVI. Cap. xix. Sect. ii.
[7] Nimrod, Vol I. p. 319.   [8] Ibid. p. 319.

three others—to Venus, Hermes, and Luna. The circuits were marked by posts, and the charioteers threaded their way through them guided by the eye and memory. " The water of " *the ocean*, coming from heaven upon mount Meru, is like Amrita, (amber or Ambrosia,) and " from it arises a river which through seven channels encircles Meru." [1] The circuits of the circus were called Euripi. An Euripus was a narrow channel of water: ductus aquarum quos illi Nilos et Euripos vocant. [2] The three Gods, on the pyramid, had reference to the three Gods in the capitol, called Συνναιοι, [3] or *the dwellers together*, for these three were the Dii Magni Samothraces—Θεοι μεγαλοι, Θεοι δυνατοι, Θεοι, ΧΡΗΣΤΟΙ. But the Θεοι χρησοι, though three were all one, and that one the Sun or the higher power of which the Sun was the emblem: and Tertullian says, that the three altars in the circus were sacred—trinis Diis, magnis, potentibus, valentibus: eosdem Samothracas existimant.

The city of Troy also had its labyrinth. The Pergamus, in which Cassandra was kept, was in the shape of a pyramid, and had three altars—to Jove, Apollo, and Minerva; but the Capitolium of Rome and all her sacred things were avowedly but revivals of the religion of Troy. Her founder arrived in Latium,

Ilium in Italiam portans victosque Penates.

The seven tracts or channels of the sky, through which the planets move, are called in the Homeric Greek τειρεα—

Αρις υτειμπιτα . . . . πυραυγεα κυκλον ιλισσον
αιθιρος ιππατοριος οι τειριειν— [4]

a word which has nothing to do, Nimrod says, with τερας, a portent, but implies merely the common idea *terere iter*, and of τριβος, via trita, or, as the Brahmins say, the paths of the planets. With the teirea agree the euripi of the circus, and the seven main streets which, taking the square as a round, circuit the seven-fold city. [5] These latter are called its αγυιαι, and Apollo Ergates, the architect God, who built the walls of Troy, was therefore called Αγυιιος, and because he traced the walls of the great seven-streeted city or πολις ευρυαγυια in the shape of an exact square, or superficies of a cube, the idol or sculptured form of the God Aguieus was a cube, σχημα τετραγωνον. [6] Orpheus describes the city of Aiaia as consisting of seven circles of walls and towers, one within another; and Gnossus, in Crete, was the alleged site of the Labyrinth of Minos, of which Ariadne possessed the clue. [7] The celebrated fair Rosamond had her underground labyrinth, near Woodstock, and *her bower from which the labyrinth did run.* [8]

In the isle of Lemnos there was a labyrinth of which some remains existed in the time of Pliny. It is very remarkable for having been surrounded with 150 columns, which were revolving cylinders, so movable that a child could spin them round. These are evidently what we call rocking-stones. [9] The maze of complicated circles near Botallek, in Cornwall, described in plate

---

[1] Asiat. Res. VIII. pp. 322, 323, 357.   [2] Cicero de Legibus, Lib. ii. Cap. i.
[3] Serv. in Æn. Lib. ii. ver. 225.   [4] Hom. Hym. Mart. ver. 6, 7.
[5] The Olympian course of Jupiter, at Pisa, was 600 feet long, as were all the running courses of Greece: this was instituted by Hercules. Stanley's Hist. Phil. Part ix. Ch. iii.
[6] Pausan. Lib. viii. Cap. xxxii. Sect. 3.   [7] Nimrod, Vol. I. pp. 247, 315.
[8] Drayton, note A, on Ep. of Ros. p. 81, Ed. London, 1748; Percy's Relics, Vol. III. p. 146.
[9] The Asphodel was called by Theophrastus the Epimenidian plant. The name As-phod-el is the Asian God Phod or Buddha, whose name rings every change upon the vowels, and upon the two variable consonants B. F. P. V. and D. T. Th. Nimrod, sup. Ed. p. 18. This was the plant used to move the celebrated Gigonian rocking-stone, (which I have noticed in my Celtic Druids,) which stood near the Pillars of Hercules, not far from the Straits of Gibraltar.

No. 29, of my Celtic Druids, was also, in some way, allusive to the planetary motions. The labyrinth of the Fair Rosamond could be nothing but an astrological emblem, allusive to the planets.

There are also histories of labyrinths in Egypt, seen by Herodotus; in Andeira; at the Lake of Van; Præneste, &c. The etymology of the word labyrinth is unknown, therefore probably Hindoo or Oriental; but Nimrod has some interesting speculations concerning it. From its form exactly corresponding to the sacred mount, &c., of India, and of the cities formed after its pattern, they probably were meant to be in one sense representations of the paradise, &c., *in inferis*, as we know these sacred matters on earth were supposed to be exactly imitated in the Elysian regions.

I have before observed, that each city had its ten years' war, its conquest and dispersion, I therefore need not here repeat them.

4. No one who has reflected much on the names of Grecian Gods and Mythoses, can deny, that their etymologies are in general most unsatisfactory. This is caused by searching for them no where but in the Greek language. The spoken language of Greece was, like that of all other nations, the child of circumstance. It was composed out of a mixture brought by Celtæ, by Ionians, if they were not the same,—by Pelasgi from Phœnicia,—from the second race of Celtæ, called Scythians,—and perhaps by others; so that it is evident, from the nature of the case, as Plato truly said, recourse ought to be had for, probably, all the old names, to the Barbari. The state of the case, as I have already intimated, is the same with respect to all ancient nations. Their spoken language was a general mixture, and the sixteen letters were common to all, and were used to record this mixture, or heterogeneous compound. This admitted, we see the reason why in etymology we ought not to be bound to any one nation for the origin of words, but why we ought to seek them wherever we can find them. They are exactly like the present English; but who would think of seeking the meaning of all English words in one language?

In addition to these reasons it must not be forgotten, that all the ancient names of towns and persons had a meaning, and, as their early histories were all mythological, this meaning was astrological. Egypt was divided, as every one knows, in its names, with a reference to the heavenly bodies: and, as I have just observed, Sir William Drummond has shewn, that most of the names of the towns and persons recorded in Joshua had an astrological meaning. It is, therefore, reasonable to believe that those which we cannot explain would be shewn to be the same, if our ignorance of their meaning could be removed. The history of every ancient state was a mythos: with such trifling variation as change of place and change of time produced, they were all the same. Such towns as were erected *de novo* were built astrologically, or with a reference to the prevailing mythos: such as arose by degrees were, when their inhabitants became rich, assimilated as far as possible to the prevailing and universal superstition. This, I think, satisfactorily accounts for the mixture of mythology and true history, and it is only by a careful attention to separate the two—an attention which has never yet been properly paid,— that any thing like a rational history can be formed. The learned author of Nimrod could not avoid seeing the universal character of the mythos; but, bound by religious prejudice, he has most absurdly exerted his great learning and talent after the example, and in aid, of Mr. Faber, to make it fit to his own superstition. He assumes that his own mythos is true literally, and as the mythoses are all fundamentally the same,—as a general, generic, or family character runs through the whole,—it is no difficult matter to give a certain degree of plausibility to his scheme. But these gentlemen never perceive that their literal systems involve consequences utterly absurd, and contrary to the moral attributes of God.

The districts of Canaan appear to have been allotted or divided according to astronomical or astrological rules, in the same manner as was practised with the *nomes* of Egypt. The tenth chapter of Genesis is an example of the same kind—a division of the world into *seventy-two* countries or nations, under the mask of a genealogy. Every chapter of Genesis exhibits an esoteric and an exoteric religion. The same persons named in the tenth chapter of Genesis are found in Ezekiel, and also in Job—a sacred book of the Jews, in which the destroyer makes a great figure.

The following passage exhibits a pretty fair example of the mist which superstition sometimes raises before the eyes of men of learning and talent, and also, in no small degree, tends to confirm what Sir W. Drummond says in his Œdipus Judaicus, viz. that the astronomical meaning, which almost all the early names in the book of Joshua contain, prove it to have an allegorical meaning: " The names of the Patriarchs of the line of Shem had a significancy " prophetic of events which should occur in their lives. ·I conceive that Salah flourishing, the " people were sent forth: Heber flourishing, they crossed or transgressed the mighty river " Euphrates or Tigris: Peleg flourishing, mankind were split by the great schism: Rehu " flourishing, the Patriarchal Unity was broken, and the kingdom of Ione, or Babel, erected in " opposition to that of Ninus: and, lastly, Serug flourishing, the confusion of tongues took " place." [1]   When I consider the fact, that the names of the towns and places described in the Jewish books, as well as the names of the persons, have all meanings like those above, I am surprised that any one who knows it should hesitate a moment to admit that an allegory is used —in fact, a mythos described.

Nimrod takes Babylon for his standard, as I have before said, not because it is more convenient or because it was the original, but because he thinks it is necessary to the religion in the belief of which he happens to have been educated; and he is probably unconscious of the fact, and will strenuously deny it, and be very angry with me for stating it. But no philosopher or unprejudiced person, reading his book, will ever raise any question about it. In our endeavours to explain the ancient mythoses, great care ought to be taken not to confound two cases which must be, in their nature, extremely difficult to separate,—the ancient mythological or allegorical histories, and the idle stories invented by the Greek or Roman priests of comparatively modern times, to conceal their ignorance,—and this is so very difficult a matter, that our success, exert whatever care we may, must always be attended with considerable doubt.

5. The account which is constantly given of the attempt of Alexander and others to declare themselves Gods, has never been satisfactory to me. With Christian priests it has always been a favourite theme, and if they have not striven to disguise the truth, we may safely say they have not taken much pains to discover or explain it. I have shewn, that in the latter times of the Roman republic an eminent person to be a general benefactor of mankind was expected to arrive along with a new and more happy sæculum.[2] This was the renewal either of the Neros or of the cycle of 608—ΥΗΣ. On the beginning of every one of these new ages a person of great merit was supposed to come, endowed with a portion of the Divine Spirit, of the ἁγιον πνευμα or the Ερως, which was the protogenos or first-begotten of the Supreme Being. It was correctly the new incarnation of the mythologists of India. It was correctly the Christian inspiration. The Supreme First Cause was generally believed to overshadow, or, in some other mysterious manner, to impregnate the mother of the favoured person, by which she became pregnant. This was done

[1] Nimrod, Vol 1. p. 16, Sup. Ed.

[2] This cycle was what the Romans called *sæculum*, at the end of which the Ludi Sæculares were celebrated—when black victims were sacrificed. These sacred and unascertained periods were professed to be known only to the keepers of the Sibylline books, from which they were learnt. Nimrod, Vol. III. p. 191.

in various ways. When any person became very eminent as a benefactor of mankind, his successors generally attributed this inspiration to him; and he was said, by the vulgar, to have a God for his father: but the initiated understood it as first stated, which was a doctrine too refined for the understandings of the populace, and was never confided to them; and which, for the most part, we only know by halves—by collecting trifling facts that have unintentionally escaped from the mysterious adyta of the temples—in which, perhaps, in later times, the whole doctrine was not known, but in great part lost. The periods of the renewal and the actual length of the cycle were unquestionably lost. It is the natural and, I take it, inevitable consequence of all secret doctrines of this kind, unwritten and handed down by tradition, that they should either be lost or become doubtful. It was a knowledge of this natural and inevitable effect, probably, which caused the priests in several countries to commit the doctrines to writing in the guise of ænigmas or allegories or parables, and experience has shewn that this is equally unavailing; or perhaps it is of worse consequence, as the allegory being at length believed to the letter, the secret meaning has not only been forgotten, but the belief of it, or the allowance of its existence, has been denounced as heretical—a crime—and the persons entertaining it, subjects of persecution. This is a great evil, but evil, less or more, is always a necessary consequence of disingenuous and deceitful conduct in man. Plato and Pythagoras, among the Gentiles, were both examples of eminent men supposed to be the produce of divine influence or inspiration, as I have shewn in B. IV. Ch. II. Sect. 6. Their mothers were believed to have been overshadowed or obumbrated by an Apolloniacal spectre, to have been *afflata numine* filled with the קרש רוח *qds ruh*, and to have produced their respective sons without connexion with man. This, in fact, was correctly Hindoo incarnation. All the extraordinary births recorded in the two Testaments, such as those of Samson, Samuel, John Baptist, &c., were examples of the same kind.

Persons wishing to obtain power often attempted to induce a belief that *they* were the effects of this kind of divine interference. This was the case with Alexander the Great,[1] who was feigned to be begotten by Jupiter Ammon in the form of a Dragon. This was the case also with Augustus Cæsar, whose mother fell asleep in the temple of Apollo, and who (when she awaked) saw reason quasi a concubitu maritali purificare se, et statim in corpore ejus extitisse maculam, velut depicti draconis......Augustum natum *mense decimo*, et ob hoc Apollinis filium existimatum.[2] When Scipio Africanus aspired to be the tyrant of his country, a similar story was told of his mother, and of him—but the Romans discovered his object, and he was banished for it,—he failed. His mother was said to have been impregnated by a serpent creeping over her body when she was asleep. In the same manner Anna, the mother of the Virgin Mary, was said, in one of the spurious Gospel-histories, to have been impregnated, when an infant of only three or four years old, by the Holy Ghost, in the form of a serpent, creeping over her body when asleep; the produce of which was Mary, the mother of Jesus. And as Jesus was in like manner the produce of the Holy Ghost, they declared Mary to be both the mother and the daughter of God. The Serpent was the emblem of divine wisdom equally in India, Egypt, and Greece.

An attempt was also made by Sylla to establish himself as the object in honour of whom the Ludi Sæculares were celebrated; but if such were his object, it does not seem to have succeeded. He appears not to have been supported by the priests, and therefore probably gave it up. "Sylla " was born in the year of Rome[3] 616, but it is uncertain what year the Sæcular Games were cele- " brated, whether in 605, in 608, or in 628. It was a matter of the most occult science and pon- " tifical investigation, to pronounce on what year each Sæculum ended, and I am not satisfied

[1] Nimrod. Vol. III. pp. 366, &c.   [2] Suet. Octav. Cap. xciv., Nim. Vol. III. p. 458.
[3] Thuscæ Historiæ cit. Censorin. p. 84; Plut. Sylla.

" whether the decemviri did not publish the games more than once, when they saw reason to
" doubt which was the true Sibylline year."[1] It is quite clear that these difficulties would not
apply to so short a period as 110 or 120 years. The nails driven annually by the consuls with
great ceremony, from a time long anterior to that here alluded to, must have readily fixed
the time for the celebration of feasts of such short periods.

6. Perhaps in ancient times there never was a more remarkable example of this superstition
than that of Seleucus Nicator, who founded the city of Antioch, which was finished by Antiochus,
who was called EPIPHANES, perhaps on that account. The original name of this city, situated
on the Orontes, was Iona or Iopolis, the city of Io, the beeve *Ie.* (Io was sometimes the name of
a male, sometimes of a female; and the Syrians, we are told, were in the habit of changing the
Chaldaic א *a* and ה *e* into the *y o*.) It was said to have been built by Triptolemus, i. e. Enyulius
or Mars, as a funeral monument to the cow Io, which died there when she fled from Jupiter
Picus (Pi-chus ᴛʜᴇ black); but it was called Antiochia by Seleucus in honour of his son Antiochus Soter.[2] The name of the kings of Antioch sufficiently explain the fact. The *first* was called
Soter or the Saviour; the *second*, Theos or the Holy, or the God; the *third*, who finished the city,
Epiphanes, or the Manifestation of the Deity to the Gentiles. One of them, in furtherance of
this scheme, endeavoured to place his image in the Temple at Jerusalem, but was defeated by
the religious zeal of the Jews, to the uninitiated of whom he would appear but as an enemy to
their local God Iao or Ieue. To these Jews the secret meaning could not be explained without
letting out all the mysteries of the religion to the vulgar. The Seleucidæ governed almost all
southern and central Asia, including part of Upper and Lower India, and here they probably
learnt anew many of the ancient mysteries then lost to the Western nations. This may have
caused Seleucus Nicator to build a magnificent temple in Antioch or Iona to *Jupiter Bottius*, that
is Jupiter Buddæus, whose high-priest he called Amphion—Om-phi-on. The Christians are said
to have received the name of Christian at Antioch. At first they were every where considered
by the Gentiles as Jews, as they really were, and the God of Seleucus was called Antichrist by
the Jews. This would be in the Greek language Αντι Χρησος, or an opponent or second Χρησος,
meaning against the good or holy one, the holy one of Israel, and this would cause the Christians,
the servants of the God of the Jews, to call themselves followers of the Χρησος, or of the good
dæmon, the opposite of Antichrist. And from this it was, that Theodoret and other fathers
maintained that the city of Antioch was a type of Antichrist. The Antichristian Antioch, *Antichristian* before the birth of Christ, unravels the mystery. Nimrod has most clearly proved, that
the Seleucidæ meant to convert the city of Antioch into a sacred place, and to found their empire
upon a close connexion between church and state:[3] but he has not observed that Buddha and
the grand Lama of Tibet were their model.[4] The grand Lama, successor of Buddha, was at that
time probably an efficient monarch, and not reduced to the inanity of the present one by the
priests. Jerusalem was set up by the *Antichrist* David, as the Samaritans would call him, in opposition to the old worship on Gerizim,[5] and Antioch was the same, in opposition to Jerusalem.
Thus we discover the origin of Antichrist, with whom modern Christians have so long amused or
tormented themselves. But of the Χρησος more hereafter. Another reason why they called
Antioch by the name of Antichrist was, because the king of it usurped the name of Epiphanes,

---

[1] Nimrod, Vol. I. p. 462, Sup. Ed.   [2] Vide Nimrod, from pp. 370 to 490, Vol. III.
[3] As all politic modern kings do.   [4] The Jupiter Bottius proves this.

[5] According to the first religion of Moses, Gerizim, not Jerusalem, was the place *chosen by God to place his altars
there.* The text of Joshua contains satisfactory, internal proof of its corruption by the Jews to favour the claim of
Jerusalem, as is admitted by the first Protestant divines.

or the Manifestation of God to the Gentiles, which belonged only to their God. Notwithstanding the destruction of the books at Antioch, under the superintendence of the Apostles, and of the Christian priests, systematically continued to the present day in all other countries, enough has escaped to prove it was the doctrine of the ancient religion, that a saviour should come at the end of the Sæculum.

The system of renewed incarnations seems to offer a strong temptation to ambitious spirits to declare themselves to be emanations of the Deity, as we have seen it was attempted by Alexander the Great and several others. Mr. Upham, in his history of Buddhism,[1] has given an account of a successful attempt of this kind in the kingdom of Ava. From this example it does not seem unlikely that similar attempts, in other places, Ceylon for instance, may have been made. In this way, at the same time that the system of incarnations which I have described, is supported, the absurd and degraded state of Buddhism in Ceylon and other places may be accounted for. Mr. Upham admits, as every one must, a primeval Buddha of great antiquity. His existence he does not attempt to explain, except so far as to admit that he was the Sun. Mr. Upham's is the account of modern Buddhism; with this I do not concern myself, except in some few instances, where the ancient truth hid, under the modern trash, seems to shew itself: as for instance, in the cycles noticed by Loubère and Cassini. From the lapse of time and other circumstances, the view of the Hindoo avatars has become indistinct; yet they are still so visible that almost every Christian who has of late carefully looked into the early history of them, is obliged to admit them. Thus the Rev. Mr. Townsend says,[2] " As this incarnate being was considered as a divine person, and " the son of God, and as Nimrod claimed the authority and titles of the incarnate, it is evident " that his father or his ancestor must, from some cause, have been also considered as divine." I can have no doubt that Mr. Townsend is right, and that Nimrod was Bala-rama, an avatar, probably Maha-Beli,[3] or an avatar of Buddha. Nimrod and Bala-Rama were both grandsons or sons of Menu, i. e. ʋ Nu. But since these most learned and orthodox gentlemen are obliged to admit the fact, I beg I may not be called fantastical and paradoxical, at least, unless they be coupled with me.

7. It is quite impossible to believe that all the striking marks of similarity between the names of towns, the modes or plans of building them, the names of persons, and the doctrines of the Orientals and the Western nations, can have been the effect of accident; and I can see no other way of accounting for them than by supposing that they were brought by the first race of people who travelled Westwards from India, and who all had, with various sectarian differences, fundamentally the same religion, and gave the same names to their towns as those they had left in their own North-eastern countries. This practice we know has always prevailed among emigrating people, and prevails to this day, and it rationally removes all the difficulties. It cannot be expected that at this late day, amidst the ruins of cities which have almost disappeared, we should find in each *all* the traits or marks of the system, or a whole system, complete. It is as much as we can expect, if we can find, in each, detached parts of the system: for example, suppose I found the head of a man in Babylon, the leg of a man in Troy, and the hand of a man in Rome; though I did not find a whole man in any of them, I should be obliged to believe that all the towns had formerly been occupied by men. It is the same with the universal system. In every city some of the débris are to be found, quite enough to enable us to judge of the remainder, with as much certainty as we should in the case of the limbs of a man, or of an animal.

An actual example of this kind took place in Ireland: in one place the back-bones of an elk

---

[1] Pp. 110, 111.   [2] Class. Journ. No. XLVIII. p. 236.   [3] Ib. p. 237.

were found, in another thigh-bones, in a third legs, and in another the magnificent antlers, and so on till all the bones of a perfect animal were found. They were collected, put together, and now form that most beautiful and majestic skeleton standing in the Hall of the Institute in Dublin. Does any one doubt that the elk was in former times an inhabitant of these places in Ireland? Just so it is with the mythological system of the ancients, with the adoration of the Sun and the host of heaven, the Lord of Hosts. Every where the same system with, in part, the same ceremonies prevailed, from Iona in Scotland to Iona at Athens, or Iona at Gaza, Iona at Antioch, or the Ioni or Argha in India.

I think it probable that the natives of central Asia, in the times of which we are treating, were nearly in the situation of the Afghans, inhabitants of the same country described by the Hon. Mr. Elphinston at this day.[1] They are in a great measure nomadic and divided into tribes, but yet are more located than the Arabians of the deserts. Wars often take place between them, and one tribe drives out another, who quit their country not in a state of distress and weakness, but of power—compared with the countries into which they come. The celebrated Baber is an example of this; he was expelled from his country about Balk into the South, where he attacked the empire of Delhi and conquered it.

8. In the old books of the Hindoos, as it was before stated, we meet with accounts of great battles which took place between the followers of the Linga and those of the Ioni, and that the latter in very early times were expelled from India under the name of Yavanas. After the sun had left Taurus and entered Aries, or about that time, it is probable that the war above alluded to arose. Whether the question of the precedence of the Linga and Ioni had any connexion with the transit from Taurus to Aries I know not, but the two events appear to have taken place about the same time. The Buddhists or Yavanas were expelled; their priests were Culdees; and they were Jaines. They passed to the West. In their way they built, or their sect prevailed in, the city of Baal, Bal, or Babylon—as Nimrod says, probably the old Iona:

Et quot *Iona* tulit vetus, et quot Achaia formas.[2]

They built, or their sect prevailed in, the city of Coan or Aiaia, if ever there were such cities—the city of Colchis or of the golden fleece, if ever there was such a city, to which the Argonauts are feigned to have sailed—the city of Iona which afterward became Antiochia—and the city of Iona called afterward Gaza, where they were Palli or Philistines, and near to which Jonas was swallowed up by a whale—and the city of Athens, called Athena, (a word having the same meaning as Iona,) with its twelve states and Amphictyonic council. They dwelt in Achaia, they built Argos, they founded Delphi, or the temple of the navel of the earth, where they were called Hellenes and Argives. They founded the state of the Ionians, with its twelve towns in Asia Minor. They built Ilion in Troy, or Troia or Ter-ia, i. e. *country of the Three.* They carried the religion of Osiris and Isis, that is Isi and Is-wara, to Egypt; they took the Deity Janus and Jana or Iana to Italy, where their followers were called Ombri: they founded the city of Valentia or the city of Rama or Roma:—they built Veii or the city of *Uei* (read from right to left Ieu), if ever there was such a city:—they built the temple of Isis, now called *Notre Dame* or the Queen of Heaven, at Paris; and, as it might be called, Baghis-stan now St. Dennis, and were called Salarii from their attachment to and practice of the sacred Mazy dance:—they left the Garuda at Bourdeaux:—they founded the most stupendous monument in the world called Carnac,[3] of the same name as the temple of Carnac in Egypt, and the Carnatic in India:—they built Stonehenge, or Ambres-stan, and Abury or Ambrespore:—they founded Oxford on the river

---

[1] Hist. Cabul.   [2] Nimrod, Vol. I. p. 287.   [3] See Celtic Druids.

which they called Isis, and Cambridge on the river Cam, Cham, HAM, Am or Om :—they built Iseur or Oldborough, and called the Yorkshire river by the name Om-ber or Umber or Humber, and called the state, of which Iseur was the capital, Brigantia, the same as the state which they had left behind them in Spain or Iberia, and Valentia a little more to the North, and Valentia in Ireland the same as the Roma and Valencia in Italy and Spain: and finally they founded a college like Oxford or Cambridge or the island of Ii or Iona, or Columba, which remained till the Reformation, when its library, probably the oldest in the world at that time, was dispersed or destroyed.[1]   These were the people, Jains or Buddhists, whom, in my Celtic Druids, I have traced from Upper India, from Balk or Samarcand, one part between the 45th and 50th degree of North latitude by Gaul to Britain and Ireland, and another part by sea, through the Pillars of Hercules, to Corunna, and thence to Ireland, under the name of Pelasgi or sailors of Phœnicia.

APPENDIX TO BOOK VII.

In the history of Brutus· and his three sons, noticed at the end of Chapter VI., we have the universal mythos in Britain, in imitation of Adam, Cain, Abel, and Seth—Noah, Shem, Ham, and Japhet.   The Welsh game of Troy, noticed by Pliny, in Ch. VII. Sect. 3, proves the Trojan mythos in Britain before the time of the Romans.   With this may be classed a medal of the Saviour found in Wales with the Hebrew inscription, in Fig. 26, described by Roland in his Mona Antiqua,[2] which may rank with the Crucifix, the Lamb, and the Elephant, or Ganesa at Brechin,[3] in Scotland; and with a ring having its Ling-ioni, its Bulls and Cobra, found in the same country, exhibited by the Earl of Munster to the Asiatic Society, and described in Volume II. art. xxvi. of their Transactions (vide my plates, Fig. 27); and with the Indian Gods Samnaut, Bood, Om or Aum, Eswara, Cali, Neith or Naut, and Creeshna, in Ireland, described in Chapter V. Section XXVI. of the Celtic Druids; and with the Trimurti of Ireland, Criosan, Biosena, and Sheeva,[4] and with the Culdees or Chaldæans in every part of the British isles.

---

[1] It is known that part of it went to Douay in Flanders.

[2] Plate V. p. 93, add. p. 298.   [3] Vide Celtic Druids, plate 24.   [4] Class. Journal, Vol. III. p. 179.

BOOK VIII

CHAPTER I

Jewish Pentateuch: Publication forced—Jews a Hindoo or Persian Tribe—Name of Phœnicia and Syria—Reason of Abraham's Migration—Abaris, meaning of—Yadus a tribe of Jews—God called by Gentile Names, but always Male—Difficulty in the Metempsychosis—Dr. Hyde shews Abraham to have been a Brahmin

1. It is scarcely necessary to remind any person who has read the preceding part of this work, of the very extraordinary manner in which the Jews appear to have been, as it were, insulated amidst the surrounding nations. If we may believe the literal sense of the Bible, (for a short time, *the Persians* excepted,) they were always at secret enmity or open war with their neighbours, the Gentiles, or the *idolaters*, as, by way of reproach, they are generally called. By the Greeks they were scarcely noticed; known they certainly were; but probably their doctrines were first made public by the translation of their Pentateuch, in the time of Ptolemy Philadelphus, and its consequent publication, which was so abhorrent to the feelings of the Jews, that a solemn fast to atone for the sin was established on the anniversary of the day that the translation was finished. This fast continues to be observed annually throughout all the world, where there are any of the Jewish nation. Notwithstanding what is said of Jesus reading in the synagogue, which admits of explanation so as not to be adverse to my opinion, I believe that anciently the Pentateuch was kept strictly secret by the Jews, and would probably have been lost like similar works of different temples,—Diana, Eleusis, Delphi, &c.,—had it not been for the translation forced by Ptolemy. In Athens they had a prophetic and a mysterious book, which they called the Testament, to which they believed the safety of the republic was attached. They preserved it with so much care, that among all their writers no one ever dared to make any mention of it; and the little we know of this subject has been collected from the famous oration of Dinarchus against Demosthenes, whom he accuses of having failed in the respect due to this *ineffable* book, so connected with the welfare and safety of the state.[1] Manetho notices a sacred book in the grand Egyptian library of Osymandias, said to be written by Pharoah Suphis.[2] This is Pharoah, Σοφος, the Wise. This was probably a similar book to that of the Athenians.

No doubt every division of the universal religion had its secret and sacred writings as well as the Jews, only they were never made public, and thus were lost. To the peculiar circumstance which caused Alexandria to be almost filled with Jews and Samaritans, and to the necessity which Ptolemy found of causing their books to be translated in order that he might know how to decide between them in their squabbles, and to a wish, perhaps, to govern them by their own laws, we are, probably, indebted for our knowledge of the books of the Old Testament. After they were once translated into Greek, there could be no longer any object in concealing the originals.

---

[1] Spinetto on Hierog. p. 123.   [2] Ibid. p. 304.

Of the reality of the translation there can be no doubt; but whether it was made from the copy of the Samaritans or from that of the Jews cannot be certainly known: against the Samaritans, Josephus is not evidence: but as the Jews allow the Samaritan to be the sacred character, from that it was probably taken: in consequence of the unintentional corruption of the LXX. by Origen, nothing can be deduced by comparison of the versions.

Calmet says, the Samaritans allege that "their translation was preferred before that of the "Jews, and laid up in the library of Alexandria." This seems not improbable. The Samaritan is said to be the sacred language of the Jews by Josephus, who, *in this case*, must be allowed to be an unquestionable authority, because it is evidence against himself and his sect. He says that the Petalon,[1] or gold plate on the forehead of the high priest, had on it "the name of God is "*sacred characters*." This plate was in existence in the capitol of Rome in the time of Origen, who relates that the letters were Samaritan. Josephus was here the most unwilling of witnesses, consequently his evidence is good,[2] and Origen's is the same.

2. Christians and Jews will find no difficulty in accounting for the insulated state or the singularity of the Jews, to which allusion was made in the last Section. They will say the Israelites were singular because they were the elect of God—God's chosen people. But philosophers will not be so easily satisfied, and perhaps they may reply, that this is an assumption made by the priests of almost every nation in its turn. A wish may also exist on their parts to discover the cause of this singularity combined with the general family likeness which, notwithstanding their peculiarity, may be perceived in their ceremonies and doctrines to those of the other nations. This wished-for cause I shall now proceed to shew may be found in the probable fact, that they were a tribe of Hindoo or Persian nomades or shepherds, for a wandering tribe they certainly were—one of the sects of the Hindoo religion after it divided into two, i. e. those of the Linga and Ioni, or Buddha and Cristna, or perhaps of the sect of the Linga after the separation, but before the reunion of the two. I think this theory will account for most of the difficulties with which we meet, and that there will not be a disagreement from the Hindoo religion, *in its probable original purity*, greater than may be expected to have arisen from the lapse of time, the change of place, revolutions, and other circumstances. I incline to the opinion that it was of the religion of the followers of the Linga after the separation. Thus they were the followers of the God Ie-pati or Iaw, in opposition to the Goddess Parvati or Venus, Astarte or Asteroth, &c. They were the followers of the *male* Io, in opposition to the *female* Io, of Syria; for the Io, as we have seen, was of both sexes. The Io of Syria, was probably nothing more than the Iη or Ιεω of Moses, with the peculiar Syriac dialect, which changed the ε into the o.

We are told that Terah, the father of Abraham, originally came from an Eastern country called Ur, of the Chaldees or Culdees, to dwell in a district called Mesopotamia. Some time after he had dwelt there, Abraham, or Abram, or Brahma, and his wife Sara or Sarai, or Sara-iswati, left their father's family and came into Canaan. If the letter A be changed, by metathesis, from the end of the word Brahma to the beginning, as is very often practised in the oriental languages, we shall have correctly Abrahm; or the A might be only the emphatic Chaldee article, making *the Braham* or Brahmin. The word *Iswati*, in the second name, is now said to be merely a term of honour, like *Lady* Sarah.[3] The identity of Abraham and Sara with Brahma and Saraiswati was first pointed out by the Jesuit missionaries.

---

[1] I apprehend that the use of the word Πεταλον here, exhibits a remnant of the first style of writing on leaves. The sacred word must have been written on a golden leaf—folium or עלה *ole*.

[2] Antiq. B. iii. Chap. vii. Sect. 6.   [3] I shall explain it hereafter.

" Mr. Paxton, in his illustrations of the Holy Scriptures, describes the striking similarity of " manners, habits, and customs, observable between the Israelite and Hindoo nations. Abraham " is said to be the son of a Hindoo Rajah, who, abandoning his caste and native land, which was " Mesopotamia, went to reside in a foreign country."[1] This Mesopotamia, as it was intimated in the last book, must evidently be the country called Doab,[2] or the Mesopotamia of India, the same as the Greek, Μεσος ποταμος. This is probably meant for Matura on the Jumna, in the country between the Indus and the Ganges. They came ultimately into a country which they called Canaan, probably from a place in India, which had the same name, noticed by Dr. Buchanan.[3]

3. In Isaiah xxx. 4, the city of Maturea, or Heliopolis, is called חנס hns; in the Vulgate, Hanes, and in the LXX. Heliopolis. Mr. Bryant observes that the place called Hanes is, by Stephanus Byzantinus, called Inys or Ινυσσος, and by Herodotus Ιηνισος. Now it is remarkable that this was the very city, to which the ΦHN or Φ hnn or Phœnix, came at the end of every 600 years to burn itself, on the altar of the temple of the sun. But under the circumstance of the Hebrews having no letter which answered to the Coptic or Egyptian letter Φ, the word, by them, may have been rendered by the letter ח h. This must also suppose the Egyptian language, when the name Phanes was given to the city, to be older than the Syrian of the time of Isaiah. But when what I have said and shall say respecting the antiquity of the language of African Ethiopia is considered, this will be found to be of no consequence. As Phœnicia was imagined to have had its name from a hero, Phœnix, so Syria is said to have had its name from a man called Syrus,[4]

---

[1] Franklin on Buddhists and Jeynes, p. 10.

[2] In the Indian language ab means river, like aub in Danaub, and Do is the Latin duo. The whole means, in the Indian language, *country of the two rivers*. Here in the *do* is a beautiful and incontrovertible example of the necessity of having recourse to mixed etymology.

[3] Franklin on the Jeynes, p. 3. I have said, in my Celtic Druids, that Canaanites meant *traders*. I have changed my opinion on this subject. They were traders no doubt, but they were called from the Hebrew כנ knn, and כין kin. Natura, omnium genetrix, et directrix. Hence the *Kann* or Diana of the Etruscans, and the כינ kivn or round cakes, in honore Reginæ Cælorum ; hence the Chann or the Jana of the ancient Romans ; as Chiun became Juno. (Ouseley's Collect. Vol. III. No. II. p. 120.) It was closely connected with the Chaones or Caones, and had the same meaning as the Apollo Cunnius. The Sun God of Egypt is called Kan, by Diodorus Siculus : and Col. Tod has observed, that the Lotus is equally sacred to the Kan of Egypt and Kaniya of India. (Hist. Raj. p. 538.) In Deuteronomy Moses orders the Israelites to destroy the names of the divinities of the land. Solomon Jarchi says, this was done by giving them a contemptible name. This was the origin of Babylon—city of Confusion. In the same way, and for the same reason, probably, Canaan was a sectarian name of reproach with the Jews. In Greece Βηλος (vide Etym. M. in voce) signified Mount Olympus or Heaven, and Βα-Βηλος any place abominated or unholy. (Nimrod, p. ii. Sup. Ed.) Hence *Babylon* perhaps. The great disorder in ancient history has arisen, in some measure, from the custom of calling princes by new names—by titles of honour. This is carried to such an extent in the Birman empire, that a native of that country shudders at the idea of calling his prince by his proper name. (Asiatic Res.) Nothing can be more clear than that this, or something very similar to it, and equally embarrassing to the historian, was practised in the East in ancient times. We find Abraham, Jacob, Joshua, and many others, changed their names ; and in these cases the text of the history tells us why, or at least when, they changed them ; but what should we have done if we had not had that information ? We should then have known these people by their new names at one time, and by their old ones at another—in fact, not have known them at all. Thus it may well be supposed to be with Persian and other names, in the Persian histories, in which it cannot be expected that the explanation can be given. There must always have been a great difficulty in distinguishing between father and son in historical accounts, and different nations had recourse to different expedients. I have no doubt that judicial astrology had a great influence in this matter, for it seems to have been a practice in all nations to give children names in reference to their horoscope, or the calculation of their nativity according to the planets, which were sacred names, and were borne in addition to their paternal names.

[4] Syncellus, p. 150.

one of the earth-born people. But Mr. Bryant[1] says, *Sur*, *Sour*, whence was formed Συρος, signified the sun. It was the same as Sehor of Egypt, called Σειριος by the Greeks. The city of Ur in Chaldea was sometimes called Sur, and Syncellus says Abraham was born in the city *Sur*. Stephanus says *Sur* was common to many places. From this it seems that Abraham may have come from an oriental Sur or Suria.

But Abraham or the Brahmin came from Ur of the Chaldees, (this may have been the peninsula of Saurastra or of Zoroaster or Sura-stan,) which has been supposed to mean the fire of the Chaldees, alluding to their fire worship. Fire worship, however, was not objected to by Moses, but was continued by him as much as by other nations; for it was adopted by no nations, in their temples, except merely as an emblem of a superior Being. We have seen just now, that Abraham was said by some authors to have come from a place called *Sur* as well as Ur; and Sur meant Beeve or Bull: see Book IV. Chap. I. Sect. 8. All this is consistent, for Sur was called from the Bull, Ur in the old language being the origin of the word Urus or Beeve. After what has been said respecting the identity of the ancient languages of Italy and India, I feel no hesitation in locating Latin words in India. And thus I am led to the conclusion, that Abraham's family may have come away from his country to avoid the adoration of the Bull, as well as that of the Yoni.[2] We have found the Agnus or Aries in the Yajna sacrifice—the Agni construed to mean Fire, the Agnus *Lamb* overlooked. In the same manner we find the word Ur called fire, the meaning of Urus or bull being overlooked. The circumstance of the Agni being only known at this time to mean *fire* is a proof that the Sanscrit language has been changed, and that we ought to go to an older language, its parent, or rather to it before its change. No one, I think, who looks at the word AGNI and considers that, in the Yajna sacrifice or the sacrifice of the Agni, a lamb is slain, and that the Agni always rides a lamb, or if on foot carries a standard bearing a lamb, and the other circumstances pointed out by me in Book V. Chap. X., can doubt that the word Agni has originally meant lamb. I do not think that the least appearance of the worship of the Bull can ever be perceived in the tribe of Abraham until their return from Egypt. But the sacrifice of the Ram is ordained by God in lieu of the human sacrifice of Isaac. There was a district of India called Ur or Urii or Uriana on the Jumna, which we shall find was the place from which Abraham came.

4. Abraham and his family or clan probably left their country on account of what he truly considered the corruption of the religion, viz. the reconciliation or the coalition which the Brahmin books say took place between the followers of the Linga and those of the Ioni. He seems to have been of the sect of the Linga alone. When he first came into Canaan, the natives with their Canaanitish king-priest Melchizedek, were of his religion—that of Brahma and Persia. When his tribe returned from Egypt under the command of Joshua or the Saviour, to which only they had been driven by famine, and where it is evident that they never were comfortable, they found the Canaanites with their *Ionic* cities (Iona at Antioch and Iona at Gaza) had become corrupted, they had fallen into the heresy of Babylon and the Culdees, the measure of their iniquity was full, and they conquered them. The Canaanites forfeited their dominions, and the Israelites seized them, and under the Saviour, the son of Nave, restored the temple of Melchizedek on Gerizim,[3] which was afterward removed by David and Soleiman or Solomon to Jerusalem.

---

[1] Anal. Vol. III. p. 446.   [2] Bulls of Bashan, Calves of Bethel and Dan.

[3] Har-Gerizim, probably, was so called after some sacred Mount in India. Ar, in the old language of Upper India as well as in Hebrew, is constantly applied to sacred mounts, indeed to all mounts—as Ar-buddha. Ar, in Sanscrit, means hill, and Gir *circle*. Azim, in Arabic, means *greatness*, a title of eminence: hence Ar-ger-izim might mean *hill of the great circle*. The great circle consisted of the circle of stones set up by Joshua, and was the Proseucha, the remains of which Epiphanius found on Gerizim, as I have already mentioned. Hebrew names are not uncommon in India: the Baithana of Ptolemy is so clear that it cannot be mistaken. Asiat. Res. Vol. IX. p. 199.

This shews us why the Israelites were a peculiar people in the midst of nations of enemies on every side—hating all nations except the Persians, who, in the time of Cyrus and Ahasuerus, were of their own religion, and who, without minding their domestic feud, restored their temples both on Gerizim and at Jerusalem. The Israelites exhibit several remarkable points of resemblance to the followers of Brahma and Cristna at this day. Their religions are mutually intermixed with many of the rites and ceremonies of their predecessors, the Buddhists. The first book of Genesis is Buddhist; the sacrifice of the Lamb at the vernal equinox or at the passover, is clearly the sacrifice of the Yajna, offered by the followers of Cristna or Brahma. This accounts for the hatred of Moses to the Bull, and his partiality to the Lamb. Jeroboam and the Samaritans fell off to the Bull and the Queen of heaven—into the union—and thus, to the Ioudahites, became heretics.

I have said above, that Abraham came from India or Persia. It is very possible that the tribe might originally have come from India and have resided a long time in Persia, before it moved forwards into Canaan. It is very possible that great numbers of persons constituted the tribe and came into Syria, and went thence into Egypt, though the history of the family of Abraham only is given. I think this is not contrary to the fair meaning of the history, and removes some difficulties.

Although the ancients of the West do not seem to have known much of the doctrines or sacred books of the Jews, yet Abraham was well known to them; several persons, both Greek and Oriental, having written respecting him. They all agree that he was not a native of Syria, but that he came thither from the East. If we can believe Mr. Faber and the Desatir, which must, I think, be genuine, (however much it may have been corrupted by Moshani in rendering it out of the old language into Persian,) the adoration of the Bull and Buddhism first prevailed in Persia; but this, there is reason to believe, was succeeded by Cristna and the Lamb which might have come in with Gemshid. The ancients would say that from Brahma, who came into Persia, came Brahminism, and the Brahmins, but yet there would have been no Brahma. Thus, when the Israelitish tribe, who were a sect of Brahmins, came into Syria, they would merely say that *Abram* came. The whole history of Abram or Abraham, that is אברם *Abrm* or אברהם *Abrem*, has a most mythological appearance. The reason given for changing his name in Gen. xvii. 5, is very unsatisfactory,[1] and I am induced to think that it looks very like the reason of a person writing and not understanding the meaning of the name; or, which is still more likely, *not choosing* to give the meaning of it, under the change of which some mystery was probably concealed. The word הם *em* means *multitude,* and the word אב *ab* may mean *father:* but אבר *abr* never means father. Now suppose the letter א *a* after the manner of the Chaldee to be emphatic, to mean *the,* and the word ברם *brm* to mean the same as the Brahm of India, whatever that might be: and suppose this בר *br* the first syllable of the Brahme-Maia to mean, as Mr. Whiter says it does mean in all old languages, *creator* or *former,* giver of forms; then, by adding to it the word הם *em,* we get the meaning given by the author of Genesis, and this in a way in perfect keeping with the remainder of the book, though perhaps mystical enough. I again repeat, that according to the *common idiom* of the Hebrew, Abraham cannot mean *father of a multitude.* Dr. Hales says, that Ab-ram meant " a high " father," and Abraham " a father of a multitude of nations :" from אב *ab* " a father," רב *rb* in Chaldee " great," and הם *em* the abridgment of המון *emun,* " multitude."[2] It has been thought

---

[1] The change made in the name of Abraham was by the addition of the vowel ה *e,* the first name not having a vowel. This is evidently mystical. I have a strong suspicion that, formerly, the vowels were only used when it was necessary to distinguish one word from another which had the *same* consonants, but a different *meaning.* In this case the vowel in one of the words was inserted to distinguish it, as the modern Jews have since done with their points.

[2] Chron. Vol. I. p. 131.

that the word Abraham had the meaning of *stranger*. This will apply to the Brahmins as well as to Abraham, because they are considered to have come into India from the North. The reader must remember that I am supposing Moses to have written many hundred years after the arrival of the tribe from the East, and that, in the course of the events of which I treat, time enough had passed for the languages to have materially changed—an event which we know to have taken place. Then I think there is nothing against our going back to a language common to both for the origin of the word: for the farther back we go, the nearer, of course, all the languages would be to one another.

Let me not be called a wicked atheist for seeing the likeness between Brahma and Abraham; for what says the Rev. and learned Joseph Hager, D. D.?[1] "As the Indian alphabets are all syllabic, "and every consonant without a vowel annexed is understood to have an ʌ joined to it, there is no "wonder if from *Abraham* was made Brahma; and thus we see other Persian words in the Sans- "crit having an *a* annexed, as *deva* from *div*, *appa* from *ab*, *deuda* from *deud*," &c.[2] Dr. Hyde says, that Ibrahim or Abraham, by the Persians, is never called otherwise than Ibrahim or *Abra- ham Zerdusht*,[3] that is evidently Zerdusht the Brahmin. All this I think is confirmed by a fact which we learn from Damascenus, that Abraham first reigned at Damascus; and Alexander Poly- histor, who lived about ninety years before Christ, and Eupolemus, who lived about 250 years before Christ,[4] say that he came and resided in Egypt at Heliopolis, that is Maturea, and there taught astrology, which he did not profess to have invented, but to have learnt from his ancestors, of course in the East. This is confirmed by Artapanus. It seems not unreasonable to suppose that by means of Abraham, Maturea acquired its Indian name,—the name of the birth-place of Cristna.

5. Mr. Bryant thinks[5] that Abaris in Egypt had its name from the word עבר *obr*. This seems not unlikely: as it was here that the Israelites dwelt, it does not seem improbable that it had its name from them—as I have shewn, in my CELTIC DRUIDS, that they had their name from the word עבר *obr*.

"The city of Abaris was called *Sethron* and *urbs Typhonia*: Seth being (as Plutarch assures "us) the Egyptian name of Typhon, the great enemy of their Gods."[6] It seems to me to be dif- ficult to say that Abaris was not the city of Maturea of Abaris, or עברי *obri*, the strangers—of Heliopolis of On, or of destruction, as it was called, or Typhon. The names of this city curiously confirm my doctrines. It was called On, or the city of the generative power of the sun; it was also called the city of Typhon, or of destruction, because destruction was regeneration; it was also the city of the Sun, because the sun was both Creator and Destroyer. The sacred books tell us why Abraham went into Egypt, and the Gentile authors find him there, and thus confirm the fact, and the finding this Brahmin and his tribe at Maturea is very striking. All this is confirmed in various ways by Eupolemus, Berosus, Philo, and Josephus, and indirectly also, I think I may say, by Sanchoniathon.[7] When Alexander says that the Heliopolitan priests made use of the astrology of Abraham, it is the same as to say of the astrology of the Brahmins.[8] And when the Greek Orpheus says, that God of old revealed himself to one Chaldæan only, I quite agree with Hornius,[9] that it is probable the person called Abraham is meant, whether he was really a person, or a sect, or a system. I beg leave to observe, en passant, that from Sanchoniathon we have in substance the same Cosmogony for the Phœnicians as is found in Genesis. On this account the genuineness

---

[1] Diss. Bab. Ins. Lond. 1801.
[2] See Paolino's Amarasinha, p. 12; Symes's Embassy to Ava, ch. xiv.
[3] Hyde de Rel. vet. Pers. Cap. ii. et. iii.
[4] Maurice, Anc. Hist. Vol. I. p. 438.
[5] Vol. III. p. 238.
[6] Cumb. Orig. Gen. p. 47.
[7] Gale, Vol. II. Book i. Ch. i. § 8, 9, &c.
[8] Ib. § 9
[9] Hist. Philos. Lib. ii. Cap. x.

of his work has been doubted, but I think without sufficient reason, as the reader must perceive. Josephus and Plutarch think, that the Phœnician shepherds, said to be driven out of Egypt, were the Israelites; but what Bishop Cumberland has written upon Sanchoniathon's account, has nearly satisfied me, that these people must have been expelled more than three hundred years before. The circumstance of these Phœnicians being able to conquer and hold possession of Egypt, shews that Phœnicia (and, I suppose, of course, its capital Sidon) must have been a very great and power-ful state before the time of Abraham.[1] I think these shepherds must have been the Palli, or Phi-listines, who came from the border of the Ærethrean sea, and at first from the peninsula of Sau-restrene or Saurastra, which perhaps means *country of Zoroaster*.

6. I will now state another fact, which, coming from the quarter whence we have it, cannot be disputed on account of any interest or system. The tribe of Cristna had a name, noticed by me before in Book V. Chap. X. Sect. 2, which is very remarkable. Captain Wilford says, "The " *Yadus*, his own tribe and nation, were doomed to destruction for their sins, like the descendants " of YAHUDA or YUDA, which is the true pronunciation of JUDA.[3] They all fell, in general, by " mutual wounds, a few excepted, who lead through *Iam bu-dwípa*, a miserable and wretched life. " There are some to be found in *Guzarat*, but they are represented as poor and wretched."[4] Mr. Maurice says, "The *Yadavas* were the most venerable emigrants from India; they were the " blameless and pious Ethiopians,[5] whom Homer mentions, and calls the remotest of mankind. " Part of them, say the old Hindu writers, remained in this country; and hence we read of two " Ethiopian nations, the Western and the Oriental. Some of them lived far to the East; and " they are the Yadavas who stayed in India, while others resided far to the West."[6] The fact of part of the tribe yet remaining in existence, is one of the pieces of circumstantial evidence which I consider invaluable. It cannot be the produce of forgery, and couples very well with the two Sions, two Merus, &c., &c. It is on circumstances of this kind that I ground my system. They surpass all written evidence, for they cannot have been forged. This emigrating tribe of Yadu or Yuda, we shall find of the first importance, for they were no other than the Jews.

Porphyry, in his book called Περι Ιυδαιων, quoted by Eusebius,[7] makes Saturn to be called Israel. His words are these: Κρονος τοινυν, ον Φοινιχες Ισραηλ προσαγορυωσι. Then he adds, that the same Saturn had by a nymph called Ανωβρετ, an only son, ον, δια τυτο, Ιευδ εχαλυν, whom, for this, they call *Ieud*, as he is so called to this day, by the Phœnicians. This only son, he adds, was sacrificed by his father. Bochart[8] says, "Thus Ieud amongst the Hebrews is יחיד " *(ihid) Iehid*, which is the epithet given to Isaac,[9] concerning whom it is evident that Porphyry " writes." Bochart is followed by Stillingfleet,[10] who says, "Abraham is here called by the " name of his posterity, *Israel, Isaac Jeoud*. So Gen. xxii. 2 : *Take thy son:* יחיד *ihd* is the " same with the Phœnician Joud." This is again confirmed by Vossius.[11]

There is, I think, no difficulty in finding here the Iudai or tribe of Yuda of the Hindoos long before the Jews of Western Syria could have taken that name from one of the sons of Jacob, called Judah,—a name which cannot have been first derived from him, because it is clear that they had the epithet long before he was born—his grandfather Isaac having borne it.

[1] Montfaucon, Vol. II. p. 245, thinks Sanchoniathon a forgery, and doubts of his translator Philo Byblius. But his reasons seem feeble: it must remain doubtful. The work of Sanchoniathon was thought spurious by Basnage, Hist. Jews, Book iii. Ch. xxvii. p. 251.

[2] Cum. San. Rem. I. p. 109.　　　[3] It ought to be יהודה ieude or ieu-de, which means *the holy Ieu*.

[4] Asiat. Res. Vol. X. p. 35.　　　[5] Hist. Hind. Vol. II. p. 262.　　　[6] Asiat. Res. Vol. III. p. 368.

[7] Præpar. Evang. Lib. i. Cap. ix.　　　[9] Can. Liv. ii. Ch. ii. fol. 790.　　　[8] Gen. xxii. 2.

[10] Origin. §. B. iii. C. v.　　　[11] Vide Gale, Court Gent. Vol. I. Book ii. Ch. i.

Stillingfleet and Bochart observe that ענברת-חן *hn-onbrt*, αναβρετ, means *conceiving by grace*. Respecting the Anobret of Sanchoniathon, Vallancey has given a copy of a very extraordinary Irish MS. with a translation of it, in which an Irish king's wife is said to bring forth a white lamb, whence she was called Uanabhreit, i. e. *bringing forth a white lamb*. This distressed her very much; but she again conceived and brought forth a son, when she was told by the priest that her womb was consecrated, and the lamb must be sacrificed as *her first-born, for her ceaniu* (קנין *qnin*) *cion-iuda* or *purification of her first-born*. [1] I quite agree with Vallancey that this can be no monkish forgery of the eleventh century. I think it decidedly proves, first, that the Irish did really come from Phœnicia; and, secondly, that Sanchoniathon is not a forgery. But the proper meaning of קנין *qnin* Cion-Iuda is evidently not what Vallancey gives above, viz. *for the purification of the first-born*, but *for the salvation of Juda of Sion*. The whole story is exceedingly curious. The son she brought forth was called Aodh-Slaine, i. e. *because he was saved from the sacrifice*. I think Aodh-Slaine is the same as יצץ *izhk*, though it is so much corrupted as scarcely to be discoverable. That the history of the sacrifice is of the nature of a mythos, or fable, or parable, for the purpose of teaching a doctrine is, I think, very clear, and I think the doctrine also is clear. The first object was to abolish *human sacrifices* by the substitution of the Lamb, which Moses afterward did better by a redemption-price; the next object was to inculcate the absolute necessity of obeying without any, even the slightest, doubt or hesitation the orders of God—in other words, the order of the priest.

That we should find the name of Iudai of the sect, in the father of the twelve tribes, is not surprising, and accords well with what I have suggested. The word Jew is a mere Anglicism, and the word Yudi or Iudi is more correctly the Hindoo name, come from where it would. No doubt it might come from the name of a son of Jacob; but still this must have been at second-hand, after the division of the tribes. It is most probable that it came from the tribe of Iudia, as the head of the tribe seems to have been known by that name, as I have before stated, many years before the son of Jacob was born, and who was probably so called after his ancestor. When Porphyry called Isaac by the epithet Ioud, he, perhaps, meant Isaac the Ioud-ite, or Isaac of the tribe of Ioud or Yuda. The name given to Jacob, Israel or ישראל *isrul*—notwithstanding Cruden's attempt to explain it by improperly changing one of the letters—is evidently unknown. ישר *isr* is the name of the book of Jasher, which has been construed *the correct book*. As this word gives name to the whole tribe, it is a very important and desirable thing to ascertain its meaning. I expect it will be discovered in the East. But, perhaps, it may only mean the same as ישרון *isrun*, *an upright person*: then it might be, *the great upright one*.

Bochart, Gale, and many other of our learned men, think the Phœnicians derived their letters, learning, &c., from the Jews. This is easily explained. When the Israelitish tribe arrived in Canaan they found the natives professing their religion in all its first principles. It might be of the Indian religion before the division about the Linga and Yoni took place, or when it partook of both, or before the division had travelled so far westwards. However this might be, the name of *Iona*, borne by the towns of Gaza and Antioch, pretty well shews that it became, if not entirely, yet in a great measure, Ionian afterward. This easily accounts for the idea of Gale and Bochart, to which, without it, there would be opposed the striking fact, that we scarcely know of the Phœnicians from the Jews except as their enemies; and this makes greatly against the Phœnicians having borrowed their learning from them. People are not often willing to learn of their enemies. Abraham is said, by oriental historians, to have brought the knowledge of astronomy to the Cana-

---

[1] Coll. Hib. Vol. IV. p. 430.

anites and Egyptians. It may have been the astronomy of the Brahmins which he brought. It is not unlikely, that though the Egyptians and Phœnicians may have had much knowledge before Abraham, or his sect or tribe, arrived, he may have brought them an increase, and this would be quite enough to authorize his successors to say and to believe, that he was their first instructor. And this theory accounts for the similarity between the writings of Sanchoniathon and the book of Genesis.

Porphyry (lib. iv. adversus Christianos) says, "that Sanchoniathon and Moses gave the like ac-" count of persons and places; and that Sanchoniathon extracted his account, partly out of the " annals of the cities, and partly out of the book reserved in the temple, which he received from " Jerombalus,[1] priest of the God Jeuo, i. e. Jao, or Jehovah."[2] The words of Porphyry are, as given by Eusebius, τα ὑπομνημαία παρα Ἱερομβαλυ τυ ἱερεως τη Θευ Ιαω. All this shews that the *fundamental* doctrines of the tribe of Abraham and the Phœnicians were the same, though they themselves might be of different sects. The system established by Moses confirmed the line of separation between them. His great anxiety was *to prevent his people from falling into the* Tauric and Ionian heresy, the heresy of Babylon, of Iona, ancient Antioch, and of Iona of the Philistines of Gaza, his bitter enemies. To prevent them from relapsing into the worship of the Bull-headed Baal and Baaltis, and Bull-eyed Juno or Asteroth, the queen of heaven, he endeavoured to keep them to the religion professed by Melchizedek, to the worship which Abraham brought, and which his tribe followed at Maturea or Heliopolis of Egypt, to the worship of the Saviour or Messiah, typified by the Lamb of the Zodiac, in India, called the Saviour or Heri-Cristna; in short to the worship of the *Male* generative principle. We have seen that Yadu was said in India to be the father of Cristna.

7. It has often appeared to me an extraordinary circumstance that the God of Moses should be called by the same names as the Gods of the Gentiles—Adonis and Baal, for instance. I have read that the Jews count in the Bible thirty-two names of God; but I believe in no case whatever will he be found by the name of one of their Goddesses. Though he is called Baal, he is not called Baaltis. If I be right, this is easily accounted for. When Abraham arrived in Canaan the Ionian heresy did not prevail, and he had no objection to his God being called *after the names of the Gods* of the *single* male principle, or perhaps of the *double* principle; but he utterly rejected the Ionism and the idolatry, its general concomitant, into which Canaan or Syria fell, between the time of his tribe going into Egypt and returning, as the Hebrew text says, after upwards of four hundred years. When the tribe left Canaan the Ionic principle might be gaining ground, but not have become the prevailing superstition. When the Jews returned, increased in strength and sword in hand, the name of the towns Iona, shew that Ionism prevailed. As I have stated before the close similarity between Paganism and Judaism is not only admitted by Mr. Faber, but is descanted on by him at great length; and, after shewing the absolute insufficiency of all theories yet promulgated to account for it, he says, "Judaism and Paganism sprang from a common source; hence their close " resemblance, in many particulars, is nothing more than might have been reasonably antici-" pated."[3]

If it be said that we do not find such clear marks of this resemblance in the books of the Jews as we ought to do, I reply, we every where find the worship of the female generative power reprobated, under the name of Astaroth of the Sidonians, Queen of heaven, בעלשמים *bolesmim*, and מלכתשמים *mlktesmim*; and the Male Jou, or Jupiter,[4] extolled. If I be right, it is evidently the

[1] Jerombalus is probably Ἱερας-ομφαλος.
[2] Gale, Court of Gent. Book iii. Ch. ii. §. i., Vol. II. Book. i. Ch. iii. § viii.   [3] Orig. Pag. Idol. Vol. I. p. 106.
[4] These were mere dialectic variations, but of the same name.

object of the Israelitish books, to conceal the secret doctrine under an allegorical history; and it is very possible that the real truth might be soon forgotten by the Jews, who contemplated their histories with only the narrow views and eyes of sectaries.[1] In the whole of the Jewish books I cannot discover a single passage indicative of a tendency to tolerate the worship of the Queen of heaven. If ever any thing like an attempt was made, as in the case of Solomon, it was met with the bitterest intolerance on the part of the priests; witness their violence against him for his toleration of the Sidonians; not his adoption of their religion I believe, but only his toleration of it.

With respect to the adoration of the female generative principle, the Israelites and the neighbouring Gentiles seem to have been situated exactly like the Papists and the Protestants. The Israelites adored the Phallus or Linga, as is evident from the stone set up and anointed with oil by Jacob. But no where can an emblem of the female principle be discovered. The festival of the Ram, the Yajna sacrifice, the emblem of the *I am that I am*, or the *I will be what I have been*, in the masculine gender, is apparent in a variety of ways: but no where can any emblem of the female principle be discovered, except as an object of reprobation. The Gentiles adored both; examples of which need not be given. The modern Romists adore the Ram, the Lamb of God, and also the Virgin, the mother of God, the Queen of Heaven, the Regina Stellarum: the Protestants adore the Lamb of God; but they, like the Israelites, can scarcely be found in any case to pay the least respect to the Queen of heaven. At Antioch-ian-Iona, at Delphi, at Rome, both are adored; at Jerusalem and London, only one—the Lamb. The Ioni was and is detested in the last-named places. The fact cannot be denied. Was it the effect of accident, or of a secret religion? Probably the same cause—some cause arising from the character of man in certain classes—which produced the dislike to Ionism or the adoration of the *female* anciently in India, produced the same in our Calvins and Luthers, of the real nature of which they might be themselves unconscious.

It will, perhaps, be objected to this, that there is no more particular account of the distinction in the Scriptures. But the case in this respect is exactly the same as it would be with us, if all the writings of our time were lost except the sacred ones, as were those of the Israelites. But the worship of the Queen of heaven is reprobated many times by the prophets, particularly by Jeremiah, and that in the strongest terms. My reader must recollect that, according to the Hindoo history of the religion, the first worship was paid to a double object, and that the worshipers were afterward divided into those who adored the *male* and those who adored the *female* principle.

It is notorious, that there are in India great numbers of sects divided from each other, like the sects of the Christians; sometimes by important, at other times by trifling and perfectly unimportant, distinctions. With this well-known fact before them, it is perfectly astonishing that our Indian philosophers should expect to find the different astronomical or astrological mythoses explained by one key. There are, probably, great numbers of systems, all having, perhaps, the same kind of foundation, but differing in the superstructure. The system of the *ten* ages, which I have explained, is one; the system of the *fourteen* Manwantaras, is another.

8. I have been told in reply to my arguments in favour of Abraham and his tribe of Iudai being Brahmins, that if it were so, we should find the metempsychosis in Judaism. I am ready to acknowledge that this seems a fair objection; but this tenet may have constituted part of the esoteric doctrine, as alleged by Mr. Maurice,[2] and as some other equally important doctrines appear to have done. For instance, the immortality of the soul is so little apparent in the Penta-

---

[1] I trust I am writing for the eyes of philosophers, taking an enlarged and bird's-eye view of all sects and nations, and as I shall favour none, I shall be favoured by none. A few philosophers are all that I ever expect to read my work.

[2] Ind. Ant. Vol. II. p 288.

teuch, that many of the most learned Christian divines have denied that it is there at all : a great Bishop has written *twelve* volumes to prove it is not there. And I reply, that whatever caused the concealment of the one, caused the concealment of the other ; or, whatever caused the one to be little apparent caused the other to be little apparent. They are in their nature closely allied. The most learned of the old Jewish Rabbis, and the first and most learned fathers of the church, I suppose, thought that they could see them in the Bible as they maintained both the doctrines; which they would scarcely have done unless they had thought they had authority for their opinion.

Learned Christian divines have found no small difficulty, in the fact just named, that in the Pentateuch there is not the least appearance of the doctrine of a future life, or of a place of punishment after death. The cause of this is to be found in the circumstance that the Jews secretly held the doctrine of the metempsychosis, and the perpetual renewal of worlds,—doctrines thought to be too sublime for vulgar comprehension. The doctrine of a *hades*, or *hell*, arose in times long after those of Moses, among the Persians, when the doctrine of two principles came to be formed, and the sublime Hindoo *trimurti* was forgotten. It is evident that the doctrine of a hell is quite inconsistent with the metempsychosis. This simple consideration removes all Bishop Warburton's difficulties. At first, when Christianity was unsettled, the transmigration of souls, and the millenium, or renewal of worlds, were received by the Christian fathers; but as the more modern doctrine of two principles, *good* and *evil*, gained ground, the other declined and was forgotten. The two doctrines were totally incompatible. The failure of the prophecies of the millenium greatly aided in producing this effect; but of all this I shall treat hereafter. At first the Gnostic and Manichæan doctrines, which possessed much sublimity, were, with a very trifling exception, universal. At that time mankind retrograded rapidly; and as they became degraded, the degrading doctrines of the Greek and Latin sectaries prevailed, till the world was overrun with Thaumaturgists and Devil-drivers, and all the absurdities which Protestantism has unveiled.

9. The likeness between Abraham and Brahma, and between their wives and histories, was observed by Dr. Hyde. Indeed it is so marked, that to miss observing it is impossible. Of course he supposes that all the immense fabric of Hindoo superstition was derived from the *man* Abraham. In palliation of this absurdity, it must be recollected that in the time of Hyde the nature of the Hindoo history and religion was not at all known; but seeing the striking similarity between the doctrines of the Hindoos and those of the Christians and Jews, he pronounces that Brahma was Abraham.[1] Postellus, in commentario ad Jezirah, had long before asserted the same thing, and that the Brahmins were the descendants of that patriarch by his wife Keturah, and were so called *quasi Abrahmanes*. This doctrine is supported by the Arabian historians, who contend that Brahma and Abraham, their ancestor, are the same person.[2]

Drs. Hyde and Prideaux, perceiving the likeness between the Persians and Jews, supposed Zoroaster to have been of the Jewish religion.[3] They were certainly so far right, that the two nations were of the same religion. I have already observed, that the Persians generally call Abraham *Ibrahim Zeradust*. Hyde says, Persarum Religio in multis convenit *cum Judaicâ, et magnâ ex parte ab eâ desumpta fuit*.[4] Hyde, in his first chapter, shews that the ancient Persians had a sacred fire, precisely the same as the Jews, from which it did not differ in any respect, and that the reverence to, or adoration of, this fire was exactly the same as that of the Jews to theirs, from which, he says, the Persians copied it. He quotes Ezra vi. 24, to shew that Cyrus consi-

[1] Hyde, Hist. Rel. Pers. p. 31.
[2] Maurice, Ind. Ant. Vol. II. p. 123.
[3] Maurice, Indian Antiq. Vol. II. p. 293.
[4] Cap. x. p. 170.

dered the religion of the Jews the same as his own. For proofs of the truth of this theory my reader may refer back to Book II. Chap. IV. It is admitted that Abraham and Brahma are the same; therefore the Hindoos must have come from Abraham, or the Israelites from Brahma. Now, Christian reader, look to the Pentateuch, which you cannot dispute, and you will see the whole history of circumcision, and how and why it was first adopted by Abraham for all his descendants; and if the Brahmins had descended from him, they would certainly have had this rite; but in no part of India is this rite observed by the Brahmins. This at once proves that Abraham came from the Brahmins, if either came from the other.

Sir W. Jones, in his translation of the Institutes of Menu, renders the word *Brahmana* in the sense of Priest. And the Jesuit Robert de Nobilibus, in what have been said to be his *forged* Vedas, calls the high-priest of the Jews and his associates Yúda-Brahmana.[1] That is, the words being in regimine, *Brahmin of the holy Ie*. I suspect that in mystic words like Yúda, the last syllable ending in d and a vowel, always means *holy*, or has the meaning of the Latin *Divus*. The expression of the Jesuit shews, that he considered the word Yúda, to be the same as the name of the tribe of Abraham.

M. Herbelot, Bibliot. Orient. article Behergir, calls Abraham " un Brahman de la secte, ou de " l' ordre, de ceux que l' on appelle Gioghis (Yoygees)." From the word Yogees our word Jews may probably have come. I beg the reader to pronounce aloud the word Gioghis. The Sanscrit word *Ayudya* becomes in English *Oude*, in Javanese *Nayugya*, and in Dutch, still more barbarously, *Djoyu*.[2] Here we arrive very nearly at the words Jude and Jew, as is apparent on pronouncing the words. And here it is found in the island of Java, the mother or sister of the island of Bali, which contains a place called Madura—the same as the Muttra of Upper India, where the statue of Bala Rama, and Cristna, so often before noticed, is found. The island of Java is the island of Ieue or Jehovah.

CHAPTER II

The Dove of the Assyrians—Black Jews—Megasthenes' Account of the Jews
—Soluymi or Solomons—Judaism shewn by Eusebius to be older than Abraham
—Hellenism—Jewish Mythos in Nubia and India—High Places

1. We have seen that the dove is, in a peculiar manner, the emblem of the Ioni. With this we find the Jews at almost perpetual war. The Assyrians are constantly described in the Jewish books by the term *sword of the oppressor*. In several places where we find this it ought to be rendered *the sword of the Dove*.[3] This was the emblem, or crest, or coat of arms[4] carried by

---

[1] Asiat. Res. Vol. XIV. p. 58.   [2] Ibid. Vol. XIII. p. 357.

[3] Jer. xxv. 38, xlvi. 16; Hosea xi. 11; Zeph. iii. 1.

[4] I have a suspicion that the Armorial-bearing called Crest, arose from being originally the sectarian brand or mark to distinguish the followers of the sect which called its divine incarnation, κατ'εξοχην, the Crest or Benignus, as the sect in India called their God *Cristna* or *Cris-en*. In both sacred and profane history we meet with accounts of

the followers of the imaginary, or at least mystical, Semiramis, who was said to have been born at or near the Phillistine Iona,—of the Semirama-isi of India, of whom I shall presently treat. See Col. Wilford's essay on Semiramis.[1] Persons may have different opinions as to the cause of the Dove, or Ca-pot-Eswari becoming the emblem of the female generative power, as also of the Holy Spirit, the third person of the Trinity, but the fact cannot be disputed.

The Chaldeans, or Chasdim, or Culdees, were priests of the Assyrians, and worshipers of the Dove or female generative power, whence they called their sacred isle of the West Iona or Columba, that is, the *female* dove, not the *male* or Columbus. No person who has studied the Romish Hagiographa can doubt of the origin of the bishops *Iona* and *Columba*.

2. The Rev. Dr. Claudius Buchanan, I believe a missionary, some years ago published Travels in India, in which he states, that he found no less than *sixty-five* settlements of ʙʟᴀᴄᴋ *Jews* in different parts of the peninsula.[2] It is a great pity that these different races of people could not be examined by a philosopher. Dr. Buchanan, who found the Christians of St. Thomas (before they were what he would call *corrupted* by the Romish Church) to have been, and yet to be, correct Lambeth Christians, notwithstanding that they received the Gospel of the Infancy, and were Nestorians, could not be expected to discover much. These *black* Jews are remnants of the sect of the Iadus, who, Col. Wilford informs us, yet remain in Guzerat. I apprehend they were part of the sect of the Linga, who would not unite with, or divided from, the followers of the female principle, the Argha or Ioni, or from those of the double principle, and, on that account, were persecuted and expelled, and from them came the tribe of Abram or the Brahmin. If this were the case, they would not, of course, have all the Mosaic books *in the form* in which we have them, except they received them from the West. And this seems rationally to account for the places in Syria being called by names of places in India. We know how almost all emigrants have given the names of the countries of their births, to their new habitations.

Jeremiah Jones says, "M. La Crose, in a letter dated at Berlin, the 4th of the ides of December,
" 1718, supposes it (i. e. the Gospel of the Infancy) written by some person who was a Nestorian;
" because in a Synod, called Diamperana, held by Alexius de Menezes, Archbishop of Goa, in the
" diocese of Augamala, in the mountainous country of Malabar, in the year of Christ 1559, he
" found it thus condemned : ' The book which is entitled, *Of the Infancy of our Saviour*, or the
" ' *History of our Lady*, already condemned by the ancient saints, because it contains many
" ' blasphemies and heresies, and many fabulous stories without foundation,' &c. Instances of

---

sudden panics, or alarms having seized large bodies of men. That of Brennus the Celt, our barbarian ancestor, was accompanied by a circumstance which appears trifling, but which exhibits a proof of the great antiquity of our practice of bearing devices or coats of arms. Nimrod, Vol. I. p. 178, sup. Ed. says, " The confusion fell upon the army at the " closing in of the evening, and at first a few only were confounded in mind, who imagined they heard the tramp of " horses, and the onset of some enemy. And in a little time this alienation possessed the minds of them all. And " taking up arms, and dividing among themselves, they mutually destroyed one another, no longer understanding their " own native tongue, nor yet recognizing the countenances of each other, ɴᴏʀ ᴛʜᴇ ᴅᴇᴠɪᴄᴇs ᴏɴ ᴛʜᴇɪʀ sʜɪᴇʟᴅs." The Assyrians always carried for their standard or coat of arms a *dove;* the Romans an eagle. On the key-stone over the inner entrance of the Amphitheatre of Verona is a shield bearing a cross, evidently coeval with the building, thus—⊕. See also Nimrod, Vol. II. p. 273.

In Æschylus's tragedy of the Seven Chiefs against Thebes, the shields of six of them are charged with Armorial-bearings, expressive of their characters, and as regular as if they had been marshalled by a herald at arms. Potter says, " The impresses are devised with a fine imagination and wonderful propriety." But he has omitted to remark that even the motto is not wanting. On one was inscribed the words I ᴡɪʟʟ ғɪʀᴇ ᴛʜᴇ ᴄɪᴛʏ. The siege of Troy, if it ever took place, was a species of crusade. On the antiquity of armorial-bearings Mons. Gibelin may be consulted.

[1] Asiat. Res. Vol. IV. pp. 370, &c.   [2] Christ. Res. p. 226, Ed. 1819.

" which are produced in that Synod, the same as are in Dr. Sykes's Gospel; and it is there said,
" that it was commonly read among the Nestorians in Malabar."

From an observation which Mr. Jones has made respecting the Marcosians, a branch of the
Gnostics, and respecting a passage of Irenæus, already noticed, I think it is unquestionable that
the Gospel of the Infancy existed in the second century. There is also existing part of a gospel
called the Gospel of St. Thomas, which is evidently taken from the same source as that of the
Infancy,[1] and St. Thomas is said to have instructed the Indians. The extract from Jones shews,
that if what Buchanan says be true, that the opinions of the Malabar Christians are the same as
the present English Protestants, they must have surprisingly changed since the arrival among
them of the Portuguese. It seems remarkable, that the Portuguese Papists should have converted
these Nestorians into Protestants!

It is to me utterly incredible that any tribe of people, existing as a tribe, should exist *as Mosaic
Jews* without the Pentateuch; because the Pentateuch forms their bond of union. It is not only
their religious, but it is their civil code, which regulates the decisions of their judges in disputes
about the common affairs of life. If they ever were Jews they must once have possessed the
Pentateuch, and they must have lost it, which seems incredible, when it must always have been in
daily use by the judges. I believe the case to be this, that they were tribes of Joudi or Yadu,
which were spared when opposing sects got the better of them in the wars of the Maha-bharat,
and were left in a poor and miserable state, without books or literature,—spared, in fact, from
mere contempt, being too low to excite fear or anger; that in the course of many generations their
origin was forgotten, and meeting with Jews from the West, and comparing notes, they found a
near relationship, and accounted for it by supposing that they must have come from Western
Syria, in consequence of the revolutions which had taken place there. Their real history, in two
thousand years and upwards, might well be forgotten. The ancient civil-religious wars of India
are recorded in the books of the Brahmins, but they are totally forgotten among the mass of the
people.

From the accounts given by Dr. Buchanan of the *black* tribes, some of them having Pentateuchs,
and others not having them; and of those who have them, having obtained them from the white
tribes, it seems probable that they are indebted for them solely to the white tribes. This will exactly
agree, as might be expected, with my theory, if it should turn out to be true; because the αποιχος
or *going out* of the tribe of Judi or Ioudi from India, in all probability, must have taken place before Moses lived, and before he partly wrote, and partly compiled or collected, the tracts into what
we now call the Pentateuch. In all probability the first books of Genesis were brought from India
with the tribe—with Abraham or the Brahmin.

The more I meditate on the extraordinary fact stated by Buchanan, that there are many *black*
tribes of what are called in our language *Jews*, but evidently tribes of Ioudi, in different parts of
India, who have not the Pentateuch of Moses, the more extraordinary and important it appears.[2]
The Pentateuch is the civil law of the Jews. By what law do these tribes govern themselves? Is it
by tradition? If they be Jews, they must be descendants of Jacob or Abraham, which branched
off before the law was given; and if their law be very similar to that of the present Ioudi, it will
prove, what indeed seems pretty clear without it, that Moses adopted, into his written law, many
of the old laws which his tribe had before.

Eusebius, in his Chronicon, says, that *Ethiopians* coming from the Indus or black river settled
near Egypt. There seems to be nothing improbable in these Ethiopians being the tribe of Jews—

[1] Vide J. Jones, Vol. II. Part iii. Ch. xxiv.   [2] Jesus was a Jew, in Italy *Nech.*

the tribe of Jacob or Israel. I think these Ethiopians did come under Jacob, and did settle in Goshen, and gave the names of Maturea and Avaris to the city in which they dwelt. Avari in Hebrew would be as often written עברי obri, or the city of the Hebrews or Foreigners.

It can scarcely be maintained that the places in Egypt which have names connected with the word Judah can have been called, in that early day, from that tribe of the Jews; but if it be, I then ask, how the name of Solomon, which is found in the desert of Solyme, &c., is to be accounted for? Taken together, the two exhibit the general Judæan mythos, independently of the tribe of Jacob or Israel.[1]

Eusebius's assertion, in his Chronicon, (by Scaliger,) that about the year B. C. 1575, a tribe of "Ethiopians came from the river Indus and encamped and settled near Egypt," is but a loose kind of information, and therefore can be little depended on; but as he fixes them to about the time when the Jews are generally supposed to have come, it rather tends to confirm my idea, though I pay little attention to the dates. It is not impossible that, without knowing it, he may allude to the Jewish tribe. But if this evidence be only weak, I will now produce what will not be easily overthrown.

3. Megasthenes, who was sent to India by Seleucus Nicator, about three hundred years before Christ, and whose accounts from new inquiries are every day acquiring additional credit,[2] in a very remarkable manner confirms my hypothesis of the Jews' coming from India. He says, *That they were an Indian tribe or sect* called Kalani, and that their theology has a great resemblance to that of the Indians.[3] The discovery of this passage, after I had written what the reader has read respecting the Jews, gave me no little pleasure, because it ALMOST *proves* the truth of my theory, and is very different from founding my theory upon it. I will now produce another proof, if records by *unwilling witnesses* are proofs, for Josephus is an unwilling witness.

Aristotle gave an account of the Jews that they came from the Indian philosophers, and that they were called by the Indians Calami, and by the Syrians Judæi.[4] I think few persons will doubt that the Calami here are the Calani of Megasthenes, one of the two being miscalled. We have seen a Calani in Ceylon, where we found a Zion, Adam's foot, Mount Ararat, and Columbo, &c., and in Gen. x. 10, and Amos. vi. 2, a Calneh or Calani is also named.

Gale[5] has observed, that the information of Megasthenes is confirmed by Clearchus, the Peripatetic. I think in this question these Grecian authorities constitute good evidence. Thus for my hypothesis we have as good written evidence as can be expected. We will presently try to confirm it by circumstances.

Respecting Megasthenes, Col. Wilford says, " Megasthenes, a man of no ordinary abilities, who " had spent the greatest part of his life in India, in a public character, and was well acquainted " with the chronological systems of the Egytians, Chaldeans and Jews,[6] *made particular inquiries* " *into their history,* and declared, according to Clement of Alexandria, that the Hindoos and Jews " were the only people who had a true idea of the creation of the world, and the beginning of " things."[7] From these circumstances Col. Wilford draws the conclusion, " that there was an " obvious affinity between the chronological systems of the Hindus and the Jews."[8] And they have an obvious tendency to support my theory of the origin of the Jewish tribe.

In a former part of this work, I have noticed the assertion of Megasthenes, that the Jews and

[1] In the Map of Antis's Egypt is a hill near Maturea called Tel-el-Ihudieb, or Jewry's hill.

[2] Vide Lempriere's Class. Dict. ed. 1828.   [3] Volney's Researches, Anc. Hist. Vol. II. p. 395.

[4] Josephus adv. Apion, B. I. Sect. 22, p. 214.   [6] Court of Gent. Vol. II. p. 75.

[5] See Asiat. Res. Vol. V. p. 290.   [7] Ibid. Vol. X. p. 118.   [8] Ibid. p. 242.

Indians were the only people who had a true notion of chronology, and I have also most clearly proved that what he said was true, or, at least, that their chronologies were the same.

If I had desired to invent a piece of evidence in confirmation of what I have said respecting the emigration of the Israelitish tribe from India to Syria, I could not have had any thing better than the following passage from Col. Wilford. The Zohar Manassé, which the reader will find named, cannot, in this case, be disputed as evidence of the ancient, probably the secret or esoteric, opinion of the Jews. The seven earths one above another is a circumstance so totally inapplicable to Jerusalem, and so clearly Hindoo, that the identity of the two cannot be mistaken.

Wilford says, " *Meru* with its three peaks on the summit, and its seven steps, includes and " encompasses really the whole world, according to the notions of the Hindoos and other nations, " previously to their being acquainted with the globular shape of the earth. I mentioned in the " first part that the Jews were acquainted with the seven stages, Zones or Dwipas of the Hindus : " but I have since discovered a curious passage from the *Zohar Manassé* on the creation, as cited " by Baanage in his history of the Jews.[1] ' There are,' says the author, ' seven earths, whereof one " ' is higher than the other, for Judæa is situated upon the highest earth, and Jerusalem upon the " ' highest mountain of Judæa.' This is the Hill of God, so often mentioned in the Old Testa- " ment, the mount of the congregation where the mighty king sits in the sides of the north, ac- " cording to Isaiah, and there is the city of our God. The *Meru* of the *Hindus* has the name of " *Sabha*, or the congregation, and the Gods are seated upon it in the sides of the north. There " is the holy city of Brahma-puri, where resides Brahma with his court, in the most pure and holy " land of Ilavratta."[2] The Judæa or Ioud-ia and Jerusalem named above, are evidently compared to the North-pole and Mount Meru, which is thus called the place of Ioudi. We shall presently find that, with the Arabians, the Pole-star was called the star of Ioudi. The following passages from the Bible are very striking :

" Beautiful for situation, the joy of the whole earth, is mount Zion, on the sides of the north, the " city of the great king."[3] " The mountain of the house of the Lord shall be established in the top of " the mountains."[4] " Then Solomon began to build the house of the Lord at Jerusalem in mount " Moriah, where the Lord appeared unto David his father."[5] " For thou hast said in thine heart, I " will ascend into heaven, I will exalt my throne above the stars of God : I will sit also upon the " mount of the congregation, in the sides of the north."[6] " I will dwell in the midst of Jerusalem : " and Jerusalem shall be called a city of truth ; and the mountain of the Lord of Hosts, the holy " mountain."[7] When we consider that our Bible is merely the sacred writings of the temple upon this mountain, of Sion or Moriah, or Meru, the exaggeration above is only what we might expect to find in them. Thus the Indians say the same of their Meru. I think it probable that all these mounts were imitative of the Heavenly Jerusalem, described in the last two chapters of the very ancient work called the Apocalypse.

4. I think if my reader will look back to the preceding pages, he will now observe several circumstances, particularly respecting the Solymi, which will tend strongly to confirm an opinion to which I have come after the most patient investigation, that the Israelites were one of the tribes which emigrated from the country of the Afghans or Rajpouts, that is, from the East, to avoid persecution. This is, indeed, in substance the account given by Moses. They were, in fact, a sect which worshiped the male generative principle in opposition to the female. The circum-

---

[1] Eng. Trans p. 247.

[2] Asiat. Res. Vol. X. p. 128, Vol. VIII. 285 ; 2 Chron. iii. 1, Isaiah xiv. 13, Psalm xlviii. 2.

[3] Psalm xlviii. 2.   [4] Micah iv. 1.   [5] 2 Chron. iii. 1.   [6] Isaiah xiv. 13.   [7] Zech. viii. 3.

stances relating to the city of Jerusalem and the Solymi will be found to be very striking, and will shew clearly why we meet with a Mount Sion in India, and with another in Syria. But though I think attachment to the adoration of the Male principle, or at least the double principle, in opposition to the female singly, or to Ionism or Hellenism, was one reason for their emigration, I also think it probable that dislike to the adoration of the Bull was another. If Solomon, of Syria, THE WISE, were a Buddha, one of the fourteen Solymi, or fourteen Menus, or fourteen Maha-bads, all supposed to be incarnations of divine wisdom, we see why he was so celebrated for that virtue. He was the son of the shepherd דוד *dud*,[1] who was the son of ישי *isi*, who was the son of עובד *Oubd*. I think *Dud* was a corruption of *Yud*, as Iacchus became Bacchus, Eioneus Deioneus, Zeus Deus, Zancle Dancle, or Dancle Zancle.[2] ישי *isi*, is the male Isis of India, עובד *Oubd* is (Syriace) *Obad* or A-bad, i. e. the Buddha.

" The Persians had a title, Soliman, equivalent to the Greek Αιολος, and implying *universal* " *cosmocrator*, qu'ils ont cru posséder l'empire universel de toute la terre, and Thamurath aspired " to this rank; but the divine Argeng, in whose gallery were the statues of the seventy-two Soli- " mans, contended with him for the supremacy. This Argeng was the head of the league of " Αργειοι, and the number 72, is that of the kings subject to the king of kings."[3]

The history of Solomon bears a very mythological appearance, which is much confirmed by a passage in Strabo,[4] who asserts, that both Syria and Phœnicia had their names from India. He says, speaking of the irruption of the Greeks of the Seleucidæ, into India, " These same Greeks " subjugated the country as far as the territory of the Syri and Phanni." Casaubon supposed the Phannon of Strabo to mean Phoinicon, and so corrected it.[5] This shews that there were nations of these names in India, which could not be very far from the peninsula of Sawrastrene or Syrastrene:[6] or perhaps Rajahpoutana or Afghanistan.

The word Rajahpoutana, I think, is Rajah-pout-tana, or three words which mean *the country of the royal Buddha*—Pout being one of the names of Buddha. That Rajah is *royal* I shall shew by and by. Of Afghan I can make nothing; but in the travels of Ibn Batuta there is a place mentioned, near Delhi, called Afghanpoor.

5. The following passage I did not notice till I had written the whole which the reader has seen respecting the tribe of Iudai. I consider this *under these circumstances* as very valuable circumstantial evidence. This kind of coincidence I value more than direct authorities. " Some of the " ancient fathers, from terms ill-understood, divided the first ages into three or more epochas, and " have distinguished them by as many characteristics: Βαρβαρισμος, Barbarismus, which is sup- " posed to have preceded the flood; Σκυθισμος, Scythismus, of which I have been speaking; and

---

[1] Ruth iv. 22.

[2] " In Thessaly they have a practice of prefixing a β before the original name, which is pronounced V; as β᾿ Othry, " for Othrys; and β᾿ Alos for Alos." (Clarke's Travels, Vol. IV. p. 256, 4to.) *Thebes*, by the natives of Lebadea, is called Thiva. (Ibid. p. 215.) " Thus we have the initial digamma in *wreck*, break, from ῥηγνυω." (Ibid. p. 160.) These changes are not greater than *iud* to *dud* or *diud*. Besides David was a man after God's own heart to do his will, and might be called St. David. This would be in the old language *Di-ud*. The word *ad* or *ud* is the common name of God or eminent person among the Rajahpoots; this had the very same import among the old Syrians and Assyrians. *Adudus* is called king of Gods. Cumberland says, " For as Macrobius (Saturnal. I. Cap. xxxi.) hath informed us, " *Adad* signifies among the *Assyrians* the ONE EMINENTLY, and therefore may well be the title of a monarch, or single " sovereign, and of the sun, their deity. Hither belongs also Josephus's observation from the Damascenus, that the " ten successions from *Hadad-eser* in Syria took all of them the title of *Hadad*." (Origin. Gent. pp. 170, 171, 172, 235, 236.

[3] See Herbelot in voce Soliman; Nimrod, Vol. III. p. 12.   [4] Vol. IV.

[5] Asiat. Soc. Vol. I. p. 335.   [6] Ibid. 336.

" Ἑλληνισμος, Hellenismus, or the Grecian period; this last must appear as extraordinary as any.
" For how was it possible for an Hellenic æra to have existed before the name of Hellas was
" known, or the nation in being ?" I suppose the reader, after having read what I have said relating to the Ionians, does not require an answer to the question. To this Mr. Bryant adds in a
note,—Αι δε των αἱρεσεων πασων μητερες τε και πρωκριτοι και ονομασοι εισιν αυται, Βαρβαρισμος, Σκυθισμος, Ἑλληνισμος, Ιͽδαῖσμος[1]—" In like manner a fourth heresy is supposed to
" have arisen, styled JUDAISMUS, BEFORE THE TIME OF EITHER JEWS OR ISRAELITES."[2] Here the
tribe of Yadu, or Judai, or Ioud, of which I have treated, is evident, which these fathers could not
help seeing, but of which they could not understand the origin or meaning.

6. The existence of the Ionian or Hellenistic heresy, as well as its antiquity, is clearly recog-
nized by several of the fathers. Eusebius[3] says, Σερυχ, 'ςις πρωτος ηρξατο τυ Ἑλληνισμυ:
Serug was the first who introduced the false worship called Hellenismus. Epiphanius says, [4]
Ραγαμ γεννα τον Σερυχ, και ηρξατο εις ανθρωπυς ἡ ειδολολατρεια τε, και ὁ Ἑλληνισμος—
Ragem or Ragan had for his son Seruch, when idolatry and Hellenismus first began among men.
Johannes Antiochenus styles the people of Midian, Hellenes, and speaking of Moses, who married
the daughter of Jethro, the Cuthite, the chief priest of Midian, he represents the woman[5] την
θυγατερα Ιοθορ τυ αρχιερεως των Ἑλληνων, as the daughter of Jother, the high-priest of the
Hellenes. The introduction or adoption of Hellenism or Ionism by Serug, several generations before Abraham, is as much in favour of my hypothesis as any thing can be.

Apollodorus[6] says, Hellen was the firstborn of Deucalion by Pyrrha; though some make him
the son of Jove or Dios. There was also a daughter Protogeneia, so named from being the first-
born of women. Manetho[7] says, that the learning of Egypt was styled Hellenic, from the Hellenic shepherds, and the ancient theology of the country was described in the Hellenic character
and language. This theology was said to be derived from Agathodæmon, by Syncellus.[8] These
Hellenic shepherds, I suppose, were the Pallestini or Palli, whom we meet with in many places,
and whom, in Syria, we call Philistines. But what were the Hellenic character and language ?
I do not know. Scarcely any question is more difficult to answer (when all the circumstances are
considered) ; but yet I think it was probably only a sixteen-letter system.

7. Mr. Franklin says, "Another striking instance is recorded by the very intelligent traveller
" (Wilson) regarding a representation of the fall of our first parents, sculptured in the magnificent
" temple of Ipsambul in Nubia. He says that a very exact representation of Adam and Eve in
" the Garden of Eden is to be seen in that cave, and that the serpent climbing round the tree is
" especially delineated, and the whole subject of the tempting of our first parents most accurately
" exhibited."[9] How is the fact of the Mythos of the second book of Genesis being found in
Nubia, probably a thousand miles above Heliopolis, to be accounted for, except that it came from
Upper India with the first Buddhists or Gymnosophists? There they were found by Clemens
Alexandrinus, and there they founded a Meru, now called Meroe. The same Mythos is found in
India. Col. Tod says, "A drawing, brought by Colonel Coombs, from a sculptured column in a
" cave-temple in the South of India, represents the first pair at the foot of the ambrosial tree, and

---

[1] Chrou. Paschall. p. 23; Epiphan. Lib. i. p. 9; Euseb. Chron. p. 13.   [2] Bryant's Anal. Vol. III. p. 151.

[3] Chron. p. 13.   [4] Hæres. Lib. i. Cap. vi. p. 7.   [5] Pp. 76, 77.   [6] Lib. i. p. 20.

[7] Ap. Euseb. Chron. p. 6.   [8] P. 40; Bryant. Anal. Anc. Myth. Vol. III. p. 157.

[9] On Buddhists and Jeynes, p. 127, Note.

" a serpent entwined among the heavily-laden boughs, presenting to them some of the fruit from
" his mouth.   The tempter appears to be at that part of his discourse, when

> ———————————— his words, replete with guile,
> Into her heart too easy entrance won :
> Fixed on the fruit she gazed.'

" This is a curious subject to be engraved on an ancient Pagan temple : if Jain or Buddhist, the
" interest would be considerably enhanced." [1]   No doubt it would be enhanced, but not I think
so much as the Colonel apprehends.   The same mythos, as the Romish Dr. Geddes calls Genesis,
is at the bottom of the religions of Moses, India, and Egypt, with such small variations only as
time and circumstance may be expected to produce.   We will not forget this mythos, when we
treat, in a future book, of the religion of South India.   It is the mythos which we have just now
noticed in Upper Egypt.   In my plates, fig. 27, may be seen a copy of one of the groups of figures
in Montfaucon.   However it may differ, can any one doubt that it is allusive to the Pentateuchian
or Mosaic mythos?   See also fig. 16.

8. Although Sion or Moriah, or the Syrian Meru, was a high-place, yet we find high-places
every where reprobated in the Old Testament, in the most pointed terms.   This is because they
had become in a peculiar manner dedicated in these countries to the Ionic worship—to Ionism or
Hellenism.   This is proved by the name given them by the LXX.—πορνειον, Lupanar.   This
again confirms what I have said respecting the Jews being attached to the exclusive *male* generative power.   In these places, called πορνεια, they had cells or adyta which the Greeks called
Naïda, where the secret and licentious rites of the Ionic worship were celebrated.   I have before
observed that I suspect that from these places, built of an oblong form in imitation of the Hindoo
Argha or Nav or Kibotos or Tibe, came the naves of our churches, and that their inhabitants were
the Naïdæ ; and if in consequence of the performance of these rites a boy was born, he was considered sacred ; in a peculiar manner dedicated to the priesthood, and educated by them with the
greatest care.   These Naïdæ were nothing more nor less than the dancing girls, who are now
found in the temples of India.   In the temple of Venus at Corinth, a thousand of them were kept.
Calmet says there were dancing girls in the Temple of Jerusalem.   No doubt our prudes will be
angry with me for repeating what Calmet has let out, but for my own part I must freely confess, I
like the girls, with all their sins, better than the nasty Galli.

Throughout all the ancient world the distinction between the followers of the Yoni and Linga
may be seen.   All nations seem to have been Ionians except the Jews and Persians ; and, as the
Jewish or *male* principle prevailed, the other declined.

---

[1] Tod's Hist. Raj. p. 581.

CHAPTER III

Names of Places—Rajpouts. Rannæ of Ptolemy—Indian Chronology—Ajimere—
Mount Sion—Sion and Hierosolyma—Various Mounts of Solyma: Temples of
Solomon—Jerusalem: Jesulmer—Meaning of Jerusalem—Temple of Solomon
in Cushmere.

1. We will now examine the names of some of the states and cities in India, and in them I think we shall find conclusive proofs of the place where Judaism came from, and probably along with it the first written language.

In India, in very ancient times, there was a state of great power. Its capital was in lat. 26° 48′ N., long. 82° 4′ E., of prodigious extent, being one of the largest of Hindostan, anciently called Ayodhya or Oude. It was, and yet is, a place celebrated for its sanctity, to which Pilgrims resort from all parts of India. The Hindoo history states that it was the seat of power, of a great prince called Dasaratha, the father of Rama, and of Rama, the brother of Cristna. Dasaratha extended his conquests as far as Ceylon, which he subdued. We shall find in a future page, from the similarity of the mythos in South India to that of Oude, reason to believe this story of the conquest to be substantially true. Ayodhia or Iyodhya is nothing but Judia, and Oude, Juda. Iyodhia is Iyo-di-ia—country of the sacred Iou, or Jud. I shall return many times to this etymon.

I feel little doubt that the tribe of Iaoud was expelled from this kingdom, perhaps from Maturea, from which place they took their names. Every difficulty will be removed if we suppose that the religious wars of the sects of the Ioni and Linga were long, and had alternate successes; and this perfectly agrees with the Hindoo histories, which represent the wars to have been long, and of this description. The cities above-named are situated a little Westward of Tibet. The tribe of Ioud or the Brahmin Abraham, was expelled from or left the Maturea of the kingdom of Oude in India, and, settling at Goshen, or *the house of the Sun* or Heliopolis in Egypt, gave it the name of the place which they had left in India, Maturea. I beg my reader to look back to Book V. Ch. VIII. Sect. 1, for all the striking circumstances of connexion, for a vast number of years, between the tribe of Abraham and Heliopolis. Let him also consider what I said just now, respecting this same city of destruction, being called the city of Seth or Typhon, and of Abaris or Avaris, that is, of the Hebrews.

We have seen that the City of Avaris was probably called Abaris, which meant Strangers or Hebrews, and close to it was the mount of Ieudieh. Bryant[1] shews that this Avaris was called Cercasora, which will turn out to be the same as the Calisa-pura in the kingdom of Ioudya or Oude, in India.[2] Thus we shall connect Maturea, Judah, and Abraham together, and, as I have suggested, the doctrines of Cristna or the Lamb.

There is an account of the Hyperborean called *Abaris,* viz. that he came into Greece carrying in his hand the arrow of Apollo, which served him as a passport through all countries. Col. Tod[3] has given an instance of the arrow of a tribe from the kingdom of Oude being made use of as a passport, exactly in the same manner. Coincidences of this kind appear trifling, but they are in reality very important. They render it probable, that the same mythos is in both countries.

Abraham came from Mesopotamia of the Chaldees.[4] This precisely answers to the situation

---

[1] Vol. III. p. 260, 4to.
[2] Vide Book V. Chap. VI. Sect. 6, of this work.
[3] Hist. Rajapoutana.
[4] Acts vii. 2—4.

of Mutra or Maturea on the Jumna. It is the country of the ancient kingdom of Oude between the two rivers Ganges and Indus, and is called Duab or Mesopotamia, as I have before stated. He probably came just before the change of the worship took place, from Taurus to Aries, from Buddha to Cristna.

Let us suppose, for the sake of argument, that a tribe or sect was expelled from India. Is it not natural to expect, that when they settled in a distant country they would give the same names to their new habitations after they had conquered or acquired them, as those places bore which they left? And if this were the case, is it not probable, that though several thousand years may have since passed, the names of the new settlements should be found in the old country? Thus it is: and as this was a sect, or national religion widely extended, and not the inhabitants of a town merely, it happens that we have names of places in the country near the Mediterranean where they settled, which are found in many parts of India, in Siam, Pegu, Tibet, &c.

I beg my reader to refer to the Map which is taken partly from those of Bishop Heber and Col. Tod, and he will find the kingdom of Oude, anciently Ayodhia, in a district called Agra, in which is a city, called anciently Argha[1] or Agra. It was in ruins in the time of Akbar—and was rebuilt by him and called Akberabad.[2] He will also find a place called Daoud-nagur, that is Dud (דוד dud) or David-nagur. Nagur means fort or walled town. There is also a district called Daod-potra, that is, town of the sons of David. Thus we have a city of David and a country of the children or sons of David.

Maturea has been before noticed in Egypt and on the Jumna, or Jamuna, or Yamuna. There is also a city in the same country called Joud-poor, or Yuddapoor, or the city of Jud, where Bishop Heber says are the ruins of a magnificent city. This is called by called Col. Tod Oole-poor : it is about lat. 24½, long. 73¾. There are also several other towns of the same name. There is also, in about lat. 26½, and long. 73, a city called, by Col. Tod, Jodpoor, with a district of the same name. About lat. 27 and long. 76, may be seen a town called Jeipour, with a district of the same name. There is also, about lat. 26, long. 78, a district called Jado-ouwatti. Bishop Heber says, the king of the country of Joud or Jud-poor, is called Malek, that is, in correct Hebrew, the King.[3] All these places, as well as Delhi and Benares, were included in the kingdom of Oud, or Ayodhia, or Juda.

There are three places in a triangle between 25 and 30 degrees of latitude, and about 73 of longitude, in the kingdom of Oude or Juda—the first, called Oudipour, or Cheitore, or Meywar, or Midwar; the second, Joodpour, or Yuddapoor; the third, called Ambeer, or Amere, or Joinagur, or Jyenagur, or Jyepour.[4] I need not remind my reader that he must strike off the syllable pour or poor, which means place or town, and then he will have the real name. As we may expect from its name Midwar or Medway in English, Oudipore or Cheitore is in the middle of the other two. My reader may smile at this observation, but the farther back he goes, the more numerous he will find these kinds of extraordinary coincidences. They are the words of an universal and very old language. In some of the Northern nations Day is called Var. This is similar to Midwar and Medway, Med or Mid-day.

The river Chelum, or Jalum, or Jhylun, or Behut, or Jenaut[5] has on its West side the country of the Joudis, at the foot of the mountains of Joud. There is also a place or district in this country called Seba or Siba. There is also a tribe called Jajoohahs, which descended from the

---

[1] Heber.

[2] A district of Jerusalem was called Acra: this must have been Arga, as it is not likely that this city should have a quarter called by a Greek name.

[3] Vol. I. p. 368.   [4] See Rennell's Memoir, p. cxxxii.   [5] Rennell, p. 98.

Joudis. Here are the Jews, descended from Judah. In the mountains of Solomon are found a tribe of people called Judoons,[1] (that is, Judæans,) and a place called Gosa, (that is Gaza,) and a people called Jadrauns, and another called Jaujees (Jews).[2] The mountains of Solomon, or Solimaun, have this name in the old books, though they are not commonly known at this time by it.[3] These mountains are higher than the Andes.[4] One of the mounts of the chain is called Suffaid Coh.[5] The Sofees of Persia are called Suffarees.[6] In this country, also, is the city of Enoch, the Anuchta of Ptolemy.

Col. Tod says,[7] the traditions of the Hindoos assert that India was first peopled or colonized by a race called *Yadu*, to which they trace the foundations of the most conspicuous of their ancient cities.[8] The Yadus are in the unpolished dialect pronounced Jadu or Jadoons.[9] The *Eusofzyes*, or tribe of *Joseph*, is also called Jadoons, that is, Judæans.

2. The country of Cheitore or Oudipore belongs to the tribe called Rajpoots, their chief called by the title of Rana. In Ptolemy they are called Rhannæ.[10] They are a most warlike tribe, and, in fact, have never been permanently subdued. They are the warrior tribe noticed by Arrian and Diodorus. Not far from the above is a town called Ajimere, the Gagasmira of Ptolemy.[11]

Father Georgius admits the truth of what I have said respecting the names of the Indian places: he says, Regnum Ayiodia alias Avod (meaning Ayodia and Oude) ex depravato nomine Jehuda, seu Jeuda. He then shews that *Giodu*, Giadu, Giadubansi, are all the same as the יהודה *ieude* of the Hebrews, and he gives the following translation of a passage of the Bagavan : " Ipse (Cristna) " salvabit Gentem suam Gioda nempe Pastorum : vitam dabit bonis : interficiet Gigantes : " relinquet Gokul, et Madiapur : agnoscetur ab universo terrarum orbe : et nomen ejus invo- " cabunt omnes, Divinum est vaticinium : nec dubita, haud : sic erit." Of course all with the monk, is clearly copied from the kingdom of Juda, which Herodotus could not find. Is it possible for any proof to be more clear than this, of the truth of the theory advocated by me, of the double mythos in Eastern and Western Syria ?

3. I shall not attempt to enter into the history or chronology of India ; I consider that it is so contaminated with nonsense and fraud, that it is merely soiling paper to transcribe it. The Grecian heroic times are sense compared to it. I will give one specimen, from which a comparison may be made with all the others. Parasu Rama, who lived since the time of Christ, looking down from a hill on the sea-shore, saw some dead Brahmins. These by magic he brought to life, and from them descended the Ranas of Udaya-pur, as Major Wilford calls it, to disguise the true name, the *city of Judea*.[12] This is a fair specimen of the way in which the lost origin of the various tribes is accounted for. Ex uno disce omnes. From this I shall be told that these Rannas are of modern date, but Ptolemy's notice of them, as well as of Gazamera or Ajimere, settles this question. They were kings of one of the very old cities of the tribe of Joudi, miscalled or disguised by the name of Udaya-pur. Col. Tod gives it its proper name and calls it *Ioude*, or Oudipore. The notice of the Rannæ, by Ptolemy, shews that the tribe was in existence before the dispersion of the Jews in the time of Vespasian. In the attempt to discover the truth in questions of this kind, it is very seldom that a proof of a fact can be obtained, but I think it is obtained respecting the RANNÆ of Oudipore. They were evidently here in the time of Ptolemy, and they are yet remaining. There can be no shadow of pretence to set up that they have been destroyed by the

---

[1] Elphins. Vol. II. p. 99.   [2] Ib.   [3] Ib. Tab. Vol. I. p. 148.   [4] Ib. p. 155.

[5] Ib. p. 156.   [6] Ib. p. 257.   [7] Trans. Royal Asiat. Soc. Vol. III. pp. 1, 141.

[8] For a sketch of this race see An. Rajastan, Vol. I. p. 85.   [9] Ibid. p. 86.   [10] Rennell, p. 153.

[11] Rennell, p. 145.   [12] Asiat. Res. Vol. IX. p. 238.

Mohamedans, and the city of Oude or Oudi-pore built by Mohamedans, and since that time a new tribe of Rannæ set up. The city of Gagasmera or Ajimere confirms this. The city of Oudepore is very large, and carries on the face of it marks of extreme antiquity. If the antiquity of the city of Oude or Ioudi-pore, and its Rannæ be considered to be proved, and that they existed before the time of Christ, I think it carries with it pretty good presumptive proof, that all the other towns in its neighbourhood having Jewish or Israelitish names are the same. Then, except as I have accounted for it, how is it to be accounted for?

Delhi, was formerly called Indraprest'ha, and was founded by Yoodishtra. The *shtra* is like the *shtra* in Saurasthra, a termination which I do not understand, but it leaves the Yoodi.[1] The most ancient of the cities of this part of India, are Oude or Yodya, and Agra, the latter of which went to decay, and was rebuilt by Akbar.

Col. Tod says a colony of the Yadu dwelt in the mountains called in Rennell's map Ioudes, when they were expelled from Saurastra. No one can deny that these Yadu or Ioudi dwelt, to use a Bible phrase, in the mountains of Juda. These were the Yadus of *Jess-ul-mer*.[2] These Yadus have now got corrupted into Jadoon.[3] Speaking of Jodpoor, the Colonel says, " The " view will give a more correct idea of the ' City of Joda' than any description."[4] Here the doctrine which I teach is unconsciously adopted by Col. Tod. *Iod* means Joda or Juda.

4. In lat. 26, 31 N. long. 74, 28 E., is the city called Ajimere or Gazamere, the Gazamera of Ptolemy adjoining to a large lake. Here is Gaza, of Syria, and the old English word *mere* for a lake. We have Wittlesey *Mere* near Peterborough, Hornsey *Mere* near Kingston-on-Hull, in the kingdom of *Brigantia*, near the river *Umber*. Is all this accidental? Col. Tod says that the word *mer* in the Hindoo language means *hill*. Then it will be the *hill* of Aji. But the expression of Ptolemy shews, that the two words Aji and Gaza are the same. The word which we call Gaza, in the Hebrew is written עזה *oza*. This means Goat, the same as Aje—which tends to prove that the original must have been Aji. The lake of Potsha is close by Ajimere, and the town of Gaza being on the sea, the word *mer* must mean both hill, and the Latin Mare, or Meris, or Mæris, a lake —the Hebrew מרה *mre* or מרר *mrr*.[5]

Col. Tod explains the word Jerusalem to mean Mer-Jesul or Hill of Jessul. The double meaning of the word Mer arises from all these sacred mounts being imitative Merus. Thus they might be all called Mer. Meru, we must recollect, was a hill in a sea, or surrounded by an oceanus. And from this the two came to be confounded. But this will be more clearly shewn presently.

The river anciently called Pontus, in Thrace, is now by the Turks called *Mer*, and the lake into which it runs, Mer-mer: whence I am justified in concluding that the word Mer meant lake, in the old language, before it was changed or translated, by the Greeks, into Pontus.

No one can doubt that Casimere or Cashmere was called from the lake which probably once filled its valley. This again fixes one of the meanings of the word *Mere*.

5. The missionary Dr. Buchanan states his opinion, that the religion of Buddha arose near Tibet. He names a river of Siam, which rises near the frontiers of China, and which is in the Burman empire; and he gives a description of a most holy imaginary mountain in the same empire called Sian.[6] I think it probable that the kingdom of Siam had its name and religion from this country. Here we have the Sion referred to by Loubere, in Book V. Chap. III. Sect. 8. The Siamese, he states to be called Yoo-dă-ya, which, he observes, is nothing but Judæi.

Tod's Hist. Raj. p. 87.   • Hist. Raj. pp. 61, 62.   ' Ib. p. 86.   ⁴ Ib. p. 709.
• Littleton, Dic.   ⁶ Asiat. Res. Vol. VI. p. 242.

Mount Sion is a mystic mount, and came from the Mount Zion of the Burmese empire, or of the kingdom of Siam, or as La Loubère says of the Sions—for there seems to have been a ridge of them, like the ridge of the Alpes. It is the mount of the Gods or of happy beings,[1] in the kingdom of Siam—the mount where the Gods reside, and there were several of these mounts above one another for different orders of beings; and though I have no authority for the assertion, I have no doubt that they were *on the sides of the North.* In short, Sion meaning the holy mount was Mount Meru. There were seven heavens before the throne of God. The word צין *ziun,* in Hebrew, correctly means *a stone mount,* and has also the meaning of the stone Carn of the Western nations. Mr. Turner observed the same Carns in Tibet. They are equally found in Iona of the Hebrides. Every person in passing these mounts thinks it an act of piety to add a stone to them. There is also a mystical Zion in Ceylon, where the Samaritan Pentateuch places Mount Ararat. The Cingales' traditions state them to have come from the land of Ava, that is, of Eva.

In the Buddhist doctrines of Ceylon, the Mount Zian, or *triumphing heaven,* makes a great figure.[2] It is called a place of SALVATION. It is evidently like the Mount Zion of the Jews a mystical mount, having in reality the same name. The etymology of the word Sion I reserve to a future book.

The ancient name of Thibet or Tibet was Baltistan; that is, the place of Balti, or Baaltis, of Syria.[3]

Mr. Faber has shewn, that the city of Sidon, in Syria, where the God Dagon was adored, had its name from an oriental city on the Erythrean Sea called Sidon; but Trogus says that the Erythrean Sidon was not the original settlement of the Sidonians, *but that they came from a more Eastern part.*[4]

6. The following observations of Nimrod's will pretty well shew us the origin of the famous Mount Moriah or Sion of the Jews. Coming as they do from so good a Greek and Latin scholar, and at the same time from a devotee and unwilling witness, with the impartial inquirer they will command the greatest respect. " Belerophon fought against the female host of the Amazonians. " He fought also with the Solymi, a circumstance which tends to identify him with Memnon, who, " on his way to relieve Troy, met and overthrew

" Αργαλεων Σολυμων ιερω ςρατον. [5]

" Immediately behind Phaselis, of Pamphylia, rose Mount Solymus, and close to it (probably one " of its peaks) Mount OLYMPUS,[6] called also Φοινιχοεις, or *the red.* Also, a Lophos, or conical " hill over Termessus, of Pisidia, was called Σολυμος Λοφος, and hard by it a work of antiquity, " called the rampart of Belerophon or mound: χαραξ.[7] A mount Solymus was, like Ida to " Jove, the σκοπιη, or seat of speculation, to the Ethiopian Neptune.

Των δ εξ Αιθιοπων ανιων κρειων Ενοσιχθων
Τηλοθεν εκ Σολυμων ορεων ιδεν. [8]

" In fact, it was one of the many names used among the nations for an Olymp, or sacrificial and " oracular high place. In the maritime Syria there was a very famous city of immemorial

---

[1] Asiat. Res. Vol. VI. p. 187.
[2] Upham's History of Buddhism, p. 74.
[3] Lett. Edif. Vol. XV. p. 188.
[4] Orig. Pag. Idol. Vol. III. p. 562.
[5] Qu. Sm. L. ii. ver. 120; Herod. L. i. C. clxxiii.; Steph. Byz. in voce Milym.
[6] Strabo, L. xiv. p. 952.
[7] Vide Strabo, L. xiii. p. 904.
[8] Hom. Od. L. v. ver. 283.

" sanctity, and containing within its purlieus several mounts dedicated to the mysteries of the
" Syrian or IONIAN religion, especially the Mount Moriah or Olivet, and the Mount Sion. This
" city, founded by the Jebusite Canaanites, was called Solyma, and, by way of honour, Hiero-
" Solyma. It was taken from its subsequent possessors, the Jews and Benjamites, by Nebuchad-
" nezzar the Great, a prince of the Syrian religion, which heresy he raised to an unexampled pitch
" of splendour: and out of the spoils of Hiero-Solyma he founded a new city, Solyma,[1] in
" Assyria."[2]

Again, Nimrod says, " This place, Hiero-Solyma, was not occupied by the chosen people till
" the time of Joshua,[3] but it was solemnly consecrated to the uses of the Christian worship in
" the days of Abraham, by the symbolical offering of his son: and the same Abraham having
" vanquished a league of kings, met in the neighbourhood, with a personage named Melchisedek,
" king of Salem, who initiated him into the mysteries of the Christian sacrament. Sacrifice,
" with immolation and libation, was appointed for anticipation of an atonement to come: but the
" two latter were thought sufficient for the commemoration thereof when complete........We
" are not told what place it was that was called *Salem*, but we find the Israelites, when in pos-
" session of Hiero-Solym, invariably calling it Jeru-salem, Behold peace: and Josephus, who was
" ignorant of the nature and character of Melchisedek, and mistook him for some Jebusite
" prince,[4] informs us, that he first gave to the city, Jerusalem, its present name. Here then we
" have the truth: the name Solym was changed to Salem, and Hiero-Solym to Hieru-Salem."[5]

Notwithstanding some nonsense and several mistakes, here are several very important admissions
of Nimrod's, as we shall presently see. What I have said before respecting the change of Salem to
Jerusalem is here confirmed. The meaning of the present name Jerusalem is, according to our
divines, *he shall see peace*. But perhaps, like many other mythic words, it had two meanings.

Nimrod seems to have forgotten that Eupolemus tells us, that Melchizedek lived at Gerizim.[6]
Before I proceed further with the meaning of the word Jerusalem, we must discuss several other
circumstances connected with it.

7. The Solymi are named by Homer, and there were a people noticed of that name in Lycia, in
Asia Minor, a province adjoining to Pisidia. I suspect that they were a sect driven out of India
to the West, and the builders of Jerusalem, or Hiero-Solyma, the Sacred Solyma. I learn from
the author of Nimrod, that Memnon was said to have fought the Solymi,[7] that is, that the sun
fought them. This might mean that they were driven from the East. There were *fourteen* Bads or
Buddhas, or incarnations of divine wisdom under that name. There were also *fourteen* incarnations
of divine wisdom under the name of Menu. And there were *fourteen* Soleimans, all, perhaps,
different names for the same mythos. But in the Jewish books we only read of *one* Menu, and
one Noah, or of *one* Solomon, *the Wise*.

I now beg my reader to reflect upon the fact, of Sanscrit words being found in the Latin and
Greek languages. This done, he will probably not be surprised to find Latin words in India. He
will recollect that the temples or sacred places in Judæa were called אל בית *bit al*, or house of
God, and Solomon built a house to the Lord, by which name of house, the temple of Jerusalem,
in a very pointed manner, was called. Thus, this being premised, the next place which I shall

---

[1] Asin. Quadr. Ap. Steph. Byz. in. voce.   [2] Nimrod, Vol. I. Sup. Ed. p. 96.

[3] Joshua, that is Jesus, that is the Saviour, the son of Nave, that is *of the boat*, or the Argha, or the female generative power: note of the author's, not Nimrod's.

[4] No mistake—note by G. H., not by Nimrod.   [5] Ibid. p. 97.

[6] On this point Josephus is not evidence. He is a partisan.   [7] Vol. I. p. 98.

notice is Tucte Soliman—this, is tectum, or house of Solomon. It is one of the five sacred mounts, Merus or Olympuses or Solymi of India. It is not far from the hills called the mountain or ridge of Solyman. But the Tucte Soleymans, or houses of Soleiman, were not confined to India.

In Morier's Travels in Persia, (see plates, Fig. 28,) may be seen a building, the style of which at once proves its great antiquity. It is called Madré Soleiman. On seven towers of Cyclopean architecture, stands a square house, with pitched roof, formed of large stones projecting one over the other, like the roof of the cave at New Grange, in Ireland, the cave at Mysenæ, the walls of Tyrins, and the temple of Komulmar, described by Col. Tod, in the history of Rajapoutana. The Persians attribute it to Soleiman, but modern learned men think they have made out, that it is the tomb of Cyrus.[1] They may please themselves with this fancy; but the style, the traditional name, the seven steps, and the square building at the top, all joined together, pretty well satisfy me that it is a tecte Soleiman. If it had been the tomb of their great Cyrus, it would never have lost its name or designation. I would ask, what has a Madré Soleiman to do in Persia, according to our construction of the text of the Jewish historians? Though the Persians say that Abraham was their ancestor—they do not say his successors, a thousand years afterward, were their ancestors. Then how came they to think of Soleiman as the author of this building? I think it probable, under these circumstances, that this is not the building alluded to by Arrian, Curtius, Pliny, &c., in their account of the visit to it of Alexander the Great,[2] but one of the same nature as the Merus of India. I consider the traditional name of the building, among the ignorant natives, as better authority than Greek historians. For I again ask, how could the name of Solomon come here among the unlearned natives? Persons are struck, at first, with the connexion between Abraham, whom, as just mentioned, the Persians claim for their ancestor, and Solomon. But such persons do not attend to the circumstance of the dates, which shew that, even admitting Abraham to have been the ancestor of the Persians, this gives them no interest whatever in the son of Bathsheba, Abraham's descendant, who never was in Persia, or had any connexion with it.

The Persian romances say, that there were seventy or seventy-two rulers, called Suleiman, before Noah: this has an obvious relation to the seventy-one Manwantaras of the Hindus,[3] and evidently is the same history as the seventy-two Soleimans alluded to before in this work.

Perse-polis, or the city of Perse, in Greek, was called in Persian Tucht-i-Gemsheed; from which we may infer that this fabulous king was the Perseus of the Greeks, who was the Sun.[4]

Thus, Tucht-i-Gemsheed being the same as *city of Gemshid*, we come to the conclusion that Tucht-i-Soleiman is the same as *the city of Soleiman*. Here we arrive at an important truth by recourse to my system of applying to several languages, and going, in fact, to the first system of letters and written language, as far as we can get. No one will doubt the identity of these Tuctis.

Nimrod says, " The Mahabadian line is nothing but the succession of antediluvian patriarchs;"[5] that is, a supposed succession of re-incarnations of Buddha, or the Sun in Taurus. Maha-Bad is Great Bud. He says, *After this line* came Gemshid or Perseus, whose emblem was a Lamb, which is yet common on medals struck in his honour.

A very important observation has been made by Sir R. Ker Porter,—that he found the traits of resemblance striking and numerous, betwixt the ruins of the temples of Persepolis and the description of the temple of Solomon.[6]

---

[1] But query, was not Cyrus a Solomon?   [5] Vide Hale's Chronology, p. 111.

[3] Asiat. Res. Vol. VI. p. 524, and also Vol. X. p. 93.   [4] Nimrod, Vol. I. p. 141.

[5] Vol. I. p. 141.   [6] P. 700, Cruezer, p. 676.

In Porter's Travels[1] may be found the description of the remains of a city called *Tackt-i-Soli-mon* of very great and unknown antiquity. This city of ancient ruins has been thoughtlessly ascribed to the 15th Calif. Another of these places called *Tuckt-i-Suleiman*, or *the throne of Suliema*, may be found described in Vol. I. p. 485. Pliny calls this place Pasargada, and says, that here is the tomb of Cyrus, by whom it was built.

If my reader will consult Pococke's Travels,[2] he will see good reason to believe that Solomon's gardens and pools in Syria were gardens of Daphne or a Meru. Though Pococke did not in the least understand the subject, he could not help observing that " it is probable there were *hanging* "*gardens* on the side of the hill." The plate describes a perfect Meru with its seven hills one above another, and its mount; on which Pococke observes, "probably the house stood at the top."

In Asia Minor, near Telmessus, noticed before, there were Solymean mountains, one of these of great height, called Takhta-lu by the present Turks, was called formerly by the Greeks *Mount Solyma*. Here is, I think, the Tekte Solyma of the Hindoos of Rajapoutana. Here is also an example of the old name returning to the place. I think no one can refuse his assent to the identity of these two curious names, Tecte Solyma and Takhta-lu Solyma.[3]

Josephus says, that the Jews assisted the Persians against Greece. He cites the poet Choerilus, who, he says, names a people who dwelt on the Solymean mountains of Asia Minor, and spoke Phœnician. Bochart, not knowing what to make of this, supposes that what he alluded to was a colony of Phœnicians, who had settled in Asia Minor, near to the lake Phaselis. The colony here spoken of, I think, were from Tekte Solymi : they were Ioudi, which is confirmed by their *sooty heads, like horses' heads dried in the smoke*, and their having the Tonsure,[4] or shaven crown, which, Bochart has shewn, was prohibited to the Jews ; and, by the fact of the prohibition, shews that it had once existed. The Buddhists of Tibet have the tonsure.

It is observed by Mercator, that, by the poets, Jerusalem was called Solyma or Solumæ. From Josephus, it appears, that there was a Mount Solyma, near the lake Asphaltes, in Judea.[5]

8. About lat. 27 N. and long. 71 E. on Col. Tod's map will be found the place called JESULMER. I learn from the Colonel's work, that it is a place of very great antiquity, and in a peculiar manner sacred among the Buddhists. In one of the temples is a very large library, and in the centre of it, suspended by a chain of gold in a golden case, is a most sacred, holy manuscript, which is expressly forbidden to be read or even looked upon. It is believed that any person reading it would be instantly struck blind. Some time ago the prince of the country caused it to be brought to him, in order that he might read it ; but his courage failed, and he sent back the virgin unde-flowered, and thus it will probably remain till some *sacrilegious European* lays hands on it. These circumstances shew, I think, that the city of Jesulmer is no common place : and now I beg my reader to transpose the letters of this word Jesulmer, and he will find they make Jeruselm. Take this by itself and the fact would be of little consequence, but couple it with all the other circum-stances—with the names of the other towns which I have pointed out, and I defy the unprejudiced reader to divest his mind of a strong suspicion, that the Jerusalem of the West is the Jesulmer of the East, or vice versa.[6] Jesulmer changed into Jeruselm, is nothing but an example of the prac-tice called *Themeru* or changing, of the tribe of Ioudi of writing words in the way called anagram-matical.[7] It is quite surprising to what a length this foolish and childish practice was carried

[1] Vol. II. p. 557.   [2] Fol. Ed. Vol. I. p. 44.
[3] Drummond's Orig Vol. IV. pp. 90—93.   [4] Ibid. pp. 94, 95.   [5] Ibid. pp. 90, 93.
[6] A little to the south of Jesulmer, about lat. 26, is a town called Iunah, the old name of Antioch.
[7] Ency. Britt. voce Anagram.

even in modern times. John Calvinus called himself Alcuinus. When a person observes the variety of ways in which the names of these cities and countries are written into English by our Indian travellers from the old dialects of the country, (I do not speak of the Sanscrit,) he will be willing to allow a very considerable latitude. Scarcely any two of them use the same letters, though the striking similitude to the Jewish names is apparent in them all.

9. The meaning of Jeru-salem is *the sacred ladder*, סלם *slm* in Hebrew; סולמא *sulma* in Chaldee. The LXX.[1] render סלם *slm* solim, by κλίμαξ, and Jerom by *scala*. The Mount Climax of Strabo, in Asia Minor, was called Mount *Solim* or *Solima* by the natives; and Climax was only a Greek translation of the oriental name.[2] I *suspect* that the name of the town of the inhabitants of Tel-messus, who lived close to Mount Solyma, and who were called Solymi,[3] was a mere corruption of סלם *slm;* that, in a similar way, the word Jesulmer of India is a corruption from the same name, like the name of the Syrian Meru, called Moriah, or Sion, or Argha or Arca, or Solyma. The city of Jerusalem is spelt with a Shin and not a Samech. The Samech being one of the new letters, if the *sixteen* letter system be true, this makes nothing against my argument; for in all this I must be supposed to speak of a time, before the letters of the alphabets were increased, when the *Shin* must have been used. Our priests will tell me that שלם *slm*, or salem, means *peace*. But the passages of Strabo, Jerom, and the LXX., compared with the circumstances relating to the town in Asia Minor, shew pretty well what was the original meaning. But it is very likely that it took the meaning of *peace* from being the name of the mount of peace, Mount Sion.

Ἱερος, in Greek, means *sacred*, and I suspect it has come from some Asiatic word now lost, or at least unknown to me. And when I consider the form of Meru, step above step, the Madré Soly-man of Persia, and the rendering of the word סלם *slm* in the LXX. by κλίμαξ, and in the Vulgate by *scala*, and the same word סלם *slm* used for Jacob's ladder, seen at Bit-al or *the house of God*, on which seventy-two angels ascended and descended, I suspect that the Hiero, ירה *ire* means sacred, the sacred ladder, or the sacred mount. It is what the Greeks called Olympus. The Bit-al, Bethel, or house of God, which Jacob's place of the ladder was called, is not unlike the Tectum of the Solymi. We must also remember that Solomon, an incarnation of wisdom, is closely connected with the wisdom of the Buddhists. The observation respecting the similarity of the Tectum of Solyman or Tucte Soleyman to the בית אל *hit al* of Genesis, is the more striking, because I learn from my friend Col. Tod, (who lived at a little distance from the Tucte-Soleyman for almost twenty years, who speaks the language of the country with ease, and who actually made a survey of it,) that, in the language of the country generally, a temple is called Beeth-el, which means Edifice or House of the Sun. He says, that though the language of the country is not Sanscrit, yet entire sentences may sometimes be found which betray the Sanscrit; and that it has many words which must have come from some language of central Asia.

10. But of all the temples of Solomon, I consider none of more importance than the Tact Solomon or Tecte Soleiman, which is found in Cashmere. "Mr. Forster was so much struck "with the general appearance, garb, and manners, of the Cashmerians, as to think he had suddenly "been transported among a nation of Jews."[4] The same idea was *impressed* upon the mind of Mons. Bernier, on his visiting that country. This Cashmerian temple of Solomon will be found of great consequence. Father Georgius, who was master of the Tibetian language, quotes the story of Anobret from Sanchoniathon, and shews that the *Jeud* of Sanchoniathon is the *Jid* of the Tibe-tians. *Jid a Tibetanis Butta tributum.* יהיד *ieid Jehid* Isaaci epithetum est, Gen. xxii. 2; et *Jid* Tibetanorum *idem ac Jehid* Phœnicium et Egyptium.[5] Thus we have the mount or house or

---

[1] Gen. xxxiii 12.   [2] Drummond's Origines, Vol. IV. p. 99.   [3] Ib. p. 92.

[4] Vol. II. p. 21.   [5] Val. Col. Hib. Vol. V. p. 314.

habitation of Solomon or Solyma in India, or the country of Ioud, or of Daud-poutri, or of the sons of David; in Persia, the *Madré Solyma*, and the same also in Palestine and in Asia Minor; and all, in some way or other, connected with the tribe of Ioudi. Can any one believe all this to be the effect of accident ? Solomon was a personification or incarnation of wisdom, and the Jews of Asia Minor were a tribe or colony from India, of black Buddhists, at or about the same time with the Ioudi to Syria, under the Brahmin.

CHAPTER IV

Mount of Solomon, Mount of Cabala—Mount Olympus—Afghans. Ioudi—Turks —Afghans speak Chaldee, Pushto, and Hebrew—Arabia on the Indus—The Thousand Cities of Strabo. Peculiarities in Eastern and Western Syria

1. Mr. Bryant[1] observes, that Strabo speaks of a city of the Solymi, in Mesopotamia, called Cabalis, which he explains, *the city of the God Bal.* It may have been a city of Bal, but that was not the reason of its name. It had its name *Cbl* or *Gbl* from the secret doctrine of tradition. It had the same name as the Gabala of Western Syria. Lucian, in his treatise De Deâ Syriâ, says expressly, that "Gabala was Byblos, that is, *city of* THE BOOK or Bible, famous for the worship of Adonis." In 1 Kings v. 18, the word נבלים *Gblim* has been translated *stone squarers* or MASONS ; but it means *in- habitants of* נבל *gbl*, or Mount Gibel or Gebel. From this comes the Gabala or Cabala, or chain of traditions. It was[3] the Mountain of Tradition. It was Gabal changed into Cabal, like נמל *gml* the name of the animal changed into that of the Camel, in the western countries. But Bal was Bala-Rama, an incarnation of Buddha. Suppose Abraham or Ioud came from thence, and it was either the Mesopotamia of Eastern or Western Syria, the Cabalis would be *the city of the traditionary doctrine.* This Cabalis also looks very like Cabul. I only throw out this for consideration, with the single observation, that it is very evident the Jews do not know the meaning of the word Cabala ; and whether Christians be any wiser is very doubtful.

2. Mount Olympuses are found in many places. These, I apprehend, are the high places reprobated in scripture ; but they were all known under different names, the same as the Merus of India and the Tecte Soleimans. This is pretty well proved by the fact, that the God Jupiter, who is called Jupiter Olympus by Jason of Cyrene and Ammianus, is, by Johannes Malalas, called Jupiter *Bottius*. Bottius is equivalent to Buddæus. [3]

Salivahana was King of Pratishtana, called also *Saileyadhara*, or simply Saileyam in a derivative form. [4] An ancient treatise of authority says, that Salivahana would appear at Saileya-d'hara, or *the city firmly seated on a rock*, which compound alludes to the city of Sion, *whose* foundations are upon the holy hills ; "the city of our God, even upon his holy hill." *Saileyam* would be a very appropriate name, for it is also, in a derivative form, from *Saila*, and is really the same with *Saileya-dhara :* and the whole is not improbably borrowed from the Arabic *Dar-al-salem*, or *Dar-es-salem, the house of peace*, and the name of the celestial Jerusalem, in allusion to the Hebrew

---

[1] Anal. Vol. I. p. 106.   [2] Costa, p. 49.   [3] Nimrod, Vol. III. p. 391.
[4] Asiat. Res. Vol. X. p. 44.

name of the terrestrial one. The Sanscrit names of this city of the King of *Saileyam* or *Salem* imply its being a most holy place, and consecrated apart, and that it is firmly seated upon a stony hill.[1]

3. Not very far from the country where we find the Indian Tucte Soleyman, the country of Daud-poutri, the city and kingdom of Oude or Ioudi, &c., there is a mountainous district called Afghanistan, or country of the Afghauns, who consist of many millions of people. Their traditions tell them that they are descended from the Jews; that is, I should say, from the *Ioudi* of Oude; for they know nothing of their descent, except that they came into their present country from a tribe of Oudi or Jews. Their similarity to the Jews of Western Syria is so striking, that it could not escape the notice of inquiring orientalists. Our priests have had no small difficulty in accounting for them, as it was impossible to deny their Israelitish character; but at last they seem to have determined that they were descendants of the *ten tribes*, who were sent thither in the time of the Captivity, and who never, as the partisan Josephus says, though directly contrary to the fact, returned into Syria. On this I shall presently say a few words.

In the traditions of the Afghauns, noticed by Mr. Elphinston,[2] the name of Saul (from whom they say they are descended,) may be found, as also many circumstances similar to those in the Jewish history; but yet, in many respects, so different, that they can scarcely be believed to be a copy of them. Mr. Elphinston concludes by shewing, in opposition to Sir W. Jones, that they cannot be descendants from the Jews of Syria; that the story, though plausible, is clouded with many inconsistencies and contradictions. Sir W. Jones found that their language was *very like the Chaldaic*. If the Jews be descended from *them*, this is easily accounted for. The emigrants must have come away before the Sanscrit was brought to its present perfection, whether they came from Afghanistan or from Oude. I suspect that originally the Afghanistans were nothing but the mountain tribes of central India, having the same language and religion.

4. The Turks, who conquered the Arabians or Saracens in modern times, have, in a great measure, adopted their language. When these pagans arrived from Tartary they found the countries which they over-ran chiefly occupied by two races of men—the Christians and the Mohamedans. The mortifying fact has been concealed as much as possible, but the truth is, that the conquerors adopted the religion of the latter, not of the former. Persons who have read my *Apology for the Life of Mohamed* will easily believe me when I say this was no matter of surprise to me. But, independently of many reasons, which may be found in my treatise, why the Mohamedan, under the peculiar circumstances of the two, should gain the preference, there is yet another to be found in the language. It is reasonable to expect that (if I be right and that the Ioudi and Arabians were sectaries, from Afghanistan and Rajapoutana, which comprehend what was called the Indian Tartary or Indian Scythia) the languages of the Turks and Arabians should be nearly the same, and very different from the Greek, the prevailing language of the Christians. This *was* the fact, and it remains so to this day. The Arabic, the language of the Koran, is, in some measure, a learned language to the Turks, though they probably find no great difficulty in it, as " the *Turkish contains* " *ten Arabic or Persian words for one originally Scythian*."[3] This agrees extremely well with what we might expect to find, if I be right in my theory. I beg leave to ask my reader, why this horde of Pagan barbarians, arriving from the very distant north-eastern countries, should bring with them a language containing *ten* out of *twelve* of its words Arabic, which Arabic was undoubtedly, in ancient times, identical with Hebrew? I am now speaking of the words, not of the forms of the letters.

---

[1] Asiat. Res. Vol. X. pp. 45, 100.   [2] Hist. of Cabul, p. 248.   [3] Rev. R. Chatfield's Hist. Hind. p. 366.

In reply to the enemies of etymology I beg leave to observe, that, in the case of the Jews, my reasoning depends very little upon it, but upon the identity of the names. If those who have written the names of places and persons, had all been guided by the sixteen-letter system, I believe in almost every case the Eastern and Western names would have been the same. Though this identity might happen in a solitary instance or two, by accident, it is quite incredible that it should have happened by accident in the great number of cases which I have pointed out.

5. It is a singular and remarkable fact, that all the authors who have written respecting the Afghans, or respecting the natives of the countries near to them to the south-eastward, have noticed, not only their personal likeness to the Jews, but also the close likeness which their language bears to the Chaldaic. Michaelis[1] says, "that the dialect of Jerusalem was East Aramean, or, as " we call it, Chaldee. The Syriac New Testament is written in the same language, but in a dif- " ferent dialect." Now this language is called the Peshito, but why it has that name I know not; for I do not believe that it means *literal*.[2] But we see that the Peshito and the Chaldaic are the same. The language of the Afghans is called Pukhto or Pushto; and it seems difficult to help be- lieving that these are the same languages. This is the language of the sacred books of the Chris- tians of Malabar. Now it cannot for a moment be supposed that the Afghans and Raja-poutani emigrated with their Jewish similitudes (that is the Rannæ of Arrian or Ptolemy) after the time of Christ. I think, then, that these two languages, bearing names so nearly identical, must have been originally the same, however much they may have changed in the thousands of years during which those who spoke them must have been separated. Of this Pushto I shall have more to say here- after.

6. It is very evident from the accounts of both Dr. Dorn and Mr. Elphinston, that the whole of the fine country—Doab or Mesopotamia—from the Ganges to the Indus, and the whole valley of the latter, were once possessed by a race, the unconquered mountain tribes of which alone retain much of their ancient habits. In their intractable, unconquerable character, they very much assi- milate to their brethren or children in Arabia. They were all called Afghans. The present king- dom of Cabul is stated by Mr. Elphinston to contain thirteen or fourteen millions of people, of whom more than four millions are yet genuine Afghans. The countries of the Afghans and of the Rajpouts are so intermingled, that it is impossible, with any precision, to separate them. But in addition to the above, it is a most important fact, that a large district on the Indus was called Arabia, and its inhabitants Arabi.

If the country be examined where we find these extraordinary proofs of a Jewish population, it will be found to be almost *covered* with the remains of what, in very remote times, were great and flourishing cities, and of an extent so large, that, to suppose a tribe or two of captives brought into it would change the manners and the pristine character of its inhabitants, is so extraordinary an absurdity, that no man who considers it for a moment can believe it. Besides, when these Jewish or Samaritan captives came to people this country, fifty times as large as their own, and the cities of which they must have taken possession, what became of the old inhabitants?

7. A very learned man, Mr. Carteret Web, has given it as his opinion, that the country about Bactria was, in primitive times, the seat of the arts, and that thence science was propagated to Persia, Assyria, India, and even to China. Strabo says, that Bactria, adjoining to Aria, abounded almost in every thing.[3] Justin[4] says, that it had a thousand cities under the jurisdiction of the Greeks, after they had destroyed the Persian empire. Strabo[5] also says, that Eucratides, one of the successors of Theodotus, had a thousand cities under his jurisdiction.

[1] Marsh's Mic. Ch. vii. Sect. viii. p. 41.   [2] Ib. p. 5.   [3] Lib. ii. p. 73.
[4] Hist. Lib. xli.   [5] Lib. xv. p. 686.

Bactria[1] is the same as Bucharia, and Bochara, which Abulghazi Khan[2] says, means *country of learned men*, and was a place to which persons went from all quarters to acquire learning. It was a most beautiful country, abounding in the richest productions of the animal, vegetable, and mineral kingdoms. Perhaps, upon the whole earth, a situation more proper for the birthplace of man could not have been selected.

8. Certain circumstances of natural similarity between the places of the settlement of the Ioudi in India and in Western Syria may be observed, which raise a suspicion, that the similarity was the *occasion of the selection of the place where the emigrating Ioudi settled*, when they came to the West. In Afghauistan or the kingdom of Cabul (query, of the Cabala?) is a river which rises in what are called the mountains of Cabul, and runs into a dead-sea, called Loukh or Zarrah. One of its heads rises in a range of hills called the *Ridge of Soleyman*, not far from which is the Snow-capped mount, called Tukte Soleiman or Solomon's Throne; where the people of the country believe the Ark rested after the Deluge. Here are also mountains called Solymi and others called mountains of Ioudi. There is a place on the side of the above-named sea (which is salt, and has no outlet, and is therefore a *dead sea*), called Zoor or Zoar, the name of a city on the shore of the dead sea, or Lake Asphaltes in Western Syria. "Among the heads of tribes I found one having the "name of Lot."[3] Mr. Elphinston observes of a tribe of Afghan shepherds, that the girls had Jewish features.[4] He also observes of the Rajpouts, "They are stout and handsome, with hooked noses "and Jewish features." The mountains of Soliman run north and south, from the Indian Caucasus, to lat. 29, and are possessed by the Afghans. They are only known in *old books* (books of the Hindoos) by the name of Soliman.[5] These mountains are also called *Suffaid Coh*, which Mr. Hamilton explains *white mountains*, from their snowy tops. But I suspect the proper translation is Mount Σοφια-δι, Mounts of sacred Wisdom, of Solomon. I shall return to the word Suffaid by and by. The Arabians call the Afghans Solimanee, by which name they are not commonly known in their own country. This is a singular fact, but for which the circumstance of their being named thus only in their old books easily accounts. Several histories of the Afghans have been written by Persians and other Mohamedans, but all evidently intended to serve religious purposes; and, consequently, owing to their innate and palpable absurdity, not deserving a moment's consideration. I say this of the notice of them in the fourth Art. of Vol. II. of the Asiatic Researches. I am of opinion that the Afghans were driven out from the kingdom of Oude or Juda, (probably at the same time part of their sect came Westwards,) to the mountainous country where they are found, and from which their sectarian opponents could not expel them. Thus Jews or Ioudi are found in Afghanistan; but in Oude there are only towns formerly occupied by them.

---

[1] Bactr-ia or Boch-ara, the place of learned men, is the place of Bock or the Book.

[2] Hist. Turks and Tartars, Lond. p. 108.   [3] Tod.   [4] Introd. p. 49.

[5] Elphinston, Vol. II. p. 148.

CHAPTER V

Religion of Afghans and Rajpouts—Saul—Ferishta, Account of Indian Jews—
Arabia, its Site and Meaning—Tombs of Noah, Seth, and Job—Bentley—
Names of Places in India continued—Places in Greece—Names of old Towns
not noticed—Saba, &c.—Nile and Egypt, Names of

1. In Lower India, in Greece, and in some other countries, the Arabian and Turkish conquerors seem to have settled themselves; as it were, in fact, to have deserted their old countries, and to have become residents of their new conquests. But it appears that this was not the case with the country of the Rajpoots or Afghans. If they were conquered, a momentary pillage took place, and a tribute was exacted, but in other respects the natives were left in possession of their countries; which, in fact, they soon liberated from their invaders. But from the Afghans or the kingdom of Cabul, conquerors of Asia have repeatedly issued, and probably will issue again.

The natives of Oude or Rajapoutana are Hindoos, of the religion of Cristna chiefly. But the Afghans are followers of Mohamed. They claim to be contemporaneous with him in their religion, and to have been his earliest allies. Most certainly the way in which the Arabian and Afghanistan peoples appear to assimilate together, has never been accounted for with the least probability, or the similarity of the latter to the Jews. My theory, I think, will develop the mystery. A communication between wandering tribes of two very distant countries is easier to be accounted for, than between two that are settled in walled cities, which was what became characteristic of the natives of Syria, but not of the greatest part of the inhabitants of Arabia. And I think there is nothing improbable in a tribe, (like a tribe of Gypsies,) as the Mahomedans say, having come from upper India or the Indian Tartary to Arabia, in the time of Mohamed, and having carried back his new doctrines to the Ioudi of Afghanistan, their ancestors.

I suppose that the tribe of Ioudi were driven out of Rajapoutana when the religion of Cristna or Kanyia prevailed. In consequence of this we find the religion of Kanyia in this country; but it was not driven out of Afghanistan or the mountains, but remained there in the situation of the 65 tribes of black Jews without Pentateuchs, found by Dr. Buchanan, until the arrival of the Saracens, when they instantly accepted their religion, for which, in fact, they would be in a very peculiar manner prepared, by having the patriarchs' statues which were of old in the temple at Mecca. The country of Cristna has statues and remains of the same patriarchs, but they have not the least relation now to its religion; they are quite obsolete—only antiquarian curiosities.

" The province of Ajimere in general has ever been the country of the Rajpoots; that is, the
" warrior tribe among the Hindoos, and which are noticed by Arrian and Diodorus : and Cheitore
" or Oudipour, (which I consider as synonymous,) is, I believe, reckoned the first among the Raj-
" poot states. The whole consists generally of high mountains divided by narrow valleys ; or of
" plains environed by mountains, accessible only by narrow passes and defiles : in effect, one of
" the strongest countries in the world, yet having a sufficient extent of arable land : of dimensions
" equal to the support of a numerous population, and blessed with a mild climate, being between
" the 24th and 28th degrees of latitude : in short, a country likely to remain for ever in the hands
" of its present possessors, and to prove the asylum of the Hindoo religion and customs. Not-
" withstanding the attacks which have been made on it by the Gaznavide, Pattan, and Mogul
" Emperors, it has never been more than nominally reduced. Some of their fortresses with which

" the country abounds were indeed taken, but the spirits of independent nations do not reside in
" fortresses, nor are they to be conquered with them. Accordingly, every war made on these
" people, even by Aurengzebe, ended in a compromise or defeat on the side of the assailants."[1]
How absurd to suppose that the towns called after the names of the Israelites in these countries
can have been built by Mohamedan conquerors!

The Mohamedans seldom changed the names of towns, but they sometimes did change them :
for instance, they substituted the name of Islam-nuggur for Jugdes-pour, that is, for Jews-pour—
or, the walled town or Islam-fort for Jews-town. But if this shews any thing, it is against their
giving the Jewish names, such as Jerusalem, Solomon, David, &c., to the towns of Central
India—not in favour of it. Though they have always tolerated the Jews as well as the Christians,
yet they were as little likely to have adopted Jewish as Christian names for their towns. No
doubt, in some instances, the Mohamedans gave new names to towns which they rebuilt, which
often makes it difficult to ascertain the truth; but we see above, that they did not give Jewish
names, but abolished them.

It is very evident that the old accounts which we have of the Afghans were all written by Mohamedans in or about the sixteenth century, who found the same likeness between the Afghans
and the Jews which we find at this day—and not knowing how to account for it, they had recourse to
what they supposed probable, and squared with their sectarian ideas of religion—sectarian as
Jewish in opposition to the Samaritan. Mr. Elphinston seems most clearly to be mistaken when
he says their towns have been named by the Mohamedans, and that the oldest of them have not
those peculiar Jewish characteristics to which our attention has been drawn. Directly the contrary is the fact. It is evident that the places had the names before the time of Mohamed. For
instance, the Tecte Soloman, one of the five sacred mounts of, and so called by, the Jain Buddhists.
If the modern Mohamedans had given names to these great cities, we should have had Mecca or
Medina, which we no where find.

2. It has been thought that the story of the descent of the Afghans from Saul is true ; among other
reasons, because there was a tribe called Khyber in the East, and one, professing the Jewish religion,
in Arabia, in the time of Mohamed. Now this has a tendency directly against the head of the
tribe coming from Jerusalem ; for the head of the two tribes, if his name were Khyber, could not
occupy both places—he could not emigrate a thousand miles to the East, and at the same time a
thousand miles to the West. To make this probable, they should both have had some well-known
Jewish name, and that have been the name of some large known Jewish division, tribe, or sect.
If their tribes had been called Samaritan for instance, and their country Samaria, we might have
believed that one went one way, the other another way. But there is another reason against their
descent from Saul. If the Jewish history is to be received, the pious David murdered *all* Saul's
children by the hands of the Gibeonites.[2] From Mr. Elphinston's account, *the traditions* of the
Jews of Western Syria, and those of the Afghans of Cabul, appear, though now much varied, to
have been derived from a common source.[3]

3. Ferishta accounts for the likeness between the Jews and Afghans by saying, that " The
" Afghans were Copts ruled by Pharaoh, many of whom were converted to the laws and religion
" of Moses; but others who were stubborn in their worship to their Gods, fled towards Hindostan,
" and took possession of the country adjoining the Koh-i-Sooliman."[4] The striking likeness

[1] Rennell, Mem. p. 153.

[2] One of the most atrocious of the actions of that most profligate man. In history there is not a more horrible character than the psalm-singing David, except, indeed, it be the church-establishing Constantine the First.

[3] Elphinston, Hist. Cabul, Vol. II.   [4] Tod's Hist. Raj. p. 241.

Ferishta could not help seeing; his mode of accounting for it is absurd enough. He says, I have read that the Afghans are Copts of the race of the Pharaohs; and that when the prophet Moses got the better of that Infidel, who was overwhelmed in the Red Sea, many of the Copts became converts to the Jewish faith, but others, stubborn and self-willed, refusing to embrace the true faith, leaving their country, came to India, and eventually settled in the Soolimany mountains, where they bore the name of Afghans.[1] Here is a choice specimen of reasoning; because they would not turn Jews in Arabia, these captive slaves, without leave, I suppose, left their masters, and turned Jews in India. All that this proves is, that the identity of the natives of the Solimany mountains in India with the Jews and Ethiopians in the West, was visible to Ferishta, which he could not account for. But it is very clear that if there had been any grounds for it, he would not have failed to have pleaded that the Jewish appearances were taken from the Mohamedans. Indeed, no one, I believe, would ever think of such a thing except our priests, and even they would not think of it except from their ignorance of the nature of the case, which, in fact, they have not the means of knowing. In deriving the Afghans from the time of Moses, Ferishta admits their Jewish existence long before the time of Mohamed. Though not much in favour of my system can be learnt from Ferishta, yet the little which he has, is decisively in favour of the Israelitish names being in these countries before the time of Mohamed. And it appears also that they were equally common with the Moguls, when they first marched to attack Delhi.

4. Arabia means Western Country. If this name were given to the people of the tribe of Arabi who were situated on the Indus, by the Ioudi of Oude, they would be very properly called Arabians or Western people, ערבים orbim; Arabi-ia country of the Arabi: but they had no pretensions to have this name given to them by the Jews or Greeks. Part of the peninsula of Arabia is due South, and the remainder South-east of Western Judæa, and all of it South-east of Greece. They were a tribe from the Indus, and brought with them in the mouths of the tribe of Israelites coming from Oude, the name of Western people which they had been accustomed to call them.

5. Not far from Oude, on the banks of a river called Gagra, by Colonel Wilford, are shewn the icons of Noah, Ayub (Job), and Shis or Sish (Seth). The stories told about them are so contradictory that their history is certainly unknown. But from two of them being noticed in the Ayeen-Akberry, they are evidently very old, and the stories about them false.[2] The idea of the Mohamedans being the authors of these monuments is quite ridiculous, as they could never bear the idea of an image. Near them there was formerly a temple dedicated to Ganesa, and a well which, in the Puranas, is called GANA-PUT CUNDA. I suspect the name of the river Gagra was formerly Argha, and the well, I suspect, is similar to the fissure in the earth at Delphi. In this country Colonel Wilford observes, rich persons or persons of consequence are called Maiter, as Maiter Solomon. Here is the French Maitre and our Master, as I have already remarked.

Along with the similarity of language, of laws, of names of places and men, almost all travellers have noticed the similarity of personal character in these people to that of the Jews. The Mohamedans could not cause this. The Adim of India, which, in Sanscreet, means the first, is plainly the Adam of the first book of Genesis. The Nuh or Noah is Menu, who, after the flood, repeopled the renovated world; and the history of Noah and his family are precisely the same in the Sanscreet as in the Hebrew Bible.[3]

---

[1] Briggs's Ferishta, Vol. I. p. 6. The etymology of the word Afghan sets me quite at defiance. These persons are said to have been among the first converts to Mohamedism. Before I conclude, I shall treat of a sect called Sophees, when I shall revert to this question (first considering many things of which I shall treat). Is it not possible that the word Afgh-an may be a corruption of the word Σοφ, Soph?

[2] Asiat. Res. Vol. VI. p. 482.   [3] Maur. Ind. Ant. Vol. VI. p. 42.

6. I must stop my argument here to observe, that if Mr. Bentley be correct in his idea, that the Brahmins forged their books since the sixth century, in which the circumstances of similarity to the Christian and Jewish dispensations are to be found, it seems to me that they must also not only have given names to these ruined towns, ancient people, and mountains, &c., (many of the names of which are now obsolete, and, except in very old writings and among the remote agricultural population of peasants, superseded by more modern ones,) but they must have erected these statues of Noah, Job, and Seth, in this country, distant many hundred miles from the Christian Malabar settlement of Nestorians, to prevent the propagation of whose opinions it is alleged that the forgeries were executed: and in a country where there is not the least reason to believe that there ever was a Christian before the last century.

Beyond the limits of Judæa proper, beyond the Jordan, or the river of Adonis, as I shall presently prove its name to mean, was a country called the *Decapolis*, or country of *the ten cities*. This was in imitation of a similar arrangement and naming of the country beyond the kingdom of Oude or Juda proper, of India, called the Deccan, which is Deccan-ia, and consisted of the country to the South of the river Buddha, or נחל ner-Buddha, or Ner-mada, river of the great God. By the author of the circumnavigation of the Erythræan Sea it is called Dachanos.[1]

7. In lat. 28, 29, and long. 72, will be found an extensive country called Daoudpotra, which means Country of the sons of David. In it will be seen a town called Ahmed-poor—City of Ahmed, the name of Mohamed, and by which his followers say he was foretold. But this was an Arabian name of description before Mohamed was born, or he could not have been foretold by it. Besides, the fact of some person being foretold by it in the Prophet Haggai, shews it to be an ancient and sacred name.[2] This has a tendency to confirm the histories of the Brahmins, which say, that the Temple of Mecca was founded by a colony of Brahmins from India, and that it was a sacred place *before* the time of Mohamed, and that they were permitted to make pilgrimages to it for several centuries *after* his time.[3] Its great celebrity as a sacred place long before the time of the prophet cannot be doubted.

Not far from the Indus, in Rennell's map, will be found a place in lat. 36, long. 67, called Dura-Yoosoof; also in lat. 32, long. 71, a place on the Indus called Dera-Ismael-Khan. This is the native country of the Olive. Col. Wilford has observed that the name of Abdala is not derived from the Persian word Abdal, the servant of God; but from the name of an ancient tribe of Upper India,[4] before the time of Mohamed. This again tends to confirm the idea of the Arabians' coming from Upper India, and also shews that we must not hastily conclude that every proper name found in India, which is the same as we find among the modern Mohamedans, is taken from them.

Col. Wilford says, that there are followers of Brahma in Arabia, at this time, who are supposed to be descendants of Hindoos. The greatest part of the old names of places in Arabia are either Sanscrit or Hindi; and Pliny mentions two celebrated islands on the Southern coasts of Arabia, in which there were pillars with inscriptions in characters unknown (Col. Wilford says he supposes) to the Greek merchants who traded there, and that these were probably Sanscrit, as one of these two islands was called *Isura*, or Iswara's island, and the other Rinnea, from the Sanscrit Hriniya, or the island of the Merciful Goddess.

In the Old Testament we read anathemas in almost every page against high places. These were, I apprehend, imitative Merus. Nimrod has observed, that of this character were all the different

---

[1] Hamil. Gaz. Deccan.
[2] Asiat. Res. Vol. X. p. 100.
[3] Vide my Apology for the Life of Mohamed.
[4] Ibid. Vol. IX. p. 206.

Olympuses or sacred mounts of this and other names in Greece. There is none more striking than Pindus on its western side.

8. In or near the Bay of Ambrasius, on the Western coast of Epirus and Acarnania, in the district of Chaonia or Caonia, which word I apprehend is closely allied to the Apollo Cunnius, and to the Caonim or Cakes offered to the Queen of heaven, was situated the Temple of Dodona, which Ritter says was anciently Bodona. Here was a town called Omphalium, and another called Ambrasia, and one of Cyclopean construction called Argos or Amphilochis, or Amphipolis, that is, the city of Amphi or Omphi, or the Om; and one called Nico-polis, the city Nysi or Nysus, the same name as Bacchus, and of the mount called Sinai in Arabia, and of Jehovah Nisi, and of the famous Nysa of Alexandria in India; and one called Klissura, which seems a corruption of the Clyssobora or Klissobora or Cercesura of the Indian Doab, and one called Argyro-Kastro, that is the Castrum or fortress of Agra. This is also called Arsinoe and Acræ; and one called Phœnice.[1] There was also a town called *Amphia*, otherwise *Evora*, the name of the ancient capital of the Brigantes, and of York. There was a river called Aias, and one called Inacbus, the son of Noah. There was a mount called Olympus, and the famous Pindus: and a Mons Tricala, and a Mount LINGON, i. e. Linga. It has been observed that all the ancient cities of the districts called Caonia are Cyclopean, and were inhabited by Ionians. Herodotus says, that Dodona was αρχαιοτατον των εν Ἑλλησι χρησηριων: and Julian says, that John the Baptist was χρησος Ιωαννες: and here, upon a beautiful lake, supposed to be the ancient Acherusia, stands the town of Joannina. The Temple of Dodona has been thought to have been at the town of PROTOPAPAS. What is Protopapas, but chief priest? Near this is a river called Kalama. May I suspect that this is another Kalane?[2] Near this sacred place is a Voni-tza, i. e. Ioni-tza, and the island of *Santa Maura*, or the Holy Meru, or at present *Leucadia*, or the island of the Holy Grove or Garden; in which is a town called Leucas or Neritus, and one where was a temple of Apollo called *Ell-omenus*. On the Eastern side of Pindus we have Arg-issa, Ambrasius, Olympus, Parnassus, Larissa, (the same as the district of Larice in Guzzerat,) formerly and now again Yeni-seri. Tricala, Delphi, Eleusis, Dium the name of the sacred isle near Bombay, Pelagonia Tripolis, that is the three cities of Pelagonia, a sacred river named Peneus, called by Homer Αργυροδινη, on which is a town called Ioanuina,[3] and many other places whose names are evidently connected with this superstition. In Macedonia we have the sacred river Sirymon, with an Amphipolis, and an Eidon or Eion, and near it a town called *Dium*, at the foot of Mount Athos, or the sacred Mount or Acro-Athos, covered with monasteries, of which I shall say more hereafter.

Between the 34th and 35th degree of North latitude, and the 72d and 73d degree of East longitude, in the Hon. Mr. Elphinston's map, is a place in the mountains of Cashmere called CHUMLA. It seems to have been a pass into, or a key as it were to, the fine countries of the South. It is in Bactria or the mountains of Balk or Bactriana, or Balkan.

There is a very lofty ridge of mountains which runs from the Black Sea to the Adriatic, and defends Greece, very much in the same way as the mountains of Bactriana defend India, which the Greeks called Hæmus. It has now recovered its ancient name of BALK-AN, and the name of its chief pass its ancient name of CHUMLA. On the South of Greece we have the Peninsula of Meru or Morea, with its Mount Olympus in its centre, its Chaonian district, its Argos, its Tripolitza or Tripoly, its Nissi, &c., &c., nearly repeated.

In Asia Minor we have the district of Troy, Ter-iia, and its capital Ilium, with the sacred Ida or

---

[1] Holland's Travels, Vol. II. p. 331.   [2] Ibid. Vol. I. p. 210, 8vo.   [3] D'Anville.

the Ida-vratta of India, and its Gargarus or stone circle, Gilgal, and Tripoli, of which we have before spoken: and in Lydia we shall find the Mount of Solym, having its towns with the same remarkable names. On the coast of Africa, at the Straits of Gibraltar, we shall again find a Tripoli, a Tangiers, &c., exact copies of the Tangore, the Trichinopoly of the Carnatic on the coast of Coromandel—and the name of Mauri-tania, is probably the country or *stan* or *tan* of Meru.

It must be unnecessary to point out the Iona of Syria with its Tripoli. In short, in the Western as in the Eastern nations, the countries were divided into districts, each having its sacred mount, its trinity of towns, &c., &c. Sir William Drummond, by shewing that almost all the ancient Hebrew names of the Holy Land had astronomical meanings, has shewn that it was like all the others. It had its high place at Gerizim in Samaria, and after a schism took place in the time of the man we and his followers call Dud or David, another was set up at Jerusalem. When the Israelites took possession of Canaan they changed all the names of the towns, and gave them names having the same or similar *astrological* meanings with those which may be perceived in every part of their temple. To their enemies' towns they gave names of opprobrium.[1] I have before observed that in the same manner the Greeks, after the time of Alexander, almost always changed the names of the towns they conquered, giving them names after the places in their old countries, or after their great men or their superstitions. All this is practised by us continually in the Americas and Australia.[2] The above were originally religious names.

9. It is no unusual thing, both in Greece and in Asia, to meet with the ruins of old towns, the names of which are not known or noticed by the ancient authors, and which shew in their construction two distinct and probably very remote periods from each other. An example of this is noticed by Dr. Holland.[3] He says, " The last town appears to have been probably Grecian, but it " has been built on the foundations of an older city which has been Cyclopean." The country where these ruins were found was Chaonia, and I suspect all the cities which were of date coeval with the word Chaonia would be Cyclopean. It is impossible to account for the Cyclopean remains which are found in Greece, without admitting the existence of a powerful people long previous to Grecian history, and even Grecian fable; and long prior to the received date of the Trojan war. These were the Ionians, the Hellenes, the Arg-ives, the Amazons, the Cyclopes : of the two last of whom I shall presently treat.

No doubt a careful examination of the names in the Arabian peninsula would afford clear traces of the Indian ancestry. There is the town of Ζευς Αγρευς, or of Agra, as the author of the Universal History calls it;[4] or perhaps of the Arga, the Nysa, (in fact Mount Sinai,) the birth-place of Bacchus. And again, two cities in a southern direction called Arga and Badeo,[5] that is, Deo-bud. The river Yamana[6] and its city, the same as the river Yamuna in India, with the tribe of the Saraceni or Saracens, evidently the same as the Suraseni of the Jumna. The Mount *Merwa*, another Meru, Moriah, and Meroe ;[7] the names of Hagar and Ishmael, and many others.

If I understand Gale rightly, he and Vossius suppose that Mount Sinai was called Nyssa or Nysa. Vide Exod. xvii. 15, Jehovah Nissi.[8]

---

[1] See Book V. Chap. XI. Sect. 2.

[2] Augustine says, " An ignoras, Asclepi, quod Ægyptus imago sit cœli, aut quod est verius, translatio aut descensio " omnium quæ gubernantur atque exercentur in cœlo, ac si discendum est verius, terra nostra mundi totius est tem- " plum !" De Civ. Dei., Lib. viii. Cap. xxiii.

[3] Vol. II. p. 321.   [4] Vol. XVIII. pp. 346, 355.   [5] Ib. p. 355.

[6] Yamuna, the name of the sacred river Jumna, means Daughter of the Sun. Asiat. Res. Vol. I. p. 29; Sir W. Jones.

[7] Ib. p. 387.   [8] Gale, Court Gent. Vol. I. p. 180.

424   Nile and Egypt. Names Of

10. Saba with the Hindoos meant the host of heaven: it is also a most important word in the Bible, where it had the same meaning. It is the Sabaoth of our liturgies, which does not mean Lord God of men-killers, as our narrow-minded priests suppose; but Lord God of the heavenly bodies—of the countless millions of suns and worlds in orderly and perpetual motion. Various places are called after this word. As we have found Solomon in India, it is not surprising that we should find the Saba or Sheba of his Queen there. In Rennell's map it is called Shibi. It is in the kingdom of Cabul, just where we might expect to find it. This place was also called Pramathasi and Parnasa, whence the Greeks got their Parnassus.[1] There is a place in D'Anville's ancient map called Sava or Saba on each side of the Straits of Babelmandel. I can scarcely doubt that a colony of the same people with the Ioudi settled on the East side of the Red Sea, built Mecca and Jidde, Juda, (as the Brahmins say,) and crossed the sea to Ethiopia or Abyssinia. Hence we find the tradition among the Ethiopians that they are descended from the Ioudi. This accounts for the Israelitish names in Arabia, as we shall hereafter see more fully. The statues of the patriarchs were in the temple at Mecca when Mohamed commenced his reform. The dove was also worshiped along with them.[2] Against this Mohamed, in a very particular manner, made war. With the assistance of Ali he himself destroyed the dove, the emblem of the female generative power. Mecca has been said to have been founded by Ishmael, the son of the Handmaid or concubine Agar or Hagar. Thus he was a bastard to the Jews—Agar meaning *Arga*, and Ishmael *Apostacy* to the religion of the Dove, which was found in the Temple of Mecca or Isis.

11. Near the Indus is a river called Nile, one of the branches of which is called Choaspes and Cophes; this river is said to pass through an opening in the mountains, called Gopha. I think it probable that the Nile of Egypt was called Guptus, from the river Cophes or Gopha: and the Gupts or Copts from the same: and that they crossed from the neighbourhood of Mecca or Sheba or Saba to E-gupt-ia. They were, if I be right, correctly Ethiopians and Egyptians. The word Gupta in Sanscrit means Saviour. Then the country might have the Greek name of αια Γυπτος, the country of Guptus or the Saviour.[3] Its own name was Sr, or Sur, or Sir, at least its river and a district in its upper part, were so called. But what can be the etymon of Gopha or Cophes? We know how the G and C were changed for one another. May *Coph* be Σοφ, the C being the Greek Σ? In the country where the river Cophes is found, I have before observed that there is a mount among the mountains of Solymi called Suffaid, (which is evidently a corruption of Σοφ, or צוף *zup*,) and that the Sofees of Persia are called Suffarees.

The explanation that the Guptus or Coptos was derived from the Cophrenes of India, is confirmed by the singular circumstance that the Nile, on flowing into the Delta of Egypt, is said to flow from the Cow's belly. The Ganges is said to flow from a sacred place, a gorge in the mountains called Cow's Mouth—and the word Cophrenes, Mr. Rennell says, means Cow.[4] One of the rivers of the Punjab was called Nilab—this is evidently Nile-aub, river Nile. This I take to have been one of the names of the Cophrenes. On the names of those rivers, Mr. Rennell says, " There is so much confusion in the Indian histories respecting the names of the branches of the " Indus, that I cannot refer the name *Nilab to any particular river*, unless it be another name for " the Indus or Sinde."[5] On the Indian Nile above named, is a city called *Ishmaelistan*. We have just now observed, that the city of Mecca is said by the Brahmins, on the authority of their old books, to have been built by a colony from India; and its inhabitants from the earliest era have had a tradition that it was built by *Ishmael*, the son of Agar. This town, in the Indian language, would be called ISHMAELISTAN.

---

[1] See Asiat. Res. VI. p. 496.

[3] Ib. Vol. V. p. 286; Drummond, Orig. Vol. II. p. 55.

[2] Ib. Vol. IV. p. 370.

[4] Mem. Map Hind. pp. 115, 120.

[5] Ib. p 70.

CHAPTER VI

Arabians from India—Laws and Customs of Afghans and Jews—Rennell on the Rajpouts—Paradise. Ararat—Colonel Tod on Places in India—Jehovah, Name of, in India—Colonel Tod on the Indian Mythoses—Kæmpfer on Siam—Herodotus did not know of the Empire of Solomon

1. My reader has probably not forgotten the proofs I have adduced, that the old Hebrew, the Samaritan, and the Arabian, are the same language. From various authors it is known that when Mohamed commenced the reform of his country's religion, the statues of the old Jewish patriarchs were in the temple at Mecca; and that the Arabians deemed themselves to have descended from Abraham, or THE Brahmin, by his son Ishmael. They never had, at any time that we know of, any connexion with the Syrian Jews, and yet, in their metropolitan temple, they had statues of the Jewish patriarchs, and their languages are radically the same, and the same, Sir William Jones says, as the Afghans'. How can this be accounted for, but by supposing them, as well as the Jews, to have migrated from Tukhte Solimaun, the Indian Arabia, or the countries on the North of India? This is proved by facts innumerable, and Sir W. Jones would have had no difficulty in seeing it, if he had not been previously tied down by a dogma, which, as he *declares*, nothing should induce him to disbelieve. In the account which Mr. Elphinston[1] has given of the division of the Afghans into tribes or clans, their similarity to the ancient tribes of the Jews and of Arabia, is very apparent. This system of tribes was formed long prior to the time of Mohamed. And it may here be observed, that the moment Mohamed or his califs conquered, the clans or tribes generally disappeared: and no instance can be produced of their founding a government by tribes where it had not been before. For some time after the conquests of Mohamed, the tribes of Arabia were all confounded beneath his victorious banner. This at once answers the idle pretences of the Afghans' founding their tribes, and naming their districts and towns, from modern Mohamedans. Their governors are called *Mullik*, evidently the Hebrew and Arabic word for King; and also *Mushir*, which is a corruption of the Arabic word Mosheer *a Counsellor*,[2] or perhaps *Judge*.

The salutation of the Afghans is correctly Hebrew: Assalaum Alaikoom—Peace be with you.[3] A person accustomed to the Jewish salutation will at once perceive that in quick pronunciation the sounds of the two must be identical.

2. The Afghan mode of government by tribes, bears a striking resemblance to that of the Israelites under the Judges. They are the very pictures of what the Israelites must at that time have been. The natives have a code of criminal law different from the Mohamedan, *such as one would suppose to have prevailed before the institution of civil government*.[4] The laws and customs are in a wonderful manner similar to those of the Jews, and in cases which can be accounted for in no other way than an original identity; and this is the most important of all the circumstances relating to them, which I have pointed out.

Mr. Maurice and Mr. Halhed have observed a very close similarity between many of the institutes of Menu and the Mosaic code, and that not consisting merely in precepts of morality, but in examples of artificial refinement, which could not be discovered by the principles of common sense,

---

[1] Vol. I. p. 256.   [2] Ibid. Vol. I. p. 258.   [3] Ibid. Vol. II. p. 372.
[4] Ibid. Vol. I. p. 265.

like many moral laws—for instance the law against Murder. Of this, the order to a brother to take the widow to raise up seed to his brother, is one out of vast numbers of examples from which a judgment may be formed of the remainder, without occupying more of my reader's time.[1] The similarity is much too close to be the effect of accident, and much strengthens the position which I maintain, that the tribe of Abraham was an emigrant one from India. In the appendix to a history of India written by a man, I believe a missionary, of the name of Ward, who has much more piety than either sense or charity, may be seen *above twenty pages of close print* of similar Hebrew and Hindoo coincidences. He *calls* them illustrations of Scripture : and *proves* the former close connexion of the two, if he do not even prove their identity. The similarity was so striking that even a missionary was obliged to confess it, and explain it away as well as he was able.[2]

No doubt the allegation that the old Jewish names of ancient ruined towns and of districts have been given by Mohamedan conquerors, or the names of Jewish towns by Samaritan emigrants, or Jewish laws and customs *differing from those of the Koran*, the law of Mohamed, by followers of the prophet, will satisfy many persons who have too much faith to use their reason : but our oriental travellers, who have examined into the histories of these places, treat the idea of the building of the towns since the seventh century with perfect contempt.

3. Major Rennell will not be suspected of writing to uphold my theory, and he expressly says, that the Rajpoots of Agimere, or inhabitants of Rajpootana, who possess a country equal to half of France, preserved their independence from the conquests of Mahmood, and still preserve it to the present time.[3] He is confirmed by Col. Tod.[4] This at once puts an end to the plea that the ancient towns, whose Judaite names have been noticed by Sir W. Jones, were built by the Mohamedans. Many of them are in ruins, and were probably reduced to this state when Mahmood of Ghazni swept across the country like a tornado, not creating towns, but every where when in his power destroying them; the ruins of which, having Jewish names, remain. The Mohamedans never acquired and occupied the towns of Rajapootana, as they did many of those of Southern India. In consequence of Jewish customs being found in Tartary, (the very place where the Afghan tribes are found,) several old authors have supposed that the Jews had been carried thither at the Captivity. For instance, Philip Mornay *de verit. Relig. Christ.*, Cap. xxvi., Geneb. Chronic. *Religions du Monde*, Tome II. (vide Grot. *de Origin. Gent. Amer.*). Davity relates,[5] that there was a place called Thabor in Tartary, whence a king came into France in the reign of Francis the First. Joseph Ben Gorion states, that when Alexander the Great marched towards the North, he came to a kingdom called Arzeret, which was occupied by the captive Israelites, into which he was prevented entering by a miracle! This serves to shew that the tribe was the same then as now. Benjamin de Tudela says, that after travelling to the North-east twenty-one days, he came to the country of the *Rechabites.* Calmet[6] says from the old authors above, that the Tartars eat no swines' flesh, observe the Levitical law, which requires that the brother shall marry the brother's widow if he die without children, &c., &c.; all customs now found among the nations of Central Asia, as we have seen. Dr. Giles Fletcher was envoy from Queen Elizabeth to the

---

[1] Maurice, Ind. Ant. Vol. VII. p. 834.

[2] The opinion which I formerly expressed of the disposition of the missionaries to *suppress* evidence, is justified by a proof adduced by Col. Van Kennedy (in the Transactions of the Bombay Society of Asiatic Literature) of their gross misrepresentations in their histories of India. This is confirmed, too, by Mr. Colebrook, (in the Second Vol. of Trans. Asiat. Soc. p. 9, n.,) who shews that Mr. Ward's translation of the Vedanta-sava is so unfaithful that it cannot be called a version of the original text. In the third volume of the transactions of the Society of Bombay, is a very able defence of the Hindoos against Mill, Wilberforce, &c., in which their misrepresentations are exposed.

[3] *Preface to Mem. of Map.* p. xlvii.   [4] See Trans. Asiat. Soc. Vol. II. p. 270.

[5] Etats du Turc en Asie, pp. 124, 168.   [6] Dict. in voce TRA.

people of Great Bucharia. He considered them to be the remainder of the *ten tribes* of Samaria, from the Hebrew names of their cities; and from the circumstance which he discovered—that their language, called Zagathai, contained Hebrew words. Here it was where Benjamin of Tudela found what he called the Hebrew-speaking Jews.[1] The Turks came from this country; it is, therefore, not surprising that in their language ten words out of the twelve, should be Arabic, which is Hebrew. I believe that thousands of years before the time of Mohamed, several pastoral tribes, natives of Upper India, were expelled, as the Brahmin books inform us, in consequence of religious feuds, and came and settled in Asia Minor, Arabia, and Syria. Such tribes as the Afghans, as they are described by Mr. Elphinston, were peculiarly well qualified for this species of emigration.

My suspicion respecting the nature of the faith of the Mohamedans, and the effects of it, is strengthened by an observation of Col. Tod's, that when they destroyed the Idols of all the other religions, they left those of the Buddhists and Jains[2] untouched. This was because, in their secret religion, as I shall presently shew, they were followers of the doctrine of Wisdom or Buddha, and of the Linga. If this were not the case, I ask, and I have a right to insist upon an answer to my question, before my doctrine is clamoured down; Why did the Mohamedan, that is the *Arabian* or *Saracen* followers of the Prophet, leave the icons of Buddha, the lingas in India, and the obelisks in Egypt, uninjured? I say *Arabian* or *Saracen*, because I have a suspicion that the barbarous hordes of Turcomans, who destroyed the fine empires of the Califs, were not initiated into the secret doctrines of Mohamedism, which I shall by and by develop.

We have in India, as already shewn, a mount of Solomon, a country of Juda, and another of the sons of David, and a Mount Moriah or Meru, and places and persons without number called Isis or Jesse. It is certain from notice of the Solymi in ancient authors, that they cannot have had these names given by Mohamedan conquerors. Then what must be the consequence of all this, if there be any truth in the history, if there were really any persons about the time usually ascribed to Solomon and David who governed Judæa by these names, but that they must have been thus named after their ancestors in the East, in the same manner as names were selected in all countries from sacred or mythological persons?

4. If the reader look back to Book VII. Chapter VI. Section 2, he will find, in the extraordinary mysticism of the history of Paradise, and in the name of one of its rivers, a pretty strong proof that the whole came from Upper India. When all the other circumstances which I have described, and the situation and character of Josephus are considered, I cannot conceive a stronger circumstantial proof that the Mythos came from India, than that he should describe one of the rivers of Paradise to be *the Ganges*. The river Oxus or Wolga is called by Rennell *Djion*. Thus we have clearly two of the rivers, and probably the other two had the names which are given in Genesis, though now lost. The circumstance of one of them running round the whole world shews it to be the Meru of India.

In my CELTIC DRUIDS, Chap. II. Sect. II. and VI., I have given a great many reasons to prove, that the Jewish Ararat was situate to the East of the Caspian Sea. The Sibyl placed Ararat in Phrygia, near a city called Celænes: this is evidently the Calani. If the Sibylline oracles had been a *Christian* forgery, they would not have placed Ararat in Asia Minor. The more I consider these oracles, the more convinced I become that they are genuine. It may be observed again, in confirmation of the fact that Ararat was not situate between the Black and Caspian seas, that the olive does not grow in Armenia, therefore the dove could hardly have found an olive-branch to pluck, when it was sent out.[3] Sir Walter Raleigh, in his Universal History, has placed Ararat

---

[1] Buchanan, Asiat. Res.   [2] Trans. Asiat. Soc. Vol. II. p. 285.   [3] Tournefort's Voyage, Lett. VII.

among the mountains between Persia, India, and Tartary,[1] and in this he is supported by Dr. Shuckford,[2] and by an author little known, called Goropius Becanus.[3] It appears from the Universal History, that this author uses nearly the same arguments as those used by me, particularly that of the impossibility of the nations having travelled from the East, if Ararat were in the present Armenia. Ben Gorion extends the mountain of Ararat to the Caucasus. And the Samaritan version calls it Serendib, the name of Ceylon, the place in which the Hindoos put Paradise. All this proves the uncertainty of the situation of this mountain.[4]   All these circumstances tend to prove, that there were sacred Merus, with their appurtenances, wherever there were settlements of the emigrators.

It is probable that a considerable part of the ancient religion consisted in the performing of pilgrimages to sacred places, as it does at this day in India and Italy; and as we know it did in Western Judæa—every Jew being obliged to go up to Jerusalem at least once a year: and in order to keep the people and their wealth at home, the priests of each tribe contrived to have its sacred places, its Mount Sion, &c., for the people to visit. We know that a contest took place between the Jews and the Samaritans for possession of the national high-place, its Meru or Sion, Olympus, Parnassus, Ida or Athos: for all these are of the kind of high-places referred to so often in the Bible in terms of reprobation. I do not, however, believe that they were objected to as being *high-places* so much as for their being Lupanars, or contaminated with the Hellenic rites, except those in Judæa: for the Jewish priests wished for only one in Judæa, and that, of course, at Jerusalem. Every where we see the same things repeated nearly by the same names: the Mount, the seven hills, the Tripoly, &c. This is the reason why we have so many Troys, so many Argoses, so many Larissas, so many Solymas, so many Olympuses.

5. Col. Tod says, " With Mat'hura as a centre, and a radius of eighty miles, describe a circle: " all within it is Vrij,[5] which was the seat of whatever was refined in Hinduism, and whose lan- " guage, the Vrij-basha, was the purest dialect of India. Vrij is tantamount to the land of the " Sura-seni, derived from Sur-sen, the ancestor of Crishna, whose capital, Surpuri (i. e. Sura or " Syra-pore,) is about fifty miles South of Mat'hura on the Yamuna (Jumna): the remains of this " city the author had the pleasure of discovering."[6] The Yamuna was sometimes called *black*, sometimes *blue*.[7] The river was *Yamuna;* the country would be, as in Arabia, *Yemen*. A little before, the Colonel says, " The *Yadu* B'hatti or Shama B'hatti (the Ashani of Abul Fuzil) draw " their pedigree from Crishna or Yadu-nat'h as do the Iha-riêjas of Kutch." Here the Hebrew and Greek God Ii, or I, or Jah, or IE of Delphi, is apparent enough. Cristna or Yadu is the God *Iaw*—the *du-ya*. Wherever we find the words *div* or *dev* or *du* thus used, we almost always find it meant *holy* or *deity*.

---

[1] B. i. Ch. vii.

[2] Connect. Vol. I. pp. 98, 103 I have been turned into ridicule by a shallow reviewer of my *Celtic Druids* for having there maintained what I have since discovered was taught by Raleigh and Shuckford—that Ararat was East of the Caspian Sea. But it has not yet been the fortune of that work to be reviewed by any person who can ever have read it, except by one really learned writer in North America, in the Southern Review, No. V. Feb. 1829, printed at Charlestown.

[3] Ino-Scythia, p. 473.

[4] Who brought the Olive-tree to Athens? Minerva, or divine *wisdom*, or Buddha: and where could it come from but from Oude, or Tucte Soleyman, or the house of Solomon or of Wisdom, in India ITS NATIVE PLACE? Thus Minerva, or Pallas, brought it. Vide Univ. Hist. Vol. I. B. i. Ch. i. p. 240.

[5] Of this country Jyadeva was a poet: this is evidently a mystic name.

[6] Trans. Asiat. Soc. Vol. II. p. 286.   [7] Ibid. p. 287, n.

Col. Tod states, that the statue of Cristna is said to have been saved from Aurengzebe, and conveyed to Nat'hdwara in Mewar, but he gives no account of the figure of the God. He calls him Kaniya, that is, Kan-or Cun-iya ; and Nath-ji, and Jy-déva. Here, again, I think it is impossible to be blind to the » *ii* and the יה *ie* of the Israelites—the *ii* of the Targums and of Iona [1]—the God *Iao*, that is, Jove—and the IE of Apollo on the temple of Delphi. Bishop Heber adduces an instance of one of the Mahratta princes, though of the Hindoo faith, being called Ali Jah—*Exalted of the Lord.* [2] Thus the above doctrine is confirmed by the Bishop.

In p. 714, Col. Tod says, " This hierarch bore the title of divinity, or Nat'hji : his prænomen of " Deo, or Deva, was almost a repetition of his title : and both together, Deonat'h, cannot be better " rendered than by ' Lord God.' " Deo-Nath-ji would be then, Lord God Jah or Self-existent Lord God. This Nath'ji was Cristna. [3] Nath is the Neith of Egypt, which meant Wisdom, and the Chinese name of God *Tien,* which read Hebraicè, is Neit.

" Radha was the name of the chief of the *Gopis* or Nymphs of Vrij, and the beloved of Kaniya." [4] Radha (Ray-di-ie) was the Latin radius, or *ray of light.* The district around Mathura, which was peculiarly sacred, called Vrij, might be the district or country of Ji. » רו *ur-ii,* Ur of Ii, in the regimine of the Hebrews. And here we have the Ur of the Mesopotamia, whence the tribe of Ioudi came to the West—the Ur of the Chaldees. The district of Ur-ii is also called Hurriana. [5] The Ana is the same as *stan* and *ania* in Mauritania. I want nothing to make the demonstration complete, but the origin of the name of Chaldees, which we shall find by and by.

Col. Tod [6] remarks, the annals of the *Yadus* of *Jesulmer* state, that the Yadus and Yutis, [7] whose resemblance, he says, is more than nominal, soon after the war of the *Mahabharat,* [8] held dominion from Guzni to Samarkand ; that the race of *Ioude* was still existing near the Indus in the emperor Baber's time, who describes them as occupying the mountains in the first Do-ab, the very place the annals of the *Yadus* state them to have occupied twelve centuries before Christ, and thence called *Iadu* or *Yadu-ca-dang,* the hills of *Iadu* or *Yadu.* The circumstance of *Yadu* being said to be the father of *Cristna,* [9] seems to imply that the tribe of *Yadu* or *Ioudi* arose before Cristna, or before the Sun entered Aries. This exactly agrees with the way I have accounted for the Afghans being Mohamedans, in Chapter V.

Aod in Irish was a name of the Sun, and also of the Goddess of Fire. *Aodh baudea teine,* [10] Aodh, the Goddess of Fire, Vesta. Gen. Vallancey says, this *Aod* is probably the same as *Yadu.* [11] I take this *Aod* and Yadu to relate to the kingdom of Oude.

6. If I be right in my idea that the religion of the Jews came from India, it is natural to expect that we should find their famous God JEHOVAH among the Hindoos, and this is, indeed, the fact. But my reader must divest his mind of the barbarous corruption of the word *Jehovah,* and restore the God to his true name, [12] יהוה *Ieue* יה *Ie,* as we call it *Jah,* and as it is called in Sanscrit, that is, in meaning, *the self-existent,* but often denominated *the God of victory.* Among the Hindoo Gods there is scarcely one who has not a name which contains, in some way or other, the elements of

---

[1] Tod, Hist. Raj. pp 523, 524.   [2] Vol. II. p. 562.   [3] Tod, p. 523.   [4] Tod, Hist. Raj. p. 530.

[5] Malcolm.   [6] Trans. Asiat. Soc. Vol. II. p 295.   [7] That is, the Getæ, I suppose.

[8] i. e. the battles of Cristna.   [9] Asiat. Res. Vol. III.   [10] Cormac.

[11] Ouseley's Oriental Collections, Vol. III. p. 26.

[12] The arguments which I use, founded on the true name of the Jewish God *Ieue* or *Ie,* will, of course, have no weight with such of my learned readers as have been instructed by modern Jews to neglect the Synagogue copies and to attend to the modern Mazoretic corruptions, and who continue talking about Elohim and Jehovah. As these gentlemen will not be instructed, they must remain in ignorance. I am certain that I have cast a new light upon ancient history, and if the *old* are too prejudiced to learn, the *young* are not.

the *Ie*, or God of the Jews. Col Tod,[1] in his treatise on the religion of Mewar, the very country whence the tribe of Ioudi must have come, has given a list of the eight principal Gods of the country. He gives the names and abodes of seven of them; but the *eighth*, whose abode he does not give, except as God of the mount,[2] he says, is above all—and he calls him Nat'h-Ji, Nat'h meaning God. When the great change is considered which has taken place in the old language by the perfecting of the Sanscrit, and which must have taken place, as I shall shew, since the emigration of the tribe, and also the change in both languages which time must have produced, it will not be a matter of surprise that the perfected language should be very different from that of the emigrant tribe. But, notwithstanding, if my reader can bring himself to cast off his prejudices in favour of the Jewish corruption of the word Jehovah, and write it as it ought to be, *Ie*, or *Ii*, or *I*,[3] he will see it in the Sanscrit names, in almost every page of the Asiatic Researches. The most remarkable of his names, which perhaps may be the best understood by an unlearned reader, is that of יה *Ie*. In the Jewish notation, which, like the Greek, is done by the letters of the alphabet, the fifth letter ה E and the tenth letter י I, (the former of which stands for five, and the latter for ten,) are never used to denote fifteen; because they are the name of God; and the Jews are forbidden to take the name of the God, Iᴇ, in vain or irreverently, which it would be to use it *thus*, and therefore for *ten* and *five* they substitute *nine* and *six*.

This name IE, corrupted into *Ia, Iy, Iu, Yu, Ya*, occurs unceasingly in the Hindoo names of Gods, and often in their sacred ceremonies, where they sing or chaunt IEYE. How can any thing be more convincing than the exclamation of this word IEYE, the meaning of which they may probably have lost?

7. I suppose Col. Tod to be a believer in the actual human existence of Cristna: but I think the following passage will satisfy my reader who and what he was, as well as strongly support my theory respecting Buddha. " Crishna, Heri,[4] Vishnu, or more familiarly Kaniya,[5] was of the " celebrated tribe of Yadu, or Jadu, the founder of the fifty-six tribes who obtained the sovereignty " of India, was descended from Yayat,[6] the third son of a primeval man called Swayambhuma " Manu[7] or Mᴀɴᴜ Lord of the earth, whose daughter Ella *(Terra)* was espoused by Buddha " *(Mercury)*, son of Chandra (the Moon), whence the Yadus are called *Chandravansi* or children " of the moon. Buddha was therefore worshiped as the great ancestor *(Pitriswara or father God)* " of the lunar race; and, previous to the Apotheosis of Crishna, was the common object of devo- " tion with all the Yadu tribe. The principal shrine of Buddha was at Dwarica, where he yet " receives adoration as Buddha *Trivicrama* (triple energy—the Hermes Triplex of the Egyptians)."[8] The Indian Cristna, we find, is called *Kaniya*. He is the Apollo of India. This word is *Kan-iya*, and is the same as the word *Cunnius*, his name at Athens, and the IE the word in front of his temple at Delphi. Diodorus says, Apollo's name was *Kan*.[9] From this has come the word *Khans* of Tartary. The meaning of Kan-iya will be *self-existent generating power*. Cristna is commonly called Sham-nat'h. This is שם *sm* and the word *Nath* which means God. שם *sn* is the singular of שמין *smin*, planets, or disposers. From this may have come Samanaut or Summaut. Col. Tod says, Cristna worshiped Buddha before his deification. This explains itself. Afterward the Colonel adds, in the cave of Gaya is the inscription[10] " Heri, who is Buddha." Heri is Cristna.

---

[1] Trans. of Asiat. Soc. Vol. II. p. 316.   [2] Mount Meru.

[3] *Ii*, the same as the Hindoo Nat'h-Ji; it is always so written in the Jerusalem Targums.

[4] The Saviour.   [5] Kaniya the Colonel has before stated to be the same as the Greek Apollo.

[6] Query, *Japhet?*   [7] Also called *Vaivu-swata Manu*, " *The* man son of the sun."

[8] Trans. Asiat. Soc. Vol. II. p. 299.   [9] Ibid. p. 312.   [10] Ibid. p. 304.

We have just observed that Cristna and Buddha were the same, but that Buddha was called *Trivicrama* or *Triple Energy*. This was the Hermes Trismegistus or Triptolemos—the Aleim or Trinity of the Jews, called ‏יה‎ *IE*, or Jah. " Cristna or Kaniya lived at the conclusion of the " *brazen age,* which is calculated to have been about 1100 or 1200 years before Christ." Here I think proof enough is admitted to shew that this Apollo or Kaniya was no other than the son or successor of Buddha in one of his renewed incarnations, which of course could be no other than the Sun. It is a common practice with the natives of India, on the naming of their children, to give them the epithets of one of their minor deities, as Europeans call their children after their saints or divi (divus Augustus, divus Paulus, divus Johannes). Here we have Christian names and names of honour. From this has arisen great confusion in their histories. To remedy this, to keep up their pedigrees, and to gratify their vanity, the princes, like the old kings of Ireland, have regular Genealogists, called by the same name, Bards or Bairds, who are domestics in their families, and whose duty it is to record every thing honourable to their patrons. Of course we need not be surprised that the apparent history is clear enough, but the real, when it gets into remote periods, fabulous enough. Every prince descends from some great God, that is, from the Sun ; and all that can be made out for a certainty is, that the Sun was the first God, and the parent of the family. From this it is clear that we are not to consider every history to be false, because the actors are called by the names of God, or to consider that the first Gods were men. The first God or King is always the sun. The only difficulty is to find out where the real history ends, and the fabulous begins. This must be judged of by circumstances. The genealogies cannot be depended on. To decide with *certainty* is very difficult, because these idle genealogists, like the genealogists or bards of Ireland and Wales, have nothing to do but to forge writings and circumstances, to make the family of their patron more honourable than that of his neighbours. I suppose that the fifty-six tribes spoken of above, were the settlements or places where the religion of Kaniya had prevailed in different parts of India—in the kingdom of Panionium, or of Pandæa the daughter of Cristna, according to another history or mythos.

8. A singular and artless observation is made by Mr. Kæmpfer, in his History of Japan,[1] in his account of JUDIA, the capital of Siam : " The Gates and other avenues of the palace are crowded " with black, checquered figures, painted in the manner as they do with the images at the holy " sepulchre at Jerusalem." This observation respecting these people of JUDIA is very striking. The name of the God worshiped here is *Prah Pudi Dsiau.* But divide the last word thus, Ds-iau, and what have we ? Deus-Iau. He is also called Siaka or Saka, the Irish Sacya. The God is an exact Buddha sitting, 120 feet high. The country swarms with monks. The Idol is also called *Amida* (Om-di), a name of Buddha. He is seen standing upright on the flower Tarate, or Faba-Egyptiaca, or *Nymphæa Magna incarnata.* He is believed to be the intercessor of departed souls. The High-priest lives in JUDIA, and his authority is such, that the king is obliged to bow to him. This shews the original superiority of the priests to the kings. *Pra* in the Baly or Bali, the sacred language of *Judia* or Odian, the capital of the kingdom of *Sion,* signifies the Sun and *the great living God;*[2] that is, the creator or former, giver of forms. From this has come Pra ja-pati, or the *Lord of mankind,* which means *father, ja, creator.*[3] This *Pra* is evidently the Hebrew word ‏ברא‎ *bra,* to create or form, of the first verse of Genesis. It is singular that Park-hurst gives us the verb ‏ברא‎ *bra* to create, but no noun for Creator. But though it may be lost now, it cannot be doubted that the verb must have had its correspondent noun. I have before observed that this word PR or BR, is said, by Whiter,[4] always to mean Creator.

[1] Vol. I. p. 29.   [2] La Loubère, pp. 6, 7.   [3] Asiat. Res. Vol. VIII. p. 255.   [4] Etymol. Univ.

On the south point of Siam the Malays reside. These are the people whose language, a Hebrew friend, Mr. Salome, of Bath, understood, when he went into the depôt of the India company near Wapping, in London. But if the Mohamedans carried to India their religious names, how are we to account for the other names connected with the Hindoo and Greek superstitions being found in Greece; such as Caon or Cawnpore, Agra or Argos? How are we to account for two Syrias and two Dagons, two Matureas, two Sions, &c., &c.? These the Mohamedans did not take. How are we to account for the Sanscrit at Eleusis and in Italy; and how for the Linga and Ioni at Pæstum?[1] And, as I shall shew my reader, in a future book, for the Yoni and Linga at Aberdeen in Scotland?

No doubt it is difficult to ascertain clearly what names of towns in the countries North-west of India are ancient and what modern. This is caused by the singular circumstance of the tribes which anciently left that country to colonise the West, having returned, in modern times, to their old countries as Mohamedan conquerors and propagators of their new doctrines. The difficulty is also increased by the constant endeavours of the priests of the Jews, the Christians, and the Mohamedans, to disguise the fact, which they feel they cannot account for consistently with their received notions and their erroneous mode of explaining the sacred books. But if the Jewish names of places and persons were in these countries before the time of the arrival of the Mohamedans, there is an end of the question. The names of places enow we have seen. When Mahmud, of Gazna, the first Mohamedan conqueror, attacked Lahore, he found it defended by a native Hindoo prince called Daood or David.[2] This single fact is enough to settle the question of the places not being named by Mohamedans.

As I have before observed, when my learned friend Col. Tod visited Naples and Pæstum he saw several small figures of Ceres, which had in the hand something which the antiquarians of that capital did not understand. On looking at it the Colonel discovered, in a moment, that it was the Linga and Ioni of India. He recognized also at Pompeii, on the temple of Isis, the same effigy. I suspect the ellipses and circles of the Druids, with the stone pillar in the middle, are emblems of the same thing.[3]

I beg my reader to look at the ruins of the ancient cities of India, Agra, Delhi, Oude, Mundore, &c., which have many of them been much larger than London, the last, for instance, 37 miles in circumference, built in the oldest style of architecture in the world, the Cyclopean, and I think he must at once see the absurdity of the little Jewish mountain tribe being the founders of such a mass of cities. We must also consider that we have almost all the places of India in Western Syria. Let us also consider how we have nests of Asiatic places in Greece, in several districts the Mounts, the Argoses, Tripolies, &c., and I think no one can help seeing that these circumstances are to be accounted for in no other way than by the supposition that there was in very ancient times one universal superstition, which was carried all over the world by emigrating tribes, and that they were originally from Upper India.

9. No one can deny that it is a very extraordinary, and it is to me an unaccountable, circumstance, that Herodotus, writing the History of Babylon, of Egypt, and of Syria, and travelling across these countries, should have known nothing of the magnificent empire of King Solomon, or of the emigration of two millions of Jews from Egypt, and the destruction of the hosts of Pharaoh. How was this ignorance possible, if there be a word of truth in the Jewish histories? Did Pythagoras or Plato never hear of the glories of Solomon? Would not their followers have told Herodotus if they had known of them? The plagues of Egypt at once decide the character of

[1] See Trans. Asiat. Soc. Vol. II. p. 285.

[2] Maur. Mod. Hist. Hind. Vol. I. p. 248.

[3] See Trans. Asiat. Soc. Vol. II. p. 302.

the miscalled history of the *going out* of Moses. They do not prove it false, any more than the mythic history of Rome proves that there was no city of the seven hills; but they reduce it to the standard of rationality, by shewing that the history is a parable or mythos, the key being known only by the initiated. The Mythos, in every place, had its αστοικος: in Babylon, in Thebes, in the case of Moses, in Homer, in Rome, &c. On this Nimrod may be consulted. He has shewn this, and treated it most learnedly, and at great length. There might be, as I have no doubt that there was, *a going out* of the tribe under Moses: it was like the migration of all other nomade tribes, and might indeed be rather a large tribe. But two millions of people is a story like the other Jewish stories of their millions of soldiers, chariots, horses, talents of gold for their temple, &c., &c. Probably, in passing the end of the Red Sea, Pharaoh's army was destroyed by a tempest, of which Moses took advantage.

It has the same effect upon the glories and magnificence of the empire of Solomon. He was, probably, the prosperous king of a petty tribe, and had a mystic name given to him, though he oppressed his people, an ignorant, priest-ridden race, to erect a very fine palace and temple; and it is no way wonderful that when the energies of a whole tribe, though not a very great one, are directed for a great number of years to the raising and adorning of one building, that it should be very magnificent. The very same effect followed the same cause in the states of central India, whence the Jews had emigrated, as the prints of several of the temples in Col. Tod's history clearly prove. If any thing can be deduced from the style of architecture, the Indian temples are of the same date with the temples at Pæstum: and as the most ancient and most important of the Hindoo emblems were found there by Col. Tod, it is probable that they were erected by the same race.

The Jain temples, in Col. Tod's book, are the very pictures of the ancient temples at Pæstum, the date of which was a subject of curiosity in the time of Augustus. I shall return to this again.

CHAPTER VII

Jews hate the Female Principle—Jews and Egyptians, Blackness of—Observations on the Jews—Samaritans—General Conclusions

1. THE excessive hatred of the Jews to the adoration of the Queen of Heaven, Milcomb and Asteroth of the Sidonians, is visible every where in the Bible, as well as to that of the Bull Apis, under the names of Baal, Moloch, Thamas, &c., &c. Though the hypothesis that the Jews were a branch of a sect which arose in the disputes of India about the Linga and Ioni may be new, when every thing is considered, I trust it will not be thought improbable. It seems rationally to account for circumstances which, as far as I am aware, have not been explained before, and to remove many difficulties. And I think when it is well understood and duly considered, it will be found to be in favour of the Christian and Jewish religions, and not against them.

2. " Major Orme[1] reckons eighty-four castes in India, each of which has a physiognomy
" peculiar to itself. The more civilized tribes," he says, " are more comely in their appearance.
" The noble order of the Brahmins are the fairest and the most comely. The mountaineers most
" resemble Negroes in their countenances and their hair. The natives of the hilly districts of
" Bengal and Babar can hardly be distinguished by their features from the modern Ethiopians."[2]
All this accords very well with my theory respecting the black Buddha. Probably at the time
the black Jews divided from their countrymen, they were black—and, from being always few in
number and low in rank, and breeding entirely in their own caste, they have kept their ancient
sable complexion. It has been observed, that the figures in all the old caves of India have the
appearance of Negroes.[3]   This tends to prove not only the extreme antiquity of the caves, but
also the original Negro character of the natives.

Dr. Pritchard has most clearly proved, as I have stated in Book V. Chap. XIII. Sect. 2, that the
ancient Egyptians were Negroes. He observes that " the Greek writers always mention the
" Egyptians as being *black* in their complexions. In the Supplices of Æschylus, when the
" Egyptian ship is described as approaching the land, and seen from an eminence on the shore, it
" is said,

" Πρεπουσι δ᾽ ανδρες νησι μελαγχιμοις
" Γυιοισι λευκων εκ πεπλων ιδειν—

" The sailors too I marked,
" Conspicuous in white robes their sable limbs :

" And again,

" Εκλυσαν δ᾽ σειτυχει κατψ
" Πολει μελαγχιμψ συν ςρατψ.

" Herodotus, who was well acquainted with the Egyptians, mentions the blackness of their com-
" plexions more than once. After relating the fable of the foundation of the Dodonean oracle by a
" black dove which had fled from Thebes in Egypt, and uttered her prophecies from the beach-tree
" at Dodona, he adds his conjecture of the true meaning of the story. He supposes the oracle to
" have been instituted by a female captive from the Thebaid, who was enigmatically described as a
" bird, and subjoins [4] that, by representing the bird as *black*, they marked that the woman was an
" Egyptian."[5]

3. I now beg my reader to reflect upon what was said in Book IV. Chap. I. respecting
Cristna and his adventures ; to cast his eye upon the plates of Cristna treading on the head of the
serpent described in Genesis, and of the serpent in return biting his foot—and, as Dr. Clarke has
shewn, biting it in a way which proves that the oriental author did not copy from Genesis,
though the author of Genesis may have copied from him ; and then, I think, he will be obliged to
admit that there must have been a mythos common to Eastern and Western Asia. Let him then
consider the history of and the facts relating to circumcision, and the other particulars dilated
upon by me, and he can hardly scruple to allow that the Western mythos was copied or derived
from that of the East.

For the truth of the theory which I have advanced—that the Jews *did* originally come from
India, in addition to the circumstantial evidence, I have as good proof as it is possible for written

[1] Indostan, Introd.   [2] Pritchard, Phys. Hist. p. 392.
[3] Hunter, in Archæologia, Vol. VII. ; Dr. F. Buchanan, Asiat. Res. Vol. VI.
[4] Herod. Lib. II.   [5] Pritchard, Phys. Hist. p. 377.

records to afford. This I say roundly of the testimony of Magasthenes. He cannot be supposed to have had any prejudice against the Jews: his observation respecting their being an Indian tribe seems to have fallen from him merely as illustrative of the character of the Hindoos. The *Hindoos* were the object of the book, not the *Jews*. He had no interested motive to induce him to misrepresent or to deceive; and the priests cannot here set up even their hackneyed argument of hatred to the Jews to account for or obviate any thing which is unfavourable to them, as his assertion is merely confirmatory of Moses's narrative—that they came from the East, and is in praise of them or their system. The passage, which I have noticed before, where he observes that the Iudians and the Jews were the ouly people who had a true idea of chronology and the nature of the creation of the world, is very striking, when coupled with what I have just laid before the reader. It all tends strongly to prove the close connexion between the Indians and the Jews.

I now beg my reader to make a visit to Duke's Place, or to any settlement of Jews, and to look them in the face and deny if he can, that they have *oriental black* written on them in the clearest characters. Let him look at the long black hair and fine aquiline nose of the handsome Cristna, and then let him deny, if he can, his likeness to the tribe of Abraham. Let him look at the beautiful black-eyed, black-haired, half-bleached Jewish girls, and deny it, if he can. If I be right in my theory, the Jews were one of the latest emigrations from India to the West: we have no symptoms of any after them, except one of which I shall immediately treat: and this accounts for their being not so much *whitened* as the remainder of the Western nations. All this exactly agrees with the theory which I have advanced respecting the change in the features of Buddha in Book V. Ch. XIII. Sect. 2. Of course, as I suppose the Ioudi did not depart from India till about the time of the suu's entrance into Aries, or the time of Cristna, they would have the advantage of the improvement to his time, and though *black* would not have *curly* hair or *flat* faces.

Another reason for the continuance of the dark complexion of the Jews, and their marked national character, is to be found in their ancient law, which forbade them from marrying out of their own tribe. This law was long anterior to Moses, and was only re-enacted by him. We have, perhaps, the first appearance of it, in the esoteric history of Jacob and Esau. The idle story of *the mess of pottage* is very good as a subject for the priests to make sermons upon; but probably the real reason for Jacob's conduct to Esau, may be found in the fact that Esau had forfeited his birthright by marrying out of the tribe, and *he* was excluded that his children might not inherit.[1] The same thing happened to Moses, who married an Ethiopian woman, as I have before pointed out, and therefore his children did not inherit; but the supreme power and the priesthood descended to the sons of Aaron, his nephews. In the case of Esau and Jacob the truth is disguised under the parable or ænigma of a mess of pottage. It is surprising that persons do not see that almost every part of Genesis is ænigmatical or a parable. The system of concealment and of teaching by parable is the most marked characteristic of the religion. I suspect that there is not a sentence in Genesis which is not consistent with good sense, if its true meaniug could be discovered. I feel little doubt that such passages as that of God wounding Jacob in the thigh, and his failing in his endeavours to kill Moses at an inn, are wholly misunderstood.

The Jews, as a race, are very handsome; they take after their ancestor Cristna. Nothing is more easy than to distinguish a thorough-bred Jew or Jewess. And it is very greatly to the honour of the Jewish matrons that the family likeness or national peculiarity should have continued so long. It gives me great pleasure to see this hitherto oppressed and insulted race re-

---

[1] Vide Gen. xxvi. 34, 35.

gaining their station in society. I hope that all distinction in civil rights will very speedily disappear.

I shall here add no more on this theory respecting Abraham and the Jews. Its probability must be left to the reader. If he do not approve it, let him account for the fact of Abraham and his wife, Sarah, being found in India; but he must not do this by telling me that the Brahmins copied from the Pentateuch, because this is an assertion which he knows he does not himself believe. Let him also account for the two Matureas, and for the *sixty-five* tribes of *Black* Jews intermixed with the tribes of *White* Jews in India, and the similarity in the names of places and identity of manners and laws: and let him shew some good reason why Megasthenes should have told a falsity. Let him also account, in a better manner, for the peculiarities which I have pointed out above, in the character and history of the Jews. But, above all, let him rebut the decisive argument which I have drawn from the circumcision of Abraham and his tribe, that the Judi of the West must have come from the East, not the Judi of the East from the West.

4. In consequence of the allegation that the Afghans were derived from the Samaritans, it becomes necessary to say a few words on the Jewish account of them; but I will compress them into as small a space as possible. The only account our priests have permitted us to have, respecting the division of the kingdom of Israel and Juda, comes from the sect of the latter. But enough transpires from the Jewish books to see that the sacred place appointed by the *Pentateuch* for the grand place of worship of the nation was Gerizim in Samaria, not Jerusalem; and that, in order to conceal the fact, the Jews have been obliged to corrupt the text, which they have done most awkwardly—substituting *Ebal* for Gerizim, and *Gerizim* for Ebal. This corruption has been admitted by some of the first divines of the Protestant Church. I believe, myself, that the great cause of the division of the kingdom, was the removal of the sacred place from Samaria to Jerusalem.

The Samaritans were carried into captivity before the Jews, and returned a little before them. A violent contention, it appears from the Jewish books, took place between the people possessing Samaria at the time of the return of the Jews, and the latter—each wishing to have only one national temple, and that temple at its own capital. Now the Jews say, that the Samaritans never returned—but that in lieu of them, Cuthite idolaters were sent by the King of Babylon, —these idolaters, the reader will observe, being the people who were so eager to have the temple of this foreign religion in their own capital, and to prevent the rebuilding of it at Jerusalem, for the promotion of a religion *not* THEIRS *in another country!* To account for these evident absurdities, the Jews tell a story, in good keeping with many of their other stories —that in consequence of the Cuthite idolaters having been plagued with LIONS sent by God, the King of Babylon forwarded them a priest to teach them the old law of the land, and that thus they became possessors of the law of Moses. Josephus being ashamed of this story of Lions, says, it was a *plague* which God sent. But it is easy to see, as the Samaritans, on the contrary, say, that the whole story of Cuthites and Lions is an interested lie of their enemies', and that they were carried into captivity by the Assyrians, and were returned from their captivity by the Persian Monarchs precisely the same, and for the same reasons, that the Jews were. The reader will not forget that we might have had the whole Samaritan history and books, if the archpriest Usher had thought proper. For, if he did not procure the whole and suppress them, (many of which I believe he did,) he had the power to do both. This is clearly proved. The whole of what I have here said, may be found in the Prologomena of Walton, in Prideaux, and in the works of Bishop Marsh. The learned have bestowed immense labour to discover the place where the *ten tribes* went to, after their country was conquered. They have sought them in every part of the world in vain. If they had consulted any persons except the *sectarian enemies* of the SAMARITANS and the LIONS, they might have saved themselves the trouble of travelling so far. The simple case was this: the kings of Babylon, after wasting the country, took away the *chief persons* of each nation to Babylon; and after the Persians took that city, they, finding a number of captives of their *own sect there*, sent them home again.

But there is yet one more consideration which at once overthrows the fancy of the *ten tribes* having given names to the places in India and Rajapootana. They would never have called the city or mount by the name of David, of Solomon, or of Jerusalem, men and a place they hated; nor countries nor districts after the name of the *tribe of Judah*, which they also hated; but Gerizim or Samaria. This at once settles the question of the *ten tribes* having founded the places in India. It is surprising that religious prejudice should blind men like Sir W. Jones, to such obvious considerations. But though the presence of the Jewish names proves that the towns cannot have been denominated by Samaritans, the names of the Samaritans, which they bore before the division of the tribes, if they should be found, will not prove the contrary.

Thus there is an end of the ridiculous pretence of the *ten tribes* in India. The fable can deceive none but Jewish sectaries and their followers. And the story of the *ten tribes* being disposed of, I have a perfect conviction that there is no other way of accounting, rationally, for the similarity between the tribes of Upper India and the Syrians, Arabians, and Ethiopians, than that which I have pointed out, viz. emigration from the East to the West, the emigrators taking with them their religion and their laws.

5. The result of all my inquiries comes to this: that about the time of the change of the Vernal Equinox from Taurus to Aries, several emigrations took place from the Mesopotamia of India to the West, in consequence of the great civil wars which then prevailed. One of these emigrations was that of the tribe of Ioudi, who constituted the Jews, Arabians, and African Ethiopians. Another emigration about the same time, but probably a little earlier, was that of the sect of the Ionians. These, I think, also came from the Duab or Mesopotamia. Long after these succeeded the tribe of Tartars or Scythians, mentioned by Ezekiel, who came down from between the Black and Caspian seas, and overran southern Asia. These probably came from the North of the Duab spoken of above. After a long series of years, the Arabian descendants returned, under the Mohamedan Califs, and reconquered India, crossing the Duab or Mesopotamia in their progress, and partly conquering it. Here they found the rudiments of their language, and the names of towns similar to those which their ancestors had carried to the West, and a mythology in great part similar to their own—the Judahs, Jacobs, Noahs, Shems, Japhets, &c., &c. This makes it impossible, without very great care, to distinguish in the Eastern Mesopotamia the works of the ancient Mythologists from those of the modern ones; but, with care, in most cases it may be done with certainty. Again, after the lapse of another long series of years, the descendants of the North-eastern Tartars, spoken of above as having come down from the North of the Duab under the name of Scythians, advanced towards the West—and, under the name of Turks, conquered the Saracens or Arabians in Syria, Arabia, and Greece, and took Constantinople, and Mount Hæmus, which has retaken its old name of Balk-an and Chumla. These people brought with them a language radically the same as that of the Arabians, yet, as might well be expected after a separation of so many years, considerably changed; nevertheless not so much changed, but that, with very little difficulty, they understand the Arabians. The close similarity of the Turkish and Arabian languages is a striking proof of my whole theory. The outlines of the history of the extended empires, which I have here exhibited, would have been much more conspicuous had our makers of maps and histories recorded the names of places as they must have appeared to them. But from their native religious prejudices and necessary ignorance of the nature of the history, it has seemed to them absurd to

believe, that there should be places or persons in the East having exactly the same names as places and persons in the West; and to avoid the feared ridicule of their contemporaries, which in fact (in opposition to the plainest evidence, and which they themselves could not entirely resist) they thought well-founded, they have, as much as possible, disguised the names. Thus, that which otherwise they would have called David-poutri, they call Daud-poutri; Solomon, Soleiman; John-guior, Jahan-guior; &c., &c. In the same way, without any wrong intention, they have been induced to secrete the truth, in many cases, from themselves, by hastily adopting the idea that the old Jewish names of places have been given by the modern Saracens or Turks, the erroneousness of which a moment's unprejudiced consideration would have shewn. All this, I think, I have proved; but in the course of the following books I flatter myself I shall strengthen my proofs by a great variety of circumstances. I therefore beg my reader, on no account, to consider my argument to be concluded. I shall here merely add, that in Chapter IV. Section 8, I have observed, there appears in the examples of the Dead Sea, &c., a great similarity in the countries where the tribes of Judah were settled in the East and in the West. The Western country seems, as much as possible, to have been accommodated to the Eastern; from this it is not unfair to suppose, that when we read, in the Jewish books, of the immense armies of horsemen and chariots, of the immense sums expended in building their temple, &c., these were meant secretly to describe the armies, cities, and temples, of the Eastern tribe of Oude, or of the Eastern Judah and Solomon. What is perfectly ridiculous, as applied to the mountain tribe of Western Syria, is quite otherwise when applied to the armies, cities, and temples, of India. The Western temple of Solomon, exclusive of the squares, or courts for the residence of the officiating priests, was only of very moderate size.

CHAPTER VIII

Pandion. Pandeus. Pandæa—Pandeism—Gypsies—Recapitulation.

1. I must now make a few observations respecting a certain person called Pandion; but whether there ever was such a person, or the stories told respecting him were mere mythoses, it is extremely difficult to determine. His residence at the birthplace of Cristna, where he reigned, is very suspicious. Mr. Maurice says, " But superior to both, in grandeur and wealth, in this southern " division of India, soared the puissant sovereign, named Pandion, whose kingdom extended quite " to the southern point of Comaria or Comarin, and who was probably of the ancient race of the " renowned Pandus. He also is said, about this time, to have sent an embassy to Augustus, but " no particulars of that embassy have descended to us. The residence of this monarch was at the " city of Madura, and the extent of his power is evident from the whole of that district being de-" nominated from him Pandi-Mandalam, literally the circle or empire of Pandion. Arrian expressly " says, that the Indian Hercules (Chrisna) worshiped at Mathura, on the Jobares, (Jumna,) left " many sons, but only one daughter, Pandæa, to whom he gave a vast army and kingdom, and " ordered, that the whole of her empire should be called by her name. In this and a few other " instances do the classical confirm and illustrate the native accounts,"[1] In not a few, I think, my reverend old friend Maurice. But I beg to observe that *Pan-di-Man-dalam* means, the circle or district of the *holy Pan*, or the district sacred to the Catholic God.

---

[1] Maurice, Hist. Hind. Ch. vi.

The temple of the Ionians of Asia Minor, built by the *twelve* tribes, at the place called Pan-Ionium, would mean, temple of the universal or catholic Ioni, or the Ioni-an Pan. The Indian palace of one of the great kings or Gods—Pandion, i. e. Pandu—was at Madoura, i. e. Mat'hura.[1] Here I think we have the *female* principle in Asia, and the *male* in India, at the birthplace of Cristna. Cunti or Prit'ha was the wife of Pandu, and mother of the Pandavas, and she was the daughter of Sura, king of the Surasenas. Sura, the most illustrious of the *Yadus*, was the father of Vasudeva.[2] Here is Pandu, the universal God, having for wife Cunti, the female generative power, &c. Can any one doubt the mythos here? Bishop Heber says, "King Pandoo and his four brethren " are the principal heroes of the celebrated romance [the Mahabarat; and the apparent identity of " his name with that of the *Pandion*, of whose territories in India the Greeks heard so much, is too " remarkable to be passed unnoticed."[3] Pliny says, there was a Panda—ultra Sogdianos, oppidum Panda: and Solinus ultra hos (Bactros) Panda, oppidum Sogdianorum. The same authorities mention a *gens Panda* or *Pandea gens*, whom Pliny places low down on the Indus. Ptolemy fixes the Pandions in the Punjab. There is at the South point of India a Madura Pandionis, and a Regio Pandionis.

Pandion was king of Athens,[4] whose son, by the famous Medea, was called Medus, and became king of the Medes. Perseus was the cousin of Medus, and the nephew of Pandion.[5]

When I consider all the circumstances detailed above respecting the Pans, I cannot help believing that, under a mythos, a doctrine or history of a sect is concealed. Cunti, the wife of Pandu (du or God, Pan), wife of the generative power, mother of the Pandavas or devas, daughter of Sura or Syra the Sun—Pandæa only daughter of Cristna or the Sun—Pandion, who had by Medea a son called Medus, the king of the Medes, who had a cousin, the famous Perseus—surely all this is very mythological—an historical parable!

2. I think Pandeism was a system; and that when I say the country or kingdom of Pandæa, I express myself in a manner similar to what I should do, if I said the Popish kingdom, or the kingdoms of Popery: or, again, the Greeks have many idle ceremonies in their church, meaning the Greeks of all nations: or, the countries of the Pope are superstitious, &c. At the same time, I beg to be understood as not denying that there was such a kingdom as that of Pandæa, the daughter of Cristna, any more than I would deny that there was a kingdom of France ruled by the eldest son of the church, or the eldest son of the Pope.

The country through which the Indus runs has been called by the moderns Panjab or Panjaub. The word *Panj* means *five*, and the word *Aub* means *river*, i. e. *the country of the five rivers*. But this is, in fact, not strictly true, for the country is in reality full of rivers. Rennell says,[6] "The " river called by Europeans Indus, and by the natives generally Sinde (or Sindeh), is formed of " about *ten* principal streams." In Ptolemy this country is called *Regio Pandoniorum*—the country of the Pandus. We have seen that though Cristna was said to have left many sons, he left his immense empire, which extended from the sources of the Indus to Cape Comorin, (for we find a Regio Pandionis near this point,) to his daughter Pandæa: but, from finding the icon of Buddha so constantly shaded with the nine Cobras, &c., I am induced to think that this Pandeism was a doctrine, which had been received both by Buddhists and Brahmins.

Col. Tod says, "But we must discard the idea that the history of Rama, the Mahabharat of " Cristna, and the five Pandua brothers, are mere allegory; an idea supported by some, although

---

[1] Tod's Account, Trans. Asiat. Soc. Vol. I. p. 326.   [4] Wilson's History of Cashmir, p. 97.
[2] Vol. III. p. 111.   [5] Diod. Sic. Lib. iv. Cap. lii.
[3] A female Pan may be seen in the second volume of the *Monumenta Vetusta*.
[6] Memoir of Map, pp. 68, 69.

" their races, their cities, and their coins, exist."[1] " Colossal figures cut from the mountain, " ancient temples and caves inscribed with characters yet unknown, attributed to the Pandus, " confirm the legendary tale."

The case, I apprehend, was this: in early times the Gods were known by their names of Bala, Rama, Cristna, &c.: by these holy names the princes, (as we know was the fact in later times,) were called, and the bards or family genealogists filled up the picture. Thus we have great numbers of princes who trace their pedigrees from the same Gods. I think there can be no doubt that sects may be traced by their significant names. Thus we find Ionas every where. We have them in India, in Syria, in Asia Minor, in Thrace, in Britain. Can any body believe that this peculiar and significant name is found in all these places by accident? Again: we have Pandions, Pan-dis, Pan-deas, Pandus, at Cape Comorin and Tanjore, in Upper India, in Asia Minor, and at Athens. This means Universal God—but can any one believe that this daughter or son of Cristna, in India, means only *red*, as some orientalists would persuade us? Every very ancient town has two or three names. Every ancient person of eminence has the same. He has one, which is his patronymic name, another his sacred, astrological, or lucky, name; and he has generally a third given him from his supposed qualities or character. This added to the frauds of genealogists, renders all history a riddle. The princes of Mewar, now living, trace their pedigrees back *two thousand* years before Christ—princes of a country which, for violent revolutions, as far as we can look back, has been exceeded by none.

Many persons have thought that this *Pan* related to what has been called Pantheism, or the adoration of universal nature, and that Pantheism was the first system of man. For this opinion I cannot see a shadow of foundation. As I have formerly said, it seems to me contrary to common sense to believe, that the ignorant, half-savage would first worship the ground he treads upon,— that he would raise his mind to so abstruse and so improbable a doctrine as, that the earth he treads upon created him and created itself: for Pantheism instantly comes to this. Against this, all our senses revolt. But all our senses lend their aid to forward the adoration of the glorious Sol, with his ministers and attendants, the planetary bodies, which appear to await his commands, and to obey his orders. No, indeed! Pantheism was the produce of philosophy, and excess of refinement, of, comparatively speaking, a recent date. I suspect that the old Pantheism is first found in the history of Pan-dæa, the only daughter of Cristna, and in Pan-dion, the first king of Athens; and these histories, like many others of the same kind, are only mystical representations of a sect of devotees, or of philosophers. An Oriental friend doubts this; he says, because Pandu means *red*, and has no relation, in meaning, to any of the Pans above noticed. I think no one who has attended to the surprising change which must have taken place in the Sanscrit language, in bringing it to its present perfection, will consider this of much consequence, particularly when he attends to a remark which he will find made by Col. Van Kennedy, in the next chapter, that the Sanscrit roots have been formed solely by grammarians, and of course artificially; and that they have in themselves no signification. But this, to the extent to which he goes, is evidently not true. Had he said *many* or *most* Sanscrit roots, I should not have disputed his authority; but my eyes tell me every moment that when he speaks of *all*, he goes much too far. However, I think his observation is enough to account for the change in the meaning of a word having taken place, without such present meaning being sufficient to obviate the arguments advanced above. The question seems likely to remain in doubt—for I do not pretend to decide it. Had Col. Van Kennedy excepted proper names of Deities, Persons, and Places, his observation would have been more correct. But this matter will be discussed in the next book.

---

[1] Hist. Raj. p. 44.

It is the received opinion, I believe, of all the first professors of comparative anatomy, that the human race originally consisted of only one genus and one species. Were it not for this received opinion, the marked distinction which may be observed in the different colours in the pictures of the Hindoos, and of the ancient Egyptians, might induce a suspicion that it was meant to indicate different species. At any rate, the distinction must be held to mark varieties—varieties readily accounted for, by the examples of peculiarity exhibited by the Jews and some other tribes, which have been, in a great degree, confined to propagating the species within their own little nation. Now I suggest, for the consideration of the learned, whether it may not be probable that the Pandus may have formed a Northern sect, which at length became *fair*-complexioned, by the same cause, whatever it might be, which made the Athenian Pandions *fair;* and whether from this yellowish-white complexion, the word Pandu may not have come to mean *red* or *yellow.* Thus a thing might be said to be of the Pandu colour, as we say a thing is of the Negro colour.[1]

If my reader will cast back his imagination over what he has read in this and the last chapter, he will find that the doctrines which I have laid down respecting the origin of the Ionians and Jews, are supported almost entirely by *evidence* and not by *theory.* The system may be said to be formed out of a great number of loose, detached parcels of a whole, brought together and fitted to their respective places, thus forming them anew into a whole again—the parts, while scattered about, offering nothing but a chaotic mass of odd materials, or the leaves of the Sibyls blown about by the winds. I shall not add any thing more here relating to the ænigma or parable: but one thing is clear—the Mythos of the Hindoos, the Mythos of the Jews, and the Mythos of the Greeks, are all, at the bottom, the same; and what are called their early histories are not the histories of man, but are contrivances under the appearance of histories, to perpetuate doctrines, or perhaps the history of certain religious opinions, in a manner understood by those only who had a key to the ænigma. Of this we shall see many additional proofs hereafter. The histories of Brahma, of Genesis, and of Troy, cannot properly be called *frauds,* because they were not originally held out as histories; but as the covers for a secret system. But in later times they were mistaken for history, and lamentable have been the effects of the mistake. The history of Lazarus in the Gospel is not true, but it is not a fraud.

Though I have said that the Ionians were the Buddhists, traced by me in my Celtic Druids, this is not perhaps quite correct; for I think it probable that, in the 2160 years which the worship of Buddha or the Bull preceded that of Cristna, the Buddhists had actually in part settled the Western countries. The modified religion of the Ioni or Jains would not find much difficulty in making its way among them, as it was virtually the same—and perhaps it might be the religion only, and not the tribes of people, which latterly came. But this can never be known. From the expressions in the old Greek writers it seems probable, that when the Ionians arrived they found Buddhists—shepherds perhaps—peaceable, unarmed people, called aborigines, whom they easily conquered.

3. A few pages back, I said that the Jews were the latest emigrants from India, with one exception, of which I should presently treat. I shall now fulfil my promise. The subject to which I alluded was that of the Gypsies. Numbers of persons have treated of the Gypsies; but as yet nothing has been written respecting them that is quite satisfactory. It is now acknowledged by all, that they are of oriental origin. I have been told by two gentlemen who had returned from

[1] *Pen* lingua Ægypt. est Osiris. (Diod. Sic.) *Phen* or *Phaneus* was one of the names of Apollo, (Macrob.) *Phaneus* Deus Sol. (Alex. ab Alex.) *Sum, Balim, Talaca,* CaishNa, *Arun,*. are common names of the sun with the Irish Druids The Sanscrit *Vahni* fire, is probably the root of *Fen* or the Phœnician פן (pn) *phen,* a cycle. From this word the Druids made up their Phenniche, or Phœnix. Phœnis Ægyptiis astrologiæ symbolum, was clear to B chart. (Ouseley's Orient. Collect. Vol. III.)

India, that they understood the language of the Gypsies when they spoke it, and that it was the Hindostannee. A strong circumstance of corroboration of this is given by a German called Grellman, [1] who has written the best account of them which I have seen, though mixed with much nonsense. Mr. Marsden has proved the language of the Gypsies to be mostly Hindostannee and Bengalee. [2]

Thus I think there cannot be a doubt that the language of the Gypsies is one of the vulgar dialects of Hindostan. Grellman states the Hindoo languages to be ALL radically the same, which is what we might reasonably expect, and gives a vocabulary of words in both the Hindostannee and the Gypsy languages. Among other similar circumstances he observes, that they have each only two genders, that the cases of their nouns are made by the addition of an article, &c. This the reader will recollect is exactly like the Synagogue Hebrew. A learned German, called Wagenseil, has quoted near fifty of their words, which he maintains are pure Hebrew. Other Germans have shewn that many of their words are those of the Mongol Tartars, with whose language theirs has a great affinity. This is the language of the Afghans, which Sir W. Jones found so like the Chaldee. These facts tend strongly to prove that they have a language in fact originally the same as all those languages, and that those languages have all originally been the same.

Their complexion, like that of the Jews, proves the Gypsies also to be oriental. When they first appeared in Europe, or by what route they came, is quite unknown. I consider them to be a tribe, like that of the Jews, from India. The difference in the fortunes of the two tribes is this: one continued together till it became strong enough to create jealousy, which caused its expulsion from Egypt, and it continued united, having fortunately a leader skilled, by accident, in all the learning of the Egyptians, who took the command, and under whom it conquered and became a nation. The other was not so fortunate. It had no child accidentally adopted and educated by a princess, or other circumstances favouring it as they did the Jewish tribe; it has, therefore, continued miserable and dispersed. The Christian will say the one was a favoured tribe for peculiar reasons. Very well. This makes nothing against my argument, or against the facts. That the Gypsies were a Buddhist tribe is proved, in part at least, by one singular remnant of the religion of Buddha, which they yet retain. It is contrary to their faith to kill animals to eat, but if they find them dead, they are permitted to eat them. Thus a dead ox or sheep is a grand feast to them. For though, as there are Mohamedans who drink wine, there are always among them some who kill and eat, yet they prefer the feast that is free from sin. Like the Jews, they couple only in their own tribe, and thus their national cast of countenance continues.

The Jews were originally believed to have a peculiar power of extinguishing fire: this is continued to the Gypsies. [3] The Jews were believed to eat children: this was formerly also believed of the Gypsies. The oldest accounts which we have of them, given by themselves, state them to be emigrants on account of religion. [4] If ever their history shall be sought into diligently by a philosopher, which has never yet been done, I think they will be found to be a tribe from Upper India—Afghans perhaps. [5] When I first began to study the Hebrew language, I received instruction from a Jewish gentleman, of the name of Salome, at Bath. I never had the least reason to entertain a doubt of his veracity. He told me that passing the depôt of the Malays, near our India House, his attention was called to it by an affray, and on going into it he found people speaking a language which, from his knowledge of Hebrew, he understood. This was an Indian or Malay language, which must have been a close dialect of the Hebrew; to this I shall return.

[1] P. 171, Eng. Ed.
[2] Grel. p. 37.
[3] Archæol. Vol. VII. p. 252; Vall. Col. Hib. Vol. V. p. 310.
[4] Ib. p. 121.
[5] For more information see Asiat. Res. Vol. VII. p. 476.

In the Morning Herald for the 16th or 17th of April, 1827, is a paragraph stating, that the Bible societies were giving Hebrew Bibles to the native Irish, as it was found that they were better understood than the English. This, in a very remarkable manner, supports what General Vallancey has maintained, but which has been much ridiculed by weak people, that Ireland was colonised by a tribe from the East, and particularly from Phœnicia. All this seems to confirm the very close connexion which there must have been in some former time, between Siam, Afghanistan, Western Syria, and Ireland. Indeed I cannot doubt that there has been really one grand empire, or one Universal, one Pandæan, or one Catholic religion, with one language, which has extended over the whole of the old world; uniting or governing at the same time, Columbo in the island of Serendive, and Columbo in the West of Scotland. This must have been Buddhist, whether it ever really existed as one empire, or was divided into different states. A friend has observed that " The priests will have a great triumph over you, for they will endeavour to revive the almost ob-" solete doctrine that the Hebrew was the language of Adam." I reply, they will have no triumph over me here, for if they do triumph, it will not be *over me*, but *with me*. For I maintain, and believe that I shall prove, that the Arabian-Hebrew, as it may be called, has of all languages the best pretensions to be the first.[1] But in my next book, when I shall treat of Sanscrit and the Hieroglyphics, I shall discuss this more at large.

RECAPITULATION

I think it now expedient to recall to my reader's recollection a few of the subjects which I have discussed, and to consider the progress which I have made in my work; but I shall not at present notice the Preliminary Observations, because I have not yet come to that part, for the use of which they were made. After a few remarks on the cosmogony of the ancients and the abuse of his faculties by man, I commence my work with stating the doctrine of the existence of the Oriental Triune God of the ancients, and with explaining his supposed nature; and then endeavour to shew the way in which the refined system of emanations or abstractions must have arisen out of the natural perceptions of the human mind. At the same time I shew that several of the most important of the ancient doctrines were intimately connected with it, and naturally arose out of it; viz. the Androgynous nature of the Deity, the Metempsychosis, and the Immortality of the Soul, by its final absorption into the substance of the Supreme First Cause.

I next shortly point out the circumstance, that Genesis consists of three distinct works, the 1st called *the book of Wisdom*; the 2nd (B. I. Cb. II. Sect. 12) *the book of the generations* or *regenerations* of the *planetary bodies*; and the 3rd *the book of the generations* or *regenerations of the human race.* After this I proceed to shew that the sun either as God himself or as the Shekinah of the higher triune principle, (which is only known to us by its attributes, and which, when attempted to be subjected to a closer examination, vanishes from our grasp like a dream or illusion,) was the object of adoration of all nations—that all the Gods and Goddesses of idolatry resolve at last into this one principle.

In the fourth chapter of the first book I shew that there were two Ethiopias, and that the doctrine of Sir William Jones is probably true, that a great *black* nation once had power and preeminence in Asia, and that it is also probable that this was the empire of the black curly-headed Buddha.

In the beginning of the second book I endeavour to prove that the religion of Abraham was the same as that of the Persians, and that he held, like all other nations of the earth, the existence of the triune God: and that the word Aleim used in the first verse of Genesis is a noun in the plural number, and used in that number for the express purpose of describing this Being. In the third

---

[1] I speak not of the *from top to bottom written* Chinese, because I know nothing about it.

chapter this leads to an examination of the secret meaning of *Genesis*, and of course to the meaning of the first word, Berasit : when I come to the development of the sublime esoteric doctrine of WISDOM, and an exposure of the dishonest means adopted by the priests to conceal it from modern Christians : and in these assertions I shew that I am supported by almost all the most eminent men of antiquity. I also prove, that the oriental doctrine of Emanations is clearly maintained in the Pentateuch. The remainder of this book is chiefly taken up with shewing the identity, with some few exceptions made for particular purposes, of the religions of the Israelites, the Persians, and other nations, neighbours to the Jews—with the origin of Sacrifices—the reason of the restoration of the Jews to Palestine by Cyrus—the allegorical nature of the Old Testament, and the history of the Jewish Cabala—so far all tending to prove that the secret doctrine of the Jews was the secret doctrine of all nations, which was, in fact, the system of the celebrated Christian eclectic philosopher, Ammonius Saccas.

The third book discusses the origin of the famous word *Om* of India and Greece—the systems of Pythagoras, of Orpheus, and of the Greeks ; and I there shew that the doctrine of the Orphic or Platonic trinity differed in no important respect from that of the Christians : and I feel confident that I have proved it to have been universally held by all nations, Jew and Gentile, from the earliest period. The proofs of its existence before the time of Christ are numerous and incontrovertible. The observation of Mr. Maurice, that Plutarch and the Gentile authors drew their information from old writers before the Christian æra, is conclusive evidence that the doctrines were not copied from the Christians ; but that they were taken from the records of the philosophy of Orpheus and Zoroaster. The substantial identity of the two trinities I consider so clear, that I shall not waste a moment upon the subject. It is too late now to renew the nonsensical controversy between the *homoiusians* and *homoousians*.

When in the fourth book we come to the God of the Hindoos, the celebrated Cristna, we are drawn to the consideration of the question of the priority of the Indian or of the Egyptian mythology : and I here think the great mass of small circumstances, as well as of direct written evidence, amount to as good a proof as the nature of the case will admit, that India was the *parent* and not the *child* of Egypt. I then observe, that such facts as that of the discovery of the Cobra Capella, on almost every monument in Egypt,—as that of the discovery and adoration by the Seapoys of their God Cristna in the ruins of Thebes, are decisive of the question—and are infinitely more valuable than any written evidence whatever. The notice taken by Mr. Maurice of the descent of Cristna into Hell and his return to his proper paradise, in Book IV. Ch. I. Sect. 3, is striking : it can scarcely be believed that he did not know of the crucifixion noticed by M. Creuzer. To the crucifixion of the Avatar of Cristna, called Balajii or Wittoba, I shall return hereafter. What shall I say of the *black Christ* among the *white* Italians, Swiss, Germans, and French ? Is it necessary to say any thing ? Does it not speak for itself ? Can any thing more be wanted to shew whence the corruptions, in the religion of the Ktētōsopher[1] of Nazareth were derived ? I shall not recapitulate the particulars of the life of the most amiable and interesting of the Gods of antiquity, the playful Cristna ; my reader must remember them ; they are much too striking to be forgotten.

The lives of Buddha and Cristna are so similar, that to tell the story of *one* is to tell the story of the other. The publication of the plate of the *crucifixion* and *resurrection* of INDRA or BUDDHA, by the learned Jesuit, with the permission of the Roman Censor, is, however attempted to be explained away by him, a credit to both.

The history of Buddha, in the Fifth Book, supplies to the list of the corruptions of Christianity

---

[1] Κτητωρ-Σοφιας, *Possessor of Wisdom*. Will my reader pardon my coining this designation—admissible, perhaps, from its appropriateness?

what was wanting in the history of Cristna. There I have shewn that from Buddha came the immaculate conception of Maia or Maria,—immaculate conception being first, in the West, ascribed to the mother of Pythagoras, and from him, perhaps, handed over to the Christian devotees. A miraculous birth having been attributed to Pythagoras and Plato, shews that it was no *new thing* when Papias and Irenæus laid hands upon it.

In this book, the history of Buddha introduces us to perhaps the most important part of the system, and to the origin of the whole—the ancient cycles: and I think that the arithmetical proofs which I have given of their meaning, leave nothing wanting to the proof of the truth of my theory. The ancient doctrine of the millenium of the Jews, the secret meaning of the cross, the mysterious numbers of the stones at Stonehenge, Abury, &c., the prophecies of Isaiah, Zoroaster, Virgil, and the Druid of Ireland, all connect and bind together, as with a chain, the mythoses of antiquity.

The evidence to the truth of my theory, afforded by La Loubère and Cassini, is more than could have been expected: and the reality of the system of cycles, arising from the arithmetical proofs, I apprehend, is clear and satisfactory as far as we have gone; but they are only *trifling* compared with the proofs which I shall bring, when I come to the chronological finale of the system.

I could scarcely wish for any thing more opportune for my theory, than the mode in which the two monograms, the ΥΗΣ and the ΧΗ which stand for Christ, for the ancient sacred number of the East, and for one of the cycles, viz, 608,—and the X alone standing for 600, the other cycle, connect together the two systems. No pretended accident can account for such a coincidence. The circles at Abury, the monograms at Rome, the prophecies, the ten Avatars, eight of which I have already explained, and the expected Millenium, prove the existence of an universal system—and that, as far as it has yet been stated, I have developed it.

The theory which I have formed for the origin of the sacred numbers of the ancients, 600, 608, 650, is, I think, more than plausibly supported in Book V. Ch. IV. by the monograms. And the records supplied by the number of pillars in the temples, and particularly by the number of 650 pillars in Abury, the number sacred to Bacchus, unknown to me when I published the CELTIC DRUIDS, is a striking circumstance, confirmatory of its truth. At first, when my attention was drawn to the ancient cycles, I by no means observed their great importance to the early generations of man. In fact, in the whole circle of science, there is not, perhaps, one object which must have been of equal importance. They were not only of consequence to mankind in all their temporal affairs, their seed-times and their harvests, but as the first religion consisted, as much of religion does yet, almost entirely of ceremonies and festivals, the cycles became of the greatest consequence as points of faith. Even within a short period of the present time, the question whether the devotees were to keep Easter on the fourteenth day after the new moon, or the Sunday afterward, caused terrible and bloody wars. In short, almost all the spiritual and temporal concerns of life were implicated in the cycles—and to this must be added their paramount importance in the nonsensical science of judicial astrology. To all these matters I request particular attention.

Most of my readers will be surprised at the explanation of the *Om* of Isaiah. The proofs I have yet to produce in its justification are almost innumerable. The passage from Martianus Capella, Book V. Chap. II. Sect. 8, rescues the Gentiles from the charge of worshiping many Gods, but my reader will be kind enough in the first line for the word *calls* to read *invokes*. The universal prevalence of the adoration of the Cross cannot be denied. The generality of my readers, I believe, will begin to be much surprised at finding in the Lama of Tibet, nearly an exact counterpart of the Pope of Rome—in whose fisherman's *poitrine* we shall find many things little suspected.

The identity of Hercules and Samson cannot, I think, be disputed, or that Bacchus was Buddha and the sun in Taurus, and that Hercules was Cristna and the sun in Aries.

Mr. Bentley's discoveries, finished by his recantation to Dr. Marsham, have taken from under the priests their last strong support; but much relating to this matter is yet to come. The Jewish *passover* found in the *Yajna sacrifice* of the Hindoos, is surely very interesting.

I flatter myself that I have explained the ænigma of the Negro God, and that the curly-head of Buddha, the Triune God of Wisdom, will no more be a reproach and disgrace to his followers. The resolution of numbers of Indian names into Hebrew roots, must begin to operate on the mind of my reader, to make him think it not so great a paradox to say, that the Hebrew is the *oldest* of languages. The wars of the Maha-barat are explained in the *fifth* book. It is not easy to refer to a proof of the truth of that part of my system, (which depends upon the change of the equinox from Taurus to Aries,) as scarcely a page can be pointed out in which some proof of it may not be found; but perhaps there is nothing more striking than the fact stated in Book V. Chap. XI. Sect. 3, that at a certain period, all the heads of the Gods and Goddesses changed from that of the Bos or Beeve, to that of the Agnus or Sheep.

When all the curious circumstances which have been developed are considered, an unprejudiced person will, I think, be obliged to admit that the ancient epic poems are oriental allegories, all allusive to the same mythos, and that many of those works which we have been accustomed to call histories, are but allegorical representations of mythologies, of the secret doctrines of which I am in pursuit, and which have been endeavoured to be concealed and perpetuated for the use of the elect, the initiated, under the veil of history—to which, as the first object was the doctrine or mythos, *the history* in every case was sacrificed or made subservient, and that Herodotus, from being the first historian was, in fact, as well as in name, the father of history. Thus we find in the East, as well as in the West, whenever an attempt was made to discover the meaning of any of the ancient ceremonies by the uninitiated, the inquirer was always put off with a story or history; and the great doctrine of the Creator, the Preserver, and the Destroyer, which was the foundation of the mythos, from incapacity or unwillingness in the priest, was never explained.

In the concluding chapter of Book V., I flatter myself that I have done an act of justice to the Gentile nations, and shewn that, however their different religions in time became corrupted, a very fine and beautiful system of morality, the morality in fact of the philosopher of Nazareth, was at the bottom of them all. I also flatter myself that, in the same chapter, I have only done an act of justice to Mons. Volney. The first chapter of the *sixth* book on the flood or floods, the Pyramids, the Delta of Egypt, the theory of Mr. Gab, and the Geological fact in Yorkshire, will suggest room for many queries. The history of the Virgin of the Sphere will, I fear, make many of my Catholic friends angry.

I think the history of *Bacchus* and *Iao*, in Book VI., will leave no room for doubting about who they were.

This book will have opened to my reader some new views of the origin of the ancient inhabitants of Greece, and the mythical meaning of the beautiful Lotus. The passage in the note on Chapter III. respecting Roger Bacon and his knowledge of the *modern* inventions or discoveries, as we call them, will surprise my reader, as the fact surprised me.

In this book also, the origin of the Hellenes or Ionians, and of the ancient Greeks, is traced— and their fable of the Argonauts is shewn to have come from India. The circumstance of the two Moriahs or Merus, two Sions, &c., prepares the way for the complete proof of the origin of the ancient Jews in the next book. The Gods Janus and Ganesa are also shewn to be the same; and what has been said before respecting the allegorical poems and histories, is confirmed by many observations respecting Homer, Troy, the hanging gardens of Babylon, &c., &c.—the whole tending to prove one universal system to have been at the bottom of all the ancient mythologies.

In the *eighth* Book I have made an attempt to explain the hitherto inexplicable peculiarity of the

Jewish nation, and I flatter myself with success. Here comes into great use the system of the *sixteen* letters, which I have established in my *Celtic Druids*, as the original system of all nations that had the use of letters. The authorities on which my explanation of the history of the Jews is founded I think cannot be impugned; they are chiefly unwilling witnesses,—the admissions of such men as Eusebius, Bryant, Faber, &c., all very learned, but most unwilling supporters to my cause. But their admissions are *confirmed by circumstances which admit of no other explanation.* Can any one doubt the existence of the Jewish mythos in India? The same names of God, of men, and of places? The two Ararats, the two Moriahs, two Sions? And, above all, the various Suleimans or Solomons—the mountains of Solomon—the Tucti Solumi of Cashmere and of Northern India—and of Persia, and of Syria, and of Telmessus? What I have said on all these subjects, will receive almost innumerable additional proofs hereafter. But I think that, at last, the origin of this singular and interesting people has been shewn in a way which a philosopher need not feel ashamed to receive. Indeed I contend, that the existence of Judaism before the time of Abraham, proved by Eusebius, and the Israelitish names found in the names of the countries, the mountains, the cities—like *Ioud-ia*, the capital of a mighty empire, in North or Central India, amount to as good proof as the nature of the case will admit, that the Judæan history is a mythos brought to the West by a tribe of Afghan Shepherds, probably conquered or driven out of India, from the country of Oude or Juda, in the wars of the Mahabarat. In a future page I shall shew, that when the same people established themselves, not as conquered emigrants, but as conquerors, in other foreign countries, they in a similar manner established their mythos and their religion.

I think my reader will now begin to perceive in the general prevalence of the Trinitarian doctrine, and the renewal of cycles, and in many other circumstances, an approximation to proof that what the Eclectic philosopher, Ammonius Saccas, said, was true, viz. that one universal and very refined system originally pervaded the whole world; which only required to be divested of the meretricious ornaments, or the corruptions with which the craft of priests, or the infirmities of men, had loaded it in different countries, to be every where found; that, in fact, in the Christian and Gentile systems, there was fundamentally no difference. I feel little doubt that in the remainder of this work I shall abundantly prove the truth of this doctrine of Ammonius, and upon this object, in fact the great object of my work, I must beg my reader to keep his eye steadily fixed.

Note. During the time that the part of this work which the reader has seen has been printing, I have met with several matters which would have much elucidated different points on which it has treated, only part of which I can conveniently insert hereafter, and indeed the insertion of such part will be rather misplaced. It is therefore my present intention, if health and circumstances permit, to publish a volume, or perhaps more than one, occasionally, called *Commentaries on the Anacalypsis and on Ancient History*. This will give me an opportunity of further elucidating the subjects which I have discussed, and of following up the important discoveries made by General Vallancey, which the priests have contrived to consign almost to oblivion, but which, I am of opinion, are of inestimable value for the discovery of ancient science. In this work I shall be able to answer objections of opponents, and to correct oversights and mistakes, which, as I have not the gift of infallibility, must necessarily occur.

Nov. 1831.

LaVergne, TN USA
22 September 2010
198008LV00001B/22/A